DON MILLER'S
HOLLYWOOD CORRAL
A COMPREHENSIVE B WESTERN ROUNDUP

EDITED BY
PACKY SMITH AND ED HULSE

Riverwood Press • Burbank

HOLLYWOOD CORRAL copyright © 1976 by Film Fan Monthly, and reprinted herein by permission of Jessiefilm, Inc.

THE SINGING COWBOY: An American Dream, appeared in a slightly longer form in "The Journal of Country Music," vol. VII, no. 2, May 1978; copyright © 1978, by Country Music Foundation. Reprinted herein by permission of the author and the Country Music Foundation.

DON MILLER'S HOLLYWOOD CORRAL:
  A Comprehensive B Western Roundup
Copyright © 1993 by Riverwood Press

  First Edition

Neither in whole nor any part of the textual material contained in this book may be reproduced or transmitted in any form, electronic or mechanical, including photocopying, micro-filming, and audio-recording, or by any information storage and retrieval system, without written permission from the publisher.

Published by Riverwood Press • Burbank, California

ISBN 1-880756-03-X

Manufactured in the United States of America.

**This book is dedicated to
Pat Buttram**

*a sidekick to one. . .
a friend to all. . .*

*You've kept the banner of the B Western flying
when others would've let it fall. . .*

*Through your efforts, the Golden Boot Awards
help preserve the legends of the "cowboy pictures."*

May this book continue your efforts.

CONTENTS

	INTRODUCTION	ix
	FOREWORD by Gene Autry	xi

PART I
HOLLYWOOD CORRAL

Preface:	WHAT ALL THE SHOOTIN'S FER	3
1.	ALARUM AND EXCURSION	7
2.	THE BIG GUNS SPEAK: Gibson, Maynard, Mix	15
3.	THE BIG GUNS SPEAK: Jones, McCoy	31
4.	BATTLING BOB AND OUR TOM: Steele, Tyler	43
5.	THOSE BRAWNY MEN IN STETSONS	53
6.	BIG JOHN: THE BEGINNING	69
7.	HOW TO MAKE GOOD WESTERNS: Fox, RKO, and O'Brien	79
8.	…OR ANYWAY, BETTER WESTERNS THAN MOST: Keene, Holt, & other guys at RKO	91
9.	HOPPY	105
10.	THE MEN FROM MUSIC MOUNTAIN: Autry & Rogers	117
11.	HAVE SONGS, WILL WARBLE	137
12.	MEMBERS OF THE POSSE	151
13.	DURANGO	159
14.	THREE FOR THE PRICE OF ONE: Mesquiteers & Range Busters	173
15.	FUZZY'S FRIENDS	185
16.	TRAILS NORTH	193
17.	TRAILS SOUTH	203
18.	SAGEBRUSH EMPIRE	211
19.	WILD BILL	225
20.	HIRED HANDS	235
21.	LAST HURRAHS	245
22.	BROWN OF ALABAMA	253
23.	THE DECLINE OF THE WEST	263
24.	"BUT FIRST A BRIEF WORD FROM OUR SPONSOR…"	273
25.	HEROES, HEROINES, HEAVIES, & HARLEQUINS	281

PART II
REFLECTIONS ON THE B WESTERN

SILENT GUNS: The Early Western Stars *by Robert S. Birchard*	293
"GO INDEPENDENT YOUNG MAN": The Maverick Producers *by Sam Sherman*	309
LIFE AMONG THE "400": Hollywood's Cowboy Colony *by Robert S. Birchard*	321
THE SINGING COWBOY: An American Dream *by Douglas B. Green*	331
THE SONS OF THE PIONEERS: "Guns On Their Hips, Songs On Their Lips" *by Ken Griffis*	375
WRITERS OF THE PURPLE PAGE: Zane Grey and Other Literary Influences *by Ed Hulse*	385
"GEE DAD, IT'S A MONOGRAM!" Styles and Signatures In The B Western *by William K. Everson*	397
THE BOTTOM LINE: Low Finance In The Reel West *by Karl Thiede*	407
A ROCK IS A ROCK: Going On Location *by Dave Holland*	427
APPASSIONATO DRAMATICO: Music In The B Western *by James King*	441
GALS OF THE SADDLE: The Lovely Leading Ladies *by Ed Hulse*	449
THE MIRACLE RIDERS: Cowboys and Cliffhangers *by Alan Barbour*	461
CUT TO THE CHASE: Sagebrush Short Subjects *by Richard W. Bann*	471
HEADING FOR THE LAST ROUNDUP: Twilight Years Of The Cowboy Greats *by Alex Gordon*	481

WHATEVER HAPPENED TO THE SINGING COWBOY?
   Life After The Movies
   by Laurence Zwisohn
	489

BEST OF THE WEST: Top Ten and Fan Favorites *by Richard W. Bann*	505
AFTERWORD *by Roy Rogers*	521
ANNOTATED BIBLIOGRAPHY *by Packy Smith*	523
TRAIL DUST: A Film Preservation Postscript *by Richard W. Bann*	533
CONTRIBUTORS	535
INDEX	537

INTRODUCTION

In the pre-video days of the '60s, hundreds (if not thousands) of nostalgic B Western devotees embraced the hobby of film collecting as a means of preserving the memories and reliving the experience of attending the Saturday matinees of a bygone era. Galvanized by fan-founded periodicals such as *The Classic Film Collector, The Western Film Collector, Film Fan Monthly,* and *The Big Reel,* Western-movie aficianados sought out each other, bought and traded 16mm prints, formed new fan clubs, reactivated old ones, started their own magazines and, essentially, reignited long-dormant passions for a film genre already moribund for a generation.

When Don Miller's *Hollywood Corral* was originally published in 1976, it was eagerly embraced by the thriving core of Western film fans that had coalesced during the preceding decade. There had already been several historical surveys of the genre—most notably George Fenin and William K. Everson's seminal *The Western: From Silents to Cinerama*—but none had focused exclusively on the low-budget series Westerns of the '30s, '40s, and early '50s. Miller, a film scholar and TV professional with an encyclopedic memory, adopted the task following the success of his book *B Movies,* an exhaustive overview of non-Western cheapies aimed at the bottom half of the double bill. While his memory occasionally failed him, Don nonetheless turned out a highly entertaining and informative volume on series Westerns, effectively describing an era that encompassed more than 2,000 movies.

As an overview, *Hollywood Corral* touched on an amazing number of the low-budget horse operas produced during the sound era; it was studded with more references to stars, directors, and individual films than any Western lover could have hoped for. It's been out of print for many years now, and has been eagerly sought after by other fans and hobbyists who, thanks to the proliferation of old movies on videotape and cable TV, have discovered the joy of watching B Westerns.

We felt it was time that Don's book was back in print. At first, we planned to reissue the Miller book as a standalone product, with the mistakes corrected and photos replaced with newly chosen scenes. It was veteran film collector and Western fan Richard W. Bann who suggested that Don's overview be augmented with additional material gleaned from other Western-movie scholars to make this edition of *Hollywood Corral* the definitive work on the genre.

Rather than interpolate new material directly into Miller's text, we elected to make this volume an anthology, staying with Don's frame of reference but expanding upon themes, stars, and movies to which he gave short shrift, and adding essays on aspects of B Westerns he never mentioned.

For example, while *Hollywood Corral* offered a broadly sketched view of quickie Western production, it failed to hone in on specific aspects of the craft: writing, directing, choice of locations, music scoring, and so on. And while Don compared certain low-budget Westerns to certain big-budget Westerns, he never supplied budgetary figures or grosses to lend context to the comparisons. Moreover, he sometimes mentioned, then quickly brushed aside, stars and films that deserved more extensive commentary.

We gave plenty of thought to the right mix of supplementary essays with which to annotate *Hollywood Corral*—and once we'd established the topics, we set about assigning the most knowledgable writers available, and we think we succeeded admirably. Who could be better qualified than historian William K. Everson to evaluate the different styles affected by the respective studios involved in B Western production? Who knows more about Western movie locations than Dave Holland, who's already written his own book on the subject? Musician/composer/conductor Jim King has already released three collections of newly recorded music cues from the great Westerns and serials; who better to sing the praises and the neglected talents who penned background music for the Bs? And who could be more appropriate than Alan G. Barbour, who started chronicling the history of the sound serial while the last chapterplays were still making the rounds in theaters, to lend his personal recollections of classic cowboy cliffhangers?

In short, every author we picked is an expert on the topic he's covered in these pages. The collected knowledge and expertise represented between these covers, we believe, is unsurpassed in any special-interest filmbook you're likely to find. For that reason, we feel justified in subtitling this collection "A Comprehensive B Western Roundup." We think that, instead of just providing lengthy filmographies with endless credit lists, we've put together a reference work that illuminates not only the making of the films themselves, but also the people who made and marketed them.

One thing you *won't* find is any case-making for the B Western as an "art form." Our contributors all recognize that Westerns were, and are, simply an entertainment form. That doesn't preclude acceptance of the fact that some highly skilled, even "artistic" individuals worked in the genre. A beautifully photographed Hopalong Cassidy film, shot on location in Lone Pine, California, featuring a cast of highly competent actors, has a certain "artistic" quality about it. But an art form? No way. These pictures were made for the enjoyment of three generations of kids, and a lot of grownups who wouldn't admit it. More importantly, they were cheaply made and showed a profit.

As for the original *Hollywood Corral:* although we have corrected obvious mistakes, typos, and misstatements of fact, the text of Don's book is essentially the same one published by Popular Library's Big Apple imprint in 1976. The opinions he expressed, and the words he used to express them, remain intact and untouched. We felt that *Hollywood Corral* is a lively, vastly entertaining book, and that Don's prose should be maintained as it originally appeared.

What we *have* changed is the photo selection. Richard W. Bann and Robert S. Birchard, two of the country's leading still collectors (and incidentally, two of our essayists) have loaned us some of the rarest photographs in their archives. Most of our other contributors furnished rare photos and documents to illustrate their essays. As a result, many of the 450-plus pictures in this book are seeing publication for the first time. We think you'll agree with our judgment that few, if any, film books published in recent years sport the percentage of candid and behind-the-scenes shots you'll see herein. Even if one collector *could* amass a selection of stills like these, he'd have to spend many times the cost of this volume to purchase them.

As with any work of this size and magnitude, many people have contributed "above and beyond" the call of duty:

Mike Bifulco did double duty as both typesetter and layout artist, and managed to keep his sanity while dealing with two editors who love to work "on the fly." Many times, long after he thought a section was "put to bed," a sudden inspiration (usually a new photo, or discovery of a previously unknown tidbit of information) led to a phone call that began, "You're gonna *love* this…"

Les Leverett spent many hours composing and hand-coloring our cover…

Mike Royer contributed the lettering found on our cover and title page…

And finally, Tony Thomas, writer, colleague and friend, whose question, "Have you ever thought about reprinting Don Miller's book?" led to all of this…

So sit back, relax, and enjoy *Hollywood Corral*. Whether you're an old fan of Don's book, or a B Western neophyte approaching it for the first time, we can safely say that you're in for a treat. In fact, we dare say that even the most knowledgable Western buffs will find in the succeeding pages many facts and figures of which they are totally unaware. It's our fervent hope that our efforts have resulted in the definitive work on this long ignored, yet fondly remembered film form.

FOREWORD
by Gene Autry

A heartfelt hello to all the friends who have supported my movies, recordings, radio and television shows, and personal appearances ever since I started in show business over 65 years ago, singing on the National Barn Dance and making records.

A book like the excellent *Hollywood Corral,* with its many fine contributors, all of whom obviously share my great love and respect for Western movies and songs, brings back so many fond memories that it is hard to be brief in an introduction that is followed by so much well-researched detail and observation.

As a kid in Achille, Oklahoma, putting up posters and then running the projector at the Dark Feather Theater, I first became aware of Western movies and their stars, watching the likes of Harry Carey, Hoot Gibson, and Buck Jones on the screen. I never dreamed that I would eventually end up being one of them, but when I did, it became a very serious and responsible job for me. Whether it was wearing cowboy outfits in public so as not to disappoint the fans, or making certain that no offensive act or action ever appeared in one of my pictures, there was a constant effort always to play fair with those who would spend their time and money to attend my shows. After all, I felt like I was the babysitter for what would become several generations of kids, and I wanted parents to feel secure knowing that the kids were spending a morning or afternoon with Gene Autry, and that they could go about their business until it was time for the family to reunite. (Of course, in many cases the parents would attend the movies, as well!)

I was aware that my films were different from the straightforward Westerns that had gone before, from the authentic-looking, austere pictures of William S. Hart to the flamboyant action-adventures of Tom Mix, and the fine early-talkie work of Buck Jones, Tim McCoy, Ken Maynard, and their compadres. When Warner Baxter, in his Academy Award-winning role of The Cisco Kid, sang in *In Old Arizona,* music was introduced into the Western. Songs were featured in many outdoor movies, but they were not, strictly speaking, musical Westerns. It was not until 1934 that, through producer Nat Levine, I introduced the format of the musical Western to the screen, first in the serial *The Phantom Empire* and then in the 1935 Republic production *Tumbling Tumbleweeds.*

Much has been written about the "fantasy" elements of my musical Westerns, but often forgotten in those critiques are several things that I would like to point out here. First, in virtually all my movies, I played myself—Gene Autry—a recording star or rodeo performer or rancher or farmer or cattle inspector or whatever, thus having a reasonable excuse to wear fancy shirts and other embellishments that a working cowboy might not employ. Fans familiar with my movies know that in later years, in the Gene Autry productions released by Columbia, the outfits became largely working clothes and the flashy elements of the Republic pictures were strongly minimized.

The fact that most of my stories were set in the "modern" West, employing cars, trains, airplanes, radio, and even television (long before that medium took hold), did not restrict the plots from including ecological and other problems that are more prevalent today than ever.

Overproduction of logging (leading to flooding of range land), hoof-and-mouth disease, quarantine of cattle and sheep, dangers of devil weed, chemical spraying from the skies, overflowing of rivers, devastated ranchers, crooked lawyers, bankers, and politicians, land sharks, use of cattle grazing areas for Army maneuvers, big-city gangsters in the West, rustling of cattle by modern means with refrigerated trucks, fur and gold smugglers—these are only a few of the still-potent plot elements and characters used in my movies. My leading ladies were hardly helpless females, but were spirited young women with minds of their own, wanting to sell inherited ranches to the detriment of employees, or engaging in "taming of the shrew" tugs of war with the characters I portrayed (often the foreman authorized to uphold the will or decision of a distant or deceased father or uncle).

Later, when I had more control over my pictures, I emphasized problems of Native Americans—land and water rights, unscrupulous Indian agents or white politicians out to cheat the Indians—as well as harmonious relations between Americans and Latin American characters often initially misunderstood. With my pictures being shown all over the world, I felt strongly that their fair and honest depiction of the situations and problems would best personify the American image on foreign as well as domestic screens.

It's comforting to know that, thanks to television, home video, satellite, cable, and other technologies still in development, future generations will be able to enjoy the Westerns we all so enjoyed making long after we've gone to that Gold Mine in the Sky. And from the way it looks to me, that will continue forever.

In this regard, my legacy to my fans and lovers of all things Western is the culmination of my dream: The Gene Autry Western Heritage Museum in Griffith Park, Los Angeles, representing the authentic history of the West from the Conquistadors to the modern cowboys, from the Native Americans to the romanticized movie West, and embracing all aspects of this uniquely American era.

In closing, I want to thank all my friends for their support for so many years, and express my hope that their dreams, also, will come true.

Gene Autry
November 1992

PART I
THE HOLLYWOOD CORRAL

Charles Starrett and director Folmer Blangsted on the set of Westbound Mail *(1937).*

PREFACE: WHAT ALL THE SHOOTIN'S FER

First, an apology. The reader expecting to find new insights into the psychological motivations of the characters in *Stagecoach, High Noon, Red River* and *Shane* within these pages will be disappointed. It isn't that kind of a book.

Nor will the statisticians find much to evaluate. Kernels of wisdom pertaining to production expenditures, the weather conditions during the big gunfight scene, and what the star ate for breakfast on the second day of shooting his last film, are missing from the manuscript. It isn't that kind of catalogue.

Well, all right then. This is about a particular type of Western movie. It was made quickly, cheaply, and much of the time not very well. However, when one of them did have the brand of talent stamped upon it, no other type of film could be more enjoyable. The preceding statement may seem to be contradicted as the book progresses, for there are many favorable mentions of individual Western movies. Please allow the author some indulgences. Writing favorably about Westerns brings back fond memories of them. Besides, applying the rap to a film is the easiest writing in the world. If you don't think so, just count the number of critics getting paid for what they scribble today.

Westerns, or in the vernacular, "cowboy pitchas," would star a current stalwart hero, or sometimes a trio, as with The Three Mesquiteers. After 1935, this stalwart hero would upon occasion lift his voice in song, an event not always accepted in the best of humor by the audience. Gene Autry built a fortune upon it, Roy Rogers was billed as "King of the Cowboys" and none dared challenge the claim, and Tex Ritter's vocal cords outlasted his six-gun. On the other hand, Jack Randall would be drowned out by vile suggestions from the darkened arena, and the group known as the Sons of the Pioneers, nice fellows all, fostered audible reactions of twitching in the seat followed by thundering hoofs of a stampede to the candy counter during their renditions. No matter. If a cowboy star could ride and fight convincingly, his indiscretions with guitar would be gladly overlooked.

For it was the hero—The Hero, who was most important in the Western movies. He'd have a character name, but it would always be ignored by the fans. Charles Starrett fell into a long succession of adventures in which his screen name would invariably be Steve something-or-other, for reasons known only to the Columbia scriptwriters. But to his devotees in the dark, he would be Charles Starrett and no other— unless the rabid fan identified him as the Durango Kid, a personification he popularized. The screen actor William Boyd so completely immersed his identity that it became easy for him. He was Hopalong Cassidy, and no further arguments. Tom Mix was Tom Mix, Buck Jones was Buck Jones, no matter the official cast credits.

This in itself explains more about the nature of the films than any long-winded dissertation. When called upon to tell what they saw at the local picture show, one would not say, for example, *Gun Lords of*

HOLLYWOOD CORRAL: A COMPREHENSIVE B WESTERN ROUNDUP

Director Les Orlebeck (seated with script in lap), Mesquiteers Livingston, Steele, Davis, and crew relax between shots on Pals of the Pecos *(1941).*

Stirrup Basin. No, indeed; the simple reply would be: "Bob Steele," and all would understand. For these were the true star vehicles. From the beginning of the sound era well into the '30s, and even the '40s, this type of Western was just about all we had. There were exceptions, the epics and the extravaganzas, notable because they were so few. For the rest, each motion picture studio would have one, or several cowboy stars turning out a series of four, six, eight, or more Westerns per season. M-G-M didn't bother and Warner Bros. tried only occasionally, but the rest of them maintained their Western units. Audiences expected them. The kids loved them and vast audiences in small town and rural areas doted on them. They had fans in the big cities too, but the rentals were paid mainly from the outer vistas. Because they were produced cheaply, they turned in profits. When they stopped being profitable, as they did in the '50s, the studios ceased making them. The motion picture industry is after all an industry—or was.

For those who came along too late to witness the phenomenon, the weekly ritual displayed on the Saturday matinee screens is not easily explained, or justified. Those of tender sensibilities found it difficult to appreciate Westerns because they would be viewed under trying conditions. The matinees were full of screaming children, making concentration next to impossible, while the evening performances were populated by adults, most of whom found it a lark to chortle or satirize the proceedings. So, Tim McCoy could shoot a gun from an outlaw's hand even though he appeared to be aiming his gun somewhere in the vicinity of the lowest hanging cloud. So, Jack Hoxie was entirely capable of delivering a haymaker to the chin of a desperado, and no matter if he seemed to miss the guy's chops by about five feet. The Western was an exhibition of bravery and cowardice, crime and punishment, adventure and romance. To the devotees, it was as familiar, and beloved, as the ancient Chinese plays were and are to their audiences.

Accept this offering then, as a sort of casual tour through the era of the low-budget, or Grade B Western, from talkies to television. The strands of the cowboy star's career are hopefully followed, but at the same time the narrative provides a more or less chronological history of the genre. Quite a few Westerns with plot predominating over star name are examined, but this is not their story, especially the many individual Westerns released since the late '40s to date. The name of the director is given

Preface / WHAT ALL THE SHOOTIN'S FER

after the title. It may be a useful identification for the auteur-minded, although the work of the director is pretty cut and dried on Westerns—always with the usual exceptions, which will be noted.

No claims are made as to the importance of the low-budget Western, or its impact upon cinema history, American history or any other kind. The author believes it had little if any influence, while conversely milestones like *Stagecoach* had considerable influence upon the low-budget Western. Critically, it is not only unjust but foolish to compare them with any but their own. There were good and bad Westerns, and then there are the rest of the movies. Even within the studio release schedules they were segregated, given their own production numbers listed separated from the rest of the product. To some this might mean that they were inferior films. Not at all. Sort of special, maybe.

There has always been a lot of palaver about how the cowboy star would be a paragon of clean-living, manliness and everything a little boy could hope to be when he grows up. The truth is, cowboy stars are human beings and have their offscreen foibles and defects just like everybody else. And anybody who tries to emulate a screen image is ready for a rubber room anyway. Actually, I've met only a few cowboy stars and without exception they were decent, courteous, intelligent, and often witty gentlemen; I can't say the same for a lot of writers I've met. Stories about bottle bouts, wenching, pettiness and similar indecencies persist—but maybe I met the wrong cowboys. Most of them are quite serious about their screen work and tend to have recall of details, unlike some high-ranking actors and directors. One gets the feeling that they are proud of their careers, not for the examples they've set for future generations, but rather as working stiffs, who've labored hard and diligently, often at ungodly hours, under miserable weather conditions, against artistic and economic odds, and for not enough money. Like you and me. As actors, they are pleased when remembered. But at that, it does no harm if doting parents would want their child to mature into the screen image of Roy Rogers. After all, too many of them have evolved into the screen image of Roy Barcroft.

El Rancho Richmond
Staten Island, NY
May 1973–January 1974   **Don Miller**

Tom Mix

> You don't need to act. You're a Western star.
> You've just gotta have two expressions—hat on and hat off . . .
> Norman Panama & Melvin Frank: *Callaway Went Thataway* (1951)

1
ALARUM AND EXCURSION

Stately, plump Leo Maloney came from Hollywood, bearing a roll of celluloid on which his fortunes lay crossed.

It was the autumn of 1929. Maloney, a veteran of the photoplay dating back to the days of Ince, had weathered the intricacies of many a Western drama in capacities of star, producer and director, often concurrently. Now he had journeyed across the country to New York, on a selling mission. Maloney had made another independent Western, starring himself, written by Ford Beebe and entitled *Overland Bound*. The completed feature film had one distinguishing facet to separate it from the rest of the low-budget Westerns currently on view. *Overland Bound* was a full-fledged talking picture. Only one other outdoor story could make that statement, the Fox production of *In Old Arizona*, with Warner Baxter portraying the Cisco Kid. Currently in release were a few Westerns with hastily inserted scenes containing dialogue or musical numbers. Otherwise, motion pictures with sound were progressing in uncertain steps, and the Western, more a visual type of movie than any other, was in a state of eclipse. Maloney had come east to persuade some enterprising distributor to take a chance on this novelty, completed after great difficulty because of unfamiliarity with the new-fangled sound medium, and the budgetary necessity of using cheap sound-recording equipment. Could the film be sold?

The position of the horse opera was indeed precarious in late 1929. If it had been possible to stress the "opera" part and shoo the "horse," many a Hollywood executive would have slept easier, since the musical film was fast becoming the rage, and open throats were vastly preferable to open ranges. Not that there wasn't a demand for Westerns. They maintained popularity in the bastions of side-road bucolic locations and the broken battlements of urban areas. But the seats in these emporiums were apt to be splintery and the bill of fare changed daily, unlike many of the patrons. Nor were these flea-pits wired for sound; soon they would be forced to follow the trend, or perish.

With the diminishing market for Westerns, it was no longer home on the range for the cowboy-movie star. Many of them had heard a discouraging word, and were idle, or on display in Wild West shows and circuses and carnivals. Only Universal Pictures had been bold enough to take a flyer on sound sequences in their series Westerns and, as had been mentioned, the talkie sections of these films were haphazard at best, regarding story construction. A bit of judicious editing could remove them with scant loss for those theaters still *sans* sound, but with or without these sound scenes the pacing tended to slow down considerably. Nevertheless, it was the best of a sticky situation for Universal. Sound had temporarily victimized the Western film.

In a little more than 25 years, the Western had become a cinematic synonym for physical movement, fast-moving stories. The Western was also the most authentically American contribution to the

HOLLYWOOD CORRAL: A COMPREHENSIVE B WESTERN ROUNDUP

motion-picture form. Its uniqueness was popular internationally. Flesh-and-blood heroes of mythological proportions had been created within its sphere, fostering sublime if fanciful legends of the American frontier. It appealed to the little boy in every adult male, and the adult dreamer in every little boy.

The Western film was, it seemed, always with us. The *Cripple Creek Bar-room Scene,* a vignette of frontier life lasting a few seconds, was filmed by Edison associate W. K. L. Dickson shortly before the turn of the century. It depicted the inhabitants of a contemporary saloon, and is the first known example of a Western setting on film. The Western story occurred a few years later, in 1903, with Edwin S. Porter's filming of *The Great Train Robbery,* also for the Edison company.

Appealing to the spirit of adventure imbued in all, tall tales of the West had long been popular on the printed page, whether accounts of the taming of the Western wilderness, largely factual if garnished generously with fancy, or exciting entertainments of the dime-novel, Ned Buntline variety; largely fanciful if garnished with a certain air of realism. Distinction and stature were added to the Western story in 1902 with the publication of *The Virginian,* by Owen Wister. His novel has since become a classic. In 1905, novels by B. (for Bertha) M. Bower and Zane Grey appeared, vanguarding a popular form of literary relaxation. They were soon joined by Clarence E. Mulford, William McLeod Raine, Dane Coolidge, Stewart Edward White and later Max Brand, Luke Short and others, with annual sales of Western books totaling in the millions. Many of these authors provided story material for the screen, either written directly for it, or adaptations of their literary works. *The Virginian* alone has been filmed several times, not including the long-running television series based loosely on the book and its characters.

No wonder then that *The Great Train Robbery* proved immediately popular. The title itself came from a successful stage presentation then touring the country, although the relationship between stage and screen ended there. The West was a source of interest to readers and playgoers. Now it captured the imaginations of the nickelodeon audiences. Not only was the spell of the West exciting, it was immediate. For in 1903, the West was still in part untamed. Arizona had not achieved statehood in 1903. Nor New Mexico. Nor Oklahoma. Frontiers remained to be conquered. *The Great Train Robbery* was made on the frontier of New Jersey.

As fortune would have it, the wilderness in the vicinity of Paterson served passably well. More important than the scenery and its authenticity was the fact that, in less than a quarter of an hour, a drama of absorbing simplicity unfolded, one that retains the rudiments of raw power as the passage of time nears the century mark. Bandits halt a train through a ruse, board, and proceed to rob the express car safe; the engineer is subdued, the fireman callously killed; passengers are robbed; the bandits attempt escape, and are tracked down by a hastily formed posse. This unadorned outline was to provide the backbone for not only Westerns but documentary-style contemporary crime yarns for years to come.

Porter either by accident or design had introduced a strong and logical method of telling a story with *The Great Train Robbery.* His use of visuals not only progressed the narrative but also enhanced the excitement via incident within the scene, such as the fight between bandit and fireman, culminating with the bandit braining the hapless railroad man with a lump of coal and, in an obvious but effective switch photographically from human to dummy, tossing the body from the speeding train ("forty miles an hour," attest the advertisements originally issued with the film). Legend has it that said dummy, thrown from a bridge as the train crossed the Passaic River, landed in front of an approaching street car on the road

Broncho Billy Anderson in "civvies."

William S. Hart on "Fritz" in Travelin' On *(1922).*

below, scaring hell out of the unsuspecting passengers.

By 1904, after it had been in circulation for a few months, *The Great Train Robbery* was a resounding success. In city areas it was actually the reason why theaters were opened, for the express purpose of exhibiting this phenomenal motion picture, and subsequently other motion pictures. It was shown in country, small town and rural vicinities as a traveling presentation, a sort of primitive road show. By mid-1904, the Lubin company went into competition with Edison by producing practically a carbon copy of the film, different only in minute details. The following year the Edison company made a parody, surely a singular sign of success of the original, enacted by a group of children and called *The Little Train Robbery*.

Films grew in technique and stature. Curiously, Edwin S. Porter failed to capitalize on his contribution. If anything, his filmmaking constituted a regression from *The Great Train Robbery*. Whatever his place in cinema history, Porter can be rightfully regarded as the mentor of the Western.

One attribute lacking in *The Great Train Robbery* was an identification with any of the characters. A hero, Max Aaronson, a minor actor in the film, was soon to fill that void and become the first of the breed, a full-fledged cowboy star.

Aronson, now known as G. M. Anderson, appeared in a number of short Western films thereafter, to a reception best described as indifferent. Besides, Anderson was more interested in the machinations on the other side of the camera as a producer. He formed a partnership with George K. Spoor, and Spoor and Anderson became Essanay Pictures. Essanay endured for years as a production company; among their roster of players was a young comedian formerly of the Karno troupe of the London Music Halls, and the Mack Sennett fun factory, named Charlie Chaplin. But that is another story. Perhaps equally important is the fact that Anderson, still a somewhat reluctant actor, took the leading role in a Western story based on a Peter B. Kyne tale, whose hero was named Broncho Billy. Thus was the cowboy star born.

Anderson kept a terrific pace in his output of films, grinding out one short film (one or two reels in length) per week for nearly five years. Far from a matinee idol in looks, Anderson performed with a rugged sincerity that made an immediate hit with audiences everywhere. The Broncho Billy films, while not smashing artistic achievements, were substantially well made, and those that have survived stand the test of time rather well. Perhaps of more import historically, Anderson had brought the Chicago-based Essanay outfit West to Niles, California. The Western was now where it belonged.

First the seminal film, now the cowboy hero. To detail the genesis of the silent Western would take a separate volume, with not only the players, but directors such as Griffith, DeMille, Ford and many more deserving attention. However, for purposes of continuing our saga, the progression of the Western, and the Western star, can be signified by three stalwart men; Anderson, or Broncho Billy; William S. Hart; Tom Mix. There were many others, but these three were the titans.

Broncho Billy Anderson eventually starred in feature-length films, but by that time his popularity had been superseded by a granite-jawed, steely-eyed, sentimental son of the plains—though born in Newburgh, New York, he had known the frontier—named William Surrey Hart, former legitimate stage star, now Western idol number one, through the teens into the early '20s. Anderson put Broncho Billy to rest, quietly produced some comedies (with Stan Laurel) and even more quietly faded from the cinema scene.

William S. Hart was a veteran of Shakespeare on the stage, and his most renowned role was that of Messala in *Ben-Hur,* the adaptation for the footlights of the epic Lew Wallace novel. His films for producer Thomas Ince were immediately successful and Hart became a movie star overnight. Hart represented a progression of the Anderson characterization, the strong, silent "good-bad" man, more often than not an outlaw redeemed by a woman's love, willing to sacrifice himself and his ways for the straight life. His stories, especially during the forepart of his ten-year tenure on the screen, were commendably mature, thoughtfully developed (the majority of them by C. Gardner Sullivan, an inspired silent scenarist) and brought to the screen with full appreciation of their values by directors Lambert Hillyer, Cliff Smith and most notably Hart himself. Additionally, no small contribution to his films was made by Hart's regular cameraman, the superb Joseph H. August. Hart also developed the Western further with his insistence upon realism and accuracy in Western minutiae. Of his films, the general opinion seems to be that the best is *Hell's Hinges,* or at least the best of the films he made under Ince's Triangle banner. *Hell's Hinges,* made in 1916, tells the parallel tale of the redemption of a badman (Hart) and the degradation and fall of a preacher; the narrative is still valid, and the film is a true "adult Western."

Hart's tendency toward sentiment eventually did him in. His views of manners and mores were certainly laudable, but were unavoidably dated by the time the Roaring '20s took hold. Hart maintained popularity, mixing in some change-of-pace roles with his Westerns, such as a factory worker, or policeman. But his outdoor dramas smacked of another day, a world war ago. The elders stood by him, but in the day of the flapper and the lounge lizard he was an anachronism. And he refused to update his films, despite pleading from several well-intentioned quarters. He made one last Western on his own, and it was a dilly. *Tumbleweeds* was produced in 1925 and summarily thrown away by the distributor, United Artists. Aging and disillusioned, Hart had reached trail's end. Financially comfortable, he retired to his ranch in Newhall, California to write. His last, *Tumbleweeds,* was reissued in 1939 with an added musical score adeptly enhancing the silent action. Hart appeared in a specially filmed prologue, addressing the audience in a theatrical but undeniably moving speech.

Tom Mix had entered the movies before William S. Hart and had had a life that could well have made an action-packed adventure picture, provided you were willing to believe all the exploits attributed to him. Whatever the facts about his early Army career and U.S. Marshaling days heretofore, Mix did possess an authentic aura of the Western teller of tall

ALARUM AND EXCURSION

tales. His films were everything that Hart's weren't—brash, showy, abounding with spectacular horsemanship, stunts and action. They were light on the dedication which marked Hart's efforts with distinction and, let's face it, light on intellect. But they entertained. They gave the audience their money's worth. And so the cowboy crown passed from Hart to Mix.

Although he was in the movies before Hart, Mix had labored unspectacularly for the Selig organization, sometimes directing as well as starring in his films. When he joined the Fox Film Corporation in 1917, his film career took an upswing. When the '20s blew in with a rush of frenzied activity, the Mix Western suited the times perfectly.

Mix was duly coronated and proceeded to live like the King of the Westerns. His films literally kept Fox solvent through the period. The magnificent Mix steed, Tony, approached his master in popularity, at least in the area of fan mail (just as Hart's pony Fritz had been adored). Humorist Will Rogers made a short comedy, *Uncensored Movies,* a portion of which kidded the Mix Westerns unmercifully. But Will and Tom were old friends, and besides, the Mix films were really produced with care and effort; directors such as Emmett Flynn, John Ford and Lynn

Mix-ing it up in Hands Off *(1921).*

Reynolds well knew what a Mix Western should contain and saw to it that the proper ingredients were in place. Scenic values were top-notch, with often breathtaking locations excellently photographed by Ben Kline and Frank B. Good in the early Fox days, then Dan Clark on a steady basis.

Mix stepped out of his element once to play Dick Turpin, the English highwayman. Critics liked the picture but the Mix multitudes didn't. Actually, the film was the usual formula of fights and chases in a different setting, but his fans would have none of it. Thereafter, Mix stayed West where he belonged.

As has been said, there were others, many others. Gibson, Jones, Bell, Custer, McCoy, Hoxie, Maynard, all made it to the sound era with varying degrees of success, and will be dealt with later. Mix himself did talkies, also of later concern. William Farnum and William Desmond, William Duncan and William Russell—some continued their careers in the talkies in the character vein. Art Acord, a tremendous favorite in the '20s, was out of things completely before they were through. They said his voice didn't register, but there were further complications. Fred Thomson might well have been the greatest of them all had he lived to talk. Harry Carey, Steele and Tyler, Wally Wales, Bill Cody, Buddy Roosevelt, Buffalo Bill, Jr., Jack Perrin, Edmund Cobb, Yakima Canutt... all lasted into the talkies, although some of them forsook heroics and began to thwart the law. Ted Wells, Fred Humes, Jack Padjeon, Don Coleman, Leo Maloney....

Leo Maloney. Back where we started. Maloney was a film veteran, a stocky, down-to-earth actor whose Westerns were like his physique—hardly streamlined but easy to take. He served as his own director, and directed others as well (Don Coleman).

Fred Thomson and "Silver King."

ALARUM AND EXCURSION

Leo Maloney (center) embarking on his Overland Bound *tour. At his left stands cutter and future director Joe Kane (in pinstripe suit and cap).*

He stayed astride his horse with alacrity but, as the saying goes, tended to fall off the wagon. Homerically. But this periodic encountering of *spiritus fermenti* had little outward effect upon his capacity to make a picture. His Westerns had been a staple of the Pathé distributing organization until 1929 when, as recounted, Maloney set out to film *Overland Bound*.

It was deemed to be a good Western with a rather noticeable drawback. The sound was lousy. Apparently Maloney had been forced to use bootleg equipment, and the results, while audible, were definitely not up to snuff. But at that, the recording was not too much worse than the norm for those early days of sound. The people in New York who took a look at *Overland Bound* liked it. It received a nice trade review from *Harrison's Reports,* and it was duly noted that it was the second all-talking Western on the market. Presidio Pictures put it into release on the indie circuit. Hot on its heels in the all-talkie Western derby came Paramount's first sound version of *The Virginian,* with Gary Cooper. But *Overland Bound* was first in one respect. It was the talkie era's initial low-budget cowboy movie, a genus soon to brighten many a day at the Saturday matinee for the kiddies, and quite a few adult evening performances too.

Leo Maloney didn't live to see it happen.

Flushed with victory, he celebrated, and celebrated mightily. The demands were too much for his heart. At the age of 41, on November 2, 1929, Leo Maloney lay dead at the Astor Hotel.

This is where our story begins.

Ken Maynard

2
THE BIG GUNS SPEAK:
GIBSON, MAYNARD, MIX

"Daddy dear, won't you step over here and say a few words to your many fans?"

Tanned brow furrowed, dark eyes cast apprehensively at the old-fashioned microphone dangling with grim menace at his face, Tom Mix seemed to speak from the heart:

"Aw, Ruthie honey, you know I never wuz much for talkin', and besides, that thing scares me...."

The above paraphrase occurred in an early talkie short, part of a series called The Voice of Hollywood (broadcasting over station S-T-A-R), released by Tiffany Pictures. Most of the entries in this series were sure bets to inflict ten minutes of ennui upon an unsuspecting audience, featuring as they did mainly second-rank and less members of the Hollywood troops. Also, the dialogue given these performers to complement their Screen Snapshottish gambols was puerile enough to cause great regret at the coming of sound to the movies. But this particular clip denoted not only realism, but cause and effect. Ruth Mix, herself an accomplished equestrienne, was introducing her more famous father to the talking-picture world, and Tom wasn't liking it a bit. Nor did his emotions appear prepared; if he was acting a part, he should have been the recipient of one of the early Academy Awards.

Mix had been absent from the screen for over a year. After leaving the Fox studios in 1928, he had made a series of Westerns for FBO. But the Western was in a decline, Mix failed to receive the plush Fox production values, and more than one film critic had been so impolitic as to suggest that the bloom was off the sage. Thenceforth Mix had confined his talents to the circus, and personal appearances.

Eventually, as will be related, Mix would return to films, and talk. But his initial sentiments in all probability reflected the attitudes of most cowboy actors. The public indicated that it preferred the sound of crooning thespians to mooing cattle. Gunshots all sounded alike. As for diction, the only acceptable dialect was English legit. *Howdy, pardner, thataway* and *ma'am* were uncouth.

Alone of the major studios, Universal decided to take a chance on the production of sound series Westerns. An amazingly prolific supplier of silent releases to theaters comfortable with outdoor and action dramas, most of their stable of cowboy heroes had been gently cast adrift by the end of 1929. Remaining was their ace in the saddle, Edmund (Hoot) Gibson, a long-time contractee and, during the golden days, runner-up in popularity to the great Mix in the Western sweepstakes. To complement their schedule, Universal acquired the services of Ken Maynard, fresh from a meritorious series for First National, one whose quality had catapulted him from a relatively unknown cowboy lead in the independents to a top contender for honors in the Western polls, all in a few short years. Now that Mix was off the screen and the rest of the posse far in the background, Universal in 1930 could be said to possess the best, and only, one-two punch in Westerns.

Parenthetically, Universal would see nearly every

HOLLYWOOD CORRAL: A COMPREHENSIVE B WESTERN ROUNDUP

Hoot Gibson restrains Sally Eilers in Trigger Tricks *(1930).*

Hoot resists getting a tooth pulled in Sunset Range *(1935).*

important Western name on the lot at one time or another during the ensuing five years. Gibson, Maynard, Mix, Jones, McCoy. Rex Bell. Tom Tyler. John Wayne and the post-sound era heroes would come later. Only Bob Steele in his heyday failed to appear under the Universal banner, and Steele was obviously far too busy at the time to lend himself out.

But Gibson and Maynard started the drive. At first, their films were cautiously part-talking, with dialogue—and perhaps as important, cowboy musical interludes—used tentatively. By mid-1930, the films of both stars were all-talking. Each used sound according to his particular needs, for no two cowboy actors could be more dissimilar than Hoot Gibson and Ken Maynard.

Both had had working knowledge of the milieu before their entrance into the motion-picture game, both were superb horsemen, both were showmen. There the parallel ends.

Hoot Gibson was a genially homely man who looked like the hired hand; the reliable neighbor; the funniest man in the weekly poker game; or a combination of all three. Sartorially, the Hooter was probably the sloppiest hero ever to adorn the Western screen. One always suspected his shirttail would be hanging out in back, and his attire would often be a masterpiece of nondescript general store goods. Once or twice, as in *Trailin' Trouble* (1930), he would be seen in a business suit and the pleasing effect would give away the modernity behind the rube façade. But for the most part, Hoot was just folks, which is one of the reasons why he remained so popular over the years. The theater audience cottoned to him, because he was one of them. Not a fancy Hollywood movie actor, rather a workin' man who might well be enjoying himself along with the rest of the Saturday-night crowd. Which is why he was a favorite with the elders, as much if not more than he was with the kids.

Another reason for Gibson's popularity was that he had hit upon the right formula, one that suited him and sustained him through the '20s. His films contained as much comedy as action; not infrequently, the humorous moments superseded the exciting ones. It didn't hurt his films, because Gibson had the comedy approach and timing of a master. Not only his mobile face, but his chunky, seemingly awkward body could play for and obtain laughs. Gibson's attitude toward action was reflected in the way he would wear his gun, if at all—shoved carelessly down into his belt, without a holster, or else stuck in his boot.

Not that Gibson would eschew the action elements, nor was he incapable of participating. Quite the contrary. An early effort, *Dead Game* (Edward Sedgwick, 1923), contains a sequence wherein Gibson, left in the desert to expire, suddenly spies a solitary untamed horse, whose capture would constitute his only means of reaching civilization, and safety. The whole conception of the sequence, as horse and potential rider eye each other; the stealthy approach; the mount; the wild ride as the desperate cowboy attempts to break the spirit of the beast, is so carefully planned, shot and cut, as well as performed by Gibson, it remains a gem of suspense and excitement.

But Gibson felt at home with the lighter facets of Western plotting, and thus played variations on the happy-go-lucky cowpoke who would usually land in the middle of trouble not by his own design but by sheer accident, and when pressed, would overcome the trouble by some ingenious means. From the standpoint of the audience, a good time would be had by all, and the faces leaving the auditorium at the conclusion of the performance would be smiling.

In his first starring role, the independently made *$50,000 Reward* (Clifford S. Elfelt, 1924), Ken

Gibson and canine companion.

Maynard is introduced in the midst of a whopping brawl, bouncing adversaries off the walls like so many rubber balls. It set the pattern for his career, with action from the outset. His First National series, under the guidance of Harry Joe Brown, stressed action, staged it on a lavish scale, and ably represented the ancient simile, "more fun than a circus." There was literally something going on every minute, and it was all done with a technical know-how and a flair peculiar to the silent film.

When sound came in, Maynard was still youthful in appearance, and a handsome devil to boot. He had Indian-straight black hair, piercing eyes, and clearcut, almost collegiate features. His figure was trim in those days before the extra suet was gained, and his range regalia fancy but stopping somewhere short of the ostentatious—a bit later, one would remember That Shirt Design, with the arrows pointing in both directions forming breast pockets, but Maynard wore everything well, including a cavalry uniform. He had this magnificent horse, Tarzan, a haughty palomino, which he rode in the manner royal, adding those little extra flourishes and hand-signals—not show-offy, mind you, but with an air that told us life was one big adventure and if you were on the right side you'd overcome all the bad guys and get the girl (in those medieval times, getting the girl meant just that—no youngster would ponder over just exactly what one would do with her after she'd been gotten). However, the Maynard films were so well done that any lack of realism was gladly overlooked.

When Maynard moved to Universal, he brought several key members of his production team with him, including supervisor, often director Brown; his frequent scenarist Marion Jackson; and photographer Ted McCord. Likewise, the credits of the Hoot Gibson talkies contained associates of long standing with the star; directors Breezy Eason and Art Rosson, both of whom contributed to the scripts, and photographer Harry Neumann.

Sound presented no outward problems for either

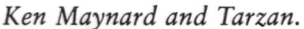

Ken Maynard and Tarzan.

THE BIG GUNS SPEAK: Gibson, Maynard, Mix

star, for their voices registered well on the imperfect, often outrageously discriminatory early recording equipment. Gibson's voice fit the physical rest of him: twangy, pleasingly resonant, able to deliver bantering dialogue expertly. As it developed, his talkie Westerns differed from his silents only in the addition of sound. Stories, approach and pacing displayed the same Gibson as before, and since his films tended to move in leisurely fashion anyway, the slowdown demanded by the pioneer talkies did not interfere with the Gibson effectiveness to any great extent. In two of his six 1930 releases, *Roarin' Ranch* and *Trigger Tricks*, starlet Sally Eilers was his leading lady and soon assumed the role in real life, meaning not much to the films themselves but providing happy paragraphs for the fan magazines of the day.

Meanwhile, Maynard had to adjust somewhat more drastically to the necessities of sound. While his vocal tones were perfectly adequate, his dialogue delivery was another matter. Maynard clipped out his phrases in pinched, squirty little spasms, and it wasn't at all certain that what he was saying was what had been written in the script. Call it ad libbing or whatever, it would often result in some odd stretches of conversation, although it did work well for purposes of an awkward romantic interlude, when Ken would fumble verbally in the presence of an attractive belle of the prairie. Throughout the remainder of his career, he never managed to come to grips with this facet of play-acting, and during the early stages, when critical eyes were contemplating the future of the sound Western, it certainly must have done him ill.

One definite Maynard contribution to the fortunes of the Western while at Universal was the introduction of, and emphasis upon, songs and range ditties. Of his eight 1929–30 season Universals, five of them were only part-talkie. The remaining trio, *Mountain Justice, Song of the Caballero* and *Sons of the Saddle,* contained a goodly amount of musical and vocalistic material during their all-talking lengths. Maynard himself joined in the caroling, even though he deprecated his singing abilities—which was entirely correct, for while his vocalizing may have been authentic, it was a strain on the ear. The era of the Singing Cowboy was several years away, but from an historical standpoint it was Ken Maynard who spawned the breed.

Otherwise, the Universal Maynards tried to capture the sense of sweep and excitement embellished in the First Nationals, although the bugaboo of sound prevented reaching the same high plateau of quality. Nevertheless, the Maynard unit had nothing of which to be ashamed, nor did the Gibson outfit. But 1930 was far from over when Carl Laemmle, head of the studio, abetted by offspring Carl, Jr., and plagued by diminishing profits brought on by the financial depression, made the fateful decision. Westerns were a risk, an unsure gamble. The studio that had once had more galloping hoofs going than any other company would now discontinue cowboy pictures completely. The contracts of Hoot Gibson and Ken Maynard were not renewed.

For Gibson it was an especially tough blow. He had been with Universal for over 13 years, had literally grown with the studio. He had been happy there, working conditions had been to his liking, and he had nurtured and perfected a screen characterization that was both comfortable and highly profitable. Now he was forced by prevailing conditions to adjust elsewhere. It would not be easy.

No attractive overtures came from the major studios. An offer did come from independent producer M. H. Hoffman, but its attractiveness was a matter of judgment. The money didn't approach the Universal days, and the allotments for the films themselves were far from the budgets of yore. But at least it would mean, back in the saddle. Gibson accepted, and over the next three years starred in a total of 11 Westerns under the banner of Allied pictures, released on a states' rights basis.

Hoffman was in the usual independent fix, with multitudinous problems revolving around time, money and wherewithal. For all that, he managed to produce some minor but respectable features, and the Gibsons were no exception. Sally Eilers played opposite him in the initial entry, *Clearing the Range*, made available in 1931; her fortunes would shortly ascend with a Fox contract, a film entitled *Bad Girl*, and instant stardom, just as Hoot's were on the downgrade. Needless to say, their brief marriage was on the rocks. The series inaugural was directed by the capable Otto Brower and sufficed as a fairly good beginning, even if the general level of production was not on a par with Universal.

Hoot's followup film was *Wild Horse*, which plainly shows how new conditions can cause pitfalls. While at Universal, Gibson was wisely steered clear of heavily dramatic situations and dialogue by Eason, Rosson and contributing scenario writers. On *Wild Horse*, Richard Thorpe and Sidney Algier shared directorial credit, and one or the other unknowingly was responsible for a brief bit that called for a delivery that Gibson was simply incapable of responding to convincingly.

HOLLYWOOD CORRAL: A COMPREHENSIVE B WESTERN ROUNDUP

As indicated in Jack Natteford's script, a minion of the law, played by Jack Rockwell, would be discovered by Gibson prone on the prairie, mortally wounded and gasping his last breaths. Their exchange of dialogue was meant to be simple and succinct, culminated by the expiration of Rockwell. It didn't get far before Gibson let it slip completely out of hand.

Gasps Rockwell, anent his wound: "Is... it bad?"

"Yeah, pretty bad," replies Hoot, the way he would say, "You gotta pretty bad hangnail there, pardner." Mix, Jones, McCoy, even Ken Maynard could have done it with the proper solemnity, even perhaps with dignity. Old Hooter just couldn't get too dramatic, and since the scene occurred fairly early in the film, it just never got back on an even track.

With his next, *Hard Hombre,* Gibson re-acquired the photographic talents of Harry Neumann (the preceding two had been photographed by Ernest Miller), Otto Brower returned to direct, and a pleasant general pattern formulated for the remainder of the Hoffman series, very much akin to the Gibson Westerns of the Universal days, minus the higher budgets and the extra polish that separates the superior product from the merely good. In this one he

Gibson clowning between takes.

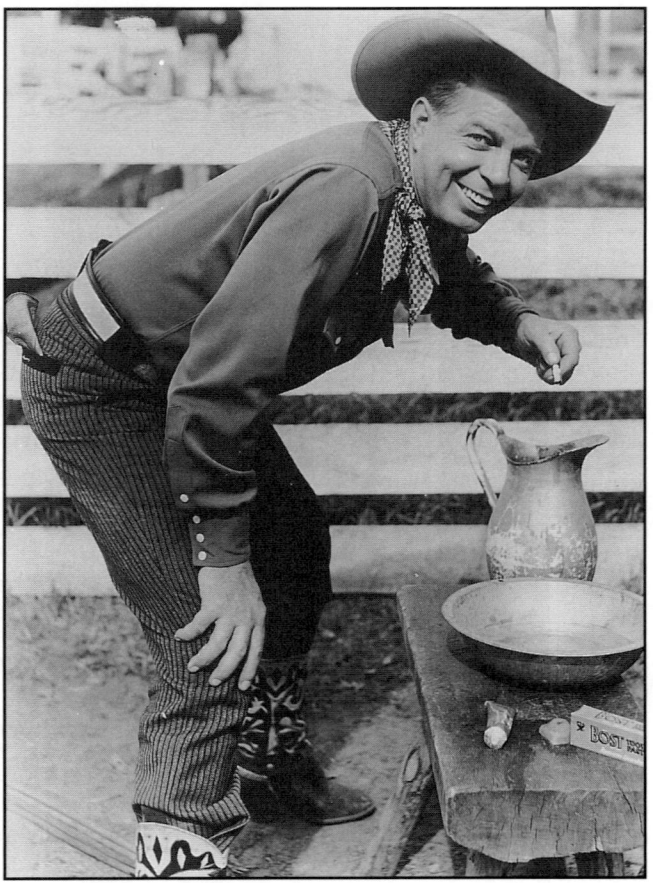

proves a cowboy's best friend is his mother, by coming to her aid in times of need. The features that followed were constructed around typical Gibson plot elements.

In *The Boiling Point* (George Melford, 1932), he has to hold his temper in check and stay out of trouble to win a bet. In *Dude Bandit* (Melford, 1933) he saves a ranch in his own inimitable way. In *The Fighting Parson* (Harry Fraser, 1933) he is mistaken for a clergyman, with appropriate mistaken-identity escapades. As before, the lighter side was stressed, while action sequences were downplayed. Along the way, Gibson had used one "Skeeter" Bill Robbins, a lanky waddy, as what passed for comedy relief, which was strange because if ever a cowboy star didn't need comedy relief it was Gibson. Robbins died in 1933, the year of Gibson's termination of association with Hoffman and Allied.

The finalities were hardly amicable. Reportedly, Gibson had been offered an opportunity to return to the Universal fold. From Hoot's standpoint, the move would be entirely understandable, considering his long and happy tenure there, while Hoffman had given him, if usually adequate vehicles, a lack of the niceties he was used to at the larger studio. On Hoffman's side there is the undeniable fact that he had Gibson under contract legally, and was loath to let him go. When the dust had settled, Universal was without the services of Hoot Gibson (but with the services of Ken Maynard), while Gibson was tied up in legal red tape and as a result off the screen for over a year.

By the time Hoot had shed himself of the contractual boundaries, Allied was no more, Hoffman having changed the trademark to Liberty Pictures, and no longer associated with any Western series. Gibson did appear in two RKO Westerns, but not as the solo star. *Powdersmoke Range* was a gilt-edged oddity from a sagebrush box office view, with just about every cowboy player otherwise not engaged in the cast. *The Last Outlaw* was a Harry Carey vehicle with Hoot relegated to a relatively minor supporting role, although he was billed second—ahead of veteran hero Tom Tyler, by the way. Concurrently with these two, Gibson starred in eight final Westerns. They represented a sad and evident decline from his Allied set, and a gloomy reminder that popularity wanes swiftly enough with the ordinary passage of time, and even faster when a performer has been away from the public eye for any great length of time.

After *Sunset Range* and *Rainbow's End,* both in 1935, and both slightly better-than-fair entries in

THE BIG GUNS SPEAK: Gibson, Maynard, Mix

Gibson, Henry B. Walthall and Harry Carey in The Last Outlaw *(1936).*

what was becoming a glutted Western market, the Gibson films ran into snags stemming mainly from an absence of the tried and true Gibson elements—namely, light comedy and the facility for not taking anything in the plot too seriously. Production values (they were made by Walter Futter's Diversion Pictures) were considerably lower than those provided by Hoffman of Allied, and the technical crew would change often, including some directors (Robert McGowan, Ray McCarey) and cameramen (Gil Warrenton, Paul Ivano) unaccustomed to the peculiarities of the horse opera. Sometimes, the ambition of the script writer would be thwarted by the unavailability of funds to execute his work (*Cavalcade of the West,* 1936); at others, plot and execution would be all too familiar (*Swifty,* 1935). But primarily, it would be Gibson operating in a milieu not his own, and trying his best to overcome obstacles over which he had no control. There were a few compensations. In *The Riding Avenger* (Harry Fraser, 1936), Hoot initiates a chase (with himself as the quarry) in a Buster Keaton-like way, starting with furtive walk, graduating to brisk canter, finally to all-out running flight. But these moments were all too few. In 1937, Gibson was featured in a Republic serial, *The Painted Stallion*; but his role was a passive one, and the chapterplay belonged to Ray

"Crash" Corrigan, in both the amount of screen time and dominance of the action. Thereafter, Gibson's name was but a memory, and it was that only to veteran Western fans. Soon there would be a new generation, a few of whom would vaguely know his name from legend, and many more who would know him not at all. Once, briefly, it was announced that he would return in a series based on the Hashknife Hartley tales of W. C. Tuttle, and he would have been ideal for those humorous outdoor yarns. But it came to naught.

If Gibson's output was restricted during the early '30s, then Ken Maynard unleashed a veritable flood of releases after he left Universal. Breaking it down to bare statistics, Maynard starred in 11 Tiffany Westerns (like Hoot, he had trouble achieving that round dozen); then eight for World Wide release; eight more upon his return to Universal; a serial and a feature for Mascot; another set of eight for Columbia; four for Grand National, culminating in a series of four for the independent Colony Pictures in 1939–40. In all, Maynard was on the screen twice as much as was Gibson.

While Gibson made do with his free-and-easy formula, usually centering around mistaken identity (Hoot posing as a bandit; a lawyer; a parson), Maynard lost an important part of his cowboy-story

HOLLYWOOD CORRAL: A COMPREHENSIVE B WESTERN ROUNDUP

equipment when he departed Universal at the end of his 1930 schedule. The Maynard productions, both the First National silents and the Universals, featured showmanship, sweep, and a superior saddle star. When Ken signed on with Tiffany, he was still well up to his saddle tricks, but the other two facets were sacrificed to the budget department.

Tiffany was an independent company, but they had been making noises like one of the majors since sound. They had some fairly impressive names on their roster, on both sides of the camera, and when Maynard was acquired it gave them a bona fide Western star of proven ability—and the Tiffany production minds were not so fearful of the Western's demise, as were the Universal Laemmles. The Maynard films, made under the banner of Tiffany, were reissued by Amity Pictures in 1934. Phil Goldstone was in charge of production.

Compared to the other independently made Westerns around at the same time, the Tiffany Maynard series rated quite favorably. They contained none of the howlers abundant in the inept bottom-rung product. The scripts were serviceable, if hardly exploratory in content. Supporting casts were generally well-chosen, with attractive and familiar feminine leads and hissable villainy, making much use of that sterling rascal, Charles King. The veteran Phil Rosen directed the majority of the films, unspectacularly but efficiently, with Breezy Eason, William Nigh and Forrest Sheldon chipping in occasionally. Maynard himself, in his mid-thirties, was still agile, personable, and very much the convincing heroic type, performing in a manner to keep his screen image untarnished.

But the production values were not there, as with First National and Universal. The sets looked economical, and while Maynard's other films probably had a watchful eye on the budget, at least it wasn't obvious. Another place the budgetary lack showed was in the paucity of dress extras, and the stories to accommodate them. Plenty of interior shooting, with two and three participants; crowd scenes were taboo. Instead of a mass Indian attack, as in the silent *The Red Raiders* of a few years ago, the big climax at Tiffany would be a set-to between Ken and King, satisfying in its own way, but vastly different in scope.

Nor would the fisticuffs be in the true realm of realism. Maynard always handled his dukes with more energy than skill, attacking his adversary with flailing arms and roundhouse rights and lefts. One would harbor the suspicion that his opponent, King or whomever, would be as much whisked away by the resulting eddies of air currents stirred up by the human windmilling of Maynard than from any solidly landing punches. At least Ken swung mightily, with none of the girlishness afflicting many of his battling contemporaries.

On the technical side, Maynard had been fortunate in having some fine photographers heretofore, notably the great Ted McCord. Chief cameraman on the initial Tiffanys was Arthur Reed, no stranger to the Western field, having done some of the M-G-M Tim McCoys, among others. But Reed was prone to photograph all the action scenes at silent speed, fistfights and riding sequences alike, and this would detract considerably from the credibility. Reed was not alone in this peculiarity. Too many cameramen, or directors, or both, mistakenly believed the speeding up of the action would increase excitement, when all it did was to give the impression of a lot of skittering waterbugs doing a Mack Sennett routine. Nevertheless, they persisted, and many an otherwise valid action scene would be marred in many a Western movie for many years to come, right up through the '40s.

Maynard's Tiffanys were also deficient in picturesque locales, another mainstay of his previous work. Few if any grand vistas with the often breathtakingly beautiful cloud formations were in evidence. Instead, Ken would often be seen galloping off along some flat, gray back-lot road, where probably stands today some urban housing project or other. Despite the lack of scenics, Ken's horsemanship lost none of its crowd-pleasing dash—an elegant leap into the saddle and Tarzan would be off at top speed (alas, the skittering silent speed of Reed), with Ken frequently giving a slight wave of salute in flight, not so much to the performers in the scene but to his spellbound audience sitting, enthralled in movie houses throughout the world. It was in the grand manner, and it was something he never lost.

If one were to select a typical Tiffany, not the best or worst, but near the general average, *Range Law* (Phil Rosen, 1931) might be it. Earle Snell wrote it and broke no new ground, but all the customary ingredients were in place properly, including hero (Ken), villains (Frank Mayo and the redoubtable Charlie King), girl (Frances Dade, fresh from her triumph as a victim of Count Dracula at Universal), and lovable comedy relief (in the somewhat surprising presence of Lafe McKee, an ageless codger usually more at home playing fathers and kindly sheriffs). In classic tradition, sides of good and evil were set up; hero Ken was unjustly accused of a crime and imprisoned, only to escape with the help of McKee, improbably dressed in drag for the sequence and sporting a below the border accent; leading up to the final confrontation, climaxed by a brawl wherein Ken and King wreck a lot of furniture. Happy fadeout, with a clinch between Maynard and Dade. An average Maynard, better than some (the preceding *Arizona Terror* and the ensuing *Branded Men*), not so good as others (*Alias—the Bad Man*), and sufficient to maintain his boxoffice popularity without materially adding to it, or bolstering the cause of Westerns to any extent.

By the time Maynard #11 was due, Tiffany was foundering on the rocks of the Great Depression, shortly to go under for good. *Hell-Fire Austin* (Forrest Sheldon, 1932) received a bit more production than the previous Maynards, including a climactic rally that hinted at, if not quite equalled, his films of yore. Other encouraging developments were some supporting players not normally found in prairie sagas, like Nat Pendleton and Alan Roscoe, and the return of Ted McCord behind the cameras. Without breaking stride, Maynard moved from Tiffany to World Wide for release. After two seasons at Tiffany, he spent only one season, 1932–33, in his new stamping grounds. World Wide was also shaky, and was to become a victim of the bad times by mid-1933. But while there, Maynard and his films regained form. Gone was the tentativeness marring the Tiffany product. Productions were still on the economical side, but were exceptionally well-knit in story and presentation. Maynard evidently had more to say about what went into his films than before, and he found a director who worked well with him, Alan James. As Alvin J. Neitz, director James had been active steering many a second-echelon cowboy star through the paces in the silent days. With a simplification of cognomen came a distillation of talent. James directed five of the World Wide May-

Maynard romances Ruth Hall as skeptical Wallace MacDonald watches in Between Fighting Men *(1932).*

nard octet, and directed admirably. *Come On, Tarzan* and *Fargo Express* (both 1932) had almost continuious action of a liveliness not found in Maynard's Tiffany product, while *Tombstone Canyon* (1932) had one of those gimmicks dear to the palpitating hearts of all youngsters, a mysterious, dark-cloaked villain, standard equipment in serials but not often found in range fare. In addition to the good work by James, a different angle using the Boy Scouts was deftly directed by J. P. McGowan in *Drum Taps* (1933), which also had a small role for Ken's brother Kermit Maynard, of whom more later. Jack Young photographed the latter entry in fine fashion, with McCord and Jackson Rose sharing credits on the rest of the series.

Ken's leading ladies were again well-chosen, since they included such as Helen Mack (*Fargo Express*), Ruth Hall (*Dynamite Ranch* and *Between Fighting Men*; a former Eddie Cantor ingenue, she married top cameraman Lee Garmes and retired from the screen, too soon), and the very young Cecilia Parker (*Tombstone Canyon*). In all, the World Wide series sent Maynard on the upswing.

So much so, in fact, that Ken must have felt he'd achieved an ironic victory of sorts, when he was resigned by Universal for the 1933–34 season. Not only that, but the studio which had ungraciously set him adrift because they had no faith in the future of the Western was now offering him not only starring vehicles at increased budgets, but also his own production unit. The World Wide deal had worked out well, but was nothing compared to the present setup. Always in contention for number one Western star, Maynard looked a sure bet to solidify the position before the season was over.

It is the Ken Maynard of Universal, 1933–34, most vividly and fondly remembered by veteran cowboy-watchers. Of his sound films, they were the most elaborate, for he made a decided effort to return to the grand manner of his First National days. If the plots were on the outlandish side, and at times bizarre in the extreme, and the action situations would often tax the credibilities, then the overall effect would nevertheless be one of intense enjoyment. Where the World Wides were tightly constructed, the Maynard productions for Universal were not loosened, but broadened. It was back to the circus showmanship.

As if to underline this, the first Universal release, *King of the Arena,* had a circus background—Ken's pre-movie career had been involved with circus life, and he apparently liked the atmosphere. *Arena* also had a fast pace, and a goofy plot concerning smug-

gling, a particularly nasty type of new-fangled bullet causing a grim sort of demise, and a couple of outrageously skulking meanies in Michael Visaroff and Bob Kortman, playing it Russian-style. Curiously, Kortman was the more believable of the two. The opener seemed to set the pattern for the series, to wit: Ken may not be the most realistic cowboy, but he's sure lots of fun... as it was before.

Fiddlin' Buckaroo was released second but might well have been made first. Maynard directed it himself and it was not good. Once more, Ken was starting to use songs in his films. They had been notably, and happily, absent from his previous series. Thereafter, Alan James handled directorial chores on the Universal Maynards, with Ted McCord contributing his customary expert photography.

Most popular of the Maynards at the time was *Strawberry Roan* (1933), which had an identifiable title (and song) to help it, and excellent wild-horse shots to sustain its length. Both *Trail Drive* (1933) and *Wheels of Destiny* (1934) had the epic sweep of the silent days—the titles are self-explanatory—and undoubtedly were the best-looking Westerns, dollar for dollar, seen around in a long time. As for Maynard, he seemed to be enjoying his free production reins, and while his acting was still hogtied he knew his limitations and performed smartly within his own limited range. Toward the end of the series he started to display a slight paunch but was otherwise a seemingly good risk for the romantic aspirations of his feminine leads.

Maynard's last Universal release was entitled *Smoking Guns* (1934), and his contract was not renewed. There's been a lot of criticism of *Smoking Guns* and most of it is justified. The plot would have one believe that Maynard could pose as Walter Miller and return to Miller's home town without anyone the wiser. There are other involvements, but this is the main stumbling block, since in the early scenes between the two actors, they resemble each other not at all. But the feeling persists that this morsel could have been made palatable if Maynard had only essayed both roles, since the Miller character is conveniently eliminated before the second reel is through. Ken could have saved some budget money by doing this, too. But maybe Miller needed the job, or Ken was too preoccupied to take on extra acting burdens. Anyway, it was his last under the contract, so if Uncle Carl didn't like it....

Reportedly, Maynard was not happy with his series of eight for Universal. Be that as it may, the series had been well received, and his reputation was higher than it had been at any time during the sound

THE BIG GUNS SPEAK: Gibson, Maynard, Mix

Maynard beats Walter Miller (r.) to the draw in Gun Justice *(1934).*

era. Unfortunately, he had not only lost a series but a production unit, so his brief tenure at Mascot must not have been pleasant for either Maynard or his co-workers. To put it succinctly, Ken had always been known to be able to lift one with the best of them, and the sauce along with the rest of the indignities, real or imagined, was becoming apparent.

As it happened, *In Old Santa Fe* (1934), although received as "just" another Ken Maynard Western by the reviewers, was given generally favorable notices. It's an interesting film, not so much for what it is, but for what it foreshadowed. A modern story with a dude-ranch setting, it had the usual Mascot penchant for using established familiar players in supporting roles, in this instance Evalyn Knapp and H. B. Warner, and executive Nat Levine's cautious use of a tight budget, getting the most for the least. It also had a young radio yodeler named Gene Autry, his chubby sidekick named Smiley Burnette, and a character actor named George Hayes appearing in his umpteenth horse opera. All would be heard from in the future, in Autry's case emphasis on "heard." David Howard directed smartly. Maynard was also inveigled into Mascot's specialty, a 12-chapter serial, *Mystery Mountain* (Otto Brower & Breezy Eason, 1934), which vitiated much of the class reputation Maynard had acquired previously—serials were no longer the drawing cards they once were and were considered strictly for the kiddies. An appearance in them was tantamount to several steps downward on the prestige scale.

Downward it was. Maynard landed a series for Columbia release, 1935–36, but the series was produced by Larry Darmour independently, with all the indie rough edges rapidly becoming prevalent in contrast to the smoothly functioning major studio product. *Western Frontier* (Al Herman, 1935) gave Ken a chance to make a little music, and perform some rope tricks as part of a medicine show. It also had the attribute of a better-than-usual role for Nora Lane as a baddie. But whatever was good about the first of the series soon settled into a routine trench,

HOLLYWOOD CORRAL: A COMPREHENSIVE B WESTERN ROUNDUP

Ken rescues Fay McKenzie from Charlie King in Death Rides the Range *(1940).*

or, as with *Western Courage* (Spencer Bennet, 1935), third in the set, a tedious attempt to modernize Maynard and to devote all too much footage to his vocalizing. It substituted attempted lightness for action, and although he had a good grasp of comedy values, Maynard could easily become slightly ridiculous when called upon to be kittenish. He was also inclined to laugh at alleged jokes rather too emphatically, snapping his head away from the actors and guffawing, almost as if he were imitating Tarzan after a lump of sugar. The remaining half-dozen for Columbia were adherants to the strict Western formula. There was enough movement to get by, but they were indistinguishable from the myriad of Western product emanating from the other producers—and not so good as some.

Off the screen for nearly a year while touring with a circus, Maynard returned for Grand National in 1937 in *Boots of Destiny* and *Trailin' Trouble*. Both were produced by M. H. Hoffman, who had done the Gibson series several years before, both were directed by Arthur Rosson, Gibson's former director and more recently an aide to Ben Hecht and Charles MacArthur at their Astoria, New York headquarters, and to Cecil B. DeMille in Hollywood. Both represented a further decline for Maynard, being deficient in content and performance. Hoffman died, and two additional Maynards for Grand National were produced by Max and Arthur Alexander. *Whirlwind Horseman* (Robert Hill, 1938) and *Six Shootin' Sheriff* (Harry Fraser, 1938) were rush jobs filmed in a few days, and looked it. The Alexanders, for their Colony Pictures, produced four more with Maynard, releasing them territorially on a states' rights basis. *Flaming Lead* (Sam Newfield, 1939) was a slight improvement over the previous pair, with Maynard again performing his lariat tricks in the opening sequence. But *Death Rides the Range* (Newfield, 1940) was one of those early World War II yarns that attempted to plant foreign agents on the prairie, with even less effective results than customary. The film is notable otherwise for the absolute running amok of Charlie King as one of the baddies; King waylays every actor in sight at about the three-quarter mark, becoming a one-man blitzkreig and taking the action honors away from Ken completely, if indeed there were any honors to take. Maynard's finale for Colony had him doing a semi-Lone Ranger act equipped with domino mask and all, but the pennies for budget showed all over the screen and Ken was putting on weight rapidly; he was fast approaching middle age, spread and all. Newcomers on the range had approached and passed him by, as they had other cowboy heroes from the silent days. A lengthy and active film career seemed about to be terminated, just as it had happened to Hoot Gibson.

After Gibson and Maynard had departed Universal in 1930, the studio made no series Westerns the following year. When it became apparent that the death of the Western, like Mark Twain's, had been greatly exaggerated, Carl Laemmle and son, the latter in charge of production at the studio, set out to recapture the outdoor audience they had ignored. What better way than to hasten the return of the Greatest Cowboy Star of Them All?

Tom Mix was apprehensive about the rigorous demands of the microphone, but he had been out of films for three years and his popularity had been on the wane even during the last films at Fox and the brief series for FBO. True, the Mix magic was still imbued in the name, and the personal apearances had kept the legend alive. But the only way to reach a movie audience was to make movies, and it was about time Tom took to the saddle with Tony again. Universal made him an offer, and he didn't refuse.

During 1932–33, Tom Mix starred in nine Universal Westerns. Taken as a whole, it was a good series. Indeed, very good, comparatively speaking. Critics reviewed them who ordinarily wouldn't bother to take up space with Westerns, and reviewed them favorably. Technically, the productions were fine. Mix evidently didn't take any active part in the operations behind the cameras, but he did manage to land his longtime photographer, Daniel B. Clark, on loan from Fox. Clark was an expert, so the scenics and lighting in the Universal Mixes were first-rate. His supporting players were notches above the Western norm and the stories allotted him were sturdy. All the experience and skill that had gone into the making of a cowboy star at Fox and a world figure of the silver screen were again put to use. And yet, from a distance of years, it might be difficult to explain, from the evidence presented, just what it was that had made Mix so famous and loved.

It has been said that Mix had throat trouble and was incapable of speaking too long and too often, but this seems part of the sweeping corn field of press agentry that had sprouted around Mix, covering his birthplace, questionable early adventures and sundry other dubious aspects of his screen personality. In any case, some place the blame on his voice, that it diminished his effectiveness as a talkie performer. More to the point, the Mix voice was perfectly adequate and he delivered his lines well, with force and a nice sense of humor. The only trouble with his voice was that it was a 50-year-old voice, and one which reflected every minute of those 50 years. Underneath the cowboy duds was a scarred body that had lived fast and hard, weathered many injuries, endured a lifetime of knocks, bumps, jolts, thuds and crashes. Cloth covered the scars, leather salved the wounds, but it all came out in the vocal timbre. Makeup couldn't disguise it, and the recording devices only accentuated it. Tom Mix was no longer a young man.

Mix made nine Westerns for Universal, and had eight diferent directors, with only Art Rosson doubling up on *Hidden Gold* and *Flaming Guns*. The first five Mixes were as good as could be found in those days. *Destry Rides Again* (Ben Stoloff, 1932) got Tom Mix off with a fast start, saving most of the action for the conclusion but adeptly keeping

Tom Mix assists a drygulched tenderfoot in My Pal, the King *(1932).*

the plot unfolding at a gallop. This is not the Max Brand novel, by the way. Nor for that matter did the subsequent versions use Brand's story. Universal apparently bought the work and used only the title, so the original Brand novel is still there, waiting to be filmed.

My Pal, the King (Kurt Neumann, 1932) was reminiscent of the Tom Mix ballyhoo style while at Fox, made with an eye for the adult and kiddie audiences alike. It puts Mix in a mythical-kingdom setting as he comes to the aid of a young monarch (Mickey Rooney) and saves him from dastardly plotters. In addition to Rooney, the cast included the gorgeous Noel Francis, and venerable oldtimers Stuart Holmes and Paul Hurst. Amiable hokum, it had the extra advantage of being accommodated as a "different" sort of Western.

Both *The Texas Bad Man* (Edward Laemmle, 1932) and *Rider of Death Valley* (Al Rogell, 1932) had superior scripts by Jack Cunningham, and impressive performances by the villainous Fred Kohler and Willard Robertson. In the former film, which has somewhat sombre overtones akin to William S. Hart's efforts, Robertson delivers a performance in an unsympathetic role that would stand up well in any kind of movie, much less a Western; the latter has a strong climax superbly photographed by Clark, as well as players of prestige like Lois Wilson (formerly of *The Covered Wagon,* also scripted by Cunningham), Otis Harlan, Mae Busch, Forrest Stanley, and the tyke Edith Fellows. *The Fourth Horseman* (Hamilton MacFadden, 1932) is in the more conventional outdoor mode, but with a nicely filmed train robbery sequence at the outset.

Thereafter, the quality lessened. *Hidden Gold* (1932) has a bit of ring action as Mix enters a prizefight to give matters a twist, and Rosson steers it capably, but the general results are just average.

Forrest Stanley (l.) and Fred Kohler, trying to sneak off with a fortune in gold, are stopped by Tom Mix in Rider of Death Valley *(1932).*

THE BIG GUNS SPEAK: Gibson, Maynard, Mix

Tom Mix subdues Ernie Adams in The Miracle Rider *(1935), Mix's last film.*

Flaming Guns was a mistake, looking like an old Hoot Gibson script picked up inadvertently and handed to Mix. It didn't suit him, and the lack of action was appalling. The two Mix 1933 releases, *Terror Trail* (Armand Schaefer) and *Rustler's Roundup* (Henry MacRae) were pleasing but relatively commonplace. And both Schaefer and MacRae were normally associated with lesser Western product, and serials.

Tom took a spill while filming *Roundup,* and old bones heal slowly. He called it a day at Universal, which is where Ken Maynard re-entered. Nat Levine enticed Mix back to the screen in 1935 to make a Mascot serial, but *The Miracle Rider* (B. Reeves Eason and Armand Schaefer) was pedestrian and Mix curtailed his screen career. In 1940, his automobile failed to negotiate a curve, and thus ended a cowboy legend.

Tim McCoy

3
THE BIG GUNS SPEAK:
JONES, McCOY

It is not recorded whether Carl and Junior Laemmle were present at any advance screenings of the new Columbia series of Buck Jones Westerns for the 1930–31 season. If they were, they would have had second thoughts about the wisdom of abandoning Universal's outdoor output. As it was, a full year and more would elapse before Universal would be able to get the six-guns barking again. And by that time, Columbia had added a top name star to their roster, Tim McCoy. And his series also started promisingly, giving Columbia, a studio not noted for Westerns, an unquestioned lead in star personalities and production quality.

As a backup man to Tom Mix at Fox, Charles (Buck) Jones had earned no mean reputation as a cowboy crowd pleaser. At another company he undoubtedly would have been recognized as the leader of the outdoor pack in his own right; even at Fox, although necessarily one rung down from the insuperable Mix, his star was undimmed. More than Mix, Jones would occasionally step out of Western roles and appear in dramas, most of them with a bucolic or pastoral setting but non-Western nevertheless. In the '20s, directors of Buck Jones pictures read like a roll of future giants, including John Ford, William A. Wellman, W. S. Van Dyke and Frank Borzage, among others.

After his contract with Fox had expired in 1928, Jones had made some bad business deals, including an independently made Western feature that misfired and an in-person touring attraction that fizzled because of naive management. He was off the screen altogether in 1929, and by the following year was happy to accept the offer from Columbia, even if it did mean a considerable loss in revenue, compared to what he had been paid while at Fox. From the standpoint of Columbia, it was a gamble too—the public has short memories and Buck had not been seen for well over a year, and then too he had never made a talkie, so there was the question of his voice being acceptable.

Louis King directed the first three Buck Jones Columbia Westerns, which were produced by Sol Lesser. The first one, *The Lone Rider,* was ready for release in June 1930, and it was good. *Shadow Ranch* and *Men Without Law* followed in quick succession, and they were good, perhaps even better. After the first set of eight, which Lesser had produced independently for Columbia release, the company took over the production of the Jones films directly. Counting the Lessers, Jones appeared in 27 Columbia Westerns, plus two non-Westerns. By 1934 he had become the top Western star in the movies, achieving a peak of popularity surpassing his best days in the silents.

There was about Buck Jones a mystique, an intriguing quality far apart from the rest of the cowboy performers. Physically he was in the accepted tradition—good-enough looking in a rugged way, trim of body without the obvious muscular characteristics of a Tom Tyler or George O'Brien. His range regalia was neat without being gaudy. Overall, he

HOLLYWOOD CORRAL: A COMPREHENSIVE B WESTERN ROUNDUP

presented a picture of quiet strength. When he confronted an adversary and threatened: "I'll squeeze yore Adam's apple 'till you taste cider," one fully believed he was more than capable of carrying out the threat. He was one of the best of the early-sound stars in a brawl, mighty fists hammering opponents into submission realistically. Astride his impressive mount Silver, silhouetted against some picturesque California cloud formations, he presented one of the more satisfying outdoor portraits.

But there was more than the mere physical to Jones. Of all the Western players before and after, the feeling persists that the respect for and devotion to his milieu and his craft ran deepest in Jones. He had observed and learned the art of film from many inspired teachers. He had obviously had considerable voice in the production of his Columbia product; when he moved to Universal in 1934 his films did indeed become Buck Jones Productions, and his hand was all the more in evidence. He directed a few of his Universals and they were not among his better efforts, but he had the ability as a director, and would have made a good one eventually, had he received further opportunities.

Beyond the outward leadership, there was a spirit prevalent in the Buck Jones Westerns, which sometimes took divergent paths. Paradoxically, Jones chose stories and scripts with a sobriety in them that was almost Hart-like, yet he also had a penchant for a rube sort of comedy, with himself as the butt of the jokes, that would contrast sharply with the severity of his serious roles. He would never show both aspects in the same film, fortunately. While his lighter Westerns were entertaining, his more serious ones were remembered longer, left a more lasting effect.

His initial Columbias made solid use of conventional plots, and were far ahead of their time in that they blissfully ignored any problems in getting the bulky, balky sound equipment to acclimatize itself to outdoor recording. Smooth of pace, vigorous of action, technically on a par with the average non-Western of 1930 and superior to many in that respect, they were winners. Perhaps most enjoyable was *Men Without Law,* whose early reels had a slight change of pace, with Jones introduced as a World War I soldier returning to his ranch to encounter more trouble. Jones had a rather touching scene with his mother (Lydia Knott) that could have easily turned mawkish but somehow didn't, as he played the son home from the wars. Incidentally, both Jones and Hoot Gibson tended to stress the bonds of mother and son in their early talkies, in an unforced and gallant manner.

One of the more interesting, and certainly one of the more curious Jones Westerns was his sixth for Columbia, *The Avenger* (Roy William Neill, 1931). Jones seemed to like his stories with a setting below the border, to the extent that he would attempt to impersonate a Mexican character, none too successfully. He did it in *The Avenger* and he did it in *South of the Rio Grande* (Lambert Hillyer, 1932), and while his efforts were a laudable attempt to be versatile, his dialect was about as Mexicano as Vincennes, Indiana, where he was born. Native costuming topped by a sombrero would cover the impersonation up to a point, but when Buck had to passionately proclaim *"Mi amore!"* as he did to Dorothy Revier in *The Avenger,* the jig was up; Buck just couldn't convince.

Otherwise, *The Avenger* had a fascinating low-key, arty look that enhanced the plot, which was a version of the Joaquin Murietta legend, about a Robin Hoodish bandito. Neill had directed some silent Jones Westerns for Fox, and this was his last film with the cowboy star. Using clever camera angles (by Ted Tetzlaff and Charles Van Enger) and a terse, crisp editing style, Neill packed many elements not usually found in Westerns into the brief hour's running time. Aside from the lapses in language, Jones played his role in straightforward fashion and presented an impressively mysterious figure as he took revenge upon those dastards who had done him wrong in bygone days, by plaguing their gold shipments and eventually meting out justice. The Jack Townley-George Morgan script was redone in 1942 under Lambert Hillyer's direction as *Vengeance of the West,* a vehicle for Bill Elliott, but the results fell short of the original.

South of the Rio Grande also had its moments, and a stronger-than-usual plot, with prominent footage given to Mona Maris in an unsympathetic role. Americanized, Jones again essayed the below the border Robin Hood theme in *California Trail* (Lambert Hillyer, 1933) to slightly lesser effect, because of a simple fault—too much footage, too little action.

Superior Jones Columbia Westerns with conventional elements included *The Texas Ranger* (D. Ross Lederman, 1931), *The Deadline* (Lambert Hillyer, 1931) and *The Fighting Ranger* (George B. Seitz, 1934). The humorous side of Jones was aptly presented in *Hello Trouble* (Lambert Hillyer, 1932). An offbeat plot well directed by Hillyer was found in *Unknown Valley* (1933), which dealt with a strange religious sect.

If one were to choose films of the Columbia group

THE BIG GUNS SPEAK: Jones, McCoy

Buck Jones working undercover in McKenna of the Mounted *(1932).*

Glenn Strange, Hank Bell and Frank Ellis (foreground) are bowled over by Buck in The Thrill Hunter *(1933).*

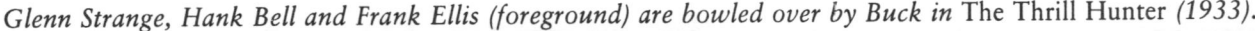

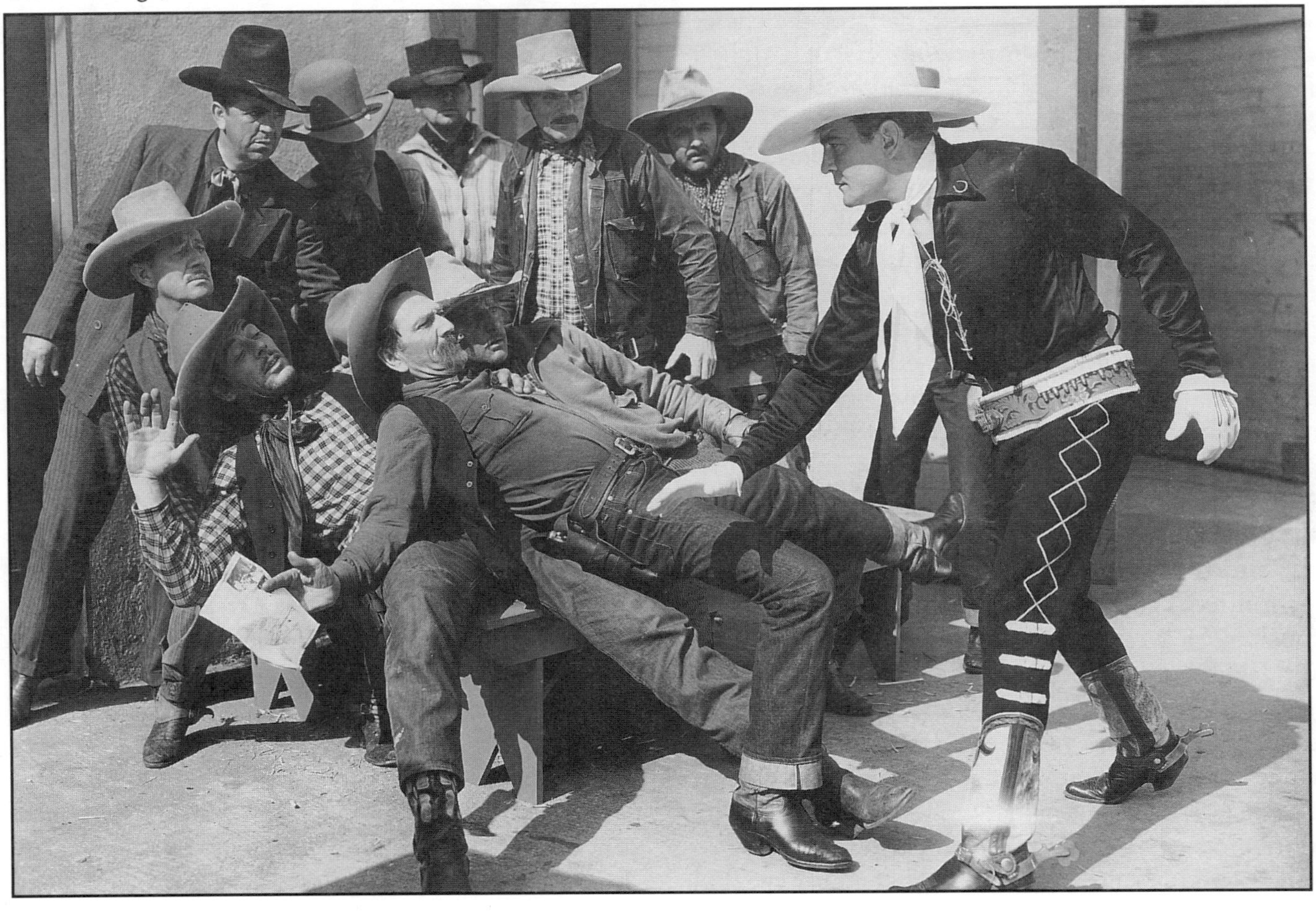

Paul Fix gets the drop on Buck while Polly Ann Young watches in The Crimson Trail *(1935).*

which showed Jones at his best, perhaps the choice could be narrowed down to *White Eagle* (Lambert Hillyer, 1932) and *The Thrill Hunter* (George B. Seitz, 1933). The former is crammed with action, a meaty script by Fred Myton, and as a bonus, a rare and well-valued understanding of the problems besetting the Indian nation at the time of the story's unfoldment. Two Columbia films, made concurrently, touched upon the injustices and intolerances heaped upon the Indian, both done in powerful fashion. *White Eagle* was one, Tim McCoy's *End of the Trail* was the other. The Jones film, although constructed along more traditional lines with action and adventure predominating, in lieu of a more thorough (and more pessimistic) view of the problem found in the McCoy story, was in itself a novel and praiseworthy effort.

In direct contrast, *The Thrill Hunter* didn't look much like a Western at all, but by breaking tradition for laughs provided a vastly amusing hour or so. Jones played a blowhard whose tall tales of heroics got him into hot water when a movie company comes to town and he's forced to back up his claims. Buck's interest in mechanics was brought to the fore, since most of his yarns in the film deal with his auto-racing and flying prowesses. His ability to kid himself genially, and his comedy timing that approached Gibson's on occasion, served him well, and made one of his most entertaining features. One Jones non-Western starring film, *High Speed* (Lederman, 1932), also had a racing background. His other non-Western appearance was in the adaptation of the Preston Sturges play, *Child of Manhattan* (Eddie Buzzell, 1933), with Nancy Carroll and John Boles. Jones played a down-to-earth cowboy tycoon who almost, but didn't, get the girl. In later years at Columbia, his role would have undoubtedly been played by Ralph Bellamy. For this appearance, he billed himself as Charles Jones, without the informality of "Buck."

Buck Jones left Columbia in 1934 and became a resident producer-star at Universal, replacing the Ken Maynard series. To fill out their schedule, Columbia reissued some of the early Jones films, since Buck had left with only three out of the eight in the hopper. As a sidenote to ponder, both *White Eagle* and *The Thrill Hunter* were released at the end of their respective seasonal schedules, as if Columbia were saying in effect, here's the best we have to offer, so sign up quickly for next season's series and play 'em off to a profit. Exhibitors invariably responded, in view of the impressive evidence.

It took about two features to get Jones in the groove at Universal. Both *Rocky Rhodes* (Al Raboch, 1934) and *When a Man Sees Red* (Alan James, 1934) might have been scripts left over for Ken Maynard; certainly the production staff, including the ubiquitous photographer Ted McCord, were remnants of the second Maynard Universal tenure. But with *The Crimson Trail* (Raboch, 1935), the Jones production stamp made itself evident. Stories became slower-paced, more introspective. There was action, but the sequences became more isolated, so that when the action did erupt, it did so with even more impact. There was increased attention to detail and atmosphere, as in *For the Service* (1936), personally directed by Jones; the opening scenes convey an all-too-real sense of a heat wave, including an accurately observed shot of blisters of humidity popping from the blazing ground like so many minuscule volcanoes. Nor was Jones fearful of ending on an overly ambiguous note. In *The Ivory-Handled Gun* (Ray Taylor, 1935), which revolves around a long-standing feud, both Buck and the villain are shot during the climactic hand-to-hand struggle. The last scene in the film is of the gun of the title, the prize of possession, mounted on the wall, signifying that the feud is over. Whether Jones perishes or recovers is not shown, leaving up to the audience, and presumably their own preference, the nature of his fate.

Recurring Jones themes found their way into *Sunset of Power* (Taylor, 1936), wherein Buck once more dons the cloak and mantle of a mysterious do-gooder, and *Ride 'Em Cowboy* (Les Selander, 1936), with Buck tackling an auto-racing yarn again, and returning to his comedy routine, none too successfully this time, as a practical joker. Beginning with the latter film, Selander was to direct six Jones releases in a row. He had known Jones a long time, having been an assistant director with the old Fox unit. Lately he had worked with Woody Van Dyke on some of the M-G-M successes, including *The Thin Man*. Jones gave him the chance to become a full-fledged director, and upon leaving the Jones production unit Selander went with Harry Sherman to work steadily on the Hopalong Cassidy films as well as some of Sherman's more lavish outdoor productions.

Upon occasion, Jones would include some bizarre or unusual aspect in his films, such as the weird, ghostly opening of *Empty Saddles* (Selander, 1936). Mostly, the remainder of his Universals were good, no-nonsense Westerns with action carefully counterbalanced by sensible script treatments of traditional plots, with little touches here and there to notch them above the average. An instance would be in *Left-Handed Law* (Selander, 1937), in a sequence between Jones and a mortally wounded cowboy, who whispers to Buck that he'd like to die with his boots off. There on the open range, Buck grimly sets about the task, only to pause in the middle, glance glumly at the man, and mutter to himself, "Got one of 'em off, old-timer."

By the time *Sudden Bill Dorn* (Taylor, 1938) was released, Buck Jones had already left Universal and was back at Columbia. Jones reportedly was dissatisfied when Universal persisted in trying to persuade him to up his schedule to eight Westerns per season instead of the half dozen he had been producing, so Jones didn't sign a new contract. Instead, he joined L. G. Leonard (Leonard Goldstein) and Monroe Shaff of Coronet Productions for a series of six for Columbia release. The first two were playing in late 1937, in direct competition with his later Universal releases still going the rounds.

Buck didn't have the control he had over his 22 Universals, but the first two Coronet-Columbias gave promise that they were staking out new story

Silent-film star Louise Brooks with Buck in Empty Saddles *(1936), one of her last movies.*

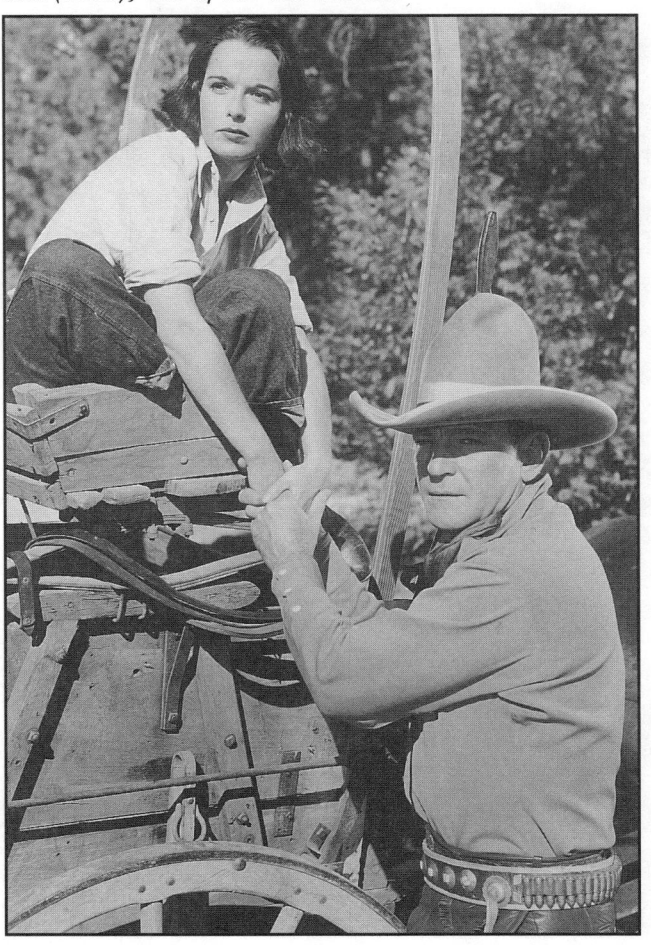

claims for the star. Both *Hollywood Roundup* and *Headin' East* were directed by Ewing Scott, and both tried a different approach. As is evident from the title, the former had a movie-making background, with Jones cast as the stunt stand-in for a conceited cowboy star, played by Grant Withers. The star, jealous, manages to get Buck into plenty of hot water before all's right by the finish. The novel angle made it different, if a bit placid for Jones, and an additional point of note was the return to the screen of Helen Twelvetrees' after a spot of retirement, as the romantic interest. *Headin' East* was a reverse Western, with Buck journeying to the big city to confront racketeers who've been messing with the lettuce crop. As before, the novelty was the key to success, and one wondered how long Coronet could keep it up without running out of ideas.

Not long, as it turned out. *The Overland Express* (Drew Eberson, 1938) was set back in the days of the pony riders and had 56 minutes of horsemanship well photographed by Jones' regular cameraman Allen Thompson, but very little else. The last three Coronets were directed by Elmer Clifton, and budgetary problems were well apparent. *The Stranger from Arizona* gave Jones some pseudo-snappy dialogue to deliver, and although Jones was good at comedy this wasn't his kind of fun. As a result, the film suffered. *Law of the Texan* and *California Frontier* abounded in saloon fisticuffing and general milling about, but the abundance of action failed to compensate for a lack of true story values and production niceties so essential for Jones to be successful. Columbia did not renew the Jones series after 1938.

Buck went civilian again for *Unmarried* (Kurt Neumann, 1939), a Paramount remake of *Lady and Gent* with Jones in the role created by George Bancroft, a pug, according to the trailer promotion, "as loud as a Times Square traffic whistle." Opposite him again was Helen Twelvetrees, and the cast had such sturdy personnel as Robert Armstrong, Sidney Blackmer, Buster Crabbe and a

Buck relaxes in his North Hollywood home.

young Donald O'Connor, but fans wondered what the hell Buck was doing in a movie called *Unmarried*. The following year his fans were mortified to see Buck cast as a crooked sheriff in a Republic fiasco, *Wagons Westward* (Lew Landers, 1940). When he was billed as Louis Friedlander, Landers had directed Buck in a serial, *The Red Rider* (1934), at a time when Jones was making a chapter-play each year for Universal (1933–36). Now he returned to join the mob in *Riders of Death Valley* (Ford Beebe and Ray Taylor, 1941); he was given third billing, after Dick Foran and Leo Carrillo, ahead of Charles Bickford, Lon Chaney, Jr., Noah Beery Jr. and Big Boy Williams, but was still merely one of many. He also made an inferior serial for Columbia at about the same time, *White Eagle* (James W. Horne, 1941). The first chapter used footage from the 1932 Jones Western feature of the same title. Buck had changed so little that it was possible to borrow a full close-up of him from the earlier film and insert it in the new footage, with few the wiser. More important, Buck Jones needed a boost for his waning reputation. It was to be provided later in 1941 by his old friend, director and agent, Scott R. Dunlap. And it would involve Tim McCoy.

With credentials more impressive than most, Tim McCoy, Col., U.S. Army (Ret.), had arrived in Hollywood in 1923 to attend to technical details on *The Covered Wagon*. He knew a lot about Indians, was in fact an authority on Indian lore. He had once led a military expedition to the site of the Custer massacre at Little Big Horn to gather any remaining evidence concerning the sad and bloody affair. It evolved that McCoy was also photogenic, and behaved with commendable ability in front of a camera. He became M-G-M's first and only cowboy star in a series of 16 features, 1926–29. With Westerns at low ebb, he managed to land the lead in a Universal serial, the all-talking *The Indians Are Coming* (Henry MacRae, 1930) that was highly profitable, as well as a non-Western chapter-play, *Heroes of the Flames* (Robert Hill, 1931). Universal was still hesitant about producing a Western series, but Columbia was having good luck with their Buck Jones unit, and so signed McCoy for a series. McCoy appeared in 16 Westerns over two seasons, 1931–33, and thereby added to his already considerable reputation.

McCoy's silent Westerns for M-G-M had been economically but ingeniously produced and usually received praise from the critics. Audiences were not quite so enthusiastic—there was something chilly about the McCoy personality that would prove a barrier. Perhaps it was the military bearing. Whatever it was, it wasn't McCoy's fault, for he supplied all the dash, hustle and action required by the scripts. He had a sense of comedy, if relatively little feeling for it, and was physically without flaw, with steely gaze for the dramatic and action sequences, and tender look for the clinches. Metro scenarists would provide him with the unusual upon occasion, such as a bit of swordplay in conquering the villain, or setting the tale in the era of the American Revolution. And he did acquire a following, despite the occasional chirps of complaint.

Columbia set right to work and humanized McCoy extensively. Gone were the little production extras provided by M-G-M. Harry Cohn made the pennies count at Columbia, so it was get down to business and prove yourself, or else. McCoy came through in fine fashion. The plots were formula, but the action didn't cease. D. Ross Lederman directed half the McCoy 16 and did some of his best work, seeming to team well with McCoy. Films like *Daring Danger*, *The Riding Tornado* and *Two-Fisted Law* (all 1932) were tailor-made for the Western market, each with constant action and no let-up in pace. Lederman also directed McCoy's one genuinely dramatic and heart-felt effort, *End of the Trail* (1932).

Cast as a cavalry officer who is instrumental in preventing an all-out war between the Arapahoes and the white man, McCoy uses much of his extensive knowledge of the Indian during the film, including sequences involving the authentic sign language. This early sound, unassuming little film, part of a Western series and probably considered as a mere throwaway by Columbia execs, dealt with the historic tragedy of Indian vs. white in an adult, thoughtful manner. Stuart Anthony's original script employed many quite daring ideas and incidents, especially for a Western produced on a minor scale. Whites were shown as largely to blame for the plight of the Indian, although exemplified by the customary villain Wheeler Oakman, as a fellow officer who had been running guns to the tribes and the primary cause of all the trouble. As it was, Anthony gave McCoy some rather forceful speeches in which he takes the white man to task in general. There are also sequences depicting the Indian as noble human beings, rather than the blood-thirsty savages of many a Western. This aspect would not be treated so effectively until *Broken Arrow* many years later. Nor did scripter Anthony flinch from tragedy. During the course of the narrative, McCoy's foster son (Wally Albright) and his best friend (Wade Boteler) meet their deaths (it was unusual in itself even to intimate that a Western star could claim parenthood, even by

HOLLYWOOD CORRAL: A COMPREHENSIVE B WESTERN ROUNDUP

Tim McCoy "speaks" to Chief Yowlachie as Wade Boteler and Luana Walters look on in End of the Trail *(1932)*.

proxy). In the original version, McCoy himself is senselessly killed, but Columbia chickened out before the film's release and inserted a finale showing McCoy recovering from his "fatal" wound. Despite the weak conclusion, *End of the Trail* was a deeply felt, powerful film, more than just a Western. Naturally, it passed unnoticed, merely an entry in Columbia's Tim McCoy schedule, just as did the Buck Jones Indian yarn *White Eagle*.

And it did seem as though there was a lessening of quality in the McCoys thereafter. Of the major Western stars heretofore, McCoy had probably the least influence over his productions; he had not outwardly given any indications that he would care to direct a film, nor did he serve in any supervisory capacity on the production end. But *End of the Trail* was obviously his personal statement, to whatever extent he was involved in it, and anything further could only be a letdown. At that, his previous release, *Fighting for Justice* (Otto Brower, 1932) showed signs of production corner-cutting, as well as some gaucheries not ordinarily inflicted on the McCoys. Of the ensuing films, *Man of Action* (George Melford, 1933) was entertaining, but the remaining three, all directed by Lederman, were below average. It was as if Lederman too had been drained by the demands of *End of the Trail,* and was now directing by rote instead of by conviction.

For the 1933–34 season somebody, McCoy or one of the Briskins or somebody, persuaded Harry Cohn to allow the Western star to go Eastern, which proved to be a mistake. McCoy appeared in eight action thrillers cast variously as a cop, fireman, auto racer and the like. It turned out badly for the studio, for Buck Jones jumped the corral to mosey over to Universal at this time, leaving Columbia without a cowboy to roam the range. Nor did the experiment serve McCoy well, for while as a cowboy, he was unique; as an action player in civvies, he could act the part of a demon reporter or policeman, but so could a number of Columbia players. Putting it bluntly, McCoy lost his gimmick, and became just another "B" hero. Film seasons began around September in those days. By the Fall of 1934, McCoy was back to the boots and saddle.

His final series of eight Westerns stacks up fairly well, compared to his pre-experimental series. The stories may have been a bit threadbare and the productions, if not of increased economy, then say streamlined. But they were head and shoulders above the various independently produced efforts cluttering the states rights market; Columbia always had a sort of stock company through the years, and one would find players of the dependability of Ward Bond, Walter Brennan, J. Carrol Naish, Joseph Sauers (Sawyer) and others. David Selman, an assistant director, was given full directorial credit on seven of the eight, with Ford Beebe handling one called *Law Beyond the Range*. In three of them, McCoy was given a young, handsome, personable gent named Robert Allen (*Law, The Revenge Rider, Fighting Shadows*) as a helpmate. Allen was leading-man material, and for a while it seemed as if Columbia was grooming him to step into McCoy's boots, or at least to give him a series of his own. Allen wound up on the receiving end of Grace Moore's coloratura trills while Ken Maynard replaced McCoy for Columbia, as has been related. But Allen did achieve his own Western series later.

With his Columbia contract at an end, McCoy decided not to renew and signed instead with the independent Puritan Pictures for ten Westerns. The first two boded well for the series, but then this is usually the case with most series, often lulling performer and spectator alike into a sense of false security. *The Outlaw Deputy* (Otto Brower, 1935) and *The Man from Guntown* (Ford Beebe, 1935) may have been slightly ragged in physical look, but both had plenty of action, well-scripted stories, familiar and congenial directors, plus two leading ladies who had played opposite McCoy before to advantage in Nora Lane and Billie Seward.

Sam Newfield took over direction of the Puritans, getting off to an okay start with *Bulldog Courage* (1935). Newfield, a tremendously prolific director if not an inspired one, was responsible for some good McCoy entries thereafter—and some in which, one might say, the shod had slipped. *Roarin' Guns* (1936) was a dull affair in which the one amusing scene was unintentional, as McCoy is supposed to leap astride his mount at the end, misses the stirrup and has to ease into the saddle; Newfield lets it run without bothering for a retake. To Newfield's credit, *Border Caballero* (1936) is an hour of good, strong Western storytelling, while *Aces and Eights* (1936), though deadeningly slow, brings some interesting

McCoy, Shirley Grey and John Wayne in Texas Cyclone *(1932).*

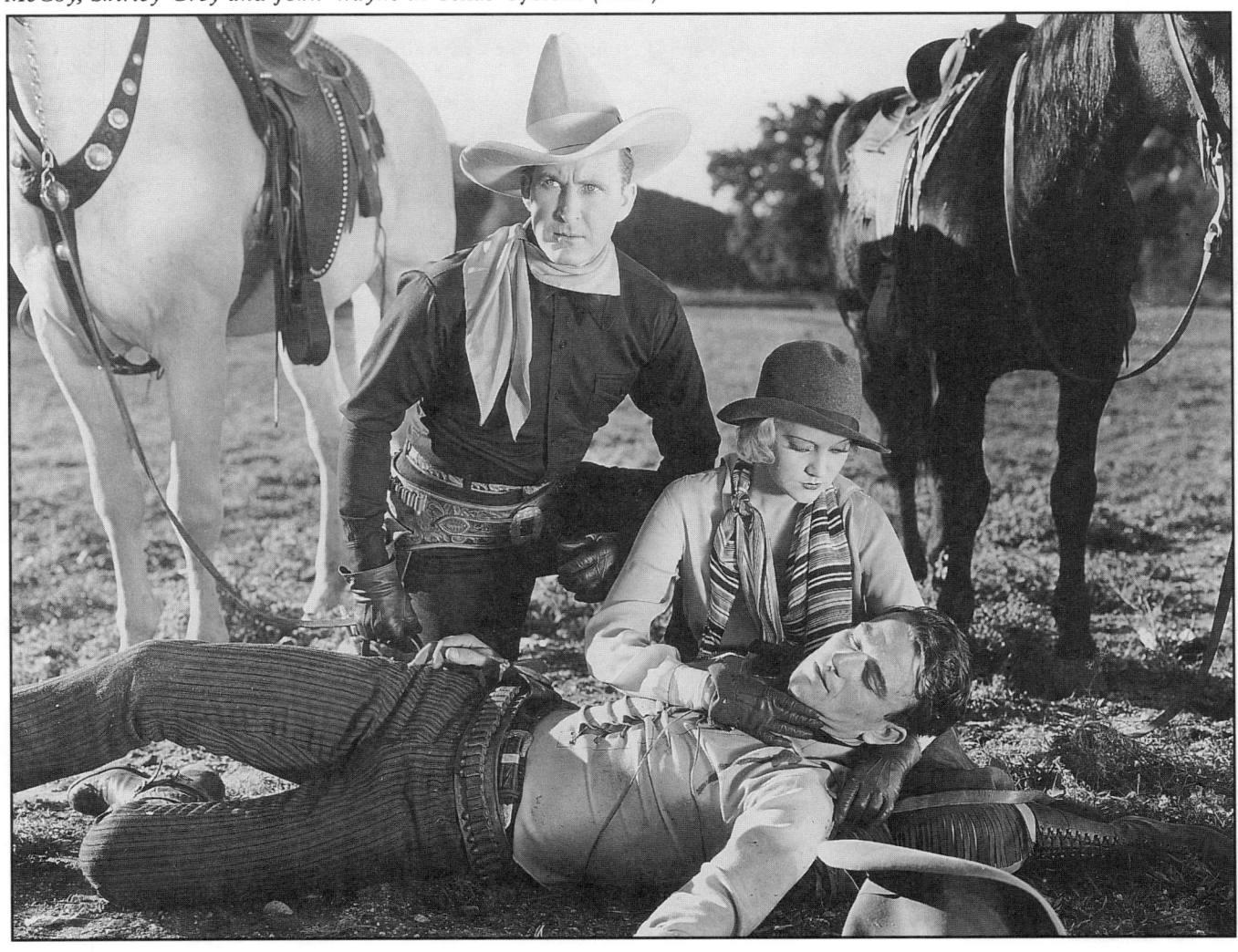

HOLLYWOOD CORRAL: A COMPREHENSIVE B WESTERN ROUNDUP

facets of McCoy's character to the fore as he plays a gambler.

In 1937, McCoy got trapped in a deal whereby he was to have starred in a series for another independent company, but the project never materialized, lawsuits flew around, and McCoy took haven with a circus tour, just as had Maynard and Mix at various times. The next year, he returned to the screen in four Westerns produced by Maurice Conn for Monogram release, taking up the slack caused by the departure of Tom Keene after his first four for the studio. Alan James directed two (*West of Rainbow's End, Two-Gun Justice*), Sam Newfield two (*Code of the Rangers, Phantom Ranger*). Conn knew his outdoor stuff, McCoy was still in good form, and the brief series, while not exceptional by any means, was a serviceable one and undoubtedly increased McCoy's Western rating. The only note of protest among fans was found in McCoy's tendency to use a snapdraw—when a director would use a wrong camera angle, as would happen, McCoy would seem to be firing at the ceiling, while the baddies would be collapsing face down on the bar room floor.

Monogram got Tex Ritter, and Victory Pictures got Tim McCoy for 1938–39, for a series of eight. They also got Sam Newfield in the bargain, and he steered McCoy through the entire series. Sam Katzman, formerly of Puritan, produced. McCoy had made one for Puritan entitled *Lightnin' Bill Carson* (1936), in which he essayed the role of an undercover G-Man adept at disguises. For Victory, the role was revived for McCoy. But it was no victory. Shooting schedules were short, budgets were low, ineptitudes crept in. McCoy probably had a good time since his continuing role allowed him to assume some disguises; Mexican, gypsy, even Chinese in *Six-Gun Trail* (1938). His Mexican act was better than Buck Jones', discounting the piercing light blue eyes; his gypsy was tolerable, but his Oriental would cause Charlie Chan no worry. He was further burdened with a comedy sidekick, Magpie, played by Ben Corbett. The Victory series, in short, was McCoy at low ebb.

Producers Distributing Corporation, a new company making noises in 1940, next presented McCoy in *Texas Renegades*, and it wasn't bad at all. Strong plot, the dependable Nora Lane as heroine, and capable direction from one Peter Stewart, who was

McCoy complements Lois January as Slim Whitaker (l.), John Merton and Ralph Byrd (seated with pipe) look on in Border Caballero *(1936).*

Frank LaRue (l.) chides McCoy in front of Hal Price (in chair), Lou Fulton and Forrest Taylor in Frontier Crusader *(1940).*

Sam Newfield by any other name. Shortly after its release, the company altered its name to Producers Releasing Corporation (PRC), and McCoy appeared in seven more, all of them directed by Stewart-Newfield. *Frontier Crusader* (1940) continued the good impression left by *Texas Renegades*, with a lively scenario (by William Lively, that is) and an atmosphere reminiscent of better days at Columbia. *Gun Code* (1940) passed muster, but then the inevitable blight set in, and quality decreased. *Arizona Gang Busters* (1940) may be of historic interest because of its introduction of fifth-column activities on the range, with guttural-sounding foreign agents to be rounded up by Marshal McCoy. But the modernization had little lasting effect. McCoy had acquired the singing services of rotund Art Davis for the last of the series, *Texas Marshal* (1941). Everybody said the same thing about Davis—if he'd lose some weight, he'd make a promising Western lead. This only emphasized the fact that they weren't talking much about McCoy, the star of the show. By that time, Tim McCoy had received an offer from Monogram. It would mean second billing for the first time, but it just might be worth it, especially in view of his unlamented PRC venture.

Buck Jones and Tim McCoy, once double aces from Columbia ranch, were about to meet onscreen.

Tom Tyler in Battling with Buffalo Bill *(1931).*

4
BATTLING BOB, AND OUR TOM:
STEELE, TYLER

While the top hands on the Western ranges were battling it out for saddle supremacy in the early and middle '30s, two further Hollywood cowboys were steadily, prolifically going about their business. Their business was starring in horse operas, the quicker filmed the better, or at least the cheaper; for ofttimes they were not better, indeed not very good at all. But Bob Steele and Tom Tyler endured, triumphed, over their respective substandard materials, and their period work is looked back upon today with, if not admiration, then understanding.

Bob Steele came to the movies first, and also made his first talkie before Tom Tyler. Steele's real name was Robert Bradbury Jr., son of director Robert North Bradbury. As a teenager, he appeared with his brother in a series of short subjects which consisted of shots taken by the elder Bradbury of the boys on camping and fishing expeditions. Released by Pathe in the early '20s as "Adventures of Bill and Bob," the shorts were popular, and young Bob Bradbury continued in films, changing his name to Steele. By the time sound arrived, Steele had acquired a following as an action star for FBO (later RKO).

Steele possessed several assets, obvious and otherwise, which enabled him to overcome production obstacles. Compared to many of his contemporaries, he was young, without that settled appearance that comes to all, even he-man actors, as they reach the 40-year mark. He was immediately recognizable, his intense features topped by the unmistakable mop of curly dark hair. Perhaps his most striking asset, in more ways than one, was a paradoxical one. He was of small stature, yet he could participate in a filmic scrap with the best of them.

Contrary to popular belief, movie fistfights are difficult to film, and consume valuable production time if something should go amiss. Done in a perfunctory manner, they give the appearance of phoniness. They must be timed accurately, and be exciting without becoming ridiculous. Early talkie brawls were hit-and-miss affairs, in all senses; this was before Wayne, Yak Canutt and later Republic studio specialists perfected pretty picture-encounters, as delicately choreographed as any Astaire dance routine. The best of his day, practically unchallenged in the flying fist department, was Steele.

He looked especially good from the back, this compact, diminutive young man with exceptionally broad shoulders for his stature, swinging long looping lefts and rights with piston-like rapidity and precision. He was a welterweight contender smashing after the heavies, or heavyweights. Veteran Charles King was more often than not on the receiving end of the Steele wrath throughout their careers, and King must have spent leisure time figuring out how to receive yet another Steele flurry of blows in a different manner. What made Steele's task all the more difficult was his lack of size. It was necessary for him to make his audience believe that he could knock about some huge bear of a baddie without getting squashed in the process. That he invariably did so was perhaps his highest achievement in West-

HOLLYWOOD CORRAL: A COMPREHENSIVE B WESTERN ROUNDUP

A pensive Bob Steele (seated left) wonders if Francis McDonald (c.) and Harry Semels (r.) have pulled a fast one on him in Texas Buddies *(1932).*

erns. It also gave every little kid hope, in a world that seemed at times peopled with big bullies.

Steele had spent 1929 at Syndicate Pictures, after leaving RKO. There, he appeared in a number of silent Westerns, directed in a veritable torrent by J. P. McGowan. Since McGowan was also directing Westerns with Tom Tyler and Bob Custer for the same company, his days and nights must surely have been passed standing before a treadmill, assuring cameraman Hap Depew to start grinding whilst one of the three stars were in view, going through their well-worn paces. Steele was contracted for his first set of sound pictures for the Tiffany outfit, his voice having been found more than adequate. His first, *Near the Rainbow's End* (1930), was directed by the same J. P. McGowan of the busy previous year. Last in the series, *Near the Trail's End* (1931), was directed by Wallace Fox, who had guided young Steele through some of his early silent starring vehicles. In between, there were six Westerns directed by John P. McCarthy.

It would be hard to justify any quality imbued in these initial Steele talkies. Historians might ponder over the state of things to come in the appearance of Al St. John in a few of them as comedy relief, while Archie Stout's photography did have its moments. But the production hands guiding the films through the awkward stages of early sound were unsure, and production work was hindered by the necessity to rush. Perhaps worth a brief look is *Headin' North* (1930), not because of its merit, which is dubious. Rather, it shows all too well how Hollywood was oriented in those days. After one of his customary slam-bang set-tos, Steele is forced to flee from a trumped-up charge. For the remainder of the hour, he hides out by posing as a dudish song-and-dance man, dressed in garish store clothes and miming through some of the most puerile vaudeville turns to blight the talkie screen. When discovered by his girl, played in an emphatic manner by Barbara Luddy, she voices what is in the minds of the audience: "Bob... WHERE did you get those FUN-NY CLOTHES!" Poor Steele looks embarrassed throughout the entire long sequence, and gets back into character only when he redeems himself by participating in a concluding man-to-man slugfest. What the film is, essentially, is a terrible vaude show sandwiched between two marathon fisticuff sessions. Since director McCarthy did the script himself, it saved him the labor of devising extended dialogue scenes.

Since it was proven beyond doubt that the name of Bob Steele would be unlikely to grace any further attempts at Western musicals, his next series, six features for World Wide, saw him settling down into what would soon be a familiar Western groove for him. By moving from Tiffany to World Wide, Steele was blazing a trail soon to be followed by Ken Maynard. Steele's first, *South of Santa Fe* (1932), boded well for the star. Nothing exceptionally original about the G. A. Durlam screenplay, but it was put across with more than the customary neatness and dispatch by Bert Glennon, a top cameraman turned director for a while. Glennon's adeptness in the direction of this and other features causes wonderment at why he returned to his cameras, but after one or two directorial assignments he did. As he did with the Tiffany Steeles, Trem Carr handled the production reins for the World Wides, and the improvement was more than noticeable. The remaining five were made a family affair, with Robert N. Bradbury directing each. Given adequate material, Bradbury could often turn in quite impressive jobs, as will be related on future pages. Working with his son, the results ranged from entertaining, *Riders of the Desert* (1932), with its exciting gun battle at the climax, to so-so, as with *Son of Oklahoma* and *Man from Hell's Edges* (1932). In general, however, the World Wide half dozen represented a considerable step forward from the Tiffanys, and solidified Steele's entrenchment as a Western star of popularity.

As the fortunes of World Wide sank slowly in the West, and into receivership, producer Carr and star Steele moved to Monogram for eight. Actually, it was in the nature of a return, since Monogram formerly had been the old Syndicate Pictures, where Steele had labored so diligently at the end of the silent era. In 1933, continuing well into the following year, Westerns had once more come under a cloud. Where once producers had been afraid of their aptitude for the sound medium, now it was deemed that there were just too damn many of them. Complaints were heard from exhibitor country. In an effort to alleviate the situation, makers of Westerns did not curtail their schedules so much, but instead resorted to subterfuge. The result was that there were a lot of Westerns around that didn't sound like Westerns, and once one got past the title, there were certain non-Western elements inserted into the scripts. However, the disguises were of only temporary effect, for once a Western, always a Western—the hero, the villain, the girl, the chase, the happy windup, all had to be adhered to. At Monogram, Steele fell heir to several of these "underground" Westerns, and it is to the credit of writers like the inventive Wellyn Totman, Harry O. Jones and poppa Bradbury himself, that for the most part they came off. Once the plots evolved, it was familiar territory, but the Monogram Steeles did have generous amounts of topical material, or attempted new slants. *Hidden Valley* (1932) had some aerial sequences, preparing Steele for his non-Western serial for Mascot the following year. Bradbury directed, as he did *The Gallant Fool* and *Galloping Romeo* (1933). The latter tried for sly humor in the Hoot Gibson manner, but among Steele's many screen accomplishments, the deft light touch was missing. However, George Hayes was alternating villainous and funny-codger roles, and walked away with the chuckles, and the picture. Other Steele oddities of the time included a change of locale in *Trailin' North* (J. P. McCarthy, 1933), some adult tangents involving the morals of a bad girl in *Young Blood* (Phil Rosen, 1932), and some boxing episodes in *The Fighting Champ* (McCarthy, 1932).

Trem Carr stayed at Monogram to oversee the destinies of John Wayne, while Bob Steele wound up eventually with A. W. Hackel, of Supreme Pictures, where the budgets were lower than before, and the pictures were ground out two or three at a time, with casts of ever-familiar faces, particularly if one had seen the previous few Steeles. At the pace set and followed, the Supreme group boils down to not so much a matter of critical appraisal, as simple arithmetic. In a bit less than five years, Bob Steele starred in a total of 32 Westerns for Hackel. Many of these were directed by his father, and some were assuredly more than adequate for their purpose, such as *Alias John Law* (1935), *Kid Courageous* (1935) and *The Last of the Warrens* (1936). But ultimately they were conventional Westerns, made for and played in lesser theaters.

At the midway point in the '30s, the states' rights market refined and clarified somewhat, with small distributors not so numerous as before, and some larger companies taking over distribution of independent product. Hackel signed a deal with Republic for the 1936–37 season, with that company handling the details on getting the Steeles–and the Johnny Mack Brown series also produced by Hackel at the time–into an increased number of showcases. Hackel's leadoff Steele for Republic release was *Cavalry* (Robert N. Bradbury, 1936), a rather ambitious yarn, post-Civil War variety, with a slightly improved physical look than Hackel had been accustomed to giving. And it might be said that the general quality of the Steeles did rise, both in 1936–37 and 1937–38. Joining Bradbury on the Steeles had been S. Roy Luby, a former film editor who had obviously learned how a movie was put together and directed stylishly, but was destined to bounce back and forth from the shooting location to the editing rooms. His *Border Phantom* (1936), with its aura of Oriental mystery, and *The Red Rope* (1937), a Johnston McCulley tale well spun, can be counted among the better Steeles of the period. Early in 1937, Sam Newfield joined Hackel to replace Bradbury, who headed to Grand National and Monogram. Newfield directed the last bunch of Steeles, including *Doomed at Sundown,* with its suspenseful situation referred to in the title, and *Paroled to Die,* with a straightforward, uncluttered action touch, worthy of Steele, and generally good Westerns by any standards. For some unknown reason, Republic tended to use the routine *Colorado Kid* as an icebreaker to persuade reluctant exhibitors to play the Steeles. Not helping matters was the fact that although released by Republic, the Steeles were not directly made by the studio, and suffered in comparison to the ultra-efficient, smoothly-honed Autrys and Mesquiteers. The Hackel association was terminated at the end of the 1937–38 season. Steele didn't miss a beat and immediately signed for a new series.

It was a fall from grace, comparatively. Metropolitan Pictures was the company of Harry S. Webb and Bernard B. Ray, who took turns producing and directing and by this time were excelling in neither function. Their former company had been known as Reliable Pictures, which belied its name, and they had been responsible for Tom Tyler's drop in prestige. No sooner had Republic released Steele's *Durango Valley Raiders* late in 1938, when he was on the Western screens in *Feud of the Range* (Harry S. Webb, 1939). It got off to a great start, real honest to gosh symbolism, as Charles King and his gang were seen in montage raiding, plundering and pillag-

Steele and Hal Price in Sundown Saunders *(1936).*

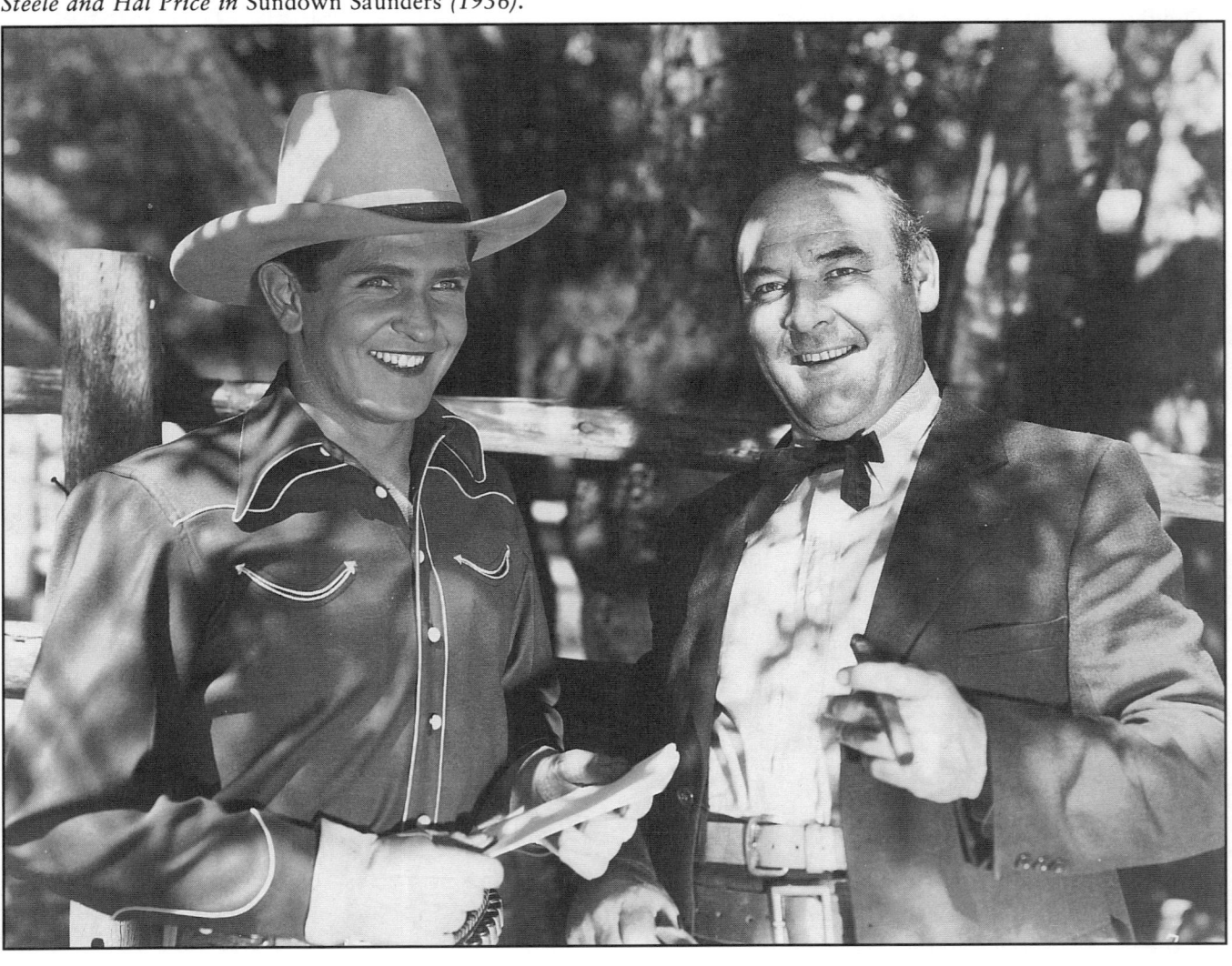

BATTLING BOB, AND OUR TOM: Steele, Tyler

Lois January (l.) stops one in the shoulder; Steele pops Charlie King as Joan Barclay watches in The Trusted Outlaw *(1937).*

ing, with the scenes interspersed with shots of lightning flashes to signify, etc. This was the beginning and the end of any pretense of motion-picture art for the Metropolitan set. The rest of the set of eight went from a profusion of aged library footage in *Mesquite Buckaroo* (Webb, 1939) to roaring ineptitude in *El Diablo Rides* (Webb, 1940), culminating in sheer tedium in *Pinto Canyon* (Raymond K. Johnson, 1940). When even the most unassuming Western series was showing signs of improving, the Metropolitan Steeles were a regression to the past, and conceivably could have harmed the future of the most indestructible cowpoke. However, Steele appeared in another film, released at the very beginning of 1940, and it was to offer him new laurels.

Lewis Milestone directed the screen version of John Steinbeck's crushingly powerful *Of Mice and Men*, and cast Bob Steele as the nasty-tempered Curley. In their glowing reviews of the film, critics included Steele with the rest of the fine performers, just as if they had known all the time that he was an accomplished thespian. In truth, Steele had never been known for his acting ability, and in fact had been occasionally taken to task for not summoning the right emotion at the right time, being handier with a right cross. But he played the demanding role as if Steinbeck had originally written it with him in mind, which wasn't the case at all, and which made his performance all the more satisfying. From then on, Steele would take occasional non-Western roles, many of them unsympathetic, and do them superbly. He was a fine dirty-dispositioned fighter in Cagney's *City for Conquest* (Anatole Litvak, 1940), and even more memorable as the hood who crosses off poor Elisha Cook in Howard Hawks' *The Big Sleep* (1946). Meanwhile, undaunted by the Metropolitan series, he continued his range riding on the screen.

The recently formed PRC outfit was endeavoring to build a Western audience, and Steele was given a series of six wherein he impersonated Billy the Kid. Any resemblance to the young outlaw of legend who died before he reached legal maturity was coincidental. Reunited with Steele was Sam Newfield, who directed the sextet as both Peter Stewart and Sherman Scott, forsaking his own name. The Billy the Kid series was old-fashioned, but for Steele repre-

HOLLYWOOD CORRAL: A COMPREHENSIVE B WESTERN ROUNDUP

Carleton Young (l.), Steele, Fuzzy St. John rein up in Billy the Kid Outlawed *(1940).*

sented a far better tenure than previously. The series also rounded out the comic character of Al St. John's "Fuzzy" and he would be known and beloved by this moniker thereafter.

Then it was one after another for Steele, leaving Billy the Kid to Buster Crabbe. He became one-third of the Three Mesquiteers, then outlasted Ken Maynard as a Trail Blazer member when the Mesquiteers were interred. He even starred in a couple of tinted jobs. Finally, he returned to PRC to fill out an expired series and starred in a quartet of minor Westerns all directed by Harry Fraser and produced by Arthur Alexander. Production, direction, plots and supporting casts were all a bit tattered about the edges, as if they had been thumbed a few times too many. But through it all came Bob Steele, still a relatively young man, performing at his best–in Westerns, since he was saving the dramatic for more worthy causes–while pummeling the usual bunch of dastards. He even gave us something different in the last, *Thunder Town* (1946). Steele presented a hero who wore a mustache, putting him on a sartorial par with his longtime opponent Charles King. Then Steele became a character actor in Westerns and otherwise, and one of Hollywood's better ones.

Tom Tyler was the physical antithesis of Steele. Tyler was huge, and he wore this gigantic ten-gallon hat that made him even taller. His real name was Vincent Markowski and he had been a strong man before entering films. Like Steele, he had been seen in a well-received series for FBO-RKO, and before sound landed on the cowboy machine at Syndicate. He made his feature talkie debut there, but first appeared in a Mascot serial talkie, *Phantom of the West* (D. Ross Lederman, 1931). His initial Western feature for Syndicate was *West of Cheyenne* (Harry Webb, 1931), and when after two more Syndicate metamorphosed into Monogram, Tyler starred in a series of eight for the new company.

It would be the blight of Tom Tyler's career, in one opinion, that he never received the care and attention he needed, and merited, to become a top-ranking cowboy star. Like Bob Steele, Tyler was unique, but his stronger qualities were not so immediately apparent, and ran deeper. As mentioned, he was imposing in appearance. His acting was restrained, and more than satisfactory even in the most desperate inept situations, and he would have more than his share of them. The intriguing thing about Tyler was his somewhat sinister attitude, underlined by piercing eyes and a deep but repressed speaking voice, as if the sounds were coming from the shadows. More than any other range hero, Tyler gave the impression of tensile, quiet menace–that if he were on the prod for an adversary, that bad one's fate would not be a pleasant one to witness. Oddly enough, Tyler was not adept with the punches, and it was usually a disappointment to see Tom fanning the villain to slumber, when it was expected that he would break him like a matchstick.

Someone at Monogram, maybe supervisor G. A. Durlam, might have recognized the potential in Tyler. For there was a definite if unsuccessful effort to make a Western series slightly offbeat. The first, *Partners of the Trail*, released during the summer of 1931, dealt with regeneration and didn't sound much like a Western at all, with Reginald Sheffield landing a role nearly equal in footage and importance with Tyler. Wallace Fox directed Durlam's script, resulting in a slow but interesting tale. Durlam himself tried his hand at directing Tyler in *Two Fisted Justice* (1931); assigned production manager Charles A. Post to direct *Single-Handed Sanders* (1932); and employed Lloyd Nosler, a film editor, to direct *Galloping Thru* (1931) and *The Man from Death Valley* (1931), the latter a co-scripting effort of Durlam and Nosler. The Nosler films were quite good, with more than normal care reflected in his direction. The rest of the series left a feeling of unfulfillment.

Tyler then joined John R. Freuler's Monarch organization for four unmemorable outdoor shows, with the two J.P.'s, McCarthy and McGowan, directing. McCarthy's *The Forty Niners* (1932) had a slightly more ambitious theme of Western exploration, unfortunately not developed with finesse, while the three McGowans, all released during 1933, were unable to rise above the routine.

In 1935, Tyler appeared as Sundown Saunders in RKO's *Powdersmoke Range*. Bob Steele was also in the cast, and it was an early Three Mesquiteers yarn from the pen of William Colt MacDonald. Both Tyler and Steele were to join the Mesquiteer ranks eventually, as Stony Brooke and Tucson Smith respectively, but here the roles were taken by Hoot Gibson and Harry Carey. The film is still possessed of its reputation as a sort of landmark among the smaller Westerns, stemming mainly from the truly all-star cast. In truth it is a slow-paced job, on the dull side, and not too ingeniously plotted. Nor are the performances anything to brag about, except Tyler's. As a cold-eyed gunman who is persuaded to come over to the side of the law, Tyler was legitimately good, and showed here what, in proper

Gino Corrado (l.), Tom Tyler and Betty Mack in The Man from Death Valley *(1931).*

HOLLYWOOD CORRAL: A COMPREHENSIVE B WESTERN ROUNDUP

Tyler in Partners of the Trail *(1931).*

hands, he was capable of doing. Perhaps director Wallace Fox worked well with Tyler, for his direction of the film was otherwise not too alert. Again, Tyler took an unsympathetic role in another RKO teaming of Carey and Gibson, in *The Last Outlaw* (Christy Cabanne, 1936), and did well with it.

A year prior to *Powdersmoke Range,* Tyler had signed with Harry Webb and B. B. Ray's Reliable company to make a Western series. From 1934 to 1936, he starred in 19 of them, beginning with the passable *Tracy Rides* (Webb, 1934). One or two of the early ones were similarly adequate, such as *Unconquered Bandit* (Webb, 1935); the remainder consisted of bottom-of-the-barrel caliber in every respect, save perhaps the photography, usually by oldtimers like Pliny Goodfriend or J. Henry Kruse, pleasingly clear and uncomplicated. Unfortunately, the pleasing eye appeal was vitiated by jumbled storylines, aimless meandering about in quest of an excuse to start the action, and supporting performances of often amateur stature. Through it all, Tyler's manly presence did much, if not enough, to overcome the pall. Even Tyler was victimized by sloppy staging of the action scenes.

Victory Pictures, in its pre-Tim McCoy period, saw Tyler move in and labor through eight Sam Katzman-produced ventures during 1937–38. Katzman sometimes directed, which was no boon. The others were done by Robert Hill. An occasional note of relief was afforded by Sammy Cohen, a Yiddish comic seen all too seldom in sound films, possibly because of the stereotype angle, but who knew his way around a broad laugh and enhanced the films in which he appeared. Mostly though, it was on the order of *Brothers of the West* (Katzman, 1937). At one juncture during the tatty narrative of this epic, Tom and the heroine are found searching a cabin, for unimportant purposes of plot. One of the villain's henchmen furtively sneaks up and spies upon them from outside the cabin; Tom's horse whinnies nervously.

"Wait a minute!" cautions Tom, tiptoeing to the window. "There's someone out there spying on us. That was my horse... he always tips me off!"

This tasty morsel of dialogue cannot be chalked up to scenarist Basil Dickey, nor can Tyler be blamed for hapless ad-libbing. For that matter, it wouldn't be fair to pin the wrap on Katzman either. It was just one of those things that happened in the Tyler Victory series, and happened all too often. He usually played the part of Tom Wade, of the Cattlemen's Protective Association; a cynical trade reviewer began referring to him as "Our Tom" as he would give a blast to each succeeeding effort.

At low ebb, Tyler received a good role, just as had Bob Steele. In the small but effective part of one of the deadly Plummer boys in John Ford's epochal 1939 production of *Stagecoach,* Tyler made his few minutes on screen count for all they were worth, and more. He also developed the stylized "long walk" after getting plugged, although Ford didn't show it–just Tyler ambling into the saloon after the (unseen) gunfight, smiling benignly at the gathered tipplers, then keeling over. Six years later, David Butler had him actually walk a city block after getting gun-shot by Errol Flynn early in *San Antonio.* His screen death scenes were noted for their longevity, if nothing else.

In contrast to his villainous duties, Tyler made quite a splash in serials, both of the Western and other variety. In addition to his first experience with sound films, he appeared in the Universal chapterplay *Battling with Buffalo Bill* (Ray Taylor, 1931), as well as *Clancy of the Mounted* (Taylor, 1933). His most famous serial appearances came when he portrayed the comic strip heroes, Captain Marvel and the Phantom. His excursion into the realm of horror,

BATTLING BOB, AND OUR TOM: Steele, Tyler

Jim Corey takes it on the chin from Tyler in Brothers of the West *(1937).*

The Mummy's Hand (Christy Cabanne, 1940), paved the way for a profitable shock series with Lon Chaney assuming Tyler's original role of a gruesome bandaged being back from the dead. A noteworthy Tyler role in a big-budgeted Western was as an Indian in *Valley of the Sun* (George Marshall, 1942); a noteworthy non-Western role was as a strikebreaker in *Talk of the Town* (George Stevens, 1942).

Tom Tyler made his swan song as a Western lead when he joined Bob Steele for the Three Mesquiteers series. He turned to character roles thereafter, most of them in Westerns, most of them badmen. Arthritis overtook him, crippled him, eventually killed him. His tenure as a cowboy star stretched back to the silents, and was long and noble. The feeling persists that with creative and intensive guidance, the attributes of Tom Tyler, buried as they were under an avalanche of neglect and carelessness, could have been tranformed into a screen image approaching the highest plateaus. That it didn't happen is too bad. We still have the rudiments in quite a few of his films.

Harry Carey

5
THOSE BRAWNY MEN IN STETSONS

Overland Bound had led the way in blazing a trail for the independently produced sound Western. Now in 1930, a few more courageous shoestring producers were determined to try their Western wares. Foremost among these were John R. Freuler, whose company was presently called Big 4, which in itself sounded more like a ranch brand than a movie outfit. The second prolific supplier of saddle sagas was Syndicate Pictures, headed by W. Ray Johnston. Johnston headed one or two other production systems as well, and would in the future merge them all into Monogram. But for the present, Syndicate was engaged almost exclusively in outdoor presentations.

Cowboy stars working for the independent producers in 1930 were relatively small in number, but they did get around, moving from company to company. The Western with songs and music was still several years away, but the scramble for the lead position in the early talkies resembled a game of cowboy musical chairs. A player would be handed the hero role in one film, then be relegated to a support job in its successor. Sometimes three or four familiar faces would grace the same film. A Big 4 production of early 1930, *Beyond the Rio Grande,* had Jack Perrin as the nominal lead, but also featured the veterans Franklyn Farnum, Pete Morrison and Edmund Cobb in supporting roles, as well as another current cowboy hero, one Buffalo Bill, Jr., in the cast. Syndicate's *Under Texas Skies* (J. P. McGowan, 1930) officially starred Bob Custer, but also had in its cast Bill Cody and Lane Chandler, both leading men and both shortly to have their own series. The same company's *Westward Bound* (Harry Webb, 1930), with Buffalo Bill, Jr. in the lead and Buddy Roosevelt billed third, after former reigning serial queen Allene Ray, was a compendium of the lowest depths of the small-budget Western. It took about a year for the filmmakers to untangle this dubious "all-star" system. Then the lines became more firmly drawn, the Western stars were securely coronated in their series, and the ones who didn't make it gradually drifted from view.

Among the first and most often on the screen, if not absolutely the best, was Jack Perrin. He was big and masculine-looking, if not particularly memorable; knew his way around the lots, since he had been in films since 1914; had had a quantity of previous experience on horseback in various Westerns for various producers, and was owner of a beautiful steed he called Starlight; and was currently at the peak of his career, having starred in a well received set for Universal. He had also shared top billing with Leo Maloney in *Overland Bound,* so Jack Perrin could claim talkie experience with the pioneers.

For Harry Webb, Perrin appeared in *Beyond the Rio Grande,* and another Big 4 outdoor saga, *Ridin' Law.* He starred in *Phantom of the Desert* for Syndicate, and in a Robert and John Tansey film, *Romance of the West,* all in 1930. These films may have secured his position as one of the first, if not the very

HOLLYWOOD CORRAL: A COMPREHENSIVE B WESTERN ROUNDUP

Jack Perrin has the drop on Tom London in Wildcat Saunders *(1936).*

first cowboy star of a regular series of low-budget Westerns. However, their quality was such that his future was severely in jeopardy, at least as a top ranking cowboy star. This dire situation was further beclouded by his next group of films, made under the aegis of Robert J. Horner, who produced, sometimes directed, sometimes wrote, and often operated in all three capacities on his product. Mr. Horner was a man with one leg, small resources, and his artistic pretensions were forthrightly nonexistent. He had made some Westerns starring Perrin in the silent era. In the interim, Perrin had peaked at Universal, and was now descending to earth as he returned to the tattered standards of his former boss. If the art of the motion picture had advanced in great strides during the few years of Perrin's absence, it was not reflected in the overall quality of Mr. Horner's contribution to the early sound film. Anyone who has seen *Wild West Whopee* (1931) or *The Kid from Arizona* (1931) can attest to that. Jack Perrin had been fortunate to be among the pioneers of the talkie Western, but his choice of films had not been so felicitous. By 1932, he was performing in featured roles in Ken Maynard productions for World Wide.

An oddity of the times, the Western featurette, was Perrin's savior the following year. He was teamed with comic Ben Corbett for a series of "Bud 'n Ben" three-reelers, each film running in the neighborhood of 30 minutes. Astor Pictures distributed these off-length efforts, which were innocuously light in conception and treatment, on the states' rights market. Perrin acted in all but a couple as the "Bud" of the series' title. His name was not mentioned in the advertisements for the series, although ironically his horse Starlight was prominently mentioned in the billing, as "The Wonder Horse." Apparently, Perrin's previous associations and inferior releases had done him little good.

Back to features for the 1934–35 season, Perrin starred in a half dozen for Reliable and producer-directors Harry Webb and B. B. Ray. An improvement over his features of three and four years ago, they were nevertheless in the lower Western bracket. Perrin's final four films as a Western star came in 1936, made for producer William Berke: *Gun Grit,*

THOSE BRAWNY MEN IN STETSONS

Wally Wales (l., on white horse) and Buzz Barton (l., on foot) in Riders of the Cactus *(1931).*

HOLLYWOOD CORRAL: A COMPREHENSIVE B WESTERN ROUNDUP

Hair-Trigger Casey, Wildcat Saunders, Desert Justice. Berke directed some of them himself, under the name of Lester Williams, while Harry Fraser did the rest. They tried to be different. They were modernized, replete with gangsters and fast automobiles—*Wildcat Saunders* had a bit of prizefight action. The casts were above par for independent product too, but despite the advantages they seemed to lack that extra finesse. As he passed the age of 40 years, Jack Perrin settled into supporting roles, where he was to remain contentedly for many years thereafter. He was among the first of the talkie cowboys, but the race is not always won by the swift.

Playing supporting roles in some of Perrin's last starring vehicles, such as the aforesaid *Hair-Trigger Casey,* was Wally Wales, soon to be re-christened Hal Taliaferro, sometimes known as Walt Williams, born Floyd Alderson: a man of many names, with a screen career similarly varied. As Wally Wales, he had been starring in independent silent Westerns since 1925, ten years after he entered films. Like Perrin, he had appeared in the transitional *Overland Bound,* and had become a fixture in early sound Westerns. Continuing the parallel, both Wales and Perrin had starred in 1930 non-Western serial dramas.

There is ample evidence that Wales, as with Tom Tyler, could have reached higher plateaus under the right discerning guidance. A true Westerner (Sheridan, Wyoming) raised on a ranch, Wales possessed that stamp of authenticity in manner, appearance and voice which set him apart from his confreres, solidified by a quiet strength and innate intelligence that shone through in his acting, even when the production odds were not favorable. On the other hand, it may be too much to ask the public to accept introspective strengths in an action performer. The early Wales is remindful of the later Ben Johnson, an actor of like qualities whom nobody seemed to use properly, except John Ford; Johnson matured well, eventually won an Academy Award for work as a character actor. Wales turned to character parts in 1936 and thereby lengthened his screen tenure by considerable years, although not hitting the jackpot as did Johnson. However, for sheer versatility in the horse opera field, Wales-Taliaferro would be hard to top. Of them all, he is presumably the only Western actor who has played hero, villain, sheriff, rancher, gang member and comedy relief—not as a stunt, but appearing in each category several times as a matter of acting course. Other achievements include of course his inaugural sound appearance, as above;

Yakima Canutt (l., with pipe) is accosted by Lane Chandler in Wyoming Whirlwind *(1932).*

THOSE BRAWNY MEN IN STETSONS

Bob Custer (center) warns Roger Williams to leave Victoria Vinton alone in The Vengeance of Rannah *(1936).*

one of the five candidates for the true identity of *The Lone Ranger,* in Republic's epochal 1938 serial; and starring in his own series of featurettes, as well as replacing Jack Perrin in another series. Quite a movie life.

Wales made his starring series for Freuler's Big 4 company in 1930–31, most of them directed by Alvin J. Neitz. Discounting the anachronisms unavoidable at the time and for the money, it can be said that they contained action to spare, though the plots may have been skimpy and some of the minor performances less than that. He then played supporting parts and appeared with practically every other working movie cowboy for the next year or two, from John Wayne to Bill Cody, from Tom Tyler to Rex Bell, from Ken Maynard to Reb Russell, and not excluding old crony Jack Perrin, as mentioned.

In 1934, Wales starred again in a series of eight three-reelers for Imperial Pictures. He also assumed the role of "Bud" in the "Bud 'n Ben" series when Perrin became incapacitated; Wales at this time appeared as Walt Williams, playing the lead in one and a supporting role in a second, when the "Bud" role was taken by Fred Humes. Wales starred in one final Western, the mediocre *Way of the West* (Robert Tansey, 1935), released by Superior on the states' rights market, then became Hal Taliaferro, the character actor. He remained in movies, primarily outdoor dramas, into the '50s, when he retired to a ranch, with enough leisure time to indulge in his hobby of sketching and painting.

Referring back to *The Lone Ranger,* the continuity centered around the identity of the masked avenger, being one of five men. Lee Powell was one. Three companion actors would change their screen names at various points in their respective careers: Herman Brix (later Bruce Bennett), George Letz (later George Montgomery) and Hal Taliaferro (formerly Wally Wales). The fifth Ranger was played by Lane Chandler, who stayed with his screen cognomen though he was born Robert Oakes. Chandler came up through the Paramount Western route, as a possible Gary Cooper type. The only trouble was that Paramount already had a Gary Cooper type, Cooper himself. By 1930, Chandler already had a couple of years' experience freelancing, mostly in non-Western roles. He starred in one Western for Big 4, *Firebrand Jordan* (Alvin J. Neitz, 1930), and essayed roles in a supporting capacity until landing a series for independent producer Willis Kent, after having been involved in a disastrous second starring effort for the Tansey brothers entitled *Riders of the Rio*. The first Kent production, *Hurricane Horseman,* directed by Armand Schaefer, appeared in 1931, with the remainder of the series of eight spread over a two-year period.

Chandler had everything a cowboy star needed; looks, riding and fighting ability, masculinity. He also had an uncommon amount of acting ability, surely not a prime requisite for range stardom although it didn't hurt. Like other worthies, Chandler was caught in the maelstrom of Western pictures, all with a shoestring producer's idea of the new Tom Mix. There were too many of them, and the odds were against an independent Western star establishing himself, unless his fans memories reached back to the silent days. In this respect, Chandler just wasn't well-known enough. Like Wally Wales, he drifted into supporting roles, mostly on the side of the law; Chandler was a bit too upstanding and stalwart in appearance to make a really convincing heavy, until some years later when a few added lines in his face and a growth of stubble on his chin provided the necessary menacing equipment. His last two starring assignments came in 1935. One of them, *Outlaw Tamer,* a Kinematrade release, was a sober, somewhat leisurely but rather dignified outdoor adventure directed by J. P. McGowan. It proved that with adequate production backing, Chandler could have been a name to reckon with. But he too soon nested in character roles.

One of Chandler's early Western supporting roles was in *Under Texas Skies,* directed by the ubiquitous J. P. McGowan in 1930 for the pre-Monogram Syndicate company. Its star was Bob Custer, who had topped the casts of a number of McGowan silents for the company and had stayed on to try talkies. Custer had been popular in the silents, and there are those who question why, especially after seeing a few of his sound films. Taken in a broad view, Custer was pleasant enough to behold, in the Ken Maynard division. His name had a lilt to it and was short for marquee purposes, easy to remember. More important, he kept working steadily through the '20s. His face was a familiar one to Saturday-matinee crowds, and sometimes familiarity breeds friendliness as well as contempt. Western devotees got used to him. But whatever it was that Custer had, the illusion was severely battered by the coming of sound. *Under Texas Skies* was a primitive, at times unpleasant affair, nor were Custer's three ensuing efforts for Syndicate much of an improvement. For 1931–32, Custer moved to Big 4, starring in a quartet of unmemorable adventures. He was the hero in a Western serial, *Law of the Wild* (Armand Schaefer & B. Reeves Eason, 1934) for Mascot. But here, his heroism was sorely tried, since he was in competition with Rex, the horse, and Rin Tin Tin Jr., the supercanine. Not to mention support comprised of such disparate talents as Lucile Browne and Sennetteer Ben Turpin. Against such an array, Custer was somewhat jostled out of the limelight. For that matter, the chapterplay itself was pedestrian. Custer gradually drifted out of the film game. His last starring vehicle was for Webb and Ray, at Reliable.

Last solo hurrah for Rex Lease also occurred at Reliable, in 1937. Like Custer, Lease had shared serial honors with Rin Tin Tin Jr., but *The Silver Trail,* directed by Webb under the alias of Henri Samuels, was an improvement over the serial, since it ran 57 minutes as opposed to 12 two-reel chapters. By way of irony, Lease had starred in a serial the year before called *Custer's Last Stand,* but we'll get to that momentarily.

Lease was being groomed as a leading man by Tiffany when he was cast in an outdoor show, *The Utah Kid* (Richard Thorpe, 1930), and from there on the die was cast. Boris Karloff had a featured role in it too, but Karloff went on to horror while Lease was confronted with horror of a different sort. For *In Old Cheyenne* (Stuart Paton, 1931) was thoroughly inept, despite the always-welcome villainy of Harry Woods. Nor did a 1932 release, *The Lone Trail* (Harry Webb and Forrest Sheldon) help much, since it was a cut-down version of a bottom-barrel serial made two years before by Syndicate, *Sign of the Wolf*. With sharp features and a not-too-forceful personality, Lease was destined for character roles, which he ultimately assumed with continuing success. The above-mentioned *Custer's Last Stand* (Elmer Clifton, 1936), a production by George Merrick and the Weiss boys, was a serial ambitious in its advertising if not in production values. A brave attempt to tie serial action to an historical background, as producers were wont to do in the old silent days, it got pretty hokey with alarming frequency. But Lease was a valorous frontier scout of a hero, and a cast filled with oldtimers was fun to watch, if not always inspiring.

Lease's one Western series had been made the year before, in 1935, and the majority of these Superior (capital "S") adventures were also directed by Elmer Clifton. Featured with Lease was young Bobby Nelson, who was to appear in *Custer's Last Stand* too. Nelson was a veteran of Westerns despite his tender years, evidence that producers were prone to err in the belief that the youthful public would accept one of them as their own. In truth, kids didn't like to see other kids riding the range on the screen—it made them envious. They always preferred their cowboy heroes full-grown. The Big 4 company tried teenaged Buzz Barton in a few of their shows, to little effect. Master Barton was a carryover from the silents, and would rank high in the longevity stakes, for he was still doing his thing in 1938 opposite Jack Luden for Columbia.

Monogram used Andy Shuford as a young pal for Bill Cody in a series of eight Westerns for their 1931–32 season. Canadian-born Cody had been starred in the silents, but had been quietly hiding out in non-Western features for the first few years of sound. Cody looked a little bit like Tim McCoy (or vice versa), except that his range regalia seemed slightly too large for him, as if he had suddenly lost weight. Before his Monogram series he had appeared in support of Bob Custer in *Under Texas Skies*. His own series was not particularly successful, not because of any lack on Cody's part, but simply for the reason that the vehicles were uninspired, and the addition of Shuford was a liability to the forward motion of the narratives. Slightly above par was *Texas Pioneers* (Harry Fraser, 1932), with its sure-fire Cavalry-vs.-Indians thematics.

Cody went on to star in eight features for Spectrum during 1934–35, if anything a descent from the Monogram series in quality. As a final indignity, he

Joan Barclay and Rex Bell in Men of the Plains *(1936).*

Bell hands a shootin' iron to Buzz Barton in Gun Fire *(1935).*

appeared in some of Robert Horner's Aywon productions. These odorous efforts were apparently produced sometime around 1935; difficult to tell, since they played in so few theaters and so little information is extant about them. Sometimes descriptions of films at the nadir are impossible, since the printed word can only fail to adequately impress upon the senses the depths to which bad filmmaking can plummet. One can only point, gagging, to *Border Menace,* directed by Jack Nelson, and run. Another Aywon debacle is *Phantom Cowboy,* directed by Horner personally, and starring former Universal silent hero Ted Wells in what must surely have been an ill-advised comeback attempt. The Wells was a single effort. Cody had the misfortune to appear in three of them.

Replacing Cody at Monogram was Rex Bell, youngest and prettiest of the group presently under discussion. Bell had gotten underway as a Westerner at Fox, at the tail end of the silent era. His films were on the wishy-washy side, afflicted with a severe case of cutes in an attempt to be offbeat. Monogram tried the novelty approach too, with a tolerable amount of success. Their gimmick was to begin the story with Bell in the East, then through plot manipulations provide him with the opportunity to move to the open spaces, and the formula Western action. In *Rainbow Ranch* (1933) he was a Navy boxing champ who exchanges his sailor suit for chaps and spurs to save the old ranch (from dastardly Bob Kortman). *The Diamond Trail* (1932) had him on the trail of valuable gems, while in *Fighting Texans* (1933) Bell was in civilian store clothes for most of the reelage, which had to do with oil-well skulduggery. *Broadway to Cheyenne* (1932) has a self-explanatory title. The Monogram Bells did deserve a bow for trying. The only trouble was that a regular viewer of the Bell series would be fairly certain of the pattern before long, thus negating the novelty value. Since there were only six in the series, the formula didn't become too intrusive. Harry Fraser directed four of them, John P. McCarthy one, *Lucky Larrigan* (1932), and Armand Schaefer helmed *Fighting Texans.*

Bell starred in four Westerns for Resolute in 1935. Featured with him were Ruth Mix and Buzz Barton, with Harry Fraser directing. Instead of some ingenuity in the scripting shown in his previous series, Bell was victimized by the writer's penchant for twisting story and dialogue into verbal knots while trying to find a reason to get the horses a-galloping. Six more for Grand National, 1936–37, produced

THOSE BRAWNY MEN IN STETSONS

by the Alexander Brothers, Max and Arthur, and Bell devoted his time to Nevada politics and to domestic matters–he was married to former screen vamp Clara Bow.

Harry Carey seemed to have been around in movies from the very beginning, which was very nearly true, since he made his film debut in 1908. He had gone through the silent era a perennial favorite, in Westerns and non-Westerns. John Ford had cut his directorial teeth on Westerns starring Carey. The coming of sound found Carey devoting his time to an African trek and *Trader Horn,* which proved a success at the boxoffice but a jinx to the careers of the performers involved–Carey, Edwina Booth, Duncan Renaldo. Carey was over 50 but still agile; with no rewarding parts coming his way, he would star in Mascot serials, two of them opposite the ill-fated Miss Booth. Or he would take the lead in an occasional Western feature, such as *Cavalier of the West* (John P. McCarthy, 1931) for Artclass, or *Night Rider* (William Nigh, 1932). But these films were cursed with production defects, and Carey was more fondly remembered for his stints in top attractions, or in retrospect by buffs for his work in *Law and Order* (Edward Cahn, 1932), Universal's singular approach to a mood piece based on W. R. Burnett's novel *Saint Johnson,* which in turn was based on the exploits of Wyatt Earp and company.

Carey's most satisfying experiences in the genre occurred in a trio of RKO attractions chronicled in later chapters. In the interim he did a series of six features for William Berke, all of them directed by Harry Fraser, which were released during 1935–36. The star was then past the mid-fifty mark in years, and had never looked youthful. Therefore, it was a scripting chore to provide the proper amount of romantic or feminine interest in his vehicles. The problem was partially overcome by introducing a significantly juvenile supporting player to take care of any romantic interest that might crop up. In *Wagon Trail* for instance, Ed Norris gained movie experience by filling in the required amount of allure. When it came to the action elements, old Harry could take care of himself. Somebody forgot to tell the writers about this, for the major drawback to the series was its lack of vigorous moments, either by brawling or riding. On the average though, they were of interest, especially for the older Western fan with memories of the Harry Carey of yore. A good representative selection would be *Last of the Clintons* (1935), with its lean and rather bleak narrative, reminiscent of the William S. Hart technique (Carey

Gertrude Messinger and Harry Carey in Aces Wild *(1935).*

was in the Hart tradition), and a powerful heavy portrayal by Earl Dwire, a villain whose villainy too often bordered on the rudimentary but was perfectly in keeping here.

Guinn "Big Boy" Williams entered the movies quite a while after Carey, but his career did stem back to the silent days of Will Rogers, which meant that Woodrow Wilson was still President. Williams didn't really make his major impression until the sound era, appearing in a variety of roles that places him nearly on a par with Wally Wales for versatility. Unlike Wales-Taliaferro, Williams' strong suit was in comedy roles, and his baffled dumbness combined with his huge frame made him a natural. He did star in six independent Westerns, beginning with *Thunder Over Texas* (John Warner, 1934) for Beacon. The production had a classier look than many low-budget jobs, but this was vitiated by a poor script and some idiotic alleged comedy relief from the hapless Ben Corbett. The other Williams films varied. *Gun Play* (Al Herman, 1935) came off fairly well, while *Law of the .45s* (J. P. McCarthy, 1935) is interesting in that it constitutes the embryo of what was to become the noted Three Mesquiteers series, furthered by Williams appearing in *Powdersmoke Range* later the same year, another pre-Republic Mesquiteers story. Even in his superior films, Williams would often inadvertently break into that simpleton grin that was fine for buffoonery, but out of place on the face of a hero.

Like a lumbering comet, Jack Hoxie had blazed across the Western sky during the silents, and zoomed from sight almost as quickly. He returned to the screen for six Majestic Pictures offerings in 1933. As with so many former favorites, audiences unfamiliar with Hoxie were hard put to understand why he had

Chuck Morrison about to bean Dave Sharpe with a chair while Carey gives Roger Williams a kick to the Adam's apple in Ghost Town *(1936).*

THOSE BRAWNY MEN IN STETSONS

Jack Perrin (l.), Tom Tyler and Jimmy Aubrey take a break on location for Mystery Ranch *(1934).*

been so popular. Hoxie was big but clumsy, and at times his vehicles gave the impression that the writers and director would go out of their way to make him out a dunce. The opening scene of *Via Pony Express* (Lewis D. Collins, 1933) must rate with the biggest unintentional laughs of its year. As Hoxie gallops through a pass formed by two large boulders, he is roped from each side by two desperadoes, and left hanging in mid-air like a Smithfield ham ripe for smoking. It was meant to be taken in earnest, but the results were more suitable for Smiley Burnette than the hero of a Western. Hoxie's fisticuffing form was a bit girlish, too. After the Majestic series, he went back to circus life, to make no more films.

Reb Russell lands somewhere between Jack Hoxie and "Big Boy" Williams on the believability scale. A gridiron hero, he appeared in one football yarn before engaging in a Western group for producer Willis Kent, 1934–35. Curious thing about the Russells is that they are impressive in casts, with prime baddies Fred Kohler, Yakima Canutt and Ed Cobb well in evidence in most of them; and the production values, while far from major caliber, are actually more than adequate. Script and directorial finesse is another matter, compounded by Russell's obvious lack of thespic ability. A potentially superior story like *Arizona Badman* (S. Roy Luby, 1934), with a good role well-played by Cobb, was marred by production gaucheries and the star's failing to hit it off with a grinding camera. *Border Vengeance* (Ray Heinz, 1934) contains the priceless scene wherein Russell is captured and bound helpless, as the villain (Kenneth MacDonald) enters in his all-too-transparent disguise of limp gray wig and deformed posture, whips off his concealment to Russell's astonished "Why… hit's Flash Purdue!" The travisty continues as MacDonald taunts our hero, who interjects at periodic intervals "Ah'll KILL yew!" Russell had a nice horse, named Rebel. He appeared as a country sheriff in a Sol Lesser non-Western doggie drama, *Fighting to Live* (Edward Cline, 1935), then retired.

A note on sons of famous fathers. Francis X. Bushman, Jr. assisted Buzz Barton in three Big 4 epics of 1931–32 and sporadically appeared in other quickies of the time, but failed to make an imprint as a cowboy leading man. Creighton Chaney, before he became Lon Chaney, Jr., had the top role in a 1932 serial made by the Van Beuren Corporation for RKO release, *The Last Frontier,* which was truncated into a feature version called *The Black Ghost* (Spencer Bennet & Tom Storey, 1932). Otherwise, Chaney's early Western experience consisted of minor unsympathetic roles in support of such as Tom Tyler (*Cheyenne Rides Again,* 1937) and Gene Autry (*The Old Corral,* 1936). Fred Kohler, Jr., offspring of the great villain, starred in two for producer William Berke, *Toll of the Desert* and *The Pecos Kid* (both Lester Williams, 1935), on the slow side but with some uncommonly good elements, especially the former. Young Kohler thereafter fit more logically into the villainous niche carved out by his father. In fact, Dad and Junior together made a fine unruly pair in the George O'Brien *Lawless Valley* (David Howard, 1938) for RKO. Finally, Noah Beery, Jr., after working with Tom Mix and in a serial or two, got a lead Western role when barely out of his teens in the Anthony J. Xydias production for Sunset Pictures, *Five Bad Men* (Cliff Smith, 1935), but the film was deficient in most departments. Beery did much better in random outdoor shows at Universal, such as *Stormy* (Louis Friedlander, 1935), a most pleasing horse story, and *Forbidden Valley* (Wyndham Gittens, 1938), another equine yarn.

Speaking of wild horses, an enterprising producer would turn out a stallion story upon occasion, such as Columbia's *King of the Wild Horses* (Earl Haley, 1933) or Grand National's *King of the Sierras* (Samuel Diege, 1938), in which the humans played distinctly second fiddle to the horseflesh and the scenery. One magnificent animal, Black King, received a mini-series of his own, consisting of *Gunners and Guns* (Jerry Callahan, 1935) and *Riddle Ranch* (Charles Hutchinson, 1935), made for producer Mitchell Leichter of Beaumont Productions. Edmund Cobb had a top role in the former film, but aside from that the horse was the main, the only, attraction. And aside from an oddity like *Fighting Fury* (Bob Hill, 1934), which featured Kazan, the canine, as well as a John King who is not the later John King of the Range Busters, the gates of the compound are closed.

This leaves us to wind up the story of the early sound independents with the work of Buddy Roosevelt, Buffalo Bill, Jr. and, certainly far from least, the amazing Denver Dixon.

Buffalo Bill, Jr. and Buddy Roosevelt appeared together in an early Syndicate talkie, *Westward Bound* (Harry Webb, 1930), the former starring, the latter in support. Both had had careers spanning the silent '20s, starring in bottom-grade features, and both made a few starring talkies: Roosevelt in *Lightnin' Smith's Return* (Jack Irwin, 1931), Buffalo Bill, Jr. in *Riders of Golden Gulch* (Cliff Smith, 1932) and others. The latter's real name was Jay Wilsey, and he also filmed under that name.

Both stars made four Westerns for Denver Dixon during the early '30s, and there the story becomes complicated. Dixon's real name was Victor Adamson, a New Zealander who came to Hollywood in the teens and quickly became a one-man studio, producing, directing, writing and starring in silent Westerns. Cashing in on the current reigning idol of the range, Adamson-Dixon concocted the character of Art Mix. At various times, Art Mix was played by Dixon; one Bob Roberts; and a George Kesterson, who eventually assumed the name as his own and appeared frequently in minor Western roles throughout the '30s. Kesterson was a smallish man who affected a towering ten-gallon hat, thus making him immediately recognizable.

Dixon made some early-sound "Art Mix Productions," including the part-talking *Sagebrush Politics* and the all-talking *West of the Rockies* for 1930 release. Then came the Wilsey and Roosevelt vehicles, with Dixon occasionally playing a bit, Hitchcock fashion. Films like *Lightning Bill* (Buffalo Bill, Jr.) and *Lightning Range* (Buddy Roosevelt) have a certain classic badness about them that becomes rather charming after one becomes attuned to their defects. Mauled lines, sudden uncalled for appearances of crew members in the backgrounds, and other sundry errors of commission and omission are prevalent. But soon, the atmosphere is one of genial amateurs having fun playing cowboy in somebody's back yard, and the films become, not dismal, but sympathetic.

Buddy Roosevelt and Buffalo Bill, Jr. received smaller and smaller roles, ending with bit parts. Dixon, like an underground river, flowed along for decades, fathering a new generation of shoestring filmmakers in Al Adamson, horror and exploitation flicks a specialty. Dixon would take a role in an occasional independent Western, and was responsible for the scripts of a Tex Ritter or two. And when

THOSE BRAWNY MEN IN STETSONS

Lucille Lund sharing her fan magazine with co-star Reb Russell in Fighting Through *(1934).*

Russell and Jack Kirk (r.) subdue crooked sheriff Alan Bridge in Outlaw Rule *(1935).*

Break time on an unidentified Buddy Roosevelt starrer.

Buffalo Bill, Jr. and unidentified player in The Whirlwind Rider *(1935).*

the money was there he would turn out another on his own, which would not be related to artistry by any distance but would receive a few playdates in obscure theaters. Today, some are rarities. Who has seen *Desert Mesa,* a 1936 drama with stuntman Wally West in the lead? It represents a type of filming, and an era, long since departed. Awful in its way, but fun.

Such were the first seven years-plus of the independently produced sound Western.

John Wayne and Marguerite Churchill in The Big Trail *(1930).*

6
BIG JOHN: THE BEGINNING

A lone horseman rides into town. The street is deserted, but the jangling sound of a ricky-tick piano emanates from the local saloon. The rider dismounts in front of the watering place, advances through the swinging doors. He is young, affable-looking; there's a smile on his face as he enters the place of merriment, ready to be convivial and join in the festivities. Immediately inside the doors he stops, smile frozen on his face. The music continues to tinkle from the automatically controlled instrument, but there will be no conviviality, no merriment in this saloon.

Bodies litter the floor, are slumped in chairs in the finality of death. The newcomer is the only one alive in the room. The rest is carnage. A massacre has taken place.

Randy Rides Alone (Harry Fraser, 1934) opens in this fashion, and after innumerable Westerns before and after, it's still the bloodthirstiest but most intriguing beginning of any low-budget Western. It's one of 16 that John Wayne starred in for Monogram between 1933 and 1935, under the general supervision of Trem Carr. The series was known as the "Lone Star" group, replete with lawman's badge for a trademark in lieu of the modernistic Monogram design of the period. Paul Malvern was the producer. *Randy Rides Alone* was written by Lindsley Parsons, who functioned as the west coast publicity representative for the studio, as well as dabbling in scenario writing. It was Wayne's seventh, coming at about midway point in the skein. After the sock start, things went predictably downhill, but not to such an extent as to leave an unsatisfactory impression. If not the best in the series, if not even typical, it indicates how Monogram, with limited resources, did make an attempt to inject some novel situations into their range product, with Bob Steele, Rex Bell, and of course John Wayne.

For the big man from Winterset, Iowa, still in his mid-twenties, the times were precarious. He had hit stardom with his first role of any dimension, and had plummeted almost as fast. The past few years had been difficult ones, but at least he was working steadily, no mean feat in a Depression year.

Wayne's story is too familiar to recount in detail here. Perhaps a pause at *The Big Trail*, however, might be pertinent. Raoul Walsh's epic of the wilderness is assuredly not a quickie Western, but it is an important one in the scheme of things regarding John Wayne; and since his performance and the film itself have been maligned, a plea in its defense might, if not set the record straight, then balance the scales somewhat. For in one opinion, *The Big Trail* is a considerable achievement for its time and stands with Victor Fleming's *The Virginian* (1929) as a landmark of the early outdoor talkie.

Released late in 1930, *The Big Trail* seemed to possess all the outward requisites to attract patronage to theaters. Its story of a great wagon trek West was epic in sweep, yet told simply and excitingly. The exterior photography was truly breathtaking in scope. In its initial city engagements, it was presented in a Fox wide-screen process; an extra attraction to enhance the talking picture, the enlarged screen was attempted as an adjunct to several current films, including King Vidor's *Billy the Kid,* another outdoor show. From a production standpoint, *The Big Trail* was obviously superior, and the reviews took full cognizance of the fact. Despite all this, the film failed at the boxoffice.

Its lack of success could be attributed to several factors. The economic depression was in full swing, plaguing the country, and the world. Wide-screen equipment proved too costly to install in theaters throughout the nation and most houses played the normal-screen version, thus losing, if not full impact, then a good deal of exploitation value of the novelty. The cast was largely unknown, including Wayne and Marguerite Churchill; comedian El Brendel was more familiar to movie audiences, and Brendel wasn't strong enough to carry the burden of a big picture on his Scandinavian shoulders.

In any case, *The Big Trail* received encouraging critical notices not reinforced by any great stampedes to the boxoffice. Until its recent uncovering and resurrection from the Fox vaults it was an unseen, forgotten, presumably lost film. The surviving material is the normal-screen version *(Editor's note: The wide-screen version was preserved subsequent to the initial publication of* Hollywood Corral*).* Apparently, the large-screen one was some minutes longer, with several sequences shortened for normal exhibition. Indications are that a depiction of pulling wagons up a precarious mountain cliff had more to it, and an Indian attack is also somewhat truncated. Reference books list two photographers, Arthur Edeson and Lucien Andriot, but only the latter is credited on the existing print, giving rise to the theory that Edeson photographed the giant-size version.

Time has not tarnished its entertainment value, nor dimmed the performance of Wayne. Said performance has been criticized, mostly after the fact, by what criteria it is hard to discern. For it is a sincere one, a fitting one, awkward only in the sense that the character has the awkward traits of youthful enthusiasm. Wayne's frontiersman is personable, masculine, refreshingly direct. His major scene, an impassioned speech delivered to recalcitrant settlers, is done with honesty and an inward conviction that makes it believable.

However sincere his performance, Wayne nevertheless was a young man with a financial flop for his big-time debut, so Fox reacted in kind. They wasted him in a couple of supporting roles, then dumped him. Columbia picked up his services, but the outcome was not much better. In fact, it was worse. A leading role opposite Laura La Plante in a tatty vehicle, *Men Are Like That,* directed by George B. Seitz and based on a shopworn Augustus Thomas drama, was an inauspicious beginning. Following were a bit in a Jack Holt sports show and minor parts in Westerns starring the studio's two current cowhands: Buck Jones, in *Range Feud* (D. Ross Lederman, 1931) and Tim McCoy, in *Texas Cyclone* and *Two-Fisted Law* (both Lederman, 1932). The films were entirely satisfactory for fans of Jones and McCoy, but Wayne had played the lead in one of Hollywood's more expensive productions not long ago, and here he was essaying kid-brother roles and anonymous range hands. His dislike for Columbia prexy Harry Cohn grew into a great hatred, which endured after Wayne left the studio.

A freelance job for Paramount didn't help much, but a couple of Mascot serials did, in more ways than one. They kept the Wayne household stocked with groceries, not a facetious remark in view of the economic times, and they strengthened his appeal as an action player. Neither of the serials was Western in locale, but somebody at Warners put two and two together and came up with John Wayne as the star of a series of six Westerns, putting the company back on the range for the first time since the First National Ken Maynard successes. At times, in fact, it was more like a reunion, since stock footage from the Maynards was frequently employed to bolster the action sequences in the Waynes.

Opening the Wayne series was *Ride 'Em, Cowboy* (Fred Allen, 1932), and it was a clever start. Not especially innovative, but clever, for it established Wayne as a studio cowboy star, and the story concerned much ado over Wayne's horse, appropriately named Duke. The Kenneth Perkins original had more meat on its bones than most Western yarns, and Warners supplied its new star with a cast of more than ordinary ability, including ingenue Ruth Hall, the impressive H. B. Walthall, and veterans Harry Gribbon, Otis Harlan, Charles Sellon and the burly Frank Hagney. With *The Big Stampede* (Tenny Wright, 1932), he was given such worthies as Berton Churchill and Paul Hurst, not to mention a villainous adversary of ripe vintage in the elder Noah Berry, who rose to the occasion imposingly. *Haunted Gold* (Mack V. Wright, 1932) probably rates as the most entertaining in the Warner set; it is fast, fervent, finely photographed by Nick Musuraca, and has a mystery angle, which seldom fails to garnish any Western.

Wayne's concluding trio of Westerns for Warners

BIG JOHN: The Beginning

Wayne and Cecilia Parker in Riders of Destiny *(1933).*

HOLLYWOOD CORRAL: A COMPREHENSIVE B WESTERN ROUNDUP

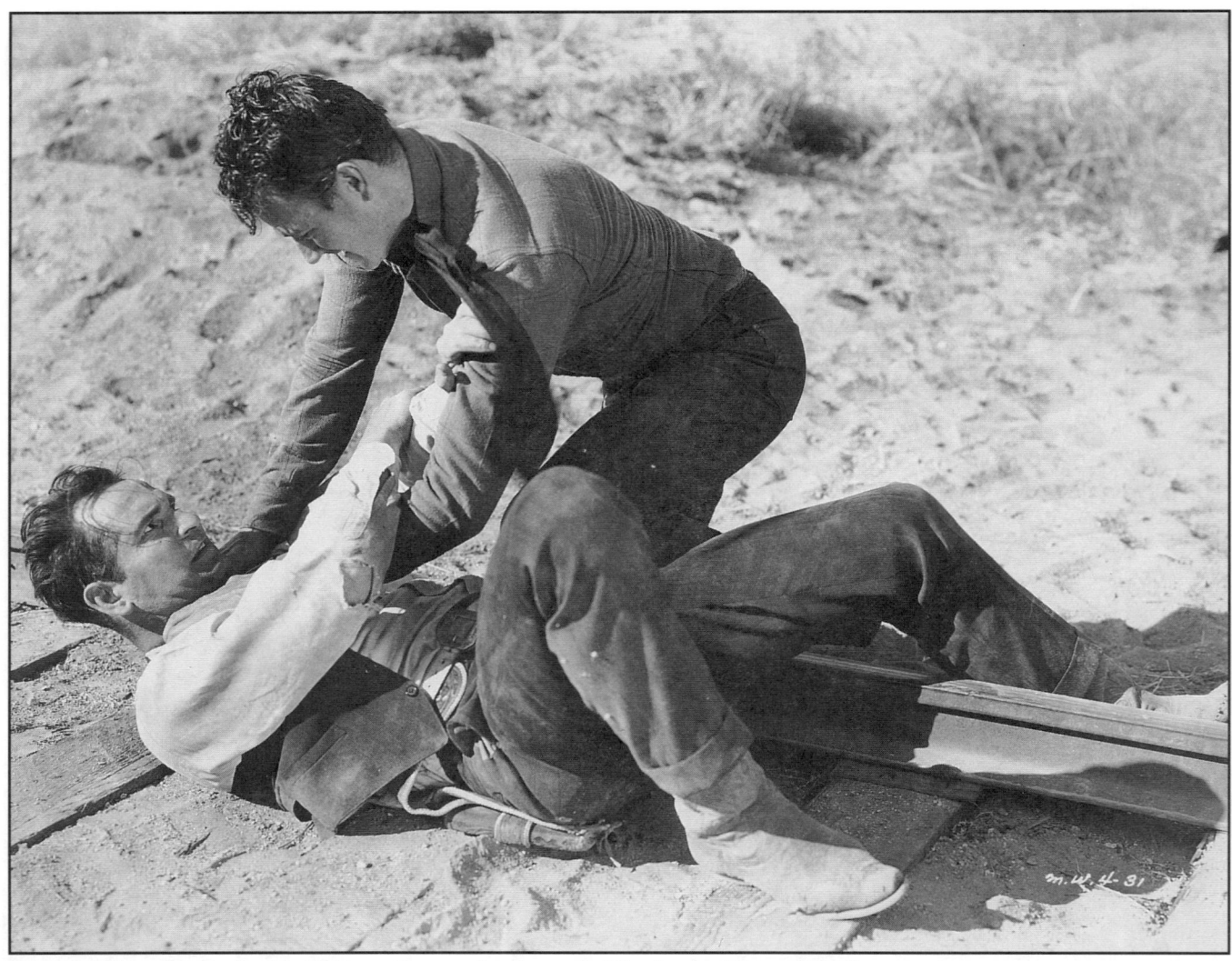

Wayne and longtime double Yakima Canutt slug it out in The Lucky Texan *(1934).*

were relatively routine, except that in *The Telegraph Trail* (Tenny Wright, 1933) he was supported by Frank McHugh and Yakima Canutt. McHugh as a cavalryman was a stranger to the plains, while Canutt was just the opposite, and would cross trails with Wayne again soon.

After *Somewhere in Sonora* (Mack V. Wright, 1933), in which he appeared with Walthall again, as well as Paul Fix, first in a long line of associations, and director-actor J. P. McGowan; and *The Man from Monterey* (Mack V. Wright, 1933), in which he was stuffed into some uncomfortable military uniforms and fancy below-the-border duds, and was ill at ease, Wayne left Warners. Like Columbia, they had shoved him into minor roles in non-Westerns too, but his own series was compensation. He had also done a third Mascot serial, and was firmly fixed in the minds of action fans. The Warner series had been well received. Even better, after the shaky times at Fox and Columbia, he was working steadily.

Came the Monogram series, 16 Westerns pro-

duced by Carr and Malvern. The Warner Westerns had been made on low budgets, but the studio facilities and know-how made the pennies count. The Monograms were even lower on the budgetary scale and, contrarily, it was inclined to show. Only when the narratives stayed outdoors did they physically display to advantage, and that was because Archie Stout was a superb cameraman who photographed most of the Monograms, and Stout could give scenic vistas a contrasty, dignified look, of a quality that might have come from an old family album, granted the family was of pioneer stock, taken by the tintype concern of a not-too-distant relative of the great Matthew Brady. This is not to overstate Stout's ability. For quickie, independent efforts, shot in a few days, the photography in the Waynes is of high caliber, especially when seen in a good 35mm print.

Though the budgets were low, Wayne's star rose higher with the Monograms. His youthfulness, ability, leisurely manner of speech blended to make him a Western favorite, if not of the top rank then securely

BIG JOHN: The Beginning

in the more elevated popularity brackets. To their credit, Carr, Malvern and company tried to find stories and ideas that would lift individual members of the series from the conventional rut, and occasionally they would succeed, as they did with their first entry, *Riders of Destiny* (Robert N. Bradbury, 1933).

Singin' Sandy was the role devised for Wayne by director-author Bradbury. Sandy was a lawman who was wont to vocalize when his dander was up and the time was ripe for gunplay. Wayne was no warbler, so his voice was dubbed—some say by Smith Ballew, though it's actually Bradbury's son Bill. The idea was different, but its execution was not of the best. The dubbed voice didn't match Wayne's, and Bradbury saw fit to include, for some inexplicable reason, an interlude of Wayne supposedly serenading heroine Cecilia Parker, accompanied by guitar. At the conclusion of the ballad, Miss Parker's ecstatic "Oooh... sing it again!" was not reflected in the attitudes of the audience. Additionally, *Riders of Destiny* contained some misplaced comedy inserted by Bradbury merely because Al St. John and Heinie Conklin were in the cast as a pair of outlaws. Their slapstick was amusing, but interrupted the flow of the narrative. On the other hand, the film did have a suspenseful gunfight between Wayne and villain Earl Dwire, given allowances for the Wayne warbling prior to the final showdown. It took place on a barren, dusty street and was filmed by Bradbury and Stout in a manner that could be described as Ford-like. There was further action to be found too, in-

Robert N. Bradbury (seated, pointing) directs a scene from Blue Steel *(1934); Wayne at left, Eleanor Hunt and Ed Peil below microphone, Yakima Canutt behind them.*

Duke with Billy O'Brien in West of the Divide *(1934).*

cluding a cliffside leap into water that would serve in the future as library footage. The series was off to a promising start.

Sagebrush Trail (Armand Schaefer, 1933) was the second series entry, more to formula but pleasing enough, as Wayne is unjustly accused of a killing, escapes and sets out to nab the real culprit (Lane Chandler), whom he eventually tracks down and befriends before the inexorable reckoning. *Lucky Texan* (Bradbury, 1934) is notable for the foreshadowing of the comedic talents of George Hayes, heretofore utility man of the indies, seen advantageously and prolifically in character roles and upon occasion a dash of skulduggery. Here he does the sidekick number, preparing himself, doubtless unknowingly, for a long tenure of lovable horseplay in the future. *West of the Divide* (Bradbury, 1934) had Wayne searching for the murderer of his father, a Bradbury stock-in-trade that he usually reserved for his offspring, Bob Steele, with little discernible variation. *Blue Steel,* with the charming Eleanor Hunt; *The Man from Utah,* with the charming Polly Ann Young; and *The Star Packer,* with the charming Verna Hillie, completed the first season's schedule. All were 1934 releases, all were directed by Bradbury, and all featured George Hayes and Yakima Canutt.

Getting the 1934–35 season off to a fine start was *The Trail Beyond,* once again directed by Bradbury, but this time adapted from a James Oliver Curwood story, the first time a Monogram Wayne had gone outside the studio gates for a plot basis. It also could boast of Noah Berry, father and son, doing their glowering act and faithful pard routine, respectively. Thereafter, the Waynes slid into a routine trench. Accustomed to working with one another, the gears

BIG JOHN: The Beginning

meshed smoothly enough, but the action became more commonplace. It has been said that during the Monogram series, Wayne and Canutt collaborated on adding an amount of realism to the fisticuffing by choosing adroit camera angles and making the punches seem to land solidly in general. The fights are admittedly perpetrated with more dash than the average Western of the period, but there is little evidence that Wayne and Canutt had come upon any great innovation as yet. One ludicrous instance has Wayne pummeling Canutt in the breadbasket for what seems an eternity, then knocking him from a second-story veranda prone upon a hitching post below, a painful descent to be sure. Midway, camera trickery is employed and a dummy substituted for Canutt, which whirls through the air with such a pinwheel-like fury that one expects to see the stuffing come spraying out. Canutt is photographically reinserted a-sprawl below. The Wayne-Canutt technique may have had its inception at Monogram, but full fruition definitely did not occur until Republic, possibly after that.

At the end of Wayne's second Monogram season, he didn't leave the studio. Quite the reverse: the studio left him. Monogram folded its tent in mid-1935, and from its ashes, along with the remains of a few other independent companies, sprang the new Republic Pictures Corp. Some of Monogram's personnel and product was absorbed by the new company, and the John Wayne Westerns gave Republic a cowboy star.

Westward Ho! (Bradbury, 1935) bore the Republic trademark, but in all other respects it was Monogram, a leftover from the old company before

Wayne shares a song with his Westward Ho *(1935) compadres, including Jack Kirk, Cactus Mack and Glenn Strange.*

75

the deluge. Somehow, it looked better as a new Republic. Stout's camerawork was up to his high standard, the action was good, and Frank McGlynn, Jr., not seen too often in Westerns, was a welcome villain. Once again, Wayne was called upon to sing, during a campfire sequence. The dubbed voice they gave him could only be described as a savage snarl, as if someone along the lines of that overbearing villain, Richard Cramer, had been cajoled into recording the number in jest. Aside from this lamentable misjudgment, the film was thoroughly okay.

Republic had Wayne for seven more features. *New Frontier* (Carl Pierson, 1935) and *The Oregon Trail* (Scott Pembroke, 1936) represented the transition period from Monogram to Republic; the latter was a bit more ambitious than the usual Wayne show, with Wayne again on the trail of dastards who've killed his father. Teenaged Ann Rutherford was the ingenue, as she was in two subsequent Wayne Westerns. Fourth in release, *Lawless Range* (Bradbury, 1936) was Monogram through and through, withheld from release until now, and below the present average.

Joseph Kane directed the next three Waynes, of which *King of the Pecos* (1936) was best, and therefore best of the series, since the Republic stamp of Western quality was now becoming assertive. *Pecos* had Cy Kendall to hiss, and Jack Marta's photography to applaud. For his last in the series, the pleasant *Winds of the Wasteland* (1936), Wayne was reunited with director Mack V. Wright from the Warner days on the range.

Trem Carr, Wayne's old boss, had moved to Universal and enticed Wayne over to star in an action series, none of them officially Westerns, so Wayne was off his horse for the 1936–37 season. He climbed right back on again when the Universal series was ended, landing in a Paramount miniature diversion entitled *Born to the West* (Charles Barton, 1937). Paramount had been continuing their Zane Grey properties right through the era, employing Randolph Scott as a standard cowboy lead for a time, then Tom Keene, then Buster Crabbe, along with some odd casting, all the way from Gilbert Roland to comic Joe Cook. The Grey name was a selling help, and the studio offered good productions to each entry. *Born to the West* contained all the attributes, plus a fine topline cast of Wayne, heroine Marsha Hunt, an actress of the highest ability; John Mack Brown, time off from his own Westerns for A.

Shooting a scene for The Lawless Nineties *(1936).*

BIG JOHN: The Beginning

Lucien Littlefield (seated), John Patterson, Wayne in Born to the West *(1937).*

W. Hackel; oldsters Monte Blue and Lucien Littlefield. The photography by Dev Jennings was fine, and the running time was short—extremely short even for a Western, at a mere 51 minutes. *Born to the West* would be reissued in later years, because of Wayne. The distributor who bought the rights from Paramount retitled it *Hell Town,* and to add heft to the footage tacked on several minutes of random footage of cattle drives, outlaws attacking and the like. This padding was spliced to the beginning, making it seem an interminable length of time before the story proper got underway.

Wayne's last Western series found him returning to Republic to replace Bob Livingston in the Three Mesquiteers series. It was a comedown for Wayne, after his action series at Universal and the Paramount effort. Livingston had been the dashing, devil-may-care member of the trio, and had played the role with a certain panache that Wayne was unable to duplicate. He delivered in the action scenes, of which there were plenty. But the script would call for some light banter with Ray Corrigan, or the ingenue of the moment, and the role fit him uncomfortably, and it showed. Paradoxically, the Mesquiteer films themselves rate among the best in that long and distinguished series, and will be examined further when the Mesquiteers have their own chapter.

At that, Wayne's disillusionment, if such it was, must have lasted fairly briefly. Ford wanted him for a picture he was making quietly for Walter Wanger called *Stagecoach,* and by the time John Wayne made his last Mesquiteer appearance in 1939, his future was assured. And it called for no more low-budget Westerns.

George O'Brien shows off a new gun he had made for Riders of the Purple Sage *(1931).*

7
HOW TO MAKE GOOD WESTERNS
FOX, RKO AND O'BRIEN

Playing "Who's on First?" has been a popular pastime since long before Abbott and Costello, when it comes to movies. It's a game fraught with pitfalls, coming up with the first to do this or that. For example, we're fairly certain that the first all-talkie Western was *In Old Arizona,* and the first all-talkie low-budget Western was *Overland Bound.* To carry on further, how about the first all-talkie Western star, and the first all-talkie Western series? Ken Maynard or Hoot Gibson? Unless records lie, as they often do, the chronological answer is George O'Brien in *Lone Star Ranger,* directed by A. F. Erickson, released during the first week in January, 1930. O'Brien continued to make Westerns for the Fox company until 1934, appearing in stories usually adapted from novels by either Zane Grey or Max Brand. All things relative, compared to the average program picture from a major studio, they hold up well. Compared to the average Western made by anyone at anytime, their quality is exceedingly high, and in one or two cases, extraordinary.

After his Fox series, O'Brien continued to star in action films for independent producers. Some of these were Westerns, a few outdoor action yarns of the non-Western variety, and in an instance or two, pleasant light comedies masquerading as action films. He joined RKO in 1938 and resumed his unswerving Western bent until 1940, when he made it clear that he was officially retiring from the screen. His work with the independents and the major studio maintained the high standards begun at Fox, and his record upon reflection was a most distinguished one in the Western field.

Not that O'Brien was a novice in the saddle when he made *Lone Star Ranger.* He had played important roles in two John Ford epics, *The Iron Horse* (1924) and *Three Bad Men* (1926), both pioneer large-scale Western dramas. However, despite the prestigious parts, O'Brien was not displayed to advantage by Ford. In the former, a saga of the railroad, O'Brien's personality was submerged by the huge sweep of the narrative; as the nominal hero, he was believable and handled his role winningly, and was able to indulge in a savage hand-to-hand climactic combat with Fred Kohler, but the story of the rails into the wilderness was the thing. He was not one of the *Three Bad Men* of Ford's latter film. Indeed, those scalawags (Tom Santschi, J. Farrell MacDonald, Frank Campeau) dominated the film, with O'Brien playing a hero's role that had little to be heroic about. But he wasn't typecast as an outdoorsman anyway, and his popularity was sustained. He was a handy leading man at Fox in films ranging from domestic comedy like the Howard Hawks 1926 *Fig Leaves,* to Ruritanian romance in *Paid to Love* (1927), again directed by Hawks, to the heavy drama of F. W. Murnau's great *Sunrise* (1927). As fate would have it, his first talkie was a Western and his future was assured.

His credentials as an actor were above reproach and his experience was on the record. Other, further attributes made George O'Brien an imposing

HOLLYWOOD CORRAL: A COMPREHENSIVE B WESTERN ROUNDUP

O'Brien, director John Ford, and J. Farrell MacDonald on location for Three Bad Men (1926).

cowboy star. First was his build. O'Brien seemed perpetually ready to burst from his shirts, and often reasons would be written into the scripts to give him cause to shed his clothing, with astounding pectorial results. Musclesville, in other words. O'Brien was living proof of the advantages of physical education, and he had done stunting in films in his salad days. The combination of mighty physique and the obvious fact that he was doing his own hard riding and fighting proved a tremendous plus in his cowboy career. Early on he had also been a cameraman's assistant, working under George Schneiderman and Dan Clark on the old Fox Tom Mix vehicles, so he was well aware of what went on behind the cameras. His contributions, if any, in this respect are not documented, but they may have been of some importance. Lastly, in addition to being heroic and convincing in action scenes, O'Brien could be a very funny man upon occasion. He had a smart delivery of lines; possessed a double-take that rivaled Jack Oakie's; and, with someone like Dan Jarrett devising clever dialogue for him, could engagingly provide chuckles for the elders as well as excitement for the kiddies. Even an ancient wheeze would assume fresh proportions in O'Brien's hands, as in O'Malley of the Mounted (David Howard, 1936). In this chestnut attributed to the pen of William S. Hart, O'Brien is the mountie who strives to get his men by going undercover and joining the gang. One of the varmints thinks he recognizes the incognito lawman, and inquires menacingly: "Say... ain't I seen your face some place before?"

Replies O'Brien with a quiet grin, "Probably the same place it is now."

What Fox had in its corporate mind concerning O'Brien is indeterminate. That he was meant to be a Western star is undoubted. But after *Lone Star Ranger,* his vehicle was a logging adventure, *Rough Romance,* also directed by Erickson. It was brief, swift, and had a breathtaking climax involving O'Brien skittering precariously over a log jam to save the heroine. Sturdy players such as Antonio Moreno and Helen Chandler appeared in prime supporting roles, and a young John Wayne could be glimpsed at a table with O'Brien in a cabaret sequence. True to the early talkie period, O'Brien is offered an opportunity to sing, dance and tinkle a tune at the piano here. He rises to the occasion bravely.

But *Rough Romance* was not strictly a Western,

HOW TO MAKE GOOD WESTERNS: Fox, RKO and O'Brien

and John Ford borrowed O'Brien again in 1931 for a World War I adventure, *The Seas Beneath*. O'Brien had made *Last of the Duanes* (1930) and *Fair Warning* (1931) for Alfred Werker previously, the former a Zane Grey adaptation like *Lone Star Ranger*, the latter based on a Max Brand novel. These and his subsequent trio would be remakes of Tom Mix films, and his next three are of particularly high interest.

A Holy Terror (Irving Cummings, 1931) is taken from Brand's *Trailin'*, and extensively modernized. The Mix version was more traditional in its Western mechanics and irrefutably more exciting. But the O'Brien has an almost documentary value in its use of authentic small town locales, including a rather impressive hotel ballroom, bowling alley and cigar counter architecture long since vanished from the American scene. Quite a bit of the story takes place in these settings, and since they are the real thing and not some studio recreation, the past comes alive again. From an action standpoint the film is relatively placid until the conclusion, and even then what develops is mild. But the running time is brief (some 53 minutes) and the players are capable, including Sally Eilers as the ingenue, James Kirkwood, Rita LaRoy, Stanley Fields, and a snarling young man in a villainous role named Humphrey Bogart, who responds to a nasty comment from a countergirl with a succinct "Aw, go chase yourself," in exactly the same manner as he would a few years later over at Warner Bros.

O'Brien's following Western was *Riders of the Purple Sage* (Hamilton MacFadden, 1931), a magnificent film for its day and still astonishingly impressive in the awesome beauty of Schneiderman's photography of the scenics, and some superb running shots of O'Brien in pursuit of a foe, as well as a remarkable trucking shot that follows O'Brien along a lengthy village street; MacFadden's incisive and occasionally inventive direction; and a formidable adaptation job by Messrs. Goodrich, Klein and Con-

Niles Welch (in vest) forces O'Brien over a precipice in The Rainbow Trail *(1932).*

HOLLYWOOD CORRAL: A COMPREHENSIVE B WESTERN ROUNDUP

nors, from a Zane Grey novel that doesn't lend itself well to the movies. The Tom Mix 1925 version had been big at the boxoffice but wasn't one of the star's better vehicles, largely because Grey's involved plot was cumbersomely constructed for the screen. O'Brien's version runs less than an hour and still manages to cram all the nuances into the yarn, except for what had to be omitted—Grey's villain was a Mormon, and a villain solely because of that, obviously taboo for Hollywood. Noah Beery's role thus becomes a crooked judge, and be done with it. But the interplay of characters is strong and the characterizations far above ordinary black-and-white delineating. A situation where Marguerite Churchill is threatened by Frank McGlynn Jr., with a timely intrusion by O'Brien, is masterfully directed by MacFadden, with adroit use of the full close-up for Miss Churchill. An undistinguished director for most of his career, MacFadden's two Westerns, this one and *The Fourth Horseman,* a Universal Tom Mix, seem to indicate that he missed his metier.

Within a few months of the release of *Riders of the Purple Sage,* its sequel, *The Rainbow Trail* (David Howard, 1932) was ready. At the conclusion of *Sage,* the hero and heroine escaped their adversaries by sealing themselves in a lost valley and obscuring its only access. The sequel begins with a search for the couple, and since O'Brien is once again the hero, he's literally chasing himself; his role in the preceding tale is now taken by a minor player. For those who failed to see its predecessor or are cursed with short memories, *Rainbow Trail* must have been difficult to follow, if not altogether incomprehensible. Counteracting this would be the fast pace, and most important, the scenery. The film was photographed in the Grand Canyon by Dan Clark, and the effects are frequently beyond description. Cecilia Parker, one of the more attractive Western ingenues, herewith made her debut, and the film marked the beginning of an association between star O'Brien and director David Howard that was to last until O'Brien's retirement.

Two pleasantries ensued. *Gay Caballero* (Alfred Werker, 1932) was based on Tom Gill's *The Gay Bandit of the Border* and co-starred Victor McLaglen, with C. Henry Gordon, Linda Watkins, Willard Robertson and Weldon Heyburn in the cast. *Mystery Ranch* (David Howard, 1932) had atmospheric camerawork from Schneiderman and Joe August, and a good piece of villainy by Charles

Weldon Heyburn (in vest) jokes with O'Brien in Gay Caballero *(1932).*

HOW TO MAKE GOOD WESTERNS: Fox, RKO and O'Brien

Middleton, as well as the beguiling Miss Parker for romance. By now it appeared that Fox was sacrificing the potential children's matinee market in an effort to attract adults. O'Brien made fewer Westerns than any other cowboy lead, and his productions were crafted with utmost care. Technical work was of the highest grade. Casts were far superior to any other Westerns. The O'Briens even had musical backgrounds, wisely but not overbearingly used, usually most effectively for action climaxes. They were not borrowings from the classics but original compositions, and thus were in the vanguard of films with substantial music scores, predating all Westerns and the large percentage of Hollywood product, large- and small-budget.

Stewart Edward White had been the source of story material for *Mystery Ranch*. Five Zane Grey adaptations in a row began with *The Golden West* (David Howard, 1932), one of the few isolated instances of a minor Western with an epic plot. In fact, there is enough story for several Westerns jammed into the 70 minutes, scanning two generations with O'Brien playing father and son, and replete with buffalo stampedes, Indian raids, and pioneering the frontier, all impressively unfolded on a restricted, but not meager budget. Howard even has a chance to film an old Southern ball and make it acceptably ornate by some fancy camera angles, such as shooting through the strings of the orchestra's harp. Action sequences are excellent, and O'Brien really shows off the physique in latter sequences calling for him to wear brief Indian garb. The next quartet of Greys kept up the good work, with even a relatively weak entry like *Robbers' Roost* (Louis King, 1933) boasting of superior technical work and a cast including Maureen O'Sullivan and Reginald Owen, some class for a horse opera.

Frontier Marshal (Lewis Seiler, 1934) ended O'Brien's Fox Westerns. It was based on Stuart Lake's account of Wyatt Earp cleaning up Tombstone, and was first in a set of periodic remakes, by Allan Dwan with Randolph Scott (1939), John Ford with Henry Fonda *My Darling Clementine* (1946), and Louis King with Rory Calhoun *Powder River* (1953), the latter the only Technicolor version.

Beginning with the 1934–35 season, O'Brien still pledged allegiance to Fox, but his films were now produced independently by Sol Lesser's Atherton Productions, and released through the Fox corporation. It was doubtless an economic move born of desperation for the financially strapped Fox concern, relieving them of the necessity of using studio facilities while at the same time providing them with a given number of outdoor pictures with an established star. Lesser, to his credit, gave O'Brien all the production adornments at his limited command, including a continuance of carefully selected supporting casts and another accomplished regular cameraman in the veteran Frank B. Good. Heretofore, the Fox O'Briens usually contained an adequate supply of action, although pure unadulterated roughhousing was never given preference over sound plotting. Action sequences were logically inserted into the scripts. With his new series, O'Brien seemed to go to lengths to avoid any emphasis on action, which was not as disastrous as it may have seemed at the outset. One look at O'Brien, and one simply knew that he was more than capable of taking care of himself, so why stress the obvious?

First in the new series was *The Dude Ranger* (Edward Cline, 1934), and its shyness when it came to excitement was temporarily disconcerting for O'Brien fans. More than making up for it was *When a Man's a Man* (Cline, 1935), not overloaded with Western action but graced with a superior story and excellent performances by O'Brien, co-star Paul Kelly and Dorothy Wilson, an attractive and talented actress who deserved stardom but never quite broke through the Hollywood barrier of press agentry over professionalism. Third in the series, *The Cowboy Millionaire* (Cline, 1935) proved mildly amusing, with some brief location scenes in London adding interest. *Hard Rock Harrigan* (1935) and *Whispering Smith Speaks* (1935) were light outdoor romances stressing comedic elements, with the former reuniting O'Brien with arch-rival Fred Kohler. *Thunder Mountain* (1935) was a Western, in costume, and on the slow side. The mountie film already mentioned and *The Border Patrolman* (1936), pleasing if routine, completed the Lesser contract. All the latter films were directed by David Howard.

Leaving Lesser, O'Brien signed with independent producer George Hirliman for four films to be released through RKO. Lesser meanwhile turned out five Westerns for Fox, now 20th Century-Fox, release, using different leads, capable performers like Ralph Bellamy, Paul Kelly, Richard Arlen and Ricardo Cortez. They may have been slated originally for O'Brien, for the scripts had that same breezy if leisurely approach. In any case, Lesser thereafter latched on to the singing Smith Ballew, who will be discussed in the section dealing with cowboys with tonsils.

HOLLYWOOD CORRAL: A COMPREHENSIVE B WESTERN ROUNDUP

George and Leroy Mason in The Dude Ranger *(1934).*

HOW TO MAKE GOOD WESTERNS: Fox, RKO and O'Brien

Hirliman started O'Brien off big, in *Daniel Boone* (David Howard, 1936). While still a low-budget production, the cash was wisely spent and RKO got behind it with some advertising, enabling it to play some better class houses. Although not the definitive word on the subject, the biographical drama has its moments, with O'Brien playing the character straight, and John Carradine adding to his rapidly increasing laurels as the dirty Simon Girty. Once again O'Brien was fortunate to have Frank Good at the cameras, and Hugo Riesenfeld and Arthur Kay contributed a zesty music score, some of which saw much service later in Republic Westerns and serials. O'Brien appeared in two more non-Westerns for Hirliman, and the pseudo-Western *Hollywood Cowboy* (Ewing Scott, 1937), diverting fluff, with Cecilia Parker once more serving as leading lady.

RKO relieved Hirliman of production duties on the O'Briens and his Westerns became authentic RKO studio efforts, produced by Bert Gilroy. The star appeared in 16 features, and as a result of RKO's complete supervision the productions returned to the old Fox form, or at least came within hailing distance of the good old days. Gone was the pretense of attempting non-Western stories, and also missing was any effort to be offbeat. The strength of the RKO O'Briens rested in their ability to be appreciably better than most other company Westerns, with a continuance of strong casting, plus a solid physical look, workmanlike screenplays and direction, and the by now expected first-rate photography from such distinguished lensers as Joe August and Roy Hunt, but mainly from Harry Wild, an outdoor specialist.

This is the George O'Brien who remains in memory: husky, never too serious, hat cocked rakishly down over one eye; the genuine article in action, and not some anonymous double or stuntman. The studio gave him some alleged comedy relief from time to time, mostly from Chill Wills. It started Wills off on the long road as a character actor, coming as he did from one-quarter of a harmonizing quartet. O'Brien didn't need the buffoonery, but it wasn't too intrusive. They also inserted Ray Whitley and his prairie musical aggregation, and at this juncture in Western cinema history musical groups only served to impede the action. But Whitley was nice, in a nasal way, and he was valuable at RKO. They also used him to head up a series of two-reel short Western comedies with songs, which were no great shakes as Westerns but did supply an occasionally welcome 20-minute addition to the program.

Gun Law (1938) had David Howard at the helm, as he was with rare exceptions during the O'Brien tenure at RKO. It was the old mistaken-identity formula, but the plot was handled carefully by scenarist Oliver Drake, as befits its age, and August's photography was top quality, especially in the opening desert sequences. Best of the early ones was *Lawless Valley* (Howard, 1938), with O'Brien once more beset by Fred Kohler, only this time with Fred, Jr. for added nastiness. Alas, for the elder Kohler it was a farewell. By the time the film was in distribution, the veteran villain had succumbed. Contending with *Lawless Valley* for top honors was *Racketeers of the Range* (D. Ross Lederman, 1939), an action-packed story of contemporary cattle rustling highlighted by a rousing climax that had O'Brien leaping from his horse on to a speeding train. It was photographed in medium close-up, so it was plain to see that O'Brien was accomplishing the stunt work himself. Keeping apace with the trend, O'Brien even indulged in a bit of jitterbugging in this one, to the Whitley jazzed-up accompaniment.

O'Brien's willingness to take risks was further exploited in *Arizona Legion* (Howard, 1939), where-

O'Brien pummels Morgan Wallace in Thunder Mountain *(1935).*

HOLLYWOOD CORRAL: A COMPREHENSIVE B WESTERN ROUNDUP

Ray Whitley takes instruction from George in The Renegade Ranger *(1938).*

in he heedlessly clambers all over a speeding stagecoach to nab the baddies during the conclusion. In *Trouble in Sundown* (Howard, 1939), a rather constricted Western yarn that takes place mostly within the confines of the local bank, O'Brien commands awe with the ease with which he blithely tosses around three or four plug-uglies, scattering them around the set like so many ornaments, again with the camera close in so there's no mistaking his personal involvement in the melee.

Whoever picked the leading ladies for the RKO O'Briens had an eye for feminine pulchritude, not to mention talent. Rita Hayworth appeared in one, Laraine Johnson in several before she changed her last name to Day. Not the least of *Lawless Valley*'s attributes was the presence of the exotic Kay Sutton, more sophisticated than the normal Western ingenue—in the lingo of the day, a real classy dish. Marjorie Reynolds appeared in a couple of O'Briens, and so did Rosalind Keith. His leading lady for his final six features was Virginia Vale, formerly Dorothy Howe of Paramount before she won one of those "Gateway to Hollywood" talent contests so thoroughly plugged by RKO at the end of the '30s. Another winner, male, who appeared in one O'Brien was Robert Stanton, a range star himself later on as Kirby Grant.

Of these final six O'Briens, two and possibly three could be counted as among the star's best. *Marshal of Mesa City* (Howard, 1939) offered a fine script by Jack Lait, Jr., again the trick of crafting a familiar plot so well that it seems almost new. Skulduggery was ably supplied by Leon Ames, and most interestingly by the sinister Henry Brandon, capital as a paid gunman out to polish off O'Brien only to lend him assistance out of respect. An excellent actor still in his twenties, Brandon of course went on to become a memorable Fu Manchu at Republic. *Prairie Law* (Howard, 1940) and *Stage to Chino* (Edward Killy, 1940) offered more of the same, Westerns so well made that it was a pleasure to just sit back and enjoy them. The latter film is generally considered as the very best O'Brien made for RKO, but the choice is not that clear cut. True, it is so expertly put

HOW TO MAKE GOOD WESTERNS: Fox, RKO and O'Brien

together it is hard to fault. A minor advantage is the comedy relief, from an actor not usually associated with Westerns, Hobart Cavanaugh, as a timid traveling salesman.

On screen in *Triple Justice* (Howard, 1940), O'Brien takes the concluding nuptial vows with Virginia Vale and quietly retires after the picture is completed. Only 40 years old, he had nevertheless put in nearly half those years as an actor, and no doubt he fully intended to concentrate on other pursuits. World War II put an end to that, since he was in the Naval Reserve. Before long he was physical instructor at San Diego, then participated in several major assault landings in the Pacific. Retirement from action movies definitely didn't mean retirement from action.

He resumed his screen career after the war, but not to the fullest extent. He assumed some supporting roles in films directed by his old boss, John Ford, and did a brief stint as a muscleman in a Dennis Morgan musical at Warners. He also returned to Western stardom once, in a dizzy affair for producer Bernard Glasser of Jack Schwarz Productions called *Gold Raiders* (Edward Bernds, 1951). O'Brien co-starred with The Three Stooges, knockabout comics, and whatever the reasoning was behind this bizarre teaming, the end results weren't too ludicrous. The film's 56 minutes were pretty evenly divided between the cowboy and the goofs, with neither intruding upon the other's specialty grounds. The Stooges indulged in their seasoned antics, and O'Brien played the hero's role straight, with a bit of his confident humor breaking through every so often. In his fifties, he had changed not a whit from the days of Fox and RKO. Encountering Lyle Talbot's double in a barroom brawl sequence, O'Brien effortlessly hoists the unfortunate aloft and heaves him across the set without even breathing hard.

RKO was stuck without a Western star when O'Brien retired in 1940, but the situation was soon

O'Brien and Rita Hayworth in The Renegade Ranger *(1938).*

HOLLYWOOD CORRAL: A COMPREHENSIVE B WESTERN ROUNDUP

O'Brien and Marjorie Reynolds in Timber Stampede *(1939).*

HOW TO MAKE GOOD WESTERNS: Fox, RKO and O'Brien

George with Virginia Vale and fellow passengers on the Stage to Chino *(1940).*

remedied. Appearing in *The Renegade Ranger* (Howard, 1938) with O'Brien—and Rita Hayworth—was young Tim Holt, who had had additional experience in a Harry Carey film at the studio as well as a small role in the landmark Western *Stagecoach*. Besides, his dad, Jack Holt, had played in many an outdoor drama, on both sides of the law. Young Holt was barely of voting age, but the studio decided he was ready and took a gamble. Tim Holt became RKO's new cowboy star.

Tim Holt

8
...OR ANYWAY, BETTER WESTERNS THAN MOST
KEENE, HOLT & OTHER GUYS AT RKO

Before Tim Holt, and before George O'Brien, RKO had established a kind of tradition of quality Western-making. Its predecessor, the old FBO production organization, had made some popular silent Westerns with Tom Tyler, Bob Steele; going back even farther, Fred Thomson; and immediately before the advent of sound, a series starring Tom Mix. The Thomsons were not only popular but exceptionally well produced, as were the Tylers and Steeles. The Mix films were not comparable to his Fox output, but the fact remained that at the time Mix was still the top cowboy draw at the boxoffice.

FBO evolved into RKO-Radio in the late '20s, and the Pathe production setup was added to the conglomerate in 1930. By 1931, they had their first talkie Western star. As George Duryea, he had been a leading man for Cecil B. DeMille and had appeared in two Western-type light romances in 1930. His name was promptly changed to Tom Keene, which is probably what a Western hero's name should sound like to the ears of a motion picture executive, and he starred in a dozen outdoor features during the following two seasons. As a result of the RKO-Pathe merger still in progress, his first two came out under the Pathe label, complete with rooster-crowing trademark.

Two things stand out about the Keene series. First, no less than five producers were involved in the 12 features, which must be some sort of record. Second, better than half of them were superior to the ordinary run-of-the-mill outdoor fare, and of those, three rate with the more original and meritorious budget Westerns made since sound, an achievement in which all concerned can take pardonable pride. Curiously enough, the major obstacle to complete success for the entire series was the star, Keene.

He was a clean-cut appearing gent of average height and weight, not especially of commanding presence in the saddle, but no tenderfoot either. Sufficiently adept in the rough and tumble, able to handle a shootin' iron convincingly, he was also a trained dramatic actor, and unfortunately it showed disadvantageously. His more emotional scenes were played blatantly, while the lighter ones were instilled with an overdose of ersatz heartiness, a bit too much of the old ho-ho-ho. In his early films, Keene had a number of scenes with children, and his false geniality was noticeably galling them, with the rather pompous camaraderie remindful of a stuffy scoutmaster. Keene managed to tone down this unfortunate aspect of his personality in time, but it was a serious drawback at the beginning.

Since Keene was as noted without a distinctive cowboy personality of his own, he was inserted into all manner of Western saga. *Freighters of Destiny* (Fred Allen, 1931) was a wagon-train yarn; *Partners* (Allen, 1932) tried the cowboy-and-the-kid formula, with Bobby Nelson as the waif; *Ghost Valley* (Allen, 1932) as the title indicates, attempted the mystery and suspense angle. These were capably produced but still lacked that extra something to make any dent in the Western market. Nor did *The Saddle*

HOLLYWOOD CORRAL: A COMPREHENSIVE B WESTERN ROUNDUP

Buster (Allen, 1932) at the time; but this one, number four in the Keene parade, shows how good a Western can be, in a potential sense. It's a rodeo story by Cherry Wilson, scripted by Oliver Drake with a good eye for defying the conventional. There is no villainy in the lawbreaking sense. Whatever difficulties are foisted upon the hero have been perpetrated because of jealousy, no more, with the wretch (Robert Frazer) being aptly penalized and properly repentant at the conclusion. What gives the picture a tremendous lift is the modern rodeo background, photographed by Ted McCord with a hard, dusty look, and peopled by a casting director briefly inspired—for once, the supporting actors, Marie Quillan, Ben Corbett, Slim Whitaker, Al Taylor, Frazer and the rest, look as if they actually belong where they are and not on some studio lot. Highlighting the film is a sequence involving the chase and capture by Keene of a wild horse, so well shot by McCord and edited by William Clemens that it's worthy of a bigger film. Again, the main fault is Keene, who overdoes the dramatics and frequently throws the entire unassuming but effective story off balance.

As stated, the producers of the Keenes were many. Charles R. Rogers started them off in an executive capacity, with Fred Allen, former film editor, also director, acting as supervisor. Harry Joe Brown took over briefly from Allen; then when David O. Selznick became production supervisor for RKO, he assigned David Lewis as his associate producer. Lewis had the best record, for under him the Keenes took a decided turn for the better. The Allen unit, including editor Clemens and photographer McCord, moved directly to Warners to work on a few of the John Waynes there. Director Robert Hill managed to work under all regimes. In fact, Hill had directed the first Keene, *Sundown Trail* (1931). His second was *Come On, Danger* (1932), with a plot gimmick that found favor at RKO through the succeeding years. It's the one about the girl who turned outlaw because she was forced to but really wasn't bad at all, with the hero galloping in to save the day and clear her name. The Keene version was lucky to have a fine young actress, Julie Haydon, in the role, and she gave it the necessary fire for additional interest. The idea was used again in the George O'Brien *Renegade Ranger* in 1938, with Rita Hayworth in the part. Three years later it was filmed again under the original title for the Tim Holt series, with Edward Killy directing and with Frances Neal doing a good job in the role. The gimmick was still unusual enough to hold up. Hill also directed Keene in *Cheyenne Kid* (1933), a W. C. Tuttle story that would have been perfect for Hoot Gibson. Here, Keene's overbearing affability was more in keeping, and the confidence of the hero, combined with a lack of any dangerous opposition to him, gave the film a nice, easy gait and made it pleasant to take.

Renegades of the West (1932) deserves mention if only because of the rather impressive direction by Casey Robinson, a writer who went on to script some of the gigantic Warner blockbusters—gigantic, and if one may comment, often quite smothering. This was apparently his only attempt at directing a feature, and he employed some intriguing ideas, photographically and dramatically, such as a subjective view of a horseman riding into town in the opening scene, and a pace that many Western directors would have deemed far too slothful, but which somehow works well, maintaining a steady interest in the story while not necessitating too much of the routine action situations. Under Robinson, Keene's performance showed improvement too. But Robin-

Tom Keene in his RKO period.

...OR ANYWAY, BETTER WESTERNS THAN MOST: Keene, Holt & other guys at RKO

Keene and Beryl Wallace in Romance of the Rockies *(1938).*

son was not destined to oversee galloping hoofs thereafter, and it is probably just as well.

Both *Scarlet River* (Otto Brower, 1933) and *Son of the Border* (Lloyd Nosler, 1933) rate with *The Saddle Buster* as Keene's best. Interestingly, they follow no set pattern, each is different. *Buster* was a rodeo story; *Border* a period piece about outlaws; *River* a contemporary, near-satiric Hollywood tale. The reliable Harold Shumate concocted a trifle concerning a movie crew on location to shoot a Western and getting some Western conniving they hadn't bargained for. Keene fit in well, and the film was graced with two leading ladies of note—the talented Dorothy Wilson and, in a comedy role, the up-and-coming Betty Furness, who had appeared with Keene in *Renegades of the West*. Edgar Kennedy also chipped in with some slow-burn humorous frustrations, Shumate's dialogue was sharp, and the whole thing turned out as a Western that could be enjoyed even by the non-addicts.

Son of the Border again demonstrated Nosler's potential as a director, and Julie Haydon's bright future as an actress. Cast in a role silimar to the one she essayed in *Come On, Danger,* she dominated every scene in which she appeared, to the betterment of the film since she was in an important role. Perhaps not morally defensible but nevertheless refreshing was the script's rationalization of banditry, made to seem a necessary way of life—or as Huston and Maddow put it in the gangster milieu later, "a left-handed form of human endeavor."

Keene's last for RKO was *Crossfire* (Brower, 1933), another Shumate script which had the hero returning from World War I to encounter some gangster tactics on the range. A good idea, evolved in ordinary fashion. Thereafter, RKO saw fit to curtail its Westerns. Keene then landed the main role in King Vidor's *Our Daily Bread*, a 1934 message film that was applauded by liberal critics when released, and avoided by general audiences. As a Western star,

Keene had developed a following, but the Vidor effort was not meant for them. To the intellectual moviegoer, if such there was in 1934, his name meant little or nothing. Nor did his performance in the film add any laurels to his career. To the contrary, the next several years meant a lot of shifting back and forth, to the independents, then over to Paramount for two more Zane Greys. Then came an offbeat, curious group of features for E. B. Derr, released on the states' rights market. Not Westerns, they could be considered as historical adventures. But since Keene's name was connoted with Westerns, they were advertised and sold as such, and invariably disappointed. As non-Westerns, they will not be discussed on these discriminatory pages.

Monogram had folded in 1935 and re-grouped in 1937, and their new production slate included a Tom Keene Western series. He did four. *God's Country and the Man* (Robert N. Bradbury, 1937) was a harkening back to the strong, silent days of William S. Hart, only Keene was not possessed of the Hart stony virility. Despite the drawbacks he did well, apparently having learned to muffle the mannerisms.

Otherwise, Charlie King excelled in a real ratty part, Betty Compson had an opportunity in the opening sequence to play her violin, and Charlotte Henry was a superior ingenue, if a long way from *Alice in Wonderland,* only a few years prior. Bob Steele's father directed the next two Keenes as well. *Where Trails Divide* (1937) had little above the norm, and all too much below; but *Romance of the Rockies* (1937) was a sterling job all around, without being especially precedent-shattering. Keene played a cow-country doctor, wearing civilian garb, but the action was Western, the battle-over-water-rights number. There was a good sequence of Keene riding a sluice on a stick, necessary to see it to believe it; and a beautiful ingenue in Beryl Wallace, an Earl Carroll show girl by inclination and a stunner. Final one in the abbreviated series was *The Painted Trail* (1938), reuniting Keene with director Robert Hill. A short one at 50 minutes, it was succinct and swift. The Robert Emmett (Tansey) script had a favorite gimmick of the author's, a climactic gun battle with the hero on one side of the border, the baddie (Walter Long) on the other. Hero plugs villain across the

Sherry Tansey pulls Keene off Jack Ingram in Arizona Roundup *(1942).*

...OR ANYWAY, BETTER WESTERNS THAN MOST: Keene, Holt & other guys at RKO

borderline. It was used several times, and always worked well. Then Keene was out, Tim McCoy was in briefly at Monogram, paving the way for Tex Ritter's arrival from Grand National.

When Ritter moved on, Keene returned to Monogram in 1941, there to appear in eight more Westerns, all directed by Robert Tansey, with Frank Yaconelli as comedy sidekick. Where he had been a major flaw at RKO, Keene was now the chief asset at Monogram. His acting was restrained, manly without being overbearing, and he had developed an impressive trait of shooting from the hip when called upon to draw. But the films were thoroughly undistinguished and the series was not renewed after the initial eight. Keene changed his name to Richard Powers and played some minor non-Western leads, starred in one Republic Western serial, and worked a lot for RKO as a character actor. He even played villains in later Tim Holt Westerns, at the studio where he had once been their first cowboy star.

Upon the curtailment of the Keene series, RKO compressed their Western production into one or two moderately big ones per year. Former *Cimarron* star Richard Dix, no stranger to the saddle, supplied one each year for three years: *West of the Pecos* (Phil Rosen, 1934); *The Arizonian*, a Dudley Nichols original (Charles Vidor, 1935); and *Yellow Dust* (Wallace Fox, 1936). Respectively, they were pleasant; pleasant; and not so. Fox also contributed *Powdersmoke Range* in 1935, the all-star job already mentioned several times and still to be examined more thoroughly, as it will be in the "Three Mesquiteers" section. Star Harry Carey returned in *The Last Outlaw* for Christy Cabanne in 1936, a charming romp in which the leathery saddle veteran played a former badman getting out of prison after many years' incarceration, and finding the old West plagued with big-city hoodlums. Tom Tyler played a bad guy again, and the story moved right along, but the big advantage was Carey, a broadly humorous and lovable rascal whose expression of resentment at being called "Pop" was a joy to behold.

Even better was *The Law West of Tombstone* (Glenn Tryon, 1938), with Carey as a Munchausen of the sagebrush whose tall tales frequently planted him in a verbal ambush. The excellent script by John Twist and Clarence Upson Young had Carey taking over a town by bluster as much as anything else, and befriending a young outlaw he was out to nab, the two teaming to rout the baddies in a finely portrayed gunfighting conclusion. The outlaw was played by Tim Holt, whose performance may have been a deciding factor when RKO came to seek a replacement for George O'Brien. The supporting cast included Evelyn Brent, Clarence Kolb, Bradley Page and Paul Guilfoyle, worthies all. The ingenue for Holt was Jean Rouverol, who later turned her talents to writing. Also in the cast was Allan Lane, soon to star at Republic.

By this time the O'Briens were in full swing at RKO, and the studio had resumed a steady Western series. A passing mention should be made at this point of *Bad Lands* (Lew Landers, 1939), about a posse after a killer, trapped in the desert by Apaches and decimated one by one. An all-character cast included Robert Barrat, Noah Beery Jr., Guinn "Big Boy" Williams, Andy Clyde, Robert Coote, Paul Hurst, Francis Ford, Addison Richards, Francis McDonald and Douglas Walton. Nobody mentioned the fact that Walton had also been seen in John Ford's *The Lost Patrol* five years before, because nobody mentioned the fact Clarence Upson Young's script sounded suspiciously like that Ford film, transposed to a different desert. That same year, Landers also directed another version of the old Willard Mack play, *The Dove*, re-titled *The Girl and the Gambler*, with Leo Carrillo, Steffi Duna, and Tim Holt, giving Carrillo plenty of opportunity for dialect and providing Holt with further seasoning.

Young Holt's schedule of RKO Westerns consisted of six for the 1940–41 season. Leading off was *Wagon Train* (Edward Killy, 1940), with a background similar to, but not a steal from, Tom Keene's early *Freighters of Destiny*, a story of freighters carrying supplies to isolated pioneer outposts on the frontier. Bert Gilroy continued his production supervision as he had on the O'Briens, and the physical look was up to the high RKO standards. For his saddle debut as a star, Holt was given a statuesque leading lady in Martha O'Driscoll and a relatively new and welcome face in the villain role, Cliff Clark, normally found ably impersonating cynical reporters or detectives in contemporary settings. Ray Whitley was to continue providing the song interludes and taffy-jawed Emmett Lynn was contracted to do the grizzled comedy bit in the continuing role of Whopper, inaugurated under O'Brien by Chill Wills.

Despite the production advantages going for it, *Wagon Train* failed to rise above the ordinary. It was felt that Holt needed more experience and would gradually assume the authority needed for a cowboy lead. He managed this in short order, but for some reason the proper ingredients, although definitely there, blended properly only upon occasion. Killy directed the first five, of varying quality with none outstanding, while David Howard, O'Brien's fre-

Martha Sleeper and Richard Dix in West of the Pecos *(1934).*

quent collaborator, directed *Six-Gun Gold* (1941), which turned out to be the speediest and most enjoyable of the Holts to date. Emmett Lynn had departed with the previous Holt, *Cyclone on Horseback,* replaced by Lee (Lasses) White as Whopper. It was a moot change.

Holt's second season of six were released throughout the 1941–42 season, but all were tradeshown to critics and exhibitors during a few weeks in the latter part of 1941. Killy directed three of them, David Howard one, and Lesley Selander, fresh from the Harry Sherman "Hopalong Cassidy" unit, handled *Thundering Hoofs,* albeit in undistinguished fashion. In general, the second group hardly constituted an improvement over the initial one. Howard's *Dude Cowboy,* with a modern setting and a plot concerning counterfeiting activities at a dude ranch, was probably the most interesting. Killy's *Land of the Open Range* could boast of some library footage from *Cimarron,* for those who had missed the big landrush scenes when the Wesley Ruggles epic first appeared ten years before. And Killy's remake of *Come On Danger,* routine in the main, did have a catchy title tune sung by the Whitley aggregation and a good actress in the girl outlaw part; Frances Neal married Van Heflin and appeared hardly at all thereafter, which was the screen's loss.

Directors were more varied for the 1942–43 Holt half-dozen, and by coincidence or otherwise the series took a sizable step forward. A major asset was the presence of Cliff Edwards, assuming the comedy relief and known by his familiar nickname of Ike. Edwards was not only a seasoned entertainer but had appeal for the kids (the voice of Jiminy Cricket in Disney's *Pinocchio*) and was experienced in the ways of saddle sagas, having just come off a Charles Starrett series at Columbia. He was a good actor, and wise enough not to force the comedy past the tolerable point, unlike all too many sagebrush sidekicks.

Holt had settled comfortably into the Western niche, and was thereby presented with something of

...OR ANYWAY, BETTER WESTERNS THAN MOST: Keene, Holt & other guys at RKO

a dilemma. As a Western star, he had amassed a following, not in the top bracket by any means, no threat to Autry or Boyd, but nevertheless an impressive coterie. Concurrently with his series, RKO gave him leading roles in two drastically different prestige productions, and in each he was cast against type. Under Orson Welles, Holt etched a sharp, realistic portrait of a spoiled brat in *The Magnificent Ambersons* (1942), then powerfully played a Nazi fanatic in Edward Dmytryk's *Hitler's Children* (1943). The Welles film was (and is) controversial critically, and a failure at the boxoffice, while the latter was economically produced and became a surprise hit, critically and financially. What if anything would have been the effect upon Holt's subsequent career is conjectural. By the time they were playing, Holt was in the Air Force and off the screen for four years.

Even if his offbeat roles had failed to advance his career, Holt's 1942–43 Westerns bid fair to solidify his rating on the open-air market. Taking into account the wartime economy increasingly making itself felt, Gilroy still managed a sturdy appearance in sets and backgrounds. Harry Wild was no longer the "house" Western photographer, but picturesque contributions were offered by J. Roy Hunt, Nicholas Musuraca, and even Jack Greenhalgh, on the lot on loan from PRC. Of the directors, the veteran Lambert Hillyer showed the benefits of his vast Western experience, from William S. Hart to Charles Starrett, on *Fighting Frontier* (1943), the one Greenhalgh photographed, incidentally; Howard Bretherton competently directed *Pirates of the Prairie* (1942); Lesley Selander did the first of the group in release, *Bandit Ranger* (1942) and the last, *Red River Robin Hood* (1943).

But the two most interesting were both directed by Sam Nelson, returning to the RKO lot where he had been an actor in the silent days. Nelson had been an assistant director, then promoted to handling the Starretts at Columbia. His style might be described as rough-and-ready. In *Sagebrush Law* (1943) he sets up one jaw-bruising slugging match and some 57 minutes of continuous excitement, and made what is perhaps the liveliest of the Holts of the period. Nelson goes a bit too far in *The Avenging Rider* (1943). An Olympic-caliber leap through a window by Holt is too much to swallow, even if deftly shaded by Hunt's nocturnal camerawork relieving the credibility somewhat. But earlier, the plot has it that Holt is wounded in the arm by a bullet. Thus encumbered, he not only challenges but bests a baddie in a saloon brawl, fighting the thug one-handed. It's one of those things—Holt engages in

Martha O'Driscoll and Tim Holt in Wagon Train *(1940).*

fisticuffing believably, Nelson choreographs the fray ingeniously, you see it, but it's still utterly far-fetched.

With Holt serving his country, RKO entered a curious phase of its Western history. The last Holt entry, *Red River Robin Hood*, was released July 23, 1943. It took the studio over a year to resume production, and even then their "little" Westerns were infrequent, although they made a number of class "A" affairs with John Wayne and Randolph Scott. Whether they were marking time, waiting for Holt to finish his military commitments, or merely idling on the range is of no matter. What is important is that when *Nevada* hit the screens at the beginning of 1945, RKO Westerns had a new producer, a new approach, and most definitely, a new star.

Robert Mitchum got his start as a heavy in

HOLLYWOOD CORRAL: A COMPREHENSIVE B WESTERN ROUNDUP

Ray Whitley, Holt and Lee "Lasses" White in Six-Gun Gold *(1941).*

Hopalong Cassidy Westerns, just one of the gang. But even thus cloaked in anonymity, there was something about him—his manner, the unusual structure of his face—that attracted and held the attention. In quick order, he worked up to the position of one of Hoppy's good guys, some further scene-stealing stints in Westerns, and several non-Western parts of note, small roles in big productions, big roles in "B" films of merit. When RKO signed him as their Western star, he was already known, and at that early date had acquired an underground reputation as one to watch.

With *Nevada,* RKO reverted to the boxoffice gimmick of using the Zane Grey tie-in for insurance. The new producer was Herman Schlom, with the faithful Edward Killy directing and Harry Wild on the cameras. Another Hopalong Cassidy recruit, Norman Houston, wrote the script; Houston was to remain on the lot and figure importantly in future Western plans. Also on hand again was composer Paul Sawtell, an underrated and prolific scorer who had worked on the Holt series from the beginning, as well as contributing Western scores for Republic, Columbia, and Universal in addition to his non-Western work. Sawtell composed some of the best and most-heard background scores for Westerns, much of the music finding its way into the studio's canned library to be trotted out and used often. Since Sawtell was seldom credited, except at RKO, his Western tracks are not associated with him, but they are melodic and enhance the action perfectly.

Mitchum had plenty of capable help in his first starring vehicle, and he carried off his role in fine style, with all the equipment needed for top billing. He could act. His horsemanship was by now entirely satisfactory. His personality came across, still with that slightly menacing tinge that suited his heavy parts, but now coupled with a leavening sense of

...OR ANYWAY, BETTER WESTERNS THAN MOST: Keene, Holt & other guys at RKO

Robert Mitchum, Thurston Hall and Barbara Hale in West of the Pecos (1945).

humor. He was fortunate in having two comedy sidekicks of uncommon ability, the engaging Guinn "Big Boy" Williams and, more important, a young and extremely interesting dialectician named Richard Martin, here inaugurating his continuing role of Chito José Gonzalez Bustamente Rafferty. Martin made himself known when Holt returned, paving the way here. For the moment however, it was Mitchum's show, and it was a good one. RKO provided Anne Jeffreys (bad girl) and Nancy Gates (good girl) to dress up the scenery, and Craig Reynolds, recently returned from duty with the Marines, and the estimable Harry Woods for the villainy. Mitchum and Woods engaged in a brawl that was one of the better ones of the season, with a muscular Mitchum revealing imposing biceps when his shirt is ripped to shreds and drawing a chorus of cooing feminine trills during at least one neighborhood theater showing.

Schlom, Killy, Houston, Wild and Mitchum collaborated again on *West of the Pecos* (1945), another version of the Zane Grey story previously filmed with Richard Dix. Unlike most Westerns, it was reviewed by New York critics upon its opening and was crowned with the rating of three stars by the *Daily News*; on a four-star scale, this was considered astronomical for a budget Western in those days. Easy to see why; it was well done, and contained some non-Western elements that were appealing, even though somewhat borrowed from Shakespeare and planted on the prairie. Barbara Hale proved attractive and adept in her role which called for her to masquerade as a boy through most of the footage, and was probably slated for better things by the time studio execs took a look at an early screening. Husband-to-be Bill Williams also had a supporting role in the film, and Richard Martin further polished his Chito Rafferty impersonation to advantage. Mitchum ambled through the heroics, making it all look a snap, which it wasn't. Released at the same time as *West of the Pecos* was a war film directed by William A. Wellman about correspondent Ernie Pyle titled *Story of GI Joe*, with Mitchum in the main supporting role as an infantry officer, Walker. As a result, he never returned to Westerns. Not low-budget ones, at any rate. RKO resumed their cowboy quest, with Holt still in the service.

They found James Warren, who may have made it had he been offered the same golden opportunities afforded Holt and in a different sense Mitchum. But Warren appeared in but one Western per year, for three years, although the latter two might have been filmed together and spread out over a period of time. Whatever the situation, it was the opener that hurt. *Wanderer of the Wasteland* (1945) had two directors, Killy and former film editor Wallace A. Grissell. Between them, conniving with scenarist Houston, they succeeded with something akin to genius in concocting a prime contender for the most actionless Western ever made. Technically, it's fine. Settings, camerawork, performances, all up to par, and superior to most. But nothing happens. Except that Warren's hero role is devised without heroics; not only that, but he is beaten at every plot turn. Hardly an auspicious debut for a cowboy star. Only Martin's role of Chito Rafferty afforded enjoyment. Otherwise, it was a complete miss.

James Warren and Debra Alden in Code of the West *(1947)*.

...OR ANYWAY, BETTER WESTERNS THAN MOST: Keene, Holt & other guys at RKO

Rumpled Richard Martin, feisty Carol Forman and Holt in Brothers in the Saddle *(1949)*.

Warren's other two were based on Zane Grey stories, produced by Schlom, and directed by William Berke. Improvements over his first, as what wouldn't be? But both *Sunset Pass* (1946) and *Code of the West* (1947) were not sufficiently out of the ordinary to advance Warren's stock. Richard Martin bowed out of these, with John Laurenz assuming the role. Casts were capable, with *Pass* featuring Nan Leslie, Jane Greer and Steve Brodie, and *Code* with Raymond Burr and, again, Brodie. But obviously, Westerns were not for Warren.

Holt was now out of the service and into a John Huston movie which was not looked upon with favor by Warner Bros., *The Treasure of the Sierra Madre*. It was held up for release for almost a year, during which time Holt had signed on with RKO to resume his Western series. Herman Schlom remained as producer, and Richard Martin returned as Holt's sidekick. The Zane Grey association was kept for the first few entries, then quietly dropped, figuring being that the Tim Holt name was by now strong enough without outside aid. Starting with the 1947–48 season, Holt appeared in 29 RKO Westerns, released in irregular groupings: six, four, seven, five, seven.

Postwar Tim Holt Westerns have the same sort of class that Harry Sherman put into the Hopalong Cassidy series. Physically, they do justice to the low budget, and look as well or better than many more costly films. RKO continued its policy of using superior supporting casts, both from the ranks of contractees and temporary visiting thespians. The studio camera department did itself proud on the Holts, with Hunt, Musuraca, George Diskant and others taking full advantage of the scenic exteriors. Anent Hunt's photography of *Under the Tonto Rim* (Lew Landers, 1947), one reviewer commented upon its "almost arty" look. Action was in more than adequate supply, especially in the initial entries, but a facet of the entire Holt series was not so much the heavy action, but the adept pacing of the action, giving a semblance of movement where often none would exist. Naturally, some Holts were better than others, and around the fourth season the strain began to show, as it would in an elongated series. But despite the uneven output, Holt never made a really poor Western. Even when the plot or pacing would falter, the performances or perhaps the scenery would offer some compensation.

Thunder Mountain (Landers, 1947), the initial

entry, bore no resemblance to the George O'Brien film of the same title, even though both were said to be based on Zane Grey's novel. In the Holt version, he returns from college and lands in the midst of a family feud. As is customary, feminine interest is provided for both Holt (Martha Hyer) and Martin (Virginia Owen), and the dirty work is in the capable hands of Harry Woods and the former Tom Keene, now Richard Powers. Landers stages a robust fight between Holt and Steve Brodie, with Holt literally knocking Brodie (or a double) off the floor with a tremendous uppercut, effectively shot by Landers with the camera at a low angle, making the blow appear even more realistic. Landers does the same thing in *Tonto Rim,* with Holt delivering a knockout punch to Robert Clarke's jaw that looks lethal, the illusion aided by Clarke's well-timed reaction.

A nice family touch was lent *The Arizona Ranger* (John Rawlins, 1948) by teaming Jack Holt with his son. The elder Holt contributed his usual steel-jawed characterization and joined in the action with gusto. Knowledge that the two were father and son in real life added to the enjoyment of the film.

All four Holts for the 1948–49 season were better-than-average Westerns, and undoubtedly represent Holt at his peak. Frank McDonald directed *Gun Smugglers* (1948), with Lesley Selander directing *Indian Agent* (1948), *Brothers in the Saddle* (1949) and *Rustlers* (1949). The cast for *Indian Agent* is well-nigh all-star for the Western ranks, with Noah Beery Jr. as a chief, Harry Woods and Richard Powers once again seeing to the villainy, Lasses White on hand for a character role, and the femininity supplied by Nan Leslie and Claudia Drake. Plotting and action were also well above the Western norm.

Writer Houston reached back to *West of the Pecos* and brushed up his girl-masquerading-as-boy

Linda Douglas listens to Holt between takes on Trail Guide *(1952).*

...OR ANYWAY, BETTER WESTERNS THAN MOST: Keene, Holt & other guys at RKO

Richard Martin, shown here with Holt in a scene from Riders of the Range (1949), *played the role of Chito José Gonzalez Bustamente Rafferty in over thirty films for RKO with three different Western stars.*

tangent for *Stagecoach Kid* (Landers, 1949). It still held together, with Jeff Donnell doing the not-too-thorough disguise. Standout of the seven 1949–50 Holts had the unoriginal title of *Riders of the Range* (Selander, 1949). Houston took the formula of the girl's brother being given a hard time by a crooked gambler and made it all seem fresh, with potent help from Selander, Holt and Martin, and Jacqueline White (the girl), Robert Clarke (the brother), William Tannen (the gambler), Reed Hadley and Tom Tyler (heavies) and Robert Barrat. The hour zoomed by rapidly.

Routine was the word for the first few of Holt's fifth and last postwar season, 1951–52. The quality improved thereafter, and the star's final two releases indicated that the series would have returned to form had it continued. *Target* (1952), directed by ace film editor Stuart Gilmore, starts in lively fashion and doesn't ebb in excitement, while *Desert Passage* (Selander, 1952) has a tight script by Houston that uses the non-Western idea of crooks trying to outwit each other while after buried loot. Players Walter Reed, John Dehner, Dorothy Patrick, Clayton Moore, Francis McDonald, Lane Bradford and Denver Pyle lent fine support to the two stars, and the series concluded on an upbeat note. At its conclusion, Holt was as boyish as when he began (he had been seen smoking a pipe in his films occasionally to add maturity; the features were nonetheless youthful). Although he had never been offered another *Ambersons*-type role, or a *Sierra Madre* for that matter, Tim Holt's Westerns endure, in their minor but craftsmanlike way, as examples of good workmanlike productions, abetting a forthright and likable outdoor personality.

William Boyd as Hopalong Cassidy in Hills of Old Wyoming *(1937)*.

104

9
HOPPY

Two things happened in 1935 that were to alter the approach of the Saturday matinee-type Western. Cowboy stars suddenly became more inclined to reach for a guitar than a shootin' iron. The era of the singing Western hero commenced. Sagebrush feature highlights, in addition to a galloping chase or a manly exhibition of saloon fisticuffs, might now include a rendition by Gene Autry of "That Silver-Hair'd Daddy of Mine," or Dick Foran assuring his fans that "The Prairie Is My Home." The other occurrence pertained to Harry "Pop" Sherman deciding to produce a series of Westerns based on the character created by Clarence E. Mulford, one "Hopalong Cassidy."

Sherman had been around the business a long time. He had been involved in the roadshowings of Griffith's *The Birth of a Nation* in the dark ages, had been a top executive of Majestic Pictures, and was generally respected as a man of tact and integrity. The independent states' rights market was fast drying up in 1935, and an independent producer didn't stand much of a chance unless he was able to acquire distribution through a major company. Sherman cooked up a deal by which he could release through Paramount. The studio had been making Westerns based on Zane Grey stories since the silent days and continued to do so, but the addition of another series was considered no liability, especially if the product was worthy.

Mulford's picture of Cassidy was a wisened, bowlegged, salty cuss with a penchant for getting into and out of trouble with clocklike regularity. The tales, of both short-story and novel length, contained as much humor as action. Like other Easterners who wrote about the West, Mulford went to painstaking detail to make sure the plots and backgrounds had some authenticity, and his literary work was highly regarded by devotees. Sherman's first choice to play Cassidy was James Gleason, who closely resembled Mulford's description of him. Negotiations with Gleason became knotty, eventually fell through. Somehow, the role dropped into the lap of William Boyd, whom Sherman had considered for the part of the heavy in the first Cassidy film.

Boyd didn't fit the Cassidy description one whit, but his powers of persuasion, or his agent's, or both, convinced the reluctant Sherman. It was a break for Boyd, for at the time he was on the verge of a washup. It had been a long trek downward for the ex-Cecil B. DeMille leading man of the silents. He was not exactly a stranger to the open spaces, having starred in a 1931 Pathe saga entitled *Painted Desert,* directed by Howard Higgin. But that film was remembered, if at all, as the one in which Clark Gable first made his mark in pictures. Boyd thereafter was demoted to program fare, then the independents, each one a little cheaper than the last. To add to the discomfort, there was another William Boyd on the screen, whose off-camera peccadilloes were unjustly attributed to him. Our Boyd could hardly qualify for sainthood himself, being a lover of wine, women and song roughly in that order, but enough was too

105

HOLLYWOOD CORRAL: A COMPREHENSIVE B WESTERN ROUNDUP

Frank McGlynn Jr. (as Red Connors), George Hayes (as Uncle Ben), Boyd and Charles Middleton (as Buck Peters) study evidence of rustling in Hop-a-long Cassidy (1935).

much. The other Boyd accepted billing as William (Stage) Boyd to alleviate matters to some degree, but it was still occasionally sticky.

Whatever misgivings Sherman might have had over Boyd's wreaking havoc on the identity of the fictional Hopalong, they were soon salved as the series rapidly became popular and successful. For Boyd had accomplished something in Westerns that had been pulled off by G. M. Anderson when he became "Broncho Billy," but seldom since then; he had created a believable character out of whole cloth. Even the cloth was important, because the Cassidy regalia was distinctive: dark blue from Stetson to boot, although changing to a lighter shade upon occasion, with a cowhead clip holding a light blue bandana. The outfit contrasted well with Boyd's delicate features and light complexion, and set off his curiously pale-hued hair in striking fashion. The rough-edged Cassidy of Mulford was transformed by Boyd into a gentler, almost genteel range rider. In time, Boyd concentrated more upon the benevolent traits of Cassidy, especially in contrast to his impetuous sidekicks played by James Ellison and Russell Hayden. The youngsters, instead of emulating their hero, looked upon Cassidy as a sort of friendly Uncle Bill, a nice guy to pay a visit several times a year, someone they'd like to be like when they grow old, say about 40. Adults cottoned to him because Boyd was mature and the films were expertly made without too much of that unpalatable Western hokum. A further present to Sherman was Boyd's pledge to calm down and become a stalwart citizen, and lay off the sauce, a promise he maintained.

To play Cassidy's youthful companion, Johnny Nelson, Sherman selected James Ellison, a new face and a handsome one. Howard Bretherton was signed to direct the initial series of six; Doris Schroeder wrote or collaborated on the scripts of each; Archie Stout, having finished the John Wayne series for Paul Malvern, was the photographer. The Sherman units through the years were noted for their permanency. Of the 66 Cassidy films, for instance, Stout photographed the first ten. Then Russell Harlan did

44 straight. Mack Stengler photographed the final dozen, as well as the Hopalong Cassidy television series, all of which were not produced by Sherman.

Hop-a-Long Cassidy appeared in mid-1935, and Paramount did its part to insure success. It received better-than-usual booking engagements, including some theaters aloof from the run of the mill Westerns. In it, we are told how Bill Cassidy acquires his nickname, or the Sherman-Schroeder-Boyd version. While recuperating following a dangerous embroglio in which he was injured, Cassidy is asked how his wound is affecting him. "Oh, I'll manage to hop along," he replies. The chief villain was portrayed by Kenneth Thomson, presumably the role originally offered to Boyd. In a character part, as Uncle Ben, a lovable codger inconsiderately dispatched by the villain toward the conclusion, was George Hayes. Among the unfavorable comments made by the reviewers, most complaints centered on the eliminating, needlessly in the eyes of the critics, of the Hayes character. Further gripes concerned the placid pace and the paucity of action, until the end. However, in the main it was received as a promising start for a new series, and the brickbats were mildly tempered.

Second in the series, *The Eagle's Brood* (1935), was deemed an improvement. Once again, most of the action was saved for the climax, complete with clifftop struggle between hero and heavy; but the preceding minutes moved faster than the previous entry, and Boyd and Ellison complemented each other adroitly, with Boyd the level-headed arbiter lending a restraining, big-brotherly hand to the youthful impetuosity of Ellison. And again, George Hayes was in the cast but not alive by the conclusion, his role here as a bartender somewhat less sympathetic and attractive than in the first of the series.

It was in the third Cassidy film, *Bar 20 Rides Again* (1935) that Hayes was called "Windy," playing a desert rat who becomes friendly with Hopalong, allowed by the scriptwriters to remain upright by the end of the picture, and is invited to join the Bar 20 bunch. He loses his identification in the following Hopalong, presumably because his popularity happened too quickly and unexpectedly for the scripters to keep abreast. But thereafter, Hayes would team with Boyd, and Ellison and his successors, to become one of the most effective comedy sidekicks.

James Ellison, Boyd and Hayes in Trail Dust *(1936).*

Bar 20 Rides Again amply showed how good the Hoppys were capable of being, and as it evolved how good they were going to be. As before, the main action was saved for the climax, but what a climax it was—a rousing pitched battle, preceded and introduced by a beautifully shot and cut montage, depicting the Bar 20 boys saddling and mounting, ready to ride to the rescue of Hopalong. The rapid cutting assumes a near documentary technique, helped by Stout's strong-angled camerawork and the musical backing of Gluck's "Dance of the Furies," a strangely apt segment of classical mood music used in many of the Cassidys, as well as a number of low-budget films lacking the price of commissioning original scores. Film editor Edward Schroeder certainly merits a full share of credit for the deft assemblage of this montage. So too, evidently, does director Howard Bretherton, trained in the cutting rooms and esteemed as one of the more resourceful practitioners of the craft. In any case, the sequence was a startler, especially in a Western. Good as it was, the entire montage was retained and used in a few later Cassidy productions to build action situations, and remained effective. Aside from the climax, *Bar 20 Rides Again* had a strong plot with a particularly intriguing villain, sharply etched by Harry Worth, a would-be rangeland dictator who keeps a bust of Napoleon in his outlaw hideaway and who gets his whilst inhaling a pinch of snuff, right between the sniff and the sneeze. The Hopalong Cassidys had hit their stride.

When the second season of Cassidys was ready in the fall of 1936, Paramount was well aware of the value of Harry Sherman's independent product. Instead of one mere popular Western star, they now enjoyed a triple treat at the boxoffice. Boyd was fast carving a sturdy characterization in the Cassidy role, while Ellison caught the eyes of the romantics in the audience and Hayes was not only doing right by the comedy chores, but chipping in with a definite portrait of his own, as the character of Windy Halliday was filled in.

The second group of Hopalongs were all directed by Nate Watt, a longtime assistant to Lewis Milestone but with only one or two full-fledged directorial efforts behind him. His first was *Hopalong Cassidy Returns,* and Watt may have been too anxious to instill some vigor into the series, or else he was haunted by *All Quiet on the Western Front;* the film was supplied with action, but of a

Billy King with Hayes, Boyd and Russell Hayden in Texas Trail *(1937).*

Boyd separates Hayden and Morris Ankrum while Andy Clyde and Eleanor Stewart watch in Pirates on Horseback *(1941).*

remarkably violent sort, verging on the sadistic. It was doubly shocking, since the first half-dozen Cassidys were on the bland side, except for the aforementioned sequences. Watt gets things off to a jarring start with a graphic scene showing an invalid in a wheelchair roped and dragged careening down a street to his doom. The dispatch of the heavies at the end also had a cold-blooded quality, as the woman behind the dirty work (Evelyn Brent) is recipient of a bullet from her dastardly henchman, who in turn is gunned down by Cassidy at point blank range— with a second pistol shot following, just to make sure. On the plus side, the script, production and other technical aspects were fine, continuing the high Sherman standard, and the part of the henchman was made memorable by a new Western face, Stephen Morris. He appeared to advantage in five more Cassidys, and returned a few years later as Morris Ankrum to become a further villainous asset to the series.

Watt distinguished himself with the rest of the 1936–37 Cassidy features, which set some sort of record for lengthiness of Western series films. *Trail Dust* (1936) had a cattle drive, fantastic scenery, and a running time of 77 minutes; *Borderland* had a strong plot, a strong villain (Morris again) and was strung out to 82 minutes, longest of all series Westerns. It was also the last appearance by Ellison as Johnny Nelson. He had been getting a buildup of sorts, including the role of Buffalo Bill in DeMille's *The Plainsman,* and his desire to step forward to greener pastures was granted by Sherman. Replacing him was Russell Hayden, with no previous screen experience, who stepped from behind the cameras where he had been a production member of Sherman's staff. Hayden first appeared in the new role of Lucky Jenkins in *Hills of Old Wyoming* (1937) and fit right in with Boyd and Hayes, just as if he'd been there all along. Less of the matinee idol than Ellison, Hayden developed a lanky, wistful charm in his role as the series ensued, in addition to being capable in the action sequences and believable in the romantic and bantering scenes. *Wyoming* was a good one considering tribulations on the Indian reservation, with the by-now customary scenic values, plus a stirring, if rather inappropriate and tinny, musical score. It ran 78 minutes. *North of the Rio Grande* was a railroad story and signified Russell Harlan's first as cameraman, expertly continuing the work so ably begun by Archie Stout. In the cast was a balding young actor from the Group Theatre in New York, out of his element as a rail tycoon but performing well anyway, Lee J. Cobb. Cobb also had a role in *Rustler's Valley,* final entry for the season, playing a badman this time. The last two Cassidys curbed their running times at 70 and 60 minutes respectively; coincidentally, neither matched the entertainment values of their predecessors, although *Valley* did have a nice zippy climax, with a rock slide flushing out the entrenched outlaws. The sequence was used intact in its remake, *Lost Canyon* (Lesley Selander, 1942). Douglas Fowley has Cobb's role, although Cobb can be clearly glimpsed in the old footage.

Hopalong Rides Again (1937) started the third Cassidy season with Lesley Selander assuming directorial duties, and the series falling heir to the Paramount musical library, dressing up the action with strains from big-budgeted studio hits of a year or two ago, notably Friedhofer's and Carbonara's tracks for Hathaway's Technicolor *Trail of the Lonesome Pine.* In time, Cassidy Westerns would be fitted with original music scores from top studio composers, including John Leipold, the above mentioned Gerard Carbonera and Paramount's ace, Victor Young. Selander went on to direct 27 more Cassidys, and his first effort held much promise, for the action was steady and sustained, the Norman Houston script was good, and Harlan caught all the grandeur of the exceptional scenic backgrounds.

George Hayes encountered some contract difficulties with Sherman and missed two in the series. Comedy relief was assigned to Harvey Clark in *Partners of the Plains* and Frank Darien in *Cassidy of Bar 20,* with Selander trying to do the best he could, but both entries were below par. When Hayes returned, the series picked up again.

Five Cassidys in a row, four of them directed by Selander, gave the series a remarkably strong run of superior Western entertainments. *Pride of the West* (1938), with script credited to former director Nate Watt, packed all the proper ingredients into 55 minutes for a speedy session. *In Old Mexico* (Edward D. Venturini, 1938) was a semi-sequel to *Borderland* and merited more than the usual amount of attention because it was not made like a Western at all, but rather resembled a suspense drama in construction and execution, with more than the obligatory number of interior sequences. Well acted and directed, it had a pert heroine in Jane, later Jan Clayton, known to Broadwayites as the poignant Julie in Rodgers & Hammerstein's *Carousel.* And also, for a time, in private life as Mrs. Russell Hayden. *Sunset Trail* (1939) afforded Boyd a chance to do a chucklesome impersonation of an Eastern tenderfoot dude while tracking down some outlaws, a role he played to the hilt with much evident enjoyment. *The Frontiersmen* (1938) strayed even farther from the Western milieu as the Bar 20 trio helped out a schoolteacher, played by the exquisite Evelyn Venable. When the action came, at the end, it was exciting. But for the preceding 70 minutes or so, comedy and human interest held the spotlight, and did so far more capably than many non-Westerns. Finally, *Silver on the Sage* (1939) had all the elements plus a fine performance in the heavy role by Stanley Ridges, another face seldom seen in Westerns.

Once more, Hayes exited the series, this time never to return. The Cassidys were dealt a telling blow, but recuperated in part. Scriptor Harrison Jacobs moved Hopalong and Lucky to Argentina for *Law of the Pampas* (1939), with Nate Watt returning to direct, Sidney Toler away from Charlie Chan briefly to supply the comedy, the sultry Steffi Duna (of Hungarian descent) adding Latin fire, and Sidney Blackmer at home in the villainy. Replacing Hayes in most of the others was Britt Wood, a seasoned vaudeville performer who played the harmonica and told mildewed rustic jokes. Wood was out of place in the Cassidys, but the ones in which he appeared had compensating attributes. Noteworthy was *The Showdown* (1940), with a highlight dear to the hearts of all poker fans, as Hoppy outwits the culprits in a rigged game.

Since Wood obviously was not an asset to the series, the search continued for a comedy sidekick. Norton S. Parker, who had written the Cassidy original that would lead off the 1940–41 season, suggested Andy Clyde to Sherman. The suggestion was a brilliant one. Clyde created the new role of California Carlson, Parker's script was a dandy, and *Three Men From Texas* (Selander, 1940) is a likely contender as the very best Hopalong Cassidy Western ("Broke every rule in the book on that one," chuckled Parker fondly, years later). In fact, the entire 1940–41 Cassidy series represents a high point in Western film history, for fans and students of filmmaking alike. There's not a weak one in the group, and several of them can take their place with the more pleasing entertainments of their day, Western or otherwise. Direction, stories, camerawork, casts, production values, all top grade. *Three Men From Texas,* aside from introducing Clyde to the series, spins an exciting tale of Cassidy and crew against land grabbers. Scenarist Parker is even so bold as to kill off the romantic interest for Lucky,

Boyd slugs Robert Mitchum in Riders of the Deadline *(1944).*

Boyd apprehends Douglas Fowley in front of Herbert Rawlinson, George Reeves (in white hat), and Jay Kirby in Colt Comrades *(1943).*

HOLLYWOOD CORRAL: A COMPREHENSIVE B WESTERN ROUNDUP

Boyd with the King's Men in Renegade Trail *(1939).*

and keeps the narrative perking every minute. Selander makes the 76 minutes seem short. Morris Ankrum excels in the villainy, as he does in several others in this group. Far from least, Clyde goes through his comedy routines, already beloved by audiences since the Sennett days, with shrewd appreciation of what makes mass patrons laugh.

Doomed Caravan (Selander, 1941) followed, and surprisingly, nearly approached its predecessor. A wagon-freighting yarn by J. Benton Cheney and Johnston McCulley (Zorro, etc.), it emphasized suspense, achieving tension seldom found in more ambitious efforts. Selander breezed it through in a fleet 62 minutes. Ankrum again attracted notice, and a fresh and appealing ingenue, Georgia Hawkins, showed promise which for some reason remained unfulfilled. *In Old Colorado* (1941) marked the return of director Howard Bretherton to the series, and he contributed expert pacing to a good script by Parker, Cheney and Ed Kelso. *Border Vigilantes* (1941) afforded assistant director Derwin Abrahams an opportunity to assume full charge, and he came through with a neat package of entertainment, with a good cast: Ankrum, Victor Jory, pretty ingenue Frances Gifford, Tom Tyler, Hal Taliaferro. *Pirates on Horseback* had to do with a hidden mine, directed for suspense by Selander.

The final entry for the season, *Wide Open Town,* was the longest at 79 minutes, the most lavish in production values, and upheld the high quality of the series. Its plot was quite similar to *Hopalong Cassidy Returns,* even to Evelyn Brent repeating her villainess portrayal. Six bullseyes in a row for the unit made one wonder how long it would last. The answer was not long in coming.

In accordance with the practice of the time, five Hoppys were screened concurrently in late 1941, then released at intervals throughout the coming months. Russell Hayden was gone, replaced by one Brad King. There was a noticeable decline in quality, too, although the set of Cassidys was not without its interesting aspects. *Secret of the Wastelands* (Derwin

Abrahams, 1941) was a fanciful concoction about Hoppy and pals discovering a hidden Chinese city, a la *Lost Horizon*. It moved in leisurely fashion, but the plot was bizarre enough to elevate its actual merit. But the rest were uneven at best. In *Outlaws of the Desert* (Howard Bretherton, 1941) the boys were localed in Arabia and in *Riders of the Timberline* (Lesley Selander, 1941) they helped the lumberjacks, but neither effort possessed more than ordinary distinction. *Stick To Your Guns* (Selander, 1941) sorely needed some compensating action, which was not forthcoming, while in *Twilight on the Trail* (Bretherton, 1941) Boyd did his dude act again, with mild results in a script co-authored by actress Ellen Corby. The sixth Cassidy entry, *Undercover Man* (Selander, 1942) was announced by Paramount; but the company sold off some of its product to United Artists, including the Cassidy opus. Thereupon, Harry Sherman moved his unit to UA for distribution. The unremarkable Brad King was replaced by the equally unremarkable Jay Kirby in the young cohort role. Kirby lasted through six. George Reeves substituted briefly, in *Bar 20* (Selander, 1943), then Jimmy Rogers, son of Will, assumed the part for the remaining half-dozen Shermans released through United Artists. The shy Rogers was not exactly a commanding presence but did manage to fill the gap, and appeared to much better advantage than he had in a truncated Western comedy series teamed with Noah Beery, Jr. for Hal Roach.

Sherman's lucky 13 for UA contained some superior series members, starting with the third, *Hoppy Serves A Writ* (1943), first for director George Archainbaud, a 25-year vet who had done everything from romantic dramas to Dorothy Lamour sarong extravaganzas. The film had pace, action, and a well fashioned Gerald Geraghty screenplay based on a Mulford story. It was the last to be so based, the rest being originals or from other sources. Robert Mitchum made his first appearance as one of the outlaws; by *Bar 20* time four Cassidys later, he was playing sympathetic parts. Highlight of *Writ* was a bruising slugging session between Boyd and Victor Jory, even if the doubles were too much in evidence; Andy Clyde also had an opportunity to deliver more than the nominal amount of foolishness, as well as more dramatic moments. *Writ* nearly represented a comeback of sorts for the Cassidys.

Resoundingly up to par were *Border Patrol* (1943), *Colt Comrades* (1943) and *Bar 20* from Selander, and *False Colors* (1943) from Archainbaud, each one sturdily produced, intelligently written and directed and capably acted. Joseph E. Henabery, who had played the role of Lincoln in *The Birth of a Nation* and who had directed a variety of thespians from Valentino to Floyd Gibbons in his time, contributed tellingly with *Leather Burners* (1943), with a good script by Jo Pagano and a standout performance by George Givot, a comedian here excelling in a dramatic role as a crazed miner. *Riders of the Deadline* (Selander, 1943), hailed as the fiftieth Hopalong Cassidy Western, was otherwise undistinguished. But *Lumberjack* (Selander, 1944), a return to the logging country, was 64 minutes of continuous action, even borrowing a fistic brawl from 1941's *Riders of the Timberline* and inserting it in the new one without undue detection. Both *Mystery Man* (Archainbaud, 1944) and *Forty Thieves* (Selander, 1944) showed signs of economy, but compensated with fast-moving action. Sherman then terminated the series.

After two years in limbo, Hopalong Cassidy returned to the screen in 1946. Boyd had obtained rights to the character from Sherman and formed his own production company, functioning as executive producer with Lewis J. Rachmil overseeing the series. Twelve new Cassidys were made, all of them directed by George Archainbaud and photographed by Mack Stengler. Andy Clyde was on hand once more, but Rand Brooks was the new Lucky Jenkins of the trio. The first two in the series, *The Devil's Playground* and *Fool's Gold,* compared favorably with the Sherman Cassidy productions, containing good casts, scripts with novel twists, not an overabundance but a sufficient supply of action, and the ever-present refreshing scenery. Boyd was still in good form, as was Clyde.

But it was as if Boyd had poured all his financial and creative resources into the openers, for the series plummeted disastrously. Scripts were constructed to avoid mass action, and thereby practically forsook any kind of movement whatsoever. As a result, although they ran little more than an hour, the films seemed to drag on for considerably longer. Two of them, *Unexpected Guest* (1947) and *The Dead Don't Dream* (1948), were more in the whodunit groove, most of the plotting taking place indoors, amid some shadowy photography. Another, *Silent Conflict* (1948), hit a low spot in the Cassidy genealogy for sluggishness, added to a ludicrous story about a quack doctor who uses hypnotism enabling him to abscond with loot. Only *Borrowed Trouble* (1948), with a good performance by Anne O'Neal as a spinsterish schoolteacher and some genial clown-

HOLLYWOOD CORRAL: A COMPREHENSIVE B WESTERN ROUNDUP

Boyd at home with "Topper" in a 1942 publicity shot.

Clyde, Boyd and Rand Brooks in Silent Conflict *(1948).*

ing by Clyde, had enough extras to relieve the tedium. There was no mourning when the United Artists series came to an end.

It was a sad conclusion to the Hopalong Cassidy saga, or would have been, had it not been for the advent of television. Then, the ancient Cassidys were resurrected, shown on the tube, and Hoppy was more popular than ever before. Boyd promptly went back into business producing a new series of half-hour Hoppys, with Brooks and this time Edgar Buchanan replacing Andy Clyde, portraying Red Connors, one of Mulford's original Bar 20 characters. There were some further changes. The old Harry Sherman Hoppys were at first shown intact, with the first one in the series, *Hop-a-Long Cassidy,* now known by its reissue title of *Hopalong Cassidy Enters.* Eventually, when NBC assumed control of the Shermans, the features were brutally hacked to 54 minutes each, usually by merely eliminating the opening reels. This wanton butchery caused many complaints, but to no avail, since the National Broadcasting Company had a financial gold mine in its distribution of the hour-long programs. Boyd retained the rights to his final dozen Hopalong features, and edited them to half-hour length to blend in with his own television series. The editing improved the meandering pace of the narratives.

Television made Boyd wealthy after being washed up. He made a guest appearance in the Cassidy outfit for his old boss Cecil B. DeMille, in *The Greatest Show on Earth* (1951); after his television series of 52 episodes, which were moderately popular, he retired, his health increasingly precarious. William Boyd died in 1972, but Hopalong Cassidy still rides; those who remember his films remember the superior ones as among the best in their field, and it is not outside the realm of possibility that newer generations will familiarize themselves with the Cassidy adventures, and enjoy them as well.

Roy Rogers

10
THE MEN FROM MUSIC MOUNTAIN
AUTRY & ROGERS

To his everlasting credit, the foresight of Mr. Nat Levine turned Westerns around in 1935. Credit, in the sense that Levine injected new life into an increasingly anemic boxoffice market—for Westerns were fast becoming a stale commodity. There were too many of them, for one thing; too many, with too little that was new, in a genre necessarily constricted in its adherence to formula plotting bordering on the ritualistic. It came so that each cowboy star seemed to be going through the same motions, covering the same trails, play-acting out the same familiar story. It wasn't true, of course, but it seemed that way. In five brief years, the low-budget Western had come full circle, from passe to popular to passe again.

Levine changed all that. He had been head of production at Mascot Pictures, a minor company turning out serials on a nearly exclusive basis. Now, Mascot was merged with some other floundering companies to form a new organization headed by Herbert J. Yates and christened Republic Pictures. Levine remained in charge of company releases. Serials were still on the bill of fare, but they were complemented by a full schedule of feature films, including Westerns. John Wayne had been inherited from the old Monogram outfit, and an additional cowboy here was urgently desired to cover the waning market.

Now Levine possessed three of the chief attributes mandatory for a Poverty-Row producer, namely parsimoniousness, frugality and thrift. He also had an eye for something different, which is why he placed Gene Autry under contract (when a near-complete unknown) and devoted time and, emphatically, money toward developing Autry's camera presence. It's why he gave Autry, a greenhorn, a starring Western series of his own. Had he miscalculated, Levine could easily have plunged the new company into serious difficulty. But the gamble paid off. In an amazingly short span of time, Gene Autry, astride his horse Champion, had galloped to the top of the list to become a champion at the boxoffice.

Prior to his first starring feature, Autry had been seen in *In Old Santa Fe,* with Ken Maynard; a Maynard serial, *Mystery Mountain;* and forthwith, Levine had cast him in the leading role of the 12-chaptered *Phantom Empire* (Otto Brower and B. Reeves Eason, 1935). The latter was a bizarre bit of weekly goofiness all about an underground kingdom and a yodeling radio star (Autry) who, it seemed, had no further mission in life other than to race back to "Radio Ranch" and from there broadcast his program of cowboy songs. This combination of sci-fi and sagebrush was a strain upon the intellect of even the most gullible, but the directors whipped up sufficient excitement to keep it moving for serial devotees. Furthermore, Autry got through the thing without too much embarrassment, projecting an unpolished but most welcome sincerity. By the same time the following year, he was firmly established as an up-and-coming cowboy star, and not long thereafter he was number one.

Autry's appeal could not, and cannot be adequately explained to many Western addicts, who from the beginning have cast aspersions upon his ability, personality and his effect upon the way of the Western, claiming that Autry did the genre no good. To the latter charge, there's no doubt that Autry kept Republic afloat, practically single-handed; Levine had departed by 1937, but the Autry slate of features had rapidly evolved into the company's prime, not to say only asset. He also improved the lot of the low-budget Western in general, simply by being an audience-pleaser himself. Standing amid the spate of singing cowboys that followed, Autry outlasted them all in the movies, judging from the standpoint of longevity. Only Tex Ritter and Roy Rogers among his contemporaries weathered the years and emerged with their accolades undiminished; and of them, Ritter had never made it quite that big in movies, although at the time of his death he had achieved near-legendary proportions in the country-music business.

What, one persists, constituted Autry's popularity, his hold on audiences? His detractors call attention to his thespic talent, of which, they say, there was none. There may be something in this, but it would be wise not to pursue it too far. For it can be said truthfully that Autry never gave a good performance; equally valid is the contention that he never gave a bad one either. Just as in the cast credits he would always be billed under his own name, Autry was in a sense always performing as himself, which isn't nearly as easy as it sounds. Once or twice he would be handed a dual role, but the scripters saw to it that the second role would be of short duration—parenthetically, Autry invariably acted more than adequately within the limited confines of these roles. But in the main, the cast list would read: Gene Autry—Gene Autry, and that's exactly the way it would come out on the screen. A pleasant, soft-spoken, rather poker-faced young man who would sing with increasing frequency in a nasal tenor. As his fame increased his action sequences became less numerous in his films, but when they did occur he was able to take care of himself nicely enough in a brawl or shootout or chase on horseback, the latter always enhanced by the magnificent steed Champion. Over all, Autry seemed a nice guy, and this transmitted itself to his fans. Of course, all the above goes with the understanding that his early films were smartly made, that Levine brought him along shrewdly during the early stages and that Republic continued to exploit him sagaciously. Add to that the fact that Autry was himself a businessman of tremendously impressive ability, as amply proven by his subsequent rise in the economic world.

Still, the question would remain unanswered to the diehards: How to explain the Autry mystique? If all other theories are discarded, ponder this: he came along at the right time. The reigning Western stars were holdovers from the silents, or were undergoing a temporary eclipse in popularity. Now that Tom Keene was no longer a factor at RKO, only John Wayne remained among the relatively newer faces, and by 1936 he would drop out of Westerns for nearly two years. Johnny Mack Brown was just starting on the independent trail, and Charles Starrett was an unknown factor at Columbia. William Boyd evidently was going to make it as Hopalong Cassidy, but Boyd was hardly a new face—only his Cassidy character was new. Autry was new, and had something different to offer, a guitar and a song. Ken Maynard had songs to sing, but Maynard never stressed the musical element to the extent that Autry did, mainly because Maynard had several cowboy tricks, ridin', ropin', fightin' and shootin' among them. John Wayne was once Singin' Sandy and wanted to forget it if they'd let him. No, Gene Autry was an original, a new cowboy star with a moderately large built-in following from radio and phonograph records, now ready to try for screen stardom.

Vehicle number one for Autry was *Tumbling Tumbleweeds,* the title taken from a ditty composed by Bob Nolan of the Sons of the Pioneers musical group. The song has since become a Western standard, as has another one rendered in the film by Autry called "Ridin' Down the Canyon." The star collaborated on this one, with his sidekick and chief laugh-rouser, the porky Smiley Burnette. Burnette and Frankie Marvin had been with Autry on his radio show and entered films with him. For Burnette, it was the beginning of a new career as a Western clown. Burnette became so adept at his broad buffoonery that he contributed new directions to the course of comic relief, and emphasized the advantage of the hero having a court jester. Burnette's popularity was at times on a par with Autry's and overshadowed Burnette's genuine talent and facility for composing.

Tumbling Tumbleweeds also marked the feature directorial debut of Joseph Kane, a film editor of heavy experience and high ability. Understandably concerned about his first feature job, Kane breathed easier when Ford Beebe, an old friend and working companion, was assigned to do the script. Armand Schaefer, who had directed a number of Westerns in

THE MEN FROM MUSIC MOUNTAIN: Autry & Rogers

Gene Autry, flanked by Frankie Marvin (l.) and Smiley Burnette, gets the drop on a badguy in Guns and Guitars *(1936).*

his time, was to produce, thus commencing a long association with Autry. Producer, director and scenarist did themselves proud. A better start for a new cowboy star, and a new Western series, couldn't have been hoped for. The construction of *Tumbling Tumbleweeds* was perfect to dispel any premature grumblings about Autry's possible lack of virility in the action field. The traditional plot—Autry leaves home, joins a medicine show, returns home to uncover his father's killer—was neatly divided by Beebe into three sections. The initial portion of the film consists of nearly continuous action, with Autry (and doubles Cliff Lyons and Tracy Layne) pitching in heartily with fights, gunplay and some especially vigorous hard riding. The central section advances the story and eases up to allow Autry and company to indulge in some songs, and ditties presented logically as part of the traveling show background. Then the finale reverts back to the action motif, and a slam-bang set-to between hero and heavy in a runaway wagon. Kane's years of editorial experience were evident in the pace of the film, with the opening and closing having that edgy, fast-moving flow of action that would come to represent the director at his best. The production outlay was far from lavish, which must have pleased Nat Levine, but entirely within the demands of the piece, which certainly made everyone happy, Levine included.

Hot on the heels of *Tumbling Tumbleweeds* came *Melody Trail*, with Kane again directing. Just as the first signified what could be done felicitously combining cowboy songs and Western action, with the latter predominating, the second Autry release took the opposite approach, as if Republic was experimenting with an Autry formula. *Melody Trail* played down the action, played up the songs and leaned heavily upon comedy, with Burnette to the fore after being under wraps in the first one, and pulchritude, with Ann Rutherford and a bevy of starlets cavorting prominently as part of the plot. Eventually, the Autrys were to adhere to this presentation, although it wasn't definitely known at the time. The third 1935 release, *Sagebrush Troubadour*, struck a halfway point between the first two by adding a mystery

HOLLYWOOD CORRAL: A COMPREHENSIVE B WESTERN ROUNDUP

Gene draws on Sons of the Pioneers Hugh Farr and Leonard Slye (soon to become Roy Rogers) in The Old Corral (1936).

element to the action and using restraint on the musical numbers. Autry would return to this type of Western only once or twice during his career, but each time the results would be above the average.

Autry's seventh starring vehicle was entitled *The Singing Cowboy* (Mack V. Wright, 1936), by which time he personified the description. By now, Joseph Kane and Wright were alternating the directorial chores, Autry was appearing occasionally in period plots instead of the stories with contemporary settings, and the action element was pronounced. Republic had rapidly developed a style of making Westerns that was pleasing to the critics and, more importantly, devoured greedily by Western and action fans, not only the Autrys but other burgeoning Republic series too. But Autry was the studio breadwinner, so the hot property was exploited to the limit. Autry #11 was *The Big Show* (Wright, 1936), and was a further stepping stone. A major part of it was filmed at the Texas Centennial in Dallas, with the on-location shooting of the various festivities adding a production gloss impossible to obtain under ordinary budgetary restrictions. It looked classy,

and was. Autry played a dual role, a cowboy star and his double, neither part taxing the star's thespic abilities. Among the musical acts involved was a group called the Sons of the Pioneers, including Bob Nolan, whose composing talents have already been cited; Tim Spencer, also handy with the compositional pen; Hugh Farr, a demon fiddler with a resounding basso voice; and a slim youth named Len Slye, now known as Roy Rogers. The group also appeared in Autry #12, *The Old Corral* (Kane, 1936). In it, Autry tangles with the Pioneers, and Rogers, and emerges victorious. As fate would have it, it didn't quite work out that way in reality. The cast of *The Old Corral* is interesting for players past and future; former top hand Buddy Roosevelt gets billing near the bottom, and Lon Chaney, Jr., formerly Creighton Chaney, is marking time waiting for Steinbeck. The feminine lead is Hope Manning, with a classically trained voice, thus unbalancing the Autry vocalistic contributions. She later became Irene Manning at Warner Bros., there enjoying a musical tenure more in keeping with her abilities.

His singing undoubtedly accounted for much of

THE MEN FROM MUSIC MOUNTAIN: Autry & Rogers

his boxoffice success; but it is the action in the early Autrys that remains in the memory. Republic would become so adept with the action sequences that their technique would be practically a patented formula. In their formative years, action scenes may not have had the polished perfection of the Republic of the '40s, but there was a clean directness and refreshing exuberance about them, along with a breakneck manner that would look suspiciously like accident being turned into advantage. An example of the former can be found in the ingenuously titled *Rootin' Tootin' Rhythm* (Wright, 1937). For the most part it's a standard Autry picture, with perhaps a bit too much stress on songs that impede the pace. However, a sequence of Autry pursuing a runaway buckboard, the horses having been frightened by an approaching thunder and lightning storm, is so smoothly presented, with the intercutting of Autry and Champion streaking ever closer toward the conveyance with its endangered heroine (the Mexican actress Armida), and the atmospheric photography by William Nobles giving a grayish cast to the proceedings, it assumes a superb feeling of space, light and movement, made possible only by craftsmen who know their Western business. And for an instance of what seems like impromptu bravado of the wow variety, one can turn to *Boots and Saddles* (Kane, 1937), in which this occurs:

Here comes Autry, riding hell-for-leather trying to escape the clutches of two villains on his trail. Over the sage gallops Autry and Champion, and horse and rider head for a nearby tree. Aha, one thinks, the old up-in-the-branches-and-pounce-on-them-from-above trick, a venerable Western dodge, standard and approved procedure. But not so—Autry reaches for an overhanging branch all right, only to have it snap off from the tree, thwock! and off goes Autry and tree branch, hitting the ground with a crunch. Flash thought... did his double get hurt on that one? Never mind, there goes Autry holding the branch, scooting behind a clump of sagebrush and hunkering down out of sight, but right in the path of the oncoming baddies. Riding abreast, they swerve, bread and butter, to pass on either side of the sagebrush, behind which lurks Autry! Zip! out goes the tree branch from either side of the sage, the ends catching

Autry, June Storey and Burnette in Mountain Rhythm *(1939).*

the legs of both horses, down go the baddies ass over saddle horn, and Gene's got 'em covered before they roll to a halt. The whole sequence runs about 20 seconds, shorter than it takes to tell it. Since they've outlawed the "Running W" for horses in movies now, it's highly unlikely that the stunt could be repeated, if indeed it was planned that way in the first place. By accident or design, it's a stunner.

As 1937 drew to a close, Gene Autry was outdistancing his competition in the Western field, and was well aware of the fact. Businessman that he was, he started casting broad hints that he was worth appreciably more to the studio than he was being paid. Prexy Yates, a tough man with a buck and a stony bargainer, remained unswayed. This wasn't the first time that Autry had made noises not nearly so sweet as his singing. Impasse time. Autry appeared in *Springtime in the Rockies* to end out the year, and starred in *The Old Barn Dance* to begin 1938, both of them directed by Joe Kane. Then Gene took a stroll. The number one cowboy star, and Republic's meal ticket, was off the screen.

No doubt it was as deep a blow to the Yates ego, as to his purse. He was adamant, and to all logical methods of reasoning, foolhardy in his subsequent decision. So be it... Republic scored with The Singing Cowboy from nowhere, so we'll get another one and build him up too. The hell with Autry. Yates thereupon scouted around, and didn't have to go any farther than his own back lot.

Len Slye, from Duck Run, Ohio. Formerly with the Sons of the Pioneers. He had been seen in some Autrys with the group, and some Charles Starretts over at Columbia. A while back, he had done a scene in *Rhythm on the Range* (Norman Taurog, 1936) at Paramount, where practically the whole cast took turns on a Johnny Mercer tune, "I'm an Old Cowhand." What with Bing Crosby, Bob Burns,

Roy Rogers with Carol Hughes and Smiley Burnette in Under Western Stars *(1938), Roy's debut film, originally planned for Autry with the title* Washington Cowboy.

THE MEN FROM MUSIC MOUNTAIN: Autry & Rogers

Martha Raye, the Sons of the Pioneers and scat trumpeter Louis Prima joining in, no wonder the song made an impression and became a novelty hit. Anyway, he broke away from the Pioneers and was now on the Republic lot. His name was Dick Weston now, and he had a brief bit in *Wild Horse Rodeo* (George Sherman, 1937), accompanying himself on the guitar as he serenaded Mesquiteer Livingston and June Martel in a cafe. He had even appeared in Autry's *The Old Barn Dance*. Now there, deemed Yates, was your next top singing cowboy star. Only his name wouldn't be Len Slye, and it wouldn't be Dick Weston. Somehow, the powers that be arrived at Roy Rogers for the lad's new moniker. It had a lilt to it, but there was another Roy Rogers, a fairly well-known square-dance caller. It didn't matter. Before long, and quite unexpectedly, Republic's Roy Rogers was the name to reckon with.

Yates gave the new Roy Rogers the cream of Republic's Western crop for his first starring feature, *Under Western Stars,* released in the spring of 1938. Joe Kane directed, lavishing the same care that he had employed on the Autrys. Sol C. Siegel produced, and promptly moved right out of Westerns and into the production of more prestigious, if not necessarily better, Republic pictures. Smiley Burnette provided the comedy, temporarily retired when Autry ceased. The script, concerning the efforts of a young Congressman (Rogers) to obtain water power for the dust bowl area, was off the beaten track without sacrificing the necessary outdoor ingredients. It was written by the sons of veteran actor-director J. P. McGowan and former ingenue Betty Burbridge. Rogers had an attractive leading lady in Carol Hughes, and a supporting cast of capable character players.

Of course all these attributes would have gone for naught, had not Rogers come through with great potential. Trade and fan reviewers alike were favorably impressed with the boyish singer. He was cleancut, they said; his personality was refreshingly modest; he delivered his songs in a pleasing manner; he was a sure bet to go places. Whether by coincidence or otherwise, Autry and Republic came to terms. The studio now had two singing cowboys on its hands, one a proven boxoffice attraction, the other a comer after only one film.

Joe Kane directed the first two Autrys to be released since the latter's contractual difficulties, and for all the difference both could have been made prior to the troubles. But thereafter Kane was destined to guide the fortunes of the Roy Rogers unit, unfamiliar names began appearing on the Autry credits, and his films took a decided turn toward the musical, at the expense of Western action. Kane had been adept at fusing the musical and Western elements so that one wouldn't interfere with the other. But the remaining three Autrys released in 1938 were directed by Ralph Staub, who had previously done a minor musical or two but who was alien to the ways of range lore, and George Sherman, who had been handling the action of The Three Mesquiteers deftly but who was untutored in staging song numbers. As a result, the Autrys suffered, the sole relief being the presence of vaudevillian Joe Frisco in the Staub-directed *Western Jamboree*. Even Frisco's Broadway quipstering couldn't save it from what was soon to be the bane of Autry Westerns, creeping blandness.

Home on the Prairie didn't alleviate matters to start 1939. It had a director, Jack Townley, who was a comedy writer by profession, and the cast included an elephant that vied with Burnette for laughs, but that's about all. With his next one, however, Autry came up with a surprise hit, of minor league proportions. *Mexicali Rose* (George Sherman, 1939) wasn't any great shakes as a Western, but the Jack Tenney song was currently popular and Noah Beery, Sr. had a role as a lovable bandit chief which he played in a manner reminiscent of brother Wallace's characterization of Pancho Villa, only Noah laid it on thicker 'n molasses, not unexpectedly. The idea of using a current hit ditty as a film title for Autry had been done before, but this time its marquee allure was more than evident. It would be done again, soon, with even more profitable results.

B. Reeves Eason, Autry's old serial co-director, returned to steer the star back on the action track with *Blue Montana Skies* and *Mountain Rhythm,* particularly the latter with its chase sequences heavily underscored by comedy of near-Sennett industriousness. And Joseph Kane came back to direct Autry for the last time, in what was meant to be an Autry special, *In Old Monterey*. Its running time was 73 minutes, ten or 15 minutes longer than the customary Autry; George Hayes, not yet "Gabby," was added to the cast to share the comedy with Burnette; some notable cornball acts, like the Hoosier Hot Shots, were employed for variety; and the cavalry background gave Autry a chance to appear in uniform, as well as Republic to get some further mileage out of some ersatz tanks developed for a previous military story. Aside from these factors, it was up to par for Autry, but not especially special.

Hayes was now free of the Hopalong Cassidys, and a Republic regular. The studio had assigned him

Roy on Trigger in In Old Caliente *(1939).*

to some non-Westerns, and their 1939 biggie about Sam Houston. They had also booked him in to replace Raymond Hatton as sidekick to Roy Rogers. Hatton had moved over to replace Max Terhune in The Three Mesquiteers series; such were the games of musical chairs at Republic. The move was good for Rogers and good for Hayes. The new star had been developing nicely, and Hayes would be an asset. For Hayes, it meant that he would be seen in tandem with a fast-rising Western name and enable him to maintain and possibly exceed his stature accrued while with the Cassidy series. It had taken six months to get the second Rogers release on the market, but it was worth the wait. *Billy the Kid Returns* packed more into 56 minutes than three ordinary Westerns. It began with a plausible account of the death of the young outlaw at the hands of Pat Garrett, then switches to Rogers, a lookalike, who is mistaken for the Kid, and so on. It was a new angle

in 1938, although the years have dulled its originality with repeated use. Smiley Burnette handled the comedy once more before going back to Autry, and the girl was Lynn Roberts. Only, for reasons left unexplained by Republic, she was billed as Mary Hart, and was to appear opposite Rogers in six more Westerns. Perhaps Republic wanted a Western Rogers & Hart to compete with the Broadway Rodgers & Hart; or, they may have desired a short, punchy cognomen to go with Roy Rogers in a sort of sweethearts-of-the-West deal. In any case, the union was dissolved and Mary Hart became Lynne Roberts again, with an extra "e."

Popularity grew in leaps and bounds for Rogers, and with good reason. His Westerns were good, strong, crowd-pleasing stuff. Kane was producing and directing now; as director, he would guide 42 Rogers Westerns in a row, an enviable record, with relatively few missteps. Action would supersede songs in importance. Indeed, swift-paced affairs like *Rough Riders' Roundup* and *Frontier Pony Express* could stand impressively with any of 1939's Saturday matinee fare. And something like *In Old Caliente* not only had action, including a fine battle on the seashore for a climax, but dependables of the caliber of Katherine DeMille, Jack LaRue, Frank Puglia and Harry Woods on hand. As for Rogers himself, he was more assured with each release, and improving with experience.

Near the end of 1939, both Rogers and Autry were victimized by some faulty guidance. Republic's story department sent Rogers to New York in *Wall Street Cowboy;* the resulting crash was not so resounding as the one on the stock exchange ten years previously, but the endeavor was the first really substandard offering since Rogers became a cowboy star. Released almost concurrently, *Rovin' Tumbleweeds* similarly took Autry off the range, and plunked him down in Washington, a la "Mr. Smith." But where Capra's hero meant high drama, Republic's Autry fell into a precipitous drop from the preceding *In Old Monterey.* George Sherman's direction failed to help, and the usual studio slick production was missing, with some technical errors seldom found in Republic product. However, this was the difference between cowboy stars numbers One and Two—where Roy Rogers entered into a period, not of decline, but of fairly standardized entries, pleasant and unexceptional, Gene Autry won what he had been fighting for continuously, namely bigger budgets and more production dress befitting his stature. Fortuitously, his next release after *Rovin' Tumbleweeds* was a boxoffice success beyond

THE MEN FROM MUSIC MOUNTAIN: Autry & Rogers

Roy challenges Pierre Watkin while Gabby Hayes and Raymond Hatton watch in Wall Street Cowboy *(1939).*

expectations, and really was the turning point of his career.

South of the Border (George Sherman, 1939) had a ludicrous plot about some submarine bases, foreign agents, counterspies, all mixed in with a literal picturization of the title tune, unconvincingly glued together with a dozen song numbers. By all Western standards it could not be rated much higher than mediocre—by all but Autry standards, that is. Somehow, his presence, stolid, imperturbable, seemingly oblivious to the drawbacks of his vehicle, not only served as a settling factor to the jumble, but the film proved to be a draw, and not only in houses catering to the outdoor trade. Its release was timed for the Christmas season, which may have helped, and the song was a current leader on the various hit-parade lists. Whatever the argument, it spiraled Autry into a cowboy class of his own. Thereafter, his films received preferential treatment, of near A status by Republic standards.

A precocious and talented teenager, Mary Lee, was introduced in *South of the Border* and appeared in seven additional Autrys. His leading lady, June Storey, was signed on for four more roles. The Autry Westerns became less Western, but dominantly Autry. He sang, blandly let the plot proceed, sang, stood aside for Smiley Burnette's bumpkinisms, sang some more, bantered with Storey, Lee or any given character actor, resumed singing, then exerted himself after a fashion for a mild action windup. His fans didn't seem to mind, but some Western traditionalists were wincing. So were the reviewers. A dour representative of the trade paper *Variety* attacked with pad and pencil, taking *Gaucho Serenade* (Frank McDonald, 1940) as an example. In a 66-minute feature Western, reported the critic, the first horse is mounted only after 44 minutes have passed. The first fist is not flung until the 50-minute mark. No gunfire at all, until the 56th minute. What, queried our man, manner of Western is this?

His point was well taken. Nor was *Gaucho Serenade* an isolated case. *Carolina Moon* (McDonald, 1940) kept the action at the same low level, and failed to resemble a Western in numerous other ways. Republic cooked up a deal with 20th Century-Fox whereby Autry would be loaned to co-star with Jane Withers; the resulting fiasco, *Shooting High* (Alfred E. Green, 1940) did neither of them any good, the Fox hands even outdoing Republic in studiously avoiding any hint of action until it became absolutely necessary. Around this time, the old *Phantom Empire* serial was pared down to feature

Gene with Lupita Tovar in South of the Border *(1939).*

length and sent out as *Men With Steel Faces,* embarrassing Autry and company, who preferred to let sleeping dogs lie. But at least the old Levine work moved faster than the brand new actionless fare.

As if to prove they could reach a higher plateau by distorting the Western milieu, Autry was cast in a starring musical, *Melody Ranch* (Joseph Santley, 1940). For it was advertised and sold as a tune-filled extravaganza, not of the sagebrush variety. Besides, what on earth would Jimmy Durante and Vera Vague be doing in a horse opera? All things considered, it turned out pleasantly. The tapping toes of Ann Miller added zest to the musical numbers, Durante and Vague were in there pitching with the laughs, joined by George "Gabby" Hayes, and Santley, a director attuned to the musical, showed he could handle the range element in capable fashion—there was actually more movement than in several preceding Autrys. Precisely a year later, Santley directed another Autry semi-special, *Down Mexico Way,* that was also comparatively busy, in contrast to the five tame offerings that followed *Melody Ranch.* Santley scored again in 1942, with *Call of the Canyon,* an above-average Autry, returning once again after five non-Santley Autry films. This time, the star was directed by William Morgan, a former film editor with an unobstrusive style. Morgan did well with *Cowboy Serenade* (1942), a sudden and rather startling temporary return to the old reliable action formula; and *Home in Wyomin'* (1942), a reprise of the mystery angle for Autry and an interesting whodunit in its own right. Morgan's material was less felicitous on the remainder, although he tried. But it was stretching believability to the limit in *Heart of the Rio Grande* (1942), which sets up a suspense situation with the heavy lining up Autry in his rifle sights for a length of time, perched atop a hill—then missing, with Autry returning fire with a six-shooter while in mid-air in a leap from Champion, and hitting the varmint square. Audiences invariably groaned. Nor could the inclusion of "Deep in the Heart of Texas" arranged for audience participation save *Stardust on the Sage* (1942) from dullness. The talented Edith Fellows appeared in both the latter films, presumably in roles slated for Mary Lee originally; Miss Fellows did her best to instill some sparkle in the proceedings.

After *Bells of Capistrano* (Morgan, 1942), Gene Autry went into the Air Force and spent the rest of World War II, amounting to over four years, away from the screen. Or almost—Republic kept his early Westerns in constant reissue. The Western crown was passed to Roy Rogers.

Public Cowboy Number Two had recovered nicely from the letdown of *Wall Street Cowboy,* considering that his 1939 release, *The Arizona Kid,* was under average. The Rogers Westerns began to take an historic bent, with such documents as *Days of Jesse James* (1939), with a new player named Donald Barry attracting attention in the James role; *Young Buffalo Bill* (1940) and *Young Bill Hickok* (1940), with Rogers portraying both frontiersmen; and *Jesse James at Bay* (1941), with Rogers personally taking the part this time. Kane was producing and directing now, and doing creditably in both departments. The Rogers Westerns became dependable. They were not equally meritorious, but the general level was lofty and, better than that, consistent. Kane would inject some punch into the action sequences, superior scripters like Norton S. Parker and Louis Stevens would contribute more adult storylines, and the performers supporting Rogers were excellent. "Gabby" Hayes was more popular than ever. Each Rogers release would contain solid names in the cast, from Monte Blue and Herbert Rawlinson, to Bob Steele and Noah Beery, Jr., from Milburn Stone to Henry Brandon to Noble Johnson to Chief Thundercloud, as well as traditionalists Hal Taliaferro, Harry Woods and Roy Barcroft. Also, Rogers was fortunate in getting good-looking leading ladies who could act: Pauline Moore, Jacqueline Wells, Carol Hughes, Marjorie Reynolds, Gale Storm, Linda Hayes, Joan Woodbury.

Also pleasing, no doubt, to Yates and Republic was the fact that Rogers was capable of stepping out of Western-hero character and enacting featured roles in films not totally belonging to him. He did leads in a couple of properties seeded for the studio's resident rustics, the Weaver Brothers & Elviry. Better, he took the role of a hot-headed young scalawag in Raoul Walsh's *Dark Command* (1940), and more than held his own in such heady company as John Wayne, Claire Trevor, Walter Pidgeon and Marjorie Main, with an equally potent role for George Hayes. But it was evident now that Rogers was most valuable in the saddle, no longer as backup man and potential pinch hitter for Autry, but a boxoffice name in his own right.

For his last 1941 release, *Red River Valley,* Rogers acquired the services of the Sons of the Pioneers, his old singing musical group. His stories also went modern to the extent that in a couple of them, most of the trouble was caused by a vengeful gal rather than a heavy with a mustache. Unlike the Autrys, updating them didn't impede the action, since the songs, as always under Kane, had been relegated to the back seat with action to the forefront. It was a nice gesture that one film was dedicated in a way to Roy's companions and titled *Sons of the Pioneers* (1942). That it wasn't one of his better efforts was no matter.

Autry's last film before entering the service was released in September, 1942. Three months later, the first upped-budget Roy Rogers special, *Heart of the Golden West,* hit the exchanges. Wisely, no effort was made to tamper with the successful Rogers formula, other than to allow for a prestigious cast (Ruth Terry, Walter Catlett, Leigh Whipper, and Smiley Burnette to blend with "Gabby" Hayes) and slightly more latitude in fabricating interior sets. Earl Felton's script was pleasant and lively, Kane was on the ball with his direction, and all indications were that Rogers, after years waiting in the wings, was now ready, and in truth had finally arrived.

Departing was "Gabby" Hayes, for awhile. Departing also, after *Idaho* (1942), was Kane's production supervision, although he stayed on as director. Former music director Harry Grey moved over from the shuttered Autry camp to assume the duties, with Eddy White, Louis Gray and assorted others succeeding him. Standing in for Hayes was Smiley Burnette, then the comedy field was left open for Guinn "Big Boy" Williams and Pat Brady of the Sons of the Pioneers. The era of the Shrieking Rogers costumery was also ushered in, with Roy sporting some sartorial nightmares—shirts embroidered with flowering roses, snug-tight pants with provocative white piping snaking up and down the legs, and sundry questionable embellishments. It was touch and go for some time, but the unassuming Rogers personality overcame the publicity-slanted garb, and he emerged with reputation intact. And the adornment was not all subjected to ridicule. As reported by H. Allen Smith, one swanky hostess eyed Rogers at a party as he retreated from a table, and remarked yearningly, "...there goes the *purtiest* behind in Hollywood."

Categorically, the Rogers productions would now

HOLLYWOOD CORRAL: A COMPREHENSIVE B WESTERN ROUNDUP

Roy and Donald Barry in Days of Jesse James *(1939).*

fall into three parts. *Idaho* and *The Cowboy and the Senorita* (1944) stressed music and plot at the expense of action, similar to the Autrys, but these happily would be in the minority. Stressing action to a degree that bordered on the breathless would be *King of the Cowboys* (1943) and *Silver Spurs* (1943). The former, the title of which became the official Rogers billing, was of serial fleetness, with its plot concerning saboteurs and a carnival locale remindful of a chapter play. The latter film is rigged at the outset with Jerome Cowan as a murder victim and John Carradine as a heavy, just to show nobody's kidding; the last half of the film develops into nonstop derring-do, featuring breakneck tricks of physical skill, among them Yak Canutt's daredevil feat of letting a wagon pass over him, grabbing the back of it and hoisting himself up and in. It was all beautifully, professionally done, with Reggie Lanning's photography a great asset in displaying the stunts.

Third and most common of the Rogers Westerns now would be the speedy, serviceable script, swiftly leading to a wild-and-woolly action conclusion, usually a frantic chase on the order of *Silver Spurs*. Then the windup would be five or ten minutes early, to allow for a miniature musical revue with Rogers and companions administering the melodies. By all reasoning the pattern should have failed miserably, but in actuality it came off satisfactorily. The Western and action fans had been well satisfied for an hour or so, therefore they didn't mind too much the lyrical conclusions. Mass unsophisticated audiences were entertained by the tabloid presentations, and the tunes were hummable, if not in the hit category. This non-Western element also enabled Republic to obtain bookings in non-Western theaters. *Hands Across the Border, Heart of the Golden West* and *Silver Spurs* were received by New York newspaper reviewers quite favorably.

Hands Across the Border (1943) was good enough to stand on its own legs in any situation. The plot centered around Trigger, a beautiful palomino horse that was to Rogers what Champion was to Autry; rather than Western, it could be advertised,

THE MEN FROM MUSIC MOUNTAIN: Autry & Rogers

and was upon occasion, as an outdoor musical drama. *Border* was the first Rogers to go all out on the musical-revue climax. Songs were by Hoagy Carmichael, although no "Star Dust" emerged from the score; Ruth Terry delivered numbers in her own impressive style; and the finale was further graced with the Wiere Brothers, clowns extraordinaire. Prior to *Border*, Rogers had added to his laurels with *The Man from Music Mountain* (1943), one of the two titles filmed by both Autry and Rogers (the other: *Red River Valley*), albeit two titles constituted four separate plots. The Rogers *Mountain* was highlighted by some stunning exterior photography by William Bradford. With Reggie Lanning, Jack Marta and Bud Thackery, Bradford would account for a continually superb photographic standard on the Rogers black-and-white features.

Dale Evans joined the cast of *The Cowboy and the Senorita,* appeared in 20 Rogers Westerns in a row as his leading lady, and eventually married him (Rogers was a widower). She was a versatile singer-actress whose Republic contract guaranteed her a busy time in the movies, since she would be used not only for Rogers but also in the studio's assembly-line action and adventure product. However, she curtailed this extracurricular activity after 1948 and thereafter appeared only in her husband's films.

After a long tenure with Rogers, Joesph Kane received a promotion to the upper Republic echelon as a producer-director of top company product, prestige films and John Wayne bonanzas. The first non-Kane Rogers Western was *San Fernando Valley* (1944), directed by John English, a recent graduate from the chapter play division; English had style and an appreciation for the subtleties of outdoor dramas, as well as a fine eye for action. The Gordon Jenkins title tune was currently heard on all the juke boxes, everything else was well up to par, and the film was voted the number one Western at the boxoffice for 1944. The Rogers-English collaboration flowered happily with *Utah* (1945), notable again for Bradford's exterior camerawork, as well as more than the ordinary amount of feminine charms, even for a Rogers Western, with Peggy Stewart, Jill Browning and Beverly Loyd playing showgirls in support of Dale Evans. English was at his best with *Don't Fence Me In* (1945), which had the Cole Porter tune going for it, and an ingenious plot featuring "Gabby" Hayes as a retired outlaw incognito. It met with the most favorable critical response of any Rogers West-

Roy and Gabby pinned down in Sunset Serenade *(1942).*

Gabby, Dale Evans and Roy in the finale of Utah *(1945).*

ern, played some of the more sophisticated theaters on the bottom half of a dual bill (where it would be heard that it was enjoyed more than the main feature), and helped solidify the already lofty Rogers stock. John English was forthwith moved up to non-Westerns, where his career should have blossomed, but somehow didn't.

Sharing directorial honors with English during this period was Frank McDonald, primarily a dialogue man and generally on target when the script was right. McDonald had a neat one in *Bells of Rosarita* (1945), the first time Republic used a neat gimmick that paid off at the boxoffice and added some fun to the proceedings. For the big action rally at the end, Rogers, playing a movie star on location, calls upon his fellow cinema saddlemates to aid him in rounding up the villains; riding onscreen to the delighted whoops of the Saturday matinee kiddies come Wild Bill Elliott (on Thunder), Allan Lane (on Feather), Don "Red" Barry (on Cyclone), Robert Livingston (on Shamrock) and Sunset Carson (on Silver), all to do their share in thwarting the evil doers. Actually, the film was on the mild side until the climax, which was effective, and would be used again by the studio. McDonald's *Sunset in El Dorado* (1945) had a different sort of story (by Leon Abrams), nicely scripted by John K. Butler. It began in the modern-day West, then flashbacked to the frontier days to tell a story within a story. Diehards griped about the paucity of traditional Western trappings, but the novelty more than made up for it. The idea of two stories within one framework is a tricky one to handle, but Republic pulled it off again around the same time in an Allan Lane vehicle.

McDonald directed *My Pal Trigger* (1946), which was sold as a special and remains as Roy's own personal favorite film. Like *Hands Across the Border*, the plot is focused on Trigger, and once again the treatment takes the film out of the realm of normal Western fare and places it in the area of an outdoor drama. Three writers—John K. Butler, Jack Townsley, Paul Gangelin—worked on the script and it was a good one, giving Rogers another oppor-

THE MEN FROM MUSIC MOUNTAIN: Autry & Rogers

tunity to act, rather than using his admittedly effective personality. Bradford's camera effects were integrated into the story this time, instead of standing out on their own. The customary Republic villainy of the Roy Barcroft-Kenne Duncan-Leroy Mason variety was complemented by the addition of the venerable Jack Holt. Animal lovers had plenty of horseflesh to coo over, while the plot and production were sturdy enough to sway the most skeptical non-fan. *My Pal Trigger* did well financially, and Butler proved the value of the story property five years later when he revamped it for Rex Allen into a similarly strong film.

Just as Rogers had crested, Gene Autry returned from the wars. The suspense must have been terrific at Republic, since it was obvious that the old cliche was unavoidably true: the studio wasn't big enough for both of them. Autry had left while on top, but during the intervening years, Rogers had risen rapidly, not by imitating Autry, but through his own devices. The results weren't long in coming. Autry's first postwar production, *Sioux City Sue* (Frank McDonald, 1946) was an attempt to harken back to the pre-war Autry days, with emphasis on music at the expense of action. Trouble was, it looked pre-war in concept, and since the wartime Autry reissues showed the cowboy in an action mood, the general reaction was a negative one. For *Trail to San Antone* (1947), John English was recalled from civilian duty back to the old stomping grounds, to get some movement into the proceedings. He did, with a reprise of that old Yakima Canutt stunt of hanging on to a stallion's neck for dear life while the beast tries to shake loose, first exploited as far back as *The Devil Horse* at Mascot. Despite the action, there were complaints that the show could have used more. The situation wasn't remedied in *Twilight on the Rio Grande* (McDonald, 1947), and deteriorated even further in *Saddle Pals* (Lesley Selander, 1947), which had no action at all; even the comedy relief was on the gentle side, it being done by Sterling Holloway of the fluffy locks and foggy voice, who had joined Autry for the new series since Smiley Burnette was no longer at Republic. The end of Autry at Republic came with *Robin Hood of Texas* (Selander, 1947), and surprisingly, it was the best he had offered, once more using a light mystery angle to help keep the plot interesting. So Gene departed on a relatively happy note, and went to Columbia to form his own production unit, taking with him his old producer, Armand Schaefer (who had, among other things, produced *My Pal Trigger* for Rogers).

At Columbia, Autry treated himself well. Production values supervised by Schaefer were superior to the Western norm. Further raids on Republic had been made, and joining Autry at Columbia were director John English (with Frank McDonald chipping in for two), writers including John K. Butler and Jack Townley, and photographer William Bradford. Supporting casts consisted of names that could easily lend distinction to a better-grade programmer. Autry also experimented with the Cinecolor process for two films, then tried the sepia tint. His first release, *The Last Round-Up* (1947), was superior to anything he had appeared in for postwar Republic, with a sturdy plot, good English direction, and sufficient action, courtesy of library footage from a 1940 Wesley Ruggles epic, *Arizona*. *The Strawberry Roan* (1948) had color tints for the eye and a pleasant wild-horse story, although hardly in the *My Pal Trigger* class. *Loaded Pistols* (1949) was heavy on the fisticuffs, news in itself for Autry followers, while *The Big Sombrero* (McDonald, 1949) lacked action but showed off Cinecolor to advantage, also news in itself.

After four releases, all of them apparently of moderately large budget, the Autrys became more or less standardized. Not quite so lavish, but still above the average Western in production accoutrements, the series reverted to the format of playing down the action, but this time paying attention to strong stories, with the musical interlude likewise held in abeyance. More often than not the plots, although interesting in themselves, would get in the way; however, upon occasion the Autrys would show some really creative twists and turns, and always well-guided by English's direction. *Rim of the Canyon* (1949), by John K. Butler, had Autry playing his own father in an intricate and nicely balanced tale of hidden loot. Butler also managed to cram in more than the usual smidgin of action for Autry. *Indian Territory* (1950) was also better than usual, with an engaging performance by character actor James Griffith as a gunslinger. Receiving critical plaudits at the time was *Mule Train* (1950), based on the runaway song hit. Snob appeal reared its head when New York's Museum of Modern Art selected the latter film to represent Autry in its collection, complete with distinguished ceremony and special showings. Well, what does the Museum of Modern Art know from Westerns? Actually, while *Mule Train* was good, a previous Autry made to cash in on a song hit, *Riders in the Sky* (1949), was superior. It had a clever screenplay by Gerald Geraghty, and particularly noteworthy directorial touches by English, including an atmospheric depiction of the title tune enacted by Tom London as the old cowpoke who went ridin' out one dark and windy day, etc. English and Bradford teamed for some brooding photographic effects combined with apt use of the closeups of London's seamed and weatherbeaten face, to produce one of the more haunting vignettes in Westerns.

Through 1950 and 1951, the Autry Westerns appeared six times a year, competent, if unmemorable in general, still clinging to the remnants of a market that was inexorably receding. With the release of *The Old West* in January, 1952, the inevitable happened. Productions became more economical, if entirely satisfactory; running times dropped from a 70-minute average down to an hour, in line with the lower bracket Western field. George Archainbaud, formerly of the Hopalong Cassidys, directed the remaining dozen Autrys. They were all adequate for their niche, and none of them was especially standout. A poignant note was added for the final six released in 1953. Heretofore, Autry had had Pat Buttram as comedy sidekick. Now for the finale, Gene and Smiley Burnette teamed once more, lending a sense of completeness to the Autry saga. *Last of the Pony Riders* was released in November, 1953, and then Autry ceased theatrical film production. His "Flying A" company was by now heavily engaged in television work, including a series for Autry, and the theatrical Western market was all but shuttered. There was no place else to go. At that, he had outlasted Roy Rogers by over two years, Rogers having quit features in 1951, except for two appearances in Bob Hope farces, and one of those a guest shot.

A burden had been lifted from the shoulders of Rogers when Autry left Republic. Now the King of the Cowboys was top hand on the lot. His popularity was at least on a par with Autry's, except in

Gene and Pat Buttram in Riders in the Sky *(1949).*

the recording field, where Rogers had never been able to match his rival's proclivity at issuing song hits. Nor was he the businessman that Autry was. But now that matters had resolved themselves favorably, it was straight ahead. Producer Eddy White, now using the more distinguished Edward J. White, had built a cohesive unit with which to manufacture the Rogers Westerns. They were now filmed in Trucolor, a process of questionable merit in which the actors gave the appearance of suffering copper poisoning; nevertheless, it was a tinting method which enhanced outdoor scenery and added boxoffice allure. Ace photographer Jack Marta supervised the cameras, bowing out for Reggie Lanning once or twice. Film editor Tony Martinelli would be assigned the splicing duties. Sloan Nibley became a scenarist almost exclusively for Rogers, contributing lean and straightforward screenplays crammed with action opportunities and seeking out new angles on which to hang the story pegs. White had gradually phased out the mini-revues, and now the Rogers Westerns deliberately relegated the songs to the background.

William Witney, of the Witney-John English prewar serial combination, had returned from a long hitch in the service, took on another serial to exercise himself into fighting trim, and was promoted to the Rogers Westerns, directing each one for the remainder of the series. Witney had a way with action and a droll appreciation of comedy relief; he could also pace a film faster than just about any action director working, and knew when and where to move his cameras, a feat unmastered by all too many directors. His workmanship well deserves an extended study, as does the more austere John English technique.

Bells of San Angelo (1947), second of the Trucolor group, amply showed the path taken. Nibley's script, about silver smuggling, stressed the modernity of the setting and fashioned the tale in a grownup manner, yet without ignoring the important kiddie appeal. Rogers here became less the legend and more the plausible human being. The fancy regalia was toned down, as it would be in future films. The invincibility of the cowboy hero was dealt a crushing blow in this picture. At midway point, Rogers is accosted by heavies John McGuire, Dave Sharpe et al, and gets the bejabbers beaten out of him.

Following was *Springtime in the Sierras* (1947), which was even better. A fine Nibley script concerning preservation of wildlife, and splendid action sequences directed by Witney, who was always able to make the Rogers fisticuffing believable. Rogers was agile, but his frame was wiry; to have him best such

Autry with popular co-star Gail Davis in Texans Never Cry *(1951).*

beefy adversaries as Roy Barcroft, Fred Graham and the rest of the Republic baddies took more than a little finesse, which Witney supplied. The brawls in *Sierras* were real rousers. Andy Devine was in for chuckles during this period. Dale Evans was in and out; in *Sierras,* she was replaced by Jane Frazee.

Under Witney, the Rogers Westerns seemed to be accumulating a skein of expert and exciting releases. *On the Old Spanish Trail* (1947) and *The Gay Ranchero* (1948) added Tito Guizar to the cast, assuring extra profits from playdates below the border, where Guizar was a tremendous draw. He lent an air of jaunty bravado, especially in *Spanish Trail,* where Guizar was in good voice and teamed smoothly with Rogers, and Nibley's script was lighter in tone than his last two, with even the villainy on the whimsical side, supplied by Charles McGraw and, as a punchy thug who casually brushes away imaginary cobwebs, Fred Graham.

Nibley wrote a story about some lethal tampering with an estate, and *Eyes of Texas* (1948) became, under Witney's potent direction, one of the better Rogers Westerns, which by now meant of appreciably high caliber. Noticeably grim and somber, the tale is acted without flourishes by Rogers and the cast, the playing marred only slightly by some overemphasis by Nana Bryant as the villainess behind the scheme. In complete contrast, *Grand Canyon Trail* (1948) is played and directed for laughs, with some

HOLLYWOOD CORRAL: A COMPREHENSIVE B WESTERN ROUNDUP

Gordon Jones (l.) and Monte Hale collar a heavy while Roy and Rocky Lane interrogate in Trail of Robin Hood *(1950).*

Gene Autry and Pat Buttram, Valley of Fire *(1950).*

THE MEN FROM MUSIC MOUNTAIN: Autry & Rogers

Andy Devine stops a brawl between Roy and Dave Sharpe as Dale watches in Bells of San Angelo *(1947).*

clever intercutting by Witney between a comedy brawl featuring Andy Devine and parallel exterior hell-for-leather riding by Rogers. Here, the Trucolor shades show to advantage under Reggie Lanning's cameras, the night action photographing in restful pea-green tints.

Foy Willing and his Riders of the Purple Sage replaced the Sons of the Pioneers as the musical aggregation backing Rogers, but lanky Pat Brady stayed on to attend to the comedy, in turn replaced by Gordon Jones, a hulking type, then by, incongruously, ex-burlesque comic and latter video kiddie star Pinky Lee. The quality of the Rogers Westerns continued undiminished, and when they were inspired, as in *Down Dakota Way* (1949), *Bells of Coronado* (1950) and *Heart of the Rockies* (1951), they could stand comparison with any bigger-budgeted outdoor shows. All this, in a market of less handsome profits and increasing lack of care in Western production.

One of the most enjoyable Rogers Westerns in the later group was *Trail of Robin Hood* (1950), a confection by Gerald Geraghty about rustling Christmas trees(!) and an oldtime movie star, played by Jack Holt, who needs help badly. Rogers comes to his aid in a reprise of the "all-star" climax, rounding up Holt's old pals to come to his rescue. One by one they ride onscreen and introduce themselves: newcomer Rex Allen, Allan "Rocky" Lane, Monte Hale, vets William Farnum, Tom Tyler, Kermit Maynard, Ray "Crash" Corrigan, Tom Keene (forsaking for once his newer image of Richard Powers). Another rider gallops up, dismounts... and is promptly given the cold shoulder. "I'm George Chesebro," he announces, "and I've been a villain in Holt's movies for 20 years. Now I'd like to be on the right side for a change." He is accepted.

After *Pals of the Golden West* (1951), Rogers called it "Happy Trails" and concentrated on television and personal appearances. His one major starring stint for Bob Hope and Frank Tashlin in *Son of Paleface* (1952) saw him looking uncomfortable and preoccupied in unfamiliar non-Republic surroundings, and thereafter he appeared in a flash as a gag in the 1959 Hope farce *Alias Jesse James*. But it may have been consolation that even at the end, when the Western field was swiftly descending in popularity and the fortunes of Republic were far from sanguine, the Roy Rogers Westerns maintained their prestige and their quality.

Tex Ritter sings in Mystery of the Hooded Horsemen *(1937).*

11
HAVE SONGS— WILL WARBLE

Did the Autry melodic phenomenon spawn a new breed of Western star, one whose tonsils were as important as his gun hand? One would be strongly tempted to answer in the affirmative, in view of the number of singing cowboys dotting the cinema ranges between 1936 and the end of the '30s. There is also evidence that it would have happened had there been no Autry—that the Republic star served as a catalyst, but at the time, the idea of songs on the prairie was a-glimmering in the brain of more than one studio executive.

Autry was catapulted to stardom, and practically overnight renown, by Nat Levine with *Tumbling Tumbleweeds,* released in September, 1935. Immediately following in his footsteps, or hoofprints or whatever, came Dick Foran, whose debut as a movie cowboy came for Warner Bros. two months later, in November, 1935. Granted that the Warner boys were quick to perceive the impact of Autry's success with what amounted to a new form, it's dubious that they could have unearthed their own Western songbird, had the initial script on the studio floor and solidified plans to exploit this new property all in the space of a few months. The prospect must have arrived near-simultaneously in both camps. Also, Foran did not resemble Autry in the least, nor did he work like the Republic cowboy. Foran, and his later compatriots Fred Scott and Jack Randall, if they could be likened to anybody, could be said to follow the trail of M-G-M's blonde thrush, Nelson Eddy, the male half of the Jeanette MacDonald-Nelson Eddy operetta confections. The first one of these also appeared in 1935, somewhat earlier than Autry. Like Eddy, Foran, Scott and Randall possessed vocal equipment within the operatic sphere. Indeed, they would be entirely at ease with a robust rendition of "Stout-Hearted Men," but the simple bucolic pleasures of "Ridin' Down the Canyon" would be beyond them. Of course, the reverse would apply to Autry, so it was take your pick. However, the booming baritones didn't last much beyond 1940, while Autry and Tex Ritter, two of the more comfortable and idiomatic vocalizers, pursued lengthy careers in the field.

It is interesting that Warner Bros. should have been the company to follow the musical Western, since their production had been dormant after the John Wayne series was halted in 1933. A new executive lineup at the studio paved the way for the move, with an extensive schedule of low-budget features placed under the supervision of Bryan Foy. Foy once claimed he had only one plot and kept producing it over and over. He also indulged in a bit of nepotism; one of the seven sons of vaudeville great Eddie Foy, he found constant casting for brothers Charley and Eddie, Jr., and this was far from the least of his accomplishments. He found further use of stock and library footage for the Foran series, again borrowing from the silent First National Ken Maynard features, which had been done for the John Waynes; some other footage predated the Maynards and came from the ancient Vitagraph days, and by the time the last

HOLLYWOOD CORRAL: A COMPREHENSIVE B WESTERN ROUNDUP

Foran was underway and the series about to meet with curtailment, it didn't much matter whether some embarrassing close-up shots crept into the stock film, a dead giveaway that the scenes weren't exactly of recent vintage.

Aside from the corner-cutting on the old footage, Foy dressed the Forans in capable fashion. The Warner studio facilities allowed for a physical look that an independent producer would find difficult to accomplish, if not impossible. Contract players were abundant at Warners, and un-Western faces like Joe King, Joe Crehan, Addison Richards and Frank Faylen would be seen, in addition to such range stalwarts as Edmund Cobb and Yakima Canutt. A Warner contactee named Gordon Elliott appeared in several Forans, usually skulking up some villainy. Not too long after, Elliott would switch from Gordon to Bill and carve a new and long-lasting Western niche for himself.

In the matter of name-changes, Foran had undergone a modified transformation at Warners. Formerly Nick Foran, he had been used sparingly at Fox, somewhat in the manner of an ensemble singer, who was around for the big production number calling for a lusty baritone but otherwise under wraps. Nick became Dick at Burbank, and *Moonlight on the Prairie* (D. Ross Lederman, 1935) became the first Dick Foran Warner Western. It was mildly entertaining, made to seem better than that by the slick production and good supporting cast, including Sheila Mannors (the ingenue), Joe Sawyer, George E. Stone, Robert Barrat, Gordon Elliott, Joe King and youngster Dickie Jones, one of the more tolerable cinema kiddies. Foran, a burly redhead (as later Technicolor would prove), sang well, could stay in the saddle without swaying and possessed acting requisites beyond the range of what he was allotted. *Song of the Saddle* (Louis King, 1936) was an improvement if anything, and bolstered Foran's standing in the new musical Western market. The potent Louis King direction displayed the serviceable if formula William Jacobs script to advantage, Foy gave it a good production and Foran was settling comfortably into the cowboy hero territory. The Sons of the Pioneers could be glimpsed briefly, as could child actress Bonita Granville, who someday would be involved in the production of a Western series, namely TV's "The Lone Ranger." *Treachery Rides the Range* (Frank McDonald, 1936) continued the good impression made by the first two, with a fast-paced Indian yarn by Jacobs, and cast with veterans Monte Blue and Jim Thorpe.

It never failed. Whether major studio or independent shoestring producer, all the effort, financial and artistic, would invariably be poured into the first few series members, then economic blight, lack of inspiration and resulting tedium would set in. The Forans were similarly afflicted thereafter, though in not so drastic a manner. There were one or two better-than-average ones, but the chief drawback of the Forans was probably due to the fact that Warners had never been heavy on Western know-how. True, their directors and scripters had been responsible for an imposing number of the breed, and production facilities were more than adequate, as mentioned. But somehow, despite these advantages, what emerged would be unconvincing, albeit entertaining. It was a West that drew too much on false devices; there was too much emphasis upon Foran's big-brotherness to too many small fry; the Warner contract players, old faces and new, were adept performers, but not on horseback, where they seemed out of place; the tone of production was geared wrong, condescending to the youngsters, yet not adult enough to satisfy completely the grownups. Songs written for Foran were pleasant and hummable, most of them by studio tunesmiths M. K. Jerome and Jack Scholl; but even here, the sound was closer to Tin Pan Alley than the Great Divide.

Perhaps the above is too harsh on Foran, for he did accrue a considerable coterie, and during his string of 12 Westerns spread over two years, did rise to a contending position with speed and grace. Warners was using him off the range during this period as well, placing him in supporting roles in their prestige product, and in leads in lower-case features, which was another source of critical comment. One trade reviewer chastised Warners for doing so, stating that Foran was not being given an adequate chance to establish himself as a cowboy, appearing as he did in other roles.

Whatever the case, Foran did have some shining moments before the conclusion of his Warner series. *Land Beyond the Law* (B. Reeves Eason, 1937) could stand proudly with any Western of the period, with Eason directing a gunfighting climax with the same care and unmistakable camera technique he had gainfully used on the second-unit action sequences so memorable in 1936's *The Charge of the Light Brigade*. Also, any exhibitor playing Westerns late in the run would have benefitted from this one, since Wayne Morris was featured in the cast and became the subject of a studio exploitation campaign shortly thereafter. *Cherokee Strip* (Noel Smith, 1937) was notable for its heroine, the talented Jane Bryan. In it, Foran crooned a lullaby to youngster

Dick Foran (center) checks his stagecoach in California Mail *(1936)*.

Tommy Bupp entitled "My Little Buckaroo." To the surprise and delight of all, no doubt including composers Jerome & Scholl, the song received a lot of play on the radio and wound up a hit, although the film had just about played out its run and failed to cash in on the notoriety.

Critics razzed *The Devil's Saddle Legion* (1937) because the director was Bobby Connolly, a choreographer who wanted to do something besides timesteps, so received his opportunity with a horse opera. Actually, it wasn't too bad, with Foran in good form and Connolly keeping the pace going. But it signified that the end was near. Warners didn't continue their feature Western series, Foran went on to play in whatever they would give him under contract. A few years later, when he switched to Universal, Foran did return to the range in a couple of serials and a feature, *Road Agent* (Charles Lamont, 1941), as part of the Foran-Leo Carrillo-Andy Devine series that proved he had lost none of his saddle expertise. He also landed the masculine lead role in an Abbott & Costello farce, *Ride 'Em Cowboy* (Arthur Lubin, 1942), and introduced what would become a pop standard, "I'll Remember April."

Independent producers caught the singing cowboy fever, with Fred Scott, billed as "The Silvery-Voiced Baritone," first to reach the screen in a series produced by Jed Buell and released through Spectrum Pictures. Scott was no newcomer, having been evident in the early sound days in some Pathe musicals. For pure quality of voice, Scott was the best of the bunch. As an actor, he didn't fare badly, and his Western attributes such as ridin' and fightin' improved steadily. But he was a singer, not a cowboy. And the productions, while squeezing the most out of the shrinking dollar, were hardly top-grade—biggest budgetary expenditure, it seemed, was for Scott's fancy costumery. Plenty of buttons on the shirts, and buttons cost money.

Scott's first was *Romance Rides the Range* (Harry Fraser, 1936), a title hardly guaranteed to cause the kiddie hearts to beat faster. Once past the barrier of the sissy titles however, the Scotts made an earnest if limited effort to satisfy their patronage. The action scenes would be vociferously hailed in the lesser-grade theaters where the films would be booked, even if some of the heroics were on the hokey side. Scott was liked, and his song interludes would be greeted respectfully by the action crowd.

HOLLYWOOD CORRAL: A COMPREHENSIVE B WESTERN ROUNDUP

Lafe McKee and Louise Small joke with Fred Scott in Melody of the Plains *(1937).*

What was probably the most important element of the Fred Scotts was the comedy. Doubletalking Cliff Nazarro began it, but soon Scott's sidekick was Al St. John, who formulated the "Fuzzy" characterization that was to serve him so profitably in later years. Scott and St. John worked well together. With *Rangers' Roundup* (Sam Newfield, 1937), another comedy name was seen on the credit titles. Buell was still producing, but the Scotts were now officially billed as Stan Laurel Productions, the comedian cutting down on his film appearances with Oliver Hardy to function behind the scenes. Whether Laurel contributed anything to the Scotts, or to St. John's comedy, is doubtful; production quality remained the same, which was frugal, and St. John had been around as long as Laurel, so there was no cause for instruction. But the Laurel name was grist for the marquee, if needed, and the three Scott productions with Laurel's cognomen gave the illusion of improvement.

Spectrum continued to distribute the Scott Westerns, but the producing honors had shifted from Jed Buell to C. C. Burr, noted for his Johnny Hines comedy features in the silents, but more recently associated with product scraped from the bottom of the barrel. Raymond K. Johnson directed the remaining Scotts, which were not on a par with the Buells. Scott had Harry Harvey replacing Al St. John for a comedy partner, a move not slated to improve the product, and neither *Code of the Fearless, In Old Montana* nor *Two Gun Troubadour,* all of 1939 vintage, helped Scott. A fourth, *Ridin' the Trail,* did not see a release until 1942, and then through independent distributor Arthur Ziehm, Spectrum having since disbanded. Scott starred in one more film, *Rodeo Rhythm* (Fred Newmeyer, 1942), filmed in Kansas City and released by PRC. He sang some, but the picture was built around the Roy Knapp Juvenile Riders, a covey of kiddies, and was a mercifully isolated effort. In retrospect, the best one can say about the Fred Scott Westerns is that the star was the big plus factor. With good voice and screen presence, one wonders what would have been his fate had he received more commensurate production values.

Cursed with financial stresses from the very start, producer Ed Finney used his head and all the exploitational wherewithal at his command, and latched on to a cowboy comer to boot. Finney formed "Boots and Saddles Productions" for his discovery, and entered into an arrangement with the newly formed Grand National Pictures to release his Tex Ritter Western series. Ritter had what Autry had, and what Foran and Scott missed. He looked like a cowboy of the range, and not the drugstore variety. His drawl was genuine Texican, his clothes practical without being ostentatious. He was a good scrapper, rode a fine steed named White Flash and his singing, while an acquired taste, did have the echo of the plains in its timbre. Actually, Tex was a city slicker, having appeared on Broadway in plays and developed his dramatic skills doing considerable radio acting in various serial stories sent out over the ether. Finney signed Ritter, and what Finney lacked in funds he made up for in hustle. At the same time, Grand National was new and raring to go. This exuberance was reflected in the Ritters and audiences took to the star, willingly overlooking some of the production defects, if indeed they noticed them at all.

Song of the Gringo (J. P. McCarthy, 1936) was the first for Ritter and it was tolerable enough. However, Grand National chose to push the fourth in the series, *Trouble in Texas* (Robert N. Bradbury, 1937) as a shining example of what the new company was offering. It had a modern story—the Ritters would jump back and forth in time as the spirit moved, in accordance with the majority of Western series of the era—and gave Ritter signal opportunities to display riding prowess, fisticuffs, and his molasses-toned prairie pipes. It also had a nifty feminine lead, Rita Cansino. When she became Rita Hayworth, *Trouble in Texas* was disinterred by opportunistic distributors and reissued, with scant mention of Ritter but plenty of advertising featuring Hayworth. But then, theaters starting the Ritters with *Trouble in Texas* would most of the time retrace and play the earlier three. Another interesting early Ritter was *Arizona Days* (1937), because of Jack (John) English's vigorous direction and the brief appearance of Ethelind Terry, former musical comedy star whose role was ground down to a mere flash part here.

After some false comedy starts with Fuzzy Knight and Syd Saylor, the Ritter series found its groove when Finney teamed portly, pompous Horace Murphy and the bloodhound-visaged Snub Pollard of the silent slapstick era, thus giving Ritter not one but two sidekicks. In addition, Finney was mixing the latter releases ingeniously. *Riders of the Rockies* (Bradbury, 1937) was in the traditional horse opera scheme of things, with a simple plot, well-planned action, including a brawl between Ritter and the ubiquitous Charlie King, and a fast pace. *The Mystery of the Hooded Horsemen* (Ray Taylor, 1937)

Scott with Victoria Vinton in The Singing Buckaroo *(1936).*

was, as the title implies, a serial-like yarn by Ed Kelso, complete with hidden villain (until the climax) and baddies galloping hither and yon in Klannish hoods and capes. Small fry would gobble this stuff up, and they did here. Finney showed smart thinking by using a solid tie-in on *Tex Rides with the Boy Scouts* (Taylor, 1937). The film was merely passable and the scout angle was pounded home with a longish prelude, but the title was a selling point of consequence, one of Finney's ways of getting more juice out of the Ritters than the run-of-the-range Western producer.

But then the economic woes became more pronounced, and it showed in the product. *Frontier Town* (Taylor, 1938) relied more on stock shots of

HOLLYWOOD CORRAL: A COMPREHENSIVE B WESTERN ROUNDUP

rodeo events than on plot. *Rollin' Plains* (Al Herman, 1938) was the sheep-vs.-cattlemen number from the tattered cliche files, and *Utah Trail* (Herman, 1938) had some action, but not much else, except a quintet of songs for Ritter which interrupted the action, a fault heretofore not found with the series. Grand National was presently undergoing some financial difficulties, from which it would not emerge. Seeing his chance to recoup and maintain the Ritter popularity, Finney moved his unit to Monogram.

Ever since it had re-formed and made its appearance in mid-1937, the new Monogram had been in sore need of a cowboy star. The veteran Tom Keene wasn't the answer, nor did the tyro Jack Randall seem to be able to carry the burden alone. Ritter looked strong enough to fill the bill, and his acquisition was a happy one for Monogram. His films were little changed in personnel. Cameraman Gus Peterson was replaced by Francis Corby, then Marcel LePicard. Bulk of the directorial duties remained with Al Herman, with Spencer Gordon Bennet assuming the reins at intervals. A director who had comedy training, Herman bore down on Ritter's adeptness with sly humor, and the lightness of touch helped. Ritter's strongest assets were still his authentic mien and prowess in the action scenes, especially the fights—he performed most of his fist work and made it real, climaxing the frays towering over his downed opponent, angrily flicking back the long, straight hair cascading over his forehead. His singing style was a further crowd-pleaser.

Finney continued to try for offbeat plots for Ritter, and often his ambitions would outweigh his budget. Because of this, the Monogram Ritters were an erratic lot, with great expectations marred by gaucheries. The first fall release, *Starlight over Texas* (1938) had the action halted for a fiesta sequence at midpoint; it was colorful and allowed for some tuneful Ritter melodies, but the net results were only mild at best. *Where the Buffalo Roam* (1938) had the germ of an idea concerning wanton decimating of buffalo herds, but this was soon swallowed by the presentation of too many song numbers, and too obvious grainy library footage. *Song of the Buckaroo* (1938) had a good plot about Ritter running for Mayor, and a selling point in the appearance of model Jinx Falkenburg as the ingenue, but Herman

There was no standing on ceremony in making low-budget Westerns. Here supervisor Lindsley Parsons doubles as a clapper-boy on Tex Rides with the Boy Scouts. *Tex and Marjorie Reynolds prepare for Scene 251: Take 1.*

Tex Ritter and Hank Worden (with mustache) peruse wanted poster held by Ed Cassidy in Hittin' the Trail *(1937).*

paced it all too leisurely and the necessary bite was missing. Finney sent a troupe on location to the Wyoming Valley for *Down the Wyoming Trail* (1939), but as usual things went awry. There were scenes of a stampede of elk and the snowy backgrounds were certainly off the beaten path; but LePicard had experienced camera difficulties with no chance to compensate for the breakdown, and many shots included in the final print were made laughable by the skittering movement caused by photographing at silent speed. As it happened the more satisfactory Ritters for the season were the ones that played it safe and contented with the traditional formulae, like *The Man from Texas* (1939) and *Riders of the Frontier* (1939), the latter Spencer Bennet's first for Ritter.

Halfway through the 1939–40 season, the Ritters hit a patch of inferior releases; not that it was planned that way by any means. But after *Rhythm of the Rio Grande* (1940), a pleasant entry, the quality factors took a beating. The star was saddled with the unwelcome presence of a moppet named Sugar Dawn, with all the imaginable saccharinities implied; or he would be plagued with a plot that called for ever-emphatic dramatics at the expense of the narrative; or he would be handed subpar development, not aided by alert direction. Ritter had acquired a new comedy sidekick in the person of one Arkansas Slim Andrews, a gangly blowhard familiar to back-country audiences on the bucolic circuit for years. There was no in-between with Andrews; one either doted on him or loathed him. If a tally had been made, results would probably have tilted in the latter direction.

Redeeming features made *Arizona Frontier* (1940) superior to the previous several Ritters, and closed out the season on an upswing. The film was photographed around Prescott, Arizona, thus furnishing fresh scenery; the Indian tale was well-knit and Ritter was in good form. Except for a few editorial lapses by Fred Bain during the gunfight at the conclusion, technical values were capable. The next few Ritters continued the improved quality, but Finney and Ritter were near a parting of the ways. Number four for the 1940–41 season was *The Pioneers* (1941), a dismal effort in all respects. It was the last Tex Ritter film for Ed Finney, and showed all the earmarks of being hastily slapped together.

Ritter spent the next few years busily appearing in Westerns and retaining his popularity, but was

HOLLYWOOD CORRAL: A COMPREHENSIVE B WESTERN ROUNDUP

Ritter rescues Dorothy Fay from Charlie King, Hank Worden, Bud Osborne and Ernie Adams in Sundown on the Prairie *(1939).*

forced to take second billing. After leaving Monogram he signed on with Columbia to co-star with Bill Elliott, thus giving the latter star's series some added punch. A year later, in 1942, he moved to Universal and functioned in the same capacity for Johnny Mack Brown. Although Ritter lent extra value to both series, essentially both remained in the province of their original stars, with Ritter considerably more than a supporting player, but not quite achieving the status of co-star, other than officially in the billing. When Brown left Universal, the company was left somewhat stranded for a Western star, and Ritter and Russell Hayden inherited the dregs. The scripts gave evidence that they were manufactured for Brown and Ritter, and were subsequently filmed with a few minor adjustments. Fuzzy Knight stayed on for comedy. In *Arizona Trail* (Vernon Keays, 1943), it seemed that Ritter took the role originally planned for Brown, while Dennis Moore, one of those capable Western players who bounced around from studio to studio without attaining much worthwhile, was drafted for Ritter's part. The same thing could be said of *Marshal of Gunsmoke* (Keays, 1943), only with Russell Hayden operating in the Moore position. Moore returned to fill in on *Oklahoma Raiders* (Lewis D. Collins, 1944). The three vehicles showed that Ritter had lost none of his ability and the Universal productions were the best he had ever received, with the films themselves rating from good to average. But Universal was looking in other directions for a new cowboy star and found him in Rod Cameron. Ritter left Universal.

He settled at PRC, replacing James Newill to join Dave O'Brien and Guy Wilkerson in the Texas Rangers series. Ritter said later that he regretted the move eventually, for the PRCs were cheaply made and far from appetizing on the Western market. As it was, Ritter did instill some dignity into the series, and a few of them were, comparatively speaking, rather well-done. But Ritter wasn't happy, the series

HAVE SONGS—WILL WARBLE

was going nowhere, and after a season, it was farewell.

Thereafter, Ritter was off the screen for long periods, concentrating upon personal appearances and recordings. He was doing exceedingly well when he was called upon to render the theme song over the credits of the Stanley Kramer production *High Noon* (Fred Zinnemann, 1952), with resulting great fortune. He became a powerful figure in the field of country-and-western music, as performer and publisher. At the time of his death in 1972, he was nurturing political ambitions. He had come a long way, but would still recall anecdotes concerning his films of 30 years before, and fondly.

As previously touched upon, the new 1937 Monogram had big plans for their cowboy star Jack Randall, formerly Addison Randall, of RKO civilian roles. His older brother was already cutting a swath at Republic as Bob Livingston of the serials, Zorro adventures and Three Mesquiteers sagas. Randall was as handsome as brother Robert, could sit on a horse in authentic range manner, and to go one up, could sing in a professional baritone. Monogram bigwig Scott Dunlap personally supervised the initial Randalls, with Robert N. Bradbury producing and directing the first three, all released in 1937. *Riders of the Dawn* inaugurated the series and was a mixture of good and bad. The good included a fine production dress, excellent photography by Bert Longenecker, sturdy supporting performances by sidekick George Cooper and heavy Warner Richmond, and an especially exciting and well-directed climax featuring a mass gun battle between the outlaws and the lawmen, topped by a runaway stagecoach with villain brought to justice by the ultimate fate, destroyed by a bolt of lightning. On the opposite side of the production coin was an unfortunate introduction to Randall and his singing. He was victimized by inept recording, photographed in close-up bobbing up and down in the saddle as he

Jack Randall (r.) gets the drop on Warner Richmond in Riders of the Dawn *(1937).*

went through his number without a quiver or quaver. It was so patently phoney that even the smaller fry weren't fooled for a moment. Randall never managed to recover from this unimpressive musical beginning, and his other songs were greeted with audible squirming from the audience, thus taking the edge off a superior Western.

Randall's next two, *Danger Valley* and *Stars over Arizona,* failed to match the assets found in his debut and there were continuing complaints regarding his vocal efforts. From appearances, Monogram lost much of the high hopes placed in the new star, and Randall's Westerns began to change producers. Replacing Bradbury was Maurice Conn, former independent producer, here operating under the Concord trade name. *Where the West Begins* (1938) was one of the last directorial jobs by J. P. McGowan, capping a long and prolific career on both sides of the cameras, and he steered a pleasant screenplay swiftly through its 54 minutes. Or in some cases, a few minutes less than that—Randall was still given songs to sing, but in at least one engagement, the numbers had been delicately but noticeably excised from the print. Another Conn production was *Land of Fighting Men* (Alan James, 1938), an ordinary horse opera with, for those days, an extraordinary cast of Herman Brix (later Bruce Bennett), Dick Jones, Rex Lease, Wheeler Oakman, Lane Chandler and the beauteous Louise Stanley in support of the star. One more, then Robert Tansey took over the productions from Conn; by that time, if there were any songs in Jack Randall Westerns, they were sung by someone else. Randall stuck to his horsemanship, gunslinging and fisticuffing.

Sol Lesser, through his Principal company, had been furnishing one-shot horse operas for 20th Century-Fox release since George O'Brien departed in 1936. One-shot, both in the sense that Richard Arlen, Ralph Bellamy, Paul Kelly and Ricardo Cortez would try one; and also referring to the sum total of action to be found. To get back into the cowboy-star race, Lesser contracted an elongated balladeer named Smith Ballew to star in a series. Ballew was known on the vaude and nitery trails as a band singer and orchestra leader of no mean skill. He had recorded extensively, both with his own and various other orchestras. In 1936, Walter Wanger had starred him opposite Frances Langford in an Aubrey Scotto-directed frippery, *Palm Springs*. Ballew resembled Gary Cooper closely, but since Cooper was already at Paramount, that settled that; besides, the film offered nothing aside from nice tunes. But Ballew played a cowboy, he was tall and could ride. Enough credentials for Lesser.

Ballew was ill-served by *Western Gold* (Howard Bretherton, 1937), which had players like Heather Angel and Leroy Mason standing around with as little to do as the star. *Roll Along, Cowboy* (Gus Meins, 1937) was a second misstep. Ballew sang nicely and was backed up by Cecilia Parker, gruff Stanley Fields and smooth Gordon Elliott, but there just wasn't enough sock to the production. The dirty work had been done so far as Ballew was concerned, but his final trio of films showed improvement. Ray Taylor, a director more closely attuned to the Western, guided them, and Lesser and his writers came up with some decidedly offbeat story angles. In *Hawaiian Buckaroo* (1937), Ballew starts on a pineapple plantation but finishes saving a cattle ranch, with the locale in itself saving the picture from the routine. The star was also handed more action than had been customary. Next was *Rawhide* (1938), which had action, a good script by George O'Brien's old writer Dan Jarrett (his last screenplay) and a co-star of importance in Lou Gehrig, baseball great. Gehrig, New York Yankee first baseman and New York City born and bred, took to the open range like the Yankee Stadium infield, and delivered a thoroughly professional, good-humored performance, overshadowing the somewhat mild-mannered Ballew. Half the fun was in seeing Gehrig handle himself in an unfamiliar surrounding—and seeing him acquit himself so well. Had he remained in films—apart from the crippling disease which killed him two years later—Gehrig boded fair to become a threat to John Wayne, whom he resembled.

Ballew's final starring vehicle was *Panamint's Bad Man* (1938), with a clever touch provided by Stanley Fields in a baddie-turned-good-guy role and moved along by Taylor's even pacing. Smith Ballew never quite caught the Western public's fancy, and the Lesser series ended. Three out of five isn't a bad score.

Universal was left without a saddle star when Buck Jones bowed out after a disagreement in 1937, so forthwith they endeavored to cultivate their own. One Leland Weed, Army veteran, heard on the WLS National Barn Dance and numerous radio shows, was now Bob Baker, Universal cowboy star, for the Trem Carr production unit. Baker had great promise. His voice was melodious, not the booming baritone of the operetta cowboys, yet not the twang of an Autry—it was easy listenin', the most appropri-

Smith Ballew, one of the screen's less successful singing cowboys.

ate description. Baker was clean-cut, dressed not too gaudily, and was poised before the camera. His first four were directed by Joseph H. Lewis, meaning that said cameras were fancily operated, since Lewis used photographic compositions more skillfully than any Western director of the period. What wasn't provided for Baker to any satisfactory degree was an opportunity to prove he could dish it out, rangeland fashion. Plenty of formula plotting, songs, horseplay by Fuzzy Knight, good looks from heroines Lois January and Constance Moore. When director George Waggner took over from Lewis, Baker had passed the test in every department except exertion. Waggner directed eight in a row, and wrote them under his *nom-de-plume* of Joseph West. Concurrently, the already tight purse strings were clamped tighter, so by the final entry one had the distinct impression that one had seen the sets in previous Baker pictures—and one undoubtedly had. Gone was the Virgil Miller photography adorning the opening entries. Gone also was the Universal library music for background, including Waxman's chase agitato from *The Bride of Frankenstein,* no less. It all was replaced by Frank Sanucci's one-trumpet-and-a-prayer. Sanucci composed what might be termed as horse opera chamber music, for players of limited range and ability. Said trumpet often flatted flatulently, whilst the violin (singular) was put out to keep apace. Sanucci was to go on from there and plague the Tex Ritters, Range Busters, Trail Blazers and sundry Western series for the next decade. Once accustomed to it, his music did have a certain fascination.

Through it all, Baker, it must be said, performed valiantly. He proved he could come to grips with a decent screenplay, as Norton Parker had written for him in *Courage of the West* (1937), his debut. Given something like *The Black Bandit* (1938) to start his second season, he could well have quit cold and few would have held him accountable, but he hung in there. He was burdened with one of those plots about the good twin and the bad twin; the obligatory hand-to-hand encounter made it easy on the audience to tell which twin was which, because the

HOLLYWOOD CORRAL: A COMPREHENSIVE B WESTERN ROUNDUP

bad twin's double sported a noticeably protruding paunch. In *Honor of the West* (1939), Joseph West wrote some dialogue that director George Waggner should have vetoed on the spot. Real tongue twisters. Baker emerged unscathed, but the ingenue nearly ran out of breath trying to penetrate the verbal swamp. She, incidentally, was a pubescent named Marjorie Bell, real name Marjorie Belcher, later and better known as the dancer Marge Champion. With the possible exception of *Ghost Town Raiders* (1939), the Bakers failed to rise above the routine, no knock to the star.

Baker was kept on at Universal when they decided to revert to the action theory with Johnny Mack Brown. But the singing cowboy was never a factor in the new Brown series; in fact, Ford Beebe unceremoniously killed him off midway through *Oklahoma Frontier* (1939), which he wrote and directed. After a serial appearance (in support) and the Maynard-Gibson opener for Monogram (also in support), Baker left films, deserving a better fate.

Merely for the record, other aborted attempts to establish range yodelers didn't develop past the initial stages. Gene Austin, once idol of the '20s, the popularizer of "My Blue Heaven" and numerous hits, now fallen upon fragile times, made a weak attempt to become a cowboy singing star in the movies. Cruel to contemplate, but Austin could then no longer trade on his own name, but rather the shadow of Gene Autry, for success. To complement his film, he made personal appearances, along with Joan Brooks and Candy & Coco, also in the picture. But *Songs and Saddles* (Harry Fraser, 1938) was a haphazard independent that encouraged no followup, and merited none. Another musical name at one time was Art Jarrett, who had crooned "Everything I Have Is Yours" as Joan Crawford danced by at M-G-M. Now better known as Eleanor Holm's former husband, Jarrett went West with *Trigger Pals* (Sam Newfield, 1939) for Grand National. Joining him were Lee "Lone Ranger" Powell, billed that way until Republic got mad, and Al St. John, everybody's funnyman at this juncture. Powell was an excellent type who should have gone farther, but didn't sing. Jarrett showed little empathy for the prairie and the movie wasn't much, ergo finis. Grand National tried out Tex Fletcher, staunch radio favorite, in *Six-Gun Rhythm* (Sam Newfield, 1939), and Fletcher had

Bob Baker, Forrest Taylor (center) and friends foil a stage holdup in Western Trails *(1938).*

Introducing (and saying goodbye to) Tex Fletcher: Six-Gun Rhythm *(1939).*

potential. He played the guitar left-handed, which in itself was interesting; the story had some gimmicks, like some football scenes to establish Fletcher as a sportsman at the beginning, and a climactic fight in a sandstorm. Grand National went blooey as a company before anything could be done about Fletcher's film future, nor did he attempt to pursue a film career. At the end of the year came Monte Rawlins in *The Adventures of the Masked Phantom* (Charles Abbott, 1939), along with Boots, the dog, and three songs. An Equity picture. Nothing further need be said.

Bob Allen

12
MEMBERS OF THE POSSE

After 1935, or after Gene Autry, if a cowboy didn't sing he was bucking the tide. With a few notable exceptions, Western heroes making their pre-World War II debut were well advised to study harmony as well as marksmanship, guitar-playing as well as gun-fanning. The mortality rate for new cowboy series was high. Most of the novice range stars didn't make it past the first season. Some failed to advance past the initial feature. One would see the Monte Montana productions *Circle of Death* or *Gun Smoke* (Bartlett Carre, 1935), starring one Buck Coburn, then no more. Yancey Lane came and went with *Trail of the Hawk* (Edward Dmytryk, 1935), produced by Herman Wohl for about ten grand and sometimes listed as just plain *The Hawk*. Lane was forthright and credible, but the film showed its budgetary limitations all too clearly. If anything, it proved that Dmytryk, an ace film editor, could direct.

One of the more jaw-slackening excretions of the time was entitled *The Irish Gringo* (William Thompson, 1936), a debacle of such blatant ineptitude that it is a source of wonder the footage was ever assembled for public showing. In the title role was Pat Carlyle, perhaps unknown to Western devotees, but a familiar face in those peculiar sex-exploitation shows dotting the schedules of the period, always promising more than they offered. Carlyle was also listed as the director of some of these. Questionable as the steamy treatises were as regards entertainment value, it was as chief player in an outdoor saga that Carlyle reached the nadir. As can be gathered from the title, his role was of the Cisco Kid type, complete with pencil mustache, Speedy Gonzalez dialect and fancy outfit with sombrero. Far from demeaning Carlyle, he was an actor of some competence; in fact, it takes a performer of considerable adeptness to keep afloat in a sea of anachronisms such as beset *The Irish Gringo*. Carlyle waded through it all, flamboyantly exuding the devil-may-care attitude that is standard equipment with the character. He used a roguish chuckle to advantage, to point up a bit of pseudo-epigrammatic dialogue and as a cover-up when his gun misses its holster in a cavalier attempt to deposit it. The plot of *The Irish Gringo* defies description because there seem to be several separate stories, some of them drifting off into nowhere, the others not making much sense. Some oldtime faces appear and vanish without explanation throughout the narrative. Bryant Washburn seems to have the chief heavy role, but he suddenly becomes missing in action halfway through. William Farnum gets one big scene near the start, and old Bill devours it with mustard. His scene is with a kiddie, but no child actor is gonna steal a scene from Farnum, no sir—he jockeys the tyke into position with back to camera, so Farnum gets the full face close-up, then in an emotional surge buries the kid's kisser deeply into his own shoulder so he can slice juicy morsels of Smithfield's pride without interruption. No sequels to *The Irish Gringo*. None were necessary.

HOLLYWOOD CORRAL: A COMPREHENSIVE B WESTERN ROUNDUP

At the opposite end of the frontier junk parade would be *Heroes of the Alamo* (Harry Fraser, 1937), an effort laudable in purpose, execrable in execution, from the ranks of A. J. Xydias and his Sunset Productions. Xydias and Sunset had been responsible for a bevy of lower-case Westerns since the silents, all made on the thinnest of shoestrings. Apparently Xydias poured all he had into the epic story of the Texas defenders of the Alamo from the forces of Santa Anna; for an indie, the battle sequences looked as if money had been spent. However, the rest of the production aspects were considerably below even independent standards, and some ordinarily capable lesser-echelon actors were made to seem silly by the Roby Wentz screenplay, cumbersomely directed. Thus did Lane Chandler, as Davy Crockett; Rex Lease as William B. Travis; Ed Piel as Sam Houston; Earle Hodgins as Stephen Austin; and Julian Rivero as General Santa Anna, all resemble cardboard characters, with the possible exception of Rivero's earnest playing of an unsympathetic role. By a stroke of luck, and persuasiveness producer Xydias sold the melange to Columbia in 1938, after handling it on the states' rights market for some months. It received more playdates under the Columbia banner than it deserved.

Mention here might be made of *The Lone Ranger* (William Witney and John English, 1938), the Republic serial with the drawing power superior to many feature films because of the allure of the radio and comic-strip character. Well up to par according to Republic action standards, it used a neat reverse plot gimmick to keep interest on high each week, that of disguising the good guys instead of the villains. Kids and grownups alike must have had a time guessing the identity of the masked rider, from among Lee Powell, Herman Brix, Lane Chandler, Hal Taliaferro and George Letz. The 15 chapters were later edited down deftly to 67 minutes for a feature version, naturally entitled *Hi-Yo Silver!* (1940). There was no mystery about the serial sequel, *The Lone Ranger Rides Again* (1939). Witney and English directed, Chief Thundercloud repeated his faithful Tonto role, and Robert Livingston assumed the mask of the riding avenger. Jinx Falken, as she was known momentarily, was the feminine interest. Following the way of many sequels, it wasn't as good as the original, but it had enough of the Republic savvy to keep the fans coming back for 15 weeks.

Catering to special audiences were the Westerns featuring black actors. The star was Herb Jeffries,

Lee Powell socks Ray Bennett in The Lone Ranger *(1938).*

who became a vocalist with Duke Ellington's orchestra. He could ride, had acting ability, and was poised in front of the camera, with his vocal talents a proven asset. He didn't receive much support from the production end, or from his supporting casts, but it is supposed little was expected. At that, seasoned funsters like F. E. Miller and Mantan Moreland (the Miller & Mantan act) did provide some welcome intentional comedy relief. *Harlem on the Prairie* (1937) was directed by Sam Newfield and written by Fred Myton, two Western perennials, and the cast played it all entirely straight and sincere. The novelty value enabled it to be played off in non-ethnic theaters, something not accomplished with either *Two Gun Man from Harlem* (1938) or *The Bronze Buckaroo* (1940), both directed by Richard C. Kahn, both of resoundingly lesser quality.

Jed Buell, whose idea *Harlem on the Prairie* was, concocted another novelty Western shortly thereafter, teaming with Sol Lesser's Principal company to make *The Terror of Tiny Town* (Sam Newfield, 1938), with a cast of midgets. The simple tradition of hero-girl-villain was adhered to religiously and played earnestly. Disregarding one's own personal reaction to the grotesquerie, it did have some moments of charm, and quite a bit of fun to watch the way in which the players took their roles seriously. Columbia was sufficiently impressed with it to acquire it for release, showing more business acumen than with *Heroes of the Alamo.*

PRC, when it was still known as Producers Distributing Corporation, made one of the few attempts at a true "family" Western series with *The Sagebrush Family Trails West* (1940), directed by Sam Newfield under his "Peter Stewart" alias. The new company thought they had something in Bobby Clark—not the beloved broad comic, but a 12-year-old rider, roper and quondam actor. Perhaps, this was not the proper place to display his talents. William Lively's script hardly lived up to his name, Sig Neufeld's production was sparse, and the whole thing clumped along soggily for an hour. No further attempts were made to continue the Sagebrush Family adventures. Sole highlight had been Earle Hodgins, as head of the family, a medicine-show barker. Hodgins had perfected his spiel over the years in vaudeville, and would employ it frequently in films. His delivery was sharp and funny, and Hodgins might well have become a sort of prairie Bob Hope had the fates been kinder (and Hodgins younger), for his patter had the same rapid-fire technique ("... yessir, this lotion is guaranteed to give you a skin like a peach, yessir, fuzz 'n all, and I wanna tell you...").

Of the companies experimenting with new cowboy stars, Columbia was trying the hardest to find a suitable hero for their second-string series, to replace Ken Maynard, who had replaced Tim McCoy. Production values had lessened noticeably since the McCoy days, with the Maynards under Larry Darmour's unit definitely also-ran in quality. To take up the slack, Columbia and Darmour settled for Bob Allen, who had been given range experience supporting McCoy in a few of his later films, and who had been biding time in the interim essaying secondary roles in Boris Karloff thrillers and such, rising as high as suitor for coloratura Grace Moore in one of her songfests. Allen could act, and had a profile amenable to the gals in the audience. Evidently borrowing one of Maynard's shirts, the one with the arrow pockets or reasonable facsimile, Allen and Darmour commenced.

Maynard's shirt was not the only carryover. Director Spencer Gordon Bennet assumed the duties on the Allens, and so did writer Nate Gatzert. Harry Woods was much in evidence perpetrating the villainy. Hal Taliaferro made his official break with the Wally Wales name in the Allen series, and Jack Perrin was content with a supporting role in *Reckless Ranger* (1937). Each of the six Bob Allen Westerns had the word "Ranger" somewhere in the title. This uniformity may have been a major factor in Allen's relatively mild impact upon Western aficionados. See one, see them all. Allen's looks may have been a count against him, too—his collar-ad handsomeness may have been right for the ladies, but the more rugged members of the audience conceivably could have resented it. More importantly, Allen could ride, fight and emote capably, but he wasn't an authentic son of the prairie, something that Western fans could spot immediately. After six features for the 1936–37 season, Allen left Columbia to ramble around Republic and 20th Century-Fox in non-cowboy roles, ultimately returning East to appear regularly in the legitimate theater.

Columbia followed their unsuccessful Allen series with another new figure in the saddle, although Jack Luden had played roles in Paramount Zane Grey Westerns at the start of the sound era. More or less under wraps for the past several years, Darmour signed Luden for a shot at the 1937–38 seasonal Western sweepstakes. Unfortunately, the Luden project was doomed from the start, it would seem. Gatzert again worked on the scripts, and Joseph

HOLLYWOOD CORRAL: A COMPREHENSIVE B WESTERN ROUNDUP

Jack Luden threatens a heavily made-up Hal Taliaferro in Phantom Gold *(1938).*

Levering directed each entry, but after four Luden Westerns the series was abandoned. It wasn't Luden's fault—he accomplished all the necessary tasks essential to a cowboy star without looking too ludicrous, and with a bit more production finesse might have stayed around longer. Messrs. Taliaferro and Woods appeared often, as did Charles "Slim" Whitaker, whose performance as a loutish outlaw served to maintain more than the usual amount of attention to *Pioneer Trail* (1938). Despite the tolerable amount of good, the Ludens contained not one whit of that extra kick distinguishing the successful from the commonplace. The tipoff came early, when reviewers would mention Tuffy, the canine member of the cast, as the most worthy performer. It was the second miss for Columbia. Then came Bill Elliott, and the studio hit the right combination.

In his new role as a non-singing cowboy, Jack Randall appeared to be making headway at Monogram, albeit with a fast turnover in producers. Maurice Conn had met with success in setting the Randall's on the right trail, and now Robert Tansey continued the steady supervision, with occasional assists from his "Robert Emmett" screenwriter's name. *The Mexicali Kid* (Wallace Fox, 1938) was slow but enjoyable. The title role was not Randall's, but belonged to Wesley Barry, once a child star, now essaying grownup parts (similarly, Buzz Barton had appeared in a couple of Jack Ludens around this time; it was an era of the returning juvenile). *Drifting Westward* (Robert Hill, 1939) was exactly the right kind of minor fast-moving Western enabling a cowboy star to keep his status—short (47 minutes), succinct, no wasted motion. Randall had now teamed with Frank Yaconelli, who provided dialect comedy relief. *Trigger Smith* (Alan James, 1939) was four minutes longer than *Drifting Westward* and of the same level of competency. There were some duds, but the Randall series had done well for Monogram.

To show their gratitude, Monogram turned Randall over to Harry S. Webb who, with low production values and lower script and directorial skills, promptly did in the series. In a charitable mood, perhaps *Wild Horse Range* (Raymond K. Johnson, 1940) would pass muster, without adding to any laurels. The rest of the 1939–40 Randalls were disasters. Webb, Johnson, scenarists Carl Krusada, Tom Gibson et al had been in the movie business for a long, long time, but had failed to grow with the industry. Their techniques were still back in the simple silent era, or even worse, early-sound days. Thus, in *The Cheyenne Kid* (Johnson, 1940) we have the spectacle of Randall diving headlong from an impossibly high cliff into the water below, and snatching his stetson, which just happens to be floating by, before swimming away; and in *Covered Wagon Trails* (Johnson, 1940), our hero, tied with his hands behind his back, maneuvers them down over his flanks to the front, where he proceeds to gnaw at them like a hungry diner attacking a sirloin steak. Audiences chortled; Randall was finished. Without the producer trouble, he might have been at Monogram without a hitch.

Monogram's Western thinking was not on target in other respects. Adrift from Tex Ritter, Ed Finney produced and directed a little opus with, as usual, a plethora of library footage and a pennywise budget. It was a pleasing tale of three good-bad guys, horse thieves, and a *Silver Stallion* (1941). The tale and its telling brought no comparisons with John Ford, but the part of the young outlaw was played by David Sharpe, who had been in films since he was a kid, but who had been the recipient of some tasty publicity of late in *Life* magazine, showing his agility with a six-shooter. Sharpe was said to be the fastest gun in Hollywood, and had a chance to back up the claim in the film, drawing as he scurried to get out of the line of fire. No two ways about it, Sharpe was lightning-fast. Furthermore, after a period of playing kid brothers and young badmen, he acquitted himself with aplomb in his first leading Western role.

Ernie Adams, Jack Randall and unidentified corpse (?) in Riders from Nowhere *(1940).*

HOLLYWOOD CORRAL: A COMPREHENSIVE B WESTERN ROUNDUP

Dave Sharpe, stuntman-turned-star of Silver Stallion *(1941).*

His action approach, including horsemanship and gunslinging ability, was the stuff of which fans are made, and he possessed all the other attributes except a speaking voice, which remained on the thin side. *Silver Stallion* was good, granting the budgetary considerations, and Sharpe was labeled a comer by many reviewers. Worse luck, it didn't happen. Sharpe served briefly as one-third of the Range Busters trio, and never managed to capture a top spot for himself again. Of course, Sharpe at this time was also one of the most adept and creative stuntmen and action-stagers in the movies. For the record, his two cronies in *Silver Stallion* were LeRoy Mason and Chief Thundercloud, performing well. A year later Finney produced and directed a followup of sorts, *King of the Stallions* (1942), depleting further the stock-footage library of horseflesh sequences. Dave O'Brien had what passed for the hero's role, and showed anew that he was suitable Western lead material, especially since World War II was beginning to diminish the ranks of leading men. O'Brien did earn leading roles shortly thereafter, but not at Monogram. He joined James Newill and Guy Wilkerson for the "Texas Rangers" series at PRC.

O'Brien came up the hard way, from the ranks of dress extras. In 1933, he could be seen performing as a chorus boy in Warners musicals. Over the next decade he became a regular in all manner of independent and Poverty-Row productions: a crook here, cub reporter there, cop, thug, killer, victim, walk-on, supporting role, second lead. He worked both sides of the law in Westerns, and was "Renfrew's" mountie pal. A while before his PRC starring venture, he had played second fiddle to Buzzy Henry in two features headed for the indie market to display a child star in a cowboy series. Dick L'Estrange produced and Richard C. Kahn directed *Buzzy Rides the Range* and *Buzzy and the Phantom Pinto* (1941), without discernible aptitude. Young Henry was a good trooper and at home in the saddle, and O'Brien helped as much as he was able, to no avail. The latter film had restricted bookings through a small distributor, while Buzzy hardly rode the range at all, with respect to his other effort. Seven years later, Astor Pictures picked up the rights and released it as *Western Terror,* with O'Brien, now well-known to Western fans and fast becoming popular with devotees of Pete Smith comedy shorts, given top billing. Buzzy Henry went on to appear opposite Western stars like Roy Rogers; became Buzz Henry upon attaining adulthood, still in the saddle in many Western films; and finally, as Robert B. Henry, became not only a capable character player but a stunt specialist, much in the manner of David Sharpe. One of Henry's most notable achievements before his untimely death in 1971 was the staging of some action sequences for Sam Peckinpah's *The Wild Bunch*.

Charles Starrett

13
DURANGO

Charles Starrett made his first Western for Columbia Pictures in 1935. He was still at it in 1952. Imagine! At the same studio for 17 years—not only that but, with few exceptions, industriously turning out a limited film form, one which required a good deal of the emoting to be accomplished on horseback, and whilst dodging the fists of an adversary bent on destruction. It's an estimable record Starrett holds. He did it without the usual amount of off-camera publicity or fan-magazine stories, leading a quiet domestic life and letting his films speak for themselves. In doing so, he landed on the various lists of popular cowboy stars continuously. His films changed their approach many times over the years, yet Starrett would remain the same, not even showing his age as the '30s melted into the '40s, and so on. There were occasions, especially toward the end, where his Westerns would have his drawing power as sole assets. Starrett, a pro, would overcome the obstacles of seedy productions and careless technical work by the force of his personality and not inconsiderable acting skill. And when the Starrett pictures were good, they were good indeed.

Columbia had lost Buck Jones and Tim McCoy by 1935. Ken Maynard was there, working for the Larry Darmour unit, but old Ken was beginning to fray at the edges and his vehicles were not of the quality to cause a company to stand up and shout their praises. Rather than try an established saddle hero, the studio decided to develop their own, and Starrett was selected. Parenthetically, Columbia tried again with Bob Allen the next year, and failed. Such was the difference of arriving on the screen before and after the singing-cowboy era.

Ford Beebe was hired to work on the new Starrett series. Beebe was in the process of playing a major role in the development of the low-budget Western; in 1935 alone, he had 1) launched Tim McCoy's independent series for Puritan; 2) written the script for the first Gene Autry musical Western, *Tumbling Tumbleweeds;* and 3) developed the screenplays of the initial two Starretts, with more work in the foreboding future. Beebe didn't set out to startle or revolutionize the Western world with his Starrett work. Wisely, he stuck to the old, traditional and safe story trail, formulae numbers one-two-three, to wit: cattlemen vs. homesteaders, rival cattlemen, and cattlemen vs. sheepmen.

Gallant Defender (David Selman, 1935) and *Mysterious Avenger* (Selman, 1936) were the inaugural entries in the series. To add to the marquee bait, the early Starretts were advertised as "Peter B. Kyne productions," in a bow to one of the few writers to mean anything in the action market—two more being Zane Grey and James Oliver Curwood. Kyne may be credited with the original stories, but their conception and development are pure Ford Beebe. Columbia dropped the Kyne appellation when Starrett had established himself as a draw.

Without setting the cowboy field ablaze, the first two Starretts were received with moderate approval, aided by Columbia's facility with obtaining max-

159

HOLLYWOOD CORRAL: A COMPREHENSIVE B WESTERN ROUNDUP

imum bookings in the action theaters throughout the country. *Gallant Defender* did the cattlemen-homesteaders number. Harry Woods and George Chesebro supplied expert villainy, and Starrett showed he was the kind of hero who could hold his own in a shootin' fracas or saloon set-to. *Mysterious Avenger* was the two cattlemen-rivals routine. Wheeler Oakman did the heavy role in his authoritative style, and a nice-looking actor named Charles Locher was around, some years away from his notoriety in South Seas epics as Jon Hall. Similarities in the two horse operas, aside from director Selman and writer Beebe, included Edward Le Saint in roles he would repeat many times in the Starretts, that of the paternal rancher who usually stopped a bullet halfway through the third reel, and Joan Perry as the ingenue. A New York model, Miss Perry moved up to feature parts, to become the wife of Harry Cohn, prexy of the studio. Also in for tentative musical interludes were the Sons of the Pioneers, with Roy Rogers.

Starrett was at home in the saddle, but in real life was a long way from the range, Massachusetts-born, Dartmouth-educated, Broadway-trained. Until this opportunity, he had been pursuing an indifferent screen career, a mixture of action and drawing-room parts. Among his more robust efforts were *The Viking* (George Melford, 1931), filmed at great peril, and loss of life, in the frozen North, and *Undercover* (Sam Newfield, 1935), a mountie yarn also filmed in Canada. Starrett returned to Canada for his next two films, and the sad results would have stopped many a budding action career cold.

Ford Beebe went along to the Victoria, B.C. studios as writer and director. Columbia had made features in Canada before, as an economical and profitable method of satisfying British and American markets. Beebe later claimed he was the victim of studio double-dealing, the studio didn't react favorably to Beebe's location methods, there was script trouble. Whatever the cause, Beebe's *Stampede* (1936) didn't turn out well at all, and Beebe was

Wally Albright lassoes Starrett and Iris Meredith in The Cowboy Star *(1936).*

replaced on *Secret Patrol* (1936), a Mounted Police story, by David Selman. All survived, however, and Beebe even fulfilled his commitment and wrote *Code of the Range* (C. C. Coleman Jr., 1936), using file number three, cattlemen vs. sheepmen. Like the other two, it served its purpose, and was perhaps the best Starrett to date. And the star was beginning to attract attention as a cowboy hero to reckon with, more convincing than many because of his thespic abilities.

His films dating from this time in 1936 through the following year did the most to secure Starrett a firm position among Western fans. The Starretts offered good stories, efficient productions, and above all else thumping action sequences, with heavy emphasis upon the fistic encounters, exceptionally well staged. It is perhaps significant that these films were handled by new directors from the editing and assistant director ranks, unfettered by the traditions of worn cinema trails, anxious to accomplish the most with the least means, relying upon ingenuity and constant excitement to spruce up their projects. The last Starrett release of 1936 was *The Cowboy Star*, with David Selman piloting a snappy Frances Guihan screenplay about a movie cowboy who becomes a real-life hero. It was the kind of script Buck Jones must have appreciated, for the idea was one that Jones cottoned to—and Guihan had written some good ones for Jones. Starrett had a greater opportunity to act than in his earlier Western efforts and entered into the spirit of the thing. Selman gave it a breezy pace, and the opening scene established the tongue-in-cheek mood, with Starrett apparently astride a bucking bronc, until the camera pulls back to find him on a seesaw contraption as the movie cameras grind away at the illusion.

Guihan also scripted *Westbound Mail*, directed by film editor Folmer Blangsted as a maiden effort, and it got 1937 off to a good start for Starrett. Nothing new about the plot, with the hero foiling mail robbers, but the pace was fast as helmed by Blangsted; the ingenue, Rosalind Keith, was gifted with more than the usual supply of prettiness and ability, and Starrett continued to look better and better in cowboy duds. *Dodge City Trail* (C. C. Coleman Jr.) followed, and was intended to represent a higher plateau for Starrett, with a slightly more expensive-looking outlay, longer running time at 64 minutes, and the introduction of a singing cohort in the person of Donald Grayson. The musical Western was having its effect and Columbia was about to compensate for Starrett's non-vocalizing. Oddly enough, Starrett's last civilian role was in a Columbia musical, *Start Cheering* (Albert S. Rogell, 1938); required to sing, his voice was dubbed by Robert Paige. Despite the adornments, *Dodge City Trail* was a step backward, Harold Shumate's script and Coleman's direction unable to bring any kick to the proceedings. Grayson was temporarily retired, while Columbia execs mulled it over.

Trapped got the Starretts back on the track, and gave another debuting director a chance. Like Folmer Blangsted, Leon Barsha was a graduate of the cutting rooms, and he knew the value of maintaining pace. *Trapped* had the pace, and a new villainous face in Alan Sears, who was to appear in subsequent Starretts to advantage. Sears could give extra dimensions to his skulduggery because he not only looked villainous, he looked depraved—in *Variety*-ese, "a baby-scarer." His screen appearances were apparently, and lamentably, few. The Barsha-Starrett combination clicked three more times in a row, in 1937. *Two Gun Law* had the action, and some hissable plug-uglies in Charles Middleton, Alan Bridge and Dick Curtis, the latter to become a mainstay in the Starretts. It was Sears who commanded the attention in *Two Fisted Sheriff* in a crazy-type killer role. Unlike most heavies, who through familiarity or sympathy for the underdog on the part of the audience assume at times rather endearing qualities, Sears was such a dangerous rat that one sighed in relief when he was dispatched permanently. Barsha's final Starrett release, *One Man Justice*, was full of rugged action and benefitted from a Paul Perez script that had a clever amnesia gimmick woven in.

Music returned to the Starretts for the 1937–38 season. *The Old Wyoming Trail* (1937) brought back Donald Grayson, joined by the Sons of the Pioneers, and directed to good effect by Folmer Blangsted. Next was *Outlaws of the Prairie* (1937), which set a pattern that would soon turn each Starrett release into Old Home Week. Sam Nelson debuted as director. Iris Meredith portrayed the heroine. Edward Le Saint again carved a noble character role. Dick Curtis and Norman Willis supplied the dirty work, and in supporting roles appeared Edmund Cobb, Art Mix and Hank Bell. There formed the nucleus of the most-often seen movie gathering since the Jones family. Some appeared more often than others, and from time to time Hal Taliaferro, John Tyrell, Jack Rockwell, Kenneth MacDonald and Richard Fiske would appear, in interchangeable roles. Donald Grayson's crooning was out after four flicks, but the Sons of the Pioneers, led now by Bob Nolan with Pat Brady prominent in the comedy

Starrett stares down maniacal Alan Sears in Two Gun Sheriff *(1937).*

parts, stayed on into 1941. The credits would be backed by the group singing Nolan's "Tumbling Tumbleweeds," and there would be no further scoring for the chases or suspense moments, only the allotted three or four songs dotted throughout the course of the film provided by the Pioneers.

Far from being inferior, the Starretts were workmanlike jobs, sufficient to hold Starrett's growing following. They moved rapidly, except for the moments when the Pioneers sang, stopping the action and causing noticeable restlessness in the audience, even though the songs, written mostly by Nolan and Tim Spencer, were listenable. Starrett put up a whale of a fist fight, and Nelson knew how to direct them, complete with bone-crushing Columbia sound effects. Curtis was wise to the ways of being on the receiving end of a knockout blow and took his beatings in stride. But the rubber-stamp syndrome set in fast. In 1938, Starrett could be *West of Cheyenne*, *South of Arizona* or on *The Colorado Trail;* you'd find Nelson directing Iris Meredith, Dick Curtis, Eddie Cobb, Art Mix, Nolan, Brady and the Pioneers, and a story about cattle rustling. Competently done, but increasingly familiar.

Soon, one longed for even the most infinitesimal alteration in the series. Ann Doran stood in for Iris Meredith in *Rio Grande* (1938) and it was welcome, this new heroine appearing on the Columbia range, ever so briefly. Dick Curtis absented himself from *Texas Stampede* (1939), a notable Starrett for numerous reasons. It was the sheep-cattlemen file again, but dressed nicely by scenarist Charles Francis Royal. No overt villainy, with all sides friendly at the end, with even Starrett and adversary Fred Kohler Jr. shaking hands. The cameraman was Lucien Ballard, giving the film shades of light unusual for a budget Western—no matter the task, Ballard took pride in his work, and it showed. With more to work with than customary, Nelson bore down on the dramatics, and emerged with a meritorious mood piece lost in the shuffle of assemblyline Western releases.

Starrett was moved North in 1939, and would essay occasional Mounted Police adventures from time to time. Sam Nelson would be spelled by Norman Deming or C. C. Coleman Jr., but no matter. Joseph H. Lewis joined the troops in 1940 for some directorial hijinks and fancy camera angles, but the Starrett-type familiarity would be only briefly relieved. *Two-Fisted Rangers* had Lewis employing some neat tracking shots, and Bob Nolan had a speaking role in tune with his abilities (Nolan was a sure bet to star in his own series, but somebody missed the boat). Nolan and Starrett even went at it with fists, but Lewis failed to cover properly, so Starrett's stuntman had a thick middle plainly seen, and a flapping shirttail unthinkable on the neatly groomed Starrett. Such lapses were uncommon in the Columbia Starretts, but would become part of the game in the future. On a happier occasion, everybody except Starrett and the Pioneers got a day off when *West of Abilene* was filmed, and it resulted in the most interesting, if not the most action-filled series entry in some time. Marjorie Cooley had the heroine role and was made to share the implied romance not with the star, but with Bruce Bennett, another face new to the Starretts. Don Beddoe, busy Columbia contract player (although not in Westerns) was capital as the boss villain. Overshadowing him was William Pauley as a hired gun with a coiled rattlesnake friendship with Starrett. Byplay between the two was adeptly acted, and set up a suspenseful concluding gun duel. Little noticed in the scheme of things, *West of Abilene,* directed by Ralph Ceder, was one of those Westerns providing more enjoyment than many high-touted efforts. Incidentally, Ceder made no more Westerns, content to direct second-unit chases for W. C. Fields comedy epics at Universal.

Starrett's previous 1940 release had been directed by Lambert Hillyer and entitled *The Durango Kid*. It hit about average, moving well and with some okay action. There was also some far-fetched stuff too—can one well-placed bullet blow a gun belt off a man's hip? Starrett's remote-control elimination of villain Kenneth MacDonald also prompted jeers, blasting the varmint right through the side of a barn. The Robin Hood idea seemed to intrigue audiences though, and prospect of Starrett impersonating a continuing character would have its payoff later. The

Starrett rescues Iris Meredith from Al Bridge in The Man from Sundown *(1939).*

HOLLYWOOD CORRAL: A COMPREHENSIVE B WESTERN ROUNDUP

Starrett, Meredith and Bob Nolan in Spoilers of the Range *(1939).*

Sam Nelson era came to an end with *Outlaws of the Panhandle* (1941), an ordinary one. Starrett's next three would be among his best.

In mid-1941, the Starretts shifted gears. Gone were the Sons of the Pioneers. Iris Meredith relinquished the role of the lady in distress. Even the accustomed villainy of Dick Curtis was gradually phased out. Lambert Hillyer, who had directed a couple of previous Starretts and who had learned his Western lore at the side of William S. Hart, took over as director. Most important, Starrett, after years of playing the standardized, heroic if somewhat characterless cowboy lead, was finally given some identification to carry from picture to picture. Columbia had in its story files a book by James L. Rubel about a frontier physician, and it was used as a springboard for the new series, which had Starrett playing the role of Dr. Steven Monroe, a traveling sawbones who usually runs into trouble and straightens it out by using fists and guns as well as stethoscope and diagnosis.

First in the series was *The Medico of Painted Springs,* and it was a good start. The Wyndham Gittins-Winston Miller screenplay was the usual cattle-sheep feud nucleus, but the development was more mature than usual. Production values were improved over the past several Starretts; process photography to simulate an outdoor setting was used, something unheard of before under the general rule of quickie shooting, and the sets were a change from the over-familiar Columbia locales. The fresh atmosphere seemed to affect Starrett, too. Able to get by on personality alone in many instances before, he was given a role with some substance and now drew upon his thespic ability to create a flesh-and-blood character. Wheeler Oakman lent his presence for another sharply etched heavy, Terry Walker was the bland heart interest, and members of the Columbia stock company gave support capably. Second in the series, *Thunder Over the Prairie,* began with Starrett still in medical school, befriending a young Indian (Stanley Brown), and eventually helping his brother (David Sharpe) and sister (Eileen O'Hearn). Cliff Edwards also made his first appearance as Starrett's sidekick, a correspondence-school medical practitioner. The plot, about contractors using Indians as slave laborers and mulcting them of their wages, was different and more logically developed than most Westerns. Edwards was a welcome addition, since his comedy relief was not the juvenile kind but catered more to adult tastes. Eileen O'Hearn was a young actress of potential who was gaining needed experience here—unfortunately, her career proved of short duration. Brown, Sharpe, and villains Donald Curtis, Ted Adams and the rest measured up, and the new Starrett medico character was making headway. He was already at home in the role, the scripts had been strong, and the series had more appeal for non-Western moviegoers while retaining the action ingredients to keep the fans happy.

Prairie Stranger was the third in the Medico series, and it proved to be the last. It was up to the standard set by the first two, although it defied convention by casually tossing off the final chase and roundup of the villain with a fast dissolve. What had been a promising series was curtailed, it is said, because of legalities surrounding the copyright to Rubel's original material. A pity, for the brief series reflected the attention lavished on it by Starrett, Hillyer and the script department.

In a dubious bit of compensation for the loss of the Medico series, Starrett was given a co-star to share the load to start the 1941–42 season. Russell Hayden, heretofore "Lucky" Jenkins in the Hopalong Cassidys, joined the Columbia crew and pitched in opposite the veteran star. Hillyer directed them in a Mounted Police film, and an exciting one, to start. Then Cliff Edwards rejoined Starrett and his new partner for seven rip-snortin', brawlin', shootin' saddle sagas that made up in frenzied action what they may have lacked in cinema artistry. To put it bluntly, the production values were pretty cheesy, not to say sloppy. Interior sets would consist of four bare walls (three, actually, with the camera running) made of the flimsiest material, which became flimsier as wartime restrictions on building became more intense. Set-ups were hurried, and shots often wouldn't match in reverse camera angles. No matter. Action predominated from the outset, with Starrett and Hayden hitting it off well together, and sometimes hitting each other—fist fights occurred every reel or so, with the boys mixing it up with all comers. Edwards continued his pleasing foolishness. Stories tried to atone for production deficiencies by injecting some novel, and at times topical situations.

Howard Bretherton directed the first two. *Riders of the Badlands* (1941) was written by Betty Burbridge, who introduced the feminine interest (Kay

Cliff Edwards (in vest), Starrett and Russell Hayden challenge Roy Barcroft in Riders of the Badlands *(1941).*

Hughes) as Hayden's bride, then promptly dismissed her with a lethal bullet, with Hayden swearing revenge, and since Hayden thinks Starrett's the guilty party, it's hold your seats. *West of Tombstone* (1942) had scripter Maurice Geraghty reviving the legend that Billy the Kid didn't die, but lived on incognito to become a law-abiding citizen. As before, action all the way.

Producing credits on the Starretts had been more or less informal. Harry Decker steered the series for the first several years, then Jack Fier and William Berke had alternated. Berke had been producing the Starrett-Haydens, but now Jack Fier resumed production guidance, with Berke taking over the direction. Berke had directed independent Westerns of the mid-'30s, but it was as a producer, at Republic and Columbia as well as independently, that he had amassed the more imposing list of credits. Berke went right to work and directed the Starrett-Haydens, beginning with *Lawless Plainsmen* (1942), for speed and action, never mind the details. Off-the-cuff shooting became more prevalent than it had been under Bretherton, with some rather shocking boners occurring along the way, but what with the fist fights, gun battles and general pellmell pace, the audiences wouldn't mind. And they didn't.

Cliff Edwards was missing from *Down Rio Grande Way* (1942), a rather ambitious historical tale by Paul Franklin about the Republic of Texas entering the Union. Edwards was spelled by Britt Wood, harmonica and weak clowning in tandem. The threadbare production could hardly support the scope called for by the script, but Berke let the action take its course. The ingenue was Rose Anne Stevens, a band vocalist crashing the acting ranks, who should have stayed in movies longer. Edwards returned for *Riders of the Northland* (1942), which brought the series from the Alamo to Nazi spies in Alaska, with Starrett and Hayden as a pair of Texas Rangers on detached service to ferret out the swine. Paul Franklin wrote this one too, proving that he could squeeze in as much action in a contemporary plot. *Bad Men of the Hills* and *Overland To Deadwood* completed the starring duo's work together. The latter entry broke with tradition by furnishing the heroine (Lesley Brooks) with a mother, rather than the customary father; few Westerns have been so generous as to provide both.

Hayden landed his own starring series at Columbia, so Starrett continued on his way, with Arthur Hunnicutt replacing Cliff Edwards as sidekick, William Berke still directing, and a succession of musical personalities marking a return to the musical interludes of yore. The warblers included Jimmie Davis, Jimmy Wakely, Ernest Tubb and other favorites. To Columbia's credit, they were worked in well, and their acting requirements were more than adequately fulfilled. Wakely, in fact, went on to star in his own Monogram series. Davis became Governor of Louisiana. Action still predominated, and to show that they weren't just fooling around, Betty Burbridge wrote one, *Frontier Fury* (1943), which had Starrett creased by a bullet and in the hospital during the first ten minutes of the plot. That he quickly recovered and went about his business goes without saying, but it did strike a blow to anyone who thought heroes were indestructible. Berke was starting to add a few little touches to his direction that enhanced the films. Never the one for subtlety, Berke would rise to the occasion, such as in *Hail to the Rangers* (1943), with weaselly Ernie Adams in the role of a greedy crook getting laid low in a gunfight and Berke flashing a quick shot of Adams prone in death with the loot at the tips of his outstretched, stiffened fingers. Naturally, Berke wasn't destined for the Western long.

With Berke upped to civilian feature films, Columbia and Jack Fier reached behind the cameras and tapped Benjamin Kline to direct. Kline had directed some serial work for Mascot, but was mostly known as a photographer, and a good one, who had done some early Tom Mix features like *Sky High* (1921) and innumerable Columbia Westerns with Jones, McCoy and Starrett. The drawling teller of tall tales Arthur Hunnicutt left, and Dub Taylor, longtime Columbia cohort of Bill Elliott, moved to the Starrett range. The musical element with Wakely and others was retained. Under Kline, the Starretts became one marathon session of fights and assorted mayhem. World War II had taken its toll of valuable construction material, and the interior sets were even more cramped. When Starrett engaged in one of his frequent brawls, one expected momentarily an onslaught that would drive his opponent right through the pasteboard wall, presumably onto an adjacent Boston Blackie set. Also, there wasn't much room for Kline and his cameras to operate. A big set would be about the size of a broom closet, hardly room enough for the actors, much less technicians. But the fights were exciting, Kline kept the pace perking and long experience had showed him how to place his cameras. The plots were modernized and slightly different: *Cowboy in the Clouds* (1943) concerned the Civil Air Patrol in wartime; *Sundown Valley* (1944) was about war-plant workers, with the crooks owners of a gambling house stripping the workers of their wages; *Cowboy from Lonesome River* (1944) dealt with water rights, and a good dual role for Kenneth MacDonald, playing a Senator and his no-good twin brother; and *Saddle Leather Law* (1944) makes the girl the heavy, after a ranch so she can turn it into a gambling house. Vi Athens, an intriguing young actress on the hard side, handled her lines well. She was on the wrong side in *Cowboy from Lonesome River* as well, making her somewhat of a specialist.

During this period Starrett starred in what might be termed an "all-star" musical Western, *Cowboy Canteen* (Lew Landers, 1944). It had a topical plot, an effort to establish a canteen for servicemen with Western trimmings, and showed Starrett in Army uniform, a change from his cowboy clothes. With him was Dub Taylor, and the cast was filled with Western film names: Tex Ritter, Max Terhune, Guinn "Big Boy" Williams, Emmett Lynn, as well as Jane Frazee and Vera Vague, and assorted musical acts from the Mills Brothers to Jimmy Wakely and Roy Acuff. The melange blended together rather pleasantly, and its unpretentiousness made it as entertaining in its own way as some of the elephantine star-studded barges currently produced by every major studio. It wasn't that much different from the average Starrett Westerns, except for 15 minutes extra length at 72 minutes and more expensive-looking sets that weren't about to collapse. But it was sold to exhibitors apart from the regular series.

In 1945, Colbert Clark, a Mascot serial graduate too, joined the Starrett team as producer. Starrett also acquired a new saddlemate, one Tex Harding, a pleasant fellow wearing an obvious toupee but otherwise photogenic and possessed of a melodious set of vocal chords, supplementing the customary assortment of Western musical aggregations allotted Starrett. For their first, Clark turned to a character Starrett had played a few years before, the Durango Kid, and turned the prospect over to J. Benton Cheney. The scriptwriter's yarn had little relation to the earlier Starrett Western except for the idea of a

Starrett about to get slugged by Charlie King.

HOLLYWOOD CORRAL: A COMPREHENSIVE B WESTERN ROUNDUP

Robin Hoodish do-gooder, masked and mysterious. *The Return of the Durango Kid* (Derwin Abrahams, 1945) had the title going for it, but was almost the reverse of the usual Starrett opus. There was practically no action; especially noticeable was the scarcity of those jaw-bruising slugfests so common in the Starrett films. While the players, including villain John Calvert and Jean Stevens in a semi-bad girl role, were above par, the slowness was too evident. However, the Durango Kid label had something that stirred the pulses of the outdoor fans, and Columbia had Starrett impersonating him for the rest of his career. Dub Taylor, missing the inaugural one, reappeared in *Both Barrels Blazing* (Abrahams, 1945) and continued as comedy relief. Director Abrahams seemed to be paying more attention to plot than pace, and although the Durango Kids were an immediate hit at the boxoffice, one missed the hell-for-leather consequences-be-damned action of the predecessors.

Fourth in the new Durango series, *Outlaws of the Rockies* (1945) was directed by Ray Nazarro, who would eventually guide the majority of the Starrett features. Nazarro's style was enigmatic. Obviously hampered from the start by the budgets, he would manage to get a sense of movement into the Starretts beyond the capabilities of mere placid directors like Derwin Abrahams and Vernon Keays, who would occasionally spell Nazarro. Nazarro had co-directed some features, but was making his solo feature debut with the Starretts; so was photographer George Kelley. Together, they were responsible for some strange results. In their favor, none of the films was dull, whatever else they were. Nazarro's directing had a slapdash, nervous energy, the narratives pushed along bumpily. Nazarro didn't spend the time choreographing fistic encounters, which are difficult to film, but instead would settle for a fast and not too realistic haymaker from Starrett. Kelley photographed some of the action and riding stuff at silent speed, further pointing at the jerky quality of the footage. The viewer would be kept awake, but the choppiness was disconcerting.

After eight with Tex Harding, the cowboy crooner vanished, having made little impression upon Starrett audiences. Dub Taylor likewise left the series, to be replaced by none other than Smiley Burnette, once Gene Autry's musical buffoon. Burnette found a home with Durango and stayed on until the end in 1952. Burnette's first was *Roaring Rangers* (Nazarro, 1946), and concurrently, the already slim budget outlays for producer Clark became even slimmer, in direct contrast to Burnette's girth. Or perhaps it was reflected in Burnette's contract. Whatever the cause, the Durango Kid series became cheap. Not the kind of raw cheapness of the earlier, war-restricted Starretts, when the action made up for it; rather, a kind of unpleasant tackiness that skimped on sets, action and production niceties. Nazarro kept the films moving, but toward no particular goal. The Durango films soon became merely 55 minutes of milling around. Starrett had become so firmly rooted in his Western milieu that he could hardly make a false step, and indeed he became a saving grace. Burnette tried hard, but his comedy became more puerile with each film. The series deteriorated to the level of *Two-Fisted Stranger* (Nazarro, 1946), *South of the Chisholm Trail* (Abrahams, 1947) and *West of Dodge City* (Nazarro, 1947)—slightly less than an hour of ersatz Western goings-on, minus point, plan, and in some cases action.

Some unwritten rule in the Columbia scripting quarters apparently required Starrett's screen name to be "Steve" in these Durango Kids, although the last name would be diferent with each film. It made about as much sense as some of the scripts he was handed. In *Last Days of Boot Hill* (1947), a new bugaboo emerged. By now, enough stock footage had been amassed from previous Durango Kids to cut corners even more drastically, so Norman S. Hall compiled a scenario that called for approximately 15 minutes of new footage and 40 minutes of library material, or so it seemed. A lot of the plot is told in flashback as Starrett searches for loot stolen by a deceased outlaw (Alan Bridge), so as soon as a flashback begins, on comes a lot of footage from *Both Barrels Blazing,* with Bridge in old scenes. Tex Harding, long since departed from the series, is plainly in sight, too; his presence is neatly explained by the scripter who has Starrett commence one flashback featuring Harding by saying: "One day, while out riding with a friend..." Such blatant cheating on the footage had not been witnessed since the early independent days and would not be equalled until the Lash La Rue series bettered it several years later. Future Starretts would use generous amounts of old material, but not to this degree.

The mediocre trend couldn't continue indefinitely, and the first half of 1948 actually had two Nazarro-directed Durangos that were considerably more appetizing than before, though still not in the preferred Western category. Both *Phantom Valley* and *West of Sonora* had mystery angles, the former more of a whodunit than a Western written by J. Benton Cheney, the latter also with a hidden villain, deftly worked out by Barry Shipman. George Kelley had

Starrett in his most famous role, as the Durango Kid.

died, and now various cameramen were assigned to the Starretts. *Sonora* featured good lens work by Ira Morgan.

In 1949, the series was presented with another debuting director, a Columbia triple-threat man named Fred F. Sears. Sears was an actor and had appeared in several Durango adventures, including a ridiculously poor performance in *West of Dodge City*. In addition, he had been a dialogue coach. His first as a full-fledged director was *Desert Vigilante*, no great shakes. But in time, Sears became adept. He developed an eye for camera angles, and worked well with Fayte M. Browne, who became more or less a regular Durango photographer, as well as with interim Columbia cameramen like Henry Freulich. Sears also learned how to stage action sequences, surpassing Nazarro in this respect. He was aided in this by the advent of a lanky actor-stuntman with the rousing name of Jacques O'Mahoney, who of course became Jack Mahoney later on the trail and Jock Mahoney still later. Mahoney had a wild recklessness about his tricks that stamped him, whether doubling for Randolph Scott, Starrett or doing his own stunts. Ted Mapes had been Starrett's double for some time, but Mahoney supplanted him and could soon be spotted by his wild, arm-swinging knockout punches (since the Durango Kid was masked, the stand-in action stuff could be easily accomplished). A good example of the Sears directorial finesse can be found in *Across the Badlands* (1950), a good Barry Shipman script involving railroad skulduggery. *Lightning Guns* (1950) was better than average, with a meaty acting part for O'Mahoney as the romance opposite heroine Gloria Henry; for some time now, Starrett had been written out of the heart-interest aspects, although he was still a relatively young man and had retained his looks. *Prairie Roundup* (1951) further indicated that Sears was fast becoming an ace action director.

As if feeling the pressure from Sears, Ray Nazarro chipped in with an exceptionally good member of the series, *Fort Savage Raiders* (1951), with Sears in front of the camera playing a minor role. Barry Shipman's script was one of the best Starrett had had in some time, with a plausible heavy characterization of a mentally deranged former Army officer turned desperado, played by John Dehner.

Eight Durango Kid Westerns were released for the 1951–52 season, some directed by Sears, some by Nazarro. The former stuntman had now become Jock Mahoney and had assumed co-starring status opposite Starrett, although not accorded billing on the credits. But he was functioning in the same capacity as had Russell Hayden. The Durango Kid

Starrett and sidekick Smiley Burnette flank heavies Fred Sears (l.) and Steve Darrell in Frontier Outpost *(1950).*

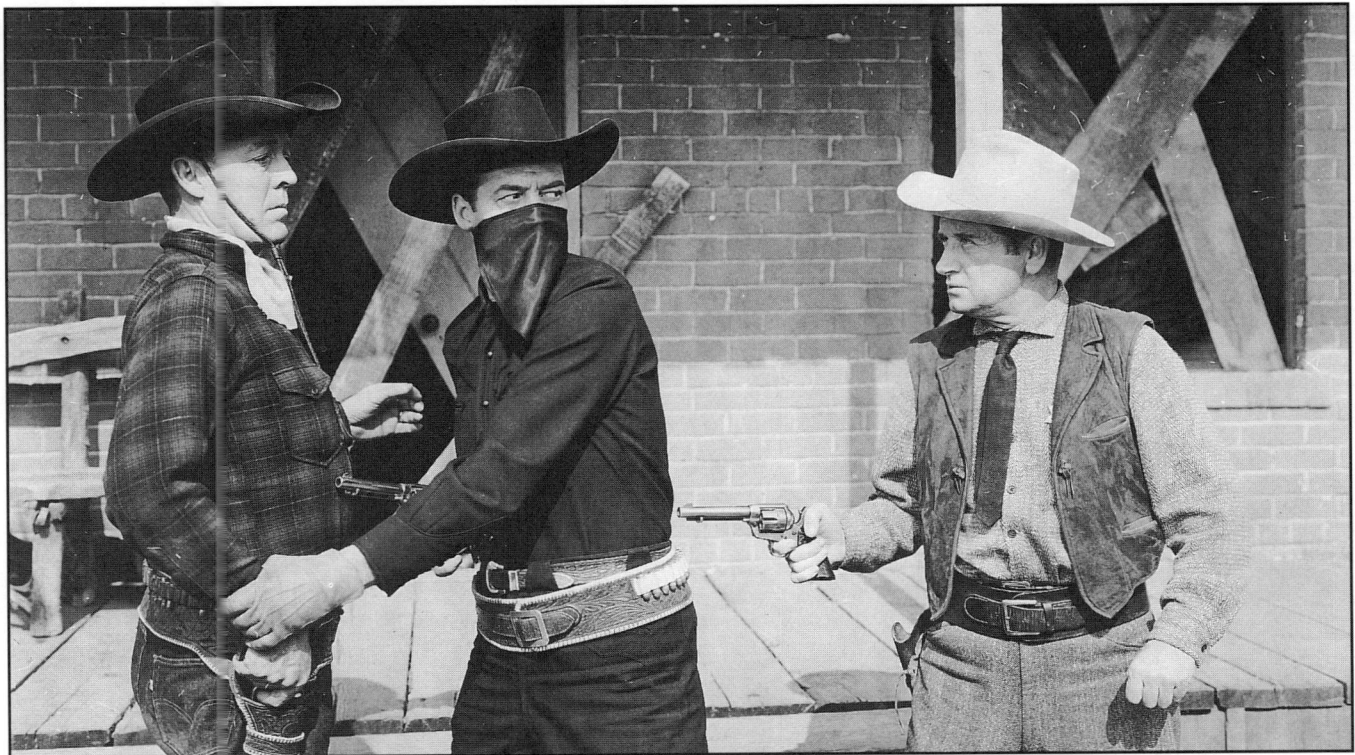
Jack Ingram sneaks up on Starrett who has Frank Fenton at bay in Streets of Ghost Town *(1950)*.

Westerns had improved noticeably, from their low point of four or five years ago. The present group was not exactly a collection of world beaters, but good enough to let bygones be bygones. After all, a fast little number like *Smoky Canyon* (Sears, 1952) was becoming rather hard to find, with so many Western series giving up and being put out to pasture. The order of release of the 1951–52 Durangos was somewhat tangled, with some appearing out of official sequence in certain areas. However, the release schedule had *The Kid from Broken Gun*, produced by Colbert Clark, directed by Fred F. Sears, written by Barry Shipman and Ed Earl Repp, starring Starrett, Burnette and Jock Mahoney, in release during August, 1952. It wasn't the best Durango Kid, but it was far from the weakest. And it was the last.

Without fanfare, Charles Starrett retired from the screen. He had been in the saddle for 17 years, had portrayed the same character for seven consecutive years. He had been busy, sometimes starring in as many as ten full-length Western features a seasonal year, and sometimes his vehicles would have been better left unmade. But Starrett had never slipped from the category of money-making cowboy stars, no matter the quality of some of his films. He had borne them with dignity, and no small talent. Had he refused to shunt aside his career as a non-Western player, he might have become just another Hollywood face. As it was, the work was steady, the pay was good, and the kids knew him by sight, either as Charles Starrett or the Durango Kid, and they admired him. There's something to be said for that.

Mesquiteers Max Terhune, John Wayne and Ray Corrigan in Santa Fe Stampede *(1938).*

14
THREE FOR THE PRICE OF ONE
MESQUITEERS & RANGE BUSTERS

Often overlooked in the course of Western cinema history is the satisfying success enjoyed by Republic with their Three Mesquiteers series, which began in 1936 and endured until 1943. The advent of the singing cowboy, and the potent individual successes of William "Hopalong Cassidy" Boyd and Charles Starrett tend to cast a shadow upon the Mesquiteer accomplishments. But the series was liked, in spite of no particular cohesion to it as a whole; numerous and frequent, often bewildering cast changes in the major roles; a slackening in quality of production handiwork toward the end; and a tendency by the studio to treat the series as the bottom of the barrel, preferring to expend time and money on their vocalizers, and subsequent upstarts like Don "Red" Barry. Furthermore, the Mesquiteer adventures spawned imitators, including a series featuring two-thirds of its family tree—the sincerest form, to coin a cliche, of flattery.

William Colt MacDonald, prolific Western story writer, created the Three Mesquiteers, a clever play on the swashbuckling Three Musketeers of Dumas fame. MacDonald's heroes were named Tucson Smith, Lullaby Joslin and Stony Brooke (the author's spelling of these names will be observed, in view of several spelling variations used through the years).

As mentioned earlier, *Law of the .45s* featured Guinn "Big Boy" Williams as Tucson and Al St. John, sans facial foliage, as Stony, with Lullaby Joslin absent from the screenplay. That same year, 1935, RKO filmed an adaptation of MacDonald's *Powdersmoke Range,* with Wallace Fox directing a most intriguing cast. Harry Carey played Tucson, Hoot Gibson was Stony, and Guinn Williams, the Tucson lead only months before, was now subjugated to the role of Lullaby. The behemoth Williams was out of proportion to the physical demands of the role; otherwise, the players closely resembled MacDonald's description, especially Hoot Gibson—it was as if the novelist had devised the character with the Hooter in mind.

RKO was not about to launch a series of Mesquiteer Westerns, but the studio packed plenty of selling angles into the moderately budgeted feature, notably a cast of familiar Western faces, new and old. Besides the starring three, Bob Steele and Tom Tyler were prominently cast, both to become Mesquiteers in the future; William Farnum, William Desmond, Franklin Farnum, Wally Wales, Buddy Roosevelt, Buffalo Bill Jr., Art Mix and Buzz Barton were all on hand, names and faces from the silent past. Sam Hardy, Adrian Morris and Ray Mayer, city types, supplied the dirty deeds, with Hardy functioning as the Big Ugly. The deep-dish Southern charm of Boots Mallory more than filled the inconsequential feminine assignment. The film was wisely advertised for its well-nigh all-star cast, received playdates in neighborhoods and theaters not usually Westernized, and even snagged some critical praise, said critics overwhelmed by the names and undernourished in the realm of what makes a good Western. Turgid direction by Fox and lethargic

HOLLYWOOD CORRAL: A COMPREHENSIVE B WESTERN ROUNDUP

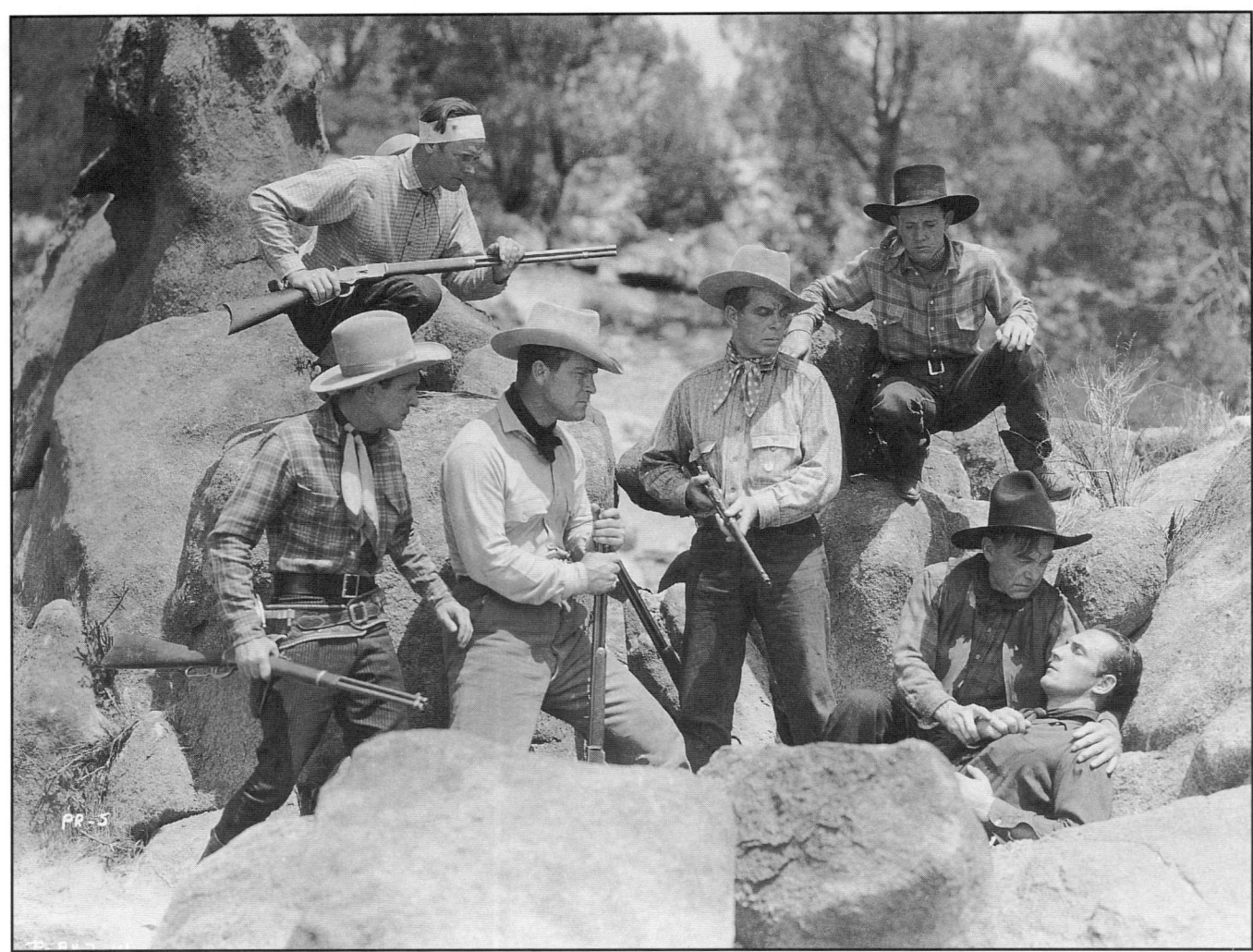

Powdersmoke Range *(1935) starred Harry Carey (kneeling over Tom Tyler), Bob Steele (l.), Guinn "Big Boy" Williams (leaning on rifle), Hoot Gibson (cradling rifle), Wally Wales (in bandage), and Buzz Barton (crouching on rock), among others.*

development in Adele Buffington's screenplay caused the hour and ten minutes to pass by too slowly, and some of the performances, Hardy's hammy villainy for example, were not up to the better independent Westerns. Exploitatively it was another matter. With plenty to sell, the RKO boys went to town, the film earned its keep, and remains a gilt-edged item for those who haven't seen it, and whose memories color their reflections.

Possibly impressed by the success of *Powdersmoke Range,* Republic busily prepared a Western series featuring The Three Mesquiteers to complement their John Wayne and Gene Autry shows. First in the series, *The Three Mesquiteers* (Ray Taylor, 1936), was ready for the 1936–37 season, with seven more on the schedule. Ray "Crash" Corrigan, a muscular stunt artist and current Republic serial hero, was Tucson Smith; Robert Livingston, ingratiating young actor groomed as a comer by Republic and currently active in Zorro-type features and serials, was Stony Brooke; and Syd Saylor, he of the bobbing adam's apple, took the Lullaby role. Results were promising. Jack Natteford's script allowed for a generous amount of excitement, capably directed by Taylor, and William Nobles contributed one of his scenically superb photographic stints. The idea of an adventuresome cowboy trio clicked, and Republic counted on a third popular Western series, judging from early returns.

Syd Saylor was replaced by Max Terhune in the second series entry, *Ghost Town Gold* (Joseph Kane, 1936). Saylor was a good comic who worked hard for, and could obtain, laughs on his own. But Terhune, a performer of long experience in vaudeville, tent shows and on the county fair circuit, although a newcomer to the screen, added the extra something needed to solidify the trio. A rapport was established among Corrigan, Livingston and Terhune immediately, and the team functioned

THREE FOR THE PRICE OF ONE: Mesquiteers & Range Busters

smoothly, if in a peculiar way. Terhune was ostensibly the comedy arm of the team; he was given the lighter scenes, and used his talents as a ventriloquist to garner chuckles with his dummy, Elmer. Neither Terhune nor his wooden friend were particularly funny. Far more enjoyable was the banter between Livingston and Corrigan, usually involving the venerable who-gets-the-girl gambit. While out of the running romantically and not quite cutting it for the yocks, nevertheless Terhune was indispensable, as the future would show.

As was apparent from the start, Livingston moved into the top Mesquiteer position on the basis of his looks and acting ability, with Corrigan amply supplying the backup dash and the muscle stuff, and Terhune making a stab at the levity. The first season's output consisted of eight good, solid Westerns for the fans who appreciated unpretentious, workmanlike action movies. What was so engaging about the trio was the almost debonair unconcern for dangerous situations. In *Roarin' Lead* (Mack Wright & Sam Newfield, 1936), the boys are accosted by Yakima Canutt and gang, minions of a would-be rangeland dictator dressed in fascistic uniformity as a sort of goon squad. The Mesquiteers merely laugh at them. Weakest of the first eight was *Hit the Saddle* (Mack Wright, 1937), wherein the romantic rivalry between Livingston and Corrigan suddenly turns serious and impedes the action. Considering that the object of their affections was Rita Cansino (Hayworth), it's understandable. The rest of the plot was about rounding up wild horses, with stock footage too evident. The remainder of the Mesquiteers was first-rate, and Republic gleefully scheduled eight more films for the 1937–38 season.

Heart of the Rockies (Kane, 1937) started the new season with a bang, and trade reviewers were moved to note Republic's authoritative manner of Westernmaking; best in the field, they said. Livingston sustained an injury that kept him out of the next, *Trigger Trio*. Standing in for him was Ralph Byrd, utility man at the studio and already spotted as the serial

Bob Livingston (l.), Syd Saylor and Ray Corrigan in The Three Mesquiteers *(1936).*

screen's Dick Tracy personification. *Trigger Trio* marked the feature-film debut of director William Witney at the ripe old age of 22. He handled it cleanly, but was shunted back to the chapter plays where he could indulge in his penchant for staging flashy action sequences. Livingston returned for *Wild Horse Rodeo,* with another debuting director, George Sherman. Sherman was an assistant director who had distinguished himself by wrapping up a George O'Brien opus when Ewing Scott was incapacitated. Now on his own, Sherman's tyro effort was auspicious, even if credulity was strained somewhat by having Corrigan bring down a strafing plane with a pistol shot, for an unlikely climax to the action. The film also presented Roy Rogers in his Dick Weston days, doing a number in a cafe sequence. Sherman directed *The Purple Vigilantes* (1938), a neat script by Betty Burbridge and Oliver Drake about a disbanded vigilante organization secretly reactivated for evil instead of good. Serial director John English followed with *Call the Mesquiteers,* a swift entry with an action situation that was surefire for the trio—in pursuit of three baddies, who each take different trails, the Mesquiteers also split and capture the fleeing villains in highly individualistic ways. The set-up for action was employed many times during the series, and never failed to provoke a response from the audience.

Sherman returned to the Mesquiteers and directed 13 in a row. *Outlaws of Sonora* gave Livingston a dual role, as a nasty killer in addition to his Stony Brooke part. *Riders of the Black Hills* had to do with a kidnapped racehorse, and *Heroes of the Hills* was one of the better ones of the series, with the boys turning their ranch into a prison farm and running afoul of a crooked contractor bent on gumming up the project. At the end of their second season, the Mesquiteers had entrenched themselves, catching the fancy of the Western devotee and upholding the high Republic standard.

Meanwhile, Livingston was being gifted with leads in other, non-Western features, to the point where it was either stay West or move on. The latter was deemed best for Livingston, and into the Stony Brooke role stepped John Wayne, already an established star who had been trying to obtain a foothold in non-Westerns, in vain. Wayne appeared in one season of Mesquiteer films, eight in all. Wayne didn't

Corrigan, Terhune, Ann Evers, Frank Melton and Livingston in Riders of the Black Hills *(1938).*

THREE FOR THE PRICE OF ONE: Mesquiteers & Range Busters

Terhune, Corrigan and Carol Landis stand by as Wayne warns Ralph Graves in Three Texas Steers *(1939).*

fit in. He was too much like Corrigan in build, and missed Livingston's debonair charm, being a bit too stolid for banter at this stage in his career. Paradoxically, some of the Wayne-Mesquiteer movies rate among the very best over the entire Mesquiteer span, and thereby with the best budget Westerns made anywhere. Strong, often ingenious scripting, backed by Sherman's steady direction and exciting action scenes, topped by production attributes in the Republic supreme style, all combined to result in a fine 1938–39 season for the series. In the round-robin scheme of Republic production duties, William Berke supervised the third Mesquiteer season. Noted without comment: each one was written or co-scripted by a woman.

Ultra-modern in treatment, *Pals of the Saddle* (1938) had foreign agents after a valuable chemical, intending to smuggle it out of the country, with the Mesquiteers thwarting their plans. Paced like a serial and full of action, it got the new series off to a flying start and served well to introduce Wayne to his new surroundings. *Overland Stage Raiders* also got off to a flying start, since shipping gold by air was its theme, with the excitement on high throughout. The heroine was portrayed by Louise Brooks, minus her famous bangs but looking nonetheless beautiful. It was the American star of German cinema's last screen appearance.

Crooks in politics was the concern of *Santa Fe Stampede,* with a rather grim turn of plot evolved by Betty Burbridge and Luci Ward; the scenarists unexpectedly kill off a precocious tyke in a runaway buckboard. Rough treatment of children was a near-taboo in Westerns. *Red River Range* was less daring but just as lively, with a dude ranch used as a focal point for a modern-day cattle-rustling ring—they herd 'em into trucks. A neat supporting cast featured Lorna Gray (later Adrian Booth), former Marie Dressler cohort Polly Moran in for additional comedy, and Kirby Grant, later Robert Stanton at RKO, still later Kirby Grant again in Westerns and mountie melodramas.

Inexplicably, *The Night Riders* (1939) transposed the Mesquiteers back to the 1880s, where they were up against another self-styled dictator and donned capes and hoods to do a triple Robin Hood act. The caped-crusaders gimmick was uncomfortably close to Klandom, but the action was fast, and former saddle stars Tom Tyler and Kermit Maynard turned up in supporting roles, on respective sides of the law

HOLLYWOOD CORRAL: A COMPREHENSIVE B WESTERN ROUNDUP

Mesquiteer doubles—including Canutt (center), for Wayne—in Santa Fe Stampede *(1938).*

(Maynard was a friendly sheriff, Tyler a baddie). Heretofore, the Mesquiteer yarns had been vaguely modern, with only the first one pinpointed in time at the close of the World War and the rest contemporary. It was somewhat disconcerting to have the trio land in the days of President Garfield's assassination, though.

Reversing the field again, *Three Texas Steers* was right up to date. It was a fast, furious and very funny story about an impoverished circus, with a wild conclusion played for laughs as the circus dancing horse is entered in a sulky race and breaks into a cakewalk in the middle of the event. Once again the cast was noteworthy, with Carole Landis the heroine, Ralph Graves the heavy and Roscoe Ates and Collette Lyons in for horseplay. With this film, Max Terhune departed the series.

Raymond Hatton appeared as Rusty Joslin in the next Mesquiteer, *Wyoming Outlaw*. Hatton was less the hayseed than Terhune and was inclined to treat his conquered adversaries with no tenderness whatsoever, booting them in the rear as they would be escorted to incarceration. Otherwise, the film was a powerful crime yarn, based on recent headlines about a young desperado played up in newspaperese as "a modern Robin Hood" but finally brought down by a rifle bullet from a small-town waiter. In the film version the outlaw was played by Donald Barry in a memorable portrayal. Barry gave the role strength, and more than the ordinary amount of depth. For a Western, it was an unusually polished job of acting, and tabbed Barry, who had been around for a few years at M-G-M and other studios, as one to watch. The waiter was played by David Sharpe. *Stagecoach* had been in release for a time by now, and it became increasingly obvious that Wayne was not about to continue going through the motions as Stony Brooke. Indeed, Republic spread the word that Robert Livingston would return in the role for the 1939–40 season. Wayne's swan song as a Mesquiteer, *New Frontier,* didn't reach the standards set by preceding entries, except for the girl, who was pretty in a fragile way. Her name was Phyllis Isley, and would be Jennifer Jones.

Not only was John Wayne about to take leave, but according to Republic, Ray Corrigan was also departing the Mesquiteer series. Livingston had been announced, and now Corrigan's replacement was said to be Don Alvarado, which raised eyebrows. A Latin Tucson Smith? *The Kansas Terrors* (Sherman, 1939) explained the situation logically, if not satisfactorily. And it wasn't Alvarado, but Duncan Renaldo, as Rico, as the third Mesquiteer. The Burbridge-Natteford scenario has Livingston and Hatton delivering horses to a small Caribbean island and hanging around long enough to aid Renaldo in combatting the local tyrant. Renaldo joins forces with the two Americans at the end, and here we go

THREE FOR THE PRICE OF ONE: Mesquiteers & Range Busters

again. On this Mesquiteer set, Harry Grey replaced William Berke as producer. Livingston was more than welcome back, Raymond Hatton grizzled up his characterization to conform with the accepted image of a prairie oldtimer (he had been relatively neat and clean-shaven previously) and Renaldo added a dash of pepper to the proceedings. But the Mesquiteers had been changed drastically, and it wasn't easy getting used to the alterations. The time element went awry again. *Heroes of the Saddle* (William Witney, 1940) was a contemporary plot about an orphanage run by crooks. In *Pioneers of the West* (Lester Orlebeck, 1940) they escort a wagon train through Indian territory, while in *Oklahoma Renegades* (Nate Watt, 1940) they come to the aid of homesteading veterans of the Spanish-American War. The films were good enough Westerns, but the series lost its appeal in losing its uniformity. Another shakeup was on the docket for the 1940–41 season, after seven Mesquiteers adventures with Livingston, Hatton and Renaldo.

Tucson Smith was back in the person of feisty Bob Steele, and bucolic comedian Rufe Davis was the new Lullaby Joslin, with Bob Livingston retaining his Stony Brooke role. Thus The Three Mesquiteers reverted to their original state. Harry Grey produced the first two, then Louis Gray took over and supervised until the end. He got off to a questionable start with *Lone Star Raiders* (George Sherman, 1940), all about rounding up horses for the government, with too much old stock footage and not enough action. Nor did the following few Mesquiteers stir any great excitement. No fault of the players, with Steele accustoming himself to his role and Livingston well settled in his. Davis was in the Terhune tradition, though younger; he was alright, and contributed a song or two innocuously. But the series had lost its zip, and was heading down hill. Republic had Autry, Rogers, and Don "Red" Barry cutting swaths through the Western markets. The Mesquiteers were relegated to last in line, and the steady tampering with the series was of no help.

Raymond Hatton, Livingston and Duncan Renaldo in The Cowboys from Texas *(1939).*

HOLLYWOOD CORRAL: A COMPREHENSIVE B WESTERN ROUNDUP

Foreground: Rufe Davis, Tom Tyler, Norman Willis, Bud Geary, Terry Frost and Bob Steele in Gauchos of El Dorado *(1941).*

Saddlemates (Orlebeck, 1941) showed a slight upswing in tempo with an Army vs. Indians theme (the series was now firmly back in the last century), and *Gangs of Sonora* (John English, 1941) benefitted from more action and English's careful direction. But after seven more Mesquiteer films and an approaching new season, another change was in the offing.

Tom Tyler signed to replace Livingston as Stony Brooke, and no great decline was felt from the move. Tyler didn't have Livingston's flair, but the veteran cowboy star was still of commanding presence, after playing villains for the past few years. Teaming him with Bob Steele was like reuniting two old friends, and they complemented each other well. Of the seven 1941–42 Mesquiteer films, three were directed by Les Orlebeck (so-so) and four by John English (entertaining). The time element was still fast and loose. *West of Cimarron* (Orlebeck, 1941) took place after the Civil War, while *Phantom Plainsmen* (English, 1942) had as its villain a Nazi agent. Thus the Mesquiteers covered 80 years with a few releases. An interesting sidelight occurred in *Gauchos of El Dorado* (Orlebeck, 1941), with former Mesquiteer Duncan Renaldo appearing in a brief role before getting killed off.

Now it was Rufe Davis who was dispatched from the series. Joining Steele and Tyler was Jimmy Dodd, as Lullaby Joslin. Dodd was a boyish singer and entertainer who restrained his personality while with the Mesquiteers and disported himself laudably. It's one of the few times that the comedy relief slot was filled by someone who looked younger than the heroes. This was to be the final season for the Mesquiteers, and the six Steele-Tyler-Dodd features represented a general improvement over what had gone before. *Shadows on the Sage* (Orlebeck, 1942) had a good plot by J. Benton Cheney. *Valley of Hunted Men* (English, 1942) cashed in on the topicality with a yarn about an escaping Nazi on the loose in the West; lots of stock footage saved the budget, but English directed it at a pace of almost continuous action. *Thundering Trails* (English, 1943) was a Texas Ranger story, with more action.

THREE FOR THE PRICE OF ONE: Mesquiteers & Range Busters

A mystery angle dominated *The Blocked Trail* (Elmer Clifton, 1943), with the novelty of a "seeing-eye" horse used by a miner who is murdered, with the animal alone knowing a way to a hidden mine. The final two Mesqiteer 1943 releases, ending the series, were directed by Howard Bretherton. *Santa Fe Scouts* and *Riders of the Rio Grande* were both unexceptional but entertaining Western fare. However, Republic thought that there was little more to be squeezed from the Mesquiteer combinations and the series was curtailed. The Mesquiteers had been portrayed in 51 Republic features by nine different trio combinations. Despite the gradual tapering off in quality, the overall record was an extremely good one, rating high with Western fans.

During their final years, the Mesquiteers had experienced competition, notably from an outfit using two former members. In 1940, George W. Weeks began producing a series called "The Range Busters," releasing through Monogram. Ray "Crash" Corrigan was the leader and Max Terhune, here known as "Alibi," assumed the same comedy position he had weathered with the Mesquiteers, with dummy Elmer in tow. Completing the trio was John "Dusty" King, approximating Bob Livingston's role, only King sang in a pleasant baritone—fortunately, not too often. It was an obvious copy of the Mesquiteers, but it was nice to have Corrigan and Terhune back. So, to the strains of "Home on the Range," scored by Frank Sanucci for what sounded like a sextet of kazoos, the first one appeared. *The Range Busters* was directed by S. Roy Luby, once of the Hackel factory, and Luby would handle 16 consecutive members of the series; his direction was, technically speaking, the chief and often the only asset of the series. The opener did hold promise. It was a whodunit by John Rathmell, and not a bad one. The mystery angle didn't restrict the action to any great degree, and though the production was far below the classy Republic brand, the tatty appearance wasn't too big a drawback.

Thereafter the trail became rocky. *Trailing Double Trouble* (1940) could have been titled "The Range Busters and the Baby," for that's what it was all about. Action was conspicuous by its absence, and this became the common complaint of the series. Weeks and the writers were trying to come up with offbeat scripts, but in the attempt the pace essential for action fans to cotton to the series was suffering. The predicament reached a crisis with *Tumbledown Ranch in Arizona* (1941), with King's son meeting Corrigan's son at college; King gets bopped on the bean and is carried back in time to the good old days, thus beginning the Range Busters story. Only

Corrigan about to heave Roy Barcroft in Trailing Double Trouble *(1940).*

by the time all the frills were out of the way and the Western properly commenced, nobody cared. There were problems besides literary ones. Sanucci's tinny music cast a pall, but was at least bearable. However, other technical departments were below par even by low-budget standards, especially the sound recording, often of tin-can telephone quality. The Range Busters were carrying the series by virtue of their own abilities, with little help from the production end.

Since their opening film had done well by a whodunit plot, the 1941–42 season of eight Range Busters opened with a similar idea in *Saddle Mountain Roundup* (1941), or, who killed the grouchy rancher? The answer was of small importance. Luby again directed each series entry. After a particularly slow and cumbersome affair, *Underground Rustlers* (1941), Luby did try to inject some movement into the films, and occasionally succeeded. *Thunder River Feud* (1942) was the usual story of the trio coming to the aid of a rancher beset by trouble. But Luby's training as an editor helped him speed the pace via several clever transitions, and he played up the friendly rivalry between Corrigan and King over a pretty face, a la the early Corrigan-Livingston Mesquiteers. The following Range Busters, like *Texas Trouble Shooters* and *Arizona Stagecoach* (1942) made up in action what they lacked in finesse. And the boys did have a fair amount of fans.

Changes abounded in the third Range Buster season, and inevitably the changes spelled demise after the series struggled through eight more Westerns. The trio was now comprised of King, Terhune and David Sharpe replacing Corrigan. Robert Tansey, off the late unlamented Tom Keene Monogram series, took over and directed *Texas to Bataan,* a novel Arthur Hoerl idea which saw the trio escorting a shipment of horses to the Philippines and matching wits with Japanese spies. The topicality kept abreast of the 1942 headlines, and Sharpe pitched in for some flamboyant derring-do in the action scenes. As a film it wouldn't win any awards, but at least it kept the patrons awake. Sharpe was one of the Range Busters for three-and-a-half films. In the middle of *Haunted Ranch* (Tansey, 1943) he was called to the colors, and the script allowed for him to join Teddy Roosevelt's Rough Riders. Rex Lease was hired to assume Sharpe's duties for the rest of the film. Further changes occurred with the next one, *Land of Hunted Men* (1943). S. Roy Luby returned as director, Corrigan returned as "Crash," and Dennis Moore joined him and Terhune, who must have had to look twice to see who his new partners were with each picture. The new threesome's first wasn't much,

John King romances Julie Duncan in Fugitive Valley *(1941).*

THREE FOR THE PRICE OF ONE: Mesquiteers & Range Busters

Dave Sharpe stares out of a dispute between King and Terhune in Trail Riders *(1942).*

but there followed two naively amusing topical Westerns directed by Luby: *Cowboy Commandos,* by Elizabeth Beecher, and *Black Market Rustlers,* by Patricia Harper. In the former, the boys round up some Nazis, a motley crew consisting of such Teutons as Bud Buster and John Merton; the latter film they crack down on wartime black marketeers. Both were juvenilia, but crammed with action, and good fun. Evelyn Finley, a movie cowgirl who could really ride, was the heroine in both films, adding a touch of expert horsemanship as well as glamour. *Bullets and Saddles* was released by Monogram on October 29, 1943, and was the last Range Busters. The series had outlasted the Three Mesquiteers by six months. The swan song was directed by an Anthony Marshall, a name unseen on credits before or since. One felt a sense of loss with the end of the series, for the boys were genial and the pace had quickened, notwithstanding the production defects. Corrigan must have been reluctant to see it all end, too. Most of the films were shot on his ranch.

Al St. John as "Fuzzy Q. Jones"

15
FUZZY'S FRIENDS

Between the years 1941–46, Al St. John, a bewhiskered comedian, appeared in 53 Westerns as regular comedy relief, known as Fuzzy Q. Jones. The 53 films in question are divided into two separate series, namely the Lone Rider adventures starring George Houston and later Bob Livingston, and the Billy the Kid features starring Buster Crabbe. Actually, St. John's total work load was even heavier, but it is these two series that are of primary concern here.

St. John had first come to attention in the days of Fatty Arbuckle (he was a relative of the obese funster), and on the threshold of the sound era had co-starred with many silent comedy lights, as well as soloing in many short subjects. He was acrobatic, could withstand falls in limber fashion, and could do tricks with a bicycle that were surefire rib-ticklers. He had a myriad of comedy wrinkles up his sleeve, and when the talkies put a temporary clamp on the short subject he found steady if undistinguished work in minor roles, and especially in Westerns. In the latter half of the '30s, as the comic sidekick became more important to the hero, St. John would be found in support of many screen cowpokes, sometimes for one or two films, occasionally for an entire series. He developed his characterization of Fuzzy in 1937 during the Fred Scott independent singing-cowboy series, and would revert to it permanently a few years later at PRC.

Two facts stand out about the Billy the Kid and Lone Rider series. St. John played the same part in each, concurrently, and nobody seemed to mind. At that, the plots in each series put no strain upon the imaginations of the scriptwriters, so if the stories all seemed alike there was no reason to complain about a capable comic doing the same act. Secondly, all the Billy the Kids and Lone Riders, save one, were directed by Sam Newfield, who while at PRC would take credit as Sherman Scott and Peter Stewart, in addition to his own name. With such a grueling schedule, it's a wonder that any of these small-budgeted quickies had entertainment value. Mainly because of St. John, Crabbe, Newfield to some extent, and a periodic screenplay of above average quality, a nugget would glimmer amid the dross. Frequently the production deficencies and off-the-cuff shooting mistakes would be good for some giggles. Through it all, St. John unfailingly plugged away, working hard for his salary. Against the odds, he came through admirably.

George Houston and Al St. John had been teamed prior to the PRC escapades. Just before the company's death throes, Grand National Pictures was engaged in trying out several fairly new Western faces with prospective series in mind. None made it and the company soon shuttered, but the Western receiving the most favorable comment starred George Houston, an opera singer gradually working his way down the scale from a Nelson Eddy-type romantic lead to an adventurous action player in indies. Houston impersonated Wild Bill Hickok in his first Western, directed by Newfield and titled

185

Fuzzy gets a lift from Slim Whitaker (l.) and Kenne Duncan while Jack Ingram and Alden Chase hold George Houston in Frontier Scout *(1938).*

Frontier Scout (1938). St. John played the comedy part, although not as Fuzzy. Interestingly enough, St. John's comedy was employed in another Grand National release, *Trigger Pals,* released shortly after *Frontier Scout,* in support of Art Jarrett and Lee Powell: for this one-shot, he did use his Fuzzy characterization.

Three years later, Houston and St. John were reteamed by Producers Releasing Corporation for the Lone Rider series. Houston had not been too active in the interim, but St. John had been working like the proverbial beaver, said beaver adorning his chin habitually now. In fact, Newfield (Sherman Scott) had directed him in a non-Western in 1940, *Marked Men,* and a clean-shaven St. John was unrecognizable in a semi-serious role—in which he was quite touching, by the way. At the time of the Lone Rider inception, St. John was already doing his Fuzzy antics in the Bob Steele Billy the Kid series, and was hustling over to Republic on off-days to lend titter assistance to the Don "Red" Barry outdoor yarns, not impersonating Fuzzy Jones, but nearly stealing the picture nevertheless.

It takes no great deduction to state that PRC was earnestly hoping for a Lone Ranger-Lone Rider similarity to present itself to the youngsters, but Houston didn't use any of the flamboyant gimmickry connected with the famous masked rider. He had some acting ability and could present a believable version of rough-and-tumble when called upon to do so. That he was possessed of a fine baritone was unquestioned—Houston was undoubtedly the best singer among the cowboys, on the basis of pure vocalistics. But he was afflicted with the curse of most opera-type belters, stolidity. Generally unsmiling and in short supply of humor, Houston often seemed preoccupied, probably musing on better days at the opera with Verdi and Puccini, rather than high noons on the PRC prairies with Charlie King and I. Sanford Jolley. In any case, he got through six

Lone Rider films for the first season and five for the second.

For the series debut, the Lone Rider was given a genesis not dissimilar to other range heroes of Joseph O'Donnell scripts. *The Lone Rider Rides On* (1941) has him returning after 20 years to find the killers of his parents and brother, only the brother isn't dead, you see, but brought up by the outlaws to become one of them, only he finds out what's what in time to save the Lone Rider, and he stops a lethal slug in doing so, but goes to the big ranch in the sky happy that he did what he did, The End. Lee Powell played the brother role, Buddy Roosevelt played in a bit, and the cast was lined with PRC saddle troops, Bob Kortman, Tom London, Karl Hackett, Frank Hagney, Frank Ellis, Curly Dresden. Hillary Brooke, a dignified blonde sorely out of place on the range, provided the femininity in this, and one or two other PRCs.

Having thus established himself, Houston ploughed through the series with unbending singleness of purpose, namely, to be done. He was happiest when given a song or three to render. The songs weren't any shining examples of melodic art, but Houston's voice gave them some distinction. Doing much to hold the remnants of the films together was St. John's broad antics. In the sixth entry, *The Lone Rider Fights Back* (1941), Dennis Moore appeared in the cast, and by the tenth and eleventh one was elevated to the position of third good guy, in the true PRC tradition, with the appellation of "Smoky" Moore. Lone Rider number eleven was *Outlaws of Boulder Pass* (1942) and it was slightly better than the usual run, thanks to St. John. It was also Houston's final Western. He retired, and died of a heart attack in 1944.

PRC decided to continue with the series, and since Bob Livingston wasn't doing anything after leaving the Mesquiteers at Republic, the choice was a logical one. Besides, Livingston had been the Lone Ranger once, so there was further hope of subliminal identification. Livingston had built a following and was a stalwart in the saddle, although his new surroundings were a far cry from the relatively plush accommodations at Republic. With no time taken for songs, the series picked up speed, if nothing else. *Overland Stagecoach* (1942) got Livingston off to an okay start, and proved to be the final appearance of

Art Jarrett, Fuzzy and Lee Powell harmonize in Trigger Pals *(1939).*

Smoky Moore, which was the best because Moore and Livingston were too much alike. Up to this point the series had been 19th century—in time, not technique, although the point is moot—but in *Wild Horse Rustlers* (1943) the villains were Nazi spies, if one can imagine Lane Chandler and Stanley Price doing their dirty deeds for Deutschland. Another hopefully modern plot gimmick was applied to *Wolves of the Range* (1943), which had Livingston getting a head-thump and developing a mild case of amnesia. When Livingston left PRC to return to Republic the next year, he brought the loss of memory bit with him in his saddlebag, for further use.

Auteurists might well compare *Law of the Saddle* (Mel De Lay, 1943) with any Sam Newfield effort, certainly a limitless expanse of celluloid from which to choose. Newfield was straight on with his cameras and meant business, which is why he lasted so long and made so many pictures. De Lay was his assistant, and assumed full helming of *Law of the Saddle* when Newfield took a breather. De Lay used panning shots, a variety of angles, instilled a lot of pace in the action and a lot of vigor in the actors, turned out one of the better PRC Westerns, and never directed another feature. You figure it out.

Livingston and the Lone Rider series called it quits after six, leaving Al St. John and his Fuzzy Jones character with but one series to contend with—until the advent of one Al (Lash) La Rue some four years hence.

St. John's association with Buster Crabbe on the Billy the Kid series began the same year as the Lone Riders, 1941, but continued until 1946, for 36 films. Not that St, John was any newcomer to Billy the Kid. The series had commenced the previous year, with Bob Steele in the lead. Steele played the Kid half a dozen times, then grabbed the opportunity to head for Republic and the Three Mequiteers. With

Bob Livingston covers Glenn Strange (in coach) while Fuzzy (climbing rear of coach) and Dennis Moore keep their eyes on driver Art Mix in Overland Stagecoach *(1942).*

Raymond Hatton and Buster Crabbe in Arizona Raiders *(1936).*

St. John and director Newfield-Stewart-Scott well seasoned on the project, and Crabbe a quick study, it didn't take long for the series to get in the groove—or rut, as you will.

Swimming is a sport where smoothness and grace are mandatory. Crabbe was an aquatic star of Olympic magnitude, but his movie career had been far from smooth, instead taking odd skips and jumps and never stabilizing enough to bring him the serious recognition he deserved. Crabbe had started at Paramount as a pseudo-Tarzan, and would actually play the jungle man in an independent serial not long after. In fact, it took no great amount of time before he was identified with an imposing number of comic-strip adventure heroes, Red Barry, Buck Rogers, and most notable, Flash Gordon. Under his Paramount contract, he was given experience in all varieties of movies, big parts and small, and perhaps that was what eventually hindered his career. For Paramount did use him, not wisely, not too well. From picture to picture, he would be Western leading man, crime-yarn heavy, Western heavy, college-boy support, Western lead, crime-heavy again, ad infinitum. Add the serial heroics and some further appearances off the Paramount lot and you have a busy career, but one that failed to take proper shape. His Flash Gordon stints were most opportune, for they kept him firmly in the memory of the action fan.

Crabbe appeared in ten Paramount Zane Grey Westerns, and starred in half of them, although his top billing in two was an act of Paramount contractual courtesy only—interloper Tom Keene had the major share of the footage, in both *Drift Fence* (Otho Lovering, 1936) and *Desert Gold* (James Hogan, 1936). But Crabbe received the big roles in truth, in *Nevada* (Charles Barton, 1936) and its sequel, *Forlorn River* (Barton, 1937), both pleasing, well made outdoor shows enhanced by excellent photographic effects and Paramount's plentiful supply of contract actors to lend fine support. Even better was *The Arizona Raiders* (James Hogan,

1936), which had more honest laughs than many comedies, with especially clever lines by Robert Yost and John Krafft. Crabbe and Raymond Hatton made a good team as a couple of not too brave cowpokes, Johnny Downs contributed a nice job as a naive dude, and Marsha Hunt and (Betty) Jane Rhodes added to the scenery and the talent as well. Crabbe had proven over and again that he could handle the action, and had become a dependable actor. Despite this, his only Western offer was villainy in a Gene Autry opus after he left Paramount. PRC started him off in the jungles briefly, then signed him for the Billy the Kids. Steele had had a partner, Carleton Young, to go along with St. John, and the threesome formula was retained for the first season, with Young, Bud McTaggart and Dave O'Brien in the part variously. After that, Crabbe and St. John had a go without any third party.

There was a certainty about the Crabbes that soon became almost comfortable. Billy the Kid was sure to be wanted for crimes he didn't commit, and Crabbe would enter combat forthwith to clear his name and pin the rap on the guilty parties. Sam Newfield was using his Sherman Scott identity, but hardly anybody's ingenuity. Aliases spilled over into the writing department, too. *Law and Order* (1942), by Sam Robins, was followed by *Mysterious Rider* (1942), by Steve Braxton—it was still Robins, no matter the name. *Billy the Kid's Smoking Guns* (1942), by George Milton, would be echoed with *Sheriff of Sage Valley* (1942), screenplay by George W. Sayre and Milton Raison (dig the first names). And during all this heavy shooting, Crabbe would still find time to do another jungle number for PRC, or sneak over to Pine-Thomas for some villainy to plague Richard Arlen.

I. Stanford Jolley thinks twice about drawing his gun under the gaze of Crabbe, St. John and Evelyn Finley in Prairie Rustlers *(1945).*

Things improved in 1943. Production would remain sloppy, but Crabbe and St. John meshed as a duo; Newfield dropped the Sherman Scott masquerade and came forth as good ol' Sam, and the confession seemed to bring added vigor to his work. Minor performers might still blow their lines without retakes and some of the interior sets looked ready for the scrap pile, but the new-found exuberance was a blessing. Crabbe was coasting in his hero role, but his easygoing manner combined with genuine skill made it look good. St. John had honed his Fuzzy character to a sharp comic point. Mugging, pratfalls, anything and everything went into the role. With trousers at crotch level and stubbled chin perpetually outthrust, he presented the picture of a Western court jester. He had developed bits of business which would never fail—the ludicrous bravado as he slithered off his horse while eyeing a potential enemy, or his reaction to a knockout blow, an unconcerned laugh as if to say it didn't hurt a bit, followed by total collapse. *Western Cyclone* (1943) was St. John at peak form, as was *Devil Riders* (1943). With the latter film, Billy the Kid became just plain Billy Carson, with all ties to the legendary outlaw severed.

Crabbe was given a dual role in *The Drifter* (1943), hero and bandit, and with some solid St. John comedy sequences balancing the plot, it was one of the better members of the series. In *Frontier Outlaws* (1944), Joe O'Donnell used one of his Tim McCoy script ideas and wrote a situation wherein Crabbe disguises himself as a Mexican cattleman. The star managed the dialect passably well, but Newfield's reluctance to indulge in retakes marred a suspense scene in which Crabbe holds the baddies at bay, slowly backs out a convenient window—and gives his head a nasty crack on the sill. Theater audiences would wince spontaneously at the accident.

PRC well knew the value of St. John's contribution as Fuzzy Q. Jones. *Fuzzy Settles Down* (1944) and *His Brother's Ghost* (1945) were designed for his talents in an unusual case of letting the star, Crabbe, temporarily take a back seat. In the latter film, St. John was handed a dual role, playing Fuzzy's twin brother Andy. To keep peace in the family, PRC gave Crabbe better billing with *Fighting Bill Carson* (1945).

Postwar blight set in. Never too strong on the production end, the films started getting quite shoddy. *Gentlemen With Guns* (1946) suffered in just about every technical department, including some painfully obvious and inept stunting scenes, with the grassy mats plainly in view as the riders were about to tumble from their horses, and some fistfights featuring clumsy misses and pulled punches. *Terrors on Horseback* (1946) was a brief return to form, a good George Milton script and little or no wasted motion. But two more films and Crabbe and St. John teamed no more. The 36 Westerns were all directed by Sam Newfield, all produced by Sigmund Neufeld (who had produced the Lone Rider series, and other PRC features), most of them photographed by Jack Greenhalgh (with occasional photography by Robert Cline or Art Reed). Even the most rabid fan might be hard-pressed to distinguish among the PRC Western output, but Crabbe and St. John did have their moments.

For Crabbe, work was comfortably steady in the movies. He'd star in some serials for Columbia, do some excellent villainous parts for Pine-Thomas, and add to the Marquee luster when he'd appear opposite fellow Tarzan Johnny Weissmuller, either for Pine-Thomas or Sam Katzman at Columbia. He added one more to his gallery of legends when he played Wyatt Earp to George Montgomery's Pat Garrett in *Badman's Country* (Fred F. Sears, 1958). He starred for Republic in *The Lawless Eighties* (Joe Kane, 1957), and notably for an Edward Small unit in two plain but satisfying moderately-budgeted outdoor dramas, *Gun Brothers* (Sidney Salkow, 1956) and *Gunfighters of Abilene* (Edward L. Cahn, 1960). He remained in top physical condition, and his performances showed a good deal of thought and depth. There were also popular TV shows, successful business endeavors, ultimately Wall Street.

In such a varied career, few would remember Buster Crabbe for his PRC Westerns; Flash Gordon would tend to be the immediate reaction. However, as a cowboy star, he lasted longer than many, and given the obstacles to surmount, could take pardonable pride in this portion of his work.

Russell Hayden

16
TRAILS NORTH

Hollywood never did right by the mounties. The challenge was there, with unlimited opportunities for adventure with fresh, picturesque locales; a group of law enforcers with a noble, proud and inspiring tradition, not to mention their distinctive redcoats; and the potential of blending rugged, Western-type action with, to non-Canadians, a tinge of the exotic allure of a foreign country. With everything at their disposal, the movies generally blew it.

Just about every cowboy star of note took a stab at playing mountie—except, by some curious quirk, the vocalizers, although Gene Autry came close a couple of times. Tim McCoy, whose military bearing would make him a natural for a Mounted Policeman tale, tried only once, in *Fighting Shadows* (David Selman, 1935). Buck Jones was a visitor in both silent and talkie adventures, while Ken Maynard and Tom Mix made silents dealing with the Mounted Police. Mountie films *Honor of the Mounted* (Harry Fraser, 1932) and *Northwest Trail* (Derwin Abrahams, 1945) afforded opportunities for Tom Tyler and Bob Steele respectively to wear the scarlet, with Steele's uniform enhanced by Cinecolor, if enhanced is the word. Tyler also headed a Universal serial, *Clancy of the Mounted* (Ray Taylor, 1933). Chapter play producers seemed to find more in Mounted Police stories than the feature filmmakers, for the theme would appear with some frequency: Columbia's *Perils of the Royal Mounted* (James W. Horne, 1942), with Robert Stevens, and *Gunfighters of the Northwest* (Spencer Bennet, 1954), with Jock Mahoney; Universal's *The Royal Mounted Rides Again* (Ray Taylor & Lewis D. Collins, 1945), with Bill Kennedy; and several Republics, including Allan Lane's two based on Zane Grey's "King of the Royal Mounted," and *Dangers of the Canadian Mounted* (Fred Brannon & Yakima Canutt, 1948), with Jim Bannon and *Canadian Mounties vs. Atomic Invaders* (Franklin Adreon, 1953) with Bill Henry. None of the above had much to recommend except the Lanes, produced during Republic's peak period and loaded with the studio's bone-breaking brand of action.

Biggest tribute to the RCMP was Cecil B. DeMille's *North West Mounted Police* (1940), which benefitted from the opulent production details and garish ballyhoo concomitant with every DeMillennium. Unfortunately, bigness and dullness go hand in hand invariably in such instances, and this was no exception. The majority of the non-series RCMP adventures couldn't afford the DeMille budget but did manage to capture the same leaden pace. One happy novelty was a Warner Bros. Technicolor job, *Heart of the North* (Lewis Seiler, 1938). It was a Bryan Foy "B" picture, with the canny Foy adding a bit to the budget for the Technicolor tints. It was well worth the expenditure, for Technicolor meant a big picture to the moviegoing public and thereby added to the boxoffice take; the process also dressed up the outdoor scenes in fine style, and the scenics were ably displayed by the cameras of L. W. O'Connell and Wilfrid Cline. Fortunately, the script

193

was a good one, allowing for no pondering and a plentitude of action and excitement. Dick Foran was given the role and had he received similar treatment while a Western star at the studio, he certainly would have lasted longer in the saddle.

Generally however, the mounties got their men on quickie schedules. Two early talkies released within two months of each other shared a common tragic bond, having nothing to do with the films themselves. *In Line of Duty* (Bert Glennon, 1931) was a Monogram rush job about a mountie adhering to his code, despite the interference of love and friendship, and *Mounted Fury* (Stuart Paton, 1931) was a gets-his-man tale with under par production treatment. James Murray was the hero in the former, John Bowers in the latter. Both were once considered sure bets for stardom; both lost to the bottle; both died by water, either accidental drowning or suicide; neither was given top billing in their respective films, even though their roles were the most important. Murray was billed fourth, behind Sue Carol, Noah Beery and Francis McDonald. Bowers bowed to Blanche Mehaffey.

Zane Grey's comic strip mentioned earlier was the basis for one feature and two serials. Sol Lesser produced *King of the Royal Mounted* (Howard Bretherton, 1936) with Robert Kent in the title part. The Lessers had a tendency to dawdle over non-essentials around this time, although they were pleasant enough, so audiences had to be content with a mild flurry of excitement for the climax, and not too much else. *King of the Royal Mounted* (William Witney & John English, 1940), Republic serial version, and *King of the Mounties* (Witney, 1942) were, to repeat, real rock-'em-sock-'em.

Showing the most affinity for the Mounted Police was Columbia's Charles Starrett, who journeyed North, in spirit if not in body, five times during his

Mountie Charles Starrett lets bearded Bruce Bennett know he means business in The Royal Mounted Patrol *(1941).*

George Regas, Ben Hendricks, Kermit Maynard and "Rocky" in Red Blood of Courage *(1935).*

saddle career. He actually did film *Secret Patrol* in Canada in 1936, with the sad results already touched upon. His subsequent RCMP adventures were Hollywood product, beginning with *North of the Yukon* (Sam Nelson, 1939) and followed in a few months by *Outpost of the Mounties* (C. C. Coleman Jr., 1939), neither causing any great stir. In fact, the latter film was awash with unbelievable coincidence and brainless brouhaha, which was greeted with jeers from audiences. Undaunted, Columbia inaugurated the Starret-Russell Hayden partnership with *The Royal Mounted Patrol* (Lambert Hillyer, 1941), to clearly improved results, with a well constructed Winston Miller script and much action. Starrett's *Law of the Northwest* (William Berke, 1943) did well with a neat Luci Ward plot idea about skulduggery attendant to building a connecting spur to the U.S.-Alaska highway under construction, a topical and offbeat theme.

Ambassador Pictures, an independent concern headed by Maurice Conn, produced the first talkie series with a mountie as hero. Signed for the lead was Kermit Maynard, Ken's brother and a splendid showman in his own right. Kermit had starred in a silent Western series for Rayart in 1927 and was billed as Tex Maynard. For the past few years he had been taking minor roles, including one in his brother's vehicle *Drum Taps*. More important than his acting roles was his stunting work. He was a superlative rider and did a lot of dangerous riding tricks for other players. He also entered rodeo events between films. Though his horsemanship was outstanding, Kermit was an all-around athlete, and performed the risky feats in his series without the aid of a double.

Maynard's first for Conn was *The Fighting Trooper* (Ray Taylor, 1934), and the series was off to an adequate start. The picture was slightly above the norm for independent product of the period, and Maynard made a good impression. His prowess on horseback was duly noted by the reviewers, and while his fisticuffing needed some work, his other physical attributes were persuasive. A six-footer with a square jaw and lean frame, he cut a dashing figure in the Mounted Police uniform.

Northern Frontier (Sam Newfield, 1935) followed, and was a definite improvement over the first. Newfield paced the action speedily, and the

HOLLYWOOD CORRAL: A COMPREHENSIVE B WESTERN ROUNDUP

Kermit faces John Merton, Stan Blystone and John Ward in Galloping Dynamite *(1937).*

supporting cast was in the better class of independent troupes, with J. Farrell MacDonald, Russell Hopton, Roy Mason and Charles King. Eleanor Hunt, formerly Eddie Cantor's leading lady, ably represented the feminine interest. In a subsequent film, the ingenue was somewhat less familiar, a youngster fresh from Paramount named Ann Sheridan. *Red Blood of Courage* (John English, 1935) was a good entry with more plot values than usual. Best of the early Maynards was *Wilderness Mail* (Forrest Sheldon, 1935), which took advantage of some heavy snowfall to instill picturesque location scenes into the narrative, obtaining realistic backgrounds difficult to recreate in Hollywood, and almost never found in low-budget independent product. Villainy was in the sinewy hands of Fred Kohler, with Paul Hurst giving a good performance in one of his squinting ratty roles. Newfield directed the rest of the 1935 Maynards save one. *His Fighting Blood* was directed by John English, and the former film editor was already showing his ability to probe a little deeper than most action meggers, and emerging with better film. Newfield's *Code of the Mounted* was uncomplicated, swift and easy to take, with photographer Edgar Lyons taking advantage of the natural backgrounds via clean, well-lit images. *Trails of the Wild* maintained the level of the series, but *Timber War,* closing out the year, fell below par. It wasn't a mountie story, but an outdoor melodrama of the logging camps, with Maynard attempting to reform a playboy (Lawrence Gray). It appeared as if Maynard and Conn were about to forsake the Mounted Police for more conventional yarns, which seemed a pity. Maynard was a most convincing mountie, and the films had an authentic look, though filmed within the California boundaries.

As expected, Maynard's first release for 1936 was a straight Western, *Song of the Trail.* It was directed by Russell Hopton, who had appeared with Maynard in *Northern Frontier,* and from the look of the interiors and the supporting cast of Evelyn Brent, Wheeler Oakman, Fuzzy Knight, George Hayes and numerous others, Conn had opened up the budget, at least this once. For most of its length, it was pretty good, with Maynard taking to the Western locale handily, and giving an exhibition (not too well staged) of Fairbanksian acrobatics trying to elude a small army of opponents within the confines of a cabaret, leaping over stairwells, up walls and down draperies cavalierly. The only serious anachronism was Arthur Reed's camerawork, which fell back on silent speed during Maynard's climactic set-to with heavy Oakman. When the latter was felled with a mighty Maynard blow, his descent to the gound was pure slapstick because of the speeded up motion, marring what would have been an entirely satisfactory Western. The slight romantic interest was entrusted to Antoinette Lees, who shortly would change her name to Andrea Leeds and have a brief praise-worthy dramatic career in the movies.

Two more mountie films followed, presumably made before *Song of the Trail* but withheld until the turn of the tide could be determined. *Phantom Patrol* (Charles Hutchinson, 1936) wasn't any great shakes, but *Wildcat Trooper* (Elmer Clifton, 1936) was a return to form, with a good performance by oldtimer Hobart Bosworth as the seemingly kindly medico in reality the brains behind the dirty deeds. Beginning with *Wild Horse Roundup* (Alan James, 1936) Maynard stashed away his RCMP uniform, hopefully in mothballs, and remained a Western lead for seven more features. Nothing fancy about these Conn productions, except Maynard's fancy riding, and it really was fancy. In *Roundup* he does this, for lack of proper terminology, climbing all over his horse (named Rocky) while at full gallop. In *Valley of Terror* (Al Herman, 1937) he approaches his steed running at full tilt and vaults what seems like 16 feet in the air, over the horse's rump, completing a perfect flying mount. No trickery, either; its done with the camera at close quarters. Although the single most enjoyable facet of his Westerns, Maynard's horseplay wasn't the sole appeal. John English returned to direct *Whistling Bullets*, and made an ordinary story seem like new. His discerning action eye also displayed Maynard's stunting most agreeably. Maynard got good treatment in the casting of his leading ladies, attractive ones like Harlene Wood, Elaine Shepard and Beryl Wallace. Strong nastiness from heavies Dick Curtis, John Merton, Charles King, Jack Ingram and others, too.

Kermit Maynard drifted into supporting roles after his Conn-Ambassador series ended, which is not understandable—he was a good actor for a cowpoke, possessed a sense of humor and his physical feats were unquestionably tops. With their accustomed lack of foresight, producers failed to follow up, so Maynard gradually faded. He was a regular at Monogram and PRC during the '40s and appeared in many TV Westerns until his retirement from the screen in 1962.

In exploiting the early Maynard mountie films, much was made of the stories being based on the works of James Oliver Curwood. Here again, as with Zane Grey and Peter B. Kyne, the Curwood name was often just that, with no connection to the scenario. But Curwood was noted for his tales of the Mounted Police, so the tie-in was made to order. No such luck graced Robert Emmett (Tansey) when he made *Courage of the North* for a 1935 release by Stage & Screen Attractions. Tansey was forced to make do with what was on hand, and that excluded the Curwood name. Also a satisfactory script, or professional direction by Emmett. John Preston was okay in the mountie hero role, and William Desmond was around for the benefit of old movie fans, but they treated Jim Thorpe badly. The Indian athletic great was now demoted to playing bits, and was unceremoniously killed off early in the footage. Preston had a nice horse, Dynamite, and a nice dog, Captain—or was it the other way around? No matter—the only asset was some fairly competent camerawork by Brydon Baker. Preston returned in *Timber Terrors* the same year, so did his four-footed companions, so did Desmond. But Emmett couldn't make anything work, and so much the better. The RCMP could do without this sort of thing.

They probably weren't too pleased when Phil Krasne started producing the Renfrew of the Royal Mounted series, either. The Laurie York Erskine books were staple adventure fare and the radio program was grist for the kiddie mill, but the budget was obviously going to be in short supply, and Grand National wasn't known as a prestige company at this stage, even though they had snagged Cagney from Warners. When *Renfrew of the Royal Mounted* (Al Herman, 1937) appeared, fears were partly justified. There wasn't much to recommend in the way of fancy production dress. But the vehicle on the whole could have been worse. Renfrew was played by James Newill, another warbler. Newill had a robust masculine baritone along the chords of George Houston—the two were friends, and Newill would sing in Houston's stage company—and delivered the specially written ditty, "Mounted Men," throbbingly over the credits of each Renfrew adventure. He also had a cleft in his chin as deep as an open mining pit, very Cary Grantish. Newill played the role with a light touch and would have been entirely satisfactory with any kind of outside accompaniment. He wasn't very fortunate in this regard.

Foiling counterfeiters passed the time in the series opener. Robbery and murder was the assignment in *Renfrew on the Great White Trail* (Herman, 1938),

James Newill (l.) as Renfrew, with partner Dave O'Brien in Fighting Mad *(1939).*

which was poor in all departments. *Crashing Through* was announced as the next Renfrew, but Grand National did a fold and the series stayed in limbo for a year, which is where it should have remained. *Crashing Thru* (Elmer Clifton, 1939) was released by Monogram. Newill continued his breezy Renfrew characterization and was given a Mountie cohort in Warren Hull. Some good performers like Milburn Stone, Walter Byron and Roy Barcroft appeared in the footage, but all concerned were stymied by the weak material, and some blatant over-acting by leading lady Jean Carmen made matters worse.

Monogram distributed five more Renfrews before Krasne halted the series. *Fighting Mad* (Sam Newfield, 1939) had Newill and pal Dave O'Brien after some American gangsters (headed by Milburn Stone again, as in *Crashing Through*). Sally Blane improved the scenery and Benny Rubin tried hard for laughs, but the film was geared for juvenile tastes, no more. Sally Blane's sister, Polly Ann Young, had the ingenue part in *Murder on the Yukon* (Louis Gasnier, 1940); if anything was certain, it was that the third acting sister in the family, Loretta Young, wouldn't be seen in the series. The present Renfrew had Newill and O'Brien investigating the murder of two prospectors. One of the victims was played by Al St. John. *Danger Ahead* (Ralph Staub, 1940) had some relieving light moments provided by Dorothea Kent, a snowy blonde with looks and comedy abilities, but was otherwise wispy as to plot and action. Finally, *Yukon Flight* (Staub, 1939) and *Sky Bandits* (Staub, 1940) looked like the same picture. Both dealt with shipping gold via airplane, and the casts were virtually identical: Louise Stanley, William Pawley, Newill and O'Brien. Newill devoted his time to off-screen engagements until 1943, when he reappeared with O'Brien for PRC.

A commendable home-grown RCMP thriller was made by Kenneth Bishop's Central Films in Victoria, B.C. *Death Goes North* had mountie Edgar Edwards and canine companion Rin Tin Tin Jr. solving a murder in the lumber country. It was ably directed by Frank McDonald with a good imported cast, including Sheila Bromley, Jameson Thomas and Walter Byron. Leading man Edwards also contributed the script, and the modest film was good enough to warrant a sequel. Warwick Films released it in the provinces in 1938, with American release by Columbia a year later.

Kirby Grant, Gloria Talbott and "Chinook" hold baddie Bill Phipps at bay in Northern Patrol *(1953).*

HOLLYWOOD CORRAL: A COMPREHENSIVE B WESTERN ROUNDUP

While under contract to Columbia, Russell Hayden had starred in a routinely competent mountie adventure, *Riders of the Northwest Mounted* (William Berke, 1943). In his later sojourn to Screen Guild, Hayden was tapped for two sets of streamlined mountie films, with running times in the neighborhood of 40-odd minutes each. The first duo, released in 1946, was directed by B. Reeves Eason. *'Neath Canadian Skies* and *North of the Border* starred Hayden and featured Inez Cooper, the Hedy Lamarr lookalike. They featured Douglas Fowley, I. Stanford Jolley, Dick Alexander, and Jack Mulhall, were allegedly based on James Oliver Curwood stories, and they looked looked like one long picture broken up into two short ones—but they were useful on double bills with long main features. A year later, Hayden and Jennifer Holt teamed for *Where the North Begins* and *Trail of the Mounties*, both directed by Howard Bretherton. Supporting casts were different, and the second duo was slightly superior, without breaking any new trails. James Oliver Curwood, who died in 1927, again received credit for the stories.

Curwood took the blame for the original story of *Trail of the Yukon* (William X. Crowley, 1949), first in a new Monogram series about the Mounted Police starring Kirby Grant and the dog, Chinook. It was an inauspicious beginning. Producer Lindsley Parsons provided a good cast: Suzanne Dalbert, Iris Adrian, Bill Edwards, Tony Warde, Dan Seymour, Jay Silverheels and more; Grant already had Western experience at Universal, and before that as an up-and-coming leading man (Robert Stanton). But as a director, Crowley was a good scriptwriter, and his scripts weren't anything to cause rejoicing. The show poked along through a long 67 minutes, the outlook was bleak, but Parsons persisted, and *The Wolf Hunters* soon followed. Oscar (Budd) Boetticher directed, players included Jan Clayton, Edward Norris, Charles Lang and Helen Parrish (husband and wife offscreen at the time). Dullsville, with a dirgelike pace and all that nice talent hanging

Kirby Grant poses against an obvious studio backdrop in this shot for The Wolf Hunters *(1949).*

Anthony Warde takes it on the chin from Russell Hayden in North of the Border *(1946).*

around with little to do. Two mountie misses in 1949 for Parsons.

Frank McDonald, who had done well years before with *Death Goes North,* directed both the 1950 Kirby Grants. *Snow Dog* was indifferent, except for the by now customary good cast, Elena Verdugo, Rick Vallin, Richard Avonde, Milburn Stone, Duke York, Richard Karlan. But *Call of the Klondike* had a better script by Charles Lang, who had appeared in *The Wolf Hunters,* all about a lost gold mine, and players like Anne Gwynne, Lynne Roberts, Tom Neal and Russell Simpson to help Grant over the hurdles. McDonald continued on in 1951 with *Yukon Manhunt* and *Northwest Territory,* at least applying a steadying influence on the films, which had turned into acceptable action product. With *Yukon Gold,* in 1952, McDonald left the series, with former assistant Rex Bailey making his directorial debut with *Fangs of the Arctic* (1953), which showed broad signs of being shot on pocket money; dim lighting, rickety sets, weak cast support. Bailey's second chance was *Northern Patrol* (1953), considerably better with a script by actor-writer Warren Douglas handicrafted to hold the interest. The series ended and Grant became "Sky King" on TV. The series had outlasted Monogram, for the company had become Allied Artists before the finale.

Duncan Renaldo as The Cisco Kid

17 TRAILS SOUTH

Once past the original movies, there's not a great deal of satisfaction to be found in the adventures of the Cisco Kid and Zorro, although the latter was adapted into a dashing action character for some vintage Republic serials. Both characters stemmed from the pens of popular American writers. O. Henry (William Sydney Porter) has come to be regarded as the master of the short story with a surprise twist—Porter had hoped to write a large-scale novel but never did, and everything that remains in print of his is complete within a few pages. Many of his short stories have earned a secure place in the realm of American literary achievements. On the other hand, Johnston McCulley was a hack writer with no pretensions other than to write adventure yarns steadily and successfully. The character of Zorro was not his sole creation. He wrote innumerable other stories and novels, of all types ranging from the detective and mystery, to the straight Western. One of the best Hopalong Cassidys, *Doomed Caravan*, was co-scripted by McCulley.

Porter's one story about the Cisco Kid is "The Caballero's Way," which first appeared in book form in the collection titled *Heart of the West*. It is no secret, since the book and collections of O. Henry works are numerous, but overlooked is the fact that, according to Porter's description of him, Cisco is not what the movies would have us believe about him— he's a *Yanqui*, name of Goodall. The Latin characterization originated with Warner Baxter's portrayal, and has remained unchanged in films. "The Caballero's Way" is about a Texas Ranger plot to catch the elusive Cisco, who has killed six men in fair fights and murdered twice that number ("mostly Mexicans," says the author). His girl friend is persuaded to trap him, but the Kid double-crosses the double-crosser and escapes.

Using the basis of Porter's story, Fox produced *In Old Arizona*, released early in 1929, and widely advertised as the first all-talking outdoor show. Raoul Walsh was to have starred and directed, but an accident which cost Walsh one of his eyes forced him to relinquish the role to Warner Baxter, who would win an Academy Award for his portrayal. Irving Cummings co-directed with Walsh. Edmund Lowe played Cisco's pursuer, the part altered to make him an Army man, and Dorothy Burgess was the treacherous paramour.

Baxter's success with the revised Cisco Kid character stuck with him. In 1930, Fox cast him as *The Arizona Kid*, under Alfred Santell's direction. The role was a carbon copy of the Cisco Kid, and proved popular with moviegoers. The following year he returned as *The Cisco Kid* (Irving Cummings, 1931), with Lowe also repeating his portrayal. It was a throwaway production running a bare hour and made little impression.

Cisco lay dormant until 1939, when Darryl Zanuck dusted him off, inveigled Warner Baxter to assume the flamboyant regalia and personality he had created, had Milton Sperling write a suitable script, assigned Kenneth MacGowan to produce,

Warner Baxter and Carole Lombard warm up while Theodore von Eltz steams in The Arizona Kid *(1930).*

Herbert I. Leeds to direct, and out came *The Return of the Cisco Kid*. Baxter's impression of the good-bad man with tabasco flavoring was still valid, and he was given two cronies, played by Cesar Romero and Chris-Pin Martin, who added some laughs. The story was one of those reformation things, with Baxter falling for the lovely lady (Lynn Bari) who loves another (Kane Richmond), attempting to rid himself of the competition by sending him into a fatal trap but changing his mind at the last minute, reuniting the lovers and riding off philosophically to more adventures. It was a "B" film with "A" pretensions, and received preferred playing time in theaters.

Series-prone 20th Century-Fox, aware of the encouraging success of the Baxter film, placed Cisco Kid adventures on its regular schedule under the supervision of Sol Wurtzel, keeper of its "Bs". Cesar Romero, who had played a Cisco sidekick, was promoted to impersonate the devil-may-care bandito, and Chris-Pin Martin was retained as a comedy companion. Romero and Martin ground out six of these Cisco sagas, beginning with *The Cisco Kid and the Lady* (Leeds, 1939). Marked similarities with the first one: Cisco still mooned over a pretty gal (Marjorie Weaver) who loved another (George Montgomery); Robert Barrat played a crooked sheriff in the previous film, and played a crook after a gold mine here. Into the chili pot was tossed an extra heart interest for Cisco, the more hardened type (Virginia Field) for spice; and an orphaned baby angle for gurgles. Well made in the approved Fox manner, it satisfied neighborhood and mid-week audiences, but Western fans registered complaints about the placidity of movement and too much trivial (to them) pondering over romantic details. This was to be the chief drawback in the remainder of the Romeros.

Second for Romero, *Viva Cisco Kid* (Norman Foster, 1940), displeased the reviewers, drawing the worst set of notices of any Cisco Kid picture, yet it was closer to the tastes of Western fans, containing more true Western trimmings and less time out for amours. The Kid tracked down a band of robbers, with some very nice, eye-catching outdoor scenery photographed by Charles Clarke. However, *Lucky Cisco Kid* (H. Bruce Humberstone, 1940) was right back in the mushy groove, with Romero trying to woo two damsels, the sweet widow (Evelyn Venable) and the tough dance-hall girl (Mary Beth Hughes). The big switch this time is that the dance-hall girl is the one who loves another (Dana Andrews), with Cisco generously bowing out. Almost as an afterthought, the plot has to do with the Kid against some land-grabbers.

Cutting production costs a bit, Fox came up with the best Cisco in the series with *The Gay Caballero* (Otto Brower, 1940). Brower was a director at home with the more vigorous approach to the Western, so the film was pared down to a brisk 57 minutes. There was nothing new about the plot—no goods (Janet Beecher and Edmund MacDonald) trying to cheat a girl (Sheila Ryan) out of some land—but the way Brower sent it humming through the course made it seem better. In the off-and-on pattern, *Romance of the Rio Grande* (Leeds, 1941) looked richer and moved slower. Romero had a dual role, also impersonating a languid fop in a plot that crossed purposes with Zorro. Patricia Morison and Ricardo Cortez were the schemers, Lynne Roberts the fair one. Last in the series, *Ride On Vaquero* (Leeds, 1941) had Cisco on the trail of kidnappers. Two gals, Mary Beth Hughes and Lynne Roberts, plus Joan Woodbury in for a bit.

Ever since his Renfrew series ended, Phil Krasne had been busy with several projects, one of them a continuation of the Charlie Chan mysteries once made by Fox. Now Krasne fell heir to a second Fox series and revived the Cisco Kids for Monogram release. Duncan Renaldo was signed for the role, with Martin Garralaga as his sidekick. The Cisco character was now a few light years away from the O. Henry original, and Krasne's productions were a long distance from the solid look of 20th Century-Fox. Actually it was a blessing in disguise, for the low budgets moved the films closer to the traditional Western. But that is grasping for straws. Renaldo's trio for Monogram were no world beaters. *The Cisco Kid Returns* (J. P. McCarthy, 1945) had him once again protecting an orphaned child, and pinning some crimes on a smoothie (Roger Pryor). *In Old New Mexico* (Phil Rosen, 1945) concerned a nurse (Gwen Kenyon) falsely accused of murder, with Cisco set to clear her. *South of the Rio Grande* (Lambert Hillyer, 1945) saw the Kid mete out justice to crooked military policia. Main trouble with the productions was that they looked about ten years older than they were, even the photography having a sort of mildewed look. But the Ciscos had a following, and Monogram was not about to forfeit their worth.

Scott R. Dunlap took over the production reins of the Cisco Kids, which was about as high as one could go at the studio then. Dunlap attended to four more Ciscos, replacing Renaldo with Gilbert Roland and assigning William Nigh to direct each entry. Oddly, Martin Garralaga, former Cisco companero, was a member of the regular cast, but no longer a sidekick. He played a different part each time, including some villainy. Cisco rode alone in the first, *The Gay Cavalier* (1946), saving the ranch owner (Garralaga) from a gang in familiar style. Roland indulged in some Zorro-type swordplay with chief heavy Tristram Coffin for a climax more exciting than usual, but aside from Roland's welcome charm there was little else to merit comment. Frank Yaconelli joined Roland for *South of Monterey* (1946) to thwart more crooked officials, including Martin Garralaga and the ace nasty Harry Woods. It moved fairly well. On the credits of *Beauty and the Bandit* (1946), Roland was listed for "additional dialogue," and it was a simple matter to spot the scenes. Everything stopped while Roland would declaim lyrically about the beauty of women, or nature, or both, or some such flowery verbiage. It didn't harm the films because Roland was so adept at dispensing the Latin charm and was so obviously having a good time with his role. Roland revived the swordsmanship for the conclusion of *Riding the California Trail* (1947), otherwise accepting the same Cisco plot gracefully and with little undue commotion.

Roland's last two outings as the Cisco Kid were produced by Jeffrey Bernard and directed by Christy Cabanne, both of whom had been active for the same lengthy spell as had Dunlap and Nigh. *Robin Hood of Monterey* (1947) was slight but short and swift at 56 minutes, and had dependable skulduggery engaged in by venerables Jack La Rue and Evelyn Brent. Chris-Pin Martin also rejoined the Ciscos for the first time since the 20th-Fox series as Roland's portly companion. The final time for Roland as Cisco came in *King of the Bandits* (1947), with Roland bringing a Cisco impersonator to justice. The girl involved was Angela Greene, one of the more photogenic sights of the year.

Phil Krasne recovered the rights to the Cisco Kid properties, and began producing them for United Artists release. Duncan Renaldo returned to the saddle and was credited as associate producer as well. Joining Renaldo was the popular Leo Carrillo as saddlemate. The new Ciscos were light on action as usual, and Renaldo didn't have Roland's poetic touch; but there were worse Westerns on the market. Supporting casts were good, and Albert Glasser

HOLLYWOOD CORRAL: A COMPREHENSIVE B WESTERN ROUNDUP

Renaldo in The Cisco Kid Returns *(1945), his first appearance in the famous characterization.*

composed some appropriate background music for the series. Wallace Fox directed *The Valiant Hombre* (1948), *The Gay Amigo* (1949) and *The Daring Caballero* (1949); *Satan's Cradle* (1949) was directed by Ford Beebe, and *The Girl from San Lorenzo* (1950) by Derwin Abrahams. The features made no great impression on the ledgers, but Krasne and Renaldo wisely moved their operation to TV. From 1951 to 1956, over 150 half-hour Ciscos were filmed with Renaldo and Carrillo. With foresight, the TV programs were shot in color, making them valuable when the tints became fashionable on television some years later.

Since the Cisco Kid was a unique and identifiable character, few imitators dared challenge him. Besides, the literary rights were securely, legally bound. A distant relative could be claimed in *The Llano Kid* (Edward D. Venturini, 1939), with Tito Guizar playing a bandit who poses as a lost heir—the story source is "A Double-Eyed Deceiver," by O. Henry. It had been filmed previously with Gary Cooper. The Guizar version was produced by Harry Sherman as a respite from his Hopalong Cassidy chores and was pleasant, with the star well supported by Gale Sondergaard, Alan Mowbray and Chris-Pin Martin. RKO sidekick Richard Martin starred in the Comet (Mary Pickford-Buddy Rogers) production of *The Adventures of Don Coyote* (Reginald Le Borg, 1947), as a Cisco-type caballero. It was photogrpahed in glorious(?) Cinecolor and was innocuously adequate, with more physical action than in most Cisco Kid films.

Zorro on the other hand was a free and easy character to fun around with. He appeared in McCulley's story "The Curse of Capistrano," then was adapted to fit Douglas Fairbanks for one of his biggest successes to date in *The Mark of Zorro* (Fred Niblo, 1920). Five years later, Fairbanks became the son of Zorro, *Don Q* (Donald Crisp, 1925), and Tyrone Power revived the original swashbuckler for the sound era in *The Mark of Zorro* (Rouben Mamoulian, 1940). The idea of an avenger posing as an effete aristocrat while masquerading as a daredevil righter of wrongs by night was appealing, the Old California setting colorful, and in the Fairbanks original the star's acrobatics and genial joshing of the story set the trend.

Each of the above films were class "A" productions, made with care. The low-budget Zorros were done by Republic starting in 1936, when Wells Root wrote and directed *The Bold Caballero*, starring Robert Livingston in the role. The plot conformed to pattern, Zorro working undercover to foil the villainous machinations of the Spanish oppressors. It was all minor, but enacted with a certain amount of verve by Livingston and the cast. Republic's color experimentation was a further asset. Livingston had just come off a serial wherein he played a role close in spirit with Zorro, called "The Eagle." *The Vigilantes Are Coming* (Mack V. Wright & Ray Taylor, 1936) might have been a warmup for Zorro.

Republic, once having employed the character of Zorro, held on to him with bulldog tenacity. The ace serial directing team of William Witney and John English collaborated for the first time on *Zorro Rides Again* (1937), with John Carroll doing the derring-do (as Zorro's great-grandson). Playing his aide was Duncan Renaldo, the future Cisco Kid, whose character identification was, inventively enough, "Renaldo." Republic was just starting to polish their chapter plays, and the Zorro serial was fast and furious, with Carroll giving a good account of himself, even getting a chance to sing briefly. Over 20 years later, the near-defunct Republic would assemble a feature-length version of *Zorro Rides Again,* and it played well at 67 minutes minus the usual gaps and jerky continuity found in most feature versions of serials.

An even better serial was *Zorro's Fighting Legion* (Witney and English, 1939), with Reed Hadley assuming the mask. It had everything to make the kiddie hearts palpitate—assorted action including swordplay, fast and often; a mystery villain, "Don

Chris-Pin Martin (l.), Gilbert Roland and Travis Kent in Robin Hood of Monterey *(1947)*.

Del Oro," in the true Republic tradition; and a stalwart and believable hero in Hadley. Production work was excellent, especially the score by William Lava and Reggie Lanning's photography, giving the film a rich look.

A few years passed before Republic cashed in on the Zorro name again, by which time 20th-Fox had made the Tyrone Power version. The relationship of Zorro to *Zorro's Black Whip* (Spencer Bennet & Wallace Grissell, 1944) is indeed tenuous. Linda Stirling does the female avenger routine and poses as "The Whip," but the Zorro connection is restricted mainly to the title. Stirling was good to look at and energetic in her action escapades. Normally a villain, George J. Lewis took care of the masculine heroics convincingly. In 1946, Adrian Booth, formerly Lorna Gray, was the *Daughter of Don Q* (Spencer Bennet & Fred Brannon, 1946), but that was as far as it went—the serial was a modern-day one, and not a particularly accomplished one either. Republic came right back with *Son of Zorro* (Bennet & Brannon, 1947), with George Turner in the title role, and *Ghost of Zorro* (Fred C. Brannon, 1949), with Clayton Moore in his pre-TV "Lone Ranger" days. Serial production was on the downgrade by this time, and the tacky trend was evident in both chapter-plays.

Retiring Zorro, Republic kept his spirit alive in two more serials, both making plentiful use of stock footage. *Don Daredevil Rides Again* (Brannon, 1951) had Ken Curtis donning the duds of Don Daredevil, his grandfather, and *Man with the Steel Whip* (Franklin Adreon, 1954) starred Dick Simmons and a lot of familiar footage from previous Republic Zorro serials.

Walt Disney revived Zorro for TV with Guy Williams in the role. The gentle Disney touch and the restrictions of children's TV shows made the TV series quite bland, but the Disney magic worked again and the weekly adventures were popular. Guy Williams played Zorro in likeable fashion, and Henry Calvin gained fans in his serio-comic role of

HOLLYWOOD CORRAL: A COMPREHENSIVE B WESTERN ROUNDUP

Yakima Canutt (doubling John Carroll) throttles Dick Alexander in Zorro Rides Again *(1937).*

Linda Stirling and George J. Lewis in Zorro's Black Whip *(1944).*

Sergeant Garcia, continually thwarted by Zorro. Some of the later episodes picked up steam, since they were directed by William Witney, but the mild, early ones garnered most of the attention. Several of these were edited into a feature and released by Disney's Buena Vista company as *The Sign of Zorro* (Norman Foster, Lewis R. Foster, 1960).

Of the Zorro-type imitations, two deserve quick mention. A mediocre swashbuckler *Don Ricardo Returns* (T. O. Morse, 1946) is of interest not for its hackneyed plot, about an attempt to regain an estate, but for the fact that the original story is by Johnston McCulley, and is "Zorro" minus the masked disguise. Also, the screenplay was co-authored by the associate producer, one Renault Duncan—or Duncan Renaldo, if you prefer. Fred Coby received top billing as the Don Ricardo of the title.

Lippert Pictures released *Bandit Queen* (William Berke, 1950), about a femme masked avenger in the Old California days. Barbara Britton took the role. From a slim idea of McCulley's, a family tree of adventurers had sprouted.

Allan Lane in his pre-Rocky days at Republic.

18 SAGEBRUSH EMPIRE

Of those who love Westerns undemandingly, most if not all pride the product of Republic Pictures highly, and not a few to a state approaching exaltation. Republic Westerns came to mean a lot of things to the Western buff, not to be found in Westerns of other companies—or if found, then in an imitative and inferior state. To their mind, Republic looked better, sounded better and were better than any comparable horse operas.

The argument used to expound this theory consists mainly of a parade of names, technicians and actors contributing to their craft, combining to make Republic's product top. The informed Republic aficionado if pressed would recite an honor roll, to wit: photographers Jack Marta, William Bradford, Ernest Miller, William Nobles (through 1941), Reggie Lanning, Bud Thackery, John MacBurnie—splendid cameramen all, giving sight values to the stories beyond compare; music supervisors Harry Grey, Alberto Columbo, William Lava, Cy Feuer, Raoul Kraushaar, Mort Glickman, Nathan Scott, Joseph Dubin, Stanley Wilson, Richard Cherwin, Dale Butts—masters of an art lost to modern audiences, that of using agitatos and sweeping themes without having it sound corny, with full orchestra (Republic had a good one, 40 fine musicians), sweating over the right notes for a serial or Western with the same care they would take with an epic; directors Joseph Kane, George Sherman, Mack Wright, Howard Bretherton, Spencer Bennet, Lesley Selander, William Witney, John English, Fred Brannon, R. G. Springsteen, Philip Ford, Thomas Carr, George Blair, Harry Keller—they knew their action, but they also knew actors and scripts, and would often get some rather amazing results when the signs were right; a special reservation for Yakima Canutt, who contributed from both sides of the camera, as an actor, stuntman, then stunt arranger and eventually director, who is the major reason why Republic Westerns run off as enjoyably as they do; Canutt's cohorts, David Sharpe, Ed Parker, Dale Van Sickel, Fred Graham, Tom Steele, Bud Wolfe, Ken Terrell, Duke Greene, Joe Yrigoyen and numerous others, who made the fistic and equine fancy work of a caliber untouched before or since—their stunt work was invariably breathtaking, and more than that plausible; steering villainy by Roy Barcroft, the all-time Big Ugly, and Bud Geary, Kenne Duncan and the legion of crooks and henchmen, who made their dirty deeds even more intriguing when at Republic because they were instructed to lace the larceny with leavening humor, making them as likeable as the assigned heroes, sometimes more so; and the heroes themselves....

Republic had hit it with Gene Autry, then Roy Rogers. They had developed the Three Mesquiteers idea into a playable and popular series, all in the first few years of their existence. In 1940, the studio began to introduce new Western names, and for 15 years thereafter showered the public with a string of minor but extremely adept second-echelon cowboy stars, worthies all.

211

Noah Beery and Don "Red" Barry in The Tulsa Kid *(1940).*

First of the new arrivals was Donald Barry, making it on pure merit. Barry hailed from Texas and was stage-trained. He had been in movies since 1933 but had made no discernible dent in the door to stardom until six years later, when he gave a performance as a sympathetic lawbreaker playing the title role in *Wyoming Outlaw,* a Three Mesquiteers adventure. Republic officials looked and approved, and Barry was shoved into a potboiler about a hoodlum who joins the Marines and turns the tables on foreign agents. The film was no better than the bare outline, but Barry again showed he had something. He was given further seasoning in two of Joe Kane's Roy Rogers Westerns, as a semi-baddie in *Saga of Death Valley* (reformed in time to stop a slug) and as the legendary outlaw in *Days of Jesse James.*

Barry projected a quiet menace, with his smallish stature by screen standards and his hushed, pleasingly raspy voice. He had the attributes for a cowboy lead, but if it did happen, he would definitely be apart from the traditional stalwart, true-blue hero. It happened, not only garnering his own series but a fancy serial introduction at the same time. Republic had purchased the rights to a popular comic strip, "Red Ryder," and hoped to continue its success experienced with *The Lone Ranger* and other sources from the funny papers. *Adventures of Red Ryder* (Witney & English, 1940) was produced in 12 chapters and released starting June 15, by which time Barry had had a couple of feature Westerns under his gunbelt. The serial and the new series complemented Barry and insured his chances of catching on with the trade. To keep the connotation in the memory, Republic soon began to bill him as Don "Red" Barry, which reportedly didn't please Barry one whit. His hair was brown, and the association forced him to sport a hairpiece in his films. The divot was uncomfortable, and it was noticeable, but Barry withstood the indignity.

Production supervision on the Barrys was handed

to George Sherman, late of the Three Mesquiteers directorial achievements, and who had steered Barry through *Wyoming Outlaw*. Sherman produced 18 Barrys in a row, directed 17 of them, with Nate Watt doing the honors for Barry #4, *Frontier Vengeance* (1940), a lesser entry. An old hand on the Republic range by now, Sherman fit into his new position as producer snugly, while his direction continued to be potent so long as the scripts were right. More often than not they were, and the Barrys rapidly became preferred fare on the Western market. After a couple of shaky starts, the Barry series hit stride with *The Tulsa Kid* (1940), highlighted by lovable old Noah Beery's portrayal of a gunfighter, together with a suspenseful climax, with Beery and Barry shooting it out. *Texas Terrors* (1940) and *Wyoming Wildcat* (1941) upheld the good work by Barry, while in something like *The Phantom Cowboy* (1941) Barry could still come out ahead, although he and Sherman were inhibited by a script that failed to allow for much movement. The weakest aspect of Republic Westerns during the period were the screenplays, not only for Barry but the rest of the Western series as well. Considering the strange manner of scenarios heaped upon the Mesquiteers, Gene Autry and, to a lesser extent, Roy Rogers, it becomes evident that Barry escaped relatively unscathed.

Barry's menacing mien contributed effectively to his success. He could come closer to the shady side of the law and get away with it, adding an extra dimension. One critic aptly described him as a sort of "cowboy Cagney." Typical of his plots is *Two-Gun Sheriff* (1941), with Barry in the dual role of a sheriff and his outlaw brother. The sheriff is held prisoner while his brother impersonates him, seeing the light in the nick of time. He poses as an outlaw in *Arizona Terrors* (1942), but only to get the goods on the gang. A novel plot twist new to West-

Roy Barcroft and Don "Red" Barry flank Helen Talbot in this scene from Canyon City *(1944).*

erns was gainfully employed here, with the only man knowing the truth about Barry's undercover work being President McKinley—who's assassinated, leaving Barry in a tight predicament with no way of proving his identity.

Sherman's good work on the Barry series earned him a promotion, and he was upped to programmers. Eddy White replaced him as producer, and his first effort was directed by William Witney. Witney started off *Outlaws of Pine Ridge* (1942) in inimitable fashion, with a barroom shooting scrape—from there on, things got rough. This rousing opener set the tone of Barry's 1942–43 season under White. *Dead Man's Gulch* (1943) had a good plot by Norman S. Hall about an ex-Pony Express rider gone wrong, benefitting from the direction of John English, equal parts action and austere mood. Oldtimer Elmer Clifton, at Republic briefly and doing some of his best sound work there, chipped in with a couple of good ones, especially *Days of Old Cheyenne* (1943), the latter with some neat touches, as when Barry, after gunning down William Haade in a bar, walks slowly out, and Clifton has the camera pan down to the spent shells on the floor.

Fugitive from Sonora (Howard Bretherton, 1943) gave Barry a comedy sidekick of durability in Wally Vernon. Heretofore, Barry had enjoyed the companionship of Dub Taylor, Emmett Lynn and Al St. John at various times—he had even been given the dubious musical pleasure of Jimmy Wakely's tunesmiths, but Sherman put the clamper on that before long, with Barry remaining musically unfettered. St. John was funny as usual, even coming close to stealing *Jesse James Jr.* (Sherman, 1942). But Barry was better when sticking to his guns sans comic relief until Vernon entered. A vaude and nitery comic, Vernon was ridiculously out of place anywhere West of Loew's Newark and his comedy approach was strictly metropolitan. Nevertheless, he teamed well with Barry. His clowning was broad enough for the kiddies, and upon occasion he'd sneak in a grownup yock, ad lib or otherwise. Like all good comedians, Vernon had the stuff of good acting in him. It showed once, in *Black Hills Express* (1943), helped along by the understanding John English. It was only a bit, as Vernon and Barry contemplate what to do about the victims of a stagecoach massacre, but Vernon carried it off poignantly. The film itself is a contender for the position of the top-rated Don "Red" Barry Western, with a fine script by Norman Hall and Fred Myton, English's direction, and action in the Barry manner.

A mistake was then committed. Barry and Vernon were beset with a third regular, horror of horrors, a tyke, female, named Twinkle Watts, tiny, blonde, precocious, blech. Little Miss Watts had received some publicity via her prowess with ice skates and a bowling ball, though not at the same time. Such versatility brought ideas of another Shirley Temple to the minds of Republic execs, and Barry drew the short straw. The kid may have belonged in the movies, but she didn't belong in Don "Red" Barry Westerns, slowing the pace and gumming up the works in general. Four of these, and the Barry series was kaput. Not that it was her fault. Barry had wanted out for a time, having been treated to leads in a few Republic non-Westerns and seeing his future as a rosier one without any saddlesores. In slightly over four years, he had climbed steadily to a lofty position, largely through his own abilities, and would be missed.

With appreciably more fanfare than usual, Republic heralded the hunt for a new cowboy star in 1943. The plans, admittedly somewhat nebulous, were to build a character named "John Paul Revere" into a Western series to be reckoned with, something that hadn't been done, in a fictional sense, by any studio for some time. After the required amount of suspenseful waiting, it was announced that the role would be filled by Eddie Dew, an actor who had been seen in several Westerns on the lawbreaking side. Dew was tall and cleft-chinned and looked a bit like Fred MacMurray. He could ride, and speak his lines with some conviction. So far, so good. For

Don "Red" Barry and "Cyclone."

laughs, Dew was partnered with Smiley Burnette, a plus in that Burnette was well known from the Autrys and could bolster the marquee until Dew became firmly established. Only it did not work out that way. The first John Paul Revere production was *Beyond the Last Frontier* (Howard Bretherton, 1943), and it missed the mark by a wide margin. John K. Butler and Norton Grant wrote an involved, slow-moving script that did not provide for enough vigorous action. Dew was hamstrung by the cumbersome screenplay, and to add insult to injury, a supporting character, a good-bad type, attracted more notice than did the new star. The role was played by the intriguingly odd-looking Bob Mitchum, he of the Hopalong Cassidy heavies. The weak start of the series was not alleviated by the second entry, *Raiders of Sunset Pass* (John English, 1943), which tried the idea of using cowgirls to round up the dogies during the World War II manpower shortage. All it was, was an idea; not strong enough to build a Western upon, especially one in a series that needed all the help it could get. During the general, inevitable dissatisfaction ensuing, Dew left the series and landed at Universal. Called back was Bob Livingston, with Burnette in place as comedy relief.

Livingston hung around for a trio of features, still weakly palmed off as "John Paul Revere" productions, but the once-great expectations were all but vanished. In contrast to what had preceded, the Livingstons were good. In fact, one was exceptionally good, making one wish for more Livingstons, which was not to be. First was *Pride of the Plains* (Wallace W. Fox, 1944), with producer Louis Gray saving the bankroll by using some stock footage of wild horses seen before. But Livingston was still a manly and believable hero, and the John K. Butler-Bob Williams script was delightfully written, with even a minor romantic tangent deftly handled by Nancy Gay and Stephen Barclay with the aid of good, natural dialogue. *Beneath Western Skies* (Spencer Bennet, 1944) used the amnesia gimmick Livingston brought over with him from PRC, and to his credit it can be said that he found at least two different ways of playing a man with a loss of memory. Here, he gave it the full treatment, complete with dazed look, nodding head and mumbled dialogue; at PRC, he simply stated "Nah, I can't remember." The final Livingston, *The Laramie Trail* (1944), was directed by John English and adapted by J. Benton Cheney from a novel by Jackson Gregory, "Mystery at Spanish Hacienda." Adaptations were the exception at Republic, writers usually doing what passed for originals. English got a lot of brooding atmosphere into the film, making it an off-beat Western in plot and treatment. Even Bud Thackery's photography had a low-keyed, almost grayish cast which enhanced the goings-on considerably. With all the atmospherics, there was still a plentitude of the expected Western action. Unnoticed at the time, *The Laramie Trail* merits a minor but deserved position on Republic's roster of preferred Westerns.

Livingston was promoted to civilian features, and Republic presented a new cowboy star. His name was Sunset Carson, but had been Michael Harrison when featured in Frank Borzage's star-studded *Stage Door Canteen* (1943) as a drawling soldier. Harrison-Carson came by the drawl naturally, and could claim credentials of impressive authenticity as an honest-to-gosh cowboy. He had won some honors at rodeos and was, said his publicity, named "Champion Cowboy of South America." He could snap a bullwhip with authority, although this facet of his accomplishments was played down in the movies. He was very young, very tall, had a baby face that the girls immediately cottoned to, and spoke slower than John Wayne, which was slow indeed, in a rather high-pitched voice. He also had to take second billing to Smiley Burnette, perhaps the first and only time in Western cinema history that a comic won the ace spot and the hero was second banana. *Call of the Rockies* (1944) got Carson off to a flying start, with director Lesley Selander going all out on the action. Carson showed that, if nothing else, he could put up a great brawl, and could take it

Sunset Carson in Sheriff of Cimarron *(1945).*

HOLLYWOOD CORRAL: A COMPREHENSIVE B WESTERN ROUNDUP

Sunset rescues Peggy Stewart in Alias Billy the Kid *(1946).*

as well as dish it out—when he fell prone after being waylaid, the thud shook the theater. Burnette received prominent attention, befitting his top position on the credits. But you can't star a comic without ladling the activity elsewhere, and Carson was getting his share and doing well by it. The scripters even gave Burnette a dual role in *Firebrands of Arizona* (Selander, 1944), but Smiley wasn't fooling anybody with a villainous portrayal. After four with Carson, the big lad was established, and Burnette wandered away from Republic to join Starrett at Columbia.

Now that he was on his own without the Burnette name, Carson made strides as an action star, emphasis on action—his action accomplishments consisted mainly of a likeable smile and boyish mobility. His first solo effort, *Sheriff of Cimarron* (1945) was also the feature directorial debut of Yakima Canutt, after a goodly amount of staging second-unit action sequences. Canutt did well, Carson did well, and Western fans were pleased. Carson received another new director in Thomas Carr for his next, *Santa Fe Saddlemates* (1945). Republic freaks would have voted Carr a special Oscar for it, had they the power—he began with three, count 'em three, fistic encounters, with Carson clobbering everybody in sight. With several more sessions of mayhem tossed in before the end, including one indulged in by heroine Linda Stirling, it was the fightin'est horse opera seen for many a moon. Carr directed Carson for the rest of his stay at Republic, ten more films, with writer Bennett Cohen serving as producer. *Oregon Trail* (1945) had some inside interest because it featured Mary Carr, of the silents; she was Thomas Carr's mother. The director also cleverly worked in a confrontation between Carson and meanie Kenne Duncan that was used by Edwin L. Marin with John Wayne and Harry Woods in *Tall in the Saddle* the previous year. It was effective, albeit familiar even to those with short memories. News was made in *The Cherokee Flash* (1945) when Carr gave Roy Barcroft a sympathetic role, after God knows how many varmints he had played so tellingly. In fact, Barcroft portrayed Carson's father, a reformation of towering consequence. Added to this miracle was the fact that another former nasty, Tom London, was hired as Carson's comedy sidekick. The last Carson for Republic was *Rio Grande Raiders* (1946), which had Bob Steele in the cast but too many stock shots, tipping off the unavoidable hint that the Carsons were about to end.

Right here, a word about Republic Western serials. In addition to those already mentioned, those of note included *The Painted Stallion* (William Witney, Alan James and Ray Taylor, 1937), with Ray Corrigan and Hoot Gibson starred; and *King of the Texas Rangers* (Witney and English, 1941), with football star Sammy Baugh in a first and last bid for

Sunset and grizzled Tom London shoot it out in Days of Buffalo Bill *(1946).*

Western fame. Baugh's thespic talents remain open to question, but the merits of the serial are unquestioned, a dozen exciting chapters of modern outdoor action in the Republic approved style, with excellent production values and a good cast of Neil Hamilton, Duncan Renaldo, lovely Pauline Moore, Roy Barcroft, Herbert Rawlinson, Monte Blue (chapter one only), Kermit Maynard and many others. Later Republic serials, the postwar ones, were not up to par, including three whitewashing the studio's favorite outlaws, Jesse and Frank James, and another, *Desperadoes of the West* (Fred C. Brannon, 1950) starring Tom Keene (now Richard Powers) and using library footage aplenty. Said footage derived largely from a 1943 serial, *Daredevils of the West,* directed by John English, and starring Allan Lane, already having seen serial service in the mounties. Now familiar through these serials, Lane was given a feature Western series of his own.

Lane's series actually replaced Don "Red" Barry. Indeed, Lane seemed to have inherited Barry's wearing apparel as well as his leftover scripts, at least for the first two entries. He also had Wally Vernon for a sidekick, which was okay, and Twinkle Watts for tot appeal, which was not okay. *Silver City Kid* (English, 1944) got the series a-flying, but Vernon left after the next one. Max Terhune and Duncan Renaldo were in the third, *Sheriff of Sundown* (Selander, 1944), making a pseudo-Mesquiteers combination. Most interesting of Lane's opening six was *Corpus Christi Bandits* (Wallace A. Grissell, 1945). Western fans must have been shocked, because for the first reel or so it was a war romance, with Lane in uniform as a returned bomber pilot. Eventually, Lane tells his kid sister (Watts) the story of their grandfather, Corpus Christi Jim, and the film thereupon flashes back to two-gun times. The idea was done that same year for Roy Rogers in *Sunset in El Dorado,* but not as well. Although taking Barry's place, Lane was not the same type of actor, being much more restrained and much less resourceful, content to underplay and let the heroics speak for him. Here however, he had a role that called for some display of emotions and gave a strong, entirely convincing performance, both in the modern part and the period section of the screenplay. Norman S. Hall's fine script drew parallels between World War II and Confederate returnees, with Lane forced to become an outlaw when he kills a carpetbagger in self-defense. His gang consisted of Tom London, Kenne Duncan (the latter a rat who doesn't reform, as does Lane) and a quiet, likeable performer named Bob Wilke, in his biggest role to date and who would swell the Republic ranks of villainy for a time before moving on to become a dependable character actor. Of course, the bona fide baddie in the film was the ever-ready Roy Barcroft. Only weak link was the so-so feminine interest represented by Helen Talbot; even Twinkle Watts was restricted to the contemporary sequences, thus not getting in the way. Lane and producer Stephen Auer halted the series after the following *Trail of Kit Carson* (Selander, 1945), a more conventional offering.

Republic's reward for services rendered was promotion to higher efforts, or anyway, a change from cowboy regalia to civilian clothes. Allan Lane was so feted at the end of his six-pack of Westerns. As often happened, the gift was snatched back shortly afterwards, and in 1946 Lane was pressed into service again. Bill Elliott had been doing well with a "Red Ryder" series, and now that Elliott had been given upped budgets in an effort to become another John Wayne, the Ryder series was open, and too valuable a property to let wither. Lane, whose acting style resembled Elliott's repressed emoting, stepped into the character—using the same costuming—and Bobby Blake continued on as his young Indian helper, Little Beaver. Martha Wentworth replaced Alyce Fleming in the third continuing role, as the Duchess.

Seven Red Ryders with Lane were produced by Sidney Picker. All were directed by R. G. Springsteen, all were written by Earle Snell, then in his sixties. Lane's first, *Santa Fe Uprising* (1946) was given the benefit of superior Western casting, with such as Barton MacLane and Jack LaRue in the cast, but was merely ordinary in other respects. Best of the seven was number three, a pleasant and different yarn entitled *Vigilantes of Boomtown* (1947). It had to do with legalizing boxing in Nevada, backgrounded by the impending championship contest between James J. Corbett (George Turner) and Bob Fitzsimmons (John Dehner). Roscoe Karns added luster to the cast as a denizen of the pugilistic world, and Roy Barcroft was there for you-know-what. Snell delivered a good script and Springsteen paced it nicely. Final entry in the series was *Marshal of Cripple Creek* (1947), which indicated that Snell was running dry, Picker wasn't opening the purse strings, the regulars were restless in their roles, and the Red Ryders were about to rove from Republic.

For the 1947–48 season, Lane was right back as if Red Ryder had never happened, this time billed as Allan "Rocky" Lane (and his horse, Black Jack). From 1947 to 1953, Lane traveled the Western route starring for Republic, his films usually being shot in about six days, sometimes less. Liberal portions of

HOLLYWOOD CORRAL: A COMPREHENSIVE B WESTERN ROUNDUP

Tom London (l.) looks puzzled as Allan Lane (holding Peggy Stewart) and young Bobby Blake explained things in the 1947 Red Ryder opus *Rustlers of Devil's Canyon. Emmett Lynn and Pierce Lyden look on.*

library footage were culled from the files to dress the action, so at times Lane would not be called upon to exert himself at all. Despite the economical productions and the rubber-stamp appearance of each release, the "Rocky" Lane series maintained a consistently high standard of entertainment, and considering the budgetary tightness, a surprisingly good physical look. If anything, it was a writer's series, notably the scripts contributed by Bob Williams and/or Richard Wormser. They would have the central plot revolve around the villainy, or some secondary characters—Lane would seldom be the focal point of the narrative, save for an occasional one like *Frontier Investigator* (Fred C. Brannon, 1949), a Bob Williams screenplay about Lane tracking down the murderer of his brother. Mostly, the scripts would set up the situation, into which Lane would ride and proceed to clean up the dirty work. The uniformity extended to the running times; each would run an even 60 minutes, later trimmed down to 54 minutes as television sales in the future made its impact upon later members of the series. The Lanes were so good in contrast to the general Western run of the time, that it becomes difficult to isolate one as a shining example. When seen in order of release, competing with routine Westerns from other companies made on low budgets, their superiority is evident.

One characteristic of the Lane scripts was to make the bad guys, if not likeable at least reasonable. Writers Williams and Wormser also gave them a sense of humor, usually played off against the thick-headedness of one of the gang's underlings. "D'ya think I'm stupid?" asks henchmen Roy Barcroft of leader Gene Stutenroth, as the latter carefully explains a scheme to him. Stutenroth gives him a long look before replying: "I'll reserve my opinion on that," leaving Barcroft with his face hanging out. It happens in *Oklahoma Badlands* (Yakima Canutt, 1948), and so did a lot of slick excitement. *Marshal of Amarillo* (Philip Ford, 1948) began with a spooky mystery plot that would have done justice to a straight whodunit, with Lane's comedy partner Eddy Waller experiencing weird happenings at a gloomy stagecoach halfway house. Waller was a character actor rather than broad clown, and his comedy landed somewhere between George Hayes and Raymond Hatton. Fortunately, it was seldom childish, a fault found with too many comics.

Little touches were incorporated into the series for the enjoyment of the fans. In *Sheriff of Wichita* (R. G. Springsteen, 1949), Lane is required to perform a headlong slide in an effort to escape an adversary. Springsteen set up the camera at ground level, and Lane makes a dive right into the lens. It's most effective, Lane forced to turn his head aside to avoid bumping it on the outer rim. Lane was a footballer (real name Harry Albershaft) in college, and could still manage the fancy physical requirements. Thereafter, he would be called upon to indulge in a skidding slide every other film or so.

Perhaps the Lane that could be chosen as most representative of the bunch is *Powder River Rustlers* (Philip Ford, 1949), with a Richard Wormser script about a kidnapping and extortion plot, with the town tailor (Francis McDonald) behind the skulduggery. Roy Barcroft has some funny lines as a gross henchman, Wormser's script gives the illusion of movement even where none exists, and Lane and Waller are in top form. The climactic struggle between Lane and McDonald is unusually realistic, with McDonald driving a pair of pinking shears into Lane's shoulder; it drew a gasp from the audience.

Minor changes occurred in the series toward the end, with Harry Keller taking over as producer, Chubby Johnson spelling Waller as comedy relief. But the Lanes adhered to the high average right up to the final entry, *El Paso Stampede* (Keller, 1953). There wasn't a weak member of the 38 in the series. And more than any other group of Westerns, its success was accountable to the writing department.

Color came to Republic Westerns in 1946. Actually, the company had tried the tint process in Bob Livingston's Zorro effort, *Bold Caballero*, nearly ten years before. In the interim, most of the non-Technicolor Western features were from the independent ranks. Telco-color had marred a Western with Grant Withers, *Lure of the Wasteland* (Harry Fraser, 1939)—not that color would have improved the blundering narrative. Cinecolor accounted for a pleasant outdoor yarn with John King, *Gentleman from Arizona* (Earl Haley, 1939) and Bob Steele had

Lane, now known as Rocky, takes aim as sidekick Eddy Waller takes cover in The Wild Frontier *(1947).*

starred in *Wildfire* (Robert Tansey, 1945), a formula show with Steele's venerability and the color process of prime concern, plus a welcome appearance by Sterling Holloway as Steele's comedy relief. Eddie Dean then commenced his Cinecolor PRC series, so Republic figured it was about time to join the rainbow, now that World War II was over and the lid was off restrictions on materials.

To star in their new tinted series, Republic chose Monte Hale, a dimpled young man who was a singer, and had appeared in a few studio horse operas of late. Hale's introduction as a lead was ingeniously titled *Home on the Range* (R. G. Springsteen, 1946). He had Adrian Booth, formerly Lorna Gray, as co-star, and Bobby Blake, lately Little Beaver of the Red Ryders, in support. He also had Bob Nolan and the Sons of the Pioneers to back the musical end. The experimental tint process was called Magnacolor and was passable, if garish. But the film itself was mild, despite the fine Republic supporting cast, nor did the second one, *Man from Rainbow Valley* (Springsteen, 1946), show improvement.

Out California Way (Lesley Selander, 1946) ran some 12 minutes longer at 67 minutes and Republic used the guest-star gimmick, with Roy Rogers (and Trigger), Dale Evans, Don Barry and Allan Lane taking brief bows. The color process officially changed its name from Magnacolor to Trucolor,

Rocky wrestles a gun from stuntman Ted Mapes in The Wild Frontier *(1947).*

though the quality remained with plenty of room for improvement. With a movie studio background and its not very villainous villainy, it looked more like a Gene Autry opus. By now, execs were faced with the fact that, if the Hales were to succeed, they needed to be tailored to his personality and not, as with the first few, stories and formats better suited to the recently departed Gene Autry. Nevertheless, Hale lasted through five more color Westerns, the final few paced toward the action market and the musical and non-rousing Western aspects played down.

Hale then starred in 11 black-and-white features and, as fate would have it, these were better than the color ones. They were not so pretentious and were helped by the better Republic scripting efforts more suitable to Monte's pleasing personality and aided with the addition of the traditionally expert studio-style action. His vocal efforts were similarly downplayed, then dispensed with.

Two of the later Hales merit comment, both forcefully directed by Philip Ford. *Pioneer Marshal* (1949) had some new wrinkles on the old dodge of having Hale pose as a desperado in order to trap the gang. Chief heavy was nicely delineated by Damian O'Flynn, and there was an offbeat version of the traditional suspense-filled gun duel at the end. *The Vanishing Westerner* (1950) has a really involved, intricate plot with a meaty role for Arthur Space as a new kind of villain. Both of the above were written by the lot's ace, Bob Williams. The Hales were good, and the star had top support, including sidekick Paul Hurst. But Hale failed to make a lasting impression; his personality was too bland, or at least not forceful enough to assume command. So the series was phased out, but in retrospect neither Hale, producer Melville Tucker nor those associated with the series had anything of which to be ashamed.

Rex Allen came along late in the Western cycle, but early enough to catch on with the fans and enjoy a fair stint. His first starring feature was *The Arizona Cowboy* (R. G. Springsteen, 1950), the tag by which he became known. He could sing, actually hailed from Arizona, could drawl through a role with ease, and generally created a pleasant impression. After a few mild entries under his belt his films began to mesh, with Bob Williams once again contributing some shrewd writing jobs. Both *Under Mexicali Stars* (George Blair, 1950) and *Silver City*

SAGEBRUSH EMPIRE

Monte Hale, one of Republic's postwar Western stars.

Hale selecting a new chapeau, with the help of Nudie, the famous Hollywood tailor to the cowboys.

Bonanza (Blair, 1951) were above average, the former with its motif of smuggling stolen gold via helicopter, the latter with a "haunted" ranch scheme to cover up dirty work. These two also introduced Buddy Ebsen as sidekick for Allen, after some false starts with Gordon Jones, Carl "Alfalfa" Switzer and Fuzzy Knight. Ebsen was in the tradition of good comedian-good actor, and he gave the young series a lift. *Rodeo King and the Señorita* (Blair, 1951) was a fine follow-up; a remake of a Roy Rogers show, *My Pal Trigger*, it still had a lot left in the John K. Butler script. Butler, once a prolific writer of sleuth stories for pulps, was another crafty craftsman at working out adult-slanted, different Western scripts. He followed *Rodeo King* with *Utah Wagon Train* (Philip Ford, 1951), with an intriguing idea of reusing a wagon train, routing it over a trail not used for 100 years, with a mystery angle worked in cleverly.

Allen had been receiving a higher budget than Allan Lane or Monte Hale, and approaching the Roy Rogers classification, though without the color. But Rogers was gone from Republic, the studio was economizing drastically, and the Allens felt the cutback. Edward J. White became the producer, taking over from Melville Tucker, and William Witney had been directing the last few, which was an asset. Allen had lost Buddy Ebsen but had acquired Slim Pickens, another reliable sidekick. The budget crunch was apparent with *Old Oklahoma Plains* (Witney, 1952), and also apparent was the devilish ingenuity of writer Milton Raison. He centered his story around the government's early experiments with tanks, thus allowing for stock footage from Republic's 1938 *Army Girl*, shot by B. Reeves Eason, to be used anew. *Old Oklahoma Plains* is the only budget Western with a definite '20s transpiration—it took place in 1926. Limited by the budgets, Witney nevertheless managed to turn out some fast, exciting Allen Westerns, including *Iron Mountain Trail* (1953) and *Down Laredo Way* (1953), the latter a Gerald Geraghty script with a circus background. Allen's last was *Phantom Stallion* (Harry Keller, 1954) and it wasn't up to par, but by then the Westerns were fading fast from the theater screens. Allen found steady work for Walt Disney as a singer-narrator after his Republic series; if he had started earlier, say, in the '40s, he may well have garnered additional laurels.

Republic's final Western series was mercifully brief, a quartet of films with two juvenile leads, Michael Chapin and Eilene Janssen. Chapin played the grandson of a sheriff (James Bell), with Janssen as his playmate. The two would invariably land in trouble but emerge with some outlaws in tow. *Buckaroo Sheriff of Texas* (Philip Ford, 1951) was the opener, and it was easy to see what the flaw was—

Slim Pickens became Rex Allen's fifth and last sidekick in his series for Republic.

Rex Allen and Slim Pickens in a scene from one of Republic's last series B Western releases.

when it came down to the necessary action, the film would have to fall back on grownups to carry it out, in this case Hugh O'Brian. Republic also erred in thinking that youngsters enjoy watching one of their own playing hero. They don't, preferring to imagine themselves as adults and transferring their allegiances to a "Rocky" Lane or Rex Allen, instead of another juvenile. With no discernible improvement shown in *Wild Horse Ambush* (Fred C. Brannon, 1952), the series was dropped.

Discounting their top series, namely the Autrys, Rogers and Three Mesquiteers, Republic Westerns brought a lot of excitement to innumerable moviegoers, children and adults alike. Not a few of them found their own particular favorites among Don Barry (29 films), Allan Lane (51 films), Sunset Carson (15 films), Monte Hale or Rex Allen (19 films each). Bob Livingston's work naturally fits in with the Mesquiteers. Perhaps there were those who even preferred the two Eddie Dew "John Paul Revere" adventures, or the Chapin-Janssen four. Whatever the case, there's no doubt that Republic did its share to make the West a safe place for movie stars.

And there was still one more cowboy who rose to prominence at Republic, but since he had started elsewhere, and finished elsewhere, he deserves a separate section. Besides, he's a peaceable man...

Bill Elliott in the first, discarded version of his Red Ryder costume.

19
WILD BILL

"I'm a peaceable man," said Wild Bill Elliott, just before whipping the stuffing out of a mean bruiser bent on no good; or prior to putting the gun to some varmint who mistakenly thought he could outdraw this cool, pokerfaced customer. Coolness became the screen character of Bill, formerly Gordon, later William Elliott. In another sphere entirely, Hemingway termed it "grace under pressure," and that's what Elliott exuded. The cool cowboy star chalked up a distinguished record for three companies and an assortment of roles, including leads in some medium-to-high budgeted productions. Behind them all was that steely, reassuring calm. You wanted him on your side.

For an actor who had specialized in villainy for much of his screen career, Elliott developed and patented his heroic characterization with astonishing rapidity. He had been a Warner Bros. stock player for a number of years, from bits to support, usually sporting a pencil-thin mustache to accent the weakness of the characters he portrayed. His supporting assignments peaked in the mid-'30s, and it was not easy to find a Warner film without his presence. He served as an opponent to Dick Foran when the redhead was ramrod of the Warner Westerns, and found time to journey to Republic where he tried to do dirty to Gene Autry. In his thirties, Gordon Elliott seemed destined to remain on the shady side of the law. Then he snagged the lead in a Columbia serial, shaved his mustache, and treated chapter play fans to *The Great Adventures of Wild Bill Hickok* (Mack Wright & Sam Nelson, 1938). Columbia was a late-comer to the serial field; this was only their fourth. But their advertising department knew all the exploitation tricks, and serials were at this time bidding for one last effort to revive the popularity and esteem they had enjoyed in the silent days. *Hickok* may have been riddled with flaws, but it made the right noises. And Elliott showed a new facet of his screen personality, one which had been thoroughly hidden under a bushel of skulduggery until now.

Columbia, in its endless search to find a second saddle star to complement its ace, Charles Starrett, was sufficiently impressed by Elliott's work, and the gratifying results of his serial, to assign him to the Larry Darmour unit to head a Western series. Ken Maynard, Bob Allen and Jack Luden had ridden before him, and stumbled. Now it was Elliott's turn, equipped with director Joseph Levering, writer Nate Gatzert, cameraman James S. Brown Jr., and other familiars of the Darmour production group. The four Darmour-Elliott Westerns had a unifying theme, the pioneering of the early West. Gatzert's scripts were founded in historical truth, even if the narratives were on the fanciful side. *In Early Arizona* (1938) was the first, a thinly-veiled account of Wyatt Earp's cleanup of Tombstone, with Elliott a fictionalized Earp, with Art Davis and, wonder of wonders, Charles King as his aides, and Harry Woods capably supplying the menace. The production showed the usual Darmour eye for economy,

HOLLYWOOD CORRAL: A COMPREHENSIVE B WESTERN ROUNDUP

Elliott mourns for Luana Walters as Iris Meredith and Frank LaRue (r.) commiserate in The Return of Wild Bill *(1940), one of Wild Bill's best Columbias.*

but the star, now officially Bill Elliott, stood out like a prize steer in a herd of sheep. Stern yet likeable, grim-jawed yet always in control, he caused even those who remembered to overlook the villainies he had perpetrated only a year ago. And the gunfight finale, with Elliott and his pards advancing down the street in wing formation ready to blast, was one of the more satisfying Western moments of the season.

Elliott consolidated his position with the rest of his series. *Frontiers of '49* (1938) was a tale of Old California, with Charles King on the lawbreaking side this time, and Elliott aided by Hal Taliaferro. *Lone Star Pioneers* (1939) took place in Texas at the end of the Civil War, while *The Law Comes to Texas* (1939) dealt with the formation of the Texas Rangers—and in this one, King was once more on Elliott's, and the law's side. All in all, the Darmours were crude but filled with action, and all Elliott needed was just a little more finesse on the production end.

He got it. Columbia took over the series from Darmour, assigned Leon Barsha to produce, and introduced the character of Wild Bill Saunders for Elliott to play. It was a clever combination of the use of "Wild Bill," as in Hickok, and at the same time establishing a new character for Elliott to make his own. The first one, *Taming of the West* (Norman Deming, 1939), set the tone of the series, with Elliott as a man of action and few words. Prior to this, Elliott had starred in a second serial for Columbia, *Overland with Kit Carson* (Sam Nelson & Norman Deming, 1939). It left much to be desired as a chapter-play, full of childish hokum, a hidden mystery villain who wasn't very mysterious or very well hidden, and some annoyingly implausible cliffhangers that even the gullible wouldn't believe.

Nevertheless, it had kept Elliott's name, and face, on the screens for 15 more consecutive weeks, so by the time his new Columbia series was ready, he was even more well-known.

Joining Elliott for comedy relief was Dub Taylor, an aggressive clown with a thick, sometimes incomprehensible deep Southern dialect. Taylor's jester antics were a matter of taste, but he did acquire adherants. Elliott also fell heir to the Columbia stock company, with Iris Meredith, Dick Curtis, Richard Fiske, Stanley Brown and sundry others, nearly as familiar as the Statue of Liberty Columbia trademark, making their entrances early and often. Discounting the serial, Elliott appeared in only four Westerns for the 1939–40 season; but at the end, after a total of eight features and two serials, he was already one of the top contending cowboy leads, a rapid rise indeed. *Pioneers of the Frontier* (Sam Nelson, 1940) had plenty of action, and an interesting female lead in Linda Winters, who reverted to her real name, Dorothy Comingore, for Orson Welles and *Citizen Kane* the following year. Both *The Man from Tumbleweeds* (1940) and *The Return of Wild Bill* (1940) were directed by Joseph H. Lewis with his eye on camerawork. The latter was also notable for a performance by Luana Walters in the part of the other woman (Iris Meredith, of course, was the lead). Miss Walters had appeared in many a Western and was always pleasant to behold. This time she was presented with a role calling for some degree of histrionics, and she gave her all. Not a performance to win awards, mind you, but a more energetic or deeply felt one would be hard to find in the annals of horse operas.

As if to make up for lost time, or else by public demand, Columbia starred Elliott in eight features for the 1940–41 season, or twice as many as he had been making. Things began slowly with *Prairie*

Elliott and Evelyn Keyes in Beyond the Sacramento *(1940).*

HOLLYWOOD CORRAL: A COMPREHENSIVE B WESTERN ROUNDUP

Schooners (Sam Nelson, 1940), but picked up a bit with *Beyond the Sacramento* (Lambert Hillyer, 1940) if only because of the presence of Evelyn Keyes as leading lady. A young actress of uncommon ability, Miss Keyes soon left Western trivialities far behind her—or anyway, low-budget Westerns. A directorial voice from the days of Jones and McCoy, D. Ross Lederman, accounted for two of the better entries of the season in *Across the Sierras* (1941) and *North from the Lone Star* (1941), the latter with a knuckle-breaking barroom brawl. Elliott had perfected a unique screen style of scrapping—fists held unusually low, at crotch level practically, waiting for his adversary to make a move, then the flurry of punches climaxed by a terrific downward chop as if the blow were a thunderbolt from the heavens, which no villain, Dick Curtis, Francis Walker or whomever, could withstand. Up to this point, Elliott had been using the Wild Bill Hickok identification again, but now portrayed figures of historical connotation, as in *The Return of Daniel Boone* (Hillyer, 1941) and *The Son of Davy Crockett* (Hillyer, 1941).

Elliott received a partner for the 1941–42 season, co-starred in eight films with him, and hit it off well. Tex Ritter took second billing, but the stories were constructed so that the two stars received nearly equal screen time. Their opener was *King of Dodge City* (Hillyer, 1941), with Elliott his usual fightin' self and Ritter chipping in with the songs and shootin'. Ritter proved admirably adept at throwing a snap-shot from his iron as he finished a song, pulling the trigger precisely on the downbeat. Dub Taylor left the series after the first, replaced by Frank Mitchell, a seemingly indestructable rag-doll of a man who had been in a roughhouse act in vaude (Mitchell & Durant) and could still take some shattering falls. Naturally, Mitchell's comedy stressed the physical, which made the series seem even more action-packed. Lambert Hillyer directed six of eight, including the better series entries: *North of the Rockies* (1942), with Elliott playing a mountie for the first and last time, and with Larry Parks and Lloyd Bridges of the Columbia stock company in the cast; *The Devil's Trail* (1942), with the always welcome Noah Beery, Sr.; and *Prairie Gunsmoke* (1942), with an accomplished horsewoman, Virginia Carroll, contributing some hard riding as well as much charm in the ingenue role, and some frantic Elliott-Ritter action scenes. Elliott then moved to

Elliott with his 1941–42 co-star, Tex Ritter, in King of Dodge City *(1941).*

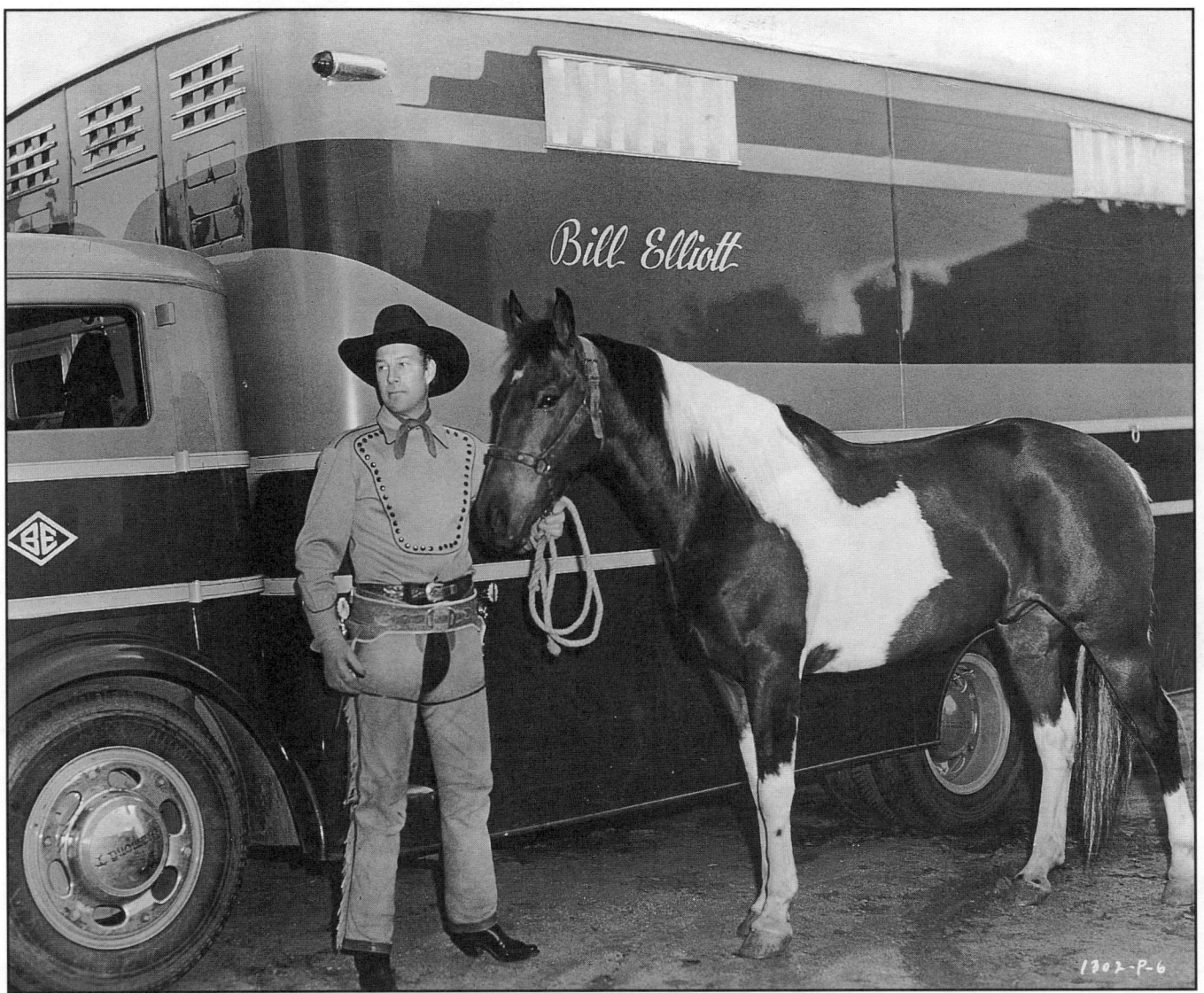

Wild Bill and pony arrive on location for The Man from Thunder River *(1943).*

Republic, but Columbia was not about to let him off easily. They shoved him into another cheaply-made serial, *Valley of Vanishing Men* (Spencer Bennet, 1942), with the lanky comic Slim Summerville providing the sole respite from the tedium.

At Republic, Elliott was considered enough of a draw to use his own name, and his first was titled simply *Calling Wild Bill Elliott* (Spencer Bennet, 1943). He was given two semi-official co-stars in Anne Jeffreys and George "Gabby" Hayes, although the films were not connected in any literary manner. Elliott appeared comfortable amid his new surroundings. The first one didn't have much in the way of a plot, but it did have continuous movement and Bennet's directorial savvy handling brawls and chases, of which there were many. The series soon became a worthy companion to Republic's other range sagas. *The Man from Thunder River* (John English, 1942) had a tidy script by J. Benton Cheney and English's strong steering to help it. *Wagon Tracks West* (Howard Bretherton, 1942) was somewhat of a rarity at the time, an old-fashioned Indian yarn well told, with Tom Tyler making a surprising but effective menace as an evil medicine man. *Death Valley Manhunt* (1943) told of oil wells and such, with English catching some unusually tense moments as Elliott has to depart from atop a well as a gusher is about to erupt. Both *Mojave Firebrand* (Bennet, 1944) and *Hidden Valley Outlaws* (Bretherton, 1944) can be described succinctly: fast and furious.

Their "Red Ryder" rights hadn't been used since the Don Barry days, so Republic reactivated the property as a series for Elliott. Bobby Blake was signed for the Little Beaver part, and Alice Fleming portrayed Ryder's motherly mentor, the Duchess. "Gabby" Hayes was held over for a non-comic strip role, but left the series after the first two films.

HOLLYWOOD CORRAL: A COMPREHENSIVE B WESTERN ROUNDUP

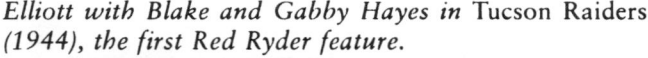

William Haade (l.), Bud Geary, Elliott and Kenne Duncan in Sheriff of Las Vegas (1944).

Elliott with Blake and Gabby Hayes in Tucson Raiders (1944), the first Red Ryder feature.

Tucson Raiders (Spencer Bennet, 1944) started the Ryder series in okay fashion, but it soon gathered momentum to become a valued item on the Republic release schedule. Elliott didn't particularly fit one's conception of Ryder, being a mite too sophisticated and austere in his portrayal, but he made the character over in his own image and nothing was lost. Young Blake was a fine Little Beaver, a child actor who wasn't obnoxious and could lend his talents to the comedy sequences. Of the first eight Ryders, six could be said to rate with the better Westerns of the season. *Marshal of Reno* (Wallace Grissell, 1944) upheld the tradition of nonstop action in the Republic manner, as did Grissell's other effort, *Vigilantes of Dodge City* (1944). *The Lone Texas Ranger* (Bennet, 1945) had a superior Bob Williams screenplay, and a fine supporting part for craggy-faced Bud Geary as a henchman with a sense of humor. It was during the Ryder series that the penchant for devising humorous heavies came over the Republic script writers, and they were often worth the price of admission. Don Costello lent both menace and chuckles to his role in *The Great Stagecoach Robbery* (Lesley Selander, 1945), by Randall Faye. Faye, who had been screenwriting in England, returned with perhaps a jaundiced continental eye for Westerns. He made the Costello character the brains of the gang who cloaked his activities as a schoolteacher. Introduced to a pair of fiendish brats, whose mother assures Costello that he'll come to love them, Costello nods and mutters as he turns away, "Ah yes, if they live that long...." W. C. Fields would have approved wholeheartedly.

Faye wrote an earlier Red Ryder which is probably the very best of Elliott's Republic Westerns, *Cheyenne Wildcat* (Selander, 1944). It's unusually bloody for a Republic Western—bloody as opposed to non-lethal action. But it's exciting, excellently made, and has plum roles for the Republic Big Three Baddies, Roy Barcroft, Bud Geary, and Kenne Duncan. Barcroft is the brains of the gang, but not the usual sneering, glowering villain. He is introduced, dandified, admiring himself in a mirror while singing *sotto voce* "Oh, Susannah." Director Selander's third Ryder of the season, *Sheriff of Las Vegas* (1944) has a leisurely buildup that makes the action at the conclusion seem all the more industrious.

Elliott didn't try to overdo the dramatics, content to remain himself and let the action occur naturally. The second season of eight Ryders gave him cause to work a little harder, for the scripts called for more plot development at the expense of the fights and chases, although these were still abundant. *Phantom of the Plains* (Selander, 1945) was all about an imposter (Ian Keith) out to fleece the Duchess, and it took a few reels to get really started. It was a harbinger of things to come. The producer, R. G. Springsteen, then took over the series as director, with Earle Snell writing most of the scripts. They were good and made good Western films—but the old buoyancy was lacking, as if Republic had been too long at the game and had become blasé about it. It was especially apparent in the villainy. Dick Curtis, a fine straight menace at Columbia, was in *California Gold Rush* (1946) and was instructed to make it funny. Curtis was not used to Republic's humorous heavies but did as told. Barcroft could have carried it off in his sleep, but Curtis merely managed to be cute about it. Instead of hitting the whimsical mark, Curtis looked stoned throughout. Elliott's staunch portrayals became the chief asset of the series, with a brief glimmer occurring in *Sheriff of Redwood Valley* (1946) thanks to Bob Steele's appearance, or a better than average plot idea by Snell for *Sun Valley Cyclone* (1946), which centers around Elliott-Ryder's horse, Thunder. The series was continued after 1945–46 with Allan Lane; Elliott had gotten out from under, and had been promoted to the upper Republic strata. He was now, formally, William Elliott, star of "A" pictures.

Republic started off by trying to make a combination John Wayne-Errol Flynn out of Elliott, and it didn't work out too well. But he soon found a groove and stayed in it for ten big-budgeted, more or less, Westerns. Worth mentioning is *The Last Bandit* (Joseph Kane, 1949), all about a train loaded with loot that apparently disappears right off the tracks, which was done in 1941 by Kane as a straight non-Western action melodrama, *The Great Train Robbery* with Bob Steele in the Elliott role. Also of note were two productions by Dorrell and Stuart McGowan, sons of veteran actor-Director J. P. McGowan, who had been writing rustic vehicles and Westerns since the early Gene Autry days. They wrote and functioned as executive producers on *Hellfire*, a Trucolor job like *The Last Bandit,* which was directed by R. G. Springsteen in the same year. It had been a strong religioso theme tailor-made for the country and small-town locations, and had a good performance by Marie Windsor as a tough saloon gal in addition to Elliott's good work. In 1950, the McGowans scripted and directed *The Showdown* for Elliott and Walter Brennan. It was an offbeat film, made in an offbeat way. Most of it was shot on a studio sound stage, with use of rear projection and process work giving the outdoor look. Most of Republic's Westerns were made in this money-saving manner at the time. Its success was open to question, but *The Showdown* had other factors, including story and cast, going for it.

With Republic severely curtailing its activities and no place for Elliott to fit in, he accepted an offer from Monogram, and appeared in 11 Westerns, many of them laudably high in quality. The budgets weren't what he had been accustomed to, but they were considerably higher than his salad days at Columbia. The first several were tinted in the sepia process, the brownish hues pleasing to the eye. More important, the story values were excellent, with scripts by Dan Ullman among the better writing jobs.

Ullman's first script was *The Longhorn* (Lewis D. Collins, 1951) and was nothing if not ambitious for a low-budget Western, concerning a trail drive from Wyoming to Oregon to cross-breed cattle. It was truly epic in scope, and amazingly the film carried it off. Sight values provided by producer Vincent M. Fennelly were entirely adequate, with no hint of skimping. Elliott was called upon to do more acting than he was before, and gave a fine performance as the rancher who forms the trail drive. It was a promising beginning for the series. The promise was fulfilled with *Waco* (Collins, 1952), also by Ullman. Elliott's characterizations began to move close to the old William S. Hart line; in *Waco* he was the good-badman, was allowed to smoke and drink contrary to nearly all Western heroes (Charles Starrett would occasionally order a beer, Tim Holt puffed on a pipe, and that was about it). He was a former outlaw again in *Kansas Territory* (Collins, 1952), an Ullman script that was the best yet, using the ancient theme of a man searching for his brother's killer and giving it many new twists. *Fargo* (Collins, 1952), by Jack DeWitt and Joseph Poland, had the new angle of barbed wire being introduced to the West, and told the story interestingly.

Thomas Carr directed three Elliotts for the 1952–53 season, *The Maverick* (1952), *Rebel City* (1953) and *Topeka* (1953). Somewhere on the lot Carr had unearthed a camera crane, and he used it on the Elliots with the gleeful exuberance of a small boy with a Christmas toy. The cameras swooped, glided, elevated, descended upon the slightest provocation, and sometimes without any, with *Topeka* especially afflicted. It may have been irritating at times, but it was noticeable how, by the simple upward gliding movement of the camera, an ordinary scene of a group of riders would assume a sense of grandeur. Obviously, Carr was experimenting, and it served him well on subsequent feature film and television assignments.

Later Elliotts for Monogram (which had become Allied Artists while the series was in progress) were not as potent as the earlier ones, but still Westerns of strength and more than the average amount of thought interposed. When the Western trails had come to an end, Elliott donned civilian clothes and appeared in a neat series for Allied Artists as a plain-clothes detective. The first in the series was written and directed by Dan Ullman. Elliott's long career had scaled the heights and experienced the

Fuzzy Knight, Elliott and Phyllis Coates in Fargo *(1952).*

Wild Bill and Marjorie Lord in Rebel City *(1953).*

depths as well—from bit player to villain to serial hero to Western hero to the star of "A" films back to Western hero, and finally a soundly-based sleuth. His Westerns were, in general, uncommonly good. Sometimes he would be better than his material, frequently he alone would hold a shaky vehicle together. He always projected integrity, and a placid, rather remote nobility. He was once quoted as saying he wanted to portray William S. Hart in a screen biography. He didn't much resemble Hart physically, but he might well have patterned his style after the great silent star. It would have been good casting.

Jimmy Wakely

20
HIRED HANDS

Once one familiarizes oneself with the top cowboy stars, and keeps going on from there, certain startling questions present themselves. For example, did Jimmy Wakely really last that long as a range hero? Just how many Bill Boyds were there, anyway? Who were The Texas Rangers—better question: Why? Like all complex answers, a simple substitute reply can be made. Yes, Wakely's starring roles began in 1944 and lasted until late 1949; there were three Bill Boyds on the screen, though not all at once; The Texas Rangers were James Newill, Dave O'Brien and Guy Wilkerson, with Tex Ritter replacing Newill. The "why" part is more difficult. The fact that any and all of these performers are remembered at all is a tribute to the devotion of Western fans. There were some others operating during the World War II era, so let's take them, gingerly and briefly, in more or less the order of their appearance.

After the end of the Cisco Kid series in 1941, 20th Century-Fox apparently had designs for George Montgomery as a potential cowboy star to continue the studio's outdoor efforts. Montgomery had had experience, notably in Republic's *Lone Ranger* serial. He was a Montana-born waddy with enough prowess in the saddle to engage in some stunting work, still in the bloom of youth, and possessed of that personality element that made the girls sigh. No sooner had Fox gotten plans underway, they were cancelled. Montgomery had starred in two Westerns directed by James Tinling, Zane Grey perennials *Last of the Duanes* and *Riders of the Purple Sage*, for late 1941 release. What had served his predecessors William Farnum, Tom Mix, and George O'Brien well, only put Montgomery at a disadvantage. The Grey plots were old-hat and not improved in their 1941 adaptations. Talk predominated, and the talk was not distiguished. The casts were fine, but out of place in the Western element. With all the factors mitigating against him, Montgomery made little impression, so 20th Century-Fox continued their buildup in other more amenable climes for Montgomery. Their Western program was given one final fling as Tinling was assigned to direct two features starring football celebrity John Kimbrough, both released in 1942. *Lone Star Ranger* was another Zane Grey standby, while *Sundown Jim* was based on an Ernest Haycox work. As an actor, Kimbrough was a superb gridiron flash, and the films themselves weren't any great shakes. Fox had obviously lost the Western touch in the Wurtzel division, and turned their attention to more salubrious matters.

PRC, Sig Neufeld and Sam Newfield, ever-ready and willing to release, produce and direct anything with the clatter of hoofbeats, conceived of a new series featuring an heroic trio, two of whom sang. The non-singer was Lee Powell, yet to receive an adequate break. Teaming with him were Art Davis, who had been seen in the Tim McCoy PRC series just ended, and a radio and recording artist of the back country repertoire named, as it happened, Bill Boyd. Now, the William Boyd of Hopalong Cassidy

HOLLYWOOD CORRAL: A COMPREHENSIVE B WESTERN ROUNDUP

George Montgomery (l.), Lynne Roberts and James Gillette in the 1941 version of Riders of the Purple Sage.

Lee Powell slips a half-nelson on Stan Jolley in Prairie Pals *(1942).*

fame had already had some confusion resulting from another actor with the same name, thereafter known as William (Stage) Boyd to avoid mistakes. As an established Western name, momentary fear arose that history would repeat itself. However, Hoppy was riding in luck. The warbling Bill Boyd headed the trio into a series of six quickies under the heading of the Frontier Marshals, and as it turned out six were more than enough. Newfield directed them under his Peter Stewart alias. All were released in 1942. The first one, *Texas Manhunt,* used the foreign agent trick, which was rapidly becoming popular on the picture prairie. But Nazis didn't belong on the range, or anywhere else, and the opener was a dud. Nor did the series improve. Boyd, Davis, and Powell failed to click together, and received no help from the production side. In the fourth entry, *Tumbleweed Trail,* Powell was forced to go through the motions of a knock-down, drag-out brawl with aging Jack Rockwell, bald and in precarious physical condition. No budgetary consideration for a double, so poor Rockwell had to puff through the charade, with Powell seemingly embarrassed by the exertion. After *Along the Sundown Trail,* the Frontier Marshals disbanded to the regret of nobody in particular. Saving graces, after lengthy and difficult searches, would be the girls involved, comely misses like Julie Duncan (another expert horsewoman), Virginia Carroll, Wanda McKay and Esther Estrella, and the Western regulars like Charles King, Kermit Maynard, Karl Hackett and Glenn Strange. One would be prompted to offer condolences once again to Lee Powell, another wasted effort. Powell joined the Marines, and was killed in action during World War II.

Still keeping the ball in play, producers Arthur Alexander and Alfred Stern rejoined two worthies from the Renfrew days, James Newill and Dave O'Brien, added a comedy sidekick, Guy Wilkerson, and thus inaugurated the Texas Rangers series. First out was *The Rangers Take Over* (Al Herman, 1942), and from the start it looked like a long, hard road. Newill and O'Brien had proven themselves before

HOLLYWOOD CORRAL: A COMPREHENSIVE B WESTERN ROUNDUP

Dave O'Brien (l.) and Tex Ritter face Stan Jolley and Kermit Maynard in Flaming Bullets *(1945).*

with weak material and production deficiencies; but Wilkerson, a cadaverous gent with a nasal twang, was no deft funster, far from it, and the dialogue written for him compounded the felony. Succeeding members of the series did nothing to cause any reassessment. Newill and O'Brien worked too much alike, and the attempted light banter between them sounded strained. When presented with halfway decent material, as in *West of Texas* (Oliver Drake, 1943), the pacing would be so slow as to vitiate the good points. Adding to the woes were the technical setbacks, below par even with a wartime excuse. The sound recording for *Trail of Terror* (Drake, 1943) is not only faulty but deficient. At one point, the sound equipment seems to have blown a gasket, and microphone thunks and thuds and crackles can be heard periodically throughout. PRC decided to stick with the series, for some unfathomable reason. But with number 14, *Brand of the Devil* (Harry Fraser, 1944), Newill's singing had been drastically cut down; and since that was why Newill was around, primarily, he left the series to return to the stage, where he was far happier. O'Brien and Wilkerson continued riding on.

Joining them was Tex Ritter, who had been around and was now nearing the end of the cinema trail at PRC. To Ritter's credit, he pepped up the series noticeably. The revamped Texas Rangers series sauntered on for eight final Westerns, four of them directed by Elmer Clifton, four by Harry Fraser. The Cliftons were released first, and were the best by far, although that doesn't mean they rated with the superior brand of Westerns. Production work was still skimpy. Interior sets were dangerously rickety, almost fire hazards. There wasn't time for retakes, therefore when Dave O'Brien would hit the floor and his toupee slip askew, just hope nobody will notice. Lee Zahler's background music was a continuing liability, snippets from ill-chosen classics with an oompah-oompah orchestration. With all this sludge, Clifton would manage to come through with an entertaining 55 minutes, mostly by using his own scripts and cannily exploiting the value of vet sagebrushers like Charles King in *Dead or Alive* (1944) and *Marked for Murder* (1944), or stirring up excitement with a good old fashioned who's-the-villain tale with *The Whispering Skull* (1944), closest to a satisfactory Western in the series. Fraser's contributions were routine by comparison, and the series fizzled out in 1945.

After having acquired Russell Hayden and putting him through the paces with Charles Starrett, Columbia separated the team and gave Hayden his own series in 1943, accompanied by Dub Taylor for comedy and the Bob Wills aggregation for music. Eight were made, all directed by William Berke and produced by Leon Barsha, but were released four at a time over two seasons. Quite naturally, since Starrett was top gun at the studio, they were played down and reviewers didn't pay them much notice—in fact, several of them weren't reviewed at all except by the trade press. But there wasn't a weak one in the bunch, allowing for some hasty production slips like mismatched shots and the like. Hayden was well-known for the Hopalong Cassidy and the Starrett series, and still possessed his boyish enthusiasm. Berke also directed him through some monumental fistic encounters, beginning with a scrap with Jack Ingram in *The Lone Prairie* (1942) and continuing for an average of roughly three fights per 55-minute film. The flair for fists was contagious. By the next-to-last Hayden entry, *Wyoming Hurricane* (1944), even Bob Wills joined in one of the donnybrooks, hopping over tables and chairs with a gleeful shout to swing away. The Haydens were fortunate in their feminine leads, too—Ann Savage lent her charms and talent to a couple, and a beauty named Alma Carroll more than dressed up the scenery when she appeared. Columbia was finding the support of two cowboy series too much, however, and Hayden landed at Universal, co-starring in some as reported, and taking care of one of his own in *Frontier Law* (Elmer Clifton, 1943). It was a good one, and was released even while his slow-playing Columbias were still being circulated. The Haydens remain underrated, and deserve to be better known by action fans.

Warner Bros. had forsaken Westerns with the

Tris Coffin gets pounded by Russell Hayden in A Tornado in the Saddle *(1942).*

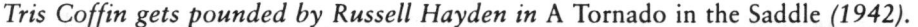

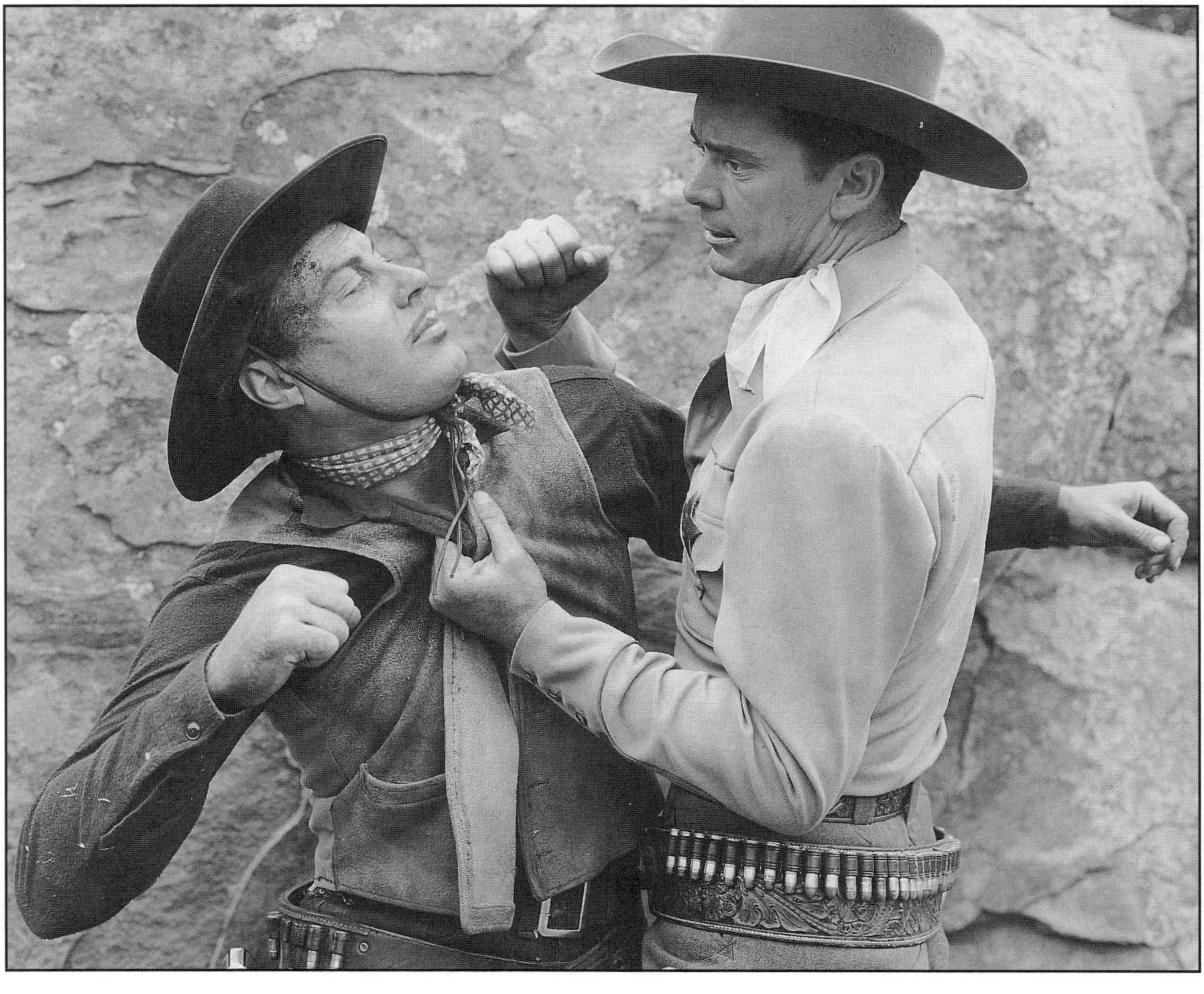

HOLLYWOOD CORRAL: A COMPREHENSIVE B WESTERN ROUNDUP

end of the Dick Forans, but did revive the genre in a series of short subjects, billed as "Santa Fe Trail Westerns." Robert Shayne, a stodgy performer, starred, and from the first one it was easy to see that the Warner stock library was going to be a busy department for the duration of the series. *Oklahoma Outlaws* (B. Reeves Eason, 1943) was about the big land rush, and one expected to see James Cagney in his *Oklahoma Kid* togs jounce out from the 1939 footage momentarily—and if one looked closely and quickly, perhaps one did. Similarly, *Roaring Guns* (Jean Negulesco, 1944) concerned hydraulic mining, bringing on thoughts of the 1938 epic *Gold Is Where You Find It*. Six of these two-reel pocket Westerns were scheduled for the 1943–44 season. The Shaynes were in sepia, and the leading man might well have been blushing—after all, it isn't easy to play most of your lines in old film. Oddly, in what looked like a mixup, a non-Shayne was inserted into the schedule, a Cinecolor tale with Dennis Moore and Louise Stanley titled *Wells Fargo Days* (Mack V. Wright, 1944). It was an outside product bought by Warners, and served no purpose except to confuse the issue. The Santa Fe series was not continued, but the missing Robert Shayne short showed up separately the next season—*Law of the Badlands* (Jack Scholl, 1945), about the Custer set-to. Shayne also appeared in a Technicolor mini-Western, *Frontier Days* (School, 1945), with Dorothy Malone as a female sheriff.

Universal's Western schedule was in a chaotic state since Johnny Mack Brown moved to Monogram. They had tried various combinations of Tex Ritter, Russell Hayden and Dennis Moore, singly or in pairs; and while the results were up to the Universal standard, there was a sense of listlessness, as if the company was scrambling for something more solid and these releases represented only temporary stopgaps. When Rod Cameron was announced as Universal's new cowboy star, it was cause for rejoicing. Cameron had endeared himself to action fans while starring in two of the sluggingest Republic (non-Western) serials ever made. He had been prominently seen in some Harry Sherman Westerns, and had been a familiar face in Paramount features for the past several years. Cameron was tall and lanky in the Cooper tradition and seemed to have all the necessary attributes. Harry Sherman had intended to star him in a large-scale outdoor show, *Wherever the Grass Grows,* but the plans hadn't panned out. Now it was Universal's turn. His first was *Boss of Boomtown* (Ray Taylor, 1944), and Tom Tyler was his co-star in a rather weak attempt to do a Quirt-Flagg impression in the old West. There was action, but it was loosely joined together. However, the mere fact that the action was plentiful was an encouraging sign. *Trigger Trail* (Lewis D. Collins, 1944) was an improvement, with Cameron backed by Eddie Dew, late of Republic. Fuzzy Knight was the house comic, as he had been ever since 1939 and the early Browns. The Universal release schedule was still in a state of flux, so the next Western out of the paddock was a non-Cameron. *Trail to Gunsight* (Vernon Keays, 1944) had Eddie Dew in the top spot, with Lyle Talbot, venerable character actor, filling in the secondary part of lawman. Fuzzy Knight was on hand, as was Ray Whitley and group, supplying the musical portions for Universal Westerns now that RKO had no further need of them. Cameron starred in four more Universals, none of them particularly noteworthy. *The Old Texas Trail* (Collins, 1944) was perhaps closest to what the studio was aiming for, with Cameron and Dew teaming nicely, Knight not too intrusive with his clowning, Whitley's music held to a minimum, and the action fast. But it was still wartime, leading men were at a premium, and Cameron was soon tapped to star opposite Yvonne De Carlo in some biggies. In his stead for the 1945–46 season was Kirby Grant, who had been on the scene for some time. Fuzzy Knight was in his usual jester spot, and the series of seven Westerns was produced and directed by Wallace Fox. The first two, released in 1945, had some sociological value for reasons disassociated from the films. *Bad Men of the Border* and *Code of the Lawless* featured Barbara Sears, who became hot news copy when she married a Rockefeller. Bobo, as she was fondly known, didn't contribute one way or another to the films. Grant appeared slightly uncomfortable at first, but soon loosened up and became a pleasantly acceptable Western lead. Fox paced the features swiftly for the most part, and his productions were a credit to Universal, with some stock footage only occasionally creeping in, as in *Gun Town* (1946). But the handwriting was on the wall for Universal, about to undergo a shakeup from top to bottom. Low-budget Westerns had no place in their future plans, so after a refreshing but relatively tepid series out West, Grant found himself at Monogram and in the RCMP. Universal became Universal-International and their Westerns were big in intent, if not in execution.

An interesting sidelight occurred in 1944 when Russell Wade, an RKO contract player specializing in weakling kid brother roles, took it upon himself to star in a Western made in 16mm, hopefully to

Fuzzy Knight (center), Hugh Prosser and Kirby Grant try to figure out why Jane Adams has that dreamy look on her face in Code of the Lawless *(1945).*

start a trend for small-gauge films for showing at clubs, schools and in the home. *Sundown Riders* co-starred Jay Kirby, a Hopalong Cassidy protege, and Andy Clyde, also late of the Bar-20 bunch. Lambert Hillyer directed, and except for the noncommercial size of the film, it was an entirely professional if routine horse opera with a cast of Western faces including Evelyn Finley, Jack Ingram, Marshall Reed, Bud Osborne, Ted Mapes, Hal Price and Steve Clark; former cowboy star Ted Wells also had a small role. Wade was said to have a piece of the action, and it was a worthy attempt to blaze a trail in a new market. But extensive use of 16mm equipment was still a few years away, and the film didn't garner too many bookings. A short time later, Planet Films was formed to produce features for a potential 16mm market. One of its few releases was a Western, modern-day type, called *Jeep Herders* (Richard Talmadge and Harvey Perry, 1945). Like *Sundown Riders* it was photographed in Kodachrome, and moved swiftly. It starred stuntman John Day; Talmadge and Perry were well versed in the stunting side of things, and the cast included risk-takers Sol Gorss, Dale Van Sickel and Tom Steele. The idea of using jeeps for a roundup was topical, and the film ran a swift 46 minutes. But once again, it was slightly in advance of its intended market.

With the intent of cultivating their own Gene Autry or Roy Rogers, Monogram picked on a popular cowboy singer, Jimmy Wakely. Wakely had been seen in some Charles Starrett and Don Barry Westerns, always to advantage, mainly because he played little part in the narratives, stayed out of the way and tended to his business, which was vocalizing. His appearance was slight but pleasant, and he could handle a line of dialogue without drastic consequences. What happened when he was seen in his first starring vehicle, however, was apparent. *Song of the Range* (Wallace Fox, 1944) was a medium-cool affair with nothing at all away from the ordinary. With a forceful personality, it might have gotten by. But Wakely in a leading role was about as exciting as Tom Mix reciting a fairy tale. When making with the songs he was in his element, and listenable. When digging into a plot, it was yawnsville. Of no great aid was Lee "Lasses" White in the alleged comedy spot, and Dennis Moore once more was stuck with playing third fiddle as the other saddle pal. The way the Wakelys were headed was made plain by the ensuing titles: *Springtime in Texas* (Oliver Drake, 1945) and *Saddle Serenade* (Drake, 1945). Not exactly the most exciting tags in the business. The series struggled on in this fashion, with songs taking precedence over the action, and technical and production values well within the economical category. Dub Taylor was added to the cast in place of Lee White in 1947, now billed as "Cannonball" Taylor in deference to his work with Bill Elliott. Dennis Moore, then John James had served as Wakely's partners, and were now gone. James, in fact, came back to do a villainous stint in one of the subsequent Wakelys. When Louis Gray, a Republic veteran, took over the production duties in 1948, the pace quickened a bit, with the musical interludes played down somewhat. But there was still little to get excited over. In *Silver Trails* (Christy Cabanne, 1948), Whip Wilson was introduced as a possibility for a new Monogram series. One could only surmise that although Wilson wasn't about to set the Western world afire, he would at least suffer little in comparison to Wakely, hence the introductory footage. The Wakelys gave way after *Lawless Code* (Drake, 1949), not to be mourned.

Columbia played straight into the hands of the country music lovers when producer Colbert Clark inaugurated a series of Western musicals, or musical Westerns. It's not quite certain what they were, exactly; what they weren't was good. *Sing Me A Song of Texas* (Vernon Keays, 1945) was the first, and the only authentic Western facet of it was the presence of Tom Tyler, billed second to Rosemary Lane, in the main role. "Big Boy" Williams and Slim Summerville were in it, as well as a bunch of musical acts like the Hoosier Hot Shots and Pinky Tomlin. Columbia made many of these over the next five or six years. They can't properly be considered Westerns, because they neither look nor sound like Westerns. Except once. *Over the Santa Fe Trail* (Ray Nazarro, 1947)

Jimmy Wakely, Dub Taylor and Steve Clark in Oklahoma Blues *(1948).*

Whip Wilson (r.), soon to be a star in his own right, alerts Dub Taylor, Robert Strange and Wakely to the danger they face in Silver Trails *(1948).*

did have a Western plot, a period one about a traveling medicine show, and it made some noises like hoofbeats and gunshots to bolster its Western claim. In the hero role was Ken Curtis, formerly of the Sons of the Pioneers and leading man in several previous musicals. Curtis wasn't about to go anywhere in this series, which gradually drifted to the point where the Hoosier Hot Shots, then country singer Eddy Arnold, were receiving top billing, and the stories became divorced from the Western milieu completely. Curtis had the makings of a strong cowboy lead. Not only could he sing, but he was adept at performing his own rough work. He starred in a couple of independent Westerns later on. *Stallion Canyon* (Harry Fraser, 1949) was filmed on location near Kanab, Utah, and the unfamiliar scenery partially atoned for the slipshod handling of the story and action. In *Riders of the Pony Express* (Michael Salle, 1949) Curtis had more of a chance to display his abilities. He did some gun-twirling, and engaged in several slam-bang fights without a double, doing some pretty fancy tricks in the process. Both the latter films were photographed in color, and the hues in *Pony Express* were so muddy it was at times difficult to distinguish the actors. But Curtis was good, when you could see him, and so was John Dehner as the villain. It was near the end of the Western cycle, so Curtis accepted some John Ford character roles and finally found a home on TV's *Gunsmoke*.

Ken Maynard and Hoot Gibson in Westward Bound *(1944).*

21
LAST HURRAHS

Neither Buck Jones nor Tim McCoy had been off the screen in 1941. Yet when they were teamed by Scott R. Dunlap and Monogram, together with Raymond Hatton to form the "Rough Riders" series, it seemed more a return from the past than the matching of two busy pros. In truth, the trials had been long and harsh for both of late. Jones had been playing in serials, but serials weren't what they used to be; and one of the chapter plays had been one of those "all-star" Universal clambakes, with Buck one of the crowd. The other serial was a reworking of his 1932 feature *White Eagle,* only the 1941 version was directed by James W. Horne and not Lambert Hillyer; Horne had done too many Laurel & Hardy comedies, and got laughs where there shouldn't be any. Other than those far from gratifying assignments, Jones had been playing supporting roles, as a crooked sheriff yet, and had resigned himself to the fact that his attempt to come back in a 1939 non-Western hadn't panned out. He hadn't been privileged to star in a Western series since his so-so Columbia set for Coronet Pictures, ending in 1938.

McCoy, on the other hand, had been top-lining several Western series. But they had been for independent producers, his last notable series being for the same Columbia releasing organization and ending in 1935. Since then he had starred for Puritan, generally well-received; for Maurice Conn through Monogram, only four replacement Westerns but of good quality; for Victory, giving him some chances to impersonate Mexicans and Chinese and indulge in fancy makeup, with the films of highly variable quality; and of late, for PRC, suffering the ignominy of a supporting songsmith and combatting unlikely characters such as enemy agents on the range.

It was Scott Dunlap's idea to team two near-legendary Western stars in a series. Dunlap had directed Jones in the silents, and had served as the star's manager; their friendship was of long standing, and based upon mutual respect. Monogram, beset with troubles caused by cowboys coming and going in revolving-door fashion, needed a strong series, and with Dunlap personally supervising, the series had prospects of developing into the company's top product.

A third member was needed, for what would pass as comedy relief. Selected was Raymond Hatton, already a veteran of the Three Mesquiteers at Republic, a handy actor to have around, and not just for working for laughs. The three stars were into their fifties when the series began—if one is to believe one's Almanac, Hatton was actually the youngest—but were in fine physical condition, with Jones and McCoy little changed since their first sound Westerns.

Eight "Rough Riders" features were made. Spencer Bennet directed the opening two, *Arizona Bound* and *Gunman from Bodie.* Robert N. Bradbury concluded a long outdoor career by directing *Forbidden Trails,* the final 1941 release. The rest of the series, all 1942 releases, were directed by Howard Bretherton. All eight were scripted by Jess

245

HOLLYWOOD CORRAL: A COMPREHENSIVE B WESTERN ROUNDUP

Buck Jones, Tim McCoy and Raymond Hatton in Arizona Bound *(1941).*

Bowers—a pen-name of Adele Buffington. Buffington-Bowers limned three identifiable characters in sharp relief. Jones played Buck Roberts, a fightin' man in true Jones tradition. McCoy was Tim McCall, steely-eyed, brains over brawn by preference but willing and able to take care of himself in a precarious situation. Hatton was Sandy Hopkins, the equivalent of what would be termed "a character," but with plenty behind that folksy facade. The three lawmen, as per script, would be called in on a case, and McCoy and Hatton would work undercover, while Jones would handle the more explosive aspects. Some of the character facets were pure hokum—Buck Roberts slowly chewing gum when riled, or the unnecessarily lengthy farewells at the end of each episode when the trio would head for different points, taking separate trails. However, the conception was a winning one, and would overcome any flaws in the design.

It would also have to surmount a malady increasingly apparent as the series went on, a tendency toward talkiness at the expense of action. This obstacle would not be made plain for a while. The first two in the series were slickly directed by Spencer Bennet, the novelty helped, and there was, if not a surfeit, enough Western action to lend a satisfactory impression. *Arizona Bound* also got Hatton's biggest and most honest laugh in the series. Being served tea by Kathryn Sheldon, she asks if he'd prefer one lump or two. "Six," responds Hatton with a twinkle in his eye. From the look on Miss Sheldon's face, it might have been an ad lib. *Gunman from Bodie* provided equal opportunities for Jones and McCoy to score, with Jones as a gunman and McCoy impersonating a gambler. *Forbidden Trails* got the action steaming ahead at the outset, placing Jones in a burning shack while outlaws fire barrages at him, blocking escape. The sequence lasts well into the second reel, and the fast pace is maintained by Bradbury.

Below the Border kept up the good work, with Jones posing as a bandit again, and McCoy as a cattle buyer. But *Ghost Town Law* slipped a bit, with too much inactivity caused by undue detail in the plot, with a mystery angle that never was as mysterious as it should have been. *Down Texas Way* changed the formula slightly, with Jones and McCoy riding to the aid of Hatton, accused of murder; otherwise, it was standard. *Riders of the West* tended to amble but sufficed, and the last in the series, *West of the Law*, moved right along, with Jones posing as an outlaw and McCoy this time impersonating a minister. If the formula had become too familiar, the fans didn't complain, for the trio worked together with super precision. The series probably drew as many adults as kids, grownups who remembered the stars from the silent flicks and desired (furtively) to relive their own youths at the Saturday matinees. Like this audience, the stars had mellowed, perhaps slowed up some, but still looked good and enjoyed themselves.

What the eventual fate of the "Rough Riders" series would have been is open to conjecture, for a couple of momentous events occurred, one a tragedy. With the onset of World War II, Tim McCoy, a long-time reservist, was placed on active duty. Jones and Hatton proceeeded to appear in *Dawn on the Great Divide* (Bretherton, 1942), still portraying their "Rough Riders" characters of Buck Roberts and Sandy Hopkins. Filling in for McCoy was former Monogram cowboy star Rex Bell, in the role of Jack Carson. Further changes were noted. Dunlap had opened the production budget, and it showed in the cast. It was a wagon-train tale, and among the passengers were Mona Barrie, Robert Lowery, Betty Blythe, names not normally associated with Westerns, as well as Robert Frazer, Dennis Moore, Harry Woods, Christine McIntyre and Tristram Coffin, all at home on the range. Buffington-Bowers based her script on a James Oliver Curwood yarn, and sup-

Hatton covers Murdock McQuarrie while Jones rounds up an unidentified heavy and Tom London, and McCoy nabs Ben Corbett in Ghost Town Law *(1942).*

plied deeper characterizations than the average Western. Running longer than usual at 70 minutes, the film was released on December 18. On the night of November 28, Buck Jones had lost his life in the horrendous Cocoanut Grove fire in Boston. The film would be his epitaph, and a majestic presence left the world of Westerns.

In the course of things, the show must go on, and at Monogram it was to go on in a manner that had proved profitable. If Buck Jones and Tim McCoy had teamed so well, why not Ken Maynard and Hoot Gibson? Well, there were some differences. Maynard had been off the screen since 1940 and Gibson since 1937. True, their names were firmly implanted in the public mind, and even the small fry had at least heard of them. But while they were a year or two younger than their predecessors, they were considerably more frayed about the edges. With Maynard, the edges had become boundaries of imposing dimensions; politely, he would be a "stylish stout." Gibson, never a contender in the Greek God sweeps, was more weather-beaten than ever—that face had seen a lot of living, and with the lines and creases it resembled a war map. Despite the physical drawbacks, producer Robert Tansey went ahead. He signed Alan James to direct the openers, then took over personally on the third and did double duty the rest of the way.

In the first release of the "Trail Blazers" series, for that is what it was called, Maynard and Gibson are called in to recover some stolen horses. At this time, 1943, wartime America was rife with sinister rumors concerning local butchers palming off horse meat as beef. Adding a topical note to a period movie, Ken and Hoot are wished luck in their assignment to retrieve the purloined equines, and Maynard assures, "Don't worry... horses're our meat!" followed by a long double-take and look at Gibson. Thereafter, *Wild Horse Stampede* stuck closely to outdoor formula, with the action lively but routine. However, the brief tongue-in-cheek business at the beginning gave rise to hopes that there would be some fun to be found in succeeding members of the series. Incidently, another wistful note was sounded upon the appearance of Bob Baker, billed third but taking a minor, non-singing part as the young marshal aided by Maynard and Gibson. Baker made no further films.

Dave O'Brien (l., with bow tie) and Luana Walters help McCoy clear Hatton while sheriff Glenn Strange, Tom London (above Hatton), Frank Ellis and others watch in Down Texas Way (1942).

Ken Maynard holds Stan Jolley at bay while Hoot Gibson restrains Kenneth Harlan in Wild Horse Stampede *(1943). Former star Bob Baker and Betty Miles observe the procedings solemnly.*

Second in the series was *The Law Rides Again* (1943), not up to, or more realistically below the standard of the first entry. Some good faces in Jack LaRue, Kenneth Harlan and Chief Thundercloud, little else of interest. Then Tansey took over direction on *Blazing Guns* (1943) and matters perked up. This is not to assert that the "Trail Blazers" series represented Westerns at their best. Far from it— everything Tansey directed looked like it had been filmed 20 years previously, and Marcel Le Picard's camerawork enforced this illusion with its flat lighting. And Tansey allowed some bizarre lapses to infiltrate the show; how to account for the strange reaction of Weldon Heyburn during a fight with Maynard? Downed by a blow, Heyburn angrily struggles up, then promptly collapses, out cold— Maynard's delayed phantom punch, perhaps. Or at another point, when Maynard is slugged and quietly passes out in a convenient corner—at one showing, snores were heard from the audience. All this complicated by Maynard's protrusion; with two guns drawn they seemed to be resting comfortably on his paunch. Gibson looked worn, but his sly sense of humor did a lot to hold the film together. Tansey's accustomed series scripter Frances Kavanaugh, came up with a rather neat plot gimmick, that of the heroes rounding up ex-convicts to help them clean up a lawless town. Tansey had used it before, and would use it again.

With *Death Valley Rangers* (1943), Bob Steele was pressed into service to make the "Trail Blazers" a trio. The result was one of the fastest Westerns of the season. Steele energetically joined in the ridin' and fightin' and also gave the ingenue a reason for being in the picture, something that could not be hoped for with Maynard and Gibson. The film featured some great sight effects, such as a terrific flying mount performed by Steele, and near-continuous chasing around. At one point, after a lengthy and acrobatic flight on horseback from the baddies, Gibson pauses to take a welcome sip from a stream. He is hardly finished when the varmints once more catch up with their prey, and when motioned by Maynard to get a move on, Gibson simply makes an expression of disgust, "Awwww," as if to say, let 'em come, I'm tired.

In *Westward Bound* (1944), Hoot demoralizes the gang by throwing dynamite at them. Only Tansey inexplicably shows the dynamite sticks landing on the ground, then the set charges go off several feet away from the dummy sticks, still in plain view. Such minor details didn't seem to bother him—or the theater fans for that matter.

After the next, *Arizona Whirlwind* (1944), Maynard bowed out of the series, after having voiced his unhappiness with the way things were going, financially and otherwise. Tansey continued the series, with Chief Thundercloud surprisingly selected to replace Maynard. *Outlaw Trail* (1944) and *Sonora Stagecoach* (1944) turned out quite well, full of action, with no waste motion, edited to the bone with all nonessentials omitted. Chief Thundercloud appeared happy to be in on the fun, and Gibson and Steele were better than ever.

Tansey dropped out of the series, having some ideas about Cinecolor and related matters. Monogram strove to keep the series going. Alas, those who took over the production duties had never scanned the previous entries, it would seem. *Marked Trails* (1944) was written and directed by J. P. McCarthy,

Trail Blazers Maynard, Bob Steele and Gibson in Death Valley Rangers *(1943)*.

Hoot and Ken watch Bob deliver the knockout blow to George Chesebro in Arizona Whirlwind *(1944).*

and could have been a reject from the Jones-McCoy "Rough Riders," plus some echoes of the past in the plot peg of a search for the killer of Steele's uncle (it was usually his father, in the old days). Steele poses as an outlaw, a la Jones, with Gibson impersonating a hellfire reformer in the McCoy mold. After the artless but exciting moments in the previous entries, the sluggish movement was even more noticeable. The "Trail Blazers" identification tag was summarily dropped. Chief Thundercloud had disappeared with *Marked Trails*, and now Steele was to be billed above Gibson. Victor Hammond, who had co-written *Marked Trails* with McCarthy, soloed on the final two, with Vernon Keays directing both. *The Utah Kid* (1944) was a mess of stock rodeo footage and a silly story about crooks who manage to take the big events. In *Trigger Law* (1944), Steele and Gibson set out to avenge the murder of—Steele's father. That was that. Steele carried on, but Gibson drifted out of pictures save for an infrequent cameo.

In their respective travels, Maynard and Tansey crossed paths briefly for a Walt Mattox production filmed in 1944, entitled *Harmony Trail*—and then *White Stallion* in 1947, when Astor Pictures states' righted it on the independent market. Tansey used his shortened Robert Emmett name as director, but the pattern followed the "Trail Blazers" series closely. Tansey used an old friend, Rocky Camron, for a marshal role. Camron, formerly Gene Alsace, had appeared in a number of Tansey productions, including the Maynard-Gibsons, and was a competent Western type. The plot had Marshal Camron calling in some friends to help track down bank robbers. Said friends were Maynard, Max Terhune and Eddie Dean, making it one Western where the good guys seemed to outnumber the crooks. Anyway, Maynard had a final opportunity to show off his prowess with a lariat, Terhune still had the dummy Elmer, and Dean really trilled "On the Banks of the Sunny San Juan." The girl was Ruth Roman, who would mean more on the marquee than all the rest in short order. Thus did some stars fade from the Western scene.

Johnny Mack Brown

22
BROWN OF ALABAMA

You might say that the career of Johnny Mack Brown is what John Wayne's would have been, if *Stagecoach* hadn't happened. Perhaps, but in cold print it looks like a putdown, which it certainly isn't meant to be. In truth, Brown's Western career began with a big splash, as did Wayne's, and both their films were unsuccessful, or disappointing, at the boxoffice. Thereafter, both floundered somewhat in dramatic roles, stiff and uncomfortable, and both gradually drifted into low-budget Westerns to attain some measure of popularity. Where Wayne carved a trail to fame, Brown became the durable cowboy star, starting at the same time as Charles Starrett with a Western series and rivaling the Columbia player for length of service, though not with one studio. If Wayne's screen work was more concentrated on the Western form, then Brown's film experience surely ranged wider in his variety of roles. If Wayne hit meteoric heights, Brown's coterie of well-wishers was no less rabid.

There was a courtly Southern charm about Brown, which was at times a help and a hinderance. In his earlier, younger days, this suggestion of graciousness and nobility would tend to overemphasize a dramatic situation and cause some stiltedness in his playing. Later on, settled and secure in his Western roles, it lent a warmth to his acting that was missing from most range heroes, even the best of them. It served to contrast his more rugged duties in films, too. This handsome, polite gentlemen could also fight like the devil, and was the meanest looking man in pictures when engaged in hand to hand combat. When Johnny Mack swung a haymaker and it connected, it was felt right to the last row in the balcony.

Brown stayed with Monogram the longest, spending over half of his 17 Western years there. He arrived in the first place to take up the slack left by the curtailment of the "Rough Riders" series, hastened by the death of Buck Jones. Brown's Monograms began as direct descendants of the Jones-McCoy-Hatton films, with Hatton inherited by Brown and playing the same role, that of Sandy Hopkins. Fans remember him most clearly from the Monograms, but lest it be forgotten, Brown had enjoyed successful series at Universal and Republic, via the independently produced Supreme Pictures product. Prior to that, he was known for his serial appearances, and in the beginning for his starring role in King Vidor's 1930 outdoor large-screen epic, *Billy the Kid*.

Gridiron fame preceeded Brown's screen career. A halfback on the University of Alabama's football team, Brown became a sports hero in the Rose Bowl game against the University of Washington in 1926, scoring the winning touchdown in movie-story style. By 1927, he was in the movies himself, and by 1928 he was contending for the cinema affections of Greta Garbo and Joan Crawford. *Billy the Kid* was his biggest and most important role to date.

Brown and *Billy the Kid* made the theaters just before Wayne and *The Big Trail*. Metro's Realife big-

Brown, starring in Billy the Kid *(1930) for director King Vidor (center), receives one of the famous outlaw's guns from former Western star William S. Hart.*

screen process thus arrived ahead of the Fox Grandeur system. Both purportedly had the effect of drawing the audience into the midst of the action. Some of the effects Vidor captured in *Billy the Kid* are startling, and have impact even on a small screen; the scenic backgrounds are magnificent. The story is a whitewash of the legendary outlaw, and far from accurate, down to the tacked-on happy ending (two conclusions were filmed, with M-G-M going with the fairy-tale approach). Brown's performance is adequate, sometimes more than that. Vidor occasionally injects little bits of business, like Brown's casualness when trapped in a burning building, pausing with flames tonguing around him to light a cigarette before making his escape. But neither the picture nor Brown's role were enough to overcome public apathy to the large-scale Western form, or the big-screen come-on. Brown's next M-G-M film was an outdoor saga, *The Great Meadow* (Charles Brabin, 1931), which attracted no more than cursory attention. His next was a gangster picture, *The Secret Six* (George Hill, 1931), in which he had the misfortune to be cast in proximity to Clark Gable, and the fledgling star so overshadowed Brown that his subsequent roles were of lesser stature, and his M-G-M contract expired and was not renewed.

Brown was cast as a Texas Ranger in a low-budget Universal trifle, *Lasca of the Rio Grande* (Edward Laemmle), and was the lead in a Paramount minor Western, *Vanishing Frontier* (Phil Rosen, 1932). Neither film was any great shakes, but if nothing else, they reinforced the theory that Brown was at his best on horseback. A large if economical step in solidifying this position occurred with the Mascot serial *Fighting with Kit Carson* (Armand Schaefer & Colbert Clark, 1933). Brown had the title role, thus playing a desperado and a frontiersman within a few years. Skulduggery was given to Noah Berry Sr., and he left no doubt that he was a dastard. Noah Jr. was also in the cast as a young brave. With its melange of marauding Indians, mystery riders and the like, it was 12 chapters of unadulterated hoke, but the kids ate it up and Brown did cut a dashing figure as the athletic fictionalized hero. Several not so fortunate roles followed, plus one diverting stint opposite Mae West that did nothing for him, although the work must have been fun. His second serial followed late that year, *Rustlers of Red Dog* (Louis Friedlander, 1935) filmed for Universal. The simple story had Brown pitted against Harry Woods for 12 episodes. Raymond Hatton played one of Brown's aides, as he would later at Monogram.

Immediately following the serial, Brown starred in his first Western series, a skein of eight features for A. W. Hackel's Supreme Pictures, released on the independent states' rights market. Hackel was also busy during this period producing the Bob Steeles, and the quality of each series was uniform, with generally sturdy plots, capable direction and a goodly share of range action. Perhaps Brown had the edge, with some balanced storytelling combined with good casting resulting in some decidedly better than average releases for an independent company.

Between Men (Robert N. Bradbury, 1935) was a shining example of what an intelligent script (Charles Francis Royal) and stout trouping can do for a horse opera. William Farnum had a role almost equal in size to the star's, playing Brown's long lost father. Farnum had a chance to swing into action with a fight recalling his *Spoilers* days, Brown's earnestness gave his role conviction, and Bradbury helmed a finale full of gunsmoke and charging riders that was most impressive for the small budget. *Valley of the Lawless* (Bradbury, 1936) had a non-comedy role for George Hayes which he handled in fine style, and Brown again showed authority in his heroics. In *The Crooked Trail* (S. Roy Luby, 1936), Brown defied convention by getting hitched in the middle of the picture. Brown was prone to matrimony—Ford Beebe tied the nuptial knot for him at Universal three years later. In addition to Brown's good work, the film had a standout nasty part for John Merton, perhaps the best of this engaging heavy's Western tenure.

Hackel arranged to release the Browns and Steeles through the new Republic organization for the next set of eight. Production quality remained steady, even though the Supremes suffered in comparison to Republic's home-made product, lacking their smoothness and technical know-how. Albert Ray directed the first two, Sam Newfield the remaining

Frank LaRue, Al St. John, Iris Meredith and Johnny in A Lawman is Born *(1937).*

half dozen. The Newfields rate among the busy director's better efforts, on the leisurely side perhaps, but with slightly more depth than the ordinary juvenile Western, aided as always by Brown's sincere thesping. Supporting casts were of help too, with Iris Meredith and Dick Curtis in their pre-Columbia days and evil-looking Warner Richmond, reptilian Ted Adams, and the perennials Karl Hackett, Charles King, Earl Dwire, Horace Murphy, Bud Buster, Steve Clark and on and on. Of more than average interest were *The Gambling Terror* (1937), with its straight forward narrative, and *Guns in the Dark* (1937), with its gimmick of Brown averse to using his artillery because he thinks he unintentionally killed his best friend.

Except for three Universal serials, *Wild West Days* (Cliff Smith, 1937), *Flaming Frontiers* (Ray Taylor & Alan James, 1938) and *The Oregon Trail* (Ford Beebe & Saul A. Goodkind, 1939), Brown didn't receive anything in the Western series line after the Hackels ended. The serials were done in typical Universal fashion, with an overabundance of library footage at times. His other Western work was limited to two Paramounts, both released at the tail end of 1937. He played opposite John Wayne in *Born to the West*, as noted previously, and was featured in Frank Lloyd's cumbersome epic *Wells Fargo*, meeting his demise early in the lengthy footage. The period spent without a series was worth the wait, for Universal then signed him for a series, teaming him with Bob Baker and comic Fuzzy Knight. It was the studio's most ambitious Western schedule since the days of Buck Jones, and high hopes rode with Johnny Mack.

Albert Ray, who had directed some Supreme releases with Brown, was entrusted with *Desperate Trails* (1939), his first for Universal. The Andrew Bennison scenario had plenty of room for action, perhaps too much. Some of it was difficult to swallow, even for a Western. For instance, as Brown is chased over hill and dale, he whips out his trusty rifle and fires back at his pursuers, one-handed, hitting the target each time. His sharpshooting was sarcastically applauded at one theater showing.

James Craig (l.) helps Johnny capture Frank McCarroll, Kermit Maynard and Bob Kortman in Law and Order *(1940).*

Johnny bops Roy Barcroft in The Old Chisholm Trail *(1942).*

Looking on the rosy side, it was a good sign that there was no stinting on the action, which boded well for the series. Knight was in there with his mushmouthed comedy for those who appreciated him, but Baker seemed unsure of what exactly he was supposed to do; it was tough to resign oneself to less prominent roles, after a starring series.

Things improved with the second entry, *Oklahoma Frontier* (1939), written and directed by Ford Beebe. Brown was presented with a bride (Anne Gwynne), even though he was incarcerated before the marriage could be consummated. Baker must have seen the handwriting on the barn door in this one—he was killed off halfway through the film. Beebe kept the plot and counterplot in rapid motion. Another early good one was *West of Carson City* (Ray Taylor, 1940), with pretty Peggy Moran enhancing the scenery and Brown delivering some crushing haymakers, one ingeniously staged set-to having Brown literally knocking the acrobatic Frank Mitchell off his feet.

With nothing but frustration in his roles thus far, Bob Baker exited the series after number six. Filling in, in somewhat peculiar fashion, beginning with *Son of Roaring Dan* (Beebe, 1940) was petite Nell O'Day, as a sort of cowgirl auxiliary. O'Day's function in the series was never properly defined, but she was featured in 13 straight, and always welcome. She was an expert equestrienne, and shots of her galloping across the flatlands, caught by Universal's camera truck, were exciting in themselves. So were the shots of Brown riding, too—Universal did the best running inserts in the business. But O'Day, although attractive, was seldom if ever considered for the romantic laurels; Brown was invariably given one of the pretty Universal contractees for that purpose alone. If any romance ever entered into the O'Day relationship, it was Fuzzy Knight who would seem to be the recipient. Anyway, the Browns continued the good work into their second season, amassing a consistently high amount of Western enjoyment. *Law and Order* (Taylor, 1940) was inter-

HOLLYWOOD CORRAL: A COMPREHENSIVE B WESTERN ROUNDUP

Left to right: Johnny Bond, Scotty Harrel, Jimmy Wakely, Fuzzy Knight, Jennifer Holt, Brown, George Eldredge (in chair), Harry Strang, Robert Mitchum (on floor in front of desk) and Tex Ritter in The Lone Star Trail *(1943).*

esting for its source, the W. R. Burnett novel based on Wyatt Earp's exploits. It had served as the basis for a 1932 Walter Huston film with the same tag. The present version was not so self-consciously arty as the early feature, but was good fun. *Boss of Bullion City* (Taylor, 1941) also had speed as a major asset, as well as Maria Montez in an early, non-exotic role. *Law of the Range* (Taylor, 1941) was a creditable refurbishing of a good Buck Jones oldie, *The Ivory-Handled Gun*. It introduced a good young villainous type, Roy Harris, who later changed his name to Riley Hill and appeared with Brown at Monogram. The photography was in the care of a master too, Charles Van Enger.

Ford Beebe contributed a different one to Brown's third Universal season. *The Masked Rider* (1941) may have stood still for a while toward the middle to allow for a fiesta with a plentitude of singing and dancing, and it added class to the production and didn't interfere with the story too much. Joseph H. Lewis directed three of the season's seven, with *Arizona Cyclone* (1941) especially noteworthy, thanks to the Lewis penchant for camera angles. It was intelligently thought out from a directorial point of view, and showed amply that Lewis was ready for the big time. His handling of the outdoor scenes in *The Silver Bullet* (1942) were also logical and eye-catching.

With the 1942–43 season, the Johnny Mack Brown series was revised to permit Tex Ritter, fresh from Columbia and Bill Elliott, to join the star. Unlike Bob Baker, Ritter wouldn't be content to sing and take a back seat for the action. His roles were written as integral to the plots, and the seven Brown-Ritters were superior. The first one had a hot song title to add to the boxoffice lure, *Deep in the Heart of Texas* (Elmer Clifton, 1942). William Farnum again played Brown's father, the action was exciting, and the new series off to a good start. The longest title was *Tenting Tonight on the Old Camp Ground* (Lewis D. Collins, 1942), but the top member of the series was the last, *The Lone Star Trail* (Taylor, 1943). Robert Mitchum had one of his early bad-guy parts, and there was a tremendously vicious, realistic barroom scrap, with Brown making his punches appear to land solidly, and sporting cuts and bruises at the conclusion, something rare in these antiseptic low-budget Westerns. Even as it was in release,

Brown had moved to Monogram and his first ones for that studio were on the market.

In keeping the strains of the Jones-McCoy "Rough Riders" series, producer Scott R. Dunlap merely eliminated the McCoy character, leaving Brown with the role of Nevada Jack McKenzie and Hatton in his customary role indulging in some impersonations when the occasion warranted. *The Ghost Rider* (Wallace Fox, 1943) was a very tentative introduction to the new series, with practically no action, a maximum of conversation. It was a Jess Bowers-Adele Buffington script, as would be a large number of the series entries. *The Stranger from Pecos* (Lambert Hillyer, 1943) had considerably more excitement including a good scrap, while *Six-Gun Gospel* (Hillyer, 1943) had practically none—but it did offer a neat trick of Brown getting the drop on a baddie by roping the gun from his holster, which almost compensated for the tedium which preceeded it. *Outlaws of Stampede Pass* (Fox, 1943) plods along, until a sudden burst of savagery which has Brown taking a heavy, Charles King, by complete surprise and proceeding to beat the living daylights out of him. It is done so realistically by Brown, and King receives the mighty blows with such uncomprehending amazement, the sympathy is all on the side of Wrong. Two non-Buffington scripts were of interest for opposite reasons. *Partners of the Trail* (Hillyer, 1944), by Frank H. Clark, didn't have much to say but took a long time in saying it. However, the dialogue was good even if there was too much of it, and the prose assumed a sort of stateliness that one could appreciate, if not admire. This was followed by *Law Men* (Hillyer, 1944), by the old comedy hand Glenn Tryon. He took a simple plot about a gang of bank robbers and tidied it up neatly. No innovations, but everything fell into place smoothly, and Brown seemed to be enjoying himself more than on some previous occasions. Brown revealed a heretofore hidden facet of his accomplishments in *Ghost Guns* (Hillyer, 1944). With the story concluded and some film still in Harry Neumann's camera, Hillyer decided to show off Johnny Mack's dexterity with a .45, so Brown nonchalantly un-

Johnny has a badguy hogtied in Frontier Feud *(1945).*

holstered and proceeded to twirl, flip and twist the gun end over end, over the shoulder, spinning round and round. It was a great flash act, and Brown repeated it once or twice in later films.

In 1945, Brown departed from his continuing role as Nevada Jack McKenzie, and starred in *Flame of the West,* produced by Dunlap on a larger scale than the series, and apparently intended as a prestige Western for Monogram. Lambert Hillyer directed with the same somber grace he had imbued in the William S. Hart silents, and Brown's role was unusual for him, playing a frontier doctor who earns the disrespect of the townsfolk because of his antipathy toward violence. Contrasted with Brown is the lawman who arrives to clean up the town, played by Douglas Dumbrille with forceful perception. The intense character studies build the narrative to a suspensefully strong climax. Adele Buffington, using her own name for this one, wrote the screenplay, and Brown and Dumbrille's fine performances were well supported by Joan Woodbury, Lynne Carver, Hatton in a minor role, and villains Harry Woods and Raphael Bennett. It was Brown's best Western, and anything coming after it would be anticlimactic.

After three more in his by-now traditional Nevada Jack role, fans of Johnny Mack must have been nonplussed to view the opening of *Drifting Along* (Derwin Abrahams, 1946), and discover Brown suddenly turned into a singing cowboy—dubbed of course, but a warbler all the same. Whatever possessed Dunlap, it was not an inspired idea, nor was the feature a world-beater. One film later, music was a major part of *Under Nevada Skies* (Hillyer, 1946), with former star Smith Ballew crooning some numbers. The fear grew that Brown was becoming confused with Jimmy Wakely in the eyes of Monogram execs. To the relief of many, the musical interludes disappeared from the Browns, but so did the characters of Nevada Jack and Sandy. Brown and Hatton played various roles thereafter.

A further attempt for the offbeat was *Raiders of the South* (Hillyer, 1947), with its Civil War back-

Douglas Evans, Brown, Kathy Frye and Raymond Hatton in Crossed Trails *(1948).*

ground. However, the Monogram budget didn't provide for the essentials, and the film was flat, despite a good job by Brown and Evelyn Brent's still-arresting smoky beauty. The Browns then assumed the dimensions of a basket of strawberries, with the viewer doing the sorting. Some were good, some were bad, and all looked pretty much alike. Raymond Hatton got one of his few legitimate laughs in the entire series in *Triggerman* (Howard Bretherton, 1948), by using an old yock device—he looked in a mirror, which promptly cracked.

Max Terhune came in to complement Hatton for *The Sheriff of Medicine Bow* (Hillyer, 1948), one of the slower ones in the series. Terhune used his old Range Busters name of Alibi and stayed on for two more with Hatton, who then called it quits and left Terhune to take care of the lighter moments. Terhune mosied around for five features, then eased off and left Johnny Mack on his own, sans laughs, which weren't too plentiful anyway. The series had assumed a rubber-stamp quality now. Brown had been putting on weight since his early Universals, and it had now, seven years later, become quite noticeable. He had been out of the romantic running for the entire Monogram series, and now used lower-echelon players like Riley Hill and Marshall Reed to attend to the yearnings of the leading ladies. The Browns were now indistinguishable.

A brief respite from the tedium came with *Colorado Ambush* (Lewis Collins, 1951). Myron Healey, an adept portrayer of meanies, wrote the script and gave himself the heavy role, and wrote a good one for Christine McIntyre. Although the dialogue resorted to "You're no good, and neither am I" cliches, it hadn't been heard in a low-budget Western too often. Healey also did the original story of *Texas Lawman* (Collins, 1951), with Joe Poland working on the screenplay.

Jimmy Ellison, looking as youthful as in his days with Hopalong Cassidy, joined Brown for six, none of which made any particular impression. In *Canyon Ambush* (Collins, 1952), Ellison's role was taken by Lee Roberts, and it proved to be the final Johnny Mack Brown Western. For the statistic-minded, the box score is as follows: for Supreme, Brown appeared in 16 Westerns, half of which were distributed by Republic. For Universal, four serials; and six co-starred with Bob Baker, 15 solo, seven co-starred with Ritter—total: 28. For Monogram, 66 features as a star, two supporting roles in Monogram-Allied Artists big-scale Westerns. He appeared infrequently thereafter, each time gaining a little avoirdupois. The latter years of his Western starring series had been mostly downhill, but he had outlasted most of the cowboy regulars. Completely in character, he departed quietly, without fanfare, and with style.

Lash LaRue

23
THE DECLINE OF THE WEST

Although the low-budget Western series lasted for a decade afterward, death knells began to toll in late 1945. Little signs, barely noticeable at first—a certain lassitude in the assembly-line productions; a hint of tiredness in the usually exuberant Republic series; most of all, a lack of appeal in the new crop of cowboy stars. No great rush to the boxoffice was inspired by the exploits of Monte Hale, James Warren, Kirby Grant or sundry others, grouped into a category that could be called the postwar crowd. While some stars like Gene Autry and Tim Holt returned from the service to take up where they had left off, and some of the Western mainstays remained just that, the potential inheritors of their mantle were proving to be not up to the task.

Not that the opportunities presented them were, at times, golden. With Eddie Dean, it was not only golden but all the colors of the rainbow—those that could be encompassed within the spectrum of glorious Cinecolor. Dean was to star in a series of tinted Westerns for PRC, with Robert (Emmett) Tansey producing and directing, and sometimes writing. Tansey was no newcomer to the color process, having directed Bob Steele in *Wildfire*, released in 1945. For that matter, the first Dean starrer, *Song of Old Wyoming*, although not officially released until November, 1945, was already being shown around in August of that year, as a sort of showcase for a new cowboy lead, a new color series, and a prestige piece for PRC. When the critical dust had settled, there was some agreement on certain issues. The color was pleasing to the eye, and enhanced the scenery; Dean had a nice, controlled singing voice; and a supporting actor named Al LaRue just about stole the picture. Taking the observations in order: Cinecolor would never replace Technicolor, but it did afford some soft, pastel shades that were refreshing; Dean had been in films for some time, and his singing ability was unquestioned; and when a supporting performer steals the attention from the debut of a new leading man, there's trouble ahead. There was LaRue, playing one of those roles calling for him to be a badman turned good long enough to stop a bullet. He was called Cheyenne in the film, was garbed all in black, and wore a perpetual snarl which was reflected in his voice. Several comments anent his resemblance to a young Bogart were heard and printed.

LaRue wasn't in the second Dean vehicle but returned for *The Caravan Trail* (1946), still depicted as on the edge of the law, but this time allowed to reform and stay upright for the conclusion. The film itself was routine, and Dean still made an impression only when he sang.

With the next, *Colorado Serenade* (1946), the role that would have been allotted to LaRue was taken

HOLLYWOOD CORRAL: A COMPREHENSIVE B WESTERN ROUNDUP

by David Sharpe, who aided with his unique specialty of performing, and presumably orchestrating acrobatic fisticuffing. Tansey's facility with directing knuckle-oriented mayhem was evident here, and Sharpe's sharpness helped the brawls no end. In this film, Roscoe Ates appeared for the first time as Dean's comedy sidekick. He replaced Emmett Lynn, he of the lolling tongue and stubby chin whiskers, and would continue with Dean until the bitter end. The color photography by Robert Shackelford was the best of the series, perennial varmint Charles King had a light-comedy role on the side of the law for a change and Dean carried himself nobly against the tide of drawbacks. A final Cinecolor Western, *Wild West* (1946) was similarly packed with action, mainly of the fistic variety, with Al LaRue returning to lend a hand, mostly by remote control since a double was used in the majority of shots. However, the effect of the Cinecolor Westerns at the boxoffice was mild, and the films were more expensive than the usual PRC release, so the color was curtailed. Tansey stayed on to direct three more black-and-white Deans, which were speedy but on a lower plane of productions than the previous ones. Then Jerry Thomas took over as producer, and Ray Taylor, late of Universal serials and Westerns, directed the rest of the Deans.

Bluntly, they weren't good. Taylor was a workmanlike action director, and probably better than Tansey when it came to handling actors and scripts. But Tansey could pace a Western like blazes and ride roughshod over the anachronisms, while Taylor most of the time could only do so much with a weak screenplay and lower-echelon talent. And the scripts did him in. In *West to Glory* (1947), there was a dream sequence wherein sidekick Ates changes places with Dean, who became the buffoon with Ates broadly playing the heroics. That's how desper-

Eddie Dean with Roscoe Ates and Dave Sharpe in Colorado Serenade *(1946).*

Eddie doesn't look happy with Roscoe as Lash warns him not to pick his teeth with a six-gun in Wild West *(1946).*

ate the situation became. Accentuating matters was the demise of PRC, absorbed by the Eagle-Lion Corporation, more money worries in tow. The Deans were already committed for the 1947–48 season, and by hook or crook Thomas and Taylor struggled through a set of eight more—or seven more, as will be related momentarily. The Deans showed no improvement, and when the schedule boiled down to *The Hawk of Powder River* (1948), it was obvious that scenes were being taken from earlier Dean films and plopped down within the new framework. Curiously, for all its cheating footage, *Hawk* was actually a bit better than several previous Deans had been. Thomas and Taylor had finished seven Deans, but the company needed another to meet the release schedule. Out came *Prairie Outlaws* in May, 1948. Trade reviewers were quite kind to it, commenting favorably upon the plentitude of action and fast pace. Nowhere was mentioned that *Prairie Outlaws* was the 1946 *Wild West,* shorn of some 15 minutes and released in black-and-white. Thus did Eddie Dean's tenure as a Western star come to an end, and thus did PRC come to an end.

While they were still operating in 1947, PRC, understandably impressed with the fan mail addressed to "Cheyenne" LaRue, wasted no time in devising a series for him. Ready and able, more chipper than ever, was Al St. John to continue his Fuzzy frolicking. In addition to his sinister appearance, part of his fascination, LaRue had become adept with a bullwhip, and PRC found it a handy exploitation peg. So he became Lash LaRue and was on his way. Thomas and Taylor did the producing and directing honors. The LaRues got by. Among the star's pre-cinema occupations had been that of hairdresser, a vocation not attuned to horsemanship, so this facet of his outdoor portrayal was on the tentative side. Nor did he handle his dukes with conviction, although Taylor covered this over with camera angles and doubles. Despite these obstacles, LaRue did present an offbeat Western figure, and St. John's clowning was a factor in helping the PRC

Lash and sidekick Fuzzy St. John in Border Feud *(1947).*

films make the grade. Best of the bunch was probably *Pioneer Justice* (1947), although something could be said for—and against—any of them.

With his eight Westerns for PRC completed, LaRue found himself without a distributor, but not for long. Screen Guild was a company that had been formed in 1945—their first release had been a pick-up of Tansey's Bob Steele Western, *Wildfire*. They had made a pass at the outdoor market with some Russell Hayden streamlined 40-minute mountie melodramas, but had not cultivated their own star of the West, until they signed LaRue and St. John. Ron Ormond was the new producer, with Ray Taylor carrying on with the directorial chores. Their first, *Dead Man's Gold* (1948) was a bit of an enigma. It was not so much written, as stitched together. The script was credited to Ormond and Ira Webb, but did one exist? If so, on who's cuff was it scribbled? The film consisted of practically no plot, scant dialogue, but much riding around, punctuated by bursts of action. To give the riding scenes some adrenalin, composer Walter Greene had his orchestra playing at fever pitch, even though nothing was occurring on the screen at the moment. It was noisy enough to keep the patrons awake, and made the action all the more welcome when it finally came. Ormond's Western Adventure company made six of the LaRues, and after the strange beginning it developed into quite a respectable little series. LaRue flourished a mean cracking whip, and these sequences were flashy enough to be worth the admission price. Somewhere along the line Taylor, or somebody, had given LaRue some fighting lessons and he had developed a wild trademark—to polish off the bad guy, he would thoroughly pummel the wretch, then deal a knockout blow by literally jumping in the air and come crashing down with a chopping right, a la Bill Elliott only more flamboyant. It was hokey, but never failed to get a rise out of the audience. Otherwise, the features were all right. *Outlaw Country* (1949) was allowed to run 71 minutes, and its overlength was never obvious because of the continuously flowing action. And *Son of a Badman* (1949), last in the Screen Guild series, boasted good names in Michael Whalen, ingenue Noel Neill and veteran Francis McDonald.

Western Adventure Productions found itself without a home, so Ormond took his LaRue property to Realart for distribution. The cast of the first of the new series, *King of the Bullwhip* (1950), was the best yet, with Jack Holt, Anne Gwynne, Tom Neal, Michael Whalen, Dennis Moore and George Lewis among the fine sagebrush talents involved. Ormond directed as well as produced, proving capable in the new capacity. The finale, an exhibition of whip-snapping as LaRue brings the (surprise) villain to justice, was excellently filmed. The future looked bright for the LaRue series, but it was the beginning of the end. Apparently, Ormond had used up a lot of coin for the first, and further expenditure was evident in his next. It was not a Lash LaRue Western—or, was it? Marquees would announce *The Daltons' Women* (Thomas Carr, 1951), with Tom Neal, Jack Holt, Pamela Blake, Raymond Hatton, Lyle Talbot, and perhaps for the more daring houses, a pin-up shot of Jacqueline Fontaine, a wide-eyed blonde with a deep singing voice, plus a chest in which to house it. All this added up to sex-on-the-range, but the film proved to be an odd mixture of loosely connected gambling-house scenes, action which didn't seem related to what was going on, and above all the sudden and surprising appearance of LaRue and St. John, lawmen out to bring to justice Dalton boy Jack Holt. Western fans, those who saw it, were confused, while the droolers were mightily disappointed at the relatively mild nature of the film.

Ormond made four more Lash LaRue Westerns. Or, if added up to a total of newly shot footage, more precisely two-and-a-half Westerns. For large hunks of footage from the LaRue Screen Guild series was used, with the flimsiest of excuses made to allow for the old material. LaRue's chase and subduing of Dan White was lifted bodily from *Outlaw Country;* action and riding scenes from *Dead Man's Gold* saw new usage. *The Frontier Phantom* (1951) tells its tale in flashback, the only legitimate introduction of stock shots. *The Thundering Trail* (1951) was practically all library material. Only *The Vanishing Outpost* (1951) managed to overcome the cheapness by adeptly editing in the retreaded action sequences. So rudely treated by production shortcomings, LaRue and St. John left the screen after suffering the indignities of the stock quartet. Both found a haven in personal appearances, often in tandem with one of their films. They were big boxoffice draws in the deep South, and they found a welcome there for a number of years. LaRue was one of the more interesting cowboys, mainly because of his offbeat approach and appearance. He was in the tradition of Don "Red" Barry, and might have enjoyed a more encompassing success had his producers been more astute.

Eagle-Lion, having emerged from the chrysalis of PRC, had acquired the rights to the "Red Ryder" comic strip for screening, and attempted to go Republic one better by filming the features in Cinecolor, resuming where the Eddie Deans had halted. To play the cowboy hero they selected a radio announcer-type, Jim Bannon. Longtime performer Marin Sais (Mrs. Jack Hoxie) played the Duchess, Emmett Lynn was in for comedy, and the part of Little Beaver was played by Don Kay Reynolds, also billed as Little Brown Jug. Jerry Thomas produced for Equity Productions, with Lewis D. Collins directing. Four new Ryder films were made. First was *Ride, Ryder, Ride* and then *Roll, Thunder, Roll.* After that the title should have been "Stop, Bannon, Stop!" because the films were poor. Two more for 1949, with the quality not noticeably improved, and the series called it quits. Bannon had been an okay lead in some Columbia non-Westerns and made a creditable horse-opera heavy, but the Ryder image was not for him.

Bannon landed a second-banana continuing character in a series of Westerns made by Monogram starring one Whip Wilson. A dozen features had already been released when Bannon joined. Wilson, as can be implied from his nickname, was adept with the bullwhip, in the style of Lash LaRue and Sunset Carson. In fact, he appeared to have all the requisites for a boxoffice cowboy, on paper. He could sing in a robust baritone, though this facet of his talent was subjugated to more strenuous pursuits; his horsemanship was superb, and his stocky but solid build added emphasis to his masculinity. He wore a hairpiece, but was able to keep his Stetson on most of the time. However, when it came to appearing on the movie screens, all the Wilson attributes seemed to misfire. No single explanation can account for it; Wilson just didn't come across on the screen. Monogram gave him a good script in *Crashing Thru* (Ray Taylor, 1949) for starters, and teamed Andy Clyde with him, which was a great advantage. But Wilson was stiff before the cameras, and wasn't

Jim Bannon as Red Ryder, Don Kay Reynolds as Little Beaver in The Fighting Redhead *(1949).*

convincing in the fighting scenes, pulling his punches. The series soon fell into a rut, with only a few managing to rise above the routine, while several hit several degrees below. *Haunted Trails* (Lambert Hillyer, 1949) was superior because of Clyde's prominence in Adele Buffington's script, and one of Hillyer's better directing jobs. *Outlaws of Texas* (Thomas Carr, 1950) had a well-devised screenplay by Dan Ullman; it was also Andy Clyde's last as Wilson's sidekick. For the next set, Fuzzy Knight and Bannon appeared as comedy relief and pard, respectively. But the series seldom rose above the ordinary. Knight drifted out, with no replacement, and Bannon was eventually spelled by Tommy Farrell or Lee Roberts. The 22nd Whip Wilson Western was *Wyoming Roundup* (Carr, 1952), and con-siderably better than most of what had gone before. Of course, it was the final Wilson entry. Wilson had never come close to challenging Johnny Mack Brown on the lot for supremacy, and remained a minor Western name. With all the factors in his favor, he should have climbed higher, even in the relatively short span allotted him.

Some already established Western names were experiencing some dusty trails. Sunset Carson Westerns, once the pride of Republic, were now the scourge of Astor Pictures. Astor was an independent clearing house for assorted oldies and shoestring independent productions. Carson had signed with producer Walt Mattox to make a few for Yucca Productions. Yucca is right. The films, directed by Oliver Drake, were terrible. *Deadline* (1948) was the most professionally made technically, and the worst. Whatever possessed Drake to stretch the narrative by inserting interminable shots of Carson and heroine Pat Starling galloping along cannot be fathomed, but the results induced a state of torpor bordering on the mesmeric. If the ennui drove one's focus upon Miss Starling, her bodily movements caused by the rhythmic pace of the steed became erotic—not enough to compensate for the other indelicacies, but a temporary stimulant. Besides, Starling was stacked. On the other hand, Carson, a towering six-footer-plus, was given opponents well below average height, and Sunset was hard put to make the brawls realistic. He exerted himself mightily to make the odds appear even, but the shrimps he battered about took the pummeling like so many bantam dolls. Carson's other three for Yucca weren't as tedious as *Deadline,* but were saddled with productions of the backyard variety. In fact, they were filmed in 16mm and blown up to 35mm for theatrical showing. Carson starred in one more independent production, filmed in Texas and also distributed by Astor, *Rio Grande* (Norman Sheldon, 1949). It was strictly amateur night on the Panhandle. In the cast was Bobby Clark, once of the Sagebrush Family and now grown older, if not wiser in the ways of acting.

Two Hopalong Cassidy proteges teamed for a quickie six for Lippert Pictures, formerly Screen Guild, in 1950. They were billed as Jimmie "Shamrock" Ellison and Russ "Lucky" Hayden, and appearing with them in each film were Fuzzy Knight and Raymond Hatton. The romantic interest, Betty (later Julia) Adams, also appeared in all six. So did Tom Tyler; so did George Lewis, and John Cason, and Stanley Price, and Bud Osborne, and Dennis Moore, and George Chesebro, and quite a few others. All six films were shot over the period of a

THE DECLINE OF THE WEST

Whip Wilson leads the posse in Nevada Badmen *(1951).*

month, using identical casts. Our friend from the Lash LaRue series, Ron Ormond, was the producer and collaborated on the scripts with Maurice Tombragel. Thomas Carr was the director. Being charitable about it, the score came out three up, three down, not a bad average for a mass rush job. *West of the Brazos* had some novel touches, such as Hayden's deafness resulting from cannon fire during the Civil War. Riding into an ambush, Hayden lopes along, blissfully unaware of the gunshots and bullets flying about him, until Ellison has to rescue him. The humorous bits, and the cohesive teamwork of Ellison and Hayden boded well for the series, and the next two, *Hostile Country* and *Marshal of Heldorado,* were fast, pleasant, and stressed the comedy. Then the others, probably afflicted by shooting late in the month, sloughed off sharply. *Colorado Ranger* got by, but *Fast on the Draw* was weak, and *Crooked River* filled in the gaps left by no budget with some Bob Steele library footage. When the series was over, Ellison and Hayden had shown they deserved better treatment.

Another Republic alumnus, Don Barry, found the going a little better than did Sunset Carson. He entered into a deal with Lippert, which allowed him to appear both in the saddle and in civilian clothes, but Barry eventually chose the Western trail. Ron Ormond (again!) produced, and Ford Beebe directed, two economical but fairly able stories in *Red Desert* (1950) and *The Dalton Gang* (1950). The former had Barry, Tom Neal, Jack Holt and some veterans in a padded but serviceable Western murder mystery; the outdoor scenes were pretty, but far too numerous, and long stretches of Barry tracking his quarry were underscored by an organ musical background, casting a funereal pallor over the proceedings. Once the plot got back on the track, it was okay, with Barry giving a typically thoughtful performance. The Dalton piece was preluded by nearly a reel of grainy stock footage while a foreword rambled on and on about the Old West. Once the library stuff was out of the way, the film became a moderately straightforward yarn with Barry as a marshal bringing the outlaws to justice. Barry made what might be termed a mini-Western series for Lippert in 1950. He was reunited with funster Wally Vernon from the Republics, and Robert Lowery also appeared in each of the four features, which William Berke directed. Patterned after higher budgeted Westerns, they missed the mark intended, but did

HOLLYWOOD CORRAL: A COMPREHENSIVE B WESTERN ROUNDUP

James Ellison as "Shamrock" in the 1950 Lippert series teaming him with Russell Hayden.

represent an earnest attempt to do something different in the lower-case Western field. All were credited as Donald M. Barry productions, in deference to the star. *Gunfire* had Barry as Frank James, coming out of seclusion when an impersonator (also Barry) starts using the James name to commit robberies. *I Shot Billy the Kid* was the outlaw (Barry) and lawman (Lowery) story over again with no variations, but was not too far from the notorious Howard Hughes fiasco about the same characters, and miles above it in the matter of taste. *Train to Tombstone* borrowed the *Stagecoach* motif and plunked it aboard a locomotive, and *Border Rangers* was in the more conventional Western groove, with Barry seeking his brother's murderer. These Barrys had their defects, but merited a nod for a good try.

Then there was John Carpenter, also known as John Forbes. Robert Tansey had used him in *Cattle Queen* (1951) in a supporting role, and then gave him a whole picture with *Badman's Gold* (1951). Carpenter was a Westerner who could ride and fight and do his own stunts and didn't look too badly, but when it came to putting a film together, he ran in bad luck. Admittedly, some of it was his own doing, since he assumed production supervision later on. But Tansey had nobody but himself to blame for *Badman's Gold,* unless it be co-scriptor Alyn Lockwood; she was a pretty girl who had been seen in several *Blondie* films at Columbia, and was now taking the ingenue role as well as indulging in literary efforts. But the film got laughs in the wrong places, and looked, as usual with Tansey, like something out of an old film library. Undaunted, Carpenter starred in *Son of the Renegade* (Reg Browne, 1953), which he produced, and wrote, and took the rap for, because it made *Badman's Gold* look good. Carpenter's company, Royal West Productions, next inflicted *The Lawless Rider* (Yakima Canutt, 1954) upon the unsuspecting public. Canutt must have had an off day, for everything indicates his thoughts were elsewhere. Considering Carpenter's script, Canutt can't be blamed. Not even the presence of Douglas Dumbrille, Frankie Darro, Noel Neill, Kenne Duncan and Bud Osborne, to say nothing of Texas Rose Bascom, a flower of the Hollywood plains, could help. As John Forbes, he starred in *Outlaw Treasure* (Oliver Drake, 1955), but as John Carpenter, he produced and wrote. Once again he had gathered a good supporting cast, Michael Whalen, Glenn Langan and Adele Jergens, Frank Jenks, Harry Lauter and others, but all were stymied by the script and production, although the present effort was slightly better than the previous atrocities. Carpenter's last along these lines was *I Killed Wild Bill Hickok* (Richard Talmadge, 1956), which endeavored to prove that the gunfighter (Tom Brown) was a skunk and deserved his fate.

In the musical Western sphere, Universal began a strange series of odd-length featurettes in 1948. At first they featured a singer known as Red River Dave, who warbled well but was painfully camera shy. He topped the cast in three, all filmed on the plains of upper New York state and directed by William Forrest Crouch, associated in days of yore with the "Soundies" juke-box reels. After three of these Universal decided there was no place to make a Western but Hollywood, so the idea was shipped coastward, Red River Dave was cast adrift, and Tex Williams, a popular Western-&-Country bandleader, took the hero roles. Nate Watt directed one or two, then producer Will Cowan, long busy on the lot with musical shorts, took over. Universal got their money's worth. Fifteen Tex Williams musical Westerns were made, running 20 minutes-plus. At the end of the string, the studio combined two of the featurettes to make a feature-length complication, which they titled *Tales of the West*. Three more *Tales of the West* features were spliced together, so that of the entire Tex Williams shorts output, half of them were used a second time for what was essentially new material in the feature schedule. The shorts were innocuous, with stress on the musical end, but Williams might have gone farther if he had started earlier.

Spade Cooley, self-styled "King of Western Swing," tried a leading role in *The Silver Bandit* (Elmer Clifton, 1949), but it was obvious Cooley would never be King of any Westerns. The production was purely amateur. Cooley tried again for director Richard Talmadge, a former acrobatic stunting star, in *Border Outlaws* (1950), but his role was secondary, with Bill Edwards doing the heroics. The film had a fast action ending, small reward for the ineptness of the preceeding 55 minutes.

Finally, Wayne Morris sort of eased into the last official Western series filmed by a regular motion picture studio, taking up the slack left by Bill Elliott's departure from the Western Milieu at Monogram. Morris had been starring in adventure films for the studio, and had made an offbeat Western, *Desert Pursuit* (George Blair, 1952), a Kenneth Perkins story that had Arabs on camels in Death Valley as the villains. This fanciful tale had been part of the Morris series for Lindsley Parsons, and went out under the Monogram label. His next was officially an Allied Artists film, since that organization was now about to envelop all Monogram product. His new producer was Vincent M. Fennelly, who had been supervising various Westerns at Monogram, including the Bill Elliotts. Dan Ullman wrote the script, and *Star of Texas* (Thomas Carr, 1953) was a novel effort that showed the influence of television's *Dragnet* series, right down to the documentary style of plot development and bridging narration by Morris as a Texas Ranger on a case. As with several Monogram Westerns of the period, there were no women evident in the cast, no time out for obligatory romantic byplay. It was a welcome change from the usual Western formula.

Ullman wrote the second Morris Western produced by Fennelly, *The Marksman* (Lewis Collins, 1953), and once again brought some new twists to the plot by using modern narrative methods, and considerably more character development than found in the run of the mill Western. Morris was inclined to be hefty and was not an authentic Western type, but his natural ability overcame the physical drawbacks. *The Fighting Lawman* (1953), script by Ullman, direction by Carr, made it three superior entries in a row. What Ullman was doing with the Morris series was to write screenplays which, with a modicum of updating, could be used just as well as modern gangster stories, with a cop or FBI man in place of a Texas Ranger or deputy marshal, and the parallel worked admirably. This time out Morris was after a gang of bank robbers, using a horse instead of a V-8. Ullman didn't write the next two for Morris; but *The Desperado* (Carr, 1954) had a strong screenplay by Geoffrey Homes and Clifton Adams, with a large role for James Lydon as a young Texan who teams with a wanted killer (Morris) to fight the head of the fascistic state police. The production was low-budget, but the results would have made the producer of any "A" film proud. Ullman wrote the last for Morris, *Two Guns and a Badge* (Collins, 1954), with Morris as an ex-con accidentally turned lawman. It was satisfactory on all counts and made a fittingly meritorious conclusion to a superior Western series—and one of the last.

Clayton Moore as The Lone Ranger.

24
"BUT FIRST, A BRIEF WORD FROM OUR SPONSOR..."

In the Spring of 1953, aficionados of Western movies might have welcomed the announcement on their favorite theater marquee of a new Western with Guy Madison and Andy Devine. If the Western devotee knew his stuff, more likely he would have grumbled under his breath and avoided the show completely—if he owned a television set. For it was at this time that Allied Artists began sticking together two unconnected episodes of the *Wild Bill Hickok* TV series with Madison and Devine, and marketing the operation as a new series of movie Westerns. It wasn't the first time that television had invaded the sanctified corridors of the local cinema; some non-Western shows had been fixed up and padded to feature length, making the transition from video to movie house with few if any complaints. But this was the first time a series of films, made for TV, had been put on the theatrical market only a short time after their run on the small screen. It typified the way the movie business was headed, and the sad state of the low-budgeted theatrical Western.

Wild Bill Hickok was one of the most popular TV series of its time. Madison and Devine appeared in 113 half-hour episodes, produced under the auspices of the old Monogram staff. Television, instead of inventing new techniques of its own, was content to borrow from the established, conventional motion picture methods. As a result, the *Wild Bill Hickok* episodes, and the innumerable TV series that preceded and followed it, were little more than low-budget horse operas accomplished in approximately half the running time of a theatrical feature. The quality of the various productions was uniformly low for most of the early TV years, improving as the rosters of the low-budget motion picture ranks diminished, and more Hollywood actors and technicians moved over to television. The *Hickok* series was studded with names which had appeared in the credits of many a "B" and low-budget Western from Monogram, including producer Wesley Barry, directors Frank McDonald and Thomas Carr, photographers William Sickner and John Martin; and the casts comprised of Western regulars. Madison's characterization was nowhere near the original Wild Bill Hickok, so the series was merely a traditional batch of short Westerns transposed to another medium. On the TV shows, even the opening credit music was taken from the old *Storm and War* agitato that introduced serials in the early '30s. The comedy relief of *Jingles* Devine was elemental, the plots necessarily cryptic, the action vigorous but routine. Nevertheless, the series was extremely popular, with adults as well as small fry, and enjoyed a seven-year production span, from 1951 to 1958. Even after the series had stopped production, syndicated reruns played constantly throughout the television world. Madison, whose star was in somewhat of an eclipse, won new popularity. If nothing else, *Wild Bill Hickok* proved the power of a TV audience in the making of a successful TV show.

Hickok was one of the first Western TV shows to make the grade. Right on its heels came *The Lone*

HOLLYWOOD CORRAL: A COMPREHENSIVE B WESTERN ROUNDUP

Andy Devine and Guy Madison on Wild Bill Hickok.

Ranger, having conquered radio and the movies, now a TV hit. The adventures of the masked man and his faithful Indian companion, Tonto, lasted through 221 episodes, 39 of which were filmed in color. Playing the title role was Clayton Moore, long a regular in Westerns, notably at Republic, where he had starred in several serials and played featured roles, from good guys to bandits. In two of his serials Moore had portrayed another legendary character, in *Jesse James Rides Again* (Fred Brannon and Thomas Carr, 1947) and *Adventures of Frank and Jesse James* (Brannon and Yakima Canutt, 1948). Moore somehow never acquired a Western series at Republic, though he was certainly entitled to one on his record, but his *Lone Ranger* series more than made up for his late arrival. Nor was Moore the only TV masked man. John Hart assumed the role for a while, but it is Moore, with Jay Silverheels as Tonto, who is most closely associated with the role. As a series, TV or otherwise, *The Lone Ranger* left much to be desired. Except for the two leads, everything about the series smacked of the second-rate. Many entire episodes were filmed within the confines of a cramped studio set, with outdoor locales ineptly imitated. Plots were juvenile, supporting performances not of the best grade, and the half-hours were tedious. But the magic of the name was still potent and the program lasted for eight prolific seasons, with the reruns still accounting for playing time via periodic revivals. The Jack Wrather company, producer of the TV show, also did two feature-length theatrical films in color with Moore and Silverheels, both of them on considerably larger budgets than their television counterparts. *The Lone Ranger* (Stuart Heisler, 1956) had "A" pretentions and "B" quality, being an ordinary horse opera except for the gimmick. In the cast was Bonita Granville, keeping an eye on the property; she was Wrather's wife, and a production associate in the company. *The Lone Ranger and the Lost City of Gold* (Lesley Selander, 1958) was more attuned to the "B" or TV demands, and thus more satisfactory within its limits. Both features were decidedly superior to the TV series. As a side-note, many of the latter were directed by

"BUT FIRST, A BRIEF WORD FROM OUR SPONSOR..."

George B. Seitz, Jr., son of the pioneer serial actor-director of the Pearl White era, and later director of the Hardy family series at M-G-M.

Another popular series of the early TV days, all but forgotten now, was *Adventures of Kit Carson*, with Bill Williams in the title role. The series lasted through 104 episodes from 1952 to 1955, and several features were compiled by joining two episodes, in the same manner as the *Wild Bill Hickok* shows; they were shown abroad, but not in the U.S. Williams was a competent if not outstanding Western lead, and the TV show can be described in the same way, allowing for the often primitive production schedules of early TV.

For a relatively short series, *Cowboy G-Men* won a lot of fans, and justifiably. The show starred Russell Hayden and Jackie Coogan as a couple of lawmen and lasted for one season, or 39 episodes (allowing for 13 repeats to fill out a year). Since it was syndicated, the 39 half-hours were stretched a long way, and the show enjoyed popularity long after Hayden and Coogan had gone on to other things. Since it was filmed in color, the series will be likely to entertain future generations as well. In all, it was a laudable project. Although slanted for the kids, it was happily without that condescending attitude that becomes the bane of the majority of juvenile programming. Hayden and Coogan worked smoothly as a team, with the latter's comedy not too broad and astutely valued. At the time it was produced, 1954–55, there were worse shows on the tube than *Cowboy G-Men*. There still are.

Hayden started his career behind the cameras on the Hopalong Cassidy features, and went behind them again for a TV series, *26 Men*. It starred Tris (Tristram) Coffin, former heavy in many a Tex Ritter, Johnny Mack Brown and numerous Monogram Westerns, and Kelo Henderson, a rangy type, in tales of the Arizona Rangers. Somehow, Hayden managed to produce 78 of these half-hours over 1957–59, and somehow the sales department got a goodly number of stations to play the syndicated series. For it was an amateurish skein, in truth. Production, stories and performances were remindful of the John Carpenter movie series of unmourned memory; in fact, Reg Browne, customary director of the first *26 men* season, had directed Carpenter's *The Lawless Rider*. Whether or not the viewers felt the series warranted a second group of 39 is not determined, but in fairness it might be said that the second half improved in some small measure over the inaugural set, which is not meant to be high praise. A better example of what could be accomplished within the same sphere can be found in *Tales of the Texas Rangers*, produced during 1955–58 by Screen Gems and starring Willard Parker and Harry Lauter. The 52 films were given a semi-documentary treatment, and the series was notable for its near-complete lack of feminine interest. Parker and Lauter were sufficiently businesslike, and the production values were in the solid Screen Gems-Columbia tradition.

Kirby Grant had tried a Western series for Universal and a mountie series for Monogram. He had been top-lined in a bunch of Columbia cornball rustic musicals beloved by fans of the Hoosier Hot Shots. Now he tackled TV, and scored his most lasting success as star of *Sky King*, nonsense about aerial adventures in a Western setting. Beginning in 1953, *Sky King* took to the air for 72 half-hour episodes. They were juvenile in concept and execution, except for Grant's serious, slightly stolid masculine presence. But the series caught on, and enjoyed a healthy run both on the CBS network and later in syndication.

Of the moveovers from the movies, Gene Autry went into television with a vengeance. His Flying A Productions were responsible for his own half-hour TV series as well as several others, including Gail Davis as *Annie Oakley*, which became a hit; *The Range Rider*, starring Jock Mahoney, one of the fastest TV series; Mahoney's co-star, Dick Jones, in a series of his own, *Buffalo Bill Jr.*; and a series for Autry's horse, Champion. The *Annie Oakley* series became prominent because of the novelty of a female Western lead, although the trick had been tried in the movies without success. Davis became a TV celebrity of sorts; she had come up through the ranks, from leading lady in theatrical Westerns. She appeared as *Annie Oakley* in 81 episodes.

Mahoney's past experience as a stuntman and double enabled him to enter into some energetic action escapades, and Jones as his partner ably kept apace. Of the 78 *Range Rider* adventures, "Let 'Er Buck!" stands out as one of the most action-packed half-hours on film. Directed by Thomas Carr, it is an unending series of athletic displays by Mahoney and Jones, which even manages to work in a plot about rodeo crooks. Jones later appeared in 42 *Buffalo Bill Jr.* shows, not quite up to the *Range Rider* action but pleasant, thanks to the exuberance of Jones. The *Champion* series entailed 26 half-hours of horseflesh, with former Red Ryder impersonator Jim Bannon heading up the bipeds.

Autry himself appeared in 85 half-hours, with Pat Buttram along as sidekick. In many ways, they were superior to the theatrical features Autry was in-

HOLLYWOOD CORRAL: A COMPREHENSIVE B WESTERN ROUNDUP

William Boyd as Hopalong Cassidy with sidekick Edgar Buchanan (playing Red Connors, Hoppy's sidekick in the books but a seldom-seen character in the features) in the TV series.

volved in at this time, 1951–54. The action was speedy, with no time out for nonessentials. Autry had hired a lot of his former co-workers away from the studios, and the surrounding experience helped him to produce TV shows which had the look of good, workmanlike low-budget theatrical Westerns. By contrast, Roy Rogers headed a production company which made 100 half-hour TV shows, starring Rogers and Dale Evans, with Pat Brady, formerly of the Sons of the Pioneers, in for buffoonery. Assorted extra gimmicks were included in the TV format. In addition to Roy's horse Trigger, there was a smart dog and Brady's jeep, but all the frills and fancies didn't help the series in elevating itself from the juvenile trench. Its popularity persevered because of the names, but Autry's TV savvy was far greater.

Screen Gems got plenty of mileage from a canine star with their *Adventures of Rin Tin Tin* series, good for 164 half-hours beginning in 1954. The series was given an Army-fort locale, which would technically place it in the Western genre. Without question is its outright catering to the juvenile audience. Lee Aaker, for the small fry, and James Brown and Joe Sawyer, the adult servicemen, handled the story portions, while the inheritor of the German shepherd star's crown convincingly woofed, whined, and wriggled on cue.

One of the most pedestrian series of the early TV days was *Steve Donovan, Western Marshal*, starring Douglas Kennedy and with Eddie Waller. NBC undertook to sell the Jack Chertok-produced series in 1953 and landed a fairly impressive number of stations, but the show hardly warranted the effort. There was little point or plan to the conception of it, with Kennedy, a dependable supporting player or heavy, quite unimpressive, and the shows cheaply made with practically no action.

In the Mounted Police field, Dick Simmons starred as *Sergeant Preston of the Yukon* for 78 episodes for Jack Wrather, and the popularity of the radio show helped no end—the TV show was weak, and probably wouldn't have gotten by without the impetus. Crawley Films offered the Canadian-made *R.C.M.P.* to much better results. Gilles Pelletier, John Perkins and Don Francks headed the weekly cast, and the show had some authenticity. However, its circulation was not wide in the U.S., compared to locally produced product, and it may have been slightly too austere and sober for some.

This then was the scan of Western-type shows paralleling the motion picture low-budget Western. In September 1955, *Gunsmoke* premiered on the CBS network and changed the course of the TV Western, and probably for the better in the long run. Speaking of long runs, *Gunsmoke* and James Arness & Co. bid fair to run forever. For *Gunsmoke* was made for adults, in two ways. The plots were mature, and the shows generally avoided the action sequences so vital a part of the low-budget Western. Succeeding series owed more to Marshal Matt Dillon than to Gene Autry or Buck Jones. Eventually, the half-hour Western would be a rarity, with *Gunsmoke* unfolding its tales in an hour's length and doing so advantageously while series like *The Virginian* would extend to 90 minutes. *Gunsmoke* made possible two of the best half-hour Western shows— and best shows of any type—in Richard Boone's satisfying, often sinister *Have Gun—Will Travel*, and what is perhaps the best of them all, the ill-fated Sam Peckinpah series with Brian Keith entitled *The Westerner*. Only 13 of these half-hours were filmed and NBC lost faith in the project because of quirky programming, but of the 13, at least ten are memorable indeed.

There are other TV shows, some of a special kind, which don't fall within the province of this report,

Duncan Renaldo as TV's Cisco Kid.

HOLLYWOOD CORRAL: A COMPREHENSIVE B WESTERN ROUNDUP

Col. Tim McCoy explaining Indian sign language on his TV show, Stories of the West.

such as the animal-oriented *Fury, Flicka* and other similar shows; the Indian yarns *Brave Eagle,* with Keith Larson and *Broken Arrow,* with Michael Ansara and John Lupton; the hour-length Disney spinoffs *Elfego Baca* with Robert Loggia and *Texas John Slaughter,* with Tom Tryon, not to mention Fess Parker's *Davy Crockett* and the already mentioned *Zorro.* The one company that would be expected to concentrate on Westerns in the early TV days was Republic, but its TV arm, Hollywood TV Service, offered *Stories of the Century,* a popular Western-crime series with Jim Davis and hordes of Republic library footage, and Rex Allen as *Frontier Doctor,* also with scads of stock, and little else. The interminable *Death Valley Days* and all its alternate titles with assorted hosts deserves mention, and a place of its own for separate study.

It was the Hopalong Cassidy feature-length theatrical films that first made a Western impact on TV. NBC started showing the features every Sunday evening in 1948, and soon had a surprise hit on its hands. At first they were shown straight through, no commercials, no interruptions, and it was grand to watch them again, since they held up so well. Then commercials started to be used, and heavily. Not long afterwards schedules became uniform and precise programming was the order of the day. The Cassidy features were trimmed to 54 minutes, usually by the simple expedient of lopping off the opening scenes and picking up the narrative often in the middle of a sentence. No matter, the films were still popular, butchered as they were. William Boyd became a celebrity once more, and went on to produce his own new Hopalong Cassidy series, a not particularly good one. The way was clear for Westerns, some of which have been mentioned above, and some, like Renaldo's *The Cisco Kid,* recounted earlier.

With the success of Hoppy, and the Western's popularity on TV, some former stars used video to their advantage. Buster Crabbe used to host a kiddie show, run some of his PRC horse operas and do a running commentary on them. *Gabby* Hayes had a 15-minute show on NBC of chatter, Western lore and snippets of old cowboy films hosted by the grizzled sidekick. Tex Fletcher, who starred in one film, hosted a Western show, and enjoyed playing his *Six-Gun Rhythm* when he could.

Noblest of all was a little 15-minute series made in 1954, *Cavalcade of the Old West,* hosted by Tim McCoy, looking sturdy as always. McCoy would tell some Western tales, but the fascinating members of the 39 episodes would be those dealing with Indian lore. McCoy was an authority, and one memorable show had the Indian actor Chief Yowlachie as guest, with McCoy interpreting the Indian sign language. McCoy was an able tutor, and the series, in color, was that rare combination, an entertaining and educational show.

And in the early days of television, when some shows were done live—that is, not on film or tape, exactly as they transpired without the advantage of retakes—there was a Western show called *Action in the Afternoon,* presented daily. It was soap-opera format, but Western in theme. Since much of it took place outdoors, the weather played an important part in the production. If it was a rainy day, then the show took place in the rain. It was difficult to compensate for the sound of an overhead airplane, but nothing's perfect. The show had a fairly decent network afternoon run. For a Western, the program originated from an unlikely source. Philadelphia, Pa.

George Hayes, pre-"Gabby," as "Windy Halliday" in Bar 20 Justice *(1938).*

25 EXTRA CHAPTER
HEROES, HEROINES HEAVIES & HARLEQUINS

So ends the saga of the cowboy star, and the series Western. As with all endeavors of this type, there are many loose ends left dangling. No alibi, but it can't be helped. Even writers are often restricted as to the number of pages they are allowed to fill. Accept this then as a last-minute attempt to tie some of the strands together, at least temporarily. Some of them call for an entire book in themselves.

Like the unclassifiable low-budget Westerns, for instance. Those without a regular saddle star in the leading role. An example: Jack Holt, although known for his Paramount Westerns in the silent period, was not especially associated with them in the talkies; he appeared more frequently in them in later life, in character parts or villainous roles. Holt did star in one Western of rather exceptional quality in the mid-'30s, *End of the Trail* (Erle C. Kenton, 1936) which was not a remake of the Tim McCoy opus with the same title, their only relationship being in the realm of merit. Both were off the beaten path and produced and enacted with unusual artistry for their milieu. The McCoy film was discussed earlier. Holt's starring vehicle cast him as a man forced to become a rustler, after having returned from the Spanish-American war and unable to adjust. Crux of the story is his friendship with a lawman, played straight and adeptly by Guinn Williams, who eventually has to turn him in for what is certainly a case of justifiable homicide. The concluding scene between Holt and Williams in Holt's cell is poignant and remarkably affecting, and the film emerged as one of Columbia's better low-budget fillers, far better than the customary nod and dismissal it received when first released. Director Kenton made a cameo appearance playing Teddy Roosevelt and contributed a well-valued job of guidance, and the Harold Shumate screenplay was a powerful one.

Shumate's script was based on a Zane Grey story, and so was just about every other non-series Western of the '30s, though ofttimes based at a great distance. The Zane Grey name on the marquee was as potent a draw as some of the actor's names, so the author-adventurer received his share of exploitation, and then some. Fox, RKO, and Paramount in particular used the Grey association often with the latter company cashing in the most. Their silent Westerns based on Grey works were elaborate, cast with top names, and even experimental to the extent that early Technicolor was used for sequences. Many of these features were remade when the talkies took hold, some of them with fairly expensive-looking production outlays, still more with an eye on the purse-strings, even fitting in stock footage of the striking action scenes filmed for the silent versions. The majority of these Grey remakes were given to Randolph Scott to star in, although the studio kept Scott one leap away from becoming a series star. While Scott starred in ten of these Grey outdoor shows between 1932 and 1935, he was also terrifically busy appearing in other, non-Western movies as well. Paramount had a large roster of

HOLLYWOOD CORRAL: A COMPREHENSIVE B WESTERN ROUNDUP

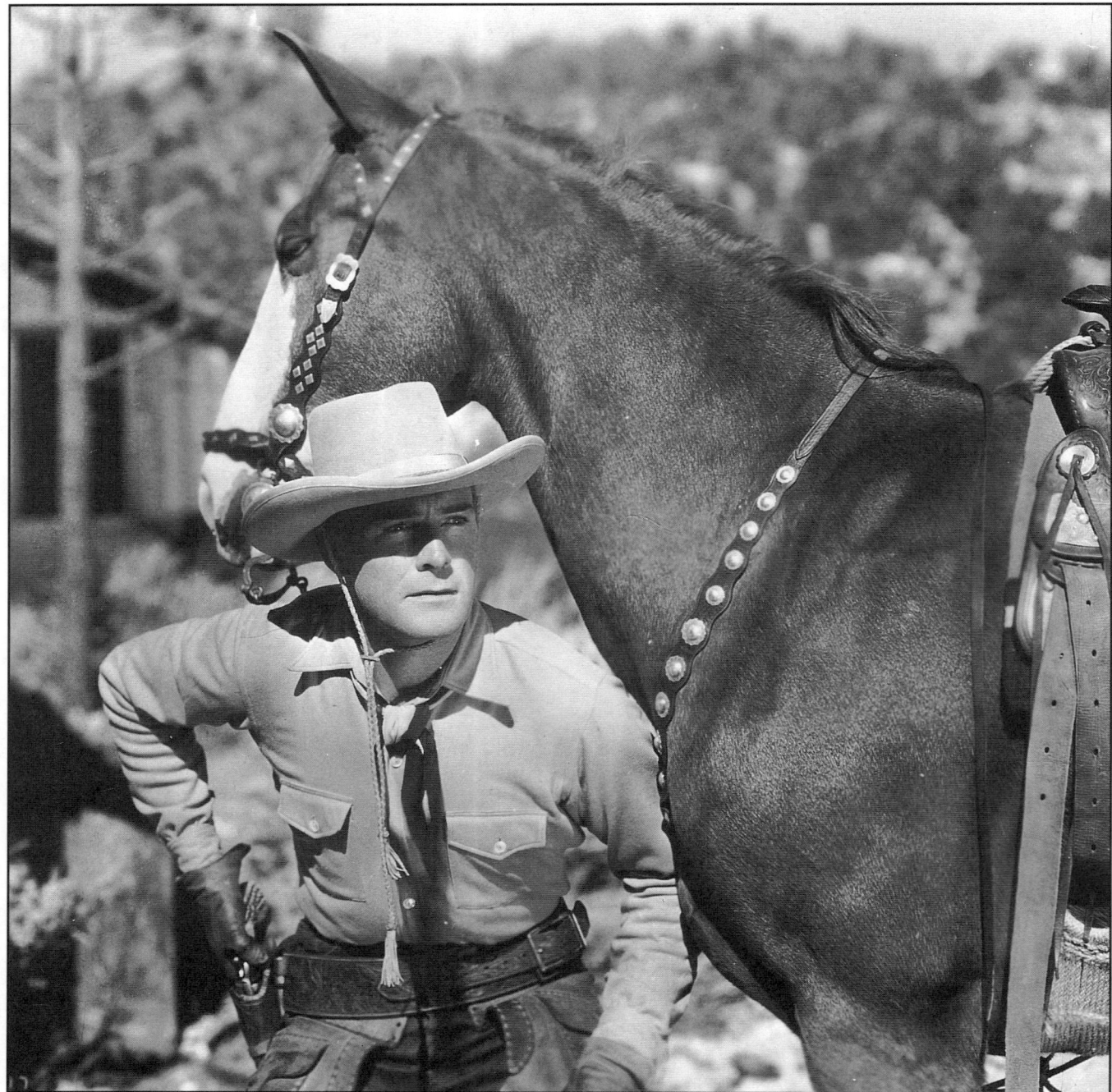

Randolph Scott in Rocky Mountain Mystery *(1935).*

contract players and would stuff their Westerns with familiars from top to bottom roles. Between the companion players and the Zane Grey name, the studio had plenty to advertise without straining themselves to push Scott as a horse opera hero. The first seven of Scott's Westerns were directed by Henry Hathaway, making his debut with the megaphone. While they are uneven, strong hints of Hathaway's virile way with an action yarn are evident, although the obvious use of library footage distracted in films like *The Thundering Herd* (1933). In others, Scott would be swamped by the "all-star" casts, notably in *To the Last Man* (1933). The novel device of introducing each character by printed titles on the screen as they made their entrance continued through nearly half the film, since the script was heavily populated. Even Shirley Temple shows up in an unbilled bit. When Hathaway was promoted to bigger and better projects, the Zane Grey's with Scott took a turn for the less robust type of Western yarn, typified by *Rocky Mountain Mystery* (Charles Barton, 1935), merely a mild whodunit in a Western setting with Chic Sale's rustic witticisms more important to the development of the plot than Scott's heroics.

Fortunately for Scott, he was yanked from the

Paramount Grey rut and nurtured from a serviceable but somewhat anonymous cowboy lead into a serviceable but somewhat anonymous leading man. Fortunately, because the pay was better. Scott would appear in an occasional Western epic surrounded by Technicolor and/or several co-stars with marquee weight, but his days as a galloping sagebrush hero where near-forgotten when he returned to the range with a vengeance in the mid-'40s, there to eventually stay. When he became his own co-producer, he really found his calling. The Westerns he starred in for producer Harry Joe Brown, of Scott-Brown, or Producers-Actors, or Ranown Productions, deserve, and will probably receive someday, full-length treatment. They have already been written about extensively in frame of reference to the work of directors Budd Boetticher, Joseph H. Lewis and Burt Kennedy; next should come the full tribute, with Randolph Scott as the main recipient. That most of them can be rightfully considered "A" pictures and thus not falling within the province of this study, is fitting. They merit closer scrutiny.

Paramount continued its Zane Grey Westerns without Scott, using such as Tom Keene and Buster Crabbe, already mentioned here, and various other well-known players. Gilbert Roland was featured in one of the better ones, *Thunder Trail* (Charles Barton, 1937), deftly portraying one of his good-badman parts. Villainy was in the capable hands of Charles Bickford, romantic interest by Marsha Hunt; behind the cameras was Karl Struss, all giving a touch of class to the fast-moving narrative.

Taking time off from the Hopalong Cassidy series, producer Harry Sherman made several medium-budgeted Westerns with Zane Grey titles, best of which was *The Mysterious Rider* (Lesley Selander, 1938), with Douglas Dumbrille in a change from his usual heavy characterization as the drifter who returns home to make right wrongs. Paramount had filmed a previous *Mysterious Rider* (Fred Allen, 1933), with Kent Taylor, which had little or no relation to the Sherman version, although both claimed to be based on Grey works. Sherman's Zane Grey Westerns had two factors in common. All were directed by Selander, and featured Russell Hayden. Victor Jory also appeared in two 1940 releases, *The Light of Western Stars* and *Knights of the Range*.

Several years before, Jory had starred in an un-

Victor Jory (on white horse) leads a posse including Eddie Dean (on his right), Noah Beery, Jr. (on his left), the King's Men, and J. Farrell MacDonald in The Light of Western Stars *(1940).*

HOLLYWOOD CORRAL: A COMPREHENSIVE B WESTERN ROUNDUP

usual outdoor adventure, the Australian production *Rangle River* (Clarence Badger, 1936). Although taking place down under, it was as Western as most horse operas, and more than some. The Grey story was the traditional tale of crooks trying to put honest cattlemen out of business, but Badger, an American director, and Jory and the rest of the cast turned it into virile entertainment with some expertly filmed thrill sequences and an exciting climactic duel with cattle whips. The parallel to the American West has been noted in quite a few Australian productions, and there have been various attempts to combine the two worlds, as in *The Kangaroo Kid* (Lesley Selander, 1950), with Jock O'Mahoney (Jock Mahoney), Veda Ann Borg, Martha Hyer and Douglas Dumbrille from the States, and Alec Kellaway, Grant Taylor and supporting Australian talent.

Until the end of World War II, the major studios were content to divide Westerns into two categories, namely the class "A" product and the low-budget series Western. Relatively few non-series low-budget Westerns were attempted, and few of those were of any special interest. A studio like M-G-M, whose "B" division bypassed Westerns, finally tried one with *Apache Trail* (Richard Thorpe, 1942), which turned out fairly well, thanks largely to a good cast including Lloyd Nolan, Donna Reed, William Lundigan and strong support. When called upon to fill their schedule with a Western in later years, Metro dusted off the old film and came forth with *Apache War Smoke* (Harold Kress, 1952), with Gilbert Roland, Barbara Ruick and Robert Horton in the roles originated by Nolan, Reed and Lundigan. The plot was altered slightly to fit the principals, but the action footage was retained from the earlier version. The studio also tried a mountie story, *Northwest Rangers* (Joe Newman, 1942), with Lundigan and James Craig, which was a retread of Woody Van Dyke's 1934 gangster opus *Manhattan Melodrama*, with William Powell and Clark Gable in corresponding roles. Obviously, the studio of the stars just went through the motions when it came to making a pass at the action market.

Non-series low-budget Westerns began to proliferate in the latter half of the '40s and the early '50s, widely variable. Worthy of brief mention are the Screen Guild-Lippert films, made on extremely skimpy expenditures but often possessing story values and occasionally scenic delights well above the norm. *Rimfire* (B. Reeves Eason, 1949) was an uneven but intriguing Western mystery about the supposed return of the ghost of a gambler (Reed Hadley), intent on doing in those who were responsible for his framing and hanging. The film caught the action of a Western and the high mortality rate of a bloodthirsty whodunit, succeeding well in both respects. Another good, sober bandit tale was *3 Desperate Men* (Sam Newfield, 1951), with Preston Foster and Jim Davis as lawmen forced to turn against the law. Orville Hampton's script probed deeper than most, with some telling insight into human frailties, and there was a fine steady performance by Monte Blue as a marshal friend of the outlaws, one of the veteran actor's last and best roles. Also meriting praise are the sepia-tinted *The Return of Wildfire* (Ray Taylor, 1948), with Richard Arlen, Patricia Morison, Mary Beth Hughes, Reed Hadley, James Millican and Chris-Pin Martin, and *Last of the Wild Horses* (Robert L. Lippert, 1948), with James Ellison, Jane Frazee, Douglas Dumbrille, Millican, Hughes and Hadley. Both are true "horse" operas with fine scenic backgrounds as well as plenty of two-fisted Western action.

These can be contrasted with some shameful product of the period, like *Buffalo Bill Rides Again* (Bernard B. Ray, 1947), with Richard Arlen in the title role awash in a plot so meandering it seems to have two separate and distinct villains enacting one role; or *Buffalo Bill in Tomahawk Territory* (Ray, 1952), with Clayton Moore similarly enmeshed in a pile of old stock footage. Or James Ellison trying vainly to pass for John Wayne in *I Killed Geronimo* (John Hoffman, 1950), which used the Indian attack from *Stagecoach* for all it was worth, and more; Charles Starrett had just played straight to the same footage in *Laramie* (Ray Nazarro, 1949), even changing his customary costume to do so. Indeed, the gap was wide in low-budget Westerns.

There can be no discussion of the Randolph Scott, Audie Murphy or George Montgomery Westerns of the '40s and '50s. What was classed as "B" at the time would be comparable to epic expenditure to the series Westerns of Tom Tyler and Bob Steele and Lash La Rue and Sunset Carson. An occasional cheap Western still will issue forth from Hollywood, but our era ceased with Wayne Morris. And there is certainly no use traveling abroad, to Italy, Spain, Yugoslavia, Germany, even Israel, to speak of the foreign-made ones. That too is another story.

It had been intended originally to devote a separate chapter to the girls of the golden West; and to the scoundrels; and to the prairie funsters. Once again, space interferes, and some of the more prominent personages have been covered. Still, no mention has been made of Dorothy Page, who tried to reign as a singing cowgirl in a series of three Grand National Westerns of 1938–39. Miss Page was pretty, carried a tune melodically and sat astride a horse believably. But when the chips were down, it evolved that, in *Ride 'Em Cowgirl, Water Rustlers* and *The Singing Cowgirl*, director Sam Diege was forced to fall back upon Dave O'Brien or Milton Frome, masculine traits abounding, to get the plot into the acceptable Western groove. A decade later, Robert Tansey tried a Western with a brittle blonde named Maria Hart in the lead. *Cattle Queen* (1951) gave Hart an opportunity to act stern and do a bit of whip-snicking, as she had done in a couple of other Tansey Westerns, on a smaller scale. But Tansey reached back for one of his favorite plots used for Maynard-Gibson and Jack Randall, the one about the convicts paroled to work for the law to clean up the town, and again the action was predominantly masculine.

Varied efforts have been made over the Western years to exploit Ruth Mix, Betty Miles, Evelyn Finley, Virginia Carroll, Nell O'Day and Reno Browne (Blair) as sagebrush queens, but always with limited results. The place for a woman, according to Hollywood, is in front of a wistful smile and adoring look saved for the finale. Some actresses made a career of horse operas, others used them as stepping stones to more satisfying pursuits. Of those who have made a home on the range, long enough to become acclimatized, undoubtedly each fan has his own special favorites. Here, unvaryingly capable and attractive, preferences include Cecilia Parker, before her adoption by the Metro Hardy family; Lois January, always the most level-headed and dependable of Western heroines; Harley Wood, usually cast in parts that called for a bit of the spitfire, antagonistic toward the hero; Julie Duncan, delicate in appearance but a better rider than many of her leading men, plus an odd voice which could have made her another Jean Arthur with the right coaching; Luana Walters, the girl with the strongest will—you'd want her on your side, anytime; Dorothy Fay, always lending dignity to her roles, often overcoming deficient scripts—and Mrs. Tex Ritter offscreen; Linda Stirling, a serial queen in her own right, breathtakingly beautiful adorning Republic Westerns of the mid-'40s, and an underrated actress; Peggy Stewart, another Republic alumnus and probably the best all-around actress of the regulars; Nora Lane, more mature than the rest, appearing opposite McCoy, Maynard, and Hopalong Boyd, always slightly tragic in her dark good looks; and for a tenth, please insert your own particular damsel, should you have one.

Peggy Stewart with director Spencer Bennet.

Dorothy Fay

HOLLYWOOD CORRAL: A COMPREHENSIVE B WESTERN ROUNDUP

Three of the outstanding villains of the early days. Harry Woods, Ralph Ince and Richard Alexander as they appeared together in Law and Order *(1932).*

Villainy can be broken down into two categories. There are those who carry on their dastardly plans in frock coats, posing as bankers or saloonkeepers, and those who have the mark of a henchman, disheveled, unshaven, and for all we know, smelly. The true test of prime villainy is the actor who can play both types with equal dexterity. Roy Barcroft was one, and he has achieved the status of legend; fortunately, he lived long enough to realize to some extent how popular he was with the fans. Barcroft once said that he learned his dirty tricks from Harry Woods, and Woods was indeed an imposing figure of evil, whether as the brains behind the outlaws or just one of the murderous boys. Fred Kohler the elder could perform well in both capacities, but he was far better on the open range, where his nasty meanness was unconfined. Alan Sears and his frightening countenance has been remarked upon. Nudging him for honors in the ugly division would be Robert Kortman, Warner Richmond and Bud Geary. The first two named verge on the psychopathic overlaying their lawlessness, while Geary had a face that could stop a clock—somebody threw. In a suaver way, Kenne Duncan and Leroy Mason could incite hatred without half trying. Charles King was great but he did work often, and his villainy became rather cuddly as the years progressed and King added more and more weight. Jack Ingram was sneaky, and George Chesebro not to be trusted. Tom London was just one of the bunch until he took his teeth out and became another "Gabby" Hayes. Norman Willis didn't do too many Westerns comparatively, but he had a built-in sneer that was delightful. So did Earl Dwire, but he was too obvious about it.

No actor could touch Noah Beery Sr. for ripe mustache-twirling monkey business—he was the villain in this picture, and he didn't let you forget it for a second. John Merton was interesting because of the way he would depict his demise, doing a little buck-and-wing dance when plugged. Zon Murray used to cough before going down, and Wheeler Oakman would clutch his hands protectively to his chest. I. Stanford Jolley could take bone-crushing falls and sometimes did so, doubly valuable because Jolley was adept at playing the dignified heavy. There were many others, but most of them spread their villainy over non-Western releases too, and cannot be considered true skunks of the frontier.

HEROES, HEROINES, HEAVIES & HARLEQUINS

Smiley Burnette

Andy Clyde

Pat Buttram

Andy Devine

HOLLYWOOD CORRAL: A COMPREHENSIVE B WESTERN ROUNDUP

Raymond Hatton

Dub Taylor

Fuzzy Knight

Eddy Waller

This is no time to go into what causes one to laugh. As far as this report is concerned, the big three of cowboy comedy are Al St. John, "Gabby" Hayes and Smiley Burnette, because they influenced the course of Western comedy, each in his own way. St. John was at it the longest; Burnette popularized the Western clown, and made the sidekick of an importance nearly equal to that of the star; Hayes refined the art of playing the foil, gave it humanity and a cantankerous dignity. Saying that, one finds it necessary to salute Andy Clyde, an inspired comedian in his own right and already established as a two-reel comedy king when he took on the Western. Clyde enhanced the Hopalong Cassidys, and saved the Whip Wilsons. Ben Corbett's name must be mentioned as a pioneer in sound-era horseplay, although at least one viewer would invariably fail to be amused at his antics. On the other hand, both Frank Rice and Si Jenks are all but unknown today, Rice because he died before the importance of the sidekick could be affirmed, and Jenks because he never really received a full opportunity to use his talents, aside from his appearances in some of the later Columbia McCoys. The grizzled Jenks countenance is remindful of both Hayes and St. John, and might have influenced either or both. But Jenks was a busy performer and in constant demand for small-town rustic roles, apart from Westerns. He did all right without them. Rice, who died in 1936, was a favorite with Buck Jones and appeared in many Western comedy roles. He had a trick of making his eyes roll counter-clockwise, but happily he didn't overdo it, a fault some found with Syd Saylor's pulsating adam's-apple. Saylor was tossed around from cowboy to cowboy and evidently nobody wanted him as a partner, but his brand of clowning was much more palatable than some.

Republic had a knack of casting able character actors as comedy sidekicks for brief spells. Thus were many of their Westerns distinguished by Olin Howlin, Irving Bacon, Gordon Jones, Eddy Waller and Chubby Johnson, as well as certified but non-Western comics like Buddy Ebsen and Sterling Holloway. Earle Hodgins had his medicine-show spiel used to good advantage by several companies, and it would be proper to repeat the contribution made by Richard Martin to the Tim Holt series at RKO. Ultimately, whether they invoked the sound of laughter or instilled deadly silence, Western comics were among the hardest working clowns in the movies.

Have we omitted the post-'40s Columbia productions directed by Fred Sears, and the A. C. Lyles Paramount Westerns with ghostly echoes of past glories in their casts? By all means, mention them. But this has been a saga of a certain kind of Western, primarily—films starring one heroic figure, or a duo or a trio, riding the familiar trails, rescuing the same heroines, besting the same villains, six, eight, even ten times a year, preferably in 60 minutes or less. Esthetes sneered, critics ignored, many moviegoers rebelled upon reaching their alleged maturity. The low-budget, series Western endured because of the support of fans and the faith of little children. The same support, the same unspoiled faith kept afloat the fortunes of Laurel & Hardy, the character of Charlie Chan and the legend of Tarzan, to offer some different areas. The day of the cowboy star is over, and will never come again. No new Starretts, Mixes, Maynards or McCoys will appear on the horizons of the screen. Generations now maturing have never experienced riding with Buck Jones at the Saturday matinee. However, while the films last, and are able to be shown, there will be those who have witnessed, and remember. William S. Hart once referred to "the thrill of it all." While Westerns are shown, even privately, and that magic works anew, those words will remain an apt description, and not an epitaph.

HAPPY TRAILS

PART II
REFLECTIONS ON THE B WESTERN

Art Acord

SILENT GUNS
THE EARLY WESTERN STARS
by Robert S. Birchard

The first edition of Don Miller's *Hollywood Corral* was offered as a survey of low-budget Westerns from the beginning of the sound era in 1929 to the coming of television in the early '50s. Miller touched briefly on the silent cowboy stars, but they were not his main interest or concern, and he opened his book by stating that Leo Maloney's *Overland Bound* (Presidio-Raytone, 1930) was "the initial low-budget cowboy movie." It would be more correct to say that it was the first independent all-talking Western.

Strictly speaking, there were no B Westerns in the silent era. The so-called B picture came into existence with the inauguration of double features in the Depression-haunted '30s, as exhibitors sought to bring the vanishing legions back to theaters. But low-budget Westerns were certainly a Hollywood staple in the days before talkies.

Bob Steele, Tom Tyler, Jack Hoxie, Ken Maynard, Bill Cody, and Wally Wales were well-established series Western stars before they ever set foot in front of a microphone, and for the most part their silent pictures were made as quickly and cheaply as their talking oaters. The difference, if there was any, is the manner in which the pictures were received in the marketplace.

Before the arrival of twin features, and especially during the silent era, short features were known as "program" pictures because they were block-booked to theaters as part of an annual studio program. The longer, higher-budgeted, and presumably more prestigious films were known as "specials" and sold individually. As the B picture became institutionalized in the mid '30s, the Charlie Chan and George O'Brien program pictures on the Fox film schedule, for instance, became Bs as budgets, shooting schedules and running times were reduced to conform to the ecomomic realities of the marketplace.

In the silent era, "budget" Westerns could compete favorably with major-studio program pictures because cowboys, horses, hats and plots were unhampered by maladroit dialogue and awkward sound recording. In fact, low-budget Westerns were largely responsible for pushing major studio Westerns off the screen in the late '20s. But we're getting ahead of our story....

From *The Great Train Robbery* (Edison, 1903) to *The Big Diamond Robbery* (FBO, 1929), the Western was the single most popular American film genre. This was a reflection of the popular culture. From the late 1800s, popular dime novels set forth the colorful exploits of Buffalo Bill and Young Wild West–the former being mere fabrication and the latter being sheer fantasy. Owen Wister and Zane Grey were among the most popular American writers in the early 1900s, and cowboy heroes loomed powerful in melodramatic plays adapted from popular novels like *The Squaw Man* and *The Virginian*. Wild West shows were also favorite attractions, and every circus was forced to offer some sort of cowboy-and-Indian show in order to compete with Buffalo Bill,

HOLLYWOOD CORRAL: A COMPREHENSIVE B WESTERN ROUNDUP

Pawnee Bill, and the Miller Brothers 101 Ranch Show.

In those years, the imaginary West was not so far removed from the real West. As Don Miller points out, New Mexico, Arizona, and Oklahoma were not yet states, and the Indian wars of the 1870s were closer in time than World War II is to us today. To give a sense of just how wild the West still was, the Universal Film Mfg. Co. could release a Western called *In the San Fernando Valley* (Nestor, 1912) without the audience associating that locale with Valley Girls and phrases like "gag me with a spoon."

The most important figure in the early Western film was G. M. Anderson (nee Aaronson). Even before he teamed with George K. Spoor to form the Essanay Film Mfg. Co. in 1907, Anderson persuaded William N. Selig of the Selig Polyscope Co. in Chicago to send units throughout the West to shoot films in real Western locations. Other producers quickly followed, and by 1910 it was common for the eastern studios to make pictures in the West during the cold winter months.

The Lubin Mfg. Co. of Philadelphia sent the multi-talented Romaine Fielding to New Mexico, Arizona, and Texas. Director D. W. Griffith went to Los Angeles for the Biograph Company, and the American Film Mfg. Co. shipped Allan Dwan and troupe to San Juan Capistrano, La Mesa, and finally Santa Barbara, California.

Anderson established a branch studio of Essanay at Niles, California, and in late 1911 he created the Broncho Billy series. For nearly four years Anderson cranked out a one-reel Broncho Billy film every week. In one film Billy might be a sheriff, in the next an outlaw. On more than one occasion he played a dude coming West to become a man. Billy was not a character so much as an established and marketable screen persona. And he was hardly a dashing screen figure. Anderson was eagle-beaked and somewhat beefy, and the appeal of his character is lost today, but one old-timer remembered that "we liked Broncho Billy because he talked out of the side of his mouth." For movie fans who were just discovering the evocative power of screen stars, a little idiosyncrasy registered heavily.

The nickelodeon destroyed the audience for theatrical melodrama, and for this reason the earliest Western stars were refugees from the "legitimate" stage. At the American Film Mfg. Co., popularly known as the Flying "A", J. Warren Kerrigan and Wallace Reid held forth. Selig's leading Western star was William Duncan, and the Bison 101 brand of the New York Motion Picture Corporation offered the dashing exploits of J. Barney Sherry. But in the background of these early films there were real cowboys among the celluloid posse. Jim and Pete Morrison played support to Kerrigan; Art Acord and Hoot Gibson could often be seen riding with Sherry; and Tom Mix worked with William Duncan.

Mix came to films in 1910, and worked as a wrangler and bit player for the Selig Polyscope Company in Flemington, Missouri; St. Augustine, Florida; Silver City, Colorado; and Prescott, Arizona, during summers between Wild West show engagements and occasional jobs as cowpuncher, bartender, physical culturalist, and lawman.

Most of what was written about Tom Mix during his lifetime was tainted with press agentry.

Born in Texas? No.

Served in Teddy Roosevelt's Rough Riders? No.

Wounded during the Philippine Insurrection? Hardly. He served in the coast artillery during the Spanish-American War, and re-upped in 1901 only to desert.

Trailed and captured the notorious Schontz Brothers while serving as a U.S. Marshal? Tom's experience as a lawman was a brief stint as night

G. M. "Broncho Billy" Anderson

marshal (city policeman) of Dewey, Oklahoma, and as lawman (security guard) in a series of construction camps.

Despite his rather spotty military and law enforcement careers, Mix was no coward. He had a great deal of physical daring, and was an excellent horseman. For a time he rode with the famed Miller Brothers 101 Ranch Show.

What Tom Mix *did* have was a sense of showmanship. He designed his own Western-cut shirts and pants with curving arrow tipped pockets and showy wrist and ankle buttons, and he instinctively understood the boxoffice value in blurring the line between his real and reel personalities.

"Few people know that Tom was responsible for the present-day cowboy clothes," director George Marshall remembered in a 1967 letter. "I have been in his dressing room when he was working with his tailor designing the tight-fitting pants, the angled pockets, and the shirts with the tight-fitting wrists with many buttons—and always very vivid colors. No question he was a real showman."

After a four-year apprenticeship in pictures, Tom Mix was finally given his own starring series of shorts beginning with *The Real Thing in Cowboys* (Selig Polyscope, 1914). Over the following two-and-a-half years, Mix starred in dozens of one, two, and three-reel pictures, and he directed many of them himself. The Mix films were crude, but they often combined comedy with action and were extremely popular with audiences. They also served as a training ground for many future Western stars. At one time or another during Tom's tenure at Selig (and later at Fox), Leo Maloney, Hoot Gibson, Lester Cuneo, Joe Ryan, Buck Jones, George O'Brien, Whitey (Art Mix) Kesterson, Floyd (Wally Wales) Alderson, and even Marion (John Wayne) Morrison worked the celluloid range with Tom Mix.

About the time Tom Mix became a Western star, William S. Hart also came to the movies, and he quickly became the leading screen cowboy of the teens. Although he had spent some time in the West in his youth, Hart was primarily a New York stage actor noted for villainous roles in *Ben-Hur, The Virginian,* and *The Squaw Man.*

In his autobiography, *My Life East and West,* Hart recalled seeing a Western film while on the road in Cleveland. He was appalled at what he saw. "Here were reproductions of the Old West being seriously presented to the public—in almost a burlesque manner—and they were successful. It made me tremble to think of it. I was an actor and I knew the West... The opportunity that I had been waiting for

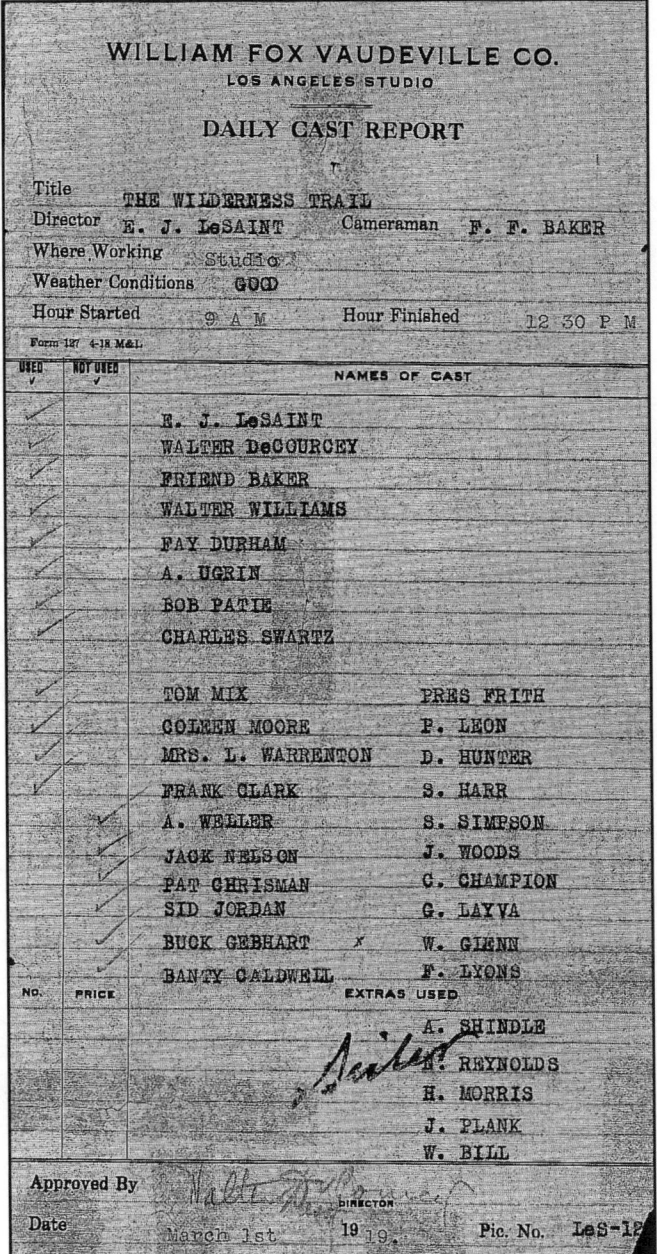

Original call report for Tom Mix's The Wilderness Trail *(1919). Notice Buck Jones (as Buck Gebhart) listed among bit players.*

years to come was knocking at my door."

While in Los Angeles with a touring company of *The Trail of the Lonesome Pine,* Hart looked up his old friend Thomas Ince, who was a supervising director for the New York Motion Picture Corporation. The actor persuaded Ince to give him an opportunity to make some Westerns, and the pictures clicked with the public.

Hart was an unlikely cowboy hero. Already well into his forties when he signed with Ince, his rugged features were more suited to the villains he played on stage. But Hart's stage training was a plus in 1914. Contrary to popular myth, the movies embraced the

HOLLYWOOD CORRAL: A COMPREHENSIVE B WESTERN ROUNDUP

On the set of Riddle Gawne *(1918): (foreground, l. to r.) Lambert Hillyer, William S. Hart, unidentified, Joseph August (1st camera), Victor Milner (2nd camera).*

theater that year. "Famous Players in Famous Plays" was the order of the day, and while not every stage star made a hit with the filmgoing public, many of the big box office favorites of the 1914-1915 period were stage celebrities of some standing, including Mary Pickford, Doug Fairbanks, Charlie Chaplin, Dustin and William Farnum, and Geraldine Farrar. Although William S. Hart was not a major star in the theater, he was several cuts above the average stock actor that comprised the N.Y.M.P.C. roster in 1914, and he brought great authority to his screen roles.

The actor also benefited from the strong screenwriters at the Ince Studio, including C. Gardner Sullivan, Lambert Hillyer, J.G. Hawks, and Richard V. Spencer. They gave Hart the role of the "good bad man," which offered a more rounded characterization than the usual stalwart hero, and this added dimension enhanced the Western actor's popularity.

Despite the fact that Hart often took credit for his screenplays, Lambert Hillyer recalled in 1954 that "... when Ince split with Triangle in 1917 [to go with Artcraft], C. Gardner Sullivan and I were sued for breach of contract and though they could not keep us from working, for a time they prevented us from using our names and taking screen credit. That is why Hart took credit for writing.... He supplied a basic idea once in awhile, but never wrote a screenplay in his life."

One of Hart's goals was to bring authenticity to the screen, but many of the cowboys who worked with him questioned his commitment to realism.

SILENT GUNS / The Early Western Stars

"He tried to live the West in every picture," wrote Lambert Hillyer. "He loved authentic detail in props and costumes and allowed me to go to any lengths to get things perfect… [but] Bill was a poor shot with any weapon, and couldn't uncoil a rope without knocking his hat off."

"He was a wonderful character," recalled Ted French, a cowboy who worked with Hart. "He was a very sincere actor, and he got onto this Western trip, but he was just the wrong type. He could maneuver himself in a Shakespearian play, but in Westerns he just wasn't it. He had the two-gun bit down pretty good, and he had that straight-brimmed hat, the big scarf, and the leather cuffs, but he was the same in every picture." Director Irvin Willat, who supervised the editing of many of Hart's early films, once said that "William S. Hart is a ham actor and belongs on 14th Street in New York and not with the New York Motion Picture Company in Los Angeles."

The moviegoing public did not share these opinions, however, and for more than five years they lined up to buy tickets to the latest Hart opus whenever it appeared. Ultimately, the sameness of the Hart Westerns took its toll, especially as Hart gained more control over his pictures and relinquished strong dramatic values in favor of bizarre star turns designed to compliment his inflated sense of his acting ability. At his best, in pictures like *Hell's Hinges* (Triangle-KayBee, 1916) and *The Toll Gate* (Paramount-Artcraft, 1920), Hart gave the screen its first classic Westerns; but at his most self-indulgent, as in *Singer Jim McKee* (Famous Players-Lasky, 1924) or *The Narrow Trail* (Artcraft, 1917), Hart's films could be tedious and border on self-parody.

Hart's closest screen rivals were William and Dustin Farnum and William Russell. After becoming stars at other studios, all three found themselves under contract to the Fox Film Corporation in the late teens.

William Farnum's first Western was an eight-reel adaptation of Rex Beach's novel *The Spoilers* (Selig Polyscope, 1914) which was famous for the big fight "staged" between Farnum and screen villain Tom Santschi. Legend has it that the fight was real, and Ted French who worked with Farnum in later years confirmed the legend.

William Farnum in Riders of the Purple Sage *(1918).*

"That old boy," the cowboy recalled of Farnum, "when he put on a fight you'd better have your hands up, because he was in there to make pictures and to make it look good and to see that he didn't get hurt."

Fox gave William Farnum the choicest Western stories, including *Riders of the Purple Sage, The Rainbow Trail* (both 1918), and *The Last of the Duanes* (1919) by Zane Grey, and *Drag Harlan* (1920), based on a novel by Charles Alden Seltzer. *Drag Harlan* appears to be the only Fox Farnum Western to survive, and it gives a glimpse of an actor who liked to work in the grand manner of the late 19th century theater. After his starring career waned in the early '20s, Farnum retained his theatrical style in hundreds of character roles nearly up to the time of his death in 1953.

Dustin Farnum (1874-1929) was two years older than his brother William, but he looked younger and possessed a more naturalistic screen technique and offered a bit more humor in his characterizations. He made his screen reputation in Westerns, playing the lead in Cecil B. DeMille's productions of *The Squaw Man* and *The Virginian* (both Lasky Feature Play Co., 1914), but like his brother he played a variety of roles throughout his career and was never typed as being strictly a Western star.

William Russell remained a popular action star until his death in 1928. He made a convincing cowboy in such films as *Six Feet Four* (American, 1919) and *Colorado Pluck* (Fox, 1921), but he too removed his chaps and Stetson to play a role in *Anna Christie* (Ince-First National, 1923) and co-star with George O'Brien in John Ford's *The Blue Eagle* (Fox, 1926).

While the Fox studio made many notable Westerns with these former stage stars, it was the arrival of Tom Mix that really set the pace for the studio's Western boom of the '20s. In 1917, the Selig Polyscope Company was on the ropes, and William Fox leased the Selig studio in Edendale, near downtown Los Angeles. Along with the studio, Fox also signed Selig's only remaining star—Tom Mix.

Fox's plan was to expand his program by producing two-reel comedies, and Mix brought a well-established following as well as a full company of players and technicians who could churn out shorts for the new studio without breaking stride. But William Fox's limited plans for Mix were short-lived. The increased distribution potential of the Fox

Tom Mix doing a stunt for Daredevil's Reward *(1928).*

organization caused Mix's already potent popularity to soar. Tom completed only a handful of shorts before the studio co-starred him in the Dustin Farnum vehicle *Durand of the Badlands* (Fox, 1917), and gave Mix his own feature series beginning with *Cupid's Roundup* (Fox, 1918).

At first the Tom Mix features emphasized the dramatic over the comic, but even in an otherwise serious film like *Fighting for Gold* (Fox, 1919), Tom's sprightly personality came through in light-hearted romantic scenes with leading lady Teddy Sampson. However, *The Untamed* (Fox, 1920) and *The Night Horsemen* (Fox, 1921), based on novels by Max Brand, were austere, even grim films that could have been William S. Hart vehicles.

As Mix's star was on the rise at Fox, Douglas Fairbanks made a handful of Westerns that became highly influential. *The Man from Painted Post* (Artcraft, 1917), *Wild and Woolly* (Artcraft, 1917), *Arizona* (Artcraft, 1918), *Headin' South* (Artcraft, 1918), *The Knickerbocker Buckaroo* (Artcraft, 1919), *The Mollycoddle* (United Artists, 1920), and *The Mark of Zorro* (United Artists, 1920). Fairbanks turned to the Western in some desperation. The actor made his reputation in a series of modern dress comedies produced for Triangle and Artcraft, but boxoffice returns began to slip as Fairbanks' pictures seemed to be rubber-stamp copies of each other. The Westerns provided a change of pace, and they also halted the steady decline in the star's grosses.

Fairbanks grew up in Denver, Colorado, in the fading days of the old West, and the cowboys who worked on his pictures respected the actor. "There were always long sessions between camera set-ups," Ted French fondly recalled, "and old Doug, he'd come down and get mixed up in a poker game with the cowboys. If he had something to do, he'd pick up 50 bucks and throw it in the game and say: 'Shoot it!' So I asked him one time, I says, 'Doug, why in the world do you always throw money into the pot and walk off and leave?'

"'Well, I'll tell you,' he says. 'When I need a cowboy I know where to get him.'

"I always liked Doug so much because he was so athletic. I seen him jump off a porch, dive over this railing, hit on the rump of the horse, and swing off into the saddle. He done that three times, and the third time he sprained one of his wrists. But I mean it was sprained. It swelled up. He couldn't work for two days. There was nothing he wouldn't try. Tom Mix was very much the same–he wouldn't let nobody double him."

Ultimately, Fairbanks turned to producing elaborate costume dramas, but the light-hearted approach he took to the traditionally serious Western feature had a liberating effect on the genre.

The Tom Mix films of the '20s expanded on the Fairbanks approach and came to be known as "streamlined Westerns," emphasizing action and comedy over plot and realistic nuance. In *Sky High* (Fox, 1922), Tom jumps from a plane into the Colorado River, fights off 20 assailants single-handed, hops on horseback and rides to the top of the Grand Canyon, while barely stopping to take a breath. *The Great K & A Train Robbery* (Fox, 1926) spent barely a reel setting up the plot, and the remaining five reels were devoted to some of the most hair-raising and hair-brained stunts ever seen on the screen.

Mix did many of his own stunts. This is confirmed by seeing the films, but the studio simply would not allow a star of his magnitude to take unnecessary risks. "Tom carried a complete stock company of cowboys from cook to wranglers, and they all doubled him at times," Lambert Hillyer wrote. "However, this fact was considered top-secret and not one of them would have admitted the fact to a stranger. Mix had guts to spare. Sometimes if he didn't like the way a stunt looked, he'd get sore and do it over himself. Better not try to stop him, either. Pat Chrisman [Tom's horse trainer, and member of the Mix stock company] and I spread lead around him in picture after picture with him always yelling: 'Come closer!'... Mix was himself a good man with a rifle, rope or six-gun. Very fast on the draw and as a stagecoach driver, one of the best."

Roscoe "Rocky" Cline was a typical member of the Mix unit. He started as a truck driver in 1921, and later became a prop man before moving into the camera department. Cline was a strong swimmer, and he was often called to do water stunts for Mix. "I did some underwater work for him on *The Best Bad Man* (Fox, 1925) with Clara Bow as leading lady. I also doubled Wallace MacDonald, who played the heavy in *Tumbling River* (Fox, 1927), on the Merced River. We had an accident and lost Ethel Hall, who doubled for leading lady Dorothy Dwan."

Many of the Mix pictures were shot on distant locations in Arizona, Colorado, and Utah, and Fox allowed 30-day schedules for the elaborate action pictures. The formula developed by Tom Mix proved a bonanza for the studio, and the star's salary reflected his popularity. In 1917, Tom earned $350 a week. By the time he signed his final Fox contract on January 14, 1925, which took effect on completion of *The Rainbow Trail* (Fox, 1925), his salary was

HOLLYWOOD CORRAL: A COMPREHENSIVE B WESTERN ROUNDUP

Buck Jones and Patsey de Forest in The Square Shooter *(1920).*

$6,500 a week through December, 1925, and $7,500 a week to the end of the contract in December, 1927. With the cost of maintaining the cowboy star's stock company, the Tom Mix films were anything but budget pictures, and the rentals charged to exhibitors reached as high as $150 per day.

One of the cowboys in the Tom Mix unit was Buck Gebhardt. In the early '20s, as Mix's popularity began to soar, Gebhardt was transformed into Buck Jones by the studio. While some have speculated that Jones was hired to keep Tom Mix in line, it is more likely the studio was merely hoping that lightning would strike twice. Fox even experimented with circus cowboy Ken Maynard, using the time-honored tradition of co-starring him with Dustin Farnum in *The Man Who Won* (Fox, 1923), before letting him drift into the independent arena. Buck Jones proved to be a fine screen actor, and Fox experimented with turning him into a straight action star minus Stetson and boots, but ultimately his silent films followed the Mix formula. While Buck Jones remained the second-string cowboy on the Fox lot in the '20s, his popularity was head and shoulders above that of other silent cowboy stars.

Universal was the one studio that rivaled Fox as a producer of Westerns in the silent era. The studio's top Western star of the teens was Harry Carey. Like Hart, the Farnums, and Russell, Harry Carey was a product of the stage. Working primarily with director Jack Ford, Carey's screen character was low-key and unglamorous. His clothes were often rumpled, and he eschewed a holster in favor of carrying his six-shooter in his waist belt.

Most of the stars on the Universal lot made Westerns at one time or another, including Herbert Rawlinson (who was English) and William Desmond (who was a Scot). Universal made its reputation churning out hundreds of short action films and comedies with only an occasional special production to bolster the studio's image. Even as feature films took over the marketplace, Universal continued to specialize in making two-reel Westerns. These shorts were cheaply and quickly made and offered a training ground for actors and directors. Among the stars developed in these pictures was Hoot Gibson.

Edmund Richard Gibson was born in Takamah, Nebraska. He got the nickname "Hoot" when he was a delivery boy for the Owl Drug Company. By 1912, when he won the title "World's All-Around Champion Cowboy," Gibson was already a movie veteran, but like many cowboys he found pictures to be seasonal work, filling in with rodeo and Wild West show work between studio engagements.

His first wife (some say the union was consummated without benefit of clergy), Helen Gibson, became a star when she took over the lead role in the Kalem Company's *Hazards of Helen* series. Hoot played extras and bits to his wife's leads, which made for a strained relationship. By the time Hoot Gibson came to Universal in 1917, they were separated, but still forced to deal with each other on a professional level.

"Hoot, Pete Morrison, and I all had the same dressing room at Universal," said Ted French, "and that was directly across from Helen Gibson, Hoot's ex-wife. And brother, I'm telling you, every time Hoot came out that door he had to duck, 'cause she was sittin' there just waitin' for him. She'd throw anything she had handy. Pete and I both got took– that old squatty Hooter would let us ride interference. He'd just sit back and laugh at us, then he'd come out when she had nothing left to throw."

Gibson began his feature film career in 1921, and

SILENT GUNS / The Early Western Stars

On location with Hoot Gibson (on horse) for The Saddle Hawk *(1925). Virgil Miller stands next to camera, Edward Sedgwick sits in director's chair while his sister Josie rests on the ground. Leading lady Marion Nixon sits on ground at far right.*

for nearly ten years was king cowboy on the Universal lot. Like Tom Mix, Gibson put a greater emphasis on comedy in his pictures, but they were generally quieter, less action-oriented films.

The success of Tom Mix and Hoot Gibson led Hollywood to look to the ranks of their cowboys and stuntmen for new Western stars rather than to the theater. At Universal, Pete Morrison, Jack Perrin, Neal Hart and Art Acord were elevated from shorts to features with varying degrees of success, and Jack Hoxie was plucked from the ranks of the independents to become a Universal star. Only Acord and Hoxie stood out from the crowd. The others quickly landed in the states rights market.

According to his official biography, Jack Hoxie was born in 1885 near Guthrie, Oklahoma; but his brother, Al Hoxie (who also starred briefly in Westerns), insisted that Jack was born five years earlier in Nebraska. Jack was a ranch cowboy in Idaho and rode with the Miller Brothers 101 Ranch Show and Dick Stanley's Wild West Show before coming to pictures. As Hart Hoxie, Jack worked with the Kalem Company on such films as *The Girl From Frisco* series (1916–17) and married leading lady Marin Sais. He continued to play supporting roles until he landed the lead in the serial *Lightning Bryce* (National-Arrow, 1919). Over the next three years he starred in more than 20 low-budget independent Westerns for such states' rights outfits as Aywon, Sunset, and Arrow. His success attracted the attention of Universal executives and he signed with the studio in 1923. Hoxie was an amiable, if somewhat stiff hero. He remained with Universal through 1927 and had a spotty film career into the early '30s.

Art Acord was a champion bulldogger who started in pictures as an extra with the New York Motion Picture Corporation in 1911. By 1915, he was starring in the "Buck Parvin" series at the Flying "A" studio in Santa Barbara, and he played with Theda Bara in *Cleopatra* (Fox, 1917). Acord served in the Army during World War I, and when he returned to Hollywood he landed at Universal starring in serials

HOLLYWOOD CORRAL: A COMPREHENSIVE B WESTERN ROUNDUP

Ken Maynard and director Al Rogell do some fancy riding on Tarzan during production of one of Ken's First National Westerns.

Fred Thomson (in sweater and plus-fours) instructs the crew of his state-of-the-art camera car.

SILENT GUNS / The Early Western Stars

Jack Hoxie in The Phantom Horseman *(1924).*

like *The Moon Rider* (1920) and *In the Days of Buffalo Bill* (1922). He moved to features in 1924 and proved to be highly popular, but his heavy drinking led the studio to let Acord go on several occasions.

Acord ended the silent era working in a series of cheap pictures for Davis Distributing. Contrary to popular belief, Acord did make at least one talking picture, playing a supporting role in one of Hoot Gibson's 1930 Universals. He was later arrested for rum-running and died in Mexico in 1931. The official death certificate said alcohol poisoning, but director Al Rogell insisted that Acord's body showed several stab wounds.

Rogell, who directed most of Universal's Western stars at one time or another, was amazed at the studio's system for budgeting its Westerns. "They used to budget the pictures by the page, and then they gave the director half of what he saved on the budget as a bonus. The system didn't make any sense at all. One page might have two people in a room, and the next page might have a cattle stampede and two dozen cowboys. I tried to get them to see how ridiculous their system was, but they wouldn't listen, so my writers and I got to putting extra pages in the script. We'd mark the extras with an 'X' up in the corner so I'd know not to shoot them. The production manager was amazed at how much I could save on a picture, and he never caught on to what we were doing. I'd take the bonus money and throw a big party for all the cast and crew and the department heads. It was worth it, because whenever I needed extra costumes, the lady in the costume department would charge me eight bucks no matter what I used and throw the overages onto director Erich von Stroheim's budgets."

HOLLYWOOD CORRAL: A COMPREHENSIVE B WESTERN ROUNDUP

SILENT GUNS / The Early Western Stars

A gallery of Silent Guns (clockwise from top of facing page): Neal Hart, Franklin Farnum, Fred Gilman, William Fairbanks, Pete Morrison, Lester Cuneo, Jack Perrin, and J. Warren Kerrigan.

HOLLYWOOD CORRAL: A COMPREHENSIVE B WESTERN ROUNDUP

Joan Crawford and Tim McCoy in The Law of the Range *(1928).*

Rogell began his career as a director making a series of Western shorts with Bob Reeves and Marion Aye in 1921. The pictures cost $1,200, and were sold to Sol Lesser for $2,500 each. On the strength of these, he was signed by Universal, but in 1924 he joined with Charles R. Rogers and Harry Joe Brown to direct a series for release through FBO (Film Booking Offices) starring Fred Thomson.

Fred Thomson was a manufactured cowboy hero. A former minister, married to one of Hollywood's leading screenwriters, Thomson was good looking and a good actor to boot. The filmmakers cast the Thomson films in the Mix mold, and Fred became an immediate sensation.

Rogell was a master at getting high production value from tight budgets, and *Thundering Hoofs* (FBO, 1924) survives as a testament to his skill as a filmmaker. Rogell and Thomson had a falling out after the star was injured shooting a stagecoach chase for that film, and he left the series after directing the first eight Thomsons. Rogell took the basic Thomson formula and scripts and re-worked them into pictures starring first Reed Howes for Rayart release, and later Ken Maynard for First National. In the early '30s the formula was re-worked again for John Wayne using liberal doses of stock footage from the Maynard silents.

Just as the popularity of Tom Mix led producers to seek out real cowboys to star in their horse operas, the success of Fred Thomson opened the floodgates to a new crop of cowboy stars. Col. Tim McCoy, Tom Tyler (Vincent Markowski), Bob Steele (Robert N. Bradbury, Jr.), Bob Custer (Raymond Glenn), Wally Wales (Floyd Alderson), Fred Humes, Don Coleman, Fred Gilman, Rex Bell (George Francis Beldam), Buddy Roosevelt, Buffalo Bill, Jr. (Jay Wilsey)—the list seemed endless as more and more Westerns were churned out by Hollywood. Much of the fun also disappeared as these new stars all seemed to present more solemn screen personalities. With this flood of horse operas, many exhibitors began to feel that a Bob Steele or a Tom Tyler was as good as a Tom Mix or a Buck Jones—or, to put it bluntly: a Western was a Western and the $10 or $15 rentals for an FBO or a Rayart picture was better spent than the high-end rentals being charged for the Fox and Universal product.

As the major studios took on the added expense of converting to talking pictures, they dropped production of series Westerns, leaving the field to the independents. Sound presented many technical problems in making outdoor pictures, but these difficulties were quickly overcome. The truth is that the smaller theaters which were the primary market for Westerns were also the last to wire for sound. The big money was to be made with talkies in the big cities, and Westerns lost some of their golden allure.

Not that the big studios ignored the market altogether. Fox re-issued a number of the Tom Mix and Buck Jones silents in 1929 and 1930, and although Universal dropped many of its second-string stars, the studio continued to make pictures with Hoot Gibson and Ken Maynard for awhile. At the same time, independent producers continued to make silent Westerns well into 1930 and were especially slow to convert to sound.

What really happened in the transition period is that all the Western stars stepped down a peg. Tom Mix went from Fox to FBO to Universal. Ken Maynard moved from First National to Universal to Tiffany-Stahl. Buck Jones and Tim McCoy shifted from Fox and M-G-M to Columbia. Bob Steele and Tom Tyler were bumped from FBO and ended up at Syndicate-Monogram. After this shakeout, which lasted into 1931, the series Western settled into a more or less comfortable market niche, and the ma-

Joe Rickson (l.), Leo Maloney and Eileen Sedgwick (billed as Greta Yoltz) in Yellow Contraband *(1928).*

jors even re-entered the field on a less ambitious scale.

The series Westerns of the sound era were not a distinct new genre, rather they offered a continuation of the themes and production techniques established in the silent era. Tom Mix even made a mute "musical" Western, disguising himself as a trombone playing drummer in *The Best Bad Man* nearly ten years before Gene Autry sang "Tumbling Tumbleweeds."

Jay Wilsey (billed as Buffalo Bill Jr.), a favorite of producer Denver Dixon.

"GO INDEPENDENT, YOUNG MAN"
THE MAVERICK PRODUCERS
by Sam Sherman

Most of the B Westerns cherished by fans and collectors were made by independent producers, some of whom later founded important B studios, while others remained confined to the depths of small-time Poverty Row. Making successful Westerns on controlled budgets required ingenuity, and in this case necessity was truly the mother of invention.

Since B Westerns were mostly shot outdoors and many locations were free to use, good locales, clever production techniques, and small dollar outlays could result in impressive-looking films. This production method for Westerns dated back to the pre-1910 days of Broncho Billy Anderson, and continued through the silent era. In the field of Westerns, budgets and production values were not what was sold to the public or the trade . . . the stars provided the sizzle. The major studios may have had Tom Mix, Buck Jones and Tim McCoy, but the independents countered with Art Mix, Buddy Roosevelt and Buffalo Bill Jr.

Everybody just assumed that Art Mix was Tom's brother, since he dressed like him and seemed to have a "family" resemblance. It couldn't be further from the truth. Art Mix was the creation of one Victor Adamson (stage name Denver Dixon), a real cowboy from Australia who produced and directed one of the first Australian short Westerns: 1910's *Stockman Joe*. He came to the U.S. in the teens, and after a stint working on films in Fort Lee, New Jersey went to Hollywood in search of fame and fortune.

Working as a wrangler in Westerns one day, producing and directing his own films the next (based on available funds), Adamson truly represented the most independent spirit of the maverick group of low-budget Western filmmakers. A lost film of the early '20s, *The White Rider,* starred Adamson himself and a novice leading lady named Jean Arthur. When Adamson worked as a bit player with Arthur in *Arizona* (1940), she chose to snub him and not admit to making such a small film many years earlier.

The Art Mix series came about in a strange way. Producer Lester Scott Jr. was planning to make a silent series of "Buck Mix" Westerns, capitalizing on the popularity of the two top Fox Western stars. He planned to farm out the production of the series to Adamson. When the plan went sour, Adamson was out his time and money spent in setting up the production plans. Seizing upon an idea, he looked up the name "Mix" in the LA phone book, found a man named Arthur J. Mix and made him president of Arthur J. Mix Productions, a company that would star wrangler George Kesterson (billed in small type). Kesterson was the Tom Mix lookalike who eventually took the name Art Mix as his own. Fox sued and lost when Arthur J. Mix testified that he could use his own name in any business venture he wanted to.

Adamson funded this series by getting money from the regional film distributors throughout the country known as states' rights distributors, as

309

HOLLYWOOD CORRAL: A COMPREHENSIVE B WESTERN ROUNDUP

Victor Adamson (a.k.a. Denver Dixon) in The Old Oregon Trail (1928).

William Pizor

Denver shakes hands with TV personality Joe Franklin before appearing on a 1965 show.

they controlled rights to films in specific states in the U.S.; they were commonly called "states' righters." The expression changed to "franchise holders" in the era of Monogram and Republic, and eventually to "sub-distributors" or "subs," of which a handful still exist (from over 125 at the peak of independent distribution in the mid-'70s).

Victor Adamson was very successful with his Art Mix series and, being independent in spirit, only wanted to work for himself. He turned down an offer from Carl Laemmle to move his production company to Universal, to his own later dismay.

By 1928 Adamson's fortunes were on the wane, so he came up with a brilliant (if desperate) idea. Taking his last $900, his wife Dee (Delores Booth), and talented cameraman Paul Allen in his car with several reels of raw stock, Adamson set out for Oregon. By dint of the clever promoting of various local ranchers and businessmen in Oregon, Adamson was able to produce an amazing mini-epic, *The Old Oregon Trail,* in which he starred (and also directed) as Art Mix. Spectacular covered-wagon scenes and beautiful locations provided the backdrop (without stock shots) for this story of the settling of Oregon. Adamson took this film on the road throughout Oregon and the northwest himself, and was soon back in the chips.

Finding an old 16mm copy of this film in a rental library back in 1960, I felt I had discovered a small gem and decided to try and find Adamson, if he still happened to be around. Meeting producer Ed Finney through William K. Everson in New York in 1961, I found out that Adamson was a close friend, was still making films with his son, and could easily be contacted. My 1962 trip to Los Angeles led to my becoming fast friends with Victor Adamson, known to me socially as "Denver," and meeting his son Al Adamson, a director-to-be. Denver taught me the ins and outs of theatrical distribution and formatted a plan whereby Al and I would have our own production and distribution company. In 1968, Al, Dan Kennis and I formed Independent-International Pictures Corp., which is still actively in business 24 years after we started it—far outlasting the early Poverty Row companies I admired, which generally lasted only a few years.

Yes, Denver Dixon was a breed apart. In the '30s he made a series of Buddy Roosevelt and Buffalo Bill Jr. Westerns on the impossible budgets of only $2500 per film, possibly a record low budget for 35mm sound feature films. He cut many corners to finish the films, and they look crude compared to most B Westerns of the period, but any comparison is unfair. Denver made these films *work,* succeeding in the depth of the Depression. Warts and all, they remain interesting museum pieces from an earlier day.

The afore-mentioned Ed Finney was another interesting independent producer. In the '30s he was a studio publicist who worked in New York as Director of Advertising and Publicity for Republic Pictures, and had held similar jobs at M-G-M, Pathe, Monogram and United Artists. Finney was part of the team at Republic that helped put Nat Levine's Gene Autry musical Westerns into the upper echelon of screen oaters. Moving over to Grand National, Finney planned to create and market his own "singing cowboy."

Tex Ritter was working in New York in radio and on the stage. Finney felt he was a sure bet for the new musical Western rage. He contacted Lindsley Parsons in Hollywood to help him set up a production unit to make these new Tex Ritter films. Parsons was also a former employee of Monogram, like Finney, and was a writer who could also produce (or act as "supervisor," as line producers were called in that era. Line producers are the actual on-the-set executives who *make* the films, as opposed to the heads of production companies who act generally in a business sense only).

The Ritter films were good, and helped put both Finney and Grand National on the map. After making 12 of these, the fortunes of Finney and Ritter looked good, but a failed film with Jimmy Cagney virtually killed off Grand National, so the Ritter series moved back to Finney's old home . . . Monogram. The Monogram series was slicker, and the films made money, but not everybody got their fair share. Ed Finney later told me: "The states' righters took all the money they collected and threw it up in the air—the part that stayed up was remitted back to the producing company."

After making 20 films for Monogram, Tex Ritter in 1941 set out to better his career and sign with Columbia Pictures. From that point on, Tex would only be a co-star with the likes of Bill Elliott and Johnny Mack Brown. He would never be a solo star again. Ed Finney's career likewise had peaked, although he made films into the '50s and '60s. I once discussed this with Tex Ritter and he remained silent on the subject with me, but did talk about it with his wife, Dorothy. Dorothy later told me: "You know, Tex was talking to me about his film career and what happened when he split with Ed Finney. He realized

Producer Ed Finney (r.) gives a special trophy to Tex Ritter on completion of The Pioneers *(1941), the last of 32 films they made together. (The inscription reads: "To Tex Ritter from His Gang in memory of 'Boots and Saddles' Days—April 1941.") Director Al Herman looks on.*

it was a big mistake. He said that you were right. 'Ed and I were a great team and we were successful together . . . we never should have split up'."

Good distribution was the key factor in the production of Westerns. Only those who had it could succeed. Denver Dixon had his foreign rights assigned to veteran international distributor William Pizor in the silent era. Pizor would later go on to form Imperial Pictures and Screen Guild Productions, the latter with exhibitor-producer Robert Lippert. Pizor's son Irwin, former president of Hemisphere Pictures Inc., became part of my own Independent-International Pictures Corp., and merged earlier Pizor and Screen Guild assets. It is obvious that many people in the film industry know and work closely with one another; that is part of film history. Take, for example, the unusual tale of Hopalong Cassidy and how he came to the screen.

Jack Trop (also known as J. D. Trop) was a fascinating character who lived in New York in the '30s. He was a writer, film editor, distributor, and sometimes producer. Like many in the New York film scene, he was a regular at Bill Pizor's office. (I was a regular at that office in a later era, when Irwin Pizor was in charge.) Back in the '30s, the regulars at Bill Pizor's office waited around to play cards or for something to happen that they might become involved with. Herman Garfield was one of those card players who also waited around for something lucky to happen to him. On one special day Garfield brought that luck to the office, but it was for somebody else—Jack Trop.

Garfield told Jack that Paramount Pictures was looking to distribute a series of B Westerns made by an independent producer. In no time Trop was over at Paramount, trying to sell them on a new

"GO INDEPENDENT, YOUNG MAN" / The Maverick Producers

On the set of an Ed Finney-produced Tex Ritter film, Hittin' the Trail, *supervisor Lindsley Parsons (l.) goes over the script with director Robert N. Bradbury in February, 1937.*

series based on the radio show *Death Valley Days*. Paramount showed interest. Jack then brought in his close friend and former partner, Harry Sherman, who was at that time down on his luck and living with his sister in Boston. Harry Sherman felt that the Clarence Mulford *Hopalong Cassidy* Western novels were a better screen bet than *Death Valley Days* and Paramount agreed. The series went forward.

Financed by independent money, the first six films were successful. Este Productions Inc. ("S" and "T" for *S*herman and *T*rop) was formed to produce the Hopalong Cassidy films, with Harry Sherman in charge of production. In the first few years under his control, the budgets went sky high and Paramount threatened to cancel the series. Trop promised to bring the budgets back in line and took over the production reins. He personally produced *Pride of the West* (1938) for about half the then-current average budget, and similarly made *In Old Mexico, Bar 20 Justice* and *Heart of Arizona,* all in 1938. Paramount was happy; Harry Sherman was unhappy. This exercise in production economy drove a wedge between the partners, which resulted in Sherman buying Trop out. Trop returned to New York to editing and distribution. A vegetarian for most of his life, Jack Trop played tennis until the age of 90, spent his time helping other people, and died peacefully at the age of 92 in 1992.

The stories of independent producers of low-budget films are generally filled with financial ups and downs, generally unrelated to the success of the films themselves. The more successful the films, the more people are siphoning off the money.

Nat Levine was a great character whose success with Mascot serials, the founding of Republic Pictures, and the creation of the Gene Autry musical Westerns certainly placed him in a special category. He started as a distributor in the silent era. When a

On location for In Old Mexico (1938). *Producer J. D. "Jack" Trop rests his hand on the shoulder of director Edward Venturini. Unit director Lesley Selander sits at William Boyd's left.*

"GO INDEPENDENT, YOUNG MAN" / The Maverick Producers

lab had an incomplete negative to a failed production, Levine bought the uncut footage for next to nothing and hired an editor to try and make some sense out of it. He hired writer Jack Natteford to help him organize this project. In the silent era, title writers were all-important; through their art new meaning could be given to scenes already filmed. Natteford performed that duty, and the final film, entitled *Every Woman's Problem* had nothing to do with the footage shot, but was a success and made Levine a distributor.

Through 1935 the success of Levine's Mascot Pictures, which cranked out B features and serials, and the classic Ken Maynard Western *In Old Santa Fe* (which introduced Gene Autry to the screen), led to the formation of Republic Pictures. In less than two years Republic became the leading producer-distributor of B Westerns, and Herbert J. Yates bought out Nat Levine's interests in the company. The reputed millions Yates paid Levine were gone in less than a year, gambled away at the Santa Anita racetrack. For the rest of his life Nat Levine was up and down making an occasional clever distribution deal, but the glory days had eluded him. He told me of the success of the first Autry feature *Tumbling Tumbleweeds* (1935), which was made for $15,000 and brought in $500,000 in $15 "flat rentals," foreign sales and such . . . it launched Republic.

Independent producers usually fell into one of two categories: those that had distribution facilities and those that didn't have them. The ones having distribution facilities generally operated through the states' righters. Unless there was a substantial distribution organization in place to police the film rentals due, small producers were better off just selling territorial rights on an outright basis.

Sol Lesser, a former exhibitor and more affluent independent producer, organized Beverly Pictures in 1930 to produce a series of Buck Jones Westerns for release by Columbia Pictures. Eventually this arrangement was renegotiated, and Columbia ended up producing the Buck Jones Westerns themselves without having to report back to Lesser as an outside producer. Although Lesser continued to produce films for his own distribution, he preferred to operate in the major leagues and have big companies distribute his independently produced product. Fox/20th Century-Fox handled the distribution on his George O'Brien series, Smith Ballew Westerns, and a variety of mixed subjects such as *Wild Brian Kent* (1936).

Following the Sol Lesser series, George O'Brien signed with George Hirliman to make a series of action films for distribution through RKO. The first of the series, *Daniel Boone* (1936), was the most elaborate. It was followed by *Park Avenue Logger, Hollywood Cowboy* and *Windjammer,* all in 1937. *Hollywood Cowboy* was notable for launching the directorial career of one of the top Western directors: George Sherman. While on location, director Ewing Scott was injured in a car accident. Three Georges (O'Brien, Hirliman and assistant director Sherman) pondered just who should take over the directorial reins. Years later George O'Brien remembered how he made the decision. "You can do it, Georgie," he told Sherman. "As an assistant director you know all about the film. You take over and direct." And so an important career was started. While on location Sol Siegel and a Republic crew were in the area. Siegel saw George Sherman directing George O'Brien, an important star, and suggested Sherman see him back at the studio, where eventually he was given a test job directing *Wild Horse Rodeo* (1937). The film proved to be one of the best of the Bob Livingston *Three Mesquiteers* series, and George Sherman stayed on at Republic for seven more years, becoming one of their top producer-directors.

In 1931 independent producer Irving Briskin organized Mercury Pictures to produce a series of Tim McCoy Westerns. With the first film in the can, Briskin planned to distribute it himself until it was suggested he screen the film for Columbia. Columbia people liked what they saw and took on the series, with Briskin to remain as producer. From that point on the Tim McCoy films were Columbia productions; Briskin himself stayed at the studio for the next three decades or so as head of one of their production units.

Of the line producers who actually made films, many only received credit as production manager or supervisor, while many received no credit, so the production company head could claim the producer's credit for himself. The real producer of the 1935–6 Bob Steele series for A.W. 'Bill' Hackel's Supreme Pictures was actually Sam Katzman, although you would never know it from the screen credits. Katzman was to make a series of Tim McCoy Westerns for Victory Pictures, a company funded by Mercury Film Laboratories head Nat Saland. That was in 1939, when a star like McCoy was still commanding good money, even from smalltime producers. One source claimed that McCoy received a $5000 salary per film, while the total budget was only $10,000 each. Former major Western stars were reaching for the immediate cash they could put

315

HOLLYWOOD CORRAL: A COMPREHENSIVE B WESTERN ROUNDUP

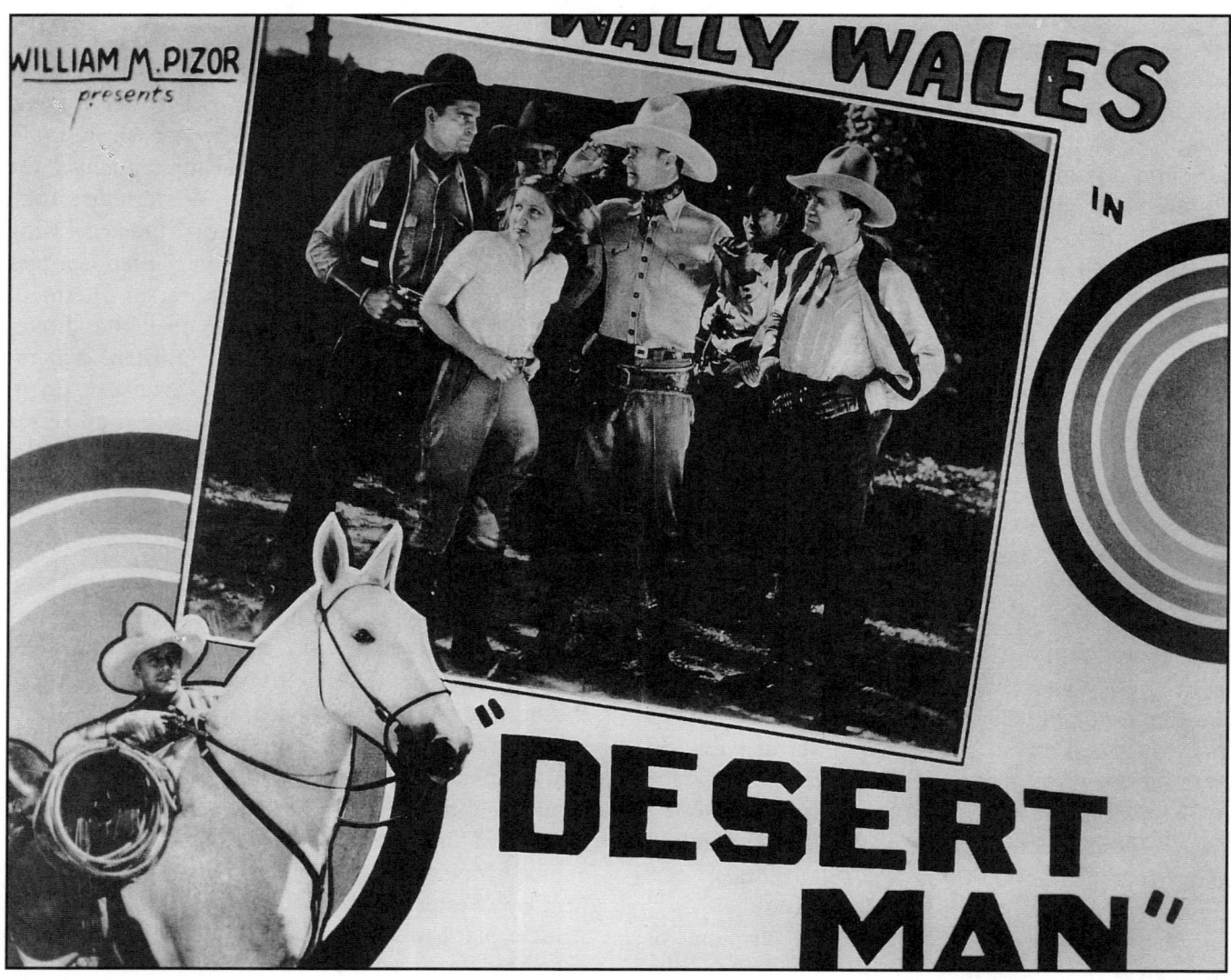

their hands on while not realizing that the cheap films they were making were helping to ruin their careers.

Ken Maynard fell into this same category. As a big star for Universal, he headed his own production unit, and although he was popular, the budgets and schedules were expanding rapidly. When Universal had enough of this, Maynard moved over to Columbia. A more budget conscious company, Columbia had to meet Ken Maynard's salary demands and still make a profit. So they farmed out the production of the Ken Maynard series to independent producer Larry Darmour. Darmour was a cost cutter from way back and made the Maynard series for Columbia, but the level was generally far below that of the Columbia-produced Tim McCoy series. In *Avenging Waters* (1936), one of the Darmour-Maynards, time-killing was the order of the day when action scenes weren't on the screen. One party scene features four or five poorly done musical numbers, one of which has Ken leading a group of cowboys in a harmonica chorus. Similarly, live recorded sound was later used in a scene where Ken plays his harmonica and Beth Marion plays the piano, another rather poorly done attempt to kill time and fill out the film.

Darmour Westerns continued to appear on the Columbia release slate with Bob Allen, Jack Luden and Bill Elliott series. Along the way some of the quality did improve, probably due to complaints from Columbia executives. Darmour operated from his studio at 5823 Santa Monica Blvd., which still stands but remains closed and unused.

In the '40s Columbia's cost cutting led them to farm out productions to Sam Katzman, who operated out of the Darmour studio. Directors at that time spoke of being "banished" off the Columbia lot to the Darmour studio. It is likely that both Darmour and Katzman were delivering finished product to Columbia for a fixed cost. The more money they saved the more they kept, regardless of the quality of the finished product.

It was the opposite at Republic, which prided itself on the quality of its Westerns. The stars were generally paid very little, and all the production budget was put into the film in which the quality could be seen. There were no $5000-per-picture Tim McCoy deals at Republic, where newer, younger stars like Roy Rogers were being brought along at salaries of $75 per week to start. Conditions like this led to Gene Autry's 1937 dispute with Republic head Herbert Yates, who eventually had to up the ante for his top money-maker.

One of the most prolific of the B Western production teams was the Neufeld brothers: Sigmund Neufeld, who produced, and Sam Newfield (with an anglicized last name), who directed. The brothers may not have achieved a level of high art in their films, but the productions were solid, professional products. Lacking were the filler scenes common to Darmour and Katzman, but in their place the well-done comedy of Al St. John, beloved "Fuzzy" of so many Neufeld PRC Westerns.

Sam Newfield was a capable director who worked to budget, finished on time, and delivered what was required of him. He directed so many films that to make it seem like the brothers employed other directors, he also took the credits of Peter Stewart and Sherman Scott. While he is rarely given any special credit for his creativity as a director, he could hold his own with the best B directors. His 1948 film noir production *Money Madness* certainly equals or exceeds the quality of more famous cult films like *Detour.*

In 1936 Sam Newfield was directing a bleary-eyed Bob Livingston in scenes for *Roarin' Lead* at Republic at three in the morning. Livingston was obviously caving in from the around-the-clock schedule the studio imposed. Newfield told Livingston, "If you ever get out of this place, look me and my brother up and we'll have some work for you that won't be under these conditions." In 1942 Bob Livingston was out of work after the expiration of his first Republic contract, so he called Sam Newfield. Newfield and his brother worked out a well-paying arrangement for Bob Livingston and starred him in a series of six *Lone Rider* Westerns for PRC, plus an additional role under his real name of Bob Randall in *The Black Raven* (1943). Al "Fuzzy" St. John was comedy lead in the *Lone Rider* series, but was more well accepted as Buster Crabbe's pal in the long running PRC Western series, which the Neufeld brothers successfully produced. (Continuing the family tradition, Sig's son Stan was head of production for Orion Pictures for many years, producing major hit films.)

Independent producers were a varied lot and their careers often as bizarre as the numerous films they made. William Berke was one of the best and most

Tourists stop to chat with Wally Wales (standing behind driver) on location for an early talkie Western.

interesting. He was a cameraman who developed cataracts on his eyes. The resulting operation required that he wear thick glasses. Due to this condition he could not get his eye close enough to the camera viewfinder and had to seek another job. He became the producer of low-budget films and series Westerns. One such series in 1935 starred Harry Carey, directed by Harry Fraser. When Berke signed Jack Perrin for a series for Atlantic (Astor Pictures), he started with Harry Fraser directing *Hair Trigger Casey* and *Wildcat Saunders,* but, possibly as a cost cutting measure, took over the directorial reins himself on *Desert Justice* and *Gun Grit* (all 1936). Berke directed under the name Lester Williams and kept things moving throughout the films. He even experimented with handheld cameras and quick cutting to make his fight scenes more exciting.

After making his own productions, William Berke moved on as producer to Maurice Conn's production unit and Republic Pictures, where he was producer on the *Three Mesquiteers* series for 1938–39. He signed on at Columbia Pictures as both producer and director, working on the Charles Starrett and Russell Hayden series.

There were other independent producers of B Westerns, and many were interrelated with one another. When you look at the production personnel who worked together, a pattern forms, showing that most of the B Westerns were made by the same people, a comparatively small group. Perhaps that's why there is a similarity to many of the films. These people invented a medium, defined the standards, and then produced to order. The hero was expected to act in a certain way, the leading lady did this and

Heavies Chuck Morrison (l.), Bob Kortman and Richard Botillier menace Harry Carey in Wild Mustang *(1935), a William Berke Production.*

"GO INDEPENDENT, YOUNG MAN" / The Maverick Producers

Jay Wilsey, Yakima Canutt (pointing) and heavies in 'Neath Arizona Skies *(1934).*

that and so on. The few films that broke those rules screen well today, being offbeat, but audiences of their day were probably not as pleased.

With the passage of time the B Western producers have been generally forgotten. These were men who struggled with the lowest budgets in the industry, and wound up producing films that appealed to the widest audiences per dollar spent, in the heyday of the movies from 1930 to 1950. And that's no small achievement.

Sid Jordan (in hat) with Tom Mix and Tony in The Heart of Texas Ryan *(1917).*

LIFE AMONG THE "400"
HOLLYWOOD'S COWBOY COLONY
by Robert S. Birchard

In 1930, a young man from Oklahoma named Bob Pillow came to Hollywood. As a boy he'd gone to the movies to see Tom Mix, Buck Jones, and Art Acord, and the idea of playing a cowboy in pictures was a dream he wanted to pursue. He had no real desire to be a star–he just wanted to work. Of course, 1930 wasn't a great time for work anywhere in America, and Hollywood was no exception. Bob Pillow worked hard at breaking into the movies, but the only film work he managed to land was a one-day job in a crowd scene for a Buck Jones picture. He quickly realized that even on Gower Gulch in Poverty Row, where labor unions were unknown, there was a closed shop when it came to hiring cowboys.

"You had to do a lot of hustlin'," recalled Ted French, one of the lucky ones who managed to make a living as a Hollywood cowboy, "'cause if you didn't get around, there was too many guys buckin' that extra board. I mean there were some pretty fair boys in there.

"The stunts we did were pretty damn rugged, and don't you ever forget it, and we took our lives in our hands if we worked with people who didn't know what they were doing.

"Back in the early '20s we had a group we called 'the 400' [like New York's social register]. We called it 'the 400' because we were so exclusive–it was just among the cowboys. If you couldn't get on a bronch', you didn't get in, and you had to have a specialty. Old Tom Smith, with his long hair, cast eye, and handlebar mustache, was noted for his ability with eight-in-hand wagon rigs; Ed 'Pardner' Jones looked like a prosperous middle-aged businessman, but he was a dead shot with a rifle; and I did bulldogging and car stunts. Once you got into 'the 400' you got a first call on the work because the studios knew you could do the job.

"In the early days we used to go down to Inceville and 'rehearse.' On our own time we'd practice buckin' horses, and bull ridin', and ropin', and all that stuff. Some of the big Western actors came out of that outfit.

"They had some real characters. There was old Slim Cole, who was just as good on a motorcycle as he was on a horse. He'd have made a good hippie–he had a full beard, and the cops would chase him up to Universal City, I think, every morning that he came into the studio. As he came up over Cahuenga Pass on his motorcycle, he might have two or more cops after him in a car trying to pick him off. Well, he'd just swing that old motorcycle off and go right up over that hill and come down in the studio back lot right above the barn. They never could get him.

"And old Murphy. He had a wife that was a squaw and, boy, she like to beat him to death. Every morning or so he'd come out and he'd have a lump on his head and a black eye and a skinned face, and we'd say, 'Murph, you don't look like you got away so good this morning.' He'd say, 'I don't know when I'm ever going to learn to keep my mouth shut, that squaw gets me every time.'"

L. to r.: unidentified player, Joe Rickson, Leo Maloney, Tom Smith and Slim Cole in "Two Gun" of the Tumbleweed *(1927).*

Ted French never became a big Western actor; he was just one of the many cowboys who came to the movies in the early days of the medium. Born Victor Edward French in New York in 1899, he moved with his family to Arizona in 1908. In later years Ted called veteran character actor Charles K. French his "father," but he actually "adopted" the old man because they had the same last name and because he never got along with his real father. (Ted recalled "that man was an artist with a horse whip, and I was his canvas.") As a boy Ted managed to find work around the King Ranch in Arizona, but his parents wanted him to finish his education so they pulled up stakes and moved to Santa Barbara, California, where he took a job driving a Wells Fargo wagon to finance his schooling. It was there that Ted met Bill Donnelly, a professional fighter and wrestler. Taking the name Teddy Starstruck to keep his parents from finding out what he was up to, Ted started wrestling and inadvertently became a professional. This made him ineligible for school athletics, and he lost much of his interest in education.

By 1915, Ted was riding on Walter and William Fudder's San Marcos Ranch, over the hill and inland from Santa Barbara. One day a unit from the American Film Company, headed by director Lloyd Ingraham, came to the ranch to shoot a stampede scene. The sequence called for the hero, Art Acord, to save the heroine from death by bulldogging the closest threatening steer and carrying the girl to safety behind a fallen tree.

"When I saw that guy bulldogging that steer," French recalled, "I got ideas. If I could learn to do that, I'd be the only guy in the valley who *could,* and that would really be something.

"I decided to teach myself how to bulldog. I got up early the next morning and went down to the manzanita corral where we kept some calves. I picked myself out a calf and went after him, but I misjudged it and got my boot caught in his horns and landed in a pile against the fence.

"The morning after that I got my determination back again, and this time I brought him down. The foreman, George Rowe, saw the whole thing and he yelled, 'Since you got so much energy, I've got a little pick-and-shovel work for you to do.'"

But Ted's determination finally paid off when he found work as a wrangler for the American Film Company's Flying "A" studio in Santa Barbara.

"There was Roy Sharpe, and the 'Dutchman' Murray, the three Morrison boys, Althouse, Jack Gilstrap, Billy Darnelly, and myself, and I tell you it was real glamorous. Two or three days a week we'd work in front of the cameras and the rest of the time we worked taking care of horses and cleaning stables. We shoveled a lot of horseshit. Pete Morrison rode his little Brownie most of the time, and he had her pretty well schooled. I had a horse up there that I called Hightower; it was a dapple grey. That son-of-a-bitch would buck at the least indication. I finally entered him in a rodeo once I knew I could ride him. After the rodeo I'd climb back on him and ride him back to the studio."

The life of a movie cowboy wasn't always as action-packed as it seemed on screen, according to French. "Those damn silent pictures, they'd take forever to shoot them. You'd go out there and sit on your butt all day long and you wouldn't do nothin', but sometimes we had some excitement.

"Once I was working on a William Russell picture in Santa Barbara. We were on a big barroom set and Henry King was the director. Now, Henry wanted me to go from the camera to the end of the bar, then turn and fire. Well, apparently I didn't go fast enough, and about halfway through Henry proceeds to shoot a quarter-load blank in my britches.

"Well, brother, it made me so mad I turned around and blasted him square in the face with my .45—and that was a full-load blank!

"I says, 'Don't you ever put one of them things in my pillowcase again, brother, or I'll put some lead in the end of this thing.' Henry and I got along real good after that."

Ted French was a consummate storyteller. He invented words, always had a punch line, and peppered his tales with innocent profanity. Early-day bulldoggers bit the lip of the steers they brought down, and as a result many bulldoggers lost their front teeth when the angry animals reared their heads. Ted's lower jaw showed a gap when he grinned, and he looked like a seven-year old waiting for his grown-up incisors. He delighted in being a "colorful character," but most of the cowboys in Hollywood tended to treat words like a rationed commodity. They kept their thoughts to themselves and didn't mix well with strangers.

While the Hollywood elite attended banquets and gala premieres, the social highlights for the real cowboys who worked in early Western movies were the semi-annual spring and fall round-ups of the Chuck Wagon Trailers. To be a member of this "Social Club for Old Cowmen," you had to be a working cowhand before 1905. Over the years the bylaws were changed to allow those with later ranch experience to join, and by the early '70s one of the older members lamented, "Now all you need to join is a pair of boots and a hat." The group, formed in the early '20s, gathered for a weekend chuck-wagon cookout which featured an unchanging menu of boiled beef, stewed prunes, baked beans and biscuits. The coffee was boiled in large vats with the time-tested recipe of one handful of grounds per cup.

The Chuck Wagon Trailers were a rugged bunch, and though many of them used to call the Columbia Drug Store at the corner of Sunset and Gower "the office," no one who valued his own physical well-being would ever think of calling them drugstore cowboys. Henry Isabell was typical of the type. Henry first worked in pictures in 1909, and as late as the early '70s, when he was well up in his eighties, he could be heard saying: "You know, it's getting to the point where if I can't do some stunts where I can make some real money, I'm just not interested in working anymore." Dressed all in black, Isabell always crouched on his haunches as he talked, and his joints seemed to be none the worse for wear after eighty-plus years of hard living—except that several of his fingers were only stubs due to roping accidents.

Joe Rickson, who entered pictures in the teens and worked in Westerns well into the '40s, actually won his wife in a rodeo contest. The fair lady, it seems, couldn't choose between Joe and another suitor; so the two cowboys challenged each other to a "Hippodrome" race—standing bareback atop two horses. Rickson was the winner, and the rivalry inspired Tom Mix to re-tell the story (with variations) in two shorts, *Roping a Bride* (Selig Polyscope, 1915) and *Roping a Sweetheart* (Selig Polyscope, 1916).

For many of the early cowboys, picture work was seasonal. They would work the Wild West shows and rodeos part of the year, work ranches at round-up time, and fill in with pictures in between.

HOLLYWOOD CORRAL: A COMPREHENSIVE B WESTERN ROUNDUP

Sid Jordan was a young man looking for a job in 1912 when he decided to go to South America to work on some of the big cattle spreads down there. Sid was the son of John Jordan, first sheriff of Washington County, Oklahoma. He met Tom Mix at the Dewey, Oklahoma Round Up in 1907, and when Mix later joined the Miller Brothers 101 Ranch Show, Sid also signed on.

Mix went into pictures in 1910, working intermittently with traveling units of the Selig Polyscope Company, first in Flemington, Missouri, and later at St. Augustine, Florida. During 1911, the film company came to Dewey, Oklahoma, where Tom's job as night marshal didn't interfere with his daytime picture work.

In 1913, Mix was working with Selig star William Duncan in Prescott, Arizona. While Sid Jordan was traveling through the state, he read a newspaper story about a film company and saw the name of his old friend. He looked up Tom, was offered a job, and never did get to South America.

Jordan had bushy eyebrows and square-cut features, and when Tom Mix was given his own starring series in 1914, Jordan was often cast as Tom's rival and he also played his share of black-hearted villains. During his early days in Hollywood it was difficult for Sid to go out in public without attracting attention. In later years Sid's wife, Alice, remembered that although Sid had the sweetest disposition away from the camera, movie fans expected that he was like his screen character. In restaurants people were known to get up and leave when Sid came into the room. Sid's reputation did have its advantages, however.

One night after shooting at Mixville in Edendale near downtown Los Angeles, Sid and Alice drove to a nearby Safeway Market to buy some groceries. It had been a long day, and Sid didn't bother to take off his costume or make-up; in fact, he still wore his six-shooter. As they pulled into the parking lot, a truck driver pulled in front of the car and yelled: "Get out of the way—can't you see I'm coming through?"

"Well, there was plenty of room," Sid later remembered. "He could have gotten by without any

Universal City in the teens saw many real cowboys forsaking the range for movie work. This group includes: (back row, l. to r.) two unidentified players, assistant director Teddy Brooks, Bill Gillis, Jim Corey, (middle row) unidentified player, Pedro Leone, Bud Osborne, (front row) Joe Rickson, Neal Hart, Harry Carey, Olive Carey, George Marshall, unidentified player.

Sid Jordan takes aim at Tom Mix's necktie in The Coming of the Law *(1919).*

trouble, but he was in this big truck and feeling like a big man. I was tired and annoyed, not to say young and stupid. I quietly got out of my car, walked over to the truck, and asked, 'What did you say to me?' Well, this poor fellow looked down and saw my gun and the collodion scar on my face, and he just withered. He stuttered, 'Oh, that's alright, boss, there's plenty of room—plenty of room—just drive on by.'"

On one picture Tom and Sid set off in Tom's car for a nearby location. On the way they decided to make several stops to do a little elbow-bending. By the time they arrived on location, they were two hours late and in no condition to follow the script, which required Tom—in real life an expert marksman—to shoot the oversized buttons off Sid's suspenders, causing Sid's pants to fall.

Tom's first shot went wide, but the second bullet passed between the suspenders and Sid's shirt. The shooting was wisely postponed for the day.

Under better conditions both men were excellent shots, and Sid was often called on to shoot a hole in Tom's hat, or shoot an object out of his hand. But not everybody had Mix's faith in Sid's ability. On one picture a comedian was brought in from the east. In his big scene, a hard hombre—played by Sid—was to shoot a glass out of his hand. Everything went fine until the crucial moment. The comic shook so hard that Sid could not make his shot. The director assured the Easterner that everything was alright, and Sid shot a glass out of the director's hand to demonstrate how easy it was. The comic watched the scene in wide-eyed amazement, but he was not convinced. When he took his mark again, he shook harder than before and the scene had to be cut from the script.

Over the years Sid became one of the most respected cowboys in the movie colony. The night before Buck Jones signed his first contract he asked Sid if it was the right thing to do, and later George O'Brien had it written into his contract that Sid was to work on all his pictures. Sid was also one of the few cowboys who dared to play a practical joke on Tom Mix.

"Tom did the most daring stunts," said Jordan, "but he got spooked at the sight of spiders and mice.

HOLLYWOOD CORRAL: A COMPREHENSIVE B WESTERN ROUNDUP

One morning we did a scene where Tom's rival put some mice in a bouquet that Tom was supposed to take to the girl.

"Some studio big-wigs came to the set for lunch, and Tom was still pretty jittery when he sat down at the card table where it was served. I found some bulk cotton and a fishing line, made a 'mouse' out of the cotton, tied the line around it, and lowered it over Tom's hat as he was eating. He jumped up and knocked the whole table over. When he realized what happened he yelled, 'It was that damn Sid Jordan that done that!' as we all doubled up laughing."

After the success of Buck Jones, who rose from the ranks of young cowboys working in the "flickers," Sid Jordan was picked by the Fox Film Corporation to be groomed for stardom, but just as the studio began to promote Sid, one of Fox's directors discovered a young trick rider named Ken Maynard. The studio worked on Maynard for quite awhile before they decided he was not suited for pictures (of the Fox variety, at least), and they finally let him go. By the time Fox dumped Maynard, the momentum to star Sid Jordan was past. But if Sid never became a star, he launched at least one future Western star on his way.

"We were up on location," Sid remembered, "and we'd hired some Indians to do a chase scene. When it came time to shoot the scene, there were no Indians, so we dressed up everyone available in blankets and feathers and swabbed 'em down with bolemaney [Bole Armenia—a skin-darkening makeup] to make 'em look like redmen. One of them was a prop boy named Marion Morrison. Well, he comes running up to me and says, 'Hell, Sid, I've never been on a horse in my life. What do I do?' And I told him, 'You just keep the horse between your legs. He'll do the rest.' He got through the scene alright, but there was a lot of daylight between him and that horse. In just a couple of years Marion Morrison became John Wayne."

As time went on, Sid made fewer appearances before the camera and worked more behind the scenes as a foreman, which meant that he was responsible for hiring the cowboys to be used on a picture. His cousin, Frank Jordan, saw the strain this caused. "I came out from Odessa, Texas, for a visit in the '30s, and Sid just couldn't sit down or take a bite without the phone ringing. All the calls were from cowboys looking for work. There wasn't enough work to go around, but Sid wouldn't hire the same crew all the time—he'd spread around what work there was so that they could all work some."

In the '30s, when all the Hollywood craftsmen started to organize unions, the cowboys attempted to form their own, The Riding Actors Association of Hollywood. The fledgling organization opened an office at 6472 Santa Monica Boulevard and tried to get better wages and working conditions for its members. The president was former Western star Neal Hart, Buck Bucko was vice-president, the half-blind cowboy-turned-lyric-writer Curley Fletcher, secretary, and Spike Spackman, treasurer. The board of directors consisted of veteran cowboys George Sowards, Walter Shumway, Vic Allan, and Jack Montgomery (the father of comedy child star "Baby Peggy" Montgomery). The organization was a logical outgrowth of the informal "400" of earlier years. Among the members of the Riding Actors Association were Art Mix (no relation to Tom, his real name was George "Whitey" Kesterson), Cliff Smith (who was a director for William S. Hart, Tom Mix and others in the '20s), Bill Patten (another fallen star from the late '20s), Tom London, Glenn Strange, and others with colorful names like Scoop Martin, Cactus Mack, Shy Thomas, and Baldy Miller. In all there were nearly 80 cowboys, ten Mexicans, and five Indians on the Association roster.

Unfortunately, The Riding Actors Association was a short-lived proposition. It seems the cowboys could never quite agree on much of anything but the name of the organization. As an adult, "Baby Peggy" Montgomery is known as Diana Serra Cary. Her 1975 book *The Hollywood Posse* was an affectionate memoir of her father and many of his fellow Hollywood cowboys. "To no one's surprise," she wrote, "the whole Riding Actors Association fell apart like a rotten saddle in a rain storm after only a few tumultuous weeks of meetings and membership drives."

Part of the problem was that the *Hollywood Posse* members were suspicious of too much organization and afraid that standing up to the producers might result in their being blackballed.

Among this group of rugged individualists was Pat Chrisman, an early member of the Tom Mix stock company. Mix's Tony the Wonder Horse was owned and trained by Chrisman. He bought the horse as a colt from a chicken-wagon driver in Glendale for a few dollars in 1914, and three years later sold the horse to Tom for $600 after the death of the star's favorite mount, Old Blue.

Tom Mix found "Dopey" Dick Crawford while working in Arizona. Crawford was an exceptional Western artist, but he was also a drug addict. Mix got Crawford "likkered up" and kept him drunk for

LIFE AMONG THE "400" / Hollywood's Cowboy Colony

Standing (center): Tom Mix, Robert Clyde "Kinney" Ruffner, Wynn Mace, Dick Hunter, Yakima Canutt, "Pee Wee" Holmes, "Bear Valley Charlie" Miller, Banty Caldwell. At far left: unidentified, Pat Chrisman, Herman Nowlin, unidentified, unidentified, Bobby Dyer, Raymond "Colorado Cotton" Smith, Earl Simpson.

three weeks to get the cowboy over the narcotic withdrawal period. After the cure, Mix gave Crawford a job, and he was never known to take dope again.

Dick Hunter, another cowboy in the Mix outfit, was the subject of a bunkhouse joke that backfired. He came in to bed down one night only to find a small boulder in his bed. Hunter didn't blink an eye. He climbed into the bunk, wrapped himself around the rock, and went to sleep. For three days the rock stayed in the bed, and for three days Hunter never said a word about his strange bedfellow. Finally, the pranksters removed the rock, and of course Hunter paid no notice to that either. Ray Smith, who went by the handle "Colorado Cotton," said it best when he opined that "When you start on a Tom Mix picture you'd best leave your right mind on the gate post."

"Yakima Canutt was undoubtedly the best Western stuntman in the business," remembered producer Lindsley Parsons, a veteran whose movie experience dated back to the teens. "I once paid him $200 for one day's work, during which he rigged a wagon to go over a cliff, had a fight with another stuntman on the seat of a racing wagon pulled by a four-horse team, fell down between the wheel horses, caught the rear axle of the wagon and pulled himself forward beneath the speeding wagon to the wagon tongue, climbed up to mount one of the lead horses, and brought the speeding wagon to a stop. He doubled one of the heavies in a fight scene, then put on the comedian's wardrobe for a fast ride away from the camera, accidentally hit his head riding under a tree limb and knocked himself out! When he came to, Yak apologized, saying that he had to do the wagon drag on unplowed ground and it had tired him out!"

Like many of his fellow cowboys, Yak liked his privacy. He built a home in the San Fernando Valley at a time when the Valley was still out in the country.

HOLLYWOOD CORRAL: A COMPREHENSIVE B WESTERN ROUNDUP

Robert Clyde "Kinney" Ruffner

"Yak was so proud of his new home," laughs Parsons, "he talked like a proud father. It got so bad that Dick Foran, 'Big Boy' Williams and some of the other cowboy actors got together and erected a 24-sheet billboard across the street from Yak's house during the night. The sign read: CHINESE LAUNDRY TO OPEN HERE SOON. You could hear Yak's anguished wail all over the San Fernando Valley, and the guffaws and horse laughs from his fellow Westerners in watering holes all around Hollywood."

Robert Clyde Ruffner, who rode with Tom Mix and Bill "Hoppy" Boyd, got his stage name when he rode with Buffalo Bill's Wild West and Pawnee Bill's Far East Combined Show. The young cowboy was about to mount a wild buffalo when a skeptic asked Pawnee Bill, whose real name was Gordon W. Lillie, "Kin 'e ride that wild buffalo?"

"Kin 'e?" yelled Pawnee Bill. "He sure kin!"

From that day on, Robert Clyde Ruffner was known as Clyde "Kid" Kinney. When he met Tom Mix in 1920 the Western star asked him, "Are you the 'Kid' Kinney I've heard so much about?"

"I'm the only 'Kid' Kinney I know," came the taciturn reply.

"Well," Mix replied, "if you're half as good as I've heard, you've got a job with me if you want it."

Kinney stayed with Mix for 14 years, and then became a foreman on the *Hopalong Cassidy* series. Although he was born in Pittsburgh, Kinney's family came to Arizona in the 1890s and he was "range raised." Arizona was 20 years away from statehood, and it was still pretty wild territory. Kinney, an adopted Apache, was known as a pretty fair hand with a gun. Years later in Hollywood his early reputation caught up with him, and an associate of Death Valley Scotty tried to hire Clyde to gun down the colorful desert rat. Kinney declined, saying that his guns weren't for sale anymore.

When Bill Boyd stopped making *Hopalong*

Cassidy Westerns, Kinney found it difficult to find work in the movies, and he went to work in a paint store. "I saw him waste away, day by day," his widow Lucinda remembered. "Every time he heard that one of the boys had gone, a little bit of him went too.

"I didn't say anything to him about his smoking and drinking. I didn't feel it was my place. I knew he wanted to live as long as he could, but he picked up those habits when he was just a boy on the range, and I couldn't see taking them from him."

Clyde Kinney died in 1962, but the real end of the trail for the "400" came in 1969, when the "Fat" Jones Stable lost its lease. Fat Jones made a career of renting horses and rigs to the movies. Originally located near Griffith Park, Jones moved his stable to the San Fernando Valley in search of cheaper rent, but after nearly 60 years of unabated popularity in movies and on TV, Westerns were suddenly out of favor and it made no economic sense to relocate the stables another time. The Milton J. Wershow Company handled the sale as horses, wagons and saddles went on the auction block. It was a hot, dry afternoon on Saturday, October 11, 1969, that the final gavel fell. In the crowd were a few of the old hands looking back over the years.

"They were a pretty salty bunch," Ted French remembered in tribute, "but there's one thing you can say—they were *cowboys*."

And what of Bob Pillow, the young man who came to Hollywood in 1930 to be a movie cowboy? He didn't make it into the "400," but he stayed in

Ted French

California and went to work for the Los Angeles Department of Water and Power. A lifelong collector of western movie memorabilia, he had his ambition partly realized in later years, when he was admitted into the Chuck Wagon Trailers.

A pre-Hollywood Gene Autry

THE SINGING COWBOY
AN AMERICAN DREAM
by Douglas B. Green

The American dream has always had the remarkably protean ability to become whatever the dreamer desired. No single goal—not fame, nor money, nor contentment—stands out as a common denominator; there are, in fact, no common denominators except for the assumption that it is right and proper for us to entertain the notion of such dreams, whatever form they may take.

The singing cowboy of films of the '30s and '40s, both the characters and the actors themselves, have long embodied a confluence of many of the aspects of the American dream, representing a sense of glamour and of adventure, a sense of the rugged individuality Americans have long prized; the fame and prestige of film stardom, the attainment of vast sums of money, the achievement of a kind of art, though an art long underrated, long appreciated by too few.

The America of today is a far different place from the nation which flocked to see the singing cowboy westerns of forty or more years ago. Yet far from rejecting these values in this enlightened age, we seem to be increasingly attracted to them, adding the warm patina of nostalgia to the inherent appeal of the embodiment of the American dreams they represent. In fact, as we become increasingly characterized by directionlessness, by a trend, if anything, to a lack of trends, the romance of the celluloid West becomes more and more attractive. This is nowhere more apparent than in the world of music, where the airwaves are filled with songs of tough but sensitive outlaws and their ladies, songs of today's cowboys written in Music Row song factories, songs listened to avidly by booted, jeaned, and hatted products of the baby-boom suburbs.

Beginnings

The singing cowboy was born of these parents: the romantic West of novels like Owen Wister's *The Virginian* (1902) and Zane Gray's *Riders of the Purple Sage* (1912), the cinematic West of *The Great Train Robbery* (1903) and a thousand subsequent films, and the musical West reaching out to America via radio and records, beginning with Carl T. Sprague's 1925 recording "When the Work's All Done This Fall." Interest in cowboy song predated records, of course. N. Howard Thorpe's *Songs of the Cowboys*, based on thirty years of research,[1] first appeared in 1908, followed closely by John Avery Lomax's *Cowboy Songs and Other Frontier Ballads* (1910). Then again, "made up" cowboy songs were nothing new: not only was some of the classic material of the genre being written while these works were being compiled, even Thorpe himself admitted in a later (1921) printing of his work that he had written one of the songs he had supposedly collected—the now-classic "Little Joe the Wrangler."[2] And, indeed, an 1891 potboiler by William Levi-Taylor called *The Cowboy Clan: or,*

Ken Maynard: the first singing cowboy?

Tigress of Texas contains a remarkably synthetic cowboy song which might have been quite at home in the worst of the '40s musical westerns:

> Lie down now cattle, don't heed any rattle
>   But quietly rest until morn.
> For if you skeedaddle, we'll jump in the saddle
>   And head you off, sure as you are born.[3]

These were the sources which existed in the years after World War I; they were galvanized by two new factors: the emergence of the "talking" film–with Al Jolson in *The Jazz Singer* in 1927–and the sudden development of the romantic cowboy song which transcended in poetry and vision the stock-in-trade tales of cowboy courage ("Utah Carrol"), cowboy pathos ("When the Work's All Done This Fall"), or cowboy humor ("Zebra Dun").

All these elements flowed together around 1930, ingredients in search of a catalyst, although the singing cowboy of fact and image did not emerge until a few years later. The emergence of this creation was hinted at, however, and it was Ken Maynard who proved to be the harbinger of all that followed, as he sang, hummed, and occasionally played the banjo, guitar, and fiddle in several of his films in the 1930–34 era. However, Maynard was to remain only a precursor; according to film historians George Fenin and William K. Everson, "perhaps due to Maynard's own limitations as a singer, and the fact that he still adhered to the traditional Western, the idea for musical Westerns did not catch on at that time."[4]

Not only did Ken Maynard introduce songs and music to the western film, he also became the first of the celluloid cowboys to sing[5] on record. In September of 1930 he cut eight songs for the soon-to-be-bankrupt Columbia Graphophone Company: "Fanny Moore," "Betsy From Pike," "Prisoner for Life," "Jesse James," "Roundup's Done," "Home on the Range," and, the only two sides ever released, "Cowboy's Lament" and "Lone Star Trail" (Columbia 2310-D).[6]

Maynard's voice was indeed a coarse one, though appealing in a rough way. He himself said, "I had this kinda high, nasal-soundin' Texas voice, but it sounded real enough, I reckon, for me to get into talkies."[7] Not only did Ken play and sing, he also displayed some flair as a songwriter, composing "The Trail Drive" and "Wheels of Destiny" for films of the same name. In addition he claimed the distinction of starring in the first film named for a popular western song, Universal's *The Strawberry Roan* in 1933, the Curly Fletcher song then popular in the Nat Vincent-Fred Howard expanded version, and recorded by the Beverly Hillbillies, Bill Boyd's Cowboy Ramblers, and a host of other string bands. Within the film Maynard not only sang the theme (twice!), but fiddled a bit in the old-fashioned style, fiddle tucked in the crook of his arm.

Though his studio press did their best to make him a Texan (Mission, Texas, was the birthplace invented for him), Ken Maynard was actually born in Vevay, Indiana, on July 21, 1895, and as early as the age of twelve he had run off and joined the circus. He became an expert horseman, a legendary stunt man, and a competent enough actor to star in dozens of films over the years, beginning with a bit part in *The Man Who Won* in 1923 and ending with *Harmony Trail* in 1944.

Maynard's major contribution to the singing cowboy genre was, in fact, neither his own singing nor his pioneering role as a singer: it was the introduction of Gene Autry to the world—in a 1934 Maynard feature called *In Old Santa Fe*—as a singer of modern cowboy songs. According to Jon Tuska, whose *The Filming of the West* stands as the most definitive work on the western film,[8] Maynard could have been the film star that Autry was to become, for Maynard himself was apparently the object of the initial effort at the creation of a singing cowboy. Tuska relates that producer Nat Levine was

THE SINGING COWBOY / An American Dream

On August 8, 1930, Tiffany released Oklahoma Cyclone, which appears to be the first series Western with what was to become the typical singing cowboy format. What makes this film truly unique is that it stars Bob Steele, a cowboy not often mentioned in discussions about the singing cowboys. Directed by John P. McCarthy, with the screenplay credited to Ford Beebe, Oklahoma Cyclone featured eight songs, five of which were sung by Steele. Although Steele sang one or two songs in a couple of other films in this series, he never did another "musical" Western.

Asked about his singing in films many years later, Steele dismissed it as unimportant and couldn't remember any particular significance put on it at the time (1930). However, he did remember a duet he did with his brother Bill Bradbury, for a film at about this time (possibly Near the Rainbow's End, another Tiffany film from 1930).

Oklahoma Cyclone was remade in 1936 as Song of the Gringo, Tex Ritter's first starring film for Grand National.

impressed with what Ken had been doing at Universal.

When Junior Laemmle ousted Maynard from his contract, Ken took... a second European voyage. Nat reached Ken via long-distance telephone in London. It was Nat's intention to produce a series of musical Westerns in both serial and feature form. He commented that he agreed with Maynard that action by itself was no longer sufficient to keep audiences interested. The proposed Mascot contract would provide Ken with $10,000 a week for each week that he worked, and Nat wanted Ken for an undetermined number of pictures. 'When I signed Ken Maynard for a serial at forty thousand dollars,' Nat Levine remarked to me, 'his name value justified the investment.' No other screen cowboy was making as much in 1933–34.[9]

For whatever reasons–his unappealing voice probably the main one[10]–Ken Maynard never "happened" as a singing cowboy. When Gene Autry appeared, fresh and free of the expectations of the past, then and there a new genre, both in music and in film, was born.

Before turning to Gene Autry's career, his influence, and his complex relationships with differing and sometimes conflicting versions of the American dream, it is important to recognize a musical trend alluded to earlier which may in itself have been largely responsible for preparing the American public to accept the emergence of the singing cowboy. This was the sudden popularity of the romantic western song. Earlier cowboy songs–"authentic," if you will–had been written before the turn of the century; extremely romantic in very specific ways, they concentrated on the rough, lonely, difficult, sometimes wryly humorous life of the cowboy. From long work songs like "The Old Chisholm Trail" to humorous dialect pieces like Gail Gardners's "The Sierry Petes" ("Tying Knots in the Devil's Tail") and reworked minstrel tunes like "The Little Old Sod Shanty on the Claim," these songs dealt in terms real or fanciful with such tangibles as housing, the art of branding or bronc riding, or a hundred other such specifics.

Few songs indeed concentrated on the beauty of the West, the romance of a generalized and dreamily appealing western life. The most notable was "Home on the Range." John I. White reports that

"Lomax had published it, with piano accompaniment, in his anthology *Cowboy Songs and Other Frontier Ballads* in 1910.... The earliest 'Home on the Range' recording of which I have any knowledge is that made by Vernon Dalhart and released by Brunswick in 1927. In 1928, Jules Verne Allen recorded it for Victor." He adds, more importantly, that "thanks largely to the sudden growth of radio broadcasting, in the early '30s America discovered and took to its heart what it thought was a genuine folksong. As the haunting, comforting strains 'Where seldom is heard a discouraging word/And the skies are not cloudy all day' miraculously came out of the air, the country somehow felt that it had a good thing going, stock market crashes and depressions notwithstanding."[11]

"Home on the Range" was not the only song causing this reaction. A rash of "new" western songs fundamentally different from their predecessors were appearing, largely from the pens of Bob Nolan and Billy Hill; these songs were concerned not with the life of the cowboy, but with the romance of the West as an entity in and of itself. Entirely apart from the life or even the existence of the cowboy except by implication, they dealt with the beauty of its haunting scenery, and in spiritual rather than earthy terms.

Billy Hill was born in Boston on July 14, 1899, the same city in which he died on Christmas Eve, 1940. As a youth he had been struck by the natural beauty of the West while living in Utah, and began writing western songs—as well as a great deal of pop material—in New York in the early '30s, often in collaboration with Peter DeRose. Beginning in 1933, a string of classic western songs reached America's ears via hit shows on Broadway, radio, record, and film, beginning with "The Last Roundup" and "The Old Spinning Wheel" and followed by "Wagon Wheels" (1934), "Empty Saddles" (1936), and a great many others, including "Call of the Canyon," "Night on the Desert," and "The Oregon Trail."[12]

As successful over a longer period of time, and artistically more effective, was Bob Nolan, a founder with Tim Spencer and Leonard Slye (later known as Roy Rogers) of the Sons of the Pioneers.[13] Nolan was born Robert Clarence Nobles on April 1, 1908, in New Brunswick, although a good deal of his youth was spent in Boston. At the age of fourteen the young student—even then a devotee of the English and Scottish poets Keats, Wordsworth, Byron, Shelley, and Burns—moved with his father to Arizona, a relocation which had a profound effect on the young man: "I came to Tucson, Arizona, right from the tall timber, out to the desert. It was awe-inspiring, to say the least, to wake up in the morning to see the desert beauty, with the sun shining through millions of drops of dew. It was just outstanding."[14] After attending the University of Arizona (where he published his western poetry in the college newspaper in a column called "Tumbleweed Trails"), Nolan eventually followed his father to California in 1929, and, after several years of roaming and occasional music-making, helped form the Sons of the Pioneers in 1933. By 1934 his song "Tumbling Tumbleweeds" had become a best selling record for Gene Autry (as "The Last Roundup" had been the year before), and Bob Nolan had established a reputation as country music's most poetic songwriter, with romantic songs like "Way Out There," "Blue Prairie," "Song of the Bandit," "Love Song of the Waterfall," and "Song of the Prairie," which both shaped and established this new image of western music. Talking about the creation of perhaps his most famous song, "Cool Water," Nolan explains this new, more romantic approach to songwriting:

I don't think there's any philosophy behind it; I was strictly trying to paint a picture of the desert, and I missed miserably, because I picked up the wrong thing to write about—a mirage—because you can't use the word mirage in a song: it just don't sing, and you can't rhyme it, and you're just up a tree, see? So I just left it out and everything was nebulous, but after I was through with it you couldn't help but know that I was talking about a mirage. You'd be surprised how many people never saw a mirage in the desert.[15]

This set of circumstances, plus the growing national interest in a romantic West, made the time ripe for something new. Though but a handful suspected it, that something was the singing cowboy.

Gene Autry, The Singing Cowboy

Into this vacuum stepped Gene Autry, the man who was ultimately to blend these disparate elements into the phenomenon of the singing cowboy, and whose career—regardless of one's sentimental favorites—is the single most important within the style.

Yet Autry's career is charged with paradox. It is a career which, like the man himself, is often nebulous, vague, and inexplicable. Gene Autry's career is surely one of the half dozen most important in country music, yet we really know little about it—just some names, dates, and facts, a bit of filmography here, a touch of discography there. We know virtually nothing of the inspiration that first fired his interest in music, the music which directed his talent (other than during his Jimmie Rodgers-influenced period) or the forces which shaped his music.

More often than not his legend and status have gotten in the way, obscuring many of the facts the country music scholar and fan seeks. For one thing, much of his legend was created in Hollywood, that land of illusion, and legends in Hollywood when written about are usually treated with reverent awe or with speculative gossip, neither of which is of much help, or interest. Writers and followers of Hollywood legends usually do not have a strong enough musical tradition on which to base their conclusions, and therefore end up concentrating endlessly on the ephemeral, the spurious, and the obvious.

A second reason Autry's influential career has been kept in an unfocused state is simply that he is a multimillionaire: nothing seems to obsess Autry historians like this most obvious manifestation of the American dream. That the compilation of his vast wealth has been his main concern since returning to civilian life after World War II is obvious. Autry is proud to recount for reporters his rapid rise from poverty to great wealth at the expense of discussing his musical origins. What about Autry's musical and film greatness?

Bill Malone spent a remarkable amount of time, given the restrictions of space, to the effects of Gene Autry's career in *Country Music USA: A Fifty Year History,* pointing out that "at the onset of the war, Gene Autry was the most financially successful and possibly the most popular country performer."[16] My own essay in *Stars of Country Music: From Uncle Dave Macon to Johnny Rodriguez*[17] was the first serious look of any length at Gene Autry's music and its considerable effects on the development of country music. Most film critics have written off his career–with a tone either of condescension or bewilderment–as a bizarre and unhealthy fluke. Only Tuska has taken the time to examine what he calls "The Autry Phenomenon" in depth, and his conclusions are remarkable and enlightening. Yet Mr. Tuska does not know country music, and his great illumination only sheds light on half a career.

Autry's own long-awaited autobiography, *Back in the Saddle Again* hardly touched upon these musical origins. As there is in Autry's estimation, equal interest in his activities as a singer, an actor, a financeer

Autry, Ann Rutherford and William Farnum in Public Cowboy No. 1 *(1937).*

("corporate cowboy" is his term) and owner of a major league baseball team, space is equally divided among these interests. He corroborates some stories, dispels others, but at the end of it all we are left with precious little more knowledge of the music that inspired him than we know now. Many musical figures of paramount importance in his career are scarcely touched upon: Johnny Marvin is mentioned a few times, as are Fred Rose and Johnny Bond; Art Satherley (his name consistently misspelled) only three times, Ray Whitley but once, and Jimmie Rodgers not at all. As one would expect, in reviewing his own life Autry sees music as but one of several careers to be touched on, and he does not devote lavish attention to any of them.[18]

Of course, the most prominent contributor to this enigma has not been the journalist unwilling to dig deep into a musical past but Mr. Autry himself. While certainly not in the Howard Hughes class, still Gene Autry is reclusive and leery of interviews, as James Horowitz's extremely amusing account in *Rolling Stone* (October 25, 1973) called "In Search of the Original Singing Cowboy" proved. If journalists are even seen at all when they come to talk with him, they come away with a few familiar stories of Will Rogers, Autry's years at Republic Studios, and his gold records; they hear about his deft combination of luck and skill in business (calculated, no doubt, to prove both his humility and business acumen), and his conservative politics. Or Autry tells of how his wife Ina persuaded him to record "Rudolph the Red Nosed Reindeer," a song he personally disliked, or how the California Angels will fare in the upcoming year's pennant race.

Although some film critics have gotten to him, apparently no music scholar ever has, for the really important musical questions remain unanswered. And with the toll age takes, it is highly unlikely now that they ever will be. Gene Autry has been singularly unreflective concerning both the origins of his inspiration and his view of the effects of his music and film careers. Whether he ever ponders these and a hundred other questions we likely will never know. It seems that Gene Autry is destined to remain both legend and enigma.

The basics of Gene Autry's early career are well-documented. Born to a rancher in Tioga, Texas, on September 29, 1907, Orvon Gene Autry learned the basics of the guitar from his mother. The family moved to Ravia, Oklahoma, when Gene was in his teens, and there he showed enough interest in music and show business to spend part of a summer with the Fields Brothers Marvelous Medicine Show, where he sang, acted, did blackface comedy, and even played the saxophone.

In his own words, "When the Fields Brothers Marvelous Medicine Show came to town one summer, looking for a local boy to sing with them, I was recommended to Professor Fields. I traveled with them for three months, softening up audiences with mournful ballads before the professor began pitching his wares: liniment and pills, and his own product, a patent medicine called 'Fields' Pain Annihilator'... I earned fifteen dollars a week. For a teen-aged boy, in the '20s, this was more than money: it was the riches of Arabia."[19]

After graduation from high school in 1925 he was hired by the St. Louis & Frisco Railroad; he worked in a variety of positions before rising to the rank of relief telegrapher. Sometime in 1928 he fell under the influence of Jimmie Rodgers, and became slavishly addicted to that sound. That year also saw the famed meeting with Will Rogers in Chelsea, Oklahoma. Rogers, in the railroad office to send a telegram, heard Autry singing and playing, whiling away the empty hours. His words of encouragement—surely they could have not been much more than a simple offhand compliment—stoked the fires of Autry's naive ambition, and taking advantage of the free railway pass available to all Frisco employees, and personal vacation time, he headed for New York, the entertainment capital of the world, where he knew absolutely no one.

Inexperienced but optimistic, he immediately set about looking up Johnny and Frankie Marvin, two of the most popular entertainers in the city. Johnny, in fact, was a toast of the town, a performer on record, on Broadway, in vaudeville (where he played with Nat Shilkret's orchestra), and on radio as "The Lonesome Singer of the Air." Frank, seven years John's junior, was a comedian and musician in his brother's act, and recorded on his own as well.

If he had nothing else, Autry did have innocent confidence. He walked up to the Marvins and introduced himself with a big smile, saying that he was Gene Autry, a fellow Oklahoman, and that he, too, wanted to make records. Legends are made of this kind of youthful optimism, this blissful naiveté, and a legend was, indeed, in the making, though it was hardly overnight. As Frank Marvin remembers it:

He was out in Butler where my folks had a little hotel and a cafe and saw Johnny's picture on the wall and my picture on the wall. I was single at the time, staying at the old Manger Hotel, and he asked Mama where I was, so he came to New York and looked me up. I was making records, so I took him down to the old Edison Company and one of the sound men there played the piano, and he tried to make a test record of "Sonny Boy." He couldn't sing "Sonny Boy" yet! I told him, when we got back to the hotel, that if I was him I'd try to do some of those western-type songs.

I asked him if he could yodel, and he said, "I don't know; I never did try." So he tried to yodel and he had just a very little falsetto voice, so I told him, "Go back home and practice your singing and yodeling and come back here and I'll get you another test record."

So next time he came back, oh, three or four months later, I was going over to the old Gennett Company in Flushing, Long Island, and he made a test record and they liked him. Then we went to Victor and Johnny and I played guitars for him. He couldn't yodel yet, but I did some yodels for him.

So we kind of helped, and Johnny even brought him out on stage at the Palace, and they liked old Gene there, by golly![20]

This is a story Autry corroborates:

I had met the mother of Johnny Marvin, then a recording artist of some popularity at Victor. I stopped off one day in Butler, Oklahoma, where the family owned a café. Mrs. Marvin told me to look up Johnny if I ever got to New York, and I took the precaution of getting his address and phone number.

When I reached Johnny, he told me his younger brother, Frankie, had just gotten into town and we had a lot in common. Like me, Frankie was broke and trying to get started. I moved into his room at the Manger Hotel, which later became the Taft.

As the weather grew colder, we took turns wearing Frankie's topcoat. It was the only coat we had between us.

The days turned into weeks as I lugged my guitar up and down Broadway, to the rhythm of the record company doors slamming in my face. At the time, there were only a handful of companies—Victor, Columbia, Brunswick, Edison—and I tried them all, day after day, hoping for an audition. My first problem was to get past the reception desk.

I had been waiting for hours in the anteroom at Victor one day, guitar across my lap, when the thought must have struck the receptionist that I might not ever leave. She glanced up, smiled nervously, and asked what kind of songs I did. "Cowboy stuff, mostly," I said, "and some hillbilly. When I can get anyone to listen."

"I'll listen" she said. "Go ahead, play something."

That was all the encouragement I needed. An audience of one. I was halfway through "Jeannine, I Dream of Lilac Time," when Nat Shilkret, the man who wrote it, by then working for Victor, strolled into the room. He stopped for a moment, then ducked into another office and reappeared with a fellow named Leonard Joy. I now had an audience of three. Joy turned out to be the Number Two man at the company, in charge of promoting new artists and their records.

An early Autry publicity portrait.

Joy asked me to come back the next morning. "We're recording a band," he said, "and if you'll be here then we'll cut a test and see what you sound like."

When they opened the offices the next morning I was waiting on the doorstep like a bottle of milk. I sang "The Prisoner's song," a weepy tune, and a Jolson hit, "Climb Upon My Knee, Sonny Boy," probably not the smartest choice on my part, and we cut the test record. After everyone listened to the playback, Nat Shilkret asked me to step into his office.

"You got a nice voice for records," he said, "but you need experience. My advice is go home. Take six months, a year. Get a job on a radio station. Learn to work in front of a microphone."

When I said good-bye to the Marvin boys, Frankie offered a piece of advice. "Forget that Jolson stuff," he said. "Learn to sing some yodel songs. That's more to you're style."

With that I rode my railroad pass back home to Oklahoma. Shilkret had given me a to-whom-it-may-concern letter, saying I had potential, and I used it to wrangle a radio show over KVOO in Tulsa. I was billed as the Oklahoma Yodeling Cowboy, backed up by Jimmy Wilson's Catfish String Band. Meanwhile, I had gone back to my job as a relief operator working up and down the Frisco Line. The idea of paying for radio talent had not yet caught on in the Southwest.

For the next six months I traveled more back roads than a bootlegger, singing at Kiwanis clubs and high schools and private parties all over the state. I was ready to try New York again. I had gained experience and exposure and the next step, I thought, was a record contract.

Backed up by the guitars of Frankie and Johnny Marvin, I cut my first record for Victor. Johnny had written one of the sides, "My Dreaming of You." Jimmy Long had composed the other, "My Alabama Home."[21]

The date of those Victor sessions was October 9, 1929, just twenty days before the wildly careening jazz age would collide head on with the Depression.

It was to be a full sixteen months before ther promising young singer would again return to the Victor microphone, for the Depression cut quickly and deeply into the booming recording business. Undaunted by the despair about him, however, Autry took advantage of another free pass and took a sixty-day leave of absence from the St. Louis & Frisco Railroad–to which he never returned–and ventured once again to New York. He soon was recording for a host of labels, exclusive contracts being rare then, including the American Record Company and its affiliate labels (Banner, Melotone, Oriole, Perfect, and Romeo), and Columbia, Grey Gull, and Gennett as well.

By the later sessions his shaky guitar playing had improved noticeably, and his voice, particularly his yodeling, had more authority. In the interim he had also come further under the spell of Jimmie Rodgers, whom he idolized and imitated, his voice at times virtually indistinguishable from Rodgers'. He began to develop his talents as a songwriter as well, although the early efforts were basically Rodgers-style blue yodels which would have fit unobtrusively into the repertoire of the Singing Brakeman. So far did this tribute go, in fact, that Autry recorded two of Rodgers' most intensely personal songs, "Jimmie the Kid" and "T. B. Blues," on Victor's budget label Timely Tunes, in the spring of 1931.

By the end of 1931, however, his records indicate that he was becoming a seasoned professional who was well aware that his own personal identity must be forged. While the Rodgers influence is quite evident, there are songs other than blue yodels, sung in a voice recognizable as a young version of the singing cowboy who would fill thousands of movie screens for three decades.

It was during this same time–October, 1931–that Autry and Jimmy Long (a guitarist and singer who not only had been his boss on the St. Louis & Frisco, but was his uncle-in-law as well) recorded a sentimental mountain tune for the American Record Company called "That Silver Haired Daddy of Mine." It was to be the first of many Autry hit records, and it radically changed his life and his recording style. It turned him into an up and coming national star, and initiated a whole series of sentimental mountain ballads firmly in the tradition of "That Silver Haired Daddy of Man."

Somewhere along the line came yet another change in the musical emphasis of his career, which in its early years displays a remarkably chameleon-like ability to shift styles. From the Jimmie Rodgers blue yodels he moved smoothly to mountain ballads, and from mountain ballads shifted once again, this time to western songs and ultimately to the development of a sound and style quite his own. When and where the singing cowboy image was originally developed is still uncertain, but as early as 1930 he was appearing on KVOO in Tulsa, and despite the dire effects of the Depression he joined the National Barn Dance in Chicago in 1931 as "Oklahoma's Singing Cowboy."[22]

In addition, he obtained a radio show of his own, "Conqueror Record Time," in which he was portrayed as a cowboy fresh off the range, ready to sing a few western songs for the folks. This format, by Autry's own admission, was the brainchild of his producer, Art Satherley, and Ann Williams of the WLS production staff. Years later, Autry recollected the sequence of these events:

Arthur Satherley made me a proposition, and told me that if I'd do exactly as he said, I'd never be sorry–an arrangement which I accepted and kept to this day.

That sort of stuff didn't sound very glamorous to me, as my recollections of ranch life included aching muscles and endless days in the sun and dust. I wanted to be a dreamy-eyed singer of love songs like Rudy Vallee, but there was my promise to Arthur, and there was Ann Williams bringing the West back East with bright talk of the wind-swept plains, of coyote howls in the moonlight, and cowboys on galloping horses.

Arthur's guidance brought me eventually to a $35-a-week job doing a daily broadcast in Chicago. There I met Ann Williams, the third influence [Johnny Marvin and Arthur Satherley were the first two] in the creation of the singing cowboy. Ann was the announcer for my broadcasts, which plugged the sale of my phonograph records. I sang cowboy songs, not because I felt the listeners liked 'em better, but because Arthur insisted upon it. Ann began to build-up my Oklahoma-Texas back-

THE SINGING COWBOY / An American Dream

Frances Grant with Gene in Oh Susannah *(1936).*

ground and sprinkled the program with talk of sagebrush and tumbleweed.

So between the three of them, Marvin, Satherley, and Ann Williams, they finally got it through my ornery skull that instead of doing poor imitations of all the popular singers of the day, I should stay in my own backyard and sing the songs I knew best.[23]

Soon Sears-Roebuck was boosting this cowboy singer's image and popularity with a host of songbooks[24] (one of which shows Autry doing a series of rope tricks) and through mail order sales of their Gene Autry Roundup guitar at $9.95. Yet it is important to note, as Malone has pointed out about this abrupt change of musical emphasis from country to western themes, that though "the subject matter was different... the style of presentation and instrumentation was substantially the same as those of most hillbilly bands of the time."[25]

Interestingly enough, as late as September 8, 1933, he wrote songwriter Raymond E. Hall ("enroute" from Marquette, in Michigan's Upper Peninsula) asking not for western songs but for "a good old southern ballad":

I received your letter a few days ago, also the songs and wish to thank you for them. I have looked them over pretty well and think they are very good. However, I am returning them all to you with the exception of "Sweetheart of the Cimarron" and I want to hold it a few days as I think I can use it and as soon as I find out about it I will let you know just what the outcome of it will be.

Clayton told me about you saying something about a song "Life's Weary Ways." I am just wondering what you ever did with it and if you would send it to me as it seems to be a very good title and might be my type of song. Also I wish you would write me some stuff such as "Mississippi River Blues" or something of a good old southern ballad. I'm sure you know what I want.[26]

There is considerably more confusion concerning the how of Autry's career than the when. As always seems to happen in the case of unexpected success, there are quite a few who step forward to take credit for it. Of many accounts, the two involving Art Satherley and Nat Levine are particularly interesting. Satherley was, of course, Autry's producer on Conqueror Records, while Levine was a film producer who headed Mascot Pictures. Two other figures

HOLLYWOOD CORRAL: A COMPREHENSIVE B WESTERN ROUNDUP

loom as large in the story: Autry, himself, who has remained characteristically vague about the sequence of events involved, and Herbert J. Yates, who not only was the head of the American Record Company—the outfit which controlled Conqueror as well as its complex of dime-store labels—but also was going about the business of consolidating a number of smaller film companies to form Republic Pictures not long after Autry's first film. Yates, who died in 1966, may have given his account of these events, but if so it has not surfaced.

Satherley firmly asserts that he was due the credit for the remarkable creation of the singing cowboy on film, bringing Gene Autry to the attention of Yates, his boss:

Herbert Yates said to me one day, "Who is this cowboy guy that you've got selling records?" I said, "Gene Autry." He said, "Let me hear some of his records." And Yates [had gotten]... amalgamated I think with someone else by the name of Nat Levine on the West Coast here, who was associated in the development of films.

So he said to me one day, "Let me hear this fellow's records." So I took them upstairs to his fabulous office, he played them, and the next day he pressed the button for Art, he said, "Art, come on up here." I won't mention the words that he said, but he looked at me and he said, "Is *that* what you're talking about?" I said, "Yeah. Don't you like it?" He said, "What is it?" I said, "That's America! Country America! That's what we're selling, and this man is a star!" And I said, "This man is going into pictures."

"How do you know he's going into pictures?"

"Because they'll be after him very shortly—he has the looks, he has everything. Therefore, you have your own picture company called Republic Studios!"

...Then he said, "Well, I can't use the stuff." I said, "Well, if you can't, let me have him!" I said, "I'll still remain with you if you like, but I could sell him tomorrow to another picture company that's already established!" "Well," he said, "how can you do that?" "Well," I said, "you just turned the guy down!" I said, "Think it over," and walked out.

About two days later he called me back and said, "Say, Art, come on up here." I won't use the words, of course, but he said, "The guy's fabulous. I don't know what the hell he's singing about, but there it is. Where is he?" I said, "He's in Chicago. He's on the air every day and he's getting fantastic publicity! Money can't *buy* the publicity that Sears-Roebuck has given to us! For the thirty bucks a week we're paying him!"

"Well," he said, "I've got a fellow at the Blackstone Hotel's just come in from Hollywood. His name is Nat Levine. Could you have Gene clean himself up a little bit and go and see him and sing a little bit of 'That Silver Haired Daddy?'" And, of course, I said sure.

I got on to the phone to Gene and said, "Gene meet this man at the Blackstone Hotel at this time. Get yourself ready, get your hair done nicely, get your pants pressed, go in there as a spic and span cowboy from the West." So he did. So Nat Levine signed him for the usual contract—I think it was a $175 a week, which was the average in those days—and Gene signed. So that was the beginning of Gene going to the West.[27]

Levine, however, tells the same story from a rather different perspective, as related by Jon Tuska:

Nat had a reputation for giving young, inexperienced talent a chance with his company. "I received a dozen letters from Autry during 1933," he wrote to me, "asking for an opportunity to work for me in anything I would suggest in pictures. Autry's name value at the time was limited to... a radio station in Chicago, practically an unknown with questionable ability. On one of my trips East, I stopped off in Chicago, not to meet Autry, but for business I had with my distributor. But I did get to meet Autry and he virtually begged me for an opportunity to come to Hollywood and work in pictures. While he was nice looking, it seemed to me he lacked the commodity necessary to become a Western star: virility! I wasn't impressed and tried to give him a nice brush-off, telling him I would think about it. For a period of six months he wrote to me continually, conveying that he would do anything for the opportunity."

Yates was enlisted by Autry to put in a good word with Levine. Yates told Nat that Gene was selling a lot of records. When Ken Maynard signed with Mascot, Levine went ahead and put Autry on salary with a five year option. He also signed Lester "Smiley" Burnette, who had worked two years with Autry, and Frank Marvin, one of Gene's backup men. Autry was hired at a hundred dollars a week, Burnette and Marvin at somewhat less. It was Levine's notion to use Autry, who could sing, to support Maynard, who really could not. "Gene was completely raw material," Levine continued, "knew nothing about acting, lacked poise, and was awkward. A couple of days after his arrival I had him at my home and invited my production staff to meet him. The next day all of my associates questioned my judgment in putting him under contract. They thought I was slipping. But I persisted, and for the first four months he went through a learning period. We had at that time, in our employ, a professional dramatic and voice teacher, and Autry became one of her pupils. He wasn't much of a horseman either, so I had Tracy Layne and Yakima Canutt teach him how to ride."

"I don't believe he ever acknowledged my contribution to his career," Nat added, "nor did I ever receive thanks."[28]

Autry's recollection of these same events—as time-hazed and self-serving as Satherley's and Levine's—is

THE SINGING COWBOY / An American Dream

Gene checks the script of Rootin' Tootin' Rhythm *(1937).*

substantially the same, yet from a significantly different viewpoint:

> It seemed clear to Herb Yates that the Western movie needed a shot in the arm. He discussed it with Moe Siegel, then the president of American Records, and they agreed that the straight, action Western was a thing of the past. So they met again with Levine, and Yates said, "Nat, I'll give you the money, but on one condition. We have a fellow who sells a helluva lot of records for us. He's on radio in Chicago, on a national hookup, does the 'Barn Dance.' Nat, it would be worth your while to take a look at Gene Autry." To get the financing for his picture, Nat Levine would have looked at a singing kangaroo. A day later I received a call from Yates and Siegel, telling me Levine was on his way to Chicago and wanted to meet with me. I had finished my show at WLS when he arrived... *blew in* is the phrase I meant to use.
> "They tell me you sell a lot of records," he said.
> "Oh, I reckon so."
> "I'm going to make this picture with Ken Maynard. Cowboy picture. Low budget. Usually, we try out a new actor, we give you a screen test, read lines, things like that. No need to bother. If you'd like to come out and appear in it, we've written in a barn dance scene. You can call the square dance, do a few songs. That can be your screen test. We'll see what kind of reaction we get when the movie plays."
> I didn't know if it was my turn to talk or not.
> "Well, Autry, how do you like it?"
> "Sounds okay to me."
> "Good. Call me before you come," He paused at the door. "You're a nice boy. You may call me collect."[29]

Regardless, Autry stole his first picture—*In Old Santa Fe* (1934)—from Ken Maynard, and an astonishing career began to mushroom seemingly out of the blue. With records aiding the success of his films and vice versa, Autry suddenly became one of the most popular film stars of the era, his films always landing near the top of boxoffice lists; at the same time he was selling a remarkable number of records.

His overwhelming success has puzzled film historians for generations; few have been able to approach it with anything more than bewilderment. According to Autry's critics, his West was so totally devoid of any shreds of reality it was ridiculous. Though he is revered in the country music field as a singer, one cannot honestly say he was the best vocalist of his day, nor even the best country singer. Although his singing has always been affecting, this is not reason enough to explain a success so overwhelming. His success could not have been based merely on the novelty of the singing cowboy, for we have seen that Gene Autry was not the first singing cowboy on film, Maynard was. In fact, he was not even the second. John Wayne, of all people, appeared as Singing Sandy in a 1933 Western titled *Riders of Destiny*, for Monogram, although his singing was dubbed in by Bob Steele's brother, Bill Bradbury.

If historians agree on anything, however, it is that this deliberate lack of realism was as much a cause for his success as any other factor or set of factors. William K. Everson, for example, writes:

> To offset expected criticisms that this new brand of musical Western was a travesty of tradition, Republic set them in their own never-never land, placing them quite apart from other Westerns. The earlier "historical" Cavalry-vs.-Indian Westerns that Autry had made—*Ride, Ranger, Ride* and *The Singing Vagabond*—were abandoned in favor of entirely modern Westerns. Autry frequently played a rodeo or radio star (and always under his own name); the props included high-powered cars, army tanks, airplanes, and radio stations; and the plots touched on contemporary politics, big business, social problems (the dust bowl), dairy farming as opposed to cattle ranching, problems of soil erosion and crop destruction by weeds. Against this thoroughly modern background, the traditional action ingredients—runaway stagecoaches and bar-room brawls, to say nothing of cowboys toting guns and engaging in full-scale range wars—were incongruous indeed, but here the musical elements came to the rescue... All of this obviously artificial glamour and song put the Autry films into a deliberate kind of horse-operetta framework which disarmed any criticism.[30]

Jon Tuska, writing with even more insight, tackles the central question:

> ...the Fantasy inspiring the screenplays and, above all, Autry himself is so fervent that it seems instead to be a demonstration of an immutable law governing human behavior. I do not doubt for an instant that Autry believed totally in the Fantasy; I think for a time that audiences believed in it too.
> I sincerely feel that Autry's massive appeal as a modest cowboy troubadour leading a uniquely charmed life, a musical magician who could turn darkness into light, sorrow into happiness, tarnish into splendor, a Pied Piper able to control men and alter the course of world events by means of a song, is the most tremendous single occurrence in the history of the American Western cinema. Gene Autry in his magnificent outfits, yodeling a pop tune, is an image so remote from the actual man of the frontier as to rival any fairy tale. If you compare Autry to Tom Mix, or even William S. Hart, of the previous generation, he appears hopelessly inept. But once you accept him on his own terms and find yourself enthralled by the Autry Fantasy, the others begin to look clumsy, plebian, vulgar....
> Gene Autry on screen met every reversal of fortune,

THE SINGING COWBOY / An American Dream

every threat of villainy, with the honest reassurance of a song. Critics of the film mock Autry or dismiss him; they try to ignore him, term him an anomaly, discredit him as a temporary lapse into lunacy, reject him bitterly, sneer at him, or are silent; but Gene Autry made more money and was more consistently popular during his time in the movies than any of his Western peers. His career was without the rise and fall of nearly every other cowboy player. The Autry Fantasy like the Mix Legend only reinforces the fact that the Western is basically an imaginative myth. Yet Autry ruined the programmer Western at the same time because, as he moved further and further into the golden reaches of the Autry Fantasy, he only intensified the grand lie about the true nature of man which World War II began to shatter with its agony of genocide, concentration camps, and total destruction. Gene Autry, although he outlived it by a few years, belongs very much to that generation of Depression-weary gentlefolk who tried to hide from the truth until it mushroomed before their startled eyes at Hiroshima.[31]

A stirring and convincing answer to the question, to be sure, but likely not the only answer. The mystery of Autry's explosive and remarkably long-lived success has yet to be answered satisfactorily. Surely it is more than the fantasy he and his producers created on screen (though Shirley Temple's simultaneous if shorter-lived career seems to have been a result of just that); it is more than his engaging singing; it is more than an idea whose time had come; it is more than Depression-era escapism; it is more than the first nationwide demonstration of the absolutely national appeal of country music, an overwhelming referendum proving country music was a major musical form and force, the ballots being 78 rpm records and theatre ticket stubs. Certainly, it was all of these, and much more.

More Singing Cowboys

Within months of Autry's first films hoards of singers and actors adopted singing cowboy roles. This is scarcely surprising, for if imitation is the

Gene shakes hands with Russell Simpson under Betty Bronson's approving eye in Yodelin' Kid from Pine Ridge *(1937).*

HOLLYWOOD CORRAL: A COMPREHENSIVE B WESTERN ROUNDUP

sincerest form of flattery, Hollywood has always gone out of its way to flatter the hell out of surprise success. What is genuinely remarkable–saying much for the idea-whose-time-has-come theory–is that singing cowboy imitations were not just extremely quick to appear on screen, they were virtually simultaneous:

Autry was catapulted to stardom, and practically overnight renown, by Nat Levine with *Tumbling Tumbleweeds,* released in September, 1935. Immediately following in his footsteps... came Dick Foran, whose debut as a movie cowboy came for Warner Bros. two months later, in November, 1935. Granted that the Warner boys were quick to perceive the impact of Autry's success with what amounted to a new form, it's dubious that they could have unearthed their own Western songbird, had the initial script on the studio floor and solidified plans to exploit this new property all in the space of a few months. The prospect must have arrived near-simultaneously in both camps. Also, Foran did not resemble Autry in the least, nor did he work like the Republic cowboy. Foran and his later compatriots Fred Scott and Jack Randall, if they could be likened to anybody, could be said to follow the trail of M-G-M's blonde thrush, Nelson Eddy.... Like Eddy, Foran, Scott and Randall possessed vocal equipment within the operatic sphere. Indeed, they would be entirely at ease with a robust rendition of "Stout Hearted Men," but the simple bucolic pleasures of "Ridin' Down the Canyon" would be beyond them... However, the booming baritones didn't last much beyond 1940, while Autry, and Tex Ritter, two of the more comfortable and idiomatic vocalizers, pursued lengthy careers in the field.

It is interesting that Warner Bros. should have been the company to follow the musical Western, since their production had been dormant after the John Wayne series was halted in 1933. A new executive lineup at the studio paved the way for the move.... Songs written for Foran were pleasant and hummable, most of them by studio tunesmiths M. K. Jerome and Jack Scholl; but even here, the sound was closer to Tin Pan Alley than The Great Divide.[32]

It was indeed clearly an idea whose time had come. John Wayne, who had experimented with songs in a couple of earlier films, and especially Maynard were the harbingers, Autry the realization. Would Dick Foran have obtained Autry's success had his series begun out two months earlier than Gene's instead of two months later?

Foran was born in Flemington, New Jersey, on June 18, 1910, and was the son of Senator Arthur F. Foran. He graduated from Princeton University, and made his screen debut in *Stand Up and Cheer* in 1934; in the following year, he became singing

Dick Foran, Warner's singing cowboy

cowboy number four with the appearance of *Moonlight on the Prairie.* His film was not, however, terribly successful, particularly compared to the rocketing success of the Gene Autry westerns. Dick Foran went on to considerable success as a singer and actor in some eighty films, many of which were major productions. By no means were all the films westerns: among his best roles was in a sophisticated comedy called *Guest Wife* (1945) with Don Ameche and Claudette Colbert. Foran also appeared on Broadway and on television in his long career, and did limited recording for Decca and Universal in both studio-western and pop styles. He died in 1979.

After Foran they came like a stampeding herd.[33] Of the thundering posse of singing cowboys which galloped across the screen in pursuit of Gene Autry in ensuing years, it is remarkable how few understood Mr. Autry's most basic gift: he was a country singer who was not only ingenuous but also believable, the qualities which not only make for great country music but also virtually define it. All too often, the prevailing feeling was that if Autry was all that popular with his country voice, then surely a "real" singer would be even more popular. It was

THE SINGING COWBOY / An American Dream

George E. Stone (l.), Sheila Mannors, director D. Ross Lederman and Foran between takes on Moonlight on the Prairie *(1935).*

tried again and again, never very successfully.

In 1935 western music began to abound in films, not only Autry's *Tumbling Tumbleweeds* and Foran's *Moonlight on the Prairie,* but in other places as well. The Sons of the Pioneers appeared in a Liberty film called *The Old Homestead,* released that same year, a further indication of this trend. In addition, they had composed the title song for Foran's film, establishing the group as actors, singers, musicians, and songwriters all at the same time. The Sons of the Pioneers in particular, and later groups like the Jimmy Wakely Trio, Foy Willing and The Riders of the Purple Sage, the Cass County Boys, Andy Parker and the Plainsmen, even Bob Wills and his Texas Playboys and Spade Cooley's Orchestra, all figure heavily in the sound and style of the musical Western film; yet, except for certain individual members of any given band who stepped into starring roles or major support roles, they lie just a bit outside the scope of this essay, though they remain an intriguing topic for a study.

At any rate, helped by his earlier Conqueror recording of the Bob Nolan classic, Autry's *Tumbling Tumbleweeds* was a great success. This was followed by *Melody Trail,* a title which distinguished this new brand of singing western from just another cowboy film. This he followed with *Sagebrush Toubadour.* Autry stayed as busy the following year, cranking out nearly twenty singing westerns, his seventh entitled *The Singing Cowboy,* a description he not only deserved, but which in a way solidified his claim to the title, as 1936 proved to be the year when other studios, realizing his early success was not just a fluke, began scrambling to discover, develop, film, and present their own singing cowboys.

Charging close behind Foran was Fred Scott, who was billed as "The Silvery Voiced Baritone." His brief appearance as a singing cowboy in RKO's *The Last Outlaw* (1936) led to his feature performance in *Romance Rides the Range,* a Spectrum Production. Thus, Scott became the first singing cowboy to be developed by an independent studio. Fred Leedom Scott, born in Fresno, California, on February 14, 1902, had had considerable experience on stage as well as in film by the time he became a singing cowboy, having appeared in silents for Pathé in the '20s. In the early '30s he performed with the San Francisco Grand Opera, returning to films with the beginning of his singing cowboy series.

Scott was a capable actor, rider, and a fine singer,

HOLLYWOOD CORRAL: A COMPREHENSIVE B WESTERN ROUNDUP

Fred Scott, the "Silvery-Voiced Buckaroo"

Ray Whitley

but in no way was he a country singer. A cowboy with a pleasant voice like Autry's (or a rough one like Tex Ritter's) seemed somehow fitting on screen, and did not endanger his credibility. A silvery-voiced baritone did, however, and Scott never found the popularity he and his producers hoped for. He drifted out of films after 1942, though he continued singing for a while before going into real estate. Interviewed some years ago, he commented that "I enjoyed making Songs and Bullets about the most of all. It had enjoyable songs written by Don Swander and his wife, June. The Swanders also wrote 'Deep in the Heart of Texas'... I don't ride anymore. I have a deal with the horses—I don't get on them and they don't sell any real estate."[34]

It was also in 1936 that the co-hosts of the WHN Barn Dance in New York City headed west—independent of each other—to seek greener pastures in Hollywood. One was Ray Whitley, whose first speaking role was in *Hopalong Cassidy Returns* (1936), and who began a series of musical shorts for RKO two years later, all firmly in the singing cowboy genre. Always a bridesmaid and never a bride was to be Whitley's lot in the film industry. Due to the success of his shorts, he was moved to singing sidekick roles with RKO through 1942, first with George O'Brien and then Tim Holt, always

with the prospect of a full-length series of his own in sight. Whitley said of the era: "RKO seemed like they were ashamed of their western program. They didn't release them–they just let them escape."[35] He continued in the same kind of role with Rod Cameron at Universal before drifting out of films with a small role in *Giant* (1956), the bulk of his time spent touring[36] with bands of various sizes which included such country music figures as Merle Travis and Jesse Ashlock from time to time. Born near Atlanta in 1901, he had a pleasant country voice and was an adept yodeler as well. He made a number of records for Decca, ARC, Okeh, and many smaller labels. He will doubtless be best remembered for having written "Back in the Saddle Again" and co-written (with Fred Rose) several other Autry hits– "Lonely River," "Ages and Ages Ago," "I Hang My Head and Cry." Why the studios he worked for never gave him his own series is mysterious, for he was as good a singing cowboy as any.[37]

Whitley's co-host on the WHN Barn Dance was Woodward Maurice "Tex" Ritter, born in Murvaul, Texas, on January 12, 1905.[38] A dedicated student of western history at the University of Texas under J. Frank Dobie, Woodward showed up in New York in 1929, intent upon a career on the Broadway stage. There he appeared in some five productions (*Green*

THE SINGING COWBOY / An American Dream

Ray Whitley (c.) appeared on the Grand Ole Opry in the mid-'30s with Pee Wee King (with accordian) and the Golden West Cowboys.

Grow the Lilacs the best known), did his first recording (October 31, 1932, for ARC), appeared on two radio shows (the other was "*Cowboy Tom's Roundup*"), and obtained the nickname "Tex."

Ritter was chosen by an independent producer by the name of Edward Finney to star in his own projected singing cowboy features, which he ultimately produced for Grand National. Finney said simply, "I wanted to make a series that would be really western with a personality who sang a good song.... I listened to some of the records he [Tex Ritter] had made for Decca, which were exactly what I had in mind."[39] He could not have made a better choice. Although Ritter was not a genuine cowboy as such, he was a Texan with great love of genuine cowboy song and lore, and his rough-hewn voice suggested authority and authenticity unmatched among singing cowboys. Though he was not a great singer, he was an extraordinarily effective one, and this quality not only helped make him a film star, but made him one of country music's most popular and most recorded performers, especially after he signed with the brand new Capitol label in 1942. As Don Miller accurately states: "Ritter had what Autry had, and what Foran and Scott missed. He looked like a cowboy of the range, and not the drugstore variety... and his singing, while an acquired taste, did have the echo of the plains in its timbre."[40]

Ritter's first film for Finney and Grand National was *Song of the Gringo*, released on November 22, 1936, quickly followed by *Headin' for the Rio Grande*, released on December 20. He was to make fifty-seven more for Grand National, Monogram, Columbia (where he co-starred with Bill Elliott), Universal (with Johnny Mack Brown), and PRC be-

347

HOLLYWOOD CORRAL: A COMPREHENSIVE B WESTERN ROUNDUP

Tex Ritter

fore closing out his B Western singing cowboy career with *Flaming Bullets* in 1945. Having signed with Capitol in 1942, after several fruitless years with Decca (1935–39), he produced a long string of hits for this label, including "Jingle, Jangle, Jingle," "There's a New Moon Over My Shoulder," "You Two Timed Me One Time Too Often," "Jealous Heart," and many others, including the Academy Award-winning "High Noon" in the '50s and "Hillbilly Heaven" in the 1960s. Ritter remained an active performer until the day of his death, January 2, 1974.

Tex was a colorful man and a kind one; his singing was far from silvery-voiced, but it was appealing, and most important of all there was a genuineness about him that was unmistakable. He was more than an actor putting on odd clothes and singing songs of roundups and ramblings: he embodied much of what the audience thought a cowboy should be, while never placing too much distance between himself and them. He was a country singer and unashamed of it; like Autry, he was a singer whose voice seemed a natural extension of his personality, rather than an obtrusive and flashy bit of business thrown in to keep apace of other studios or stars. As an actor and a singer he had the sincerity which typifies the best of country music, and this accounted for his appeal on record which even exceeded his attraction on film. A simple thing, hardly worth explaining to those who know and love country music, yet many Hollywood heads were scratched in bewilderment over the success of singers like Autry and Ritter while "finer" singers in cowboy clothes did not draw patrons to the theaters and often were even unable to scare up record contracts at all.

The Singing Cowboys: 1937

This was the situation as 1937 dawned, then, probably the most eventful year in the history of the singing cowboy: Autry, two years previously a regional star unknown in films, was now firmly ensconsed among the top western stars in Hollywood, and with a long string of hit records already behind him: "Silver Haired Daddy of Mine" (1932), "Yellow Rose of Texas" (1933), "The Death of Jimmy Rodgers" (1933), "There's an Empty Cot in the Bunkhouse Tonight" (1933), "The Last Roundup" (1934), "Tumbling Tumbleweeds" (1934), "Nobody's Darling" (1935), and "Mexicali Rose" (1936). It found him free of his $175 a week contract, making large sums of money and pursued by a number of other singers who would eventually make a musical style out of the Autry approach to the western film. It also found him increasingly irritated with Republic Studios. Some attribute it to a swelled head, others to the legendary stinginess of Herbert Yates. Johnny Bond claims[41] it was Autry's righteous indignation at finding that exhibitors were forced to buy blocks of unprofitable Republic films in order to get the money-making Autry features.[42] Whatever the cause, Autry was to ask for a great deal more money and not get it, after which he simply refused to report for the filming of his next picture. The walkout lasted some months, resulting in both one of the most amusing and tawdry set of events in singing cowboy history, culminating in the signing of Roy Rogers in October.

As the pressure built within this pressure cooker, however, a great deal was also happening all over Hollywood concerning Gene Autry and the singing cowboys. Competing studios had begun full-scale attempts aimed at entering the fray, mounting their own singing cowboy stars and series in earnest, and, consequently, a wide variety of new performers found their way to the screen.

Early among them was a tall, lanky big band leader named Smith Ballew. He was born in Pal-

THE SINGING COWBOY / An American Dream

estine, Texas, on January 21, 1902, but his background was far from country. He had his own big band at college and later in Chicago, and played and recorded with such swing bands as Joe Venuti's, Ben Pollack's, Red Nichols', The Dorsey Brothers', Benny Goodman's, Glenn Miller's, and with his own orchestra on Okeh and Columbia.[43] His first feature film was *Palm Springs* (1936), and Sol Lesser signed him for a series to be released by 20th Century-Fox the following year with *Western Gold* (1937), the first of the short-lived series. As a singing cowboy he lasted but two seasons, his films more memorable for their own intrinsic appeal than his own. *Hawaiian Buckaroo*, for example, took place on an Hawaiian cattle ranch and pineapple plantation, while *Rawhide* found him co-starred with New York Yankee first baseman Lou Gehrig. His final singing cowboy film was *Panamint's Bad Man* (1938) after which he returned to the business of vocalizing with and leading big bands.

A fellow by the name of Bob Baker was the next to enter the picture. When Universal announced in 1936 that it was auditioning for a singing cowboy, Stanley Leland Weed's mother sent a letter and photo of her son, who was a singer known as Tumble Weed on the National Barn Dance. Film historian Kalton Lahue writes "to everyone's great surprise (except Mrs. Weed's), a letter came back inviting him to make a screen test." Not only did Weed take the test, but he landed the job over the expected host of competitors including Dick Weston, formerly known as Leonard Slye, soon to be known as Roy Rogers. As Tuska relates:

> When Buck Jones decided to leave Universal... a frantic search was mounted for a suitable replacement. Two finalists emerged from all the screen tests, Dick Weston, a member of the Sons of the Pioneers, and Bob Baker. Baker was born Stanley Leland Weed at Forest City, Iowa, on November 8, 1914.[44] He first came to prominence on the National Barn Dance. Max Terhune persuaded him to try pictures and instructed him in how to act before a camera. Baker was finally chosen over Weston on the basis of physical maturity. Universal gave him the screen name of Bob Baker, with Baker opting to retain his stage name

Singing Cowboy Smith Ballew (l.) with baseball great Lou Gehrig in Rawhide *(1938).*

HOLLYWOOD CORRAL: A COMPREHENSIVE B WESTERN ROUNDUP

Tumble Weed, and starred him in a series of singing Westerns commencing with *Courage of the West* (Universal, 1937). Baker, no matter the reasoning behind his selection over Weston, projected rather an undernourished screen image. He could sing but was untrained. Universal discovered to their dismay, as did the others, that singing Westerns weren't the answer to Autry. Baker, like most of his peers, ignored the Autry Fantasy, and his writers weren't even conscious that there was such a thing.[45]

Baker, who had grown up in Colorado and New Mexico, began his musical career over KTSM in El Paso while in the Army. He joined the WLS National Barn Dance in 1935, and was featured on a program of his own as well. A good singer with a smooth, middle-of-the-road country flavor, it is a wonder to many film historians that he did not become extremely successful. Lahue says: "One would not think that a major studio like Universal would have so badly botched the new star's build-up, but they did and before long, Bob surfaced in the Johnny Mack Brown Westerns.... When his contract expired in 1943 he simply left the screen." To this Tuska adds the pungent coda, "However embittered he may have been at the time, Roy Rogers was more fortunate that he lost out to Baker and was signed at Republic instead."[46] After a small role in *Wild Horse Stampede* (1943) with Ken Maynard and Hoot Gibson—both by then rather long in the tooth—Baker left the screen for good, apparently, in the words of film historian Gerald F. Vaughn, "disenchanted with show business."

Also strange is Baker's failure to have ever recorded, even for Universal's labels which released a series of records by some of its screen vocalizers in the '40s. To the best of anyone's knowledge there were no records cut by Bob Baker or Tumble Weed or any other pseudonym. Baker moved to Arizona after his final fling in films and became a policeman, saddle shop owner, and operator of a dude ranch among other things before his death of a heart attack in 1975. Was his lack of success due to Universal's poor handling of his career, his lack of screen presence, or his inability to secure a recording contract? Whatever the reason or combination of reasons, Baker's failure to emerge as a performer of considerable dimensions is a major unanswered mystery in the curious history of the singing cowboy.

Jack Randall was yet another who met with less than smashing success in much the same way. Though his background was not terribly authentic for westerns, he was a singer of note, and began a series of some twenty-two westerns for Monogram with *Riders in the Dawn* late in 1937. Born Addison Randall on May 12, 1906, the son of West Coast Associated Press editor Edgar Randall in San Fernando, California, he was also the brother of non-singing cowboy star Bob Livingston, who encouraged brother Jack to enter films. Stepping from the vaudeville and Broadway stage to the sound stage in 1934, his first feature film was *His Family Tree* in 1935, and he played romantic leads in a number of RKO films over the next couple of years.

Monogram, like all companies at this time, realized the singing cowboys were saleable products, and apparently had high hopes that Jack Randall would rocket to the top. Once again, they assumed that a better singer was a better singing cowboy, which as previously noted, ignores both the audience and the appeal of country music. Fenin and Everson write that Randall "had a fine voice, superior to those of most of his rivals,[47] but the market was flooded with musical Westerns, and when Monogram presented Randall as one more singing cowboy, there were audible protests from exhibitor groups [and] as a result, songs were deleted from completed Randall Westerns and the bulk of the series made as normal action Westerns. This was a pity, for Randall could out-sing most of the others, and had he been introduced a year earlier he might well have become one of the top singing cowboys."[48]

Jack Randall made a few films in the early '40s before joining the Army where he spent the war years entertaining the troops. He returned to Hollywood in 1945 after his discharge, and while on location at Iverson's Ranch in Chatsworth filming a cheap serial called *The Royal Mounted Rides Again,* he suddenly slumped over in his saddle dead of a massive heart attack on July 16, 1945, just two months past his thirty-ninth birthday.[49]

Donald Grayson, a non-country crooner, was also in the process of being developed into a singing cowboy by Columbia, playing second lead and providing songs in several Charles Starrett westerns, beginning with *The Old Wyoming Trail* in 1937. His intrusion into the otherwise fine backup work of the Sons of the Pioneers was doubtless due to the dislike of some Columbia executives of Bob Nolan's voice. Grayson did not last beyond a few films, and before long Nolan was acting as second lead, as well as singing his own songs at last.[49]

Surely the most bizarre entry into the singing cowboy field trekked west in 1937: Herb Jeffries, a deep-voiced ballad singer from Detroit who had sung with Earl Hines' orchestra in Chicago and re-

THE SINGING COWBOY / An American Dream

(l. to r.) Leroy Mason, Forrest Taylor, Bob Baker and Don Barclay in Outlaw Express (1938).

Horace Murphy and Jack Randall in Stars Over Arizona (1937).

corded several Brunswick sides for them. In 1937, he moved to Los Angeles seeking bigger things than the Midwest had to offer, appearing as a singer and emcee at the Club Alabam. He was contracted by Jed Buell of the newly-formed Associated Features in the same year, and his first film was premiered at the Paramount Theatre in Hollywood and at the Rialto Theatre on Broadway in New York City, where it opened for its first run.

Just another singing cowboy story, except that Jeffries was black, and his first film, *Harlem on the Prairie,* was widely touted as "the first 'all-colored' western musical!"[50] The following year Jeffries ground out three more all-black singing cowboy films: *Bronze Buckaroo, Harlem Rides the Range,* and *Two-Gun Man from Harlem* for Hollywood Productions. Several of the films contained the musical group The Four Tones—one is tempted to think of a combination of the Sons of the Pioneers and the Ink Spots—composed of Lucius Brooks, bass, Ira Hardin, guitar and baritone, Rudolph Hunter, and Leon Buck, tenor. They also accompanied Jeffries on a promotional tour of the South in 1939 to promote his films.

Unfortunately, the standards for Jeffries' films were even shoddier than for the standard singing cowboy films:

> The producers took their small units out to excellent locations, and then lacked the knowhow to follow through... The plots were the standard western themes, with stock dialogue amplified and exaggerated until, unwittingly, it reached near-burlesque proportions. Interestingly enough, there was no inverted racism in these films. The stories took place in a totally black West; there were no whites in them at all, even as villains! Yet the prolonged and padded comedy relief invariably consisted of the kind of material (the comic pal scared of ghosts, the chicken-stealing cook, the crap-shooting, lazy roustabouts) which the Negroes understandably objected to in regular Hollywood films. Apart from the "personality" stars like Herb Jeffries, the acting level was low.... The musical element was not stressed, and Jeffries was really the only singing cowboy that this small group produced.[51]

After the southern tour with The Four Tones, Jeffries resumed his singing career, recording a good bit of material for Victor with Duke Ellington in 1940 and thereafter, and on his own on Columbia, Mercury, and other small labels.[52]

However, the big story of 1937 was the departure of Gene Autry from the Republic fold. As mentioned, there are conflicting stories for the walkout, but when it occurred in the fall of 1937 it was a major upheaval, probably *the* major upheaval in this history. Art Satherley recalls the events in this way:

> Gene Autry had found himself a manager on the Coast here, after he'd been here a year or so, so Yates said to me, "Art, you'd better go and get your boy Autry and get him off his damned pony and kick that damn manager in the ass and get him out of here. He's signing up and now wants double the money per picture! And I'm not going to pay it."
>
> So Gene, he called me and said, "I'm walking off the lot and Mr. Yates can go to hell," or something like that, and he sent me a four page telegram addressed to Art Satherley of American Records, which was owned by Yates, so it got to Yates and came down to me opened. And in there he wanted me to go down to the dock and find out how much it would cost to pack up all his show and take it to South America! And they figured about 150 animals all told, and all the trappings and everything for a boat to there. So I called Gene with the figures and said, "When do you want this done?" And he said, "Well, as soon as you possibly can!" But nevertheless I don't think he had quite that much money at the time, so I stalled it, you know, and I said, "Gene, think this over."
>
> So I went out to the Coast, went to Gene's home, we played golf, and he said, "I'm not going to work for him anymore—why the hell should I? I want double the amount!" So I said, "Gene, so far as I know you're still from Sapulpa, Oklahoma. You're not that big yet to have to force up on a guy." I tried to break that thing, but I found that he was so tightly in that I called Yates after six weeks and I said, "Herb, this guy is so tightly up I can't do anything with him. He's going to stick by that guy win or lose."
>
> So in the meantime this guy Seigel, Sol, was out on the lot working on these pictures and he said, "Well, get somebody else." So they had been employing the Sons of the Pioneers, and in the Sons of the Pioneers was Roy Rogers, so Roy Rogers was brought in to replace Gene Autry.
>
> So here comes the funny one: Yates called me up and said, "Art, I want you to record Roy Rogers quick and get a nice bunch of numbers in by him. We're going to give it to this guy Autry." I said, "Herb, you're not going to give it to Autry so quick. Number one, I've heard Roy Rogers sing. He's as much country as you are, and you're not!... I'll tell you before I record him he's not going to sell." He said, "So you won't record him?" I said, "If it's your wish I'll record him. I'm still your vice-president."[53]

Autry's own account of these events is not dissimilar, and he cites the block-buying practices as the main cause of his walkout:

> I hurried back to Hollywood and confronted Herb Yates. I wanted that practice stopped, and, while I was about it, a fairer share of the profits my pictures were producing. That was the wrong approach to take with

THE SINGING COWBOY / An American Dream

Frankie Marvin (at Gene's elbow), Autry, Robert Homans, Smiley Burnette and cowboys (including George Montgomery at Autry's back) in Gold Mine in the Sky *(1938).*

Yates. But if there was a better one I didn't know it then, and I don't now...

I had a new movie scheduled to start in two weeks, to be called *Washington Cowboy*. When I walked out of his office, we both knew I wouldn't be there when the cameras rolled. The trade papers made it sound like a range war...

Of course, when I failed to show up for the first day's shooting on *Washington Cowboy*, the studio suspended me. Yates said he would make the film without me and create a new cowboy star. That was when they gave a screen test to Leonard Slye, who had appeared in a couple of my pictures as Dick Weston, and whose name was soon to be Roy Rogers. They changed the title of the movie to *Under Western Skies*.

Yates had threatened to break me– "if you won't work here, you won't work anywhere." The studio took out an injunction to prevent me from appearing on stage until my contract had been fulfilled. We hit the road, through Arizona, New Mexico, and Texas, always one step ahead of the process server.

Back in Los Angeles, I was getting help from a powerful lobby. Republic's distributors were holding their annual convention and they climbed all over Herb Yates. It was going on six months since an Autry movie had been released. They made it sound not like a business problem, but a national famine. Many of them had gone along with the block-buying, to the extent that they would buy a package of twenty, my eight plus twelve others, and ship back the ones they didn't want without using them. Now they demanded some assurance I would be working for Republic next year. Otherwise, they warned Yates, their theaters would be in trouble.

At that point, Yates called. While our attorneys got together and worked out a compromise, we went off to play golf. In a curious way, there were no hard feelings. All he had done was call me disloyal and threaten to ruin me. In return, I had called him a cheap skate and a tyrant. In those years, in Hollywood, no one took anyone else seriously. So we played golf.

My salary was raised to ten thousand dollars a film (escalating to fifteen and twenty over the next seven years), and the clauses I found objectionable were removed. The package deals continued; they were by then too entrenched to undo.[54]

Rogers himself has a different perspective on the situation, one which remains vivid in his memory:

Talk about being in the right place at the right time. I went out to Glendale–there's a little hat shop out there with an old fellow that cleaned hats. He used to be with Stetson Company. So I went out there to get my hat and there was a guy in the shop all excited. He was about 6'4"-6'6", a big tall guy and his name was Carter. I'd

HOLLYWOOD CORRAL: A COMPREHENSIVE B WESTERN ROUNDUP

The Sons of the Pioneers (including Roy Rogers atop wagon) joined by Ray Whitley (r.) and Donald Grayson (second from r.) in The Old Wyoming Trail *(1937).*

never seen him before, and I've never seen him since, but I got to talkin' to him, and he was goin' to have a screen test the next morning. I found out that it was Republic. He said, "Yeah, they're looking for a new singing cowboy out there."

The next morning, I get up and I saddled up my guitar and went out to Republic Studios. I couldn't get in to see Sol Siegel, who was the producer of the pictures at that time. I didn't know how to make an appointment or anything, so I waited around 'till noon came and there was a bunch of extras goin' back to work, so I just walked in with them. And as I got through the door, a hand fell on my shoulder–I thought the security guard got me. And I turned around and it was Mr. Siegel, who knew me as one of the Sons of the Pioneers. And he said, "Roy, we've been testin' for a new cowboy. We tested 17 different guys, and we're lookin' for a musical singing cowboy to start a new series. And you never entered my mind until you walked through that door."

They liked the screen test, and they signed me October the 13th. I was there 14 years.[55]

Western star Bob Allen was one of those "17 different guys"–as we must assume was the tall fellow named Carter–and apparently several other established stars were contacted. Johnny Bond reports Tex Ritter was approached but turned the deal down. His contract was with his producer Ed Finney, rather than with the company, Grand National, and Republic felt they had enough staff producers, wanting only Ritter and not Finney. Bond also reports in his book *The Tex Ritter Story* that "the man" from Republic was considering not only Slye/Weston/Rogers, but "a singer back east named Red Foley... but," he said, according to Bond, "we'd rather have Tex Ritter."[56] Red Foley's candidacy may seem surprising, but it too is corroborated by Arthur Satherley, who claims he himself approached Foley, who eagerly referred him to John Lair, then acting as Red's manager. Satherley recalls being rebuffed by Lair, who claimed: "That would break up my outfit. Besides, I haven't any time to go to Hollywood!"[57]

Roy Rogers, born Leonard Franklin Slye on November 5, 1911, in Cincinnati, Ohio, grew up as a singer and mandolinist in a musical family near Duck Run, Ohio. The Slye family moved to California about 1930, and after a period of manual labor,

THE SINGING COWBOY / An American Dream

Len decided to become a professional singer, Depression or no Depression. He became a featured vocalist with several prominent West Coast cowboy bands before forming in 1933 the original Pioneer Trio, the forerunners of the Sons of the Pioneers.

The Sons of the Pioneers made their film debut in *The Old Homestead* in 1935, and by 1937 were signed to a series of westerns with Charles Starrett at Columbia, although Len appeared in only the first few before pursuing freelance efforts. Tuska maintains that "there was some friction between Roy and Bob Nolan during this period."[58] Ray Whitley, who managed the group at the time, states unequivocally that there was no such conflict.[59]

At any rate, it was Len Slye (Dick Weston/Roy Rogers) who was signed, with this revealing note appearing in the trade press in November of 1937:

ROGERS: GENE AUTRY'S WALKOUT WAS LUCKY BREAK FOR COWBOY SINGER
The row between Gene Autry, the western star, and Republic Pictures is following the familiar course of such feuds in Hollywood. Republic now has named a successor to Autry in Roy Rogers, a 25-year old radio singer who has worked in a couple of pictures. Exactly the same tactics that M-G-M used in the Freddie Bartholomew dispute. By the way, what has become of Rennie Sinclair since Freddie went back to work?....

Some of you movie-goers may wonder why all this bother about a western star. But there are 7500 theatres in the U.S. who play Hollywood "horse operas." Get a few miles out of a city and Autry and his competitors are big shots with the fans.[60]

With the release of Rogers' *Under Western Stars* in 1938, and Autry's return that fall (supported by Pee Wee King and his Golden West Cowboys in *Gold Mine in the Sky*), Republic had two singing cowboys. In one sense they were not competitive, for immediately upon his return, Autry once again got the big budgets, the best films, and the best songs, while Roy Rogers went about making solid films and surprising more than a few people with his genuine acting ability in secondary roles in major features such as *Dark Command* (1940), starring John Wayne. It was not until Autry entered the Army Air Corps in 1942 that Rogers got his real break into big budget films and adopted the inflated–but eventually accurate–title "King of the Cowboys." A career on film, on television, and on record continues to this day despite recent open-heart surgery.

Though primarily a singer, not a cowboy, another singing cowboy to emerge in 1938 was George Houston. Born in 1898 in Hampton, New Jersey,

Roy Rogers in a 1938 publicity portrait.

Houston attended the Julliard Institute of Music and after graduation joined the American Opera Company of New York City, where he had the privilege of presenting *Faust* before President Calvin Coolidge. He had a notable career on Broadway– appearing in *Shooting Star, New Moon, Thumbs Up,* and *Casanova* among others–before heading west to try films, his first major role coming in *The Melody Lingers On* (1934). Miller succinctly sums up his career:

An opera singer gradually working his way down the scale from a Nelson Eddy-type romantic lead to an adventurous action player in independents... Houston was undoubtedly the best singer among the cowboys,[61] on the basis of pure vocalistics. But he was afflicted with the curse of most opera-type belters, stolidity.[62]

Like many, Houston was tapped for singing cowboy roles for the wrong reasons. After *Frontier Scout* in 1938, a non-musical Western featuring Dorothy Fay, Tex Ritter's bride to be, Houston began a series of Lone Rider singing westerns for Producers Releasing Corporation. Known commonly as PRC, the firm was the brainchild of several "Poverty Row" producers. Beginning with *The Lone Rider Rides On* in 1941 and ending with *Outlaws of Boulder Pass* in 1942, George Houston made eleven singing cowboy films for the small producing firm before

HOLLYWOOD CORRAL: A COMPREHENSIVE B WESTERN ROUNDUP

Art Davis entertains a bevy of baddies headed by Bud Buster (hat in hand), Benny Corbett and Ted Adams (to r. with white hat) in a scene from Tim McCoy's Code of the Cactus *(1938).*

Ted Adams (l.) holds Charlie King with an assist from Al St. John while George Houston subdues I. Stanford Jolley in a scene from Outlaws of Boulder Pass *(1943).*

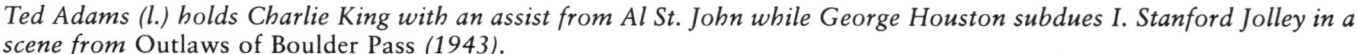

both parties realized that opera singers do not make singing cowboys. Thoroughly discouraged, George gave up films and died a couple of years later (November 12, 1944) of a heart attack.

A final entry into the singing cowboy sweepstakes of 1938 was Gene Austin, multi-million record seller of the '20s, with hits like "How Come You Do Me Like You Do?" (1924), "When My Sugar Walks Down the Street" (1924), and, of course, "My Blue Heaven" (1927). "Cruel to contemplate," writes Don Miller, "but Austin could then no longer trade on his own name, but rather the shadow of Gene Autry, for success.... *Songs and Bullets* (Harry Fraser, 1938) was a haphazard independent that encouraged no followup and merited none."[63] It was Austin's only attempt at singing cowboy films, though he did record two sides of cowboy material late in his career for the Universal label (on which Dick Foran also cut a couple of sides): "I'm Coming Home" and "Give Me a Home in Oklahoma" (Universal 131). Born in Gainesville, Texas, on July 24, 1900, Gene Austin died in Palm Springs, California, January 24, 1972.[64]

Tex Ritter left Grand National in mid-1938. Grand National was to go through several more singing cowboys and a singing cowgirl—always with the air of grasping at straws—in the ensuing years, bringing two more ill-fated songsters to the screen before the firm's demise. Repeating the miscalculation they had made with Houston, they signed on New York City-born Art Jarrett for a film called *Trigger Pals* in 1939. A big band vocalist, guitarist, and trombonist with Ted Weems who had recorded on his own for Columbia, Victor, and Brunswick, Jarrett had been in films since 1933, when he played opposite Joan Crawford in *Dancing Lady*. *Trigger Pals* was, for good reason, to be his only singing cowboy film. He was replaced by a slightly more authentic country singer who recorded extensively for Decca in the '30s and on smaller labels thereafter: Jerry Bisceglia, known as Tex Fletcher on record and radio. A left-handed guitar player, he might have had a future in films, but Grand National finally gave up the ghost in 1939, and Tex's *Six Gun Rhythm* was his only—and Grand National's last—singing cowboy film.

Grand National's final efforts may have had an air of desperation, but they proved to be ahead of their time, regardless. In 1938 they cast Dorothy Page as a singing cowgirl in a short-lived series of three westerns—*Ride 'Em Cowgirl*, *The Singing Cowgirl*, and *Water Rustlers*—all of which appeared in 1939. Ms. Page, who had worked her way up from inspired features like *Manhattan Moon*, *King Solomon of Broadway*, and *Mama Runs Wild* in the middle '30s, was a talented woman who rode, roped, shot and sang with skill and enthusiasm, but even the force of her personality and the unique premise on which her westerns were built could not overcome the ill effects of a moribund studio. *Variety* reported, "*Water Rustlers* is a western cheapie whose only redeeming feature is Dorothy Page."[65]

Wonder Woman and equal rights aside, the world was apparently not yet ready for an action heroine, and Grand National's bold and visionary step—or desperate last gasp—began no trend, and the concept of the singing cowgirl faded into the realm of the obscure. Ms. Page, despite her avant-garde role thirty years ahead of its time, apparently did not return to the screen.

It was also around this time that Bob Nolan began to have bigger and bigger parts in the Charles Starrett westerns. A handsome strapping man whose voice was not pretty but was unique, he seems to have been a natural for leading parts, an observation which has not escaped leading film historians. "[In *Two Fisted Rangers*] Bob Nolan had a speaking role in tune with his abilities (Nolan was a sure bet to star in his own series), but somebody missed the boat."[66]

"The most surprising aspect of the film [*The Durango Kid*], in retrospect is, given Bob Nolan's physical resemblance to George O'Brien, why no one ever attempted to capitalize on it and build him into a star in his own right, which had long been Nolan's ambition. Starrett, for his own part, never begrudged Nolan the opportunity, itself rather an unusual posture among Western players."[67]

Whether starring parts had been his ambition is a question still unanswered in the infrequent interviews conducted with the retiring Nolan. Ray Whitley stated flatly, "Bob was always reluctant to take any kind of leading role. Aside from his humility, I think he had reservations about his ability to act."[68] Regardless, with the completion of *Outlaws of the Panhandle* with Charles Starrett in 1941, the Sons of the Pioneers' contract with Columbia expired, and they were persuaded to make a fine series of films with Roy Rogers at Republic, beginning with *Red River Valley* in 1941. Nolan's personal roles were reduced, though the Sons of the Pioneers were featured as a group, and his candidacy for singing cowboy stardom slipped into the realm of what might have been.

In 1940 Bob Wills made his first western film. Surely the most popular country band leader of the era, Wills was cresting with the overwhelming success of "San Antonio Rose." Efforts had been made to get him into films before, but Wills finally accepted an offer from Monogram to provide musical support for Tex Ritter in *Take Me Back to Oklahoma.* Though he was forced to use an uncharacteristically small band, response was good, and Columbia signed him for *Go West Young Lady* in 1941. This led to an eight-film deal with Columbia the following year; the Texas Playboys provided musical support for Russell Hayden, with Bob himself doing a stiff but creditable job as second lead in most of these films. Except for a few shorts, however, this was the extent of Bob Wills' career as a singing cowboy.[69]

Also in 1940, a cowpoke named Dusty King rode into the Range Buster trio—trios were becoming extremely popular at this point in the western film cycle. Born Miller McCloud Everson in Cincinnati on July 11, 1909, King had apprenticed as a big band singer and announcer over WCKY and WKRC in his hometown before breaking into movies—as John King—with romantic leads in *Ace Drummond* (1936), *Charlie Chan in Honolulu,* and many others. King drifted out of films after the Range Busters series ground to a halt in 1943, and went back to singing in a style more befitting his big band training.

A new crop of hopefuls thundered on screen in 1941, though none were destined for major careers. At last, Red Foley made his debut, singing and playing guitar in support of Tex Ritter in Monogram's *The Pioneers,* released May 10, 1941. Although he would continue to appear in films from time to time, and even have both dramatic and musical television series in years to come, the times were apparently not as ripe for him as they had been in the autumn of 1937, and Red Foley never attained singing cowboy stardom. Yet another full-fledged country singer, Ernest Tubb, made his first film in 1941: *Fightin' Buckaroo,* in support of Charles Starrett. He followed this with *Ridin' West* in 1942, and *Jamboree* in 1943. Tubb was self-conscious and uncomfortable looking before the cameras, and did not pursue a film career after joining the Grand Ole Opry in January, 1943. A 1947 musical extravaganza called *Hollywood Barn Dance* was his last Hollywood

Bob Wills (l., in light shirt) shares a laugh with Tex Ritter (center), Slim Andrews (r.) and the Texas Playboys in Take Me Back to Oklahoma *(1940).*

film; his stage and recording career, for which he was better suited, occupied his energies to his dying day.[70]

Tubb was not the only one to support Charles Starrett once the Sons of the Pioneers left his films. An obscure singer named Tex Harding played in eight Durango Kid westerns with Starrett in 1945, following by several years an ex-vaudevillian named Cliff Edwards (1895–1971). Edwards, commonly known as Ukulele Ike, played the role of Harmony in several Starrett westerns before heading over to RKO and similar roles with Tim Holt. He is best remembered as the voice of Jiminy Cricket in Walt Disney's *Pinnochio*, and made a lasting impression on the national consciousness with his breathy tenor rendition of "When You Wish Upon a Star." Jimmie Davis, a major record seller of the era– "Beautiful Texas" (1934), "Nobody's Darling But Mine" (1935), "It Makes No Difference Now" (1939), "You Are My Sunshine" and "Too Late" (1940), "A Worried Mind" (1941), and "Sweethearts or Strangers" (1941)—and soon to be Governor of Louisiana was another who got a couple of shots as a vocalist in Starrett's westerns. Though his term as Governor interrupted his musical and film career, he was later to star in the story of his own life, *Louisiana* in 1947.[71]

Western swing fiddler Art Davis, a former member of Bill Boyd's Cowboy Ramblers and Gene Autry's band, also appeared on screen in singing roles. "Everybody said the same thing about Davis," writes Don Miller, "if he'd lose some weight, he'd make a promising Western lead."[72] Davis sang in Tim McCoy's last PRC feature that year, *The Texas Marshall*. He also played a singer in a film about a masked good guy, in which he sang a few songs and rode around with a special guitar-shaped saddlebag fitted for his instrument. Billed in the latter as Larry Mason, he looked trim and fit, though he did grow to unstylishly stout proportions in his later years as a western swing band leader.

Davis, a native Texan, had fiddled with Bill Boyd's Cowboy Ramblers as far back as their hit Bluebird record of 1934, "Under The Double Eagle." He was reunited with Boyd, his former employer, and actor Lee Powell (who was later killed in World War II) in a series of six PRC cheapies known as the Frontier Marshall series. All six, beginning with *Texas Manhunt* and ending with *Along the Sundown Trail*, were released in 1942. Art Davis made no more westerns of consequence, nor did Boyd, who returned to Dallas to resume his extremely successful radio, record, and stage career.

Cliff "Ukelele Ike" Edwards

Born in Fannin County, Texas, April 29, 1910, Bill Boyd recorded for RCA and Bluebird from 1934–1950; he died in December of 1977 in Fort Worth. His main legacy to the western film was added to the already considerable confusion between William "Stage" Boyd and William "Hopalong Cassidy" Boyd. None of the three were related.[73]

Such trio pictures were becoming popular at the time, in imitation of the Three Mesquiteers series dating from 1936, which featured John Wayne among its many players through the years. One member of such trios was often a singer (sometimes two, in the case of Boyd, Davis, and Powell): Bob Baker, as we have seen, ended up his career this way, and Tex Ritter was featured in more than a few. Comedians Max Terhune and Rufe Davis had both portrayed Lullaby Joslin as one of the Three Mesquiteers; in 1942 a youthful Jimmy Dodd took over the role for a few pictures, beginning with *Shadows on the Sage*. He is far better remembered as the bubbly emcee of television's *Mickey Mouse Club*. Also entering the sweepstakes in 1942 was James Newill, a baritone profundo in the George Houston school of operatic cowboys, with *The Rangers Take Over* in the Texas Rangers series. A singing Mountie (shades of Nelson Eddy) as far back as 1937, with the successful *Renfrew of the Royal Mounted* and subsequent Renfrew adventures, Newill lasted but two years with the Texas Rangers, replaced by Tex Ritter, who was more suitable for the role.

The big news of 1942 was not, however, this crop of newcomers, but the war which had a drastic effect on all American life. Singing cowboys were no less affected, least of all Gene Autry, who enlisted in the Air Force during a "Melody Ranch" broadcast in 1942, and was gone for four years from the screen, four years in which a whole new crew of hopefuls tried to fill his boots, years in which he and his audience changed drastically.

The War Years and After: 1942–1945

When he left, Gene Autry was still unquestionably at the top of the heap.[74] Tex Ritter and Roy Rogers had their following, Bob Baker was fading fast, and the operatic types were never even in the same ball park. Autry's last pre-war film was released in September, 1942, though several of his earlier films were re-released during his absence; Roy Rogers' films were immediately upgraded with the December release of *Heart of the Golden West,* and over the course of the next four years, he overtook Autry while his mentor was flying supply planes in the Far East.

It is more a matter of taste than anything else, but despite his high budget westerns, his pleasant voice and great yodeling, his acting ability, and the benefit of the Sons of the Pioneers, Rogers' pictures were not as successful as Autry's had been and would be. One reason was the unbearable gaudiness of his clothing, what Don Miller calls the "era of the shrieking Rogers costumery,"[75] stretching the willing suspension of disbelief to the breaking point. Roy told Jon Tuska that the heavy indulgence in costumes and production numbers in his wartime movies was a result of a directive from Yates himself: "Mr. Yates had gone to New York and seen the stage show *Oklahoma.* He came back to the studio and put out a memo that from then on my films were to be made in the mold of *Oklahoma.* He wanted musicals more than westerns from me."[76]

More a problem than this, however, was Rogers' basic inability to put over a country song. Gene Autry and Tex Ritter's huge record selling successes amount to more than a combination of good songs and good productions: both were country singers who took some pains to remain so. Even with a huge orchestra, Autry featured Johnny Bond's guitar runs, Frankie Marvin's distinctive steel guitar, and his own comfortable, relaxed voice. Roy Rogers with Country Washburn's Orchestra was just another good singer walking through a country or countryish tune. It is little wonder that his most successful record, "Blue Shadows on the Trail," featured the Sons of the Pioneers so heavily that it is virtually their performance.

Although it is hard to agree totally with Jon Tuska's Autry Fantasy as the explanation of Autry's success, it is the most lucid and creditable and thoughtful explanation by a film historian to date, and does cast considerable light on the fundamental differences between Gene Autry and Roy Rogers:

> Ultimately, because there was no underlying fantasy about Roy's person, as there was about Gene Autry, he remained merely a wholesome, likeable man who sang and performed and had great camaraderie with the Pioneers and who, invariably, embodied the impulse to make beautiful westerns which later filmmakers strove so earnestly to contradict.

In the meantime, Gene Autry changed drastically, turning toward a dedication to the financial. He told Tuska, "I don't think I ever appreciated money until I had been in the service. I learned what it was like to work for almost nothing, and I didn't like it." His current press release tells the same story: "In 1941 I made $600,000 with pictures, radio, records and personal appearances. Suddenly, I found myself in uniform at $115 to $125 a month as a tech sergeant. It started me thinking. If it hadn't been for royalties from things such as sweatshirts, pistols, boots and hats and records, I would have been in a mess. I knew I could make good money as long as I could work. But suppose I was incapacitated? Where would I get my income? I decided I better start investing in some business."[78]

Autry elaborates, with a folksy homily:

> I was reminded once by Johnny Bond, who toured and worked with us on radio, of a tradition of the Old West. Whenever a lone cowboy or Indian needed to take a long journey by horseback, it was customary for him to ride one saddled horse while leading another bareback. When his mount began to tire, instead of stopping for a rest, he merely slipped the saddle onto the spare horse and rode on. In just about that way I eased out of my life as a performer and began to devote my full energy to business. I just changed horses.
>
> I had discovered during the war how quickly your security can be threatened by conditions beyond your control. It was a jolt to the nervous system to find myself staring at an Air Force salary of less than two thousand dollars a *year,* after earning up to ten thousand dollars a *week.* I thought to myself, well, as long as I can work I

THE SINGING COWBOY / An American Dream

know I can make money. But what if something happened to my health? Or my voice went haywire. Times change, too. If you don't part your hair right, they, the public, will find someone who does. I knew the time had come to start looking for an interest that did not depend on my being able to perform.[79]

Because the acquisition of wealth became Autry's principal occupation after his return from war, plus the press' attention to that subject alone, Gene Autry's genuine contributions to country music have been unfairly ignored and overlooked. This is true also of his role in the history of the American film. A typical comment, largely truthful though obviously condescending and unsympathetic, is Fenin and Everson's:

> Autry actually was just a shrewd businessman who had no great interest in or respect for the Western as such. He realized that his value as a show business personality (taking in also radio, rodeos, and ultimately television and his own production companies) depended on his almost comic-opera approach to the Western. He also had the happy knack of being able to hide his shrewdness behind

Gene endorsing Wheaties, circa 1937.

the amiable facade of the hillbilly singer; he was both a popular idol of the people, in the manner, if nothing else, of Will Rogers, and at the same time a highly successful businessman.[80]

As stated, there is truth here, hidden among loaded words like "*just* a shrewd businessman," "happy knack," and "amiable facade." There is no question that Gene Autry returned from World War II a profoundly changed man; he realized he was a commodity to be merchandized to its fullest extent, and doubtless it is at this point that money became his primary concern. However, that this should in no way obscure his genuine contributions is so obvious as to hardly be worth committing to paper, except that the opposite approach has for years been so prevalent. For the moment, suffice it to say that Tuska's axiom "the acquisition of wealth itself has concerned Autry primarily in his career"[81] holds true, especially for the post-World War II phase. Whatever drove and spurred him in his rise to success in the entertainment world before the war—and this is difficult to ascertain—it is certain that with a combination of shrewdness and luck, he pursued the goal of becoming a millionaire with intensity and zeal. Wealth has preoccupied Autry, and the story of his successful pursuit of it has overshadowed his very real contributions to country music and to American entertainment.

At any rate, during his absence the pace of the world of the singing cowboy began to accelerate rapidly, not only for Roy Rogers but for a fresh new crop of hopefuls, singers, in general, who were far more authentic country singers than the George Houstons and James Newills of the recent past. The singing cowboy genre was by now nearly a decade old, and perhaps by that time the film colony had come to a glimmering of understanding that it was not the operatic projection of the singer's voice that attracted the customers, but the basic virtue of the country singer: believability.

First among the new breed was Jimmy Wakely, often unfairly accused of being an Autry imitator; the main similarity was that both were primarily country singers, and while they were able to hold their own in the action sequences, they were basically vocalists.

James Clarence Wakely was born in Mineola, Arkansas, on February 16, 1914, and raised in eastern Oklahoma. By 1937 Wakely, Johnny Bond,[82] and Dick Rhinehart had formed a western trio based on the Sons of the Pioneers called the Bell Boys, named for Bell Clothing, their sponsor in Oklahoma City. They blithely headed west in 1940, arriving in Hollywood on June 4, and by November of that year all had recording contracts—Wakely with Decca, Bond and Rhinehart with Columbia. In addition, they had become regulars on "Melody Ranch," and had appeared in their first film, *Saga of Death Valley,* with Roy Rogers.

Wakely left "Melody Ranch" after two years—replaced by Eddie Dean—as his film roles as a singer in Hopalong Cassidy and Charles Starrett movies began to grow. Due to the success of his records—"Too Late," a major hit in 1942, foremost among them—he began his own starring series for Monogram in 1944 with *Song of the Range.* After twenty-eight films for them, *Saddle Serenade* and *Song of the Sierras* among them, Wakely closed out with *Lawless Code* in 1949. He made but one more film, writing the score and playing a singing "buddy" to Sterling Hayden in a big budget A Western made in 1954 called *Arrow in the Dust.*

Wakely remarked, "I'm so glad that I was a singer, because if I hadn't been I'd have gone down the tubes."[83] Indeed, by 1949 his singing had become so popular he scarcely had the time or need for films. His Capitol records "I Love You So Much It Hurts Me" and "One Has My Name (The Other Has My Heart)" had been major successes in 1948, and in 1949–50 his duet with Margaret Whiting, "Slipping Around," sold well over a million copies. A whole series of successful Wakely-Whiting duets followed including their Christmas classic "Silver Bells" (1950). Jimmy Wakely pursued an active musical career, recording for Capitol, Decca, Coral, and his own label, Shasta, and playing the nightclub circuit in Nevada and southern California. Later on he re-released many of his older performances on Shasta along with those of Tex Ritter, Merle Travis, Eddie Dean, and others, and guided the firm into a thriving mail-order concern. Perhaps more than any other singing cowboy, his film career served not as an end in itself, but as a promotional vehicle furthering his career as a successful country singer on radio (he had his own CBS network show for some years), records, and in person.

Wakely's dedication was admirable, though at times a bit self-serving. There is no question of economic need or ego satisfaction, simply love of a form they themselves helped create, a form they did not use as a means to an end concerned only with black ink on the bottom line. Perhaps because he was first and foremost a country singer (albeit with a decided pop tinge), Wakely had much love for the music outside of the trappings of success that tend to overwhelm residents of Hollywood and its environs.

THE SINGING COWBOY / An American Dream

Jimmy Wakely (r.) warbles in Song of the Wasteland *(1947). Johnny Bond in rear with legs crossed, Lee "Lasses" White in top hat.*

Another singer of similar background is Eddie Dean, born Edgar Dean Glosup in Posey, Texas, on July 9, 1907. Though he has had a long and honorable career as a country singer, Dean has long (and rather unfairly) been scorned by film critics. Miller states that "while Dean could sing, his attributes as a two-fisted strong-willed cowboy hero were dubious... and that drawback was difficult to overcome."[84] "[His] pictures were even cheaper... than the Buster Crabbe... Westerns of 1940–45 that they replaced,"[85] claims Jon Tuska.

Dean was certainly not the greatest thespian to ever hit the screen; however, on the whole, this kind of poison-penned criticism does considerable injustice to a fine singer and a good singing cowboy. That he has survived with such grace after such abuse seems to be in itself a credit to the man.

After an early career as a gospel singer, Eddie Dean moved to Chicago in 1926, intent on pursuing a career. After appearing on stations in Shenandoah, Iowa, and Yankton, South Dakota, he and his older brother Jimmy Dean[86] joined the cast of the National Barn Dance[87] from 1933 through 1936. In 1936 he was chosen for the part of Larry Burton in the radio soap opera "Modern Cinderella," and acted and sang in that series until 1937, when he flipped a coin, heading to Hollywood or New York depending on how it landed. It came up heads, and Dean blew into Hollywood, where he quickly began to land small roles in support of other heroes. In 1942, he and his brother replaced Jimmy Wakely and Johnny Bond as Autry's backup vocal group, as Wakely left to pursue his own career and Bond was upgraded to sidekick. Dean stayed two years before going to a

363

Eddie Dean.

featured spot on Judy Canova's network radio show.

A prolific songwriter, he has at least two country classics ["One Has My Name (the Other Has My Heart)" and "I Dreamed of a Hillbilly Heaven"] and one Western classic ("On the Banks of the Sunny San Juan") to his credit, and over the years has recorded a remarkable amount of material for Decca, Capitol, Majestic, Mercury, Crystal, Sage and Sand, ARC, and Shasta. As for his entry into starring roles, he ascribes it largely to luck:

I met Pete Canova, and by meeting Mr. Bill Crespinell, who had the color [process of his own invention], who'd made all the tests for the color in my back yard. He said to me, "Eddie, why don't you do a series with my color?... We have a good color process."

Well, what they had to do, they had to run two films through at the same time... so you had one a sort of gray-blue and the other a sort of orange. And through that process they got this beautiful color, called it Cinecolor. So I went to work on it, and I told Pete Canova, and we went to Monogram, and Monogram turned us down. And then we went out to PRC, and PRC took the series. 'Course Monogram tried to buy my contract right after, but I was already on my way. And I think what happened, I got started a little late... well, I know I did, as far as what you call the picture cowboy, 'cause I only had three years. But I made the top ten moneymakers the first year! For the three years I was in the top ten moneymakers. That was '46, '47 and '48.[88]

Dean starred in twenty features for PRC and the equally unstable Eagle-Lion firm that rose phoenix-like from the ashes of PRC, although only the first few were in Cinecolor, an attractive, subdued color system which never threatened the Technicolor system because of its limited pallette.

Today Eddie Dean continues to pursue his singing career; he even managed to obtain Colonel Tom Parker as a personal manager for a time. Parker dressed him up in gold lamé and called him "The Golden Cowboy," presaging Elvis' similar costume by some years.

Next of the new breed to arrive was Ken Curtis, who had been born Curtis Wayne Gates in Lamar, Colorado, on July 2, 1916. Though he came from a pure country background–his father a fiddler, his brother a banjo player–Curtis developed a smooth, rich voice that so well adapted itself to pop music that he spent some time with Shep Field's Orchestra and replaced Frank Sinatra in Tommy Dorsey's Orchestra, recording "Love Sends a Little Gift of Roses" and "Anniversary Waltz" with them. After a stretch in the service (1942–1945) he returned to Hollywood, and having sung "Tumbling Tumbleweeds" as a guest on Jo Stafford's radio show, he was signed by Columbia Pictures, who were in the process of reactivating their singing cowboy series.

Often supported by Andy Parker and the Plainsmen (and sometimes even the Hoosier Hot Shots), Curtis made 12 films in two years. In 1945, Gene Autry returned from the Army Air Corps. Tuska describes the situation at Republic:

> Yates had been preparing himself for this moment and felt well armed... with Duke Wayne and now Bill Elliott, he was marching forward into the ranks of the majors. He was able to control Roy Rogers. Gene's first picture after his discharge was *Souix City Sue*... released in November [1946] and produced on a modest budget... Gene's contract was again coming up for renewal, and he had best not be unreasonable in his demands.[89]

However, as we have seen, Gene's focus had drastically changed during his stint as a soldier, and upon his return he opened secret negotiations with Columbia Pictures.

> Autry made four Westerns for Republic that were released in 1947... Autry felt that as a Western property he was worth more than any player on the screen. He refused to put up with Yates' attempt to humble him and negotiated himself an excellent package with Columbia. He also signed a lucrative radio contract and was able to quickly regain his preeminence in the field. Of all people, Yates understood the least, apparently, about the magic of the Autry Fantasy.[90]

Autry, with blandness so typical of his public statements, says: "There had been quite a break at that time because—well, my contract was out, and I wanted to have control over my own pictures. By that time Republic had Roy over there, and I just didn't feel that there was enough room for one company to really promote two of the same type. I made five pictures at Republic, and then went over to Columbia to set our own corporation up."[91]

He adds, becoming a bit more specific in *Back in the Saddle Again*:

> By the time *Robin Hood of Texas* had reached the movie houses, I had parted ways with Republic. The courts had upheld my suit and I was now free to make my own deals, and pick my own friends. We had offers from several studios. But I wanted to form my own company, frankly, because of the tax angles. If you earned over $100,000 in those days, 85 per cent of it was taxable. The only way to hang on to your money was to form a corporation. So I became the president and executive producer of Gene Autry Productions, and we signed a contract with Columbia to release our pictures. It was as good a deal as anyone in Hollywood had at that time. I had complete say over my films and I could take home half the profits.[92]

Autry's defection to Columbia affected a great many people, among them, of course, Ken Curtis. It was obvious that if Republic, in Autry's view, could not adequately support two singing cowboys, then neither could Columbia. After his 1947 series, therefore, Ken was cast adrift. Although he was to make a couple of independents as a singing cowboy hero, his next step was to join the Sons of the Pioneers, with whom he remained from 1949 to 1953, his lovely voice highlighted on such Victor recordings as "I Still Do" and "Room Full of Roses." Curtis settled in the Los Angeles area, working as an actor and a singer, and recording Western material through the years for Mercury, M-G-M, Capitol, and Dot. For a time, he even had his own television series, *Ripcord*, and came up with a grizzled hillbilly character called Monk in the *Have Gun, Will Travel* series. Ultimately, he brought this character to *Gunsmoke*, where he spent well over a decade portraying Matt Dillon's faithful deputy, Festus. So pervasive has this characterization been that few remember, or can even conceive of, Ken Curtis as a fine pop and western singer or a handsome western movie hero. Yet he was one of the finest.

Monte Hale was another person profoundly affected by Gene Autry's move to Columbia. Born June 8, 1921, in San Angelo, Texas, Hale became a

Autry keeps up with current events between setups on an early Republic Western.

Dale Evans and Roy Rogers give Monte Hale some pointers on folding hat brims, circa 1949.

professional singer at the age of twelve. In the early '40s, he was discovered singing on a USO tour and brought to Hollywood. His first film roles came in 1944 in such productions as *Stepping In Society* and *Big Bonanza*. When Yates moved Roy Rogers into A budget westerns with *My Pal Trigger* in 1946, Monte was promoted from supporting roles in the Sunset Carson series to his own musical series with *Home on the Range* (1946) and *Out California Way* (1946), where he was usually supported by Foy Willing and the Riders of the Purple Sage. The purpose of this move on Yates' part was not only to fill the void left by Autry's departure and Rogers' move into A Westerns, but also to provide the same kind of insurance against Rogers' demands at contract time that Rogers himself had provided against Autry years earlier.

Enough was thought of Hale that eight of his nineteen films were shot in color. After his series ended in 1949, he returned to singing, and recording for a few years before retiring from show business in the early 60s. He appeared in only two more films, *Giant* (1956) and *The Chase* (1974).

An amusing entry into the singing cowboy race in 1945 was Johnny Mack Brown, who had ridden many a trail with Bob Baker, Tex Ritter, Jimmy Wakely, and other singers in the past. An action cowboy from start to finish, Brown looked uncomfortable as a singer (with a dubbed-in voice) in *Drifting Along* (1946), an experiment that was never repeated.

The Final Days

Time was running out on the singing cowboy, however, as World War II had drastically changed America, physically as well as spiritually. Romantic, dreamy, clearly fantastic films about the old West that never was, or a new West with old West trappings, whether featuring singers or not, were no longer attractive to a public that had experienced five years of real injury and death, and was beginning to cower under the spectre of atomic attack. Then, too, the impact of television was sudden and dramatic, staggering the film industry in general, and virtually eliminating the need for new low budget westerns. In fact, this was especially true since so many of the older westerns were being edited and shown on the small screen.

Though in its waning days, the singing cowboy film showed a bit more life, however, before it finally cashed in its chips. Striving for that special something to catch the fancy of the public, it came up with some unusual solutions. For example, radio singer and modern-day balladeer Red River Dave began a series for Universal in 1948. Miller says he "warbled well but was painfully camera shy," and that the series was, of all things, "filmed on the plains of upper New York state."[93] Red River Dave—born David McEnery in San Antonio, Texas, on December 15, 1914—had appeared in singing roles in *Swing in the Saddle* (1948) with Jimmy Wakely, and returned to his native Texas and elsewhere, after *Hidden Valley Days* and *Echo Ranch* wound up his film career.[94] He was joined in films that year by another country singer, and a more popular one at that, named Elton Britt, who made the first of his three Westerns, *Laramie* in 1948. Britt then returned to the singing and yodeling which had justly made him famous.

The story was virtually unchanged in 1949: popular country singers stuffed uncomfortably into cheap singing cowboy Westerns, probably with the hope of attracting country music fans to the theatres in the ever-loyal Southern market. However, television was making its inroads into the South as well, and ultimately this latest move on the part of the film industry was a lost cause. Universal moved their Red River Dave series west in 1949 replacing Dave with vocalist-band leader Tex Williams, who made a series of fifteen musical shorts known as "Tales of the West." They were then spliced into four musical, though somewhat incoherent, feature films capitalizing on his recent 1947 hit "Smoke! Smoke! Smoke!" After years of providing musical support for many Westerns, Western swing band leader Spade Cooley—who had begun his film career as an Indian in one of those little Ray Whitley shorts for RKO, *Redskins and Redheads*—at last took a shot at starring roles in *The Silver Bandit* in 1949 and *Border Outlaws* in 1950. Although Cooley was the snappiest of dressers and a charismatic musician and band leader, his films left little mark on the genre. At the same time Eddy Arnold made a couple of what might loosely be called Westerns, though they were actually more in the "Southeastern" mold, similar to Roy Acuff's Republic features. Arnold was hot as a firecracker with staggering record sales, a fine singer and a handsome man, and his films were produced by a major studio, Columbia. For whatever combination of reasons, however—the lateness of the hour more than likely—no one ever tried to

Foy Willing (top center) and the Riders of the Purple Sage.

develop him further as a singing cowboy, and *Feudin' Rhythm* (1949) and *Hoedown* (1950) sum up his career in Western musicals.

In 1949 Monte Hale's contract was allowed to run out, and he was replaced by the last of the singing cowboys—Rex Allen. Yet another alumnus of the National Barn Dance, Allen had been a rodeo star born in Wilcox, Arizona, on December 31, 1924, and had gotten his first radio work at WTTM in Trenton, New Jersey, in 1944. He worked from 1945–1949 in Chicago at the National Barn Dance and recorded for Mercury before heading west, where he ultimately would appear in some thirty-two Western films, nineteen of them as star, beginning with *The Arizona Cowboy* in 1950.

Rex Allen was likeable, believable, a powerful singer, and a good actor; but he was also too late. Dwindling budgets had been cut further and further, nowhere more evident than in poor Rex's films: "Key action footage was repeated endlessly, and even songs were doctored—even by just one word—so that an 'old' Roy Rogers song like 'Roll on Texas Moon' would re-emerge as a 'new' Rex Allen song, 'Roll on Border Moon.'"[95]

Allen went from B Westerns into a television series called *Frontier Doctor*, and pursued his singing career, with "Crying in the Chapel" becoming his biggest hit in 1953. He has also had a unique career as narrator in a great number of Walt Disney films and television programs.[96]

HOLLYWOOD CORRAL: A COMPREHENSIVE B WESTERN ROUNDUP

Roy Rogers and Rex Allen

Thus, the cycle of singing cowboy Westerns ground to a sad halt, outmoded by changing American tastes and the advent of an exciting new medium of entertainment. Tex Ritter had made his last film in 1945, Eddie Dean in 1948, Jimmy Wakely in 1949. Roy Rogers' finale–except for a couple of guest appearances–came with *Pals of the Golden West* in 1951, while Gene Autry bowed out, appropriately enough, with *Last of the Pony Riders* in 1953. Rex Allen brought the whole thing to a close in 1954 with *The Phantom Stallion*, just a few months before Wayne Morris made his last film, *Two Guns and a Badge*, not a singing Western but still the last B Western film. Since *Two Guns and a Badge,* Western films have been produced sporadically by independent producers operating on big budgets.

As Autry himself says with some poignancy:

There were no farewell toasts, no retirement dinner with someone handing out a pocket watch for twenty years of faithful service. Actually, nineteen years, between the release in November of 1934 of *In Old Santa Fe,* when I made my first appearance with Ken Maynard, for Mascot, until Columbia released my last [*Last of the Pony Riders*] in November of 1953. It just kind of slipped up on us. I don't recall ever saying that I had quit, or that I would never make another motion picture.[97]

The passing of the B Western and the singing cowboy coincides neatly with the coming of rock, the music which made instant anachronisms of a wide number and variety of styles, sounds, singers, and musicians. It can hardly be blamed for the fall of the singing cowboy, of course; the genre had been in a state of gradual decay, despite the fact that many fine talents—among them some good country singers—appeared in its waning years. In fact, because of this new crop of country singers, the singing cowboy films probably were given a few years of added life. At last, the studios had figured out that the public wanted to see pleasant cowboy singers, not operatic baritones. Of course, there were no Hank Williams or Roy Acuffs; however, Eddie Dean, Jimmy Wakely, Ken Curtis, Monte Hale and Rex Allen all had good credentials as soft country singers, and made credible singing cowboys.

Rock and the Southeastern sound revival (in the form of Hank Williams, Kitty Wells, Webb Pierce, Carl Smith and the like) did not kill off the singing cowboy; that was already done. Worse, they tarnished its image. The raw energy of rock and the hard-hitting, gut-level realism of early 1950's country music made the dreamlike world of the singing cowboy look foolish. Consequently, the music went into such a decline that few scholars or even popular writers and historians mention it much in overviews of country music history, except to remark on the indignity of grown men wearing those funny clothes, of six-shooters which never needed reloading, or of orchestras swelling from behind cacti and rock formations. The growth of the folk movement at the end of the '50s and the early 1960s beat the dead horse with a vengeance: nothing seemed more antithetical to their notion of valuable music than made-in- Hollywood, Western music sung by guys in gaudy suits, playing $1,000 guitars on top of $5,000 saddles.

The singing cowboy represents in its most innocent manifestation an American dream, albeit a dream which has far more to do with self-image than reality. It has come to a devaluation in recent years, as America turned away first from dreams, then from heroes. It is a dream which did not sour, but staled, no longer new nor suited to its times. Yet it is a powerful dream, one in which we have all shared, for it is the nature of mankind to set his mind free to dream such dreams. The singing cowboy in his prime gave us some of those dreams, those flights of

THE SINGING COWBOY / An American Dream

Rex Allen

Jane Frazee, Roy Rogers, Estelita Rodriguez and Tito Guizar record the songs for The Gay Ranchero *(1948).*

fancy, and gave us much fine music to boot, despite the inherent artificiality of the on-screen situation. The singing cowboy gave much to country music in style, repertoire, and gifted singers, musicians, and writers, and in dignity and glamour in a time when country music was seen by outsiders and critics as possessing neither.

The singing cowboy and his version of the American dream speaks strongly of its era; Autry was in the forefront of his contemporaries in turning from the escapist mentality of the Depression-haunted thirties to the financial growth of the aggressive, victorious, booming late '40s and '50s; he simply turned his attentions from one reality to another, as he had so adroitly shifted musical styles early in his career when it was to his advantage to do so. He was the first to outgrow his own mythos–though he continued to milk its financial possibilities for some years–as a profoundly changed America turned away from the glamourous and fantastic towards harsher, realer concerns in film as well as in music.

The glamour of the singing cowboy is today nostalgic, campy; yet some of the music is very, very fine, as pure and real a type of country music as any, and as moving. The indelible legacy of the singing cowboy is a naive innocence that America has always prized in itself, a stirring version of the American dream, and a great deal of the finest music to branch from that magnificent shade tree we call country music.

Notes

1. Austin E. and Alta S. Fife, eds., *Cowboy and Western Songs: A Comprehensive Anthology* (New York: Clarkson N. Potter, Inc., 1969), p. ix.

2. John I. White, *Git Along, Little Dogies: Songs and Songmakers of thr American West* (Urbana: University of Illinois Press, 1975), p. 196.

3. Nick Tosches, *Country: The Biggest Music in America* (New York: Stein and Day, 1977), p. 112.

4. George F. Fenin and William K. Everson, *The Western: From Silents to the Seventies,* rev. ed. (1962; rpt. New York: Grossman Publishers, 1973), p. 176.

5. In strict point of fact the first records made by a cowboy film star were two poems, "Lasca" and "Big Ben" recorded by silent film star William S. Hart on Victor's Red Seal label, normally reserved for classical music and other "timeless" performances. As far as we know Bill Hart, the grand old man of the Western film, did not include singing among his talents or aspirations.

6. William Henry Koon, "The Songs of Ken Maynard," *John Edwards Memorial Foundation Quarterly,* 9 (1973), 70–77.

7. "CSR's Western Movie Hall of Fame: Ken Maynard," *Country Song Roundup,* June 1978, p. 28.

8. Jon Tuska, *The Filming of the West* (Garden City: Doubleday, 1976), p. 272. Tuska's work is also the most sympathetic to the singing cowboy, a genre which sets the teeth of most film historians on edge.

9. Tuska, p. 292.

10. Tuska reports of Maynard's later film making (1937): "Ken's singing had been off key when he worked for Darmour; in fact, he had exploded when Darmour dubbed him. At Grand National, Maynard's brand of music-making was–to put it charitably–grotesque." (p. 399).

11. White, p. 117, 153–54, 167–75.

12. Roger D. Kinkle, *The Complete Encyclopedia of Popular Music and Jazz 1900-1950* (New Rochelle: Arlington House, 1974), II, 1105–06.

13. Much of the information on the careers of the Sons of the Pioneers and its members has been gained from Ken Griffis' invaluable compilation *Hear My Song: The Story of the Celebrated Sons of the Pioneers,* JEMF Special Series, No. 5 (Los Angeles: John Edwards Memorial Foundation, Inc., 1974).

14. Griffis, p. 71.

15. Personal interview with Bob Nolan, 28 April 1976.

16. Bill C. Malone, *Country Music USA: A Fifty Year History* (Austin: University of Texas Press, 1968), p. 197.

17. Douglas B. Green, "Gene Autry," in *Stars of Country Music: Uncle Dave Macon to Johnny Rodriguez,* ed. Bill C. Malone and Judith McCulloh (Urbana: University of Illinois Press, 1975), pp. 142–56.

18. Autry, Gene, with Mickey Herskowitz. *Back in the Saddle Again.* (Garden City, New York: Doubleday & Co., 1978).

19. Autry, p. 6.

20. Personal interview with Frank Marvin, 1 April 1975.

21. Autry, p. 13–15.

22. The October, 1928 issue of *Radio Digest* contains a photo and caption of "Tiny Renier, The Singing Cowboy, who rounds up listeners with his Western songs at WDAF, Kansas City." Exactly when the term singing cowboy came into usage is uncertain, but Autry was certainly quick to adopt it.

23. Gene Autry, "Three Pals," *Country Song Roundup,* Jan. 1950, p. 15.

24. The first was called *Mountain Ballads and Cowboy Songs;* the second, significantly, was *Cowboy Songs and Mountain Ballads,* both published by M. M. Cole.

25. Malone, p. 154.

26. Gene Autry, Letter to Rayond Hall, 8 Sept. 1933, copy graciously provided to the author by Nolan Poterfield.

27. Personal interview with Arthur E. Satherley, 27 June 1974.

28. Tuska, p. 294.

29. Autry, p. 33.

30. William K. Everson, *A Pictorial History of the Western Film* (Secaucus, N. J.: The Citadel Press, 1969), p. 147.

31. Tuska, pp. 305–06.

32. Don Miller, *Hollywood Corral* (New York: Popular Library, 1976), pp. 127–128.

33. It is difficult to discover exactly who came when, but the following biographical list is presented roughly in accurate chronological order. As with all statements of fact within this essay, the dates, places, people, and events discussed are accurate to the best of the author's knowledge, but correction of any errors found by readers is eagerly welcomed by the author, as is additional information on any singing cowboys mentioned or inadvertently ignored.

34. Frank Matheny, Jr., "An Interview with Fred Scott," *Film Collector's Registry,* Sept. 1976, pp. 3–4.

35. Telephone interview with Ray Whitley, 21 April 1978.

36. Gerald F. Vaughn and Douglas B. Green, "A Singing Cowboy on the Road: A Look at the Performance Career of Ray Whitley," *Journal of Country Music* 5 (1974), 15.

37. Gerald F. Vaughn, *Ray Whitley: Country-Western Musicmaster and Film Star* (Newark, Delaware: privately printed, 1973), n. pag. Though brief, this is the definitive work on Whitley to date.

38. There has been some confusion over Ritter's birth date for years: even his plaque at the Country Music Hall of Fame reads 1907, the commonly given date. Actually the publicity department at Grand National thought that thirty-one was a bit mature for a hot new discovery, and promptly made him twenty-nine–in fact, Johnny Bond quoted Tex as saying, "They made me twenty-nine for a couple of years, and then moved me back to twenty-eight!" At least they didn't have to move his birthplace as they had with Ken Maynard.

39. Edward Finney, "The Making of a Star," *Classic Film Collector* (Fall 1975), p. 11.

40. Miller, p. 131.

41. Johnny Bond, "Gene Autry: Champion, or My Thirty Years with Gene Autry," MS, unpublished.

42. Film historians uniformly comment that the fantastic success of the Autry films was often responsible for keeping Republic in the black, and was sometimes the *only* thing.

43. Kinkle, pp. 541–42.

44. Actually 1910.

45. Tuska, pp. 419–20.

46. Tuska, p. 421.

Roscoe Ates and Eddie Dean clowning between takes on Wild Country *(1947).*

47. Not necessarily. These authors prove time and time again through their impressive landmark work that they have little sympathy for and less understanding about country music, its inherent greatness, and its strong appeal.

48. Fenin and Everson, p. 217.

49. Whitley interview.

50. Harry T. Sampson, *Blacks in Black and White: A Source Book on Black Films* (Metuchen, N. J.: Scarecrow Press, 1977), p. 63.

51. Everson, p. 148.

52. Kinkle, p. 1170.

53. Personal interview with Arthur E. Satherley, 27 April 1975.

54. Autry, p. 61-63. The layoff certainly didn't hurt his record sales—he racked up three major hits that year alone with "Gold Mine in the Sky," "Take Me Back to My Boots and Saddles," and "When It's Springtime in the Rockies."

55. James Morgan, "Conversations with the Cowboy King," *TWA Ambassador*, Oct. 1976, p. 38.

56. Bond, *Tex Ritter*, p. 56.

57. Satherley interview, 27 April 1975.

58. Tuska, p. 400.

59. Whitley interview.

60. Griffis, p. 25.

61. Again, a highly subjective judgment.

62. Miller, pp. 168-69.

63. Miller, p. 136.

64. Kinkle, pp. 524-25.

65. *Variety,* March 15, 1939, p. 18.

66. Miller, p. 147.

67. Tuska, p. 404.

68. Whitley interview.

69. Charles R. Townsend, *San Antonio Rose: The Life and Music of Bob Wills* (Urbana: University of Illinois Press, 1976), pp. 207-12.

70. Townsend Miller, "Ernest Tubb," in *Stars of Country Music,* p. 230.

71. Gus Weill, *You Are My Sunshine: The Jimmie Davis Story* (Waco: Word Books, 1977), pp. 59-60.

72. D. Miller, p. 41.

73. Bob Pinson, Jacket Notes, *Bill Boyd's Cowboy Ramblers,* Bluebird, AXM2-5502, 1975.

74. This was as true of his record sales as well, with "Back in the Saddle Again" (1939), "South of the Border" (1940), "You Are My Sunshine" (1941), "It Makes No Difference Now" (1941), the Academy Award-nominated

"Be Honest With Me" (1941), and "Tweedle-O-Twill" (1942) having all been major hits. He had also begun his extremely successful Melody Ranch radio show in 1939; it was to last until 1956.

75. D. Miller, p. 119.
76. Tuska, p. 461.
77. Tuska, p. 468.
78. Dave Distel, "The Good Guy in the White Hat or The Cowboy with the Midas Touch: A Horatio Alger Story for Our Time," Press release, Golden West Broadcasters, p. 3.
79. Autry, p. 168.
80. Fenin and Everson, p. 216.
81. Tuska, p. 480.
82. Placing Johnny Bond in the context of this narrative is a conundrum. He became a familiar face on screen and a staple of "Melody Ranch" for over a decade, one of country music's most successful record sellers of the '40s (with a career lasting until 1977 on record), and more recently the author of two valuable studies—his autobiography and Tex Ritter's biography—as well as a massive unpublished study of Gene Autry. Bond was a sidekick of sorts, an occasional singer—nearly always in trios on film—but never played any parts which called for heroics. A frequent singing cowboy player, he was never a singing cowboy star; yet his musicianship, songwriting, and prominence in the field deserve considerable mention. Autry's longtime steel player Frank Marvin is, to a lesser extent, a similar case, as is Merle Travis and most members of the vocal groups that provided musical backing and occasional speaking parts in numerous Westerns. There are another whole set of purely country music performers who have likewise made Westerns—or in Roy Acuff's case, perhaps Southeasterns. *Night Train to Memphis* (1944) opens with a shot of a train rumbling through the California mountains, ostensibly on a Nashville to Memphis run. His other films for Republic were, similarly, filmed in California but with a southeastern setting. Among Grand Ole Opry stars, Eddy Arnold made a few musical films for Columbia in the late '40s, and Zeke Clements appeared in a few films, most prominently as the voice of yodeling dwarf Bashful in *Snow White and the Seven Dwarfs*. Cowboy Copas had singing roles in a couple of cheapo Westerns like *Square Dance Jubilee* involving little or no acting. Well into the '50s country singers like Johnny Cash, Faron Young, and Marty Robbins all appeared in super cheapies as quasi-cowboys, the emphasis being more on their latest hit than in production values or stories, the films meant to play in that new phenomenon—drive-ins—in areas where these artists were popular. So vile were most of these things they made PRC Westerns of a decade earlier look like lavish productions. Country music extravaganza films enjoyed a limited vogue in the 1960s—films with titles like *Second Fiddle to an Old Guitar* and *Country Music Cavalcade*—but were basically thin plots pasted lamely around performances of current stars, the heroes played by then up-and-comers like Del Reeves and LeRoy Van Dyke. The trend is not dead—Waylon Jennings starred in a bit of hokum called *Nashville Rebel* (apt title as things turned out) in the late 1960s, while an R-rated drive-in special with Johnny Rodriguez was cranked out just two years ago: *Nashville Girl*.

83. Personal interview with Jimmy Wakely, 25 June 1974.
84. D. Miller, p. 231.
85. Tuska, p. 425.
86. His real name was, of course, James Glosup, and he went on to appear for some time as a singer and musician in southern California, especially noted for his work with Foy Willing and the Riders of the Purple Sage. He is no relation to Seth Ward, another Texan, whose professional name is Jimmy Dean and who is now chiefly noted for his sausage.
87. With Gene Autry, Eddie Dean, Bob Baker, and Rex Allen all having gone from its stages to Hollywood and singing cowboy films, the National Barn Dance proved to be an extraordinarily fertile breeding ground for singing cowboy stars.
88. Personal interview with Eddie Dean, 24 June 1975.
89. Tuska, pp. 455–56.
90. Tuska, pp. 455–56.
91. Bob Birchard, "Gene Autry: Back in the Saddle Again," *Westerner*, Sept.-Oct. 1974, p. 46.
92. Autry, p. 97.
93. D. Miller, p. 230.
94. D. Miller, p. 239.
95. Dellar, p. 147.
96. Dellar, p. 149.
97. Autry, p. 103.

A 1946 Sons of the Pioneers portrait. Clockwise from left: Hugh Farr, Pat Brady, Bob Nolan, Karl Farr, Lloyd Perryman, and Tim Spencer (seated).

THE SONS OF THE PIONEERS
"GUNS ON THEIR HIPS, SONGS ON THEIR LIPS"

by Ken Griffis

In the late '20s and early '30s, Western music was the poor step-child of a segment of American folk music generally referred to as "hillbilly." At that particular juncture of its development, most rural music fell into that classification. It later was to assume the more respectable name of "country." Of course, music performed by "The Blue Yodeler" Jimmie Rodgers, Harry McClintock, Jules Verne Allen, Carl Sprague and other "cowboy singers" of that period was widely accepted for its content, but with the premature departure of Rodgers, Western music lost a measure of its appeal.

However, three young musicians, calling themselves the "Pioneer Trio," appeared on the scene in the mid-'30s, forever changing the world of Western music. No one could possibly have guessed that with their close harmony, trio yodeling and especially their new and exciting songs—"Tumbling Tumbleweeds," "Cool Water," "Way Out There," "Over the Santa Fe Trail," "Happy Rovin' Cowboy," "Tumbleweed Trail" (with dozens more to follow)—would set the standard by which other Western groups would come to be judged.

Interestingly enough, not one of the trio was a "cowboy," or even a Westerner for that matter. The founder and inspirational leader of the new trio was a young farm lad from Ohio with the non-cowboy sounding name of Leonard Slye. Len migrated to California with his family in 1929, finding work not in music, but in picking peaches, driving a truck, or any form of common labor that would put a few dollars in his pocket to help support the family. Slye did have a strong desire to perform, not so much for the sake of being a performer, but to do something he really enjoyed, and get paid for it. In 1931, his first chance came when he and his cousin Stan wheedled their way onto an amateur program at the Inglewood, California radio station KMCS. While the pair received scant notice, Len was offered a spot as a singer with an instrumental group, the Rocky Mountaineers, then appearing on radio KGFJ. According to Len, the Mountaineers had determined that without a vocalist, the group had limited appeal.

Soon after he joined, Len, lacking confidence in doing solo work, suggested that another singer be added. One of the musicians answering his ad for "yodeler for old-time act to travel, tenor preferred," appeared with shoes in hand and blisters on his feet. The aspiring singer, Bob Nolan, explained he lived at the beach where shoes weren't often needed and the long walk from the streetcar line was more than his feet could accept. Though Nolan was not a tenor, had never sung harmony to any degree, and certainly had no experience in harmony yodeling, he impressed Slye with his natural ability to do all required, and was added to the Mountaineers. In late 1931, a beach friend of Nolan's, Bill "Slumber"

The Rocky Mountaineers

Nichols was added, completing the trio. Nichols not only possessed a good singing voice, he had training in classical music as a violinist.

In this Depression era, sponsors of the Mountaineers were few, and pay days sporadic, so it wasn't too surprising that within a few months Bob Nolan took leave of the group. In August, 1932, another ad was placed by Slye, seeking a "harmony yodeler, baritone singer, young one who plays stringed instrument preferred." Verne "Tim" Spencer was not a baritone, had never yodeled and did not play a stringed instrument, yet he responded to the ad and was hired. Like Nolan before him, Tim exhibited an unusual natural ability to harmonize and to yodel.

Within a relatively short period of time, the trio decided a brighter future lay elsewhere and joined the International Cowboys, headed by Bennie Nawahi. Failing to find their niche within this group, the trio, assuming the name O-Bar-O Cowboys, began an unprofitable tour of the Southwest. The most redeeming aspect of this trip was that both Slye and Spencer met their future wives.

A discouraged Len Slye, Tim Spencer, and Bill Nichols struggled back to Los Angeles in the fall of 1933, not at all convinced that a secure future lay ahead. But Len, ever the optimist, soon joined with an eager Spencer and a reluctant Nolan to give it one more try. The new trio took up residence in a Hollywood boarding house that had been the home of movie great Tom Mix, paying the heady sum of nine dollars a week, room and board. Slye was the only one with a job, having hooked on with a nondescript group of musicians, Jack LeFevre and his Texas Outlaws, then appearing on radio KFWB in Hollywood. When he was not on the air, Len would join

THE SONS OF THE PIONEERS

Spencer and Nolan in endless hours of rehearsal, working on a block sound that would come to be their hallmark. Within a few weeks, Nolan and Spencer joined Slye as part of the Outlaws.

Fortunately for the trio, Nolan had spent most of his spare time writing poetry to which he now added music, and what exciting music it was. Most of the early poetry was inspired by interaction with the Arizona desert in his youth. Nolan was to recall:

"You see, I was brought up in the backwoods of Canada, and I came to Tucson, Arizona, after the first World War, right from the tall timber, out to the desert. The desert and prairie country's first impact on me was an entirely new phase of life for me. I would walk right out into the desert, where at first you see and hear nothing, then the desert becomes alive with things few people ever see. It was awe-inspiring to say the least, to wake up in the morning to see the desert beauty, with the sun shining through millions of drops of dew. It was just outstanding."

As a result of their inspiring performances with the Outlaws, the Pioneer Trio was given their own time slot. Slye recalled it became readily apparent that if they were to take a break from singing, instrumental back-up was needed. Deciding to go for the best, the fellows contacted a local fiddler, Hugh Farr, only to find they weren't as irresistible as they had imagined. Hugh knew he was good and it made sense to him not to appear too eager, so he asked them to audition. Hugh remarked, "The fellows broke into their act, singing a medley of some eight songs, all written by Nolan as I recall, and when they had finished I was so greatly impressed I said, 'I'm your man.'" Hugh sensed that his jazzy style of breaks and fills would compliment and further the development of the group's sound. Farr had a feel for the music like few others of his era.

Shortly after joining the trio, Hugh recalled an unusual event taking place. At the start of one of their programs, announcer Harry Hall introduced them as the *Sons of the Pioneers!* The introduction was so disturbing they had difficulty getting the program off to an acceptable start. An indignant quartet approached Hall after the program, demanding an explanation. Hall explained that the fellows were

Sons precursors The Texas Outlaws in 1933. Left to right: Rudy Sooter, Curley Hogg, Spencer, Nolan, Slye, "Half-Pint," Jack LeFevre.

too young to be called pioneers, but they could rightfully be called sons of pioneers. The fellows readily accepted his explanation, and the first verified appearance of the Sons of the Pioneers is in a radio log dated March 3, 1934.

Another notable occurrence took place in that year. They were approached by the Standard Recording Company with a request to record a large number of songs for the label. While the financial arrangement between the series producer, Jerry King, and the fellows left a lot to be desired, the decision to go ahead and record did prove to be one of the best decisions made by the group. The Standard Transcription series, which ran from the mid-'30s into the '50s, was a major springboard to success for the fellows, and many other artists as well. The 12-inch discs, containing some three hundred Pioneer tunes, were distributed to radio stations across the country, bringing widespread attention to the Pioneers' singing talents and their songs in particular. It is difficult to adequately describe the acclaim which the songs of Nolan and Spencer were receiving at that time. Johnny Bond, noted singer/song writer, who lists the classic "Cimmaron, Roll On" among his great songs, recalled:

"I chose Western music as a career from listening to the North Texas stations in the mid-'30s. While it was the Lightcrust Doughboys with Bob Wills, Tommy Duncan and Milton Brown that initially caught my attention, it wasn't long before I began hearing the great transcriptions of the Sons of the Pioneers. As a matter of fact, we were so impressed with the Pioneer harmony that our first trio of Jimmy Wakely, Scotty Harrell, and myself patterned ourselves to a large degree after them. It is interesting to note that I sang 'Tumbling Tumbleweeds' as I auditioned for my first radio job in Oklahoma City. The Sons of the Pioneers have always had color, depth, blend, and feeling."

Part-way through the Standard Transcriptions, an outstanding guitar appears, played by Karl Farr, younger brother to Hugh. The addition of Karl, beyond question, enhanced the group's sound to a notable degree. His talent was greatly admired by other guitarists, several of whom credit him with influencing their style of playing. With Karl's join-

The Sons with KMTR announcer Jimmy McMasters (in suit) in 1936. Lloyd Perryman's (left of McMasters) first job with Sons.

ing, the group widely acknowledged as the *Original Sons of the Pioneers* was complete.

The new Decca Record Company approached the fellows in early 1935, offering them the opportunity to place several of their better-known songs on the label. The Pioneers were third among those signed by the fledgling Decca Record Company, the legendary singer and composer Stuart Hamblen was first, and part-time Western singer, Bing Crosby, was second. The Decca association was to last until 1943.

In 1935, Columbia Pictures signed the Pioneers to a supporting role for their new rising star, Charles Starrett. The fellows found Starrett a most enjoyable individual to work with. It is safe to say that while these Westerns were not works of art, the association proved invaluable as it gave the group wide exposure to a different audience, and it generated a need for a multitude of new songs, a need to which both Nolan and Spencer eagerly addressed themselves. An interesting side note to their songwriting was recounted by Nolan: "The studio gave Tim and I what they called a rough treatment of the story for the next picture. Tim and I would discuss the 'situation' in which the song is to be used. All this was dropped in the hopper and the grind began, guitars tuned, and the framework of music and lyrics would take shape. Then the rest of the gang was called in and the songs tested for harmony possibilities and instrumentation. Out of these sessions come the finished product. Believe it or not, Tim and I once turned out four tunes in 24 hours. One time Columbia's *Outpost of the Mounties* was changed right in the middle of shooting. We were asked to produce a tune as quickly as possible. We went to work and in two hours had a completely new and different original number. It was 'Timber Trail,' and Tim did the trick."

The quantity and quality of the songs written for Columbia Pictures—"A Cowboy Has to Sing," "This Ain't The Same Old Range," "Wind," "When Payday Rolls Around," "Chant of the Wanderer," "Open Range Ahead," "Blue Prairie," "Love Song of the Waterfall," to mention a few—is most impressive and, not too surprisingly, a number of these evergreen tunes are still being performed and recorded some 50 years later. The Pioneers appeared with Starrett through some 30 pictures from 1935 to 1941.

Before we leave the Columbia movie days, it may be of historical interest to touch on the vocal arrangements of the group. In the pictures, it often appeared as if the whole group was singing. However, as on their commercial recordings, most of the

The original Sons of the Pioneers in a 1936 portrait. Nolan (l.), Hugh and Karl Farr (in back), Tim Spencer, and Leonard Slye (soon to be Roy Rogers).

singing was done by the trio only. Nolan and Spencer wrote most of the arrangements specifically to three-part harmony and the group deviated from that only when they wished to include a bass part, which was sung by Hugh Farr who had a deep, beautiful, soft bass voice. But a bass part does not necessarily compliment every song. It was the trio that maintained the continuity of the "Pioneer sound" through the years, even on recordings with orchestral backgrounds. Pat Brady had a good voice, featured mainly on novelty recordings, and on rare occasions when a group sound or double-trio is featured, Karl Farr also sang. Without question, Pat Brady and the Farr brothers were of tremendous importance to the sound of the group, but the trio *was* the sound.

Following their appearance at the Texas Centennial in 1936, Tim Spencer took leave of the group, the result of an internal dispute. His leaving had both negative and positive consequences. Tim's contribution–singing and songwriting–cannot be overstated. His departure from the trio, for two years, did create a need for a new tenor, and if there

The Sons in The Durango Kid *(1940).*

was one crucial decision in the history of the Sons of the Pioneers, it undoubtedly would have been the adding of a young Lloyd Perryman to the trio in late 1936. Perryman, who had appeared with a number of groups in and around the Los Angeles area, was the added ingredient that brought the Pioneer sound to an unequaled level. A natural baritone, Perryman took over the very critical tenor role, giving it a unique, powerful sound. He was endowed with an uncommon ability to harmonize, knew all the harmony parts, and could sing them–from tenor to bass.

Columbia Records sought out the fellows for a series of recordings, which featured the trio of Slye, Nolan, and Perryman, as well as the Farr Brothers. The first session, under the direction of the legendary "Uncle Art" Satherley, took place on October 21, 1937, with Slye leaving then returning to the trio for the final session on December 14.

Shortly before leaving Columbia Pictures, and after Tim Spencer had returned to the trio, the fellows managed several cross-country tours, during which they were very well received. On one of the tours, the Pioneers landed in Chicago, where they found time to participate in NBC's Orthacoustic Transcription series. The over-200 selections recorded for this series are a prime example of the classic sound produced by the trio of Nolan, Spencer and Perryman, backed by Pat Brady and the Farr Brothers.

As he was shopping for a new Stetson in a local Western store in October of 1937, Len Slye overheard a comment to the effect that Republic Pictures was auditioning for a "singing cowboy." Slye recalled: "I saddled up my guitar and headed for the studio, fully confident that I would have no problem getting in for the audition. Although I had been through the front gate many times before, the guard told me in no uncertain terms that I couldn't enter the lot without a pass. Seeing that I couldn't change his mind, I waited around until the cast was returning from lunch. I just stepped in among the group, hoping the guard wouldn't see me. I hadn't gone ten

THE SONS OF THE PIONEERS

steps before he shouted for me to stop. As luck would have it, just as I was about to be thrown off the lot, I heard a familiar voice. It was Sol Siegel, a producer I had come to know. I explained to Mr. Siegel about the audition, and told him I would like to try out. He said he was surprised he hadn't thought of me before. He had already auditioned several other fellows, but invited me into his office for a listen. I was nervous enough, but when he asked me where my guitar was, I nearly dropped in my tracks. I had left it in my car which was parked a couple of blocks away. Mr. Siegel said he would wait, so I raced back for my guitar, returning completely out of breath. I sang 'Tumbling Tumbleweeds,' and a couple of other Pioneer songs. After what seemed an eternity, he remarked that I might just be what they were looking for. I was so excited, I couldn't remember driving home.

"I explained my situation to the fellows and they were very supportive. We discussed a possible replacement, and we all decided it should be Pat Brady, a fellow whose friendship we had enjoyed for sometime. Pat had a pretty fair voice and was a better-than-average bass fiddle player. He was a very likable guy with a great sense of humor. And I think you'll find most of the fellows feel Pat never received the credit due him. He was a great guy. Anyhow, the studio thought a name change was in order, and suggested the last name of Rogers, after Will Rogers, and feeling that Roy was a good American name that went well with Rogers, gave me the name Roy Rogers. I signed my contract with Republic on October 13, 1937."

As soon as their contract with Columbia expired, Rogers invited the Pioneers to join him at Republic in December, 1941, for the filming of *Red River Valley*. Nolan remarked that the fellows were of the opinion that the Republic movies were a notch

Roy Rogers and the Sons, circa 1941.

HOLLYWOOD CORRAL: A COMPREHENSIVE B WESTERN ROUNDUP

The reunited Sons of the Pioneers in January, 1946.

above those they had appeared in at Columbia. Again the need for songs was there and again Nolan and Spencer responded with the likes of "Cowboy Campmeeting," "Everlasting Hills of Oklahoma," "Springtime on the Range Today," "Jubilation Jamboree," "That Pioneer Mother of Mine," "Headin' For the Home Corral," "Coyote Serenade," "A Sandman Lullaby," and "Ne-Ha-Nee." The association with their old friend Roy Rogers lasted through some 40 pictures.

With the coming of WWII, both Perryman and Brady entered the service—Brady ended up in Europe, Perryman in the South Pacific. During the war years, the Pioneers were fortunate to find a replacement in Ken Carson, a fine tenor. Ken performed his trio part well, remaining with the Pioneers until 1947. Competent bass fiddle player and singer Deuce Spriggens and, later, funnyman Shug Fisher filled in for Brady until his return in 1945. Later, Fisher was to return to the group for several years.

In 1945, a recording contract with RCA Victor was signed with the first session taking place on August 8, featuring the trio of Nolan, Spencer, and Carson. With the return of Perryman and Brady in late 1945, the group was again united, and the sound that *is* the Sons of the Pioneers was once again made available to their appreciative fans. The association with RCA was to last for over 20 years, coming to an end in 1969. Countless classic Pioneer sounds are captured on those recordings.

The year 1949 was to see the first major change in the Pioneer trio. Early in the year, his voice troubling him, Spencer gave up performing but continued as manager for the group for several years. Finding a replacement for Spencer was not an easy task. Singing the critical harmony of the Sons of the Pioneers was very difficult, and a good vocalist was not necessarily a good harmony singer. But Tim's replacement, former pop singer Ken Curtis, had an excellent, strong baritone voice that blended well with those of Nolan and Perryman. Prior to his Pioneer association Ken had sung little harmony, certainly nothing to compare with that featured by the group, but with dedication and hard work, Ken made the transition with a minimum of effort. Lloyd Perryman paid Curtis the ultimate compliment when he remarked, "With Ken in the trio, I had confidence that no matter what we sang or how we sang it, it would come out right."

By mid-year (1949), Bob Nolan also decided to call it quits, the strain of traveling and performing having taken its toll. Nolan, by nature a very private person, just walked away, not wishing to meet any further deadlines. One appealing aspect of the trio's sound had been, as Spencer described it, "the bubbling baritone" sound of Nolan. Bob's distinct vibrato was particularly pleasing to Pioneer fans, and a sound that became most closely associated with the Pioneers. To find a voice with that same timbre was thought highly unlikely, but find it they did in the voice of Lloyd Thomas Doss. "Tommy," as he was called, had appeared with several groups in and around the Los Angeles area, and most fortunately for the Pioneers, he not only had the right voice, he was well versed in their music. Without question, Doss made a major contribution to the sounds and success of the Pioneers during the '50s and well into the '60s. The Perryman, Curtis and Doss trio is featured on several RCA recordings, and they were a part of the radio, TV and movie scene as well.

Ken Curtis, fulfilling an urge to get into the movies (and eventually becoming "Festus" on TV's *Gunsmoke*) departed the Pioneers in late 1952, his lead position in the trio being filled by Dale Warren. Dale, whose family had a long tradition in country music, unquestionably met the needs of the group. Warren's true, soft baritone voice blended extremely well with that of Doss and Perryman, and some of the finest Pioneer recordings were made by this trio.

In 1958, feeling he was not getting his fair share of credit for the success of the group, Hugh Farr departed. Neither the Pioneers nor Hugh benefitted

THE SONS OF THE PIONEERS

The Sons in 1952: Hugh Farr (l.), Tommy Doss, Ken Curtis, Lloyd Perryman, and Karl Farr.

from this rash decision. The creative influence of the Farr Brothers was permanently ended with the sudden passing of Karl Farr in 1961. The Pioneers were most fortunate to sign as Karl's replacement the outstanding guitarist, Roy Lanham. Roy, in addition to his splendid musicianship, was a man with a sunny, funny disposition.

With the death of Lloyd Perryman, Dale Warren assumed leadership of the Pioneers in 1977, and the group remains active today. A number of changes have taken place within the group over the past several years. Lead singer Luther Nallie, whose impressive ability must be acknowledged, joined in 1968. Other talented musicians—Billy Armstrong, Rusty Richards, Billy Liebert and Rome Johnson, as well as current group members—must be credited for their exceptional contributions to the success of the celebrated Sons of the Pioneers.

Jack Holt and director John Waters look over script changes before beginning the day's shooting on Paramount's Man of the Forest *(1926)*, based on a Zane Grey story.

WRITERS OF THE PURPLE PAGE
ZANE GREY AND OTHER LITERARY INFLUENCES

by Ed Hulse

The movie Western is so much a visual experience—with the thrilling chases, the picturesque vistas, the thundering herds, and so on—that many of us who enjoy them so much tend to forget the literary influences that shaped the content of this unique film genre. Most of the plots, themes, and characterizations that are second-nature to Western fans have written-word antecedents in the form of plays, novels, and short stories dating back to the turn of the century—and even before.

The works of prolific Western chroniclers such as Stewart Edward White, Clarence E. Mulford, Harold Bell Wright, Max Brand, W. C. Tuttle, William Colt MacDonald, Walt Coburn and many others provided fertile ground for prospecting by Western filmmakers. And even if the works themselves were not specifically adapted for the screen, themes and plot gambits were gleaned from them, forming the basis for hundreds and hundreds of B Western scripts.

Stewart Edward White, for example, was an incredibly popular, accomplished author of "outdoor romances" during the early decades of this century. His well-crafted stories, loaded with factual detail and authentic backdrops, were raided unmercifully by silent-film scenarists, some of whom lifted whole situations from his stories, then changed the characters' names, and dropped them into "original" scenarios. Of course, other filmmakers treated White with more respect. His brilliant short novel *The Killer*, about the kidnapping of a young girl by a cold-blooded, dictatorial ranch owner, was twice brought to the screen. A 1921 version starring Claire Adams and Jack Conway was generally faithful to the original, but the 1932 remake, *Mystery Ranch*, actually improved on the source material by infusing it with a sinister, Gothic style that heightened suspense and redefined the villain in quasi-horror movie fashion.

The novels of Harold Bell Wright made it to the screen in a variety of forms; some were big-budget spectaculars, others were insignificant Bs. Some were faithfully translated from printed page to film frame, others used little more than Wright's titles and character names. In many of his best-remembered stories, Wright unashamedly proffered the notion that Eastern city dwellers were, almost by definition, creatures of moral, spiritual and often physical dissipation; that those who sought redemption and regeneration could always find it in the pure, unsullied West, where nature's majesties and the inherent purity of a simple, rugged lifestyle almost invariably bred strength and character.

Independent producer Sol Lesser sensed the commercial possibilities in adapting Wright's best-selling novels to the screen, and purchased movie rights to most of them. He made, among others, faithfully adapted medium-budgeted versions of *When a Man's a Man* and *The Mine with the Iron Door* in 1924, and sold rights to *The Winning of Barbara Worth* to Sam Goldwyn for an epic 1926 filmization directed by Henry King. Lesser retained rights to the

HOLLYWOOD CORRAL: A COMPREHENSIVE B WESTERN ROUNDUP

Wright properties well into the sound era; he announced a remake of *When a Man's a Man*, to star Reb Russell, for 1933 release. It reached the screen in 1935, substantially altered in incident if not theme, with George O'Brien in the lead role. *The Mine with the Iron Door* underwent even more drastic surgery for its 1936 talkie re-do; barely more than the mine itself survived from the original story. And *Wild Brian Kent* (1936), supposedly adapted from Wright's *The Recreation of Brian Kent*, took little from its source other than the lead character's name and the theme of his regeneration.

Clarence Mulford's popular *Hopalong Cassidy* adventures, as every B-Western fan knows, were turned into movies with scarcely more than character names intact. More's the pity, in some ways, because Mulford—himself an Easterner with an abiding love of Western lore—routinely salted his stories with nuggets of authentic cowboy life, endowing them with a verisimilitude seldom equalled by subsequent Western-story scribes. It is interesting, though, that while the Hoppy movies seldom followed the Mulford novels, they *did* filch plots, themes, and characterizations from other Western tales and incorporated them into the Bar 20 legend.

Max Brand (real name: Frederick Faust) was a struggling pulp writer and poet whose first major Western story, *The Untamed,* was filmed in 1920 as a star vehicle for Tom Mix. It was the first Western film to "co-star" the cowboy's horse and dog, a practice that was still being used a generation later. Mix, as Brand's hero "Whistlin' Dan" Barry, got a major career boost from the amazing success of this thematically simple but extremely affecting story. Several more Brand stories were filmed (including *The Night Horseman,* a 1921 sequel to *The Untamed*, again starring Mix as Dan Barry) during the silent era, but it was the adaptations of *Destry Rides Again*—with Mix in 1932, James Stewart in 1939, and Audie Murphy in 1954—that cemented his reputation in Western film history. Which is more than a little odd, since none of the film versions bear much relationship to the novel.

Of all the Western-story authors whose works

William Farnum shields Mary Mersch (holding Nancy Caswell) in Riders of the Purple Sage *(1918).*

WRITERS OF THE PURPLE PAGE / Zane Grey and Other Literary Influences

inspired and perpetuated the "myth" of the Old West as viewed by Hollywood, none was more influential—or more beloved—than Zane Grey, the Pennsylvania dentist who became one of the world's best-selling authors. It's the Grey *oeuvre*, in fact, that virtually defines the entire genre.

In one of his earliest works, *Riders of the Purple Sage* (1912), Grey penned situations and created characterizations establishing many of the conventions of Western storytelling both on the printed page and the movie screen. The enigmatic, legendary gunfighter, eventually redeemed by a woman's love...the pursuit of vengeance for a crime committed many years before...the fatherless woman of indomitable character...the band of renegades posing as vigilantes...the ruthless badman with his own peculiar code of honor...the hidden valley...the mysterious masked rider whose identity is zealously guarded...the mighty stallion of seemingly limitless speed and power...all this, and much more, in just that one novel.

Of course, Grey's other stories added elements to the Western mystique as well. *Heritage of the Desert* (1910), for example, found Grey on Harold Bell Wright's turf, threading the story of a weak Easterner—ambushed and left for dead in the desert, but nursed and nurtured in the care of a proud pioneer family—into the fabric of an almost Biblical tale of violence and retribution.

The Vanishing American (1925), one of Grey's most heartfelt tales, offered a sympathetic view of the Native American and a tacit indictment of the white man for his shameful treatment of the red man.

Grey had a canny understanding of the motion picture's impact; he licensed his works to movie producers very early on, and personally produced screen adaptations of several of his novels as well. The licensing arrangements varied (Grey did, however, pioneer what became standard film-industry practice: the seven-year licensing period), with Fox Film Corporation getting rights to some of the stories, and Paramount Pictures getting rights to others.

The Grey adaptations of the late Teens and '20s were, for the most part, fairly lavish productions, befitting both the popularity of the subjects and the box-office draw of their stars: Tom Mix, Jack Holt, Richard Dix, Gary Cooper. The Paramount series in particular boasted top production values, enabling the studio to pluck spectacular sequences from them for inclusion in lower-budgeted remakes of the early sound era.

By 1930, with Grey's most prolific period winding

down, the Western had become a firmly established film genre with all its conventions familiar to millions of moviegoers. Relentless repitition of plot and character had blunted the "edge" that seminal Western stories and their earliest screen translations had had; the formularized—in fact, the *ritualized*—horse-opera had by this time distilled the form's most popular elements for incorporation into homogenized "units" of product churned out regularly by major studios and independent producers alike.

Throughout the '30s, though, the Zane Grey Western films maintained surprising levels of interest and quality, whether by accident or design. Many of them, sadly, are unavailable to the general public, although assiduous film collectors have managed to lay their hands on 16mm or videotape copies of many of them, some copied from the only surviving prints.

Just as Tom Mix had starred in '20s remakes of Grey adaptations that had originally featured William Farnum, George O'Brien won top-billing in '30s versions of the same stories, dusted off by Fox for a third go-round. *The Lone Star Ranger* (1930) and *The Last of the Duanes* (1931) were carefully produced and shot on picturesque locations; the occasional crudity of outdoor sound recording ever so slightly mars enjoyment of these well-mounted Westerns. With technological advances coming on

Harry Carey (r.) helps ward off an Indian attack in The Thundering Herd *(1933).*

an almost daily basis, Fox's sound Westerns improved substantially as 1931 progressed. O'Brien's *Riders of the Purple Sage*, arguably the best adaptation of a Grey story produced during the '30s, crammed in most of the author's plot points, reallocating some of the heroics from the subordinate character Venters to the gunfighter Lassiter (as had been the case in the 1925 Mix version), played by O'Brien in a solid black outfit that became his unofficial Western costume throughout much of the decade.

The Rainbow Trail (1932), also starring O'Brien, was even slicker than the previous three films, combining superb pictorial values and an engaging (if not wholly faithful) adaptation of the novel with much better sound recording and a well-chosen musical score consisting of recognizable silent-era cues and newly composed material. *The Golden West* (1932), only nominally faithful to Grey's *The Last Trail*, strikes today's Western scholars as a trifle too ambitious for its budgetary restrictions and B-movie running time. *Robbers Roost* (1933) benefitted from the chemistry between O'Brien and leading lady Maureen O'Sullivan, and stayed within the basic framework of Grey's original premise, but lacked real excitement. *The Last Trail* (1933) and *Smoke Lightning* (1934, allegedly based on *Canyon Walls*) owed little or nothing to their supposed sources.

When Fox turned over production of the O'Brien Westerns to the star himself and independent producer Sol Lesser, who were equal partners in Atherton Productions, several unfilmed Grey properties already purchased by the studio went along with the deal. *The Dude Ranger* (1934), like many Zane Grey Westerns of the '30s, used characters and elements from the original story—but, by this time, so many Western scripters had used the same situations that the Grey film seemed not only lackluster but derivitive as well. Moreover, for some strange reason, Lesser and O'Brien were accepting scripts that virtually eliminated the physical action that was not only a large part of the star's appeal, but also the basic element that endeared Westerns to moviegoers. This lethargy also afflicted *Thunder Mountain*

WRITERS OF THE PURPLE PAGE / Zane Grey and Other Literary Influences

(1935), the last of O'Brien's Zane Grey films and one of his weakest to boot.

With only a couple of exceptions, all the other Zane Grey Westerns released through 1940 came from Paramount. The studio had been making Grey adaptations since 1923, inheriting many of the properties—including *Man of the Forest*, *Desert Gold*, and *The Mysterious Rider*—that the author himself had produced for the screen just a few years earlier (and, hence, not included in the group licensed and renewed by Fox). As mentioned above, the Paramount silents were generally meritorious, although their quality had slipped by the late '20s, as evidenced by the lackluster *Avalanche* and *Stairs of Sand* (both 1929).

Matters didn't improve much with the coming of sound. *Light of the Western Stars*, a complicated Grey story that doesn't lend itself to screen adaptation, provided the basis for a turgid 1930 entry, the first of Paramount's talkie Greys. Both *The Border Legion* (1930) and *Fighting Caravans* (1931) were deemed to be significantly better; the first is unavailable for reappraisal, but the second—despite the presence of Gary Cooper in the leading role and some elaborate exterior work—is only marginally more engaging than *Light of the Western Stars*.

Paramount left the filming of Zane Grey novels to Fox for nearly a year before resuming production in 1932, with Henry Hathaway—then just cutting his directorial eyeteeth—wielding the megaphone. Although the Hathaway series entries—which include *Wild Horse Mesa* (1932), *Heritage of the Desert* (1932), *The Thundering Herd*, *Under the Tonto Rim*, *Man of the Forest*, *Sunset Pass*, *To the Last Man* (all 1933), and *The Last Round-up* (1934)—depend heavily on stock shots from the silent versions, they are reasonably well acted (by young Paramount contractees and venerable Western standbys),

Randolph Scott, Verna Hillie and Vince Barnett in Man of the Forest *(1933). Note the similarity of Scott's shirt and hat to that of Jack Holt on page 384.*

vigorously staged, and nicely photographed. What they are *not* is faithful to the Grey source novels.

The economy measures forced Hathaway and company to occasionally amusing extremes. In *Man of the Forest* (1933), for example, Randolph Scott, the fair-haired, clean-shaven leading man in all but one of the Hathaways, had his hair darkened and sported a thin mustache so that he'd match up with Jack Holt in stock shots lifted from the 1926 silent version. Ingenue Verna Hillie, who always appeared on screen as a blonde, wore a dark wig so she'd match up with Georgia Hale from the earlier film. And Tom Kennedy, a distinctly non-Western type who'd had a part in the silent, repeated his role in the talkie, so as to avoid restaging a scene in which he wrestled with a mountain lion.

Man of the Forest's excessive reliance on stock from its silent adaptation marks it as one of the series' cheapest, although the practice of casting veteran Western performers in the same roles they had played in earlier versions was a constant. (Both Noah Beery and Raymond Hatton, for instance, essayed the same characterizations in silent and sound versions of *The Thundering Herd*.)

To the Last Man (1933) was a happy exception, using only a few brief stock shots and allowing an unusually strong cast—Scott, Beery, Esther Ralston, Jack LaRue, Buster Crabbe, Barton Maclane, Gail Patrick, Muriel Kirkland, Fuzzy Knight, James Eagles, and even Shirley Temple—to carry a well-scripted (but, again, only marginally faithful) Grey adaptation visualizing a frontier family feud. Although the film is surprisingly light on traditional Western action (chases, fistfights, and the like), its solid story, superb staging, and skillful direction make it one of the highlights of the Paramount series.

The Paramount Zane Grey Westerns took two big hits in 1935, when both director Hathaway and star Scott departed for the greener pastures of big-budget movies. The Greys, under the supervision of producer Harold Hurley, were carried by amiable leading men Buster Crabbe and Tom Keene; although still "based" on the famous author's works, the adapted scenarios watered down Grey's plots until virtually all the interesting or recognizable elements had been dissolved. The films became standard B Westerns, still entertaining for their sturdy casts and major-studio production gloss, but hardly distinguishable from the better independently made horse operas.

Crabbe's *Nevada* (1935) and *Arizona Raiders* (1936) rate pretty high in this bunch, although the latter's goofball humor (mostly contributed by Johnny Downs), while entertaining, certainly denigrates the Grey image. The colorless *Drift Fence* and *Desert Gold* (both 1936, both starring Tom Keene, both featuring Crabbe as secondary male lead) offer very little enjoyment, and the stupifyingly awful *Arizona Mahoney* (1937), ostensibly based on Grey's *Stairs of Sand*, is actually adapted from a treatment by vaudevillain Joe Cook, who gets top billing in this dismal effort. (Somebody at Paramount felt Cook was owed a favor; using his treatment as the basis of an already-announced film got someone, possibly Hurley, off the hook without adding a new film to the studio's release schedule.)

Thunder Trail (1937) and *Born to the West* (1938) emerge as two of the best post-Hathaway entries in the series. Not surprisingly, neither resembles its credited source save for the inclusion of some character names. But *Thunder Trail* tells an oft-repeated Western story—two brothers, separated in their youth, grow up on opposite sides of the law but ultimately unite to combat the men responsible for their separation—with real flair. Director Charles Barton, saddled with Gilbert Roland as a leading man (totally removed from the character as described by Grey), plows through the story with gusto, bringing it in at a very taut six reels, immeasurably aided by the crisp photography of Karl Struss, the supporting performances of Charles Bickford, Marsha Hunt, and J. Carrol Naish, and some well-spotted musical cues lifted from big-budget Paramount movies.

Born to the West has many of the same attributes, along with two immensely likable stars in John Wayne and Johnny Mack Brown (although Wayne's top billing tips off the viewer that he'll wind up with fetching Marsha Hunt). It's even shorter and punchier, although the reissue version titled *Hell Town* incorporated meaningless stock footage to pad the picture out to a full six reels.

Paramount's involvement with the novels of Zane Grey ended on a high note, thanks to producer Harry Sherman, who brought the skill and experience of his *Hopalong Cassidy* unit (players and technicians alike) to four remakes released between 1938 and 1940. Sherman turned out his Grey films without resorting to the use of stock footage, and instructed his scripters to go back to the original novels, rather than Paramount's earlier versions, for inspiration.

So it was that Sherman's *The Mysterious Rider* (1938), starring Douglas Dumbrille in the title role, was much closer to the book than either the 1927 Jack Holt version or the 1933 Kent Taylor version.

WRITERS OF THE PURPLE PAGE / Zane Grey and Other Literary Influences

Leif (billed as Glenn) Erikson and Buster Crabbe in Nevada *(1935).*

Gilbert Roland (r.) and J. Carrol Naish in Thunder Trail *(1937).*

HOLLYWOOD CORRAL: A COMPREHENSIVE B WESTERN ROUNDUP

Heritage of the Desert (1939) doesn't sit well with most of today's B-Western buffs, primarily because they dislike Donald Woods in the lead role. And yet Woods, playing the Eastern tenderfoot left to die in the desert, is well cast in the part as originally conceived by Grey. Moreover, the utilization of non-Western players Evelyn Venable, C. Henry Gordon, Robert Barrat, and Paul Guilfoyle lends this *Heritage* more interest than it might otherwise have had, staffed with overly familiar horse-opera regulars.

Even better is *Knights of the Range* (1940), a model of what can be achieved on a limited budget with a good script, careful direction (with an eye on capturing little bits of business for added character delineation), beautiful cinematography, and an evocative musical score. Russell Hayden, doing double duty for Sherman as Hopalong Cassidy's sidekick Lucky Jenkins, came to the fore in this Grey after assuming secondary roles in *Mysterious Rider* and *Heritage of the Desert*. Jean Parker, adorable in period Western costume, contributes a feisty characterization far superior to the performances of the general run of B-Western leading ladies.

Sherman's *The Light of Western Stars* (1940), Paramount's third try at that difficult Grey property, was somewhat more entertaining but certainly no more faithful to the source than the previous two versions. Its best asset: a strong cast, led by Victor Jory and including Tom Tyler, J. Farrell MacDonald, and even Alan Ladd. That rung down the curtain on Paramount's Zane Grey series.

There were a few oddball Grey adaptations— Republic's 1940 turn at *The Border Legion*, virtually eviscerated to provide a streamlined Roy Rogers series entry, and Fox's 1941 *Riders of the Purple Sage* and *The Last of the Duanes*, the studio's fourth go-round for these venerable Western classics, both starring a handsome if colorless

Victor Jory (pointing) warns J. Farrell MacDonald (in white shirt and vest), Rad Radford, Eddie Dean, Noah Beery Jr. and the King's Men in The Light of Western Stars *(1940).*

392

WRITERS OF THE PURPLE PAGE / Zane Grey and Other Literary Influences

Robert Mitchum (l.), Guinn "Big Boy" Williams, and Richard Martin (at right) formed a heroic trio in Nevada *(1944).*

George Montgomery, and the same year's *The Lone Star Ranger* with John Kimbrough—before RKO struck a deal with Paramount (and, presumably, Grey himself) for film rights to some of the author's oft-filmed works.

It was 1944, and RKO was in a spot. With B-Western star Tim Holt in the service, but B-Western demand still high, the studio decided it needed to have a familiar marketing peg on which to hang its new oaters—until such time as a sagebrush star could be developed. Apparently, the still-potent Grey name (and recognizable titles) were felt to carry the requisite punch.

It's RKO, in fact, that we have to blame for the disappearance of Paramount's talkie versions of *Wild Horse Mesa, Under the Tonto Rim, Wanderers of the Wasteland, Sunset Pass,* and *Nevada.* As part of the deal, Paramount apparently surrendered its original negatives as well as rights to the films themselves. (Unstable nitrate prints do exist on some of these Paramounts at the UCLA Film & Television Archive—but for how long?)

Nevada (1944) kicked off RKO's cycle of Zane Grey-based B Westerns. Robert Mitchum took the title role, and was supported by sidekicks Guinn "Big Boy" Williams and Richard Martin, the latter introducing (in Westerns, anyway) his characterization of "Chito Jose Gonzales Bustamante Rafferty." It was a solid, unpretentious Western, with good action and major-studio production gloss—but it bore even less resemblance to Grey's novel than did the Paramount versions. *West of the Pecos* (1945) reunited Mitchum and Martin, and used as its storyline the scenario written for a 1934 version, produced by RKO, that had starred Richard Dix. It got good reviews—better than it deserved, actually—and helped springboard Mitchum into bigger-budgeted movies.

Still without a resident B-Western star, RKO scaled back production, but continued to utilize the Grey name on those infrequent occasions when it deigned to make a low-budget oater. James Warren, rightly pegged by *Hollywood Corral*'s Don Miller as a handsome but ineffectual leading man, appeared in *Wanderer of the Wasteland* (1945), *Sunset Pass* (1946), and *Code of the West* (1947), none of which elicited even the slightest enthusiasm.

With several Zane Grey properties still unfilmed,

393

HOLLYWOOD CORRAL: A COMPREHENSIVE B WESTERN ROUNDUP

Martha Hyer and Tim Holt in Thunder Mountain (1947).

WRITERS OF THE PURPLE PAGE / Zane Grey and Other Literary Influences

Sheila Ryan and John Kimbrough in Lone Star Ranger *(1942).*

James Warren

RKO teamed returning Tim Holt with Richard Martin and assigned the pair to producer Herman Schlom, who'd assembled RKO's current Western unit for the Mitchum pictures. Holt's Zane Grey pictures, *Thunder Mountain, Under the Tonto Rim,* and *Wild Horse Mesa* (all 1947 releases), are possibly his best; all his subsequent pictures drew on them in their use of corresponding pictorial values, directorial technique, pace, musical scoring, and so on. *Thunder Mountain* (1947), which may be the best of the three, has a curious production history. Astute Grey fans will no doubt recognize its basic plot—feuding families in the West wipe each other out, leaving the daughter of one and the son of another to marry and extinguish forever the flickering flames of the old quarrel—as that of *To the Last Man*. And, indeed, the Holt film went into production under that title; stills from it are coded "TLM," the title's initials. But sometime between conception and release, RKO learned to its dismay that *To the Last Man* hadn't been cleared in the deal with Paramount. Hence the change to *Thunder Mountain*, a meaningless substitute.

The Holt entries were very successful, reestablishing the star as a top B-Western draw and thus eliminating the need to license well-known properties in which to feature him. Exactly 100 films had been produced based—officially, at least—on Zane Grey's stories. In the intervening 45 years, only a handful of feature films have drawn on his works for inspiration.

Changing tastes, both in fiction and film, diminished Grey's appeal in the atomic age, and while many of his books remain in print, he's not nearly as popular as he was decades ago. His plots, themes, and characters, so much beloved by readers of the 20th Century's first half, have long since been assimilated into Hollywood formula screenwriting. It's all the more amazing, then, that so little of his stories were interpolated into their film adaptations. But we should never forget just how profound an impact Grey had on the Western. Without him, there couldn't have been a *Shane*, or a *Stagecoach*, or, for that matter, a *True Grit*. Simply put, without him the genre, if it had survived at all, would have been infinitely poorer.

John Wayne in New Frontier *(1939).*

"GEE DAD, IT'S A MONOGRAM!"
STYLES AND SIGNATURES IN THE B WESTERN

by William K. Everson

The perception of studio styles and differences is really two-pronged. There are the characteristics that first attracted us to a studio's product, in our childhood, when action and the charisma of a specific star guided our responses. And there are the more mature considerations of story values and production quality that meant little to us in childhood. Finally, of course, there is the complicating factor that those qualities were not always consistent, and could—and usually did—change drastically with the years, as production costs rose and boxoffice receipts dwindled.

I'm going to start on a purely personal note with my first familiarity with any kind of studio identity. I grew up in the London suburb of Hayes, a town a mile or so from what is now the huge Heath Row Airport area. In the early '30s, Hayes was split into two well-separated areas, and the main part of town, where I saw almost all of my early movies, had only one cinema; the long-extinct Regent. It boasted a rather tatty transparent black curtain from the center of which radiated golden streaks, simulating a sunburst. One of my earliest and most pleasant movie memories is of the Columbia trademark appearing behind that curtain, its shimmering, flickering lights welding with the sunburst, and being welcomed with a roar of approval from an impatient (and largely juvenile) audience to create a visual/aural impression that I can recall and savor to this day. Automatically, I came to expect the best of any Columbia movie. In those days they had Buck Jones and Tim McCoy riding their ranges—my very first Western was a McCoy—and they had Jack Holt protecting the innocent (luckily, I missed a few in which he was less virtuous) in urban settings. Within a short time, I came to know and subliminally recognize the difference in Universal, Republic, RKO Radio and Paramount Westerns (about the only ones that played that theater), but Columbia made the biggest earliest impression. Perhaps it was because they *looked* the most realistic—not that a child of three, getting his introduction to Westerns, was looking for or would understand realism. The streets were cramped and dusty, the saloons ramshackle, and the stagecoaches looked as though they'd fall apart if someone as substantial as Dick Cramer stepped aboard.

This is not the place to discuss the *merits* of the early Columbias, except to say that they were considerable, with good directors, good stars, and often strong plots. And the *look* of economy is what gave them that aura of conviction. Unfortunately, as the '30s wore on and B Westerns lost many of their inroads into adult markets, and especially after Columbia lost Tim McCoy and Buck Jones, the Columbia B Western became a more and more standardized product. Their impressive Western street was used so often—in big Westerns and small—with so little re-dressing or innovative camera angling, that it became a prop rather than a location. Their sound effects—fistic sloshings and round, mellow, non-vicious gun-shots in particular—became

397

HOLLYWOOD CORRAL: A COMPREHENSIVE B WESTERN ROUNDUP

On location with Ken Maynard, director Spencer Bennet (seated with legs crossed) and the crew of a 1936 Columbia Western.

so pat and mechanical that one could recognize a Columbia B even if the projector lamp blew before the main title.

The standardization extended even more dangerously to the casting: Iris Meredith or Ann Doran as the heroine; Edward Le Saint (who usually only made it to the end of reel one) as her father; Dick Curtis, Kenneth MacDonald and Alan Bridge as the major villains; Ed Cobb, Ernie Adams and Dick Bottiler as their hangers-on. The plots were as standardized as their casts, little more than a vaguely connected series of fights and chases.

Without exaggeration, I think you could name *any* Gene Autry, Hopalong Cassidy or George O'Brien Western at random, and without a moment's hesitation I (or any relatively experienced B Western viewer) could give you a reliable critique and synopsis of the film, even if its title had no connection whatsoever with its content. But not only would it be an impossible task with the Columbias (from 1940 on at least), it wouldn't even be worth the effort. Apart from the added quality in the first two or three entries in any new series (especially the Bill Elliotts), and those few that had unusually strong plots (Charles Starrett's *Two Gun Law*), or were directed by Joseph H. Lewis and thus had memorable editing and other stylistics, it's difficult to remember the Columbias individually–only as being good or bad, or (in later years) unacceptably full of stock footage. Plot-wise, about the only surprises they came up with was in finding new things for Charles Starrett to do in cutaways from songs by the Sons of the Pioneers: shaving in one, grooming his horse in another!

Studio economies also affected the Columbias rather too obviously: when times were good, we had excellent musical scores and plenty of running inserts; when the economic bite was on, no inserts, no music, and very often a curtailing of action or plot to lop a day off the shooting schedule. (The worst offender in that respect was the Jack Holt non-Western *Roaring Timbers*, in which *none* of the problems were solved, an action climax was avoided, and we went from a commiseration over disasters to Holt being congratulated by the heroine for having met the deadline on time after and despite all!) However, in fairness, while *collectively* the Columbias (especially of the later years) do seem a standardized bunch, *individually* most of them had the action and the entertainment value, machine-made or not, to keep both customers and exhibitors happy.

RKO Radio was the very opposite of Columbia. Quality came first with them, and even in the '50s, when the TV competition was hitting hard and everybody else was either abandoning B Westerns or cutting costs to the bone, they continued to shoot on good locations, to break up sequences into well-edited shots (rather than emulate the Monogram method of long, monotonous takes), to use good scores and running inserts, and to disregard for as long as they could the fact that this care and pride was tripling their budgets. First in the exceptional George O'Brien series (I'm not forgetting the earlier Tom Keenes, but there was little studio differential of Westerns in the early '30s) and then in the Tim Holts that followed, RKO offered above-average scripts and top production values, especially photographic.

If there was anything remotely standardized about the RKOs, it was the musical scoring, which often sounded as though it was copying the Republic style or had even entered into a secret conspiracy with them to re-orchestrate the same music. O'Briens such as *Lawless Valley* (1938) and *Racketeers of the Range* (1939), and Holts such as *Under the Tonto Rim* (1947) and *The Arizona Ranger* (1948) demonstrate best what the RKO Westerns were all about. They were never barrages of non-stop action, and took time out for comedy and serious romance—which is probably why as youngsters we *enjoyed* them, but put them in second place behind the Maynards and the Browns, their superior values becoming apparent only as we matured.

Surely no one reading *this* book needs any endorsement of Republic, which earned its bread and butter from Westerns, and knew just how to make them. True, action was the common ingredient (except in a few overblown Autrys and Rogers) and Republic knew how to slam it over in grand style, backed up by top stuntwork, superb musical scores, and—one of its major assets—the creative and exhilerating breaking up of major action sequences into almost Eisensteinian mathematical precision by the innovative directing/editing methods of its top director, William Witney.

Each Republic series (in the studio's heyday) had its own unique style, its own kind of pacing, and

Veteran assistant director C. C. "Buddy" Coleman got his first solo directorial credit on Code of the Range *(1936); he's flanked by Mary Blake and Charles Starrett.*

HOLLYWOOD CORRAL: A COMPREHENSIVE B WESTERN ROUNDUP

Ray Whitley and George O'Brien prepare to take a scene from Renegade Ranger *(1938).*

writing tailored to specific stars, so that even within a series there might be a *formula* but never a lazy standardization. Since they never slummed with their Westerns, the pains Republic took with them always showed—especially in the early *Three Mesquiteers* series and in those Autrys (*Home on the Prairie, Colorado Sunset*) and Rogers (*Heart of the Golden West, Man from Music Mountain*) made when the stars had confirmed their huge boxoffice pull and were being rewarded (and the exhibitors given bonuses) with added budgets and production values, but were not yet being swamped with *too much* size and music.

Photographic quality in the Republics of the '30s and early '40s was superb: crystal clear, atmospheric, shimmering, shot against a variety of impressive outdoor locations, and making the very most of smooth running inserts. Republic was very proud of its new camera truck in the mid-'30s, and used it to the utmost, often swinging the protagonists (and the audience) into the action from a variety of angles and vantage points, creating the same sense of participating excitement that one got from such much larger sequences as the initial clash of the aerial armadas in *Hell's Angels* or the climactic charge in *The Charge of the Light Brigade*.

Put it down to rose colored nostalgia if you like (although re-viewing of the films would seem to deny that), but it seems to me that the old Republic chose to shoot only when the sun was out (which admittedly it usually was in California locations) and the visual image would be bright and arresting. If there *was* bad weather, it was usually and creatively turned to good dramatic effect, as in the storm sequence in Autry's *Rootin' Tootin' Rhythm* (1937).

The loss of this visual beauty was the element most apparent when Republic (like other studios) began to economize drastically in the late '40s. First the large posse and gangs of outlaws were cut down to just three riders, then the stock footage sequences became more and more recognizable through over-use, the heroes tended to dress less individually (in drab if more realistic garb, the easiest to intercut with stock footage) but, worst of all, shooting went right ahead on dull, overcast days, and even the film stock used on release prints seemed to lack luster. The Monte Hales and the Allan Lanes continued to supply the action that the fans wanted, but perhaps only the Rex Allens directed by William Witney seemed to retain the exuberance and care that one once took for granted in such '30s classics (and I use the word deliberately, though within the boundaries of the B Western) as *Heart of the Rockies* (1937) and *Outlaws of Sonora* (1938). But at that, even to the end, Republic maintained a lively pace denied to the films of its nearest rival, Monogram.

Monogram always existed in the shadow of Republic. It also suffered from delusions of would-be grandeur, and slowly but constantly tried to move into the big-time, a pattern that eventually caused it to self-destruct. Westerns were important to Monogram as a reliable bread-and-butter product, but the studio didn't really *respect* them. Moreover, the European market was important to Monogram, and most European distributors, working in single-bill territories, didn't really want B Westerns, certainly not en masse.

Monogram had a good Western ranch and street, a succession of good stars (over the years including Bob Steele, John Wayne, Tim McCoy, Buck Jones, Johnny Mack Brown, Ken Maynard, Hoot Gibson and Bill Elliott), an exceptionally good (and sympathetic-to-Westerns) producer in Scott R. Dunlap, and some first-rate directors ranging from Lambert Hillyer and Spencer Bennet to Lesley Selander. But Monogram had the infuriating habit of starting off each new series with a bang, providing above-average production values, scripts and action, then cutting back drastically when the series was established, providing a modicum of quality so that audiences wouldn't abandon the series in question,

Look carefully and you'll spot the camera (in lower right) filming this chase scene with heavies Jack Shannon (l.), Monty Montague and Roy Barcroft, shot for an unidentified Republic Western of the '40s.

HOLLYWOOD CORRAL: A COMPREHENSIVE B WESTERN ROUNDUP

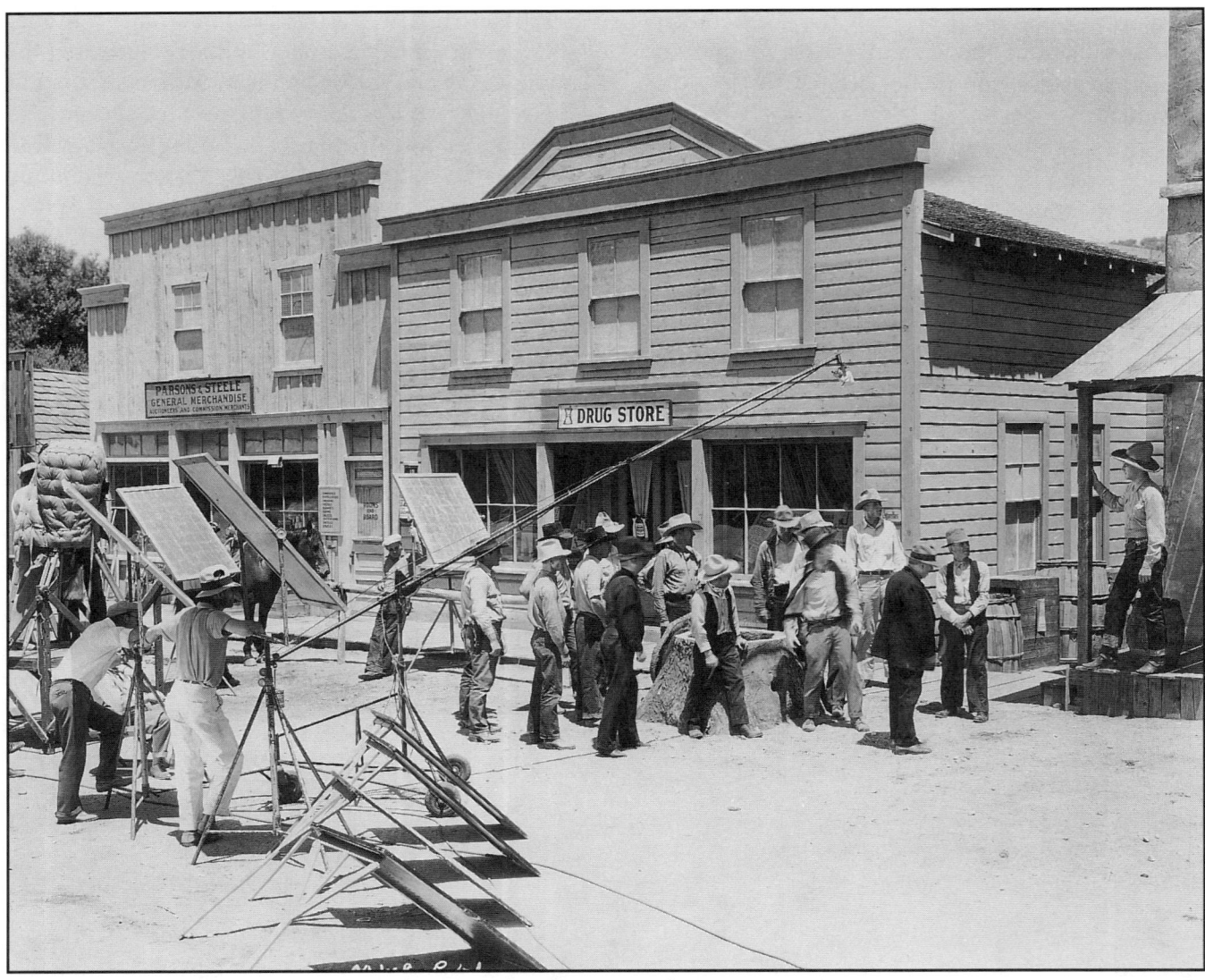

John Wayne (r., on porch) runs through a scene for The Star Packer *(1934).*

but clearly losing enthusiasm and transferring it to the next new series that came along. Nevertheless, Monogram did come up with some gems: *Beauty and the Bandit* (1946) with Gilbert Roland, *Riders of the Dawn* (1937) with Jack Randall, *The Gentleman from Texas* (1946) with Johnny Mack Brown, and the first three in the *Rough Riders* series with Buck Jones, Tim McCoy and Raymond Hatton.

The decline and rapid formularization of that last-named series (underlined by the fact that its many almost identical unused scripts were just turned over to Johnny Mack Brown when the series came to an end due to Buck Jones' tragic death) is typical of the path that most Monograms followed. Their camerawork was good but never as creative as at Republic, and while individual series—particularly *The Rough Riders*—did offer some innovative original scoring (although even the distinctive *Rough Riders* music had its roots in the music of such earlier Monograms as *Wolf Call*), the studio's Westerns relied far too much on the repetitive, formless themes of Frank Sanucci.

If it's more difficult to summarize Monogram Westerns than it is those of Republic, it's probably because the studio operated, in a sense, under the kind of producer system common at M-G-M. Anything given to Scott R. Dunlap, like the initial Rough Riders, Cisco Kid and Jack Randall Westerns, emerged as an automatically superior product. A producer like Edward Finney, whose tenure was pretty much guaranteed through his association with the popular Tex Ritter, was more concerned with proving how ingenuiously economical he could be. Conversely, independent producers used, from experience, to making a buck go further, were given a temporary berth that might turn into a longer one, and often tried much harder. Maurice Conn, who had made an excellent series of independent Westerns with Kermit Maynard, produced some of the earlier Jack Randalls, and his *Gunsmoke Trail*

(1938) is a model of how to make a thoroughly expert and *slightly* different Western on a very modest budget. Even Republic would have been proud of that one.

To its credit, Monogram *did* experiment with the format occasionally: the '50s Bill Elliotts were strong, mature, and unconventional, clearly trying to emulate the style and content of the silent William S. Harts. One of them, *Topeka,* was not only a casual remake of Hart's *The Return of Draw Egan,* but for some inexplicable reason it featured extensive use of the mobile camera, and looked like something from the Germanic heyday of Freund and Murnau!

What Monogram was to Republic, PRC was to Monogram. The less said about PRC the better, except that in its earlier days at the very beginning of the '40s, when a production dollar went much further, the charisma of Tim McCoy, Bob Steele, and Buster Crabbe helped to make the studio's horse operas fairly entertaining. But shabby sets, nonexistent plots, unrehearsed acting, unconvincing stuntwork, murky photography (with a stress on day-for-night shooting, eliminating the need for background detail) and all-around shoddiness made the bulk of their fare suitable only for the most undemanding action fans. Fights and chases there were a'plenty, but the musical scores, many of them from Lee Zahler, made even Frank Sanucci's work (by comparison) worthy of presentation at the Vienna Opera House. Only in their development of Eddie Dean into a popular new singing cowboy, and their utilization of Cinecolor for some of his early films, did they come up with some half-way decent Westerns like *Colorado Serenade* (1946). But after Dean came Lash LaRue, and a descent to the depths—and beyond—quickly followed.

Universal's characteristics are complicated by a mid-'30s change of ownership and policy. Its earlier Westerns with Tom Mix, Ken Maynard and especially Buck Jones all bore the imprint and style of those stars, with the Jones films coming off best. Also, apart from the regular production of medium-budget Westerns like *Men of Texas* (1942) and *Badlands of Dakota* (1941), Universal kept only one series going at a time, so that standardization set in rather quickly. If there was one common denominator to the Universal Bs, it was slickness, characterized by excellent (if limited and overused) musical scores, superbly (and uniquely) staged chase scenes with exceptionally fluid mobile camerawork, and frequent, expertly presented and vigorous fistfights.

Nobody could complain about the early Johnny Mack Browns, which were carefully made and full of action, with plots that were often reworkings of older Buck Jones stories. The series maintained a high level of expertise, and such films as *West of Carson City* (1940), *Riders of Pasco Basin* (1940), *Man from Montana* (1941) and *Stagecoach Buckaroo* (1942) are at least in terms of more than fulfilling audience expectations, among the best B Westerns ever made. Some of the more enterprising (like Bob Baker's *Courage of the West,* 1937, and Johnny Mack Brown's *Arizona Cyclone,* 1941) were directed by Joseph H. Lewis, and were full of innovative directorial, editing and cinematographic devices never found in the more traditional entries in the series done by Ray Taylor or Lewis Collins. Even though the energy and the budgets ran out as Universal reached the end of the B Western trail in the mid-'40s (Johnny Mack Brown by then having left for Monogram), the studio's Westerns always remained slick and streamlined, as formularized and typecast in their way as the Columbias, but in more recognizable and attractive packages.

Fox had an impressive series with George O'Brien in the very early '30s, hardly Bs despite their short running time, distinguished by an admirable use of landscape (which suddenly became rockier and more spectacular for the massed riding and cliff-fight climaxes) and a pictorial style still influenced by the low-key photography that paid homage to the Murnau period of the late '20s. However, in 1934 Fox farmed out their George O'Brien series to independent producer Sol Lesser, and the style became his rather than that of the studio.

Periodically Fox would return to the B Western, but mainly to introduce a new star, such as George Montgomery, whose rise to popularity was so rapid that he made only two Zane Greys before promotion. He passed the torch to John Kimbrough, whose decline was equally rapid (two pictures, to be precise). These four Westerns, and especially the Montgomery *Riders of the Purple Sage,* were blessed with superior production qualities and, like all Fox films, *looked* great because the studio had its own laboratory and took pains to see that skills in camerawork and art direction were not minimized by shoddy printing at the labs. However, Fox also displayed a lack of *experience* with the B Western. The 1941 *Riders of the Purple Sage,* first-rate though it was, diminished its excitement potential by the elimination of one of the most essential ingredients of the small Western, the musical score. Its *Cisco Kid* series with Cesar Romero likewise boasted top photographic and other production values, large interior sets well peopled with character actors and extras, but spent too much time on comic byplay and not enough on movement. The directors of these later Fox B Westerns were drawn from the ranks of their stock B directors—James Tinling, for example—rather than from those who had a special talent for the Western, such as David Howard of the earlier O'Brien series.

Apart from the very impressive silent Tim McCoy series (two-thirds historical Westerns, one-third historical action films set elsewhere), M-G-M made no regular B series, obviously considering it beneath their dignity. Perhaps it is just as well. For unless a major director like King Vidor made a Western for them (such as *Billy the Kid*) and insisted on major location work, M-G-M just *loved* to keep their Westerns *indoors,* the narrative unreeling in standing township sets if possible. If exteriors *were* needed, they were shot against the most obvious, stylized and unconvincing "outdoor" sets possible. 1939's *Let Freedom Ring* is an outstanding offer in this regard; so, to a slightly lesser degree, was the Wallace Beery *The Bad Man of Brimstone* (1937), which had one or two genuine outdoor scenes for punctuation, and did everything else in the studio. Too, when budget or time ran out—not a major consideration at M-G-M, but it happened—they could be as ruthless as Columbia had been on *Roaring Timbers* (1937) in saving money and time. *The Bad Man of Brimstone* has an interestingly complicated plot and a fine set of villains, all of which build up to a promising climax. But when it comes, all the chasing, showdowns and confrontations are done via one lightning *montage*—a fascinating experience for editing students, but a real downer, not to say cheater, for movie audiences. The few times M-G-M moved into medium-budget Westerns (several with James Craig), those pedestrian and studio-bound conditions prevailed.

Warner Bros. was the very antithesis of M-G-M. No sneering at the B pictures here, no false pride in a studio image. Just the opposite, in fact. Every Warner B movie looked like a Warner A movie, the only difference being in star power and length. If the 50-minute *Bullets for O'Hara* was a miniature *The Roaring '20s*, then every Dick Foran six-reeler had the pace and pep of *The Oklahoma Kid*—not necessarily by design, but because the studio machinery worked that way. But it wasn't necessarily, especially in the case of the Westerns, an asset. As a youngster, I loved the Dick Foran Westerns—perhaps because, cannily, the Warner Bros. were aiming them at youngsters. They were usually packed with action and sported easy to follow plots. Dick Foran, with ultra-simplistic dialogue, was a Big-Brother type whose roles frequently had him befriending and protecting young boys. The very first one in the series, *Moonlight on the Prairie* (1935), set up this concept, and was even smart enough to have Foran sing to the youngster rather than to the heroine.

Seeing the Forans again today, one is impressed by the skill with which the juvenile-aimed formula was applied, and amazed by their *over*-produced quality. Films like *Trailin' West* (1936) move so fast that they seem to be covering *narrative* time in an hour as well as just running time. With no footage wasted on subtleties, complications and misunderstandings arise and are acted upon and solved in nothing flat. Fights and chases are fast and furious—no stinting on quality—but all just a little shorter than they should be, as though every second is precious. The supporting casts are full of every pioneer and villain type who was not otherwise working that day, and the musical scores are so mathematically cut to the bone that their climaxes crescendo and die away just a second or two before the accompanying action does, so that one is always just a shade *ahead* of what is going on on the screen. Vastly entertaining, quite unique among B Westerns, surprisingly light on comedy relief, they are made without any apparent awareness of their lack of moments of repose, or of the state of subliminal exhaustion created by the non-stop onslaught of music and action.

I have left Paramount until last, since, just as they made some of the most economy-conscious As, so did they make B Westerns and otherwise—superior to almost anybody else's. Photographic excellence was one dependable feature: let DeMille shoot his epic Westerns in a studio with obvious back-projection screens, but not the B units. Harry Sherman's Zane Grey Westerns of the later '30s, and his Hopalong Cassidys, made fine use of the outstanding outdoor locations in the Lone Pine area. Indeed, even those Cassidys that were lax on action and overly-emphatic on boosting (very unsubtly) Cassidy's values as a role-model for youth (his self-sacrifice and rough-hewn idealism was a little hard to take at times) were a visual treat. Many of the later Cassidys did beef themselves up considerably in terms of action, and their only consistent handicap was a fairly weak record in terms of interesting and attractive leading ladies and virile villains, the latter perhaps a deliberate ploy to downplay William Boyd's inexpertise in fisticuffs.

But whatever their strengths or weaknesses, the Cassidy Westerns always *tried*: one never felt that

"GEE DAD, IT'S A MONOGRAM!" / Styles and Signatures in the B Western

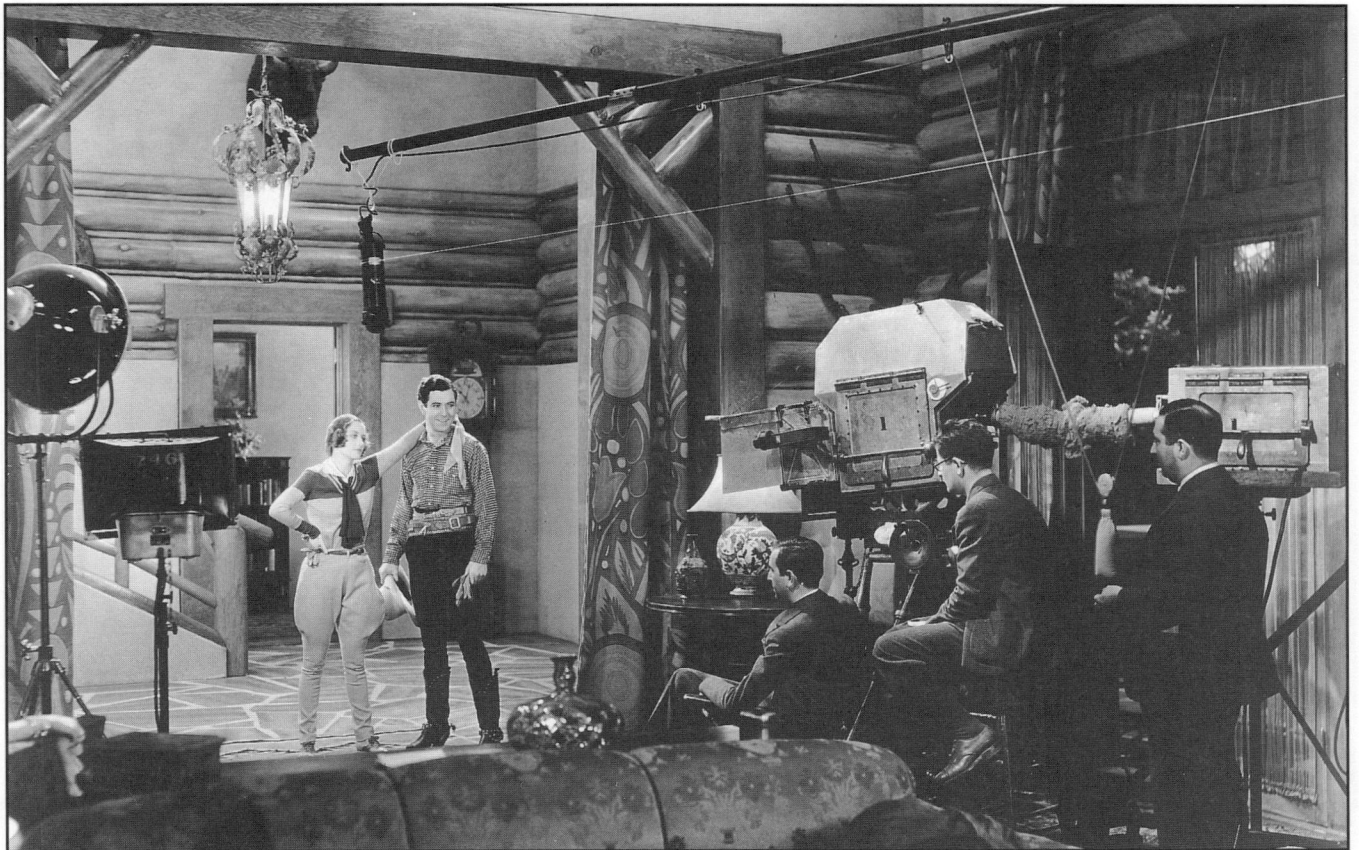

Joan Crawford and Johnny Mack Brown rehearse a scene for Montana Moon *(1930).*

they were just program fodder being churned out to meet contracts, and they were aimed at adults as much as juveniles. Their running times bore this out: if the plot warranted it, seven or eight reels as opposed to the usual five or six was not unusual. The Zane Greys from the early '30s, despite much reliance on stock footage from the silent versions, were on the whole an outstanding group, most of a very high quality, and even the relative duds still had considerable redeeming features. The casts (Randolph Scott, Buster Crabbe, Harry Carey, Noah Beery, Tom Keene, Monte Blue, Esther Ralston, Gilbert Roland) were superior; the plots, more faithful to Grey than usual, strong and unpredictable; and the photographic and other values high. Among the best: *To the Last Man* (1933), *Sunset Pass* (1933), *Nevada* (1935), the Lesley Selander version of *The Mysterious Rider* (1938) and *Thunder Trail* (1937), the last an absolute model on how to cram a top cast, action, plot, superb photography (Karl Struss) and real, loving care (not having been made before as a silent, Paramount didn't even look for stock and shot everything fresh) into only one hour. Heresy though it may be, I think there's more love of the medium and more casual craft exhibited in *Thunder Trail* than in all the overblown pretentions of *Dances With Wolves*–release print, restored version *or* Director's Cut!

William Boyd with Harry "Pop" Sherman, the producer of the Hopalong Cassidy series for Paramount and United Artists.

THE BOTTOM LINE
LOW FINANCE IN THE REEL WEST
by Karl Thiede

The ongoing interest in B Westerns and their stars—thanks to such groundbreaking books as Fenin and Everson's *The Western: From Silents to Cinerama* and Everson's *The Western*, as well as the ongoing attempts by film collectors to keep memories of the genre alive via annual Western Film Festivals—is certainly welcome, as mainstream cinema historians have always downplayed the influence of low-budget product on the movie industry. Even the best reference tomes give short shrift to the hundreds of inexpensive series Westerns that were staples of motion picture exhibition during the '30s, '40s and early '50s—an injustice at least partially rectified by authors Miller, Everson, and even the contributors to this volume.

In their enthusiasm for the B Westerns, however, many devotees forget the economic imperative that determined the production and distribution of cheapie horse operas. The driving force behind series Westerns was not the crafting of artistic works that could compete for screen time with A movies playing the big theater circuits, but rather the efficient assembly-line production of entertaining films, scaled down in both budgets and running times, that could be profitably marketed to the smaller chains and neighborhood theaters (especially in rural areas and the South). The B Westerns were made with rigid financial considerations in mind, their budgetary outlays almost exclusively based on predetermined estimates of their earning power. And, like any other mass-produced commodity, they were cranked out with little regard for individual unit quality, but just enough dedication to collective acceptability to satisfy marketplace demands.

During the latter half of the '20s, as the studio system matured and distribution patterns developed, the assembly-line approach to series Western filmmaking took root. The typical theatrical season for film distribution began on the first of September and ran through the end of August of the following year. (The summer months were not considered as important as they are now; in those years many theaters weren't air conditioned, and audience attendence fell off due to outdoor activities and vacations.) Producing companies offered series Westerns in blocks of four, six or eight per year for the most part, often pre-selling titles chosen arbitrarily for their marketability, long before scripts had been written—which explains why so many B Westerns sport titles that bear little or no relation to the film's content.

Studios that owned their own theater circuits, such as Fox and Paramount, could count on booking their films in a guaranteed number of theaters, which would produce revenue gauged as film rentals. Film rental rates, those fees paid to the distributors by the theaters, were calculated according to individual house size and the market in which the house competed. Box-office grosses were simply the totals of ticket sales. (The equation was complicated somewhat by block-booking and byzantine bookkeeping procedures, and also by revenues generated by independent theaters that booked major-studio product.)

HOLLYWOOD CORRAL: A COMPREHENSIVE B WESTERN ROUNDUP

The early years of Universal Pictures, circa 1922.

The amount of money spent on production was, to a great extent, predicated on film-rental figures. If rentals on a series of B Westerns declined, then the money spent on that series was reduced.

A surfeit of Westerns, all too many of them cheaply made, glutted the marketplace during the 1927-28 season, driving film rentals down dramatically and endangering the genre's viability. Before the plunge, Tom Mix's Fox Westerns (most of them sold as "specials") were costing around $175,000 each, and returning anywhere from $300,000 to $375,000 in film rentals. The more moderately produced Buck Jones films cost $50,000 to $75,000 and returned up to $125,000 each to Fox. (The discrepancy extended to salary as well; during this period Mix was drawing a salary of $7,500 per week, while Jones was getting $4,000 per week.) Fox's concern over the future of series Westerns, and the studio's concomitant decision to cut budgets and salaries, drove Jones to independent production and Mix to FBO.

FBO, which later metamorphosed into RKO, had been a leader in series Western production. The studio's top star in the mid '20s was Fred Thomson, who operated with autonomy by taking $85,000 for each picture and assuming responsibility for paying all salaries and producing the film. His Westerns brought in rentals of around $125,000 each. When Thomson left FBO for what he thought were greener pastures at Paramount (where, in fact, his starring vehicles, budgeted at $250,000—including his $100,000 salary—were losers), the studio promoted Vincent Markowski, a former athlete working in Westerns under the name Tom Tyler, as its new cowboy sensation. Initially signed at $75 per week, Tyler was pulling in $175 per week within a year of his starring debut, and by 1928 was the studio's top Western draw, despite the fact that his pictures were among the lower-end product in the marketplace, costing an average of $10,000 each to make.

The 1927-28 rental decline hurt Hoot Gibson over at Universal, where he'd been making movies for around $65,000 each. The 1926-27 group brought in an average rental of $130,000 each, but the next season's offerings took in only around $100,000 each. Universal management planned to cut budgets to $40,000 each; when Gibson balked at that and refused to sign a new contract, the studio compromised by offering him an independent production unit with a $75,000-per-picture limit, out of which Hoot's salary would be drawn.

A more detailed accounting of budgets and rentals during this period can be seen in Appendix I, which shows the entire profit-and-loss information on the 16 outdoor action films (not all of them Westerns) that Tim McCoy made for M-G-M during the waning years of the silent era. It's significant to note that the studio (or, to be more precise, producer David O. Selznick) responded to shrinking rentals during the 1927-28 season by filming pictures back-to-back: *Wyoming* and *Spoilers of the West* utilized the same production units and locations, and were brought in at $52,000 and $48,000 respectively, for a combined "negative cost" (the cost of actually producing a movie, minus expenditures for prints, advertising, and distribution) of $100,000. The previous series entry, *The Adventurer*, had come in at $85,000.

The highly regarded Ken Maynard series produced for First National (six entries per season for 1926-27, 1927-28, and 1928-29) has virtually vanished, much to the chagrin of Western fans and collectors. One of the two films known to survive, *The Red Raiders* (1927), shows that most of the $77,590.84 budget wound up on screen: Literally hundreds of extras are employed in this cavalry-vs.-Indians extravaganza, which sported some of the most thrilling action scenes of its day. In fact, stock footage from *Red Raiders* turned up in many sound B Westerns. Producer Harry Joe Brown got a mere $800 (or $160 per week for five weeks) and director Al Rogell only $650 (or $81.25 per week for eight weeks).

Major studios, with guaranteed playdates thanks to their theater holdings, weren't afraid to spend more on their Westerns; above-average quality and popular stars enabled them to win bookings from independent theaters and, amazingly, foreign markets as well. Shoestring producers, whose parsimonious pictures contributed to the 1927-28 product glut, couldn't compete with a Fox, First National, or M-G-M Western.

The coming of sound temporarily buffaloed the majors, who reasoned that technical problems with recording sound outdoors—plus an increased public appetite for stagebound, dialogue-heavy stories—would sink the genre altogether, leaving Western production to indie producers who could afford to service the small, rural theater chains and independent theaters whose undiscriminating patrons still craved horse-opera hokum.

Within just a couple years, independent producers were out on the range in droves. Reports of the Western's demise were, as usual, premature. Major-studio stars Jones, Maynard, and Gibson were all working in independent productions by 1930 (Jones' pictures, produced by Sol Lesser, were released by Columbia), and even silent-era lesser lights such as Bill Cody, Bob Custer, Jack Perrin, Jay Wilsey, and Buzz Barton were back in action by then. Sound-recording facilities were bought outright (seldom), rented from independent suppliers (who also provided the technicians), or bootlegged from major studios whose employees weren't above "leasing" equipment not being used on a given day (or week).

Most of the independent Westerns were distributed via the "states rights" method, by which a producer licensed his movies outright to small, independent distributors—also known as "franchise holders" and "sub-distributors" (or simply as "subs")—who paid for exclusive rights to market those films to existing theaters within their "territories," or exchange areas. The territories, which varied in size from a perimeter of several miles to several states, were generally the same in which the major studios operated. (There were at one time 36 separate exchange areas in the United States, and some independent distributors had exchanges in more than one territory.) The states righters put up "guarantees" by which a producer gauged potential profits. If he pre-sold a movie to ten territories for $1,000 each, he had $10,000 worth of guaranteed money; if he made the movie for $5,000, including a limited number of prints, he could theoretically pocket the other $5,000.

Even at that, the indies didn't have it so easy. Several film laboratories, whose own fortunes depended on a continuing flow of new movies, ensured themselves of getting business by advancing money to the "coffee-and-cake producers" (so named because that's about all they got for making indie films). If producers could present proof of states-rights deals based upon delivery of a finished negative, the lab might approve a loan of, say, $3,500 for actual production. The producer would agree to pay the lender ten percent of the loan price once it was approved. Then he'd pay an attorney roughly, say, $35 for drawing up the agreement, according to which the producer agreed to repay the lender his

HOLLYWOOD CORRAL: A COMPREHENSIVE B WESTERN ROUNDUP

Tim McCoy, Dorothy Sebastian, and director Nick Grinde check the camera mount on the dolly before shooting a scene for Morgan's Last Raid *(M-G-M, 1929).*

THE BOTTOM LINE / Low Finance in the Reel West

$3,500 plus six percent interest. In addition, the lab would get the producer's business. The producer now had $3,125 with which to make his Western.

Upon finishing the picture and securing his states-rights guarantee money, the producer could repay the loan. Thus the lab not only got the producer's business, it also made six percent (plus the ten percent paid "under the table") for loaning the money.

But could anyone actually *make* a Western for $3,125? The answer is yes, but not a very good Western. As late as 1934, independent producer/director/actor Victor Adamson (a.k.a. Denver Dixon) was making Buddy Roosevelt starrers for $2,500 each. The films were shot in three or four days, often without interiors (saving potentially costly studio rentals), and netted Roosevelt—the star, mind you—a whopping $250 each. That the films themselves are execrable is hardly the point; they were made cheaply, and they made money all around.

Independent entrepreneurs saw in cheapie Westerns an opportunity to make money easily—but their efforts weren't always rewarded with the quick payoffs they expected. William W. Hirsch, owner of the Mineral Spring Hotel near Beaumont, California, founded Beaumont Productions in 1935. He reasoned that Westerns could be shot on the picturesque terrain near his hotel, and the cast and crew could be fed and sheltered at his hotel. Hirsch spent $6,000 on *Gunners and Guns* (1935), first of what he hoped would become a series. At the time he reasoned that if he didn't make money in distribution, he'd write off production costs as an advertising/promotional expense for the hotel. Beaumont Productions didn't last out the year.

Malcolm Brown Pictures, Inc. was formed in 1938, and was reported by movie-industry trade papers to be gearing up for production of a series of eight B Westerns, budgeted at $10,000 to $12,000 each, to be released during the 1938-39 season. Only *Adventures of the Masked Phantom* was made, but not released until a year later. (By this time, Republic, Monogram and Grand National—small studios that operated their own exchanges—had usurped most of the market for indie Westerns, virtually eliminating the "coffee-and-cake producers.")

The major studios gingerly approached series Western production again in the early '30s, alternately expanding and cutting back output whenever shaky market conditions hinted that Westerns weren't in demand. These policies varied from studio to studio, of course. Universal, which had embraced talkie Westerns with full series from both the Ken Maynard and Hoot Gibson units during the 1929-30 season, let both stars go and dropped Westerns from the release slate for two years before signing Tom Mix in 1931 for a series of six to be released for the 1931-32 season. Mix's first six Universal pictures were budgeted at an average of $84,000 each, but ended up costing an average $107,000 each. The 1931-32 entries were late in arriving to the screen; the last, *Hidden Gold*, wasn't released until November of 1932. Mix had completed three films for 1932-33 when, after suffering several serious injuries while in production, and with the blessing of Universal, he decided to retire.

In 1931 Columbia assumed production of the Buck Jones series from Sol Lesser, and hired Tim McCoy to appear in a series produced by Irving Briskin. Jones, the more popular of the two stars, got slightly bigger budgets and longer shooting schedules. His 1932-33 efforts, for example, were shot on schedules of seven to 14 days. The McCoy Westerns made during the same period were brought in on budgets of about $20,000 each and were shot in four to nine days. Watching those Jones and McCoy films today, it's virtually impossible to detect differences in the production values or directorial styles of the two series.

Warner Bros. cartoon producer Leon Schlesinger handled production chores on six John Wayne Westerns for 1932-33, bought by the studio for $28,000 each (not much money by major-studio standards). By drawing on stock footage of spectacular, costly action sequences from the Warner-owned Ken Maynard silents released by First National, these films appeared much more expensive. Appendix II offers more statistics on this group. Wayne next went to Trem Carr's Monogram, where he appeared in a total of 16 B Westerns (1933-34 and 1934-35) budgeted at $15,000 each (or less), including Duke's $2,500-per-film salary.

Wayne's Monogram salary wasn't very impressive, even by 1933 standards.

The series Western, more than any other genre, was a star-driven form of movie entertainment, and the top cowboy stars made a pretty penny for their chores, even in those Depression days of the '30s. The glory days of the '20s were long gone, of course, and none of the sound-era sagebrush stars ever negotiated deals approaching Tom Mix's fabled $7,500-a-week salary at Fox.

After his fortune was wiped out by a disastrous, self-produced 1928 talkie and an ill-advised circus venture, Buck Jones signed with Sol Lesser in 1930 for $300 a week. Regaining his box-office stature within a few years, Jones won his own production

HOLLYWOOD CORRAL: A COMPREHENSIVE B WESTERN ROUNDUP

Iron Eyes Cody and Tim McCoy in an art still (above left) that evolved into the poster art shown above right.

Wheeler Oakman and Tim McCoy in another art still (below left) and the resulting one-sheet art (below right).

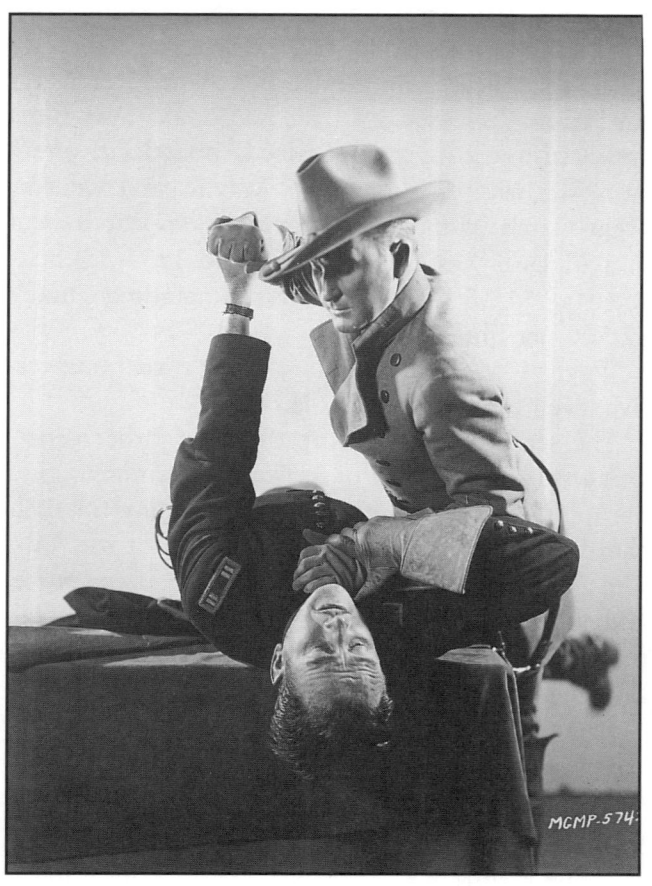

THE BOTTOM LINE / Low Finance in the Reel West

Hoot Gibson checks the sound on the set of one of the pictures he produced for Universal.

unit at Universal. His 1936-37 films for that studio were budgeted at $75,000 each; Buck got $15,000 per film plus a percentage of the profits.

George O'Brien was for a time the top-paid cowboy star in the business. After Fox stopped producing his starring Westerns, some of which had cost more than $200,000, O'Brien signed a partnership deal with Sol Lesser, who produced pictures independently for Fox release. The films were budgeted at $100,000 to $125,000 each, with O'Brien drawing $20,000 per film and a percentage of the profits—which, he later claimed, he never got from Lesser. O'Brien was reported to have been paid $25,000 each for the four 1936-37 films he made for RKO release with George Hirliman as producer. In 1938, however, he was paid $15,000 per film by RKO, which by this time had assumed production of his movies.

O'Brien's salary notched upward over the next two years. His RKO Westerns, among the slickest in the field, were made for between $80,000 and $90,000 each, a couple of them going a little over budget. They took in between $152,000 and $245,000 in worldwide revenue, but his last 1940 release showed a $5,000 loss. RKO dropped O'Brien and replaced him with Tim Holt, whose initial salary was only a fraction of O'Brien's. His pre-World War II films were made for an average of $50,000 each, although a few of his 1943 releases squeaked in at around $35,000—making them more profitable to the studio than O'Brien's later efforts had been.

Perhaps no Western star enjoyed as meteoric a rise to stardom as did Gene Autry. Hired by Mascot president Nat Levine at $75 a week in 1934, the screen's first singing cowboy appeared in Ken Maynard's *In Old Santa Fe* and the serial *Mystery Mountain* before winning his own starring series, under Levine's supervision, when Mascot merged with several other indies to become Republic in 1935. As a top-billed star, his salary was $100 per week, and his contract called for $50-a-week raises every six months that he remained at the studio.

Autry, already a canny businessman, knew that his popular films were making a lot of money for

An independent unit on location in the Arizona desert.

Republic, with whom he was splitting personal-appearance fees. After threats and counter-threats had been exchanged, Autry re-signed with Republic for $2,000 per picture (eight pictures per season) in July, 1936. He was also allowed to keep all monies earned from personal appearances and recording contracts. The following year his salary was doubled.

When Autry signed a one-picture deal with Columbia in 1938, Republic president Herbert J. Yates invoked a clause in the star's contract forbidding him from making outside pictures. The deal fell through, but Yates increased Autry's per-picture compensation to $5,000 in an attempt to keep him happy. It didn't succeed. Autry said he wanted $15,000 per picture, and failed to appear for the first day of production on the already-prepared *Washington Cowboy*, which was hastily revamped and, under the new title *Under Western Stars*, shot with Roy Rogers in the lead. Autry compromised, returning to Republic later that year with a new deal for $10,000 per picture, beginning with *The Man from Music Mountain*. Autry's first Republic Western, *Tumbling Tumbleweeds* (1935), was brought in for less than $15,000. By the time he left the studio in 1947, his starring vehicles were costing $200,000 each. That same year he signed with Columbia, where he established an independent unit, initially making pictures for $300,000 to $350,000 each, and splitting the profits with Columbia 50-50.

Along with Jones, O'Brien and Autry, Bill Boyd was one of the '30s' top-paid range riders, and his

THE BOTTOM LINE / Low Finance in the Reel West

success ultimately eclipsed their own. His once-promising career on the wane when Harry Sherman signed him to play Hopalong Cassidy in 1935, Boyd took $5,000 per picture for the first series of six, produced independently by Sherman and J.D. Trop's Este Productions for Paramount release. When Paramount took over the series in 1936, budgets were upped and Boyd's salary was doubled. His salary was "bumped" again for the 1937-38 group, this time to $12,500 per film. By 1940 he was making $25,000 per picture—which, as in George O'Brien's case, ultimately made his starring vehicles less profitable. When Boyd produced his own Cassidy series for United Artists in the late '40s, several years after the property had remained dormant, he paid himself the same handsome salary but tightened purse strings of other production aspects, which is one of the reasons why his Hoppys suffer in comparison to Sherman's.

The *Hopalong Cassidy* Westerns, on the whole, were among the most popular and profitable B Westerns ever made. The Paramount entries, 41 in all, generated worldwide film rentals of $9,240,000—an average of $225,366 each. The first six films, financed by tire magnates Nick Luddington and William Fisk, were brought in per contract for a total of $350,000, slightly less than $65,000 each. Subsequently, with Paramount picking up the tab, Sherman allowed negative costs to creep up into the $85,000-90,000 range. When the studio balked, threatening to pull the plug on the series, Sherman's partner Jack Trop personally pro-

An early '30s shot of the Mack Sennett Studio which became Mascot in 1932, and Republic Studio in 1935.

HOLLYWOOD CORRAL: A COMPREHENSIVE B WESTERN ROUNDUP

duced several of the 1938-39 entries, bringing them in for $40,000 to $45,000, mollifying the studio but earning the emnity of Sherman, who felt he'd been shown up by his junior partner. (The partnership was dissolved shortly thereafter.)

By 1942 Sherman was producing Hoppys back to back to save costs (although budgets were back up to $80,000 and more), and he'd amassed a considerable backlog when Paramount elected to sell the series to United Artists, which didn't have enough completed films to service its exchanges. In what was a terrific deal for UA, Paramount sold the Hoppys to UA for the pictures' negative costs. Appendix VI shows figures on the UA Hoppys.

During the series' heyday, Paramount was "selling" *Hopalong Cassidy* Westerns at minimum rentals of $10 per week (with some small, rural, independent theaters getting them on a per-case basis at $7.50). Upon assuming distribution of the series, United Artists raised the minimum to $12.50 a week, then raised it to $15 and, ultimately, to $20.

That these popular series Westerns could be had, as late as 1946, for $20 a week underscores the basic fragility of the B Western marketplace, and offers the best insight into why the genre lost favor in the early '50s, after television had usurped its theatrical audience. Saturday-matinee screenings and occasional runs in rural "split-week" and "daily change" theater engagements didn't make for million-dollar grosses. With few exceptions, throughout the sound era B Western rentals were $10 per seven days, less for daily-change houses. Even if distributors got 10,000 bookings (and very few series Westerns played more than 10,000 theaters), maximum film rentals would amount to less than $100,000. The films had to be made cheaply, or they couldn't be made at all. Warm memories of Saturday afternoons spent with Lash LaRue, Whip Wilson, The Durango

The Tiffany-Stahl Studio on Sunset Boulevard at Hollywood Boulevard, where many Ken Maynard and Bob Steele films were shot in the early '30s. Nothing remains of this studio today.

THE BOTTOM LINE / Low Finance in the Reel West

The cast and crew of the 1937 Crescent production Old Louisiana. *Star Tom Keene is dressed in the Army uniform and immediately to his right is leading lady Rita Cansino (Hayworth).*

Kid and other cowboy stars of the late '40s unfortunately don't obscure the reality: by the late '40s, the B Western had played out its mass-market appeal—at least as far as theatrical potential was concerned.

And yet, spending varied considerably from studio to studio. Comparisons between a major studio oater of 1938 and an independent production of 1945 show startling differences in budgetary outlay. Take RKO's *Border G-Men* (1938), for example. Star George O'Brien got $15,000 for his chores. Leading lady Laraine Johnson [Day] was paid $500; sidekick Ray Whitley got $600; veteran villain John Miljan got $1,250. Producer Bert Gilroy was compensated to the tune of $1,000; director David Howard got $2,500; production manager Lee Marcus took home $500. Oliver Drake was paid $1,600 for his script; Bernard McConville got $250 for his original story. The film, budgeted at $86,280, was completed in 12 days for $86,401.07.

By contrast, PRC's *Prairie Rustlers* (1945) was budgeted at $22,500 and was shot in six days for $23,304.12. Star Buster Crabbe was paid $3,000; sidekick Fuzzy St. John got $1,000. Producer Sigmund Neufeld received $1,200; his brother, Sam Newfield, directed the film for $1,250. Scripter Fred Myton got $1,000 for his original screenplay.

It would be ludicrous to compare the two films on a qualitative basis. Yet, each is entertaining in its own way, and each filled the market niche it was produced to fill. The O'Brien film cost four times as much, but probably played in more than twice the number of theaters the Crabbe film brightened. In both cases, production overages were kept to a minimum, further underscoring the care with which B Westerns were made, relative to the market they serviced and the revenues they were expected to generate. "Relative" is, in fact, the key word: Domestic film rental of $150,000 was considered excellent for a series Western from a major studio. Domestic film rental of $30,000 was considered very good for an independently made Western on states-rights release.

Hopefully, the statistics in this essay and in the accompanying Appendices will provide the reader with a somewhat clearer picture of the financial aspect of series Western production. Magically, many of these pictures transcend their artistic and budgetary limitations when we remember them in our mind's eye. That so many of them turned out as well as they did, on such meager investments, is little short of miraculous—and a testimony to the talented filmmakers who made the genre their primary creative baliwick throughout the B Western's halcyon days.

417

HOLLYWOOD CORRAL: A COMPREHENSIVE B WESTERN ROUNDUP

Tim McCoy, circa 1929.

THE BOTTOM LINE / Low Finance in the Reel West

The RELEASE NUMBER is the accounting number assigned by the *distributor* to each title. The PRODUCTION NUMBER is the accounting number assigned by the *studio* or *production* company. The RELEASE DATE is the date that the films were actually available to the theaters. NEGATIVE COST is the total amount of money spent to produce a film. DOMESTIC GROSS is the film rental paid to *distributors* in the U.S. and Canada. FOREIGN GROSS is the film rental for all countries *except* the U.S. and Canada. WORLD WIDE GROSS is the sum of *Domestic* and *Foreign* rentals. PROFIT AND LOSS (P & L) is arrived at by adding Negative Cost, the cost of prints and advertising, and distribution fees, and then subtracting the total from the Worldwide Gross. NUMBER OF BOOKINGS is the actual number of theaters in the U.S. and Canada that played a film. AVERAGE RENTAL is the Domestic Gross divided by the Number of Bookings. SHOOTING DAYS is the actual number of days before the cameras for each film.

APPENDIX I
TIM McCOY AT M-G-M

RELEASE NUMBER	RELEASED		PRODUCTION NUMBER	TOTAL DAYS	NEGATIVE COST	DOMESTIC FILM RENTAL	FOREIGN FILM RENTAL	WORLDWIDE FILM RENTAL	PROFIT AND LOSS
		1926-27 SEASON							
750	10/10/26	WAR PAINT	285	15	$ 82,000	$ 172,000	$ 120,000	$ 292,000	$ 84,000
752	01/15/27	WINNERS OF THE WILDERNESS	292	21	$ 86,000	$ 158,000	$ 125,000	$ 283,000	$ 74,000
754	05/07/27	CALIFORNIA	295	21	$ 124,000	$ 143,000	$ 88,000	$ 231,000	$ 5,000
755	06/11/26	THE FRONTIERSMAN	317	19	$ 96,000	$ 129,000	$ 77,000	$ 206,000	$ 22,000
		TOTAL		76	$ 388,000	$ 602,000	$ 410,000	$1,012,000	$ 185,000
		AVERAGE		19	$ 97,000	$ 150,500	$ 102,500	$ 253,000	$ 46,250
		1927-28 SEASON							
844	09/03/27	FOREIGN DEVILS	307	14	$ 74,000	$ 148,000	$ 94,000	$ 242,000	$ 71,000
845	07/14/28	THE ADVENTURER	323	13	$ 85,000	$ 126,000	$ 84,000	$ 210,000	$ 38,000
848	03/24/28	WYOMING	333	10	$ 52,000	$ 130,000	$ 91,000	$ 221,000	$ 79,000
847	12/10/27	SPOILERS OF THE WEST	341	13	$ 48,000	$ 144,000	$ 95,000	$ 239,000	$ 96,000
846	01/21/28	LAW OF THE RANGE	347	12	$ 52,000	$ 139,000	$ 102,000	$ 241,000	$ 87,000
848	04/21/28	RIDERS OF THE DARK	351	12	$ 46,000	$ 126,000	$ 88,000	$ 214,000	$ 78,000
		TOTAL		74	$ 357,000	$ 813,000	$ 554,000	$1,367,000	$ 449,000
		AVERAGE		12	$ 59,500	$ 135,500	$ 92,333	$ 227,833	$ 74,833
		1928-29 SEASON							
942	09/15/28	BEYOND THE SIERRAS	362	13	$ 44,000	$ 122,000	$ 98,000	$ 220,000	$ 81,000
943	11/17/28	THE BUSH RANGER	367	15	$ 50,000	$ 118,000	$ 86,000	$ 204,000	$ 67,000
944	01/05/29	MORGAN'S LAST RAID	377	13	$ 59,000	$ 114,000	$ 78,000	$ 192,000	$ 46,000
945	03/02/29	THE OVERLAND TELEGRAPH	384	12	$ 64,000	$ 103,000	$ 57,000	$ 160,000	$ 22,000
946	04/20/29	SIOUX BLOOD	386	11	$ 41,000	$ 98,000	$ 64,000	$ 162,000	$ 49,000
947	05/11/29	DESERT RIDER	404	12	$ 50,000	$ 91,000	$ 61,000	$ 152,000	$ 32,000
		TOTAL		76	$ 308,000	$ 646,000	$ 444,000	$1,090,000	$ 297,000
		AVERAGE		13	$ 51,333	$ 107,667	$ 74,000	$ 181,667	$ 49,500
		GRAND TOTAL		226	$1,053,000	$2,061,000	$1,408,000	$3,469,000	$ 931,000
		AVERAGE		14	$ 65,813	$ 128,813	$ 88,000	$ 216,813	$ 58,188

APPENDIX II
JOHN WAYNE AT WARNER BROS

RELEASE NUMBER	RELEASED	1932-33 SEASON	NEGATIVE COST	DOMESTIC FILM RENTAL	FOREIGN FILM RENTAL	WORLDWIDE FILM RENTAL	PROFIT AND LOSS
431	08/27/32	RIDE 'EM COWBOY	$ 28,000	$ 93,970	$ 60,000	$153,970	$ 67,478
432	10/08/32	THE BIG STAMPEDE	$ 28,000	$ 93,730	$ 61,000	$154,730	$ 68,048
433	03/18/33	TELEGRAPH TRAIL	$ 28,000	$ 87,526	$ 56,000	$143,526	$ 59,645
434	12/17/32	HAUNTED GOLD	$ 28,000	$ 88,482	$ 57,000	$145,482	$ 61,112
435	05/20/33	SOMEWHERE IN SONORA	$ 28,000	$ 80,182	$ 59,000	$139,182	$ 56,387
436	07/15/33	THE MAN FROM MONTEREY	$ 28,000	$ 78,404	$ 56,000	$134,404	$ 52,803
		TOTAL	$168,000	$522,294	$349,000	$871,294	$365,471
		AVERAGE	$ 28,000	$ 87,049	$ 58,167	$145,216	$ 60,912

HOLLYWOOD CORRAL: A COMPREHENSIVE B WESTERN ROUNDUP

APPENDIX III

RELEASE NUMBER	RELEASED		NEGATIVE COST	DOMESTIC FILM RENTAL	FOREIGN FILM RENTAL	WORLDWIDE FILM RENTAL	PROFIT AND LOSS
		DICK FORAN AT WARNER BROS — 1935-36 SEASON					
928	11/02/35	MOONLIGHT ON THE PRAIRIE	$ 76,000	$ 135,000	$ 91,000	$ 226,000	$ 73,500
929	05/02/36	TREACHERY RIDES THE RANGE	$ 84,000	$ 121,000	$ 71,000	$ 192,000	$ 40,000
930	11/14/36	CALIFORNIA MAIL	$ 82,000	$ 116,000	$ 64,000	$ 180,000	$ 33,000
		TOTAL	$ 242,000	$ 372,000	$ 226,000	$ 598,000	$ 146,500
		AVERAGE	$ 80,667	$ 124,000	$ 75,333	$ 199,333	$ 48,833
		DICK FORAN AT FIRST NATIONAL — 1935-36 SEASON					
978	02/29/36	SONG OF THE SADDLE	$ 81,000	$ 170,000	$ 75,000	$ 245,000	$ 82,750
979	09/05/36	TRAILIN' WEST	$ 66,000	$ 115,000	$ 71,000	$ 186,000	$ 53,500
980	01/02/37	GUNS OF THE PECOS	$ 77,000	$ 139,000	$ 67,000	$ 206,000	$ 57,500
		TOTAL	$ 224,000	$ 424,000	$ 213,000	$ 637,000	$ 193,750
		AVERAGE	$ 74,667	$ 141,333	$ 71,000	$ 212,333	$ 64,583
		COMBINED TOTAL	$ 466,000	$ 796,000	$ 439,000	$1,235,000	$ 340,250
		AVERAGE	$ 77,667	$ 132,667	$ 73,167	$ 205,833	$ 56,708
		DICK FORAN AT WARNER BROS — 1936-37 SEASON					
128	03/13/37	LAND BEYOND THE LAW	$ 76,000	$ 135,000	$ 91,000	$ 226,000	$ 73,500
129	06/12/37	BLAZING SIXES	$ 58,000	$ 115,000	$ 54,000	$ 169,000	$ 48,750
130	08/14/37	THE DEVIL'S SADDLE LEGION	$ 64,000	$ 106,000	$ 52,000	$ 158,000	$ 34,500
		TOTAL	$ 198,000	$ 356,000	$ 197,000	$ 553,000	$ 156,750
		AVERAGE	$ 66,000	$ 118,667	$ 65,667	$ 184,333	$ 52,250
		DICK FORAN AT FIRST NATIONAL — 1936-37 SEASON					
178	05/15/37	CHEROKEE STRIP	$ 99,000	$ 160,000	$ 55,000	$ 215,000	$ 42,250
179	07/10/37	EMPTY HOLSTERS	$ 56,000	$ 142,000	$ 47,000	$ 189,000	$ 65,750
180	09/11/37	PRAIRIE THUNDER	$ 56,000	$ 143,000	$ 43,000	$ 186,000	$ 63,500
		TOTAL	$ 211,000	$ 445,000	$ 145,000	$ 590,000	$ 171,500
		AVERAGE	$ 70,333	$ 148,333	$ 48,333	$ 196,667	$ 57,167
		COMBINED TOTAL	$ 409,000	$ 801,000	$ 342,000	$1,143,000	$ 328,250
		AVERAGE	$ 68,167	$ 133,500	$ 57,000	$ 190,500	$ 54,708
		ERROL FLYNN AT WARNER BROS					
304	04/08/39	DODGE CITY	$1,061,000	$1,688,000	$ 844,000	$2,532,000	$ 708,000
404	03/23/40	VIRGINIA CITY	$1,179,000	$1,518,000	$ 602,000	$2,120,000	$ 295,000
		TOTAL	$2,240,000	$3,206,000	$1,446,000	$4,652,000	$1,003,000
		AVERAGE	$1,120,000	$1,603,000	$ 723,000	$2,326,000	$ 501,500

THE BOTTOM LINE / Low Finance in the Reel West

APPENDIX IV
MONOGRAM

REPORTING PERIOD	APPROXIMATE NUMBER OF RELEASES	WORLDWIDE INCOME FOR PERIOD	AVERAGE INCOME PER RELEASE	PROFIT & LOSS FOR PERIOD
02/01/37 TO 12/31/37	21	$ 286,780.07	$ 13,656.19	($239,076.05)
01/01/38 TO 12/31/38	33	$ 1,494,402.00	$ 45,284.91	($180,817.00)
01/01/39 TO 06/30/39	18	$ 947,565.00	$ 52,642.50	$ 41,642.00
07/01/39 TO 06/29/40	37	$ 1,945,879.19	$ 52,591.33	($179,656.24)
06/30/40 TO 06/28/41	40	$ 2,030,459.75	$ 50,761.49	$ 10,897.69
06/29/41 TO 06/28/42	57	$ 2,186,092.00	$ 38,352.49	$ 157,103.00
06/30/42 TO 06/26/43	36	$ 2,567,187.00	$ 71,310.75	$ 99,144.00
06/27/43 TO 07/01/44	40	$ 4,300,627.00	$ 107,515.68	$ 177,823.00
07/02/44 TO 06/30/45	35	$ 4,807,446.00	$ 137,355.60	$ 165,161.00
07/02/44 TO 06/26/46	35	$ 6,235,228.00	$ 178,149.37	$ 397,474.00
07/02/46 TO 06/28/47	37	$ 8,100,205.60	$ 218,924.48	$ 375,895.53
06/29/47 TO 07/03/48	41	$ 9,030,906.00	$ 220,266.00	($497,696.00)
07/04/48 TO 07/02/49	44	$10,177,868.00	$ 231,315.18	($1,108,433.00)
07/03/49 TO 07/01/50	35	$ 9,225,793.00	$ 263,594.09	($263,342.00)
07/02/50 TO 06/30/51	39	$ 9,311,914.00	$ 238,767.03	$ 1,061,648.00
07/01/51 TO 06/30/52	35	$ 9,223,759.00	$ 263,535.97	$ 589,259.00
GRAND TOTAL	583	$81,872,111.61	$2,184,023.05	$ 607,026.93

Johnny Mack Brown, the star of Monogram's longest running series of Westerns, with sidekick Raymond Hatton.

HOLLYWOOD CORRAL: A COMPREHENSIVE B WESTERN ROUNDUP

APPENDIX V
GEORGE O'BRIEN AT RKO — CONDOR PRODUCTIONS

RELEASE NUMBER	RELEASED		PRODUCTION NUMBER	TOTAL DAYS	NEGATIVE COST	DOMESTIC FILM RENTAL	FOREIGN FILM RENTAL	WORLDWIDE FILM RENTAL	PROFIT AND LOSS
		1936-37 SEASON							
781	10/16/36	DANIEL BOONE				$191,000	$ 94,000	$ 285,000	
782	02/26/37	PARK AVENUE LOGGER				$177,000	$ 75,000	$ 252,000	
783	05/28/37	HOLLYWOOD COWBOY				$168,000	$ 55,000	$ 223,000	
784	08/06/37	WINDJAMMER				$156,000	$ 62,000	$ 218,000	
		TOTAL				$692,000	$286,000	$ 978,000	
		AVERAGE				$173,000	$ 71,500	$ 244,500	
		1937-38 SEASON							
881	05/13/38	GUN LAW	126	12	$ 78,000	$148,000	$ 45,000	$ 193,000	$ 46,000
882	06/24/38	BORDER G-MEN	133	12	$ 85,000	$146,000	$ 60,000	$ 206,000	$ 38,000
883	08/12/38	PAINTED DESERT	143	12	$ 86,000	$147,000	$ 42,000	$ 189,000	$ 33,000
884	09/16/38	RENEGADE RANGER, THE	153	12	$ 87,000	$136,000	$ 59,000	$ 195,000	$ 31,000
		TOTAL			$336,000	$577,000	$206,000	$ 783,000	$148,000
		AVERAGE			$ 84,000	$144,250	$ 51,500	$ 195,750	$ 37,000
		1938-39 SEASON							
981	11/04/38	LAWLESS VALLEY	160	13	$ 80,364.63	$159,791.27	$ 55,530.30	$ 215,321.57	$ 48,526.34
982	01/20/39	ARIZONA LEGION	169	13	$ 94,519.31	$129,980.10	$ 54,079.31	$ 184,059.41	$ 19,568.47
983	03/24/39	TROUBLE IN SUNDOWN	180	12	$ 81,847.98	$137,249.55	$ 56,642.67	$ 193,892.22	$ 28,017.16
984	05/26/39	RACKETEERS OF THE RANGE	192	12	$ 96,348.93	$117,236.61	$ 52,000.11	$ 169,236.72	$ 1,162.86
985	06/30/39	TIMBER STAMPEDE	200	12	$ 95,299.39	$133,607.31	$ 41,959.32	$ 175,566.63	$ 1,604.00
986	09/08/39	FIGHTING GRINGO, THE	217	12	$ 88,101.23	$117,568.51	$ 39,518.83	$ 157,087.34	$ 6,650.19
		TOTAL			$536,481.47	$795,433.35	$299,730.54	$1,095,163.89	$105,529.02
		AVERAGE			$ 89,413.58	$132,572.23	$ 49,955.09	$ 182,527.32	$ 17,588.17
		1939-40 SEASON							
081	11/03/39	MARSHAL OF MESA CITY, THE	226	8	$ 75,197.99	$130,910.82	$ 46,968.00	$ 177,878.82	$ 37,076.77
082	01/05/40	LEGION OF THE LAWLESS	231	10	$ 81,171.23	$121,016.32	$ 49,943.24	$ 170,959.56	$ 28,055.44
083	04/05/40	BULLET CODE	242	13	$ 83,000.00	$117,000.00	$ 20,000.00	$ 137,000.00	$ 3,000.00
084	06/14/40	PRAIRIE LAW	256	10	$ 77,000.00	$114,000.00	$ 33,000.00	$ 147,000.00	$ 15,000.00
085	07/26/40	STAGE TO CHINO	263	10	$ 84,000.00	$114,000.00	$ 36,000.00	$ 150,000.00	$ 10,000.00
086	09/27/40	TRIPLE JUSTICE	273	13	$ 85,000.00	$110,000.00	$ 19,000.00	$ 129,000.00	($5,000.00)
		TOTAL			$485,369.22	$706,927.13	$204,911.25	$ 911,838.38	$ 88,132.21
		AVERAGE			$ 80,894.87	$117,821.19	$ 34,151.87	$ 151,973.06	$ 14,688.70

George O'Brien as he appeared in his last RKO film Triple Justice *(1940).*

THE BOTTOM LINE / Low Finance in the Reel West

APPENDIX V (continued)
TIM HOLT AT RKO

RELEASE NUMBER	RELEASED		PRODUCTION NUMBER	TOTAL DAYS	NEGATIVE COST	DOMESTIC FILM RENTAL	FOREIGN FILM RENTAL	WORLDWIDE FILM RENTAL	PROFIT AND LOSS
		1940-41 SEASON							
181	10/04/40	WAGON TRAIN	281	13	$ 95,000	$114,000	$ 21,000	$ 135,000	($12,000)
182	12/06/40	FARGO KID, THE	282	14	$ 64,000	$108,000	$ 30,000	$ 138,000	$ 18,000
183	02/07/41	ALONG THE RIO GRANDE	296	13	$ 65,000	$103,000	$ 34,000	$ 137,000	$ 19,000
184	04/18/41	ROBBERS OF THE RANGE	299	11	$ 62,000	$103,000	$ 15,000	$ 118,000	$ 13,000
185	06/06/41	CYCLONE ON HORSEBACK	317	10	$ 56,000	$ 94,000	$ 32,000	$ 126,000	$ 20,000
186	08/08/41	SIX GUN GOLD	329	10	$ 49,000	$ 98,000	$ 14,000	$ 112,000	$ 22,000
		TOTAL			$391,000	$620,000	$146,000	$ 766,000	$ 80,000
		AVERAGE			$ 65,167	$103,333	$ 24,333	$ 127,667	$ 13,333
		1941-42 SEASON							
281	10/10/41	BANDIT TRAIL, THE	323	9	$ 45,000	$104,000	$ 17,000	$ 121,000	$ 33,000
282	12/10/41	DUDE COWBOY	321	9	$ 51,000	$ 94,000	$ 14,000	$ 108,000	$ 20,000
283	02/27/42	RIDING THE WIND	334	10	$ 51,000	$ 91,000	$ 17,000	$ 108,000	$ 19,000
284	04/17/42	LAND OF THE OPEN RANGE	339	10	$ 49,000	$ 84,000	$ 18,000	$ 102,000	$ 17,000
285	06/05/42	COME ON DANGER	342	11	$ 49,000	$ 81,000	$ 15,000	$ 96,000	$ 14,000
286	07/24/42	THUNDERING HOOFS	345	9	$ 44,000	$ 81,000	$ 25,000	$ 106,000	$ 25,000
		TOTAL			$289,000	$535,000	$106,000	$ 641,000	$128,000
		AVERAGE			$ 48,167	$ 89,167	$ 17,667	$ 106,833	$ 21,333
		1942-43 SEASON							
381	09/25/42	BANDIT RANGER	371	7	$ 37,000	$111,000	$ 33,000	$ 144,000	$ 60,000
382	11/20/42	PIRATES OF THE PRAIRIE	373	7	$ 38,000	$106,000	$ 30,000	$ 136,000	$ 53,000
383	01/29/43	FIGHTING FRONTIER	376	7	$ 41,000	$105,000	$ 25,000	$ 130,000	$ 49,000
384	04/02/43	SAGEBRUSH LAW	380	7	$ 36,000	$ 98,000	$ 24,000	$ 122,000	$ 46,000
385	06/08/43	AVENGING RIDER, THE	384	7	$ 35,000	$ 98,000	$ 22,000	$ 120,000	$ 45,000
386	07/23/43	RED RIVER ROBINHOOD	382	7	$ 35,000	$ 94,000	$ 29,000	$ 123,000	$ 48,000
		TOTAL			$222,000	$612,000	$163,000	$ 775,000	$301,000
		AVERAGE			$ 37,000	$102,000	$ 27,167	$ 129,167	$ 50,167

Lee "Lasses" White, Tim Holt and Ray Whitley

HOLLYWOOD CORRAL: A COMPREHENSIVE B WESTERN ROUNDUP

APPENDIX VI
HOPALONG CASSIDY AT UNITED ARTISTS

RELEASE NUMBER	RELEASED	NEGATIVE COST	DOMESTIC FILM RENTAL	NUMBER OF BOOKINGS	AVERAGE RENTAL	FOREIGN FILM RENTAL	WORLDWIDE FILM RENTAL	PROFIT & LOSS
	1942-43 SEASON							
632	10/23/42 UNDERCOVER MAN	$ 103,815.64	$ 162,214	8,639	$ 18.78	$ 67,760	$ 229,974	$ 4,273
633	12/18/42 LOST CANYON	$ 82,808.83	$ 166,076	8,628	$ 19.25	$ 70,061	$ 236,137	$ 32,187
637	03/12/43 HOPPY SERVES A WRIT	$ 83,771.24	$ 159,936	8,388	$ 19.07	$ 59,174	$ 219,110	$ 18,781
634	04/02/43 BORDER PATROL	$ 87,285.09	$ 159,255	8,468	$ 18.81	$ 70,654	$ 229,909	$ 23,427
635	05/28/43 LEATHER BURNERS, THE	$ 95,264.18	$ 162,775	8,524	$ 19.10	$ 56,670	$ 219,445	$ 9,241
636	06/18/43 COLT COMRADES	$ 101,850.15	$ 158,857	8,429	$ 18.85	$ 51,659	$ 210,516	($2,904)
	TOTAL	$ 554,795.13	$ 969,112	51,076	$ 18.97	$375,978	$ 1,345,090	$ 85,004
	AVERAGE	$ 92,465.86	$ 161,519	8,513	$ 18.97	$ 62,663	$ 224,182	$ 14,167
	1943-44 SEASON							
649	10/01/43 BAR 20	$ 85,705.93	$ 159,211	7,990	$ 19.93	$ 49,776	$ 208,987	$ 15,112
653	11/05/43 FALSE COLORS	$ 100,470.99	$ 157,841	7,993	$ 19.75	$ 44,797	$ 202,638	($4,242)
654	12/03/43 RIDERS OF THE DEADLINE	$ 106,234.43	$ 156,173	7,920	$ 19.72	$ 42,703	$ 198,876	($15,480)
659	02/18/44 TEXAS MASQUERADE	$ 102,705.80	$ 154,863	7,885	$ 19.64	$ 44,203	$ 199,066	($5,290)
662	04/28/44 LUMBERJACK	$ 117,402.22	$ 154,713	7,876	$ 19.64	$ 41,130	$ 195,843	($25,034)
664	05/31/44 MYSTERY MAN	$ 94,533.13	$ 149,927	7,829	$ 19.15	$ 42,393	$ 192,320	($1,278)
666	06/23/44 FORTY THIEVES	$ 129,925.73	$ 150,983	7,838	$ 19.26	$ 41,701	$ 192,684	($36,237)
	TOTAL	$ 736,978.23	$1,083,712	55,331	$ 19.59	$306,703	$ 1,390,415	($72,449)
	AVERAGE	$ 105,282.60	$ 154,816	7,904	$ 19.59	$ 43,815	$ 198,631	($10,350)
	THIRTEEN FILM TOTAL	$1,291,773.36	$2,052,824	106,407	$ 19.29	$682,681	$ 2,735,505	$ 12,555
	THIRTEEN FILM AVERAGE	$ 99,367.18	$ 157,910	8,185	$ 19.29	$ 52,514	$ 210,423	$ 966
	1946-47 SEASON							
1008	11/15/46 DEVIL'S PLAYGROUND, THE	$ 98,066.43	$ 233,656	12,081	$ 19.34			
1013	01/31/47 FOOL'S GOLD	$ 89,403.25	$ 228,593	11,501	$ 19.88			
1014	03/28/47 UNEXPECTED GUEST	$ 94,664.65	$ 203,802	10,640	$ 19.15			
1021	05/23/47 DANGEROUS VENTIURE	$ 85,421.41	$ 205,577	10,851	$ 18.95			
	TOTAL	$ 367,555.74	$ 871,628	45,073	$ 19.34			
	AVERAGE	$ 91,888.94	$ 217,907	11,268	$ 19.34			
	1947-48 SEASON	**BUDGET**						
1029	07/18/47 HOPPY'S HOLIDAY	$ 95,580.72	$ 205,041	10,881	$ 18.84			
1033	09/12/47 MARAUDERS, THE	$ 124,000.00	$ 194,141	10,218	$ 19.00			
1047	03/19/48 SILENT CONFLICT	$ 124,000.00	$ 181,200	9,115	$ 19.88			
1053	04/30/48 DEAD DON'T DREAM, THE	$ 124,000.00	$ 154,328	8,176	$ 18.88			
1055	06/11/48 SINSITER JOURNEY	$ 124,000.00	$ 152,452	7,928	$ 19.23			
	TOTAL	$ 591,580.72	$ 887,162	46,318	$ 19.15			
	AVERAGE	$ 118,316.14	$ 177,432	9,264	$ 19.15			
	1948-49 SEASON							
1060	07/23/48 BORROWED TROUBLE	$ 124,000.00	$ 153,144	8,108	$ 18.89			
1068	09/10/48 FALSE PARADISE	$ 124,000.00	$ 140,912	7,031	$ 20.04			
1067	10/08/48 STRANGE GAMBLE	$ 124,000.00	$ 153,844	7,486	$ 20.55			
	TOTAL	$ 372,000.00	$ 447,900	22,625	$ 19.80			
	AVERAGE	$ 124,000.00	$ 149,300	7,542	$ 19.80			

APPENDIX VII
THE CISCO KID AT UNITED ARTISTS

RELEASE NUMBER		DOMESTIC FILM RENTAL	NUMBER OF BOOKINGS	AVERAGE RENTAL
	1948-49 SEASON			
1071	01/21/49 VALIANT HOMBRE	$156,714	6,928	$22.62
1080	05/13/49 GAY AMIGO	$146,353	6,311	$23.19
1091	06/24/49 DARING CABALLERO	$132,262	5,679	$23.29
	1949-50 SEASON			
1097	10/07/49 SATAN'S CRADLE	$111,909	4,618	$24.23
1108	02/24/50 THE GIRL FROM SAN LORENZO	$ 88,953	3,838	$23.18
	TOTAL	$636,191	27,374	$23.24
	AVERAGE	$127,238	5,475	$23.24

THE BOTTOM LINE / Low Finance in the Reel West

APPENDIX VIII
GENE AUTRY AT COLUMBIA

RELEASE NUMBER	RELEASED		PRODUCTION ORDER	NUMBER	SHOOTING DAYS	TOTAL DAYS	DOMESTIC FILM RENTAL
		1947-48 SEASON					
981	NOV '47	THE LAST ROUND-UP	1	892-12	05/16/47 TO 06/07/47	20	$ 360,000
982	AUG '48	THE STRAWBERRY ROAN (CineColor)	2	889-12	06/19/47 TO 07/18/47	25	$ 397,000
					TOTAL	45	$ 757,000
					AVERAGE	23	$ 378,500
		1948-49 SEASON					
181	JAN '49	LOADED PISTOLS	3	905-12	05/04/48 TO 05/22/48	17	$ 295,000
182	MAR '49	THE BIG SOMBRERO (CineColor)	5	893-12	08/07/47 TO 09/09/47	28	$ 311,000
183	MAY '49	RIDERS OF THE WHISTLING PINES	4	911-12	06/21/48 TO 07/08/48	15	$ 250,000
186	JUL '49	RIM OF THE CANYON	6	947-12	12/06/48 TO 12/20/48	13	$ 225,000
184	SEP '49	THE COWBOYS AND THE INDIANS	7	924-12	03/14/49 TO 03/28/49	13	$ 235,000
185	JAN '50	SONS OF NEW MEXICO	9	921-12	06/15/49 TO 06/29/49	13	$ 208,000
					TOTAL	99	$1,524,000
					AVERAGE	17	$ 254,000
		1949-50 SEASON					
250	NOV '49	RIDERS IN THE SKY	10	971-12	08/08/49 TO 08/23/49	14	$ 272,000
248	02/22/50	MULE TRAIN	11	976-12	11/08/49 TO 11/23/49	14	$ 272,000
245	MAY '50	COWTOWN	8	952-12	05/02/49 TO 05/16/49	13	$ 206,000
247	JUL '50	BEYOND THE PURPLE HILLS	12	977-12	12/06/49 TO 12/20/49	13	$ 193,000
249	SEP '50	INDIAN TERRITORY	13	981-12	03/27/50 TO 04/08/50	12	$ 184,000
246	NOV '50	THE BLAZING SUN	14	967-12	04/24/50 TO 05/08/50	13	$ 171,000
					TOTAL	79	$1,298,000
					AVERAGE	13	$ 216,333
		1950-51 SEASON					
351	JAN '51	GENE AUTRY AND THE MOUNTIES	15	988-12	06/12/50 TO 06/24/50	12	$ 174,000
352	MAR '51	TEXANS NEVER CRY	16	8009-12	07/17/50 TO 07/27/50	10	$ 159,000
354	APR '51	WHIRLWIND	17	8026-12	12/04/50 TO 12/15/50	11	$ 149,000
355	JUN '51	SILVER CANYON	18	8016-12	03/12/51 TO 03/22/51	10	$ 137,000
356	SEP '51	HILLS OF UTAH	19	8032-12	04/16/51 TO 04/26/51	10	$ 129,000
353	NOV '51	VALLEY OF FIRE	20	8010-12	06/05/51 TO 06/15/51	10	$ 129,000
					TOTAL	63	$ 877,000
					AVERAGE	11	$ 146,167
		1952-53 SEASON					
473	JAN '52	THE OLD WEST	21	8045-12	08/18/51 TO 08/28/51	9	$ 128,000
475	MAR '52	NIGHT STAGE TO GALVESTON	22	8063-12	09/20/51 TO 09/28/51	8	$ 111,000
471	MAY '52	APACHE COUNTRY	23	8072-12	11/12/51 TO 11/20/51	8	$ 121,000
474	JUL '52	BARBED WIRE	24	8079-12	12/10/51 TO 12/20/51	10	$ 102,000
476	SEP '52	WAGON TEAM	25	8094-12	04/07/52 TO 04/15/52	8	$ 96,000
472	NOV '52	BLUE CANADIAN ROCKIES	26	8067-12	05/19/52 TO 05/27/52	8	$ 104,000
					TOTAL	51	$ 662,000
					AVERAGE	9	$ 110,333
		1951-52 SEASON					
571	JAN '53	WINNING OF THE WEST	27	8125-12	06/24/52 TO 07/01/52	7	$ 104,500
572	MAR '53	ON TOP OF OLD SMOKY	28	8118-12	08/12/52 TO 08/19/52	7	$ 104,500
574	MAY '53	GOLDTOWN GHOST RIDERS	29	8128-12	09/09/52 TO 09/16/52	7	$ 83,500
575	JUL '53	PACK TRAIN	30	8146-12	10/07/52 TO 10/14/52	7	$ 85,500
576	SEP '53	SAGINAW TRAIL	31	8151-12	01/05/53 TO 01/13/53	8	$ 75,500
573	NOV '53	LAST OF THE PONY RIDERS	32	8188-12	03/16/53 TO 03/24/53	8	$ 80,500
					TOTAL	44	$ 534,000
					AVERAGE	7	$ 89,000
					GRAND TOTAL	381	$5,652,000
					OVERALL AVERAGE	12	$ 176,625

Corriganville's "stunt lake" flowed in the dry wash below the huge flat rock on the left.

A ROCK IS A ROCK
GOING ON LOCATION
by Dave Holland

Remember in the Monogram Western *Sagebrush Trail* (1933), when John Wayne is ambushed in a deep canyon and he and Lane Chandler jump on a stagecoach, whip the horses into action and drive into a cave and on through a long tunnel to escape Yakima Canutt and his gunmen?

As many of you know, that did not happen on a back lot but in a real cave in the Hollywood Hills, and when you finish reading this, you will be able to visit the exact spot where it was filmed. And you will recognize it immediately because it hasn't changed one bit in all these years. Those big cave entrances are still there, the tunnel is still there, everything.

As a matter of fact, once you get there, no matter which way you turn, everything around you will look familiar since so many scenes from so many movies and TV shows were done there. This is the same canyon where Clayton Moore became the Lone Ranger in the 1949 TV series and where he was wounded and rolled down that hill in the 1956 feature. What's more, the cave opening where Robert Wilke stood to shoot the Ranger in that same picture was the same cave used as the secret entrance to the underground Murania in Gene Autry's *Phantom Empire* (1935).

This is where the Paint Horse Gang holed up in Tom Mix's *Terror Trail* (1933) and where Hopalong Cassidy discovered the secret door to the old mine in *Leather Burners* (1943). And remember when Buck Jones was tied up in that abandoned gold mine and Silver untied him in *Gordon of Ghost City* (1933)? Same place.

So where is this place? Many of you know. In fact, many of you know where to find all seven of the famous Western movie locations we are going to examine here. But for those of you new to tramping about where so many of our cowboy heroes went on location, all of the above scenes were filmed at an old Los Angeles rock quarry called Bronson Canyon, a place you can visit today, a place not 15 minutes from Hollywood and Vine.

That feeling of *deja vu*, by the way, that sensation of "having seen this place before" you will experience at Bronson Canyon, will come over you at all seven of these locations. Scenes from hundreds of movies were shot at each one and *thousands* were shot at a couple of them. So get ready. There are memories on the trails ahead. And when we're finished, you will not only know how to find these locations, but how to recognize and call them by name when you see them in films.

What are the other locations we'll be exploring?

Remember the huge stone monoliths that Roy Rogers and Gabby rode between just before Grant Withers and Hal Taliaferro ambushed them in *Utah* (1945)? Over the years, you've probably recognized that same monumented pass as the one through which Sunset Carson chased his dad's killer in *Rough Riders of Cheyenne* (1945) and where Johnny Mack Brown was ambushed in *Bury Me Not on*

427

HOLLYWOOD CORRAL: A COMPREHENSIVE B WESTERN ROUNDUP

the Lone Prairie (1941). This is the Garden of the Gods area at the old Iverson's Movie Ranch in Chatsworth, California.

Another of the popular movie ranches—which were not working ranches or farms, but vast, fenced-off areas where ostensibly nothing but movie-making went on—was Corriganville, just over the Santa Susana Pass from Chatsworth in Simi Valley, California.

Here is where the runaway buckboard carried Dale Evans off that big flat rock into the lake with Roy racing to the rescue in *Along the Navajo Trail* (1945). It was from that same man-made stunt rock that Johnny Weismuller dove into the lake as *Jungle Jim* (1948), and it's the same big gray rock in the background when Gene Autry stopped the wagon dragging Lynne Roberts in *Sioux City Sue* (1946), and when he sang the title tune in *Beyond The Purple Hills* (1950).

Literally thousands of Westerns were filmed at these two ranches alone. Before we travel further into the past, let's clarify something right here. When we say that such-and-such a picture was shot at Iverson's or Corriganville or wherever, it doesn't literally mean that all of that picture was filmed there. It doesn't even necessarily mean that all of the exteriors were shot there. Rarely all, sometimes most, always some. Don't forget that Hollywood hopped about to make movies.

In RKO's case, for instance, interiors were done on sound stages at the studio in Hollywood, street scenes on its Western street at what is now the Sepulveda Basin in the San Fernando Valley, and exteriors at any number of locations. If the story called for Tim Holt and Richard Martin to ride "two miles from the ranch to the abandoned mine," it would not be unusual in the finished film to see them leaving the Jauregui ranch house in Placerita Canyon, gallop over a hill at Lone Pine, then rein in for close-ups at Iverson's to shoot the dialogue at the mine.

On to Number Four.

Remember the huge saw-toothed rock formation that lean on the diagonal behind Roy Rogers when he sang "Ride, Vaqueros, Ride" in *Apache Rose* (1947)? The same one he scrambled up at the end of *Jesse James at Bay* (1941)? This location is just north of Los Angeles in Vasquez Rocks State Park (pronounced Vahs-KAYS, not Vass-KWEZ).

Then there are the tall, columned cliff-faces and eroded rocky canyons that surrounded Dick Foran, Buck Jones and the other *Riders of Death Valley* when they were looking for the Lost Aztec Mine in that 1941 serial. This great desert location, which Universal thought looked more like Death Valley than Death Valley, is about two hours north of Los Angeles at a place with the appropriately Western name of Red Rock Canyon. And the rocks really are red there. Look at the beginning of Warner Bros.' *Four For Texas* (1963). It was at Red Rock Canyon that Charles Bronson and Jack Elam led that filmed-from-a-helicopter attack on a really red stagecoach with Frank Sinatra on top and Dean Martin inside.

Even further north is the magnificent moonscape of huge rounded boulders with the snow-capped Sierras in the background you've seen in so many of the early Gene Autry, Roy Rogers and John Wayne movies. This is the rugged Alabama Hills area, a tangled maze of rock formations just five minutes west of Lone Pine, California.

Folks thereabouts are proud of their movie heritage. Just off a road they've named Movie Road is a place they call Lone Ranger Canyon. That's the canyon where the Texas Rangers were ambushed in *The Lone Ranger* (1938), where Roy Rogers and Duncan Renaldo tried to capture Trigger in *Hands Across the Border* (1943), where Hopalong Cassidy rode the bucking bronc at the beginning of *Outlaws of the Desert* (1941) and where Frank McGlynn Jr. saved John Wayne from the ambush in *Westward Ho!* (1935)—all filmed at the exact same spot.

Roy Rogers made his first starring feature in Lone Pine. So did Robert Mitchum. And Kirk Douglas made his first Western here. This is also where nearly half of the 66 *Hopalong Cassidy* features were shot.

Almost all of the other Hoppys were shot in and around the old town of Kernville, California. This was a very popular Western location because, in addition to great white rocks and tree-dotted hills and draws, Kernville had something none of the other close locations had. Remember when Hoppy, California and Johnny crossed the Rio Grande in *Border Patrol* (1942)? That was really the Kern River. And when we first saw the Lone Ranger and Tonto at the beginning of *The Lone Ranger Rides Again* (1939), it's the Kern behind them, too. Being the closest real river to Hollywood, it worked a lot. "Convenience" (as in closest) was usually the most important factor in selecting a location for a B Western, although if the script called for a desert, you had to shoot it in the desert.

So there they are, the seven areas we'll tell you how to find: Bronson Canyon, Iverson's, Corriganville, Vasquez Rocks, Red Rock Canyon, Kernville and Lone Pine.

But why *these* locations? What about other Western locations? Henry King shot *Jesse James* (1939) in Missouri and Tom Mix travelled all over for his films (e.g., 1926's *The Great K & A Train Robbery* was shot at Colorado's Royal Gorge) – not to mention the Spaghetti Westerns or the Mexican Westerns or the very *first* Western (1903's *Great Train Robbery*), which was shot in the wilds of New Jersey!

Interviewed as this essay was being prepared, Republic's ace action director William Witney said that "Selecting a location began very simply. We looked around town first. Why? You said 'convenience' was a reason. An even better one-word reason for working close to home is 'commercial.' The further away we went, the more it cost."

"The story didn't necessarily dictate where you shot it," I said.

"The budget dictated everything," he replied. "I can remember the writers were always saying things like 'the script says he's behind a Ponderosa pine and you've got him in the middle of all those Joshua trees!'

"And," he went on, "weather played a big part in selecting a location, too.

"I remember on one of the Rogers pictures, we set it for June 'cause it never rains in June and we had a lot of exteriors to do. So we headed out to Thousand Oaks and it started to rain. And we stayed inside for three days while it rained. Now, the costs were adding up because we had Tito Guizar and Estelita and people like that just sitting around..." (that would make the picture 1948's *The Gay Ranchero*) "...so I finally went to the production people and said we've got to go somewhere else. 'We can't afford to,' they said. 'We can't afford *not* to,' I told 'em. Now, the next closest place with good weather right then was Kernville so we went up there for five or six days and did the picture. And the looks of the two places are completely opposite: Thousand Oaks has rolling hills and oak trees and Kernville has all those gullies and white rocks and pine trees, but the sun was shinin' there so it was just what the doctor ordered.

"One of my favorite little locations is out in that canyon where the Disney Ranch is now, what was it called? Just up the canyon from Andy Juaregui's place. The Walker Ranch, that's it, in Placerita Canyon. The only thing I didn't like about it was that the running insert road there was so short."

"But it was close to town," I said.

"We always looked around town first," Witney reiterated – which is why the seven most popular B locations are the places we're talking about now.

At each of our stops, we'll cite specific films shot there, not the *only* ones shot there, remember, but ones in which the individual location is easily recognizable. And if you study these films, you'll soon learn to recognize the distinctive physical characteristics of the locations and be able to name them when you see them in other movies. And their proximity to each other makes it possible for vacationers to visit them all within a reasonable length of time. So let's hit the road. Let's go find some memories.

Bronson Canyon

Get off the Hollywood Freeway in Hollywood at Gower, go east on Franklin and turn left on Canyon. Continue past the gated picnic area, park and walk up the hill road.

The first thing you'll see is the exit of the tunnel used in *Sagebrush Trail*. Immediately to its left is where Warner Bros. built that little pool where Jay Silverheels found the wounded Clayton Moore in *The Lone Ranger* (1956). Walk on in the cave and you're where Kevin McCarthy and Dana Wynter hid when the mob was chasing them in the original *Invasion of the Body Snatchers* (1956). Also, in *Call of the Canyon* (1942), this is the tunnel the dynamite blasts drove Gene Autry's spooked cattle into, almost trampling Tadpole, while Gene was trying to stop that runaway train roaring in from another direction.

Walk deeper into the tunnel and you'll see the three cave entrances. The one on the left (from inside) is the gateway to Murania and the big middle

The cave entrance in Bronson Canyon.

HOLLYWOOD CORRAL: A COMPREHENSIVE B WESTERN ROUNDUP

This scene from Desert Vigilante *(1949) was shot inside the caves at Bronson Canyon.*

one is where, with two guns blazin', John Wayne battled the Wrecker's gang in *Hurricane Express* (1932).

Still looking out the middle cave entrance, the hill in front is the one Wayne chased Natalie Wood down in *The Searchers* (1956) and it's the hill the wounded Lone Ranger rolled down that same year. Even Marlon Brando was here in *Julius Caesar* (1953). So were TV's *Wonder Woman* and *MacGyver*.

Iverson's Movie Ranch

Head West on the 118 Freeway up in the Northwest corner of Los Angeles' San Fernando valley. Exit at Topanga Canyon, turn left under the freeway and turn right at the traffic light onto Santa Susana Pass Road. Go another three-tenths of a mile to the entrance to California West. Enter this "Private Residential Community" and you'll see the Nyoka Cliff directly to your right and against the skyline just ahead on your right is the Lone Ranger Rock where the masked man reared Silver at the beginning of all those TV shows–which was *not* the only time that rock was used, by the way. Roy, Gabby and Raymond Hatton rode by it in 1939's *Wall Street Cowboy*.

Park along here (before you get to the condos) and over on the West side of the road, you'll see a sign back by the rocks that says "Santa Monica Mountains Conservancy Parkland." Walk up that old wagon road (chained to prevent vehicle access) — the same road on which Errol Flynn stepped from his horse onto California Joe's wagon to talk to Olivia DeHavilland in *They Died With Their Boots On* (1941)–and in less than 200 yards, you'll be at the Garden of the Gods. You'll be where Gene Autry sang Tom Mix's radio theme in *Roundup Time in Texas* (1937), where Flynn captured Anthony Quinn in *Boots*, where Alan Ladd got stopped at a Japanese roadblock in *China* (1943), the pass John Wayne led *The Fighting Seabees* through in 1944 and if you look back the way you came, you'll see that you were just on the road the Lone Ranger and Tonto rode at the end of every TV episode.

You're also right where the stage picked up John Wayne in *Stagecoach*, where they rolled into that Mexican relay station in the same picture, and where two years before, Charles Starrett had turned to one of the Sons of the Pioneers in *The Old Wyoming Trail* (1937) and said, "Len, get my horse." That blur dashing across the screen to do Starrett's bidding was one of the founding Pioneers, Leonard Slye, later to change his name to Roy Rogers.

Return to Santa Susana Pass Road and turn right. Less than half a mile on the same road Cagney used on the way to hold up that train in 1949's *White Heat* will take you to the side road leading to what was called "Upper Iverson's" in the movie days. There are truly palatial mansions back there now, but behind those homes off to your right—no trespassing, please—the old stagecoach road is still there, running along side those tree-lined bluffs.

That is where Don "Red" Barry hid inside the stage to surprise the holdup men in *The Apache Kid* (1941). It was out where those huge homes are now that stuntman Tom Steele performed his thrilling variation of Yakima Canutt's so-called *Stagecoach* stunt in *Phantom of the Plains* (1945).

Playing Wild Bill Elliott playing Red Ryder, Steele jumped down onto a racing getaway stage, only to be promptly thrown forward and down between the wheel horses, falling through the traces to the ground, grabbing hold and working his way back underneath the coach where he reaches up into the boot, almost losing his momentum, but finally pulling himself up and over the top of the coach to start the fight all over again.

I said Canutt's *so-called Stagecoach* stunt because many believe the first time he did anything like that was out on the dry lake near Victorville, California, in that John Ford classic. (*Many* locations were used in making Westerns, not just the ones discussed here.) Canutt himself once said in print that he remembered first doing the stunt in *Riders of the Dawn* (1937), doubling Jack Randall (up at Lone Pine,

Indian Head Rock at Iverson's as it was in 1925. This scene is from Silver Treasures, *starring George O'Brien, a Fox Film.*

HOLLYWOOD CORRAL: A COMPREHENSIVE B WESTERN ROUNDUP

California), but you can see him doing that famous underneath drag on film as early as 1931 up at Kernville, California, doubling George Brent of all people at the end of Chapter Three in *The Lightning Warrior*. (That Rin Tin Tin Jr. serial also used Bronson Canyon as a location, by the way. It was there in everyone's favorite real-life tunnel—as opposed to the cave-tunnel set on Republic's back lot—where the cloaked Wolfman met his hired bad guys to give them orders. Ditto the cloaked Rattler in Ken Maynard's 1934 serial *Mystery Mountain*.)

Off to the left when you're facing the Upper Iverson's bluffs is where Bob Livingston as the Masked Rider jumped down onto the top of that stage to hold it up before Leroy Mason and his gang could get to it in *Rocky Mountain Rangers* (1940). Just before the bad guys started chasing Livingston, they reined in by another distinctive rock out there, the tall easy-to-spot Turtlehead Rock. It's also prominent in *Sunset in El Dorado* (1945) when Roy Barcroft tries to shoot Roy and Dale and you'll see World War II soldiers marching by it in *The Story of G.I. Joe* that same year. Tall bushes obscure its shape now but it can be found.

Of course, William Wellman's *G.I. Joe* wasn't the only A picture to do bits and pieces at Iverson's. Shirley Temple, Victor McLaglen and Cesar Romero were there on John Ford's *Wee Willie Winkie* (1937), ditto Abbott and Costello for *Ride 'Em Cowboy* (1942) and Laurel and Hardy for the laundry scene in *The Flying Deuces* (1939). And during the big battle at the end of *Lives of a Bengal Lancer* (1935), look for the Nyoka Cliff in the background through all that gunsmoke.

But back to Bob Livingston. To escape Leroy Mason, he had to jump his horse off a cliff into the water. Now, if he had really jumped off a cliff out at Iverson's, he'd have been in big trouble because there wasn't a lake out there! The Bs generally shot their water scenes at Malibu Lake or Lake Sherwood in Thousand Oaks or went North to Kernville.

There was a Western street on the ranch at one time. When Gary Cooper was producing and starring in *Along Came Jones* (1945), he built it where the mobile home park is now.

Cooper had liked Iverson's as a location ever since he and Franchot Tone had been out there for the *Bengal Lancers* battle scenes. (Cooper had also done a scene on the ranch for 1939's *The Real Glory*, that time on top of the Nyoka Cliff, right where the gorilla would later chase Kay Aldridge in 1942's *The Perils of Nyoka*, giving the big formation its name.)

In *Along Came Jones*, look for the scene where Loretta Young saved Cooper and William Demarest from being shot outside the saloon. She leads them out of town past a big stone corner building and up a long curving road with the rail fences on either side. You'll easily recognize the same area when Eddie Dean and Emmett Lynn rode into town in *The Caravan Trail* (1946).

All of the major studios had their own Western streets. Most were on the back lots—you saw Republic's in the Red Ryder pictures and the ones with Roy and Gene and Sunset and so on (and such TV series as George Montgomery's *Cimarron City*). The Paramount street is best remembered from *Bonanza*; Audie Murphy and Tom Mix and Jimmy Stewart (1939's *Destry Rides Again*) rode Universal's (not to mention James Drury as *The Virginian*); and the Fox street can be seen in *The Ox Bow Incident* (1943), as a ghost town in *Yellow Sky* (1948) and where Charlie Chan waited for the bus to take him out to the *Castle in the Desert* (1942).

The Columbia street (used so often by Buck Jones, Wild Bill Elliott and the Durango Kid) was on the Columbia Ranch (still in operation in Burbank) where the Blondie house, the Boston Blackie New York street and the *Leave It To Beaver* house are still pointed out. And this was Hadleyville in Gary Cooper's *High Noon* (1952).

Warner Bros. shot such dandies as *Dodge City* (1939) and *San Antonio* (1945) on its long-gone street in those wheat-colored hills of Calabasas. (It also had an adobe Mexican section; witness 1939's *Juarez* and Tyrone Power's *The Mark of Zorro* in 1940.)

One of the most-used non-studio streets was out in Newhall, California, on the old Monogram Ranch (called Placerita Ranch when William S. Hart first used it in 1915's *The Disciple*). Tom Keene and Tex Ritter rode there in the '30s and during the Monogram years, this was the town that Johnny Mack Brown, Jimmy Wakely and Whip Wilson cleaned up every Saturday. Gene Autry bought it in 1952, changed the name to Melody Ranch and used it for such Flying "A" Productions as *The Range Rider*, *Annie Oakley*, *Buffalo Bill Jr.*, *Death Valley Days* and his own show, plus renting it out for *Wyatt Earp* and *Hopalong Cassidy* TV shows. The opening shoot-out at the beginning of *Gunsmoke* was shot there, too.

There were also streets at Pioneertown near Indio, in Kernville and in Lone Pine where Hopalong Cassidy Productions went in with local businessmen to build Anchorville, a street set used in the later Hoppys. Another street used occasionally in the

Gene Autry, Roy Rogers and Lone Ranger TV shows was the Jack Ingram Ranch (aka the Hertz Ranch and Four-Star Ranch) in the hills south of Ventura Boulevard in Woodland Hills.

Corriganville

Continuing West on the 118 Freeway into the Simi Valley, you'll pass the Rocky Peak Road off-ramp (which leads to another Western street location, the Bell Ranch). Get off at Kuehner Drive and go left nearly a mile to the old fenced-off entrance to the one-time weekend Western amusement park. Movie companies used a gate off the next road in the early days.

Ray "Crash" Corrigan, one of the Three Mesquiteers and Range Busters trios for years, bought the land in 1937. When he rented the property to movie-makers, it was with the proviso that if you built a set on the ranch, you left it standing. Eventually, Corrigan had hide-out cabins, a wonderful cavalry fort (which John Ford built for 1948's *Fort Apache*) and a complete street called Silvertown.

There are plans to rebuild Corriganville, so someday you may again be able to walk back to the stunt rock-lake location through the giant oaks where Buster Crabbe chased Charlie King so often. The stunt rock is still there, but the lake has been drained, making it easy to see the camera ports Columbia built to shoot the underwater *Jungle Jim* scenes.

Concrete foundations are all that remain where the Silvertown buildings stood. There is nothing left of Fort Apache except the memories of Wayne and Henry Fonda and John Agar out on the parade ground. It's also easy to recall seeing Robert Taylor there in *Ambush* (1949), William Holden in *Escape From Fort Bravo* (1953) and James Brown, Rand Brooks and Lee Aaker in the *Rin Tin Tin* television series.

Vasquez Rocks

As you're leaving the San Fernando Valley on your way North on State Highway 14, you'll pass near Beale's Cut which sits back from the old Sierra Highway. This is the deep narrow defile Tom Mix and Tony are supposed to have jumped in 1923's

Bob Steele gallops along one of Corriganville's insert roads for Death Valley Rangers *(1943).*

HOLLYWOOD CORRAL: A COMPREHENSIVE B WESTERN ROUNDUP

A terrific view of Vasquez Rocks as seen in the Roy Rogers starrer Apache Rose *(1947).*

Jack Hoxie on location in Lone Pine in 1925.

Three Jumps Ahead. John Ford also used this location in *Straight Shootin'* (1917) and he started the Indian attack here in *Stagecoach.* The jungle hero, The Phantom, was even ambushed here in his 1943 Columbia serial.

Continuing on through Palmdale and Lancaster, way off out of sight to your right among the gnarled old Joshua trees is where John Wayne rode as Singin' Sandy and Gene Autry sang the title tune in *South of the Border* (1939).

Nearly 15 miles North of where Highway 14 peels off from Interstate 5, you'll come to the Agua Dulce Canyon off-ramp. Exit there and follow the signs to Vasquez Rocks.

The Lone Ranger rode here, both in *... Rides Again* (1939) and in *The Legend of...* (1981). Roy Rogers was here, too, remember; and Buck Jones and Monte Hale and Rod Cameron and Rocky Lane. *Star Trek* shot out here. So did *Fantasy Island* and *Bonanza.* And one of the countless times you can easily recognize Vasquez Rocks is at the end of *The Last Bandit* (1949) when Wild Bill (William in this one) Elliott watched helplessly as Jack Holt zeroed in on Forrest Tucker way at the top of that jagged formation. Scenes for this were also shot at our next location.

Red Rock Canyon

Another 50 miles or so on Highway 14 will bring you to Mojave and 25 miles beyond that will put you smack in the middle of these eroded red cliffs and canyons. The distinguishing characteristics here are the sometimes diagonal layer-cake tops of the cliffs and the fluted columns in the cliff faces, making them look like giant pipe organs.

You see Red Rock in Hoppy's *Texas Trail* (1937) and this is where Chief Thundercloud stripped off his buckskin Tonto outfit in the 1939 *Lone Ranger* serial so his masked friend could stuff it with brush and fool the bad guys. In *Last Bandit* (just referred to) Forrest Tucker's gang hid that gold train in a tunnel here (thanks to the miniature magic of Republic's Lydecker brothers).

And remember in the *Three Mesquiteers* movie, *Gunsmoke Ranch* (1937), when Max Terhune stretched his rope across the trail, spilling the two men chasing him from their saddles, not knowing they were his fellow Mesquiteers, Bob Livingston and Ray Corrigan? That was shot here, too. So was the Chester Morris *Three Godfathers* (1936) and 1958's *The Big Country*.

If you turn off at Abbott Drive, park and hike back over the hill to your left, you'll soon be where Audie Murphy fought soldiers and Indians alike in *40 Guns to Apache Pass* (1967), where Buster Crabbe was *Buck Rogers* and where Boris Karloff watched the archaeologists discover that tomb in *The Mummy* (1932).

Robert Fuller almost died of thirst here on a TV *Wagon Train*. In all the years *Bonanza* was on the air, there were only two two-part stories. William Witney directed both, one here and one at Lone Pine, where we're headed next.

Lone Pine

Continue North on Highway 14 'til it joins U.S. 395, which you follow on up to the small desert town of Lone Pine, where movie-makers first came in 1920. The Chamber of Commerce is now in the old Lone Pine Hotel complex where Tom Mix and Fatty Arbuckle stayed.

Turn toward the Sierras at the only traffic light and in just minutes, you're surrounded by what the sign says are the Alabama Hills. But you know better. Look around you. This is India's Khyber Pass. This is where Errol Flynn and Tyrone Power, Cary Grant and Douglas Fairbanks Jr., even Gary Cooper and Franchot Tone led all those gallant British soldiers on patrol.

This was Peru in John Wayne's *Tycoon* (1947), Argentina in *Law of the Pampas* (1939) and Arabia in *Outlaws of the Desert* (1941).

The expanded Dow Hotel (where Hopalong Cassidy and Clayton Moore stayed) is still in town, so is the expanded Best Western (where Gregory Peck, Randolph Scott and Maureen O'Hara stayed).

It's in Mix's *Flaming Guns* (1933) that someone pulled up to a gas station and said "So this is Lone Pine!" and the town actually gets screen credit at the beginning of Hoppy's *Pride of the West* (1938): "Filmed at the base of majestic Mount Whitney in Lone Pine, California."

Nearby are the sand dunes used for occasional desert pictures (including a Johnny Weissmuller Tarzan). When you head up the switchback to the Whitney Portals, you'll be where Lucy and Desi drove *The Long, Long Trailer* (1954), where the cops chased Bogart in *High Sierra* (1941) and where Hoppy first met California's outlaw pal, Pico, in *Three Men From Texas* (1940). (The pass they rode through to get to Pico's hideout–where California again identified "the mating call of the Bull Camino" –is off Whitney Portal Road at Ruiz Hill. It was El Diablo Pass in that one and Gunsight Pass when Hoppy was ambushed there in 1941's *Border Vigilantes*.)

One of the fun things about roaming Lone Pine's Alabama Hills (where Bob Steele, Tom Tyler and Hoot Gibson also roamed) is finding spots used time and time again by the movie companies. This is the ideal location to match photos to still recognizable filming sites.

You'll find that the spot where Gene Autry jumped Champ over the convertible (it was really stuntman Joe Yrigoyen in 1947's *Trail to San Antone*) is the same spot where (11 years earlier) John Wayne strung a rope across the trail and tripped the four horses and riders chasing him in *Westward Ho!* Gabby's house in *Utah* (1945) belonged to California's cousin in *Pirates on Horseback* (1941). The fort in *King of the Khyber Rifles* (1953) was Edward G. Robinson's ranch house in *The Violent Men* the next year. And the spot where Robert Preston dragged Gregory Peck out of the wagon in *How the*

HOLLYWOOD CORRAL: A COMPREHENSIVE B WESTERN ROUNDUP

The readily identifiable rocks at Lone Pine as seen in this shot from The Cisco Kid and the Lady *(1940).*

Red Rock Canyon *in 1933, this scene from* Heritage of the Desert *starring Randolph Scott.*

West Was Won* (1962) is the same place Hoppy captured Sidney Blackmer in *Law of the Pampas* (1939); where Randolph Scott waited for the stage in *The Tall T* (1957); and where Tyrone Power buried Edgar Buchanan in *Rawhide* (1951). Fortunately for movie buffs, a book on the Lone Pine movies (with photos and maps to the locations) is available in town.

The only permanent sets in Lone Pine were a real house in Tuttle Creek Canyon (still called the "Hoppy Cabin" and again, no trespassing, please) and the long-gone hacienda-mission set on the Anchor Ranch (just across from the airport). When RKO finished shooting the classic *Gunga Din* (1939), the local contact man for Hollywood bought the big sets (the eight-acre town, the temple, the fort), trucked the materials to his ranch and built the sprawling mission first used in Hoppy's *Range War* (1939) and often in the later Tim Holts. It was also at this ranch that the Anchorville street was built for the later Hoppys.

Kernville

To be accurate, we should be saying "Old Kernville" when speaking of the movie days here. It was to today's Kernville (and to Wofford Heights) where people moved when the Kern River was dammed up in the '50s to form Lake Isabella, which eventually covered Old Kernville. (With the drought of recent years, the water has receded and you can tour the old town site nowadays, finding various building locations, including where "Movie Street" was and the site of the town's old Mountain Inn where movie people usually stayed.)

To get there, take Highway 178 either West from 14 (passing through the stand of Joshuas so evident in Hoppy's 1939 *Sunset Trail*) or East from Bakersfield. Turn North at Lake Isabella.

Tom Mix shot here. And Ken Maynard. So did DeMille, they say. Joel McCrea's *Wells Fargo* (1937) was done here. That river was a great draw. In fact, even if a film crew never left the San Fernando Valley, you could still see the Kern in the movie, thanks to stock shots (filming done for previous pictures but used in a current one); i.e., in Lash LaRue's *Stage to Mesa City* (1947), when Jennifer Holt's runaway buckboard goes off that cliff into the river, that one shot is from an earlier movie. Ditto the Chapter Three ending in *Riders of Death Valley*. Those great white boulders are the giveaway.

And so many companies invaded Kernville to use its old buildings for street scenes—the town was

Roger Imhof and friend cross the Kern River in this scene from Fox Films' Wild Gold *(1934).*

The Kern River (or what's left of it), as shot in 1992.

HOLLYWOOD CORRAL: A COMPREHENSIVE B WESTERN ROUNDUP

This courthouse is a facade built at Lone Pine for Riders of the Purple Sage *(1925).*

The majestic rock formations at Lone Pine, as shot in 1992.

438

The Monogram town at Newhall.

founded during Civil War days–that a special "Movie Street" was finally built on the Eastern edge of town. To see what it looked like, take a look at Hoppy's *The Showdown* (1940) or *Doomed Cavaran* (1941). You'll recognize it by the tall church and steeple at the end of the street on the left (a real Methodist church, built in 1898).

Hardly any of the old streets or sets are left; parts of the old Columbia street are still in use, a few buildings at Pioneertown. Melody Ranch burned in 1962, Corriganville in 1970. Kernville's "Movie Street" was dismantled during World War II and moved out into the desert for Army manuevers. The Century Plaza Hotel sits about where the old Fox street was. There are condominiums where the Mexican relay station in *Stagecoach* stood with the Garden of the Gods in the background.

Many of the historic old sets had to be torn down–the Foreign Legion post at Vasquez Rocks, the Lone Ranger silver mine shack at Iverson's–because picnickers, vagrants and yes, even inconsiderate movie fans climbed all over them, hurt themselves and sued.

But the rocks remain. And the memories. At least there are still memories where the cameras used to roll... the cameras and the wagon trains and all those stages to Thunder Rock and Chino and Monterey.

So get going! Get out there and walk those dusty trails where Roy Rogers rode Trigger, Gene Autry rode Champion and the Lone Ranger rode Silver. As it says on a bumper sticker you see occasionally, "It's never too late to have a happy childhood."

William Lava

APPASSIONATO DRAMATICO
MUSIC IN THE B WESTERN

by James King
with additional material by Sam Sherman

If you've ever watched one of the very early sound B Westerns, you probably sensed that something was missing. Oh, maybe the scenery was great, the girl beautiful, the stunt work superb, and the guys in white hats real heroes... but where was the music? We're not referring here to songs, but rather, to background scores that punctuated the action, caused the viewer to cringe in suspense, perhaps bring a tear to the eye when Granny lost the ranch, or even inspire us with chords of grandeur. Those pioneer film efforts could be quite dead indeed without that magical ingredient to bring it all together... music!

Early attempts at synchronizing music to picture in the silent days were often awkward. The success or failure of such attempts depended almost entirely on the music director. Many theaters employed live orchestras in those days, ranging in number from a small ensemble to a full symphony of 75 players. Imagine, if you will, the problems involved when a sudden shift of mood occured. The orchestra, depending on the conductor to signal them when a change was about to occur, would oftentimes be required to turn a page and suddenly go from a pastorale to a chase... all in the blink of an eye! The busy conductor, working from music cue sheets, would indicate the changes as soon and as accurately as possible, but perfect synchronization was something that was years away in technology yet to be invented.

The coming of sound created new problems for the pioneers in the field, and early technology proved inadequate. Attempts to synchronize recorded sound on disc to the action on screen were only partially successful. Then in 1920, a sound-on-film process was developed out of the photo-electric cell. Its inventor, Lee DeForest, employed sound impulses that were actually comprised of fluctuating light patterns, which were recorded on a track parallel to the visual track. As technology improved, the process allowed for isolation of tracks and the recording of music and sound as separate entities. The event brought about the creation of a new era of specialization–the "mixing" or blending together the various sound elements... and thus the "mixer" became a very important technician in motion-picture production.

When Hollywood finally did get around to "scoring" B Westerns, the studios were hampered as they were in all departments relating to B product. There was very little money to devote to post production. The very early B Westerns boasted only a musical Main and End Title and, more often than not, the music had nothing to do with the true atmosphere of the film. A nondescript instrumental piece, sounding very much like the dance-band music of the day, often introduced and closed a Western that should have had a dynamic score. Some person, or persons, must have known that such a score could help a picture, and perhaps overcome a number of

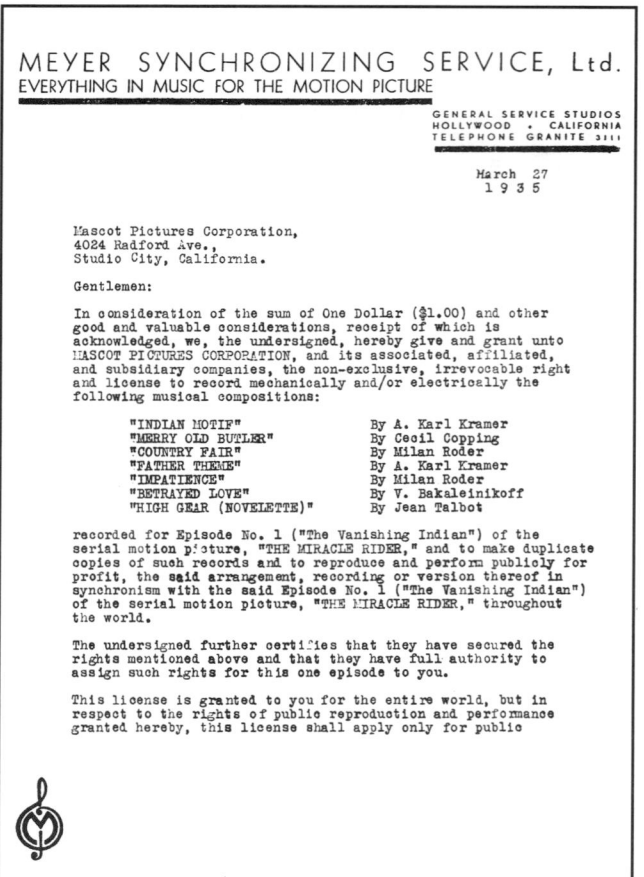

Page one of a letter of agreement from the Abe Meyer Synchronizing Service licensing music to Mascot for *The Miracle Rider (1935).*

weaknessess in production, but the economics of the situation prohibited a budget which would include a tailor-made score.

Although some early talkie Westerns (Fox's George O'Brien series, for example) had full scores, cobbled together from snippets of silent-era scores and newly written compositions, most independent Westerns, when they utilized music at all, depended upon cues sourced from independent music libraries.

The most prolific supplier of canned background music was the Meyer Synchronizing Service, Ltd., located at Hollywood's General Service Studios. Abe Meyer, an entrepreneur who'd come to Hollywood from New York in the late '20s, established his music library at the dawn of the talkie era and added to it throughout the early '30s, his high-quality library consisted of silent-era scoring cues (some of them written as early as 1915), original pieces written specifically for him, and fragments of original scores which he reused. Every serious Western fan has heard cues from the Meyer library in dozens of '30s oaters; the stirring "Dance of the Furies," actually written for a Gluck opera and used dramatically in the early Hopalong Cassidy films, was a popular piece. "Agitato #4" was another favorite of independent producers; it's used in several of the Kermit Maynard Westerns and some of the Sol Lesser pictures starring Smith Ballew and Paul Kelly. Meyer's relationships with veteran composers Hugo Riesenfeld and Heinz Roemheld, among others, enabled him to compile full "original scores" when necessary, and those consisting of old cues rearranged and rerecorded by new orchestras, plus a few custom-written themes worked in to freshen up the old supply.

Meyer charged $50 per cue to lease his music to producers. That was a relatively high sum, considering the shoestring budgets of many independent filmmakers, and it explains why the ultra-cheapie films ground out by Robert Horner, Denver Dixon, B. B. Ray, and others were devoid of music. Better-heeled producers such as Lesser and George Hirliman relied on Meyer, though, and others used him sparingly, sometimes renting one cue and using it several times in the same film.

Silent-era composer Lee Zahler worked for Meyer, at one point acting as Musical Director for Meyer Synchronizing Service. This association gave him insight into the business, and led him to start his own library in direct competition to Meyer, who closed his business in 1938 to become an agent with MCA.

Several other music libraries serviced Western producers during the '30s. One of them, the New York-based Sam Fox library, was an outgrowth of a music publishing company; it was represented in Los Angeles by Edward Kilenyi, a sometimes composer/conductor.

The close relationship between the Sam Fox Publishing Company and Fox Film Corporation (in the days before Fox's merger with Darryl Zanuck's 20th Century Pictures) led to the creation of Movietone Music Corporation, which not only serviced producers with Sam Fox cues, but also licensed cues written for Fox features (including the George O'Brien Westerns) by such composers as Louis De Francesco and J. S. Zamecnik, and even imported recordings of background music from France. The Movietone library flourished well into the '60s, old cues eventually being replaced by newer compositions when they became overly familiar thanks to repeated use in newsreels and theatrical trailers produced by National Screen Service.

Sam Fox offered cues to producers such as Sam Katzman and Maurice Conn at cheaper rates than Abe Meyer's; this explains why today's viewer can hear music in one of Conn's Kermit Maynard Westerns that was originally written for a much more expensive George O'Brien Western in the early '30s.

By the time Warners resumed B-Western production in 1935 with the Dick Foran series, the aesthetic value of rousing background music had been amply demonstrated. Not to be outdone by producers who relied on stock-music libraries, Warners created original scores for the Forans, complete with lush, even bombastic orchestrations and weaving some of Foran's songs into the scores. But the new scores often overpowered the visuals, and someone at the studio, realizing this, decided to license some old, tried-and-true Sam Fox cues and insert them into the pictures. *Guns of the Pecos* (1936) is one of the Foran Westerns that sports a score consisting of both original Warners compositions and rerecorded Fox cues. (The studio continued to use several Fox cues, including "Perilous Pursuit," in its '30s cartoons as well.)

Use of library synchronization music eventually gave way to studio "stock" music: generic cues of varying lengths and moods penned by a small staff of composers. By the late '30s, the often-predictable sound of B Western background music was being replaced by a more polished style of scoring. I can still recall the surprise and thrill I felt when I heard for the first time William Lava's stunning Main Title music for the 1937 serial *The Painted Stallion*. Used for all episodes except Chapter One, the composition was a tour-de-force for orchestra. The music punctuated the flight of the Whistling Arrow from the bow of "The Rider" of the Painted Stallion. As the title flashed on the screen, a galloping rhythm appeared in the brass, above which the strings and woodwinds repeated a fast broken chord figure in an ever-increasing crescendo. The Foreword music was no less impressive with its ominous tremolos, clarion french horn calls, and woodwinds and strings soaring to new heights. From then on, B-Western scores would never be the same. William Lava had established the standard and ushered in the "golden era" of music for the B Western.

Born in St. Paul, Minnesota, William Lava entered the Hollywood scene in 1936, whereupon he received indoctrination in film-music writing at RKO Studios, working under Nat Shilkret. Radio was still a very important entertainment factor in those days, so it is not surprising that Lava worked extensively in that field on many coast-to-coast broadcasts—composing, conducting and arranging. Probably the most notable of these shows was the Screen Directors Playhouse, which featured the top stars of Hollywood. After three years of composing and conducting at Republic, where he wrote music for nearly 150 films, Lava transferred to RKO and then, Warner Bros. Later, he scored many pictures for Universal and Walt Disney Studios. Two highly successful TV shows, *Cheyenne* and *Zorro*, were scored by William Lava and contained some of his best work. B Western fans will always remember his exciting scores for *The Lone Ranger Rides Again*, *Adventures of Red Ryder*, *Zorro's Fighting Legion*, *Three Mesquiteers* series, and many pictures featuring Don Barry, Gene Autry and Roy Rogers.

Other important names in the field of B-Western music are...

ALBERTO COLUMBO was born and raised in New York City, where he served as a cellist in the Manhattan Opera House Orchestra. Following a tour as an arranger with Paul Whiteman, he joined RKO as music director in 1934. Three years later he went to Republic, where he wrote music for *Zorro Rides Again*, *Wild Horse Rodeo*, *Springtime in the Rockies*, *The Purple Vigilantes*, *The Old Barn Dance*, *The Lone Ranger*, *Outlaws of Sonora*, *Under Western Skies* and *Gold Mine in the Sky*, among others.

Part of a sketch written by William Lava for a 1937 Gene Autry Western.

HOLLYWOOD CORRAL: A COMPREHENSIVE B WESTERN ROUNDUP

CY FEUER was born in New York City, where he received his musical education at Julliard. He played trumpet in the Roxy and Radio City Music Hall orchestras before coming to California to work for Brunswick Records, which at the time was owned by Republic Pictures head Herbert J. Yates. Through that connection, he was hired at Republic in 1938 as Music Director, a position he held until 1942. After two years of military service, he returned to Republic, which by that time had erected the finest stage in Hollywood. He composed and conducted for many B Westerns at Republic until 1947, at which time he became a partner in Feuer and Martin Productions, whose Broadway hits include *Guys and Dolls, Can-Can,* and *Silk Stockings.*

KARL HAJOS was born in Budapest. He studied at both the University and the Academy of Music. After composing operettas in Hungary, Hajos moved to New York City where he worked on staged musicals. He became a staff composer for Paramount in 1928 and served there for six years before moving to M-G-M and then to Universal. In 1936 he began a two-year stay at Republic, where he wrote stock cues with such titles as "Mechanical Montage" (used in many B Westerns), "Rushing Riders Hurry," "Light Mysterioso," "White," "Yellow," and "Gray." His score for *The Bold Caballero* (1936) became a rich source of music for many B-Western films to follow. Hajos employed a dark, somber style of orchestrating that served him well in the many scenes embodying mystery or suspense. Following his stay at Republic, he worked at M-G-M, Monogram, United Artists and PRC.

ALBERT GLASSER "I love Western music—it's big, rich, warm, and American. It pictures people ten feet tall." These sentiments are mirrored in his strong thematic score for *The Buckskin Lady,* released in 1956 by United Artists. It is, however, his music from the Cisco Kid feature films that Glasser is most remembered. From his scores for four of these feature films was gleaned the music used on 156 TV shows from 1949 to 1956.

PAUL SAWTELL's music can be heard in countless B Westerns released between 1940 and 1953 by RKO, Monogram, Republic, Universal and Columbia. A master at scoring the chase, his style closely resembles that of William Lava. Paul Sawtell studied in Berlin, Munich and Chicago and was frequently asked to be guest conductor of symphony orchestras. His vast output of movie scores include those for RKO's famous Tarzan films.

ROY WEBB was a pioneer in the use of the click-track, a metronomic device that can be heard through the headphones of the conductor and musicians, thus allowing for absolute coordination of music and picture. Roy Webb began his career as an orchestrator in New York. He came to Hollywood in the early '30s and worked for many years at RKO, Warner Bros. and Paramount. His B-Western scores include *Arizona Legion, Racketeers of the Range, The Renegade Ranger* and *Badman's Territory.*

VICTOR YOUNG is not known as a B composer, although some of his compositions have been heard in B Westerns, including several *Hopalong Cassidy* films. Possessing a great gift for melody, he would amaze studio executives by sitting down and turning out one beautiful theme after another. Born in Chicago but trained in Europe, he contributed greatly to films of the '40s and '50s. Adept as he was at composing a melody, Young was also skilled at writing exciting chase music and thunderous climactic episodes for full orchestra. Republic drew heavily on his score from *The Dark Command* (1940) for use in their cheaper Westerns. Listen to some of the larger orchestra sounds in the Three Mesquiteers Westerns of the early '40s and you'll hear the music of Victor Young. The studio also used his Emblem music from *Army Girl* (1938) to introduce many B Westerns.

CHARLES DUNWORTH was a free-lancer who was also associated with the Abe Meyer Synchronization Service. He is remembered primarily for his "Storm and War" which served as the Main Title for *The Phantom Empire* (1934). His "Stealthy Footsteps" was an oft-used mysterioso.

LEE ZAHLER originally came to Hollywood in the '20s to work as a set musician at the Thomas Ince studio. After Ince's death, Zahler was thrown out of work and free-lanced as both a set musician and as a composer (and occasional performer) of film music played live in theaters to accompany silent films. Zahler went to work for Abe Meyer as talkies became popular, and worked his way up to become Meyer's top hand. He composed music, conducted the orchestra recording it, and even on occasion, helped select and edit cues into movie soundtracks (he was even a member of the film editors' union).

When Zahler established his own music library to service independent producers such as Sam Katzman, Larry Darmour, and the Weiss brothers, he took some Meyer cues with him (under unexplained circumstances) and fleshed out his inventory with compositions written by close friend Ross DiMaggio, who was also writing music for Republic serials. Thus, DiMaggio's "Doomship" (written for Republic's 1941 serial *Adventures of Captain Marvel*) became, with the most minute alteration, Zahler's "The Decoy;" and "Mysterious Dr. Satan Main Title" became "Main Title #3." In that way, music written by DiMaggio was heard in Columbia serials produced by Larry Darmour only months (or even weeks) after it had been used at Republic.

DiMaggio was eventually hired by Columbia, where he served as conductor and musical director. Music Department head Morris Stoloff preferred to keep DiMaggio from composing, as the former violinist's soulful string-dominated themes had less effect on Stoloff than they did on B-Western and serial fans, who appreciated the weird moods they evoked.

The Zahler library outlived its founder. Son Gordon kept the service going well into the TV era (*Wild Bill Hickok* was one of the shows that used Zahler music), and leased cues to producer Sam Sherman for his 1975 B Western homage *Blazing Stewardesses*.

FRANK SANUCCI's musical background themes have probably been heard in more B Westerns than those of any other composer, and some aficionados believe his work evokes a better feeling for the subject matter than more elaborate scores written for higher-budgeted pictures.

Sanucci broke into B Westerns writing and arranging songs for the Tex Ritter oaters produced at Grand National. He performed similar chores at Universal while working for producer Trem Carr on the Bob Baker series. In addition to working on songs, Sanucci helped score the film with cues selected from Universal's considerable library. When the studio's 1938 contract with the Musicians' Union curtailed the unrestrained use of old studio library cues, Sanucci wrote chase themes recorded by the small cowboy band being used for songs in the Baker films. (A similar experiment had been performed in the 1936 Buck Jones starrer *Empty Saddles*, in which a cowboy band led by Frank Yaconelli plays an improvised chase theme during a sham battle.) A trumpet and a piano were added to the cowboy band, making up a grand total of eight musicians playing for Sanucci. It was the lowest-priced scoring in the movie industry...but it worked. Sanucci repeated the experiment at Monogram for Ed Finney's Tex Ritter series; the cues sounded better and were eventually rerecorded for later use. In fact, Sanucci received single-card, full-screen credit in Monogram's *Trail Blazers* series, putting him on a par (well, almost) with major studio composers. His music was also used by PRC and some independent producers during the '40s; the number of films utilizing his cues, if they were ever totalled, would surely be staggering.

FRANZ WAXMAN composed the cue entitled "The Gold Rush" for the 1936 Universal picture *Sutter's Gold*. It, along with "Pastorale" and "Chase" from *The Bride of Frankenstein* were used in many Universal B Westerns in the late '30s.

DAVID RAKSIN composed the Main Title for Universal's serial, *Wild West Days*. The cue was later used in many B Westerns such as *Oklahoma Frontier* with Johnny Mack Brown and *Outlaw Express* with Bob Baker.

MORT GLICKMAN was one of the first to introduce dissonance into the B-Western score. He did it, however, in combination with the more accepted melodic and traditional harmonic treatments, and thus captured the ear of the modernist and the traditionalist alike.

Many composers for B Westerns found that their efforts went uncredited on screen. Usually, the Music Director was credited with the score, although he may not have written a note of it. Actually, it was very often the work of several composers.

Of course, the studios were also producing A

First page of the cue-sheet compilation listing all the musical compositions used in Heart of the Rockies *(1937).*

REPUBLIC PRODUCTIONS, INC.			
Republic Studio		No. Hollywood, Calif.	
MUSIC CUE SHEET			
Title HEART OF THE ROCKIES		Date August 13, 1937	
Description of Picture: WESTERN ROBERT LIVINGSTON MAX TERHUNE RAY CORRIGAN		Prod. No. 711	
Sound Equipment RCA VICTOR		Producer SOL SIEGEL	
Musical Director RAOUL KRAUSHAAR			

Reel Cue			
1. Composition:	REPUBLIC SIGNATURE NR	Usage:	COMPLETE
Composer:	Al Colombo	Instrumental	X
Publisher:	Santly Bros Joy	Instrumental Visual	
Rights Secured:	RP Property	Vocal Vocal Visual	
2. Composition:	THREE MESQUITEERS M.T.	Usage:	COMPLETE
Composer:	Al Colombo	Instrumental	X
Publisher:	Santly Bros Joy	Instfumental Visual	
Rights Secured:	RP Property	Vocal Vocal Visual	
3. Composition:	THE ROUGH RIDERS NR	Usage:	COMPLETE
Composer:	Karl Hajos	Instrumental	X
Publisher:	Santly Bros Joy	Instrumental Visual	
Rights Secured:	RP Property	Vocal Vocal Visual	
4. Composition:	SHADOWS IN THE NIGHT NR	Usage:	COMPLETE
Composer:	Al Colombo	Instrumental	X
Publisher:	Santly Bros Joy	Instrumental Visual	
Rights Secured:	RP Property	Vocal Vocal Visual	
5. Composition:	LISTEN TO THE MOCKING BIRD (WHISTLING)	Usage:	COMPLETE
Composer:	S Winner	Instrumental	X
Publisher:	Public Domain	Instrumental Visual	
Rights Secured:	Public Domain	Vocal X Vocal Visual X	
6. Composition:	RUSHING RIDERS NR	Usage:	COMPLETE
Composer:	Al Colombo	Instrumental	X
Publisher:	Santly Bros Joy	Instrumental Visual	
Rights Secured:	RP Prop	Vocal Vocal Visual	
7. Composition:	PAINTED STALLION M.T.	Usage:	PARTIAL
Composer:	Bill Lava	Instrumental	X
Publisher:	Santly Bros Joy	Instrumental Visual	
Rights Secured:	RP Prop	Vocal Vocal Visual	
8. Composition:	GLORIA'S THEME	Usage:	PARTIAL
Composer:	Hugo Riesenfeld	Instrumental	X
Publisher:	Santly Bros Joy	Instrumental Visual	
Rights Secured:	RP Prop	Vocal Vocal Visual	

HOLLYWOOD CORRAL: A COMPREHENSIVE B WESTERN ROUNDUP

First page cue-sheet for South of the Border *(1939).*

pictures with tailor-made scores, and many times music would be gleaned from those pictures and used in the B Westerns. This was especially true at Universal, where editors built the entire scores of the studio's '40s Westerns from music written for *Destry Rides Again* (1939) and *Trail of the Vigilantes* (1940). In the late '30s and early '40s, a key figure emerged: the music editor, or music "cutter," whose job it was to piece together from optical track all the various cues to give the picture a custom-made sound. The process, also known as "tracking" in low-budget films, could be very creative. The editor almost became the composer as he endeavored to select musical sequences to match the action on screen. Such ability was something that could not be taught. The *technique* was, of course, something that could be learned, but the actual ability to *feel* a scene... to demonstrate a flair for the dramatic... was something not to be found in textbooks.

Technically, a machine called a Moviola became an indispensable piece of equipment. Using two sound heads, the machine allowed for dialogue on one track and music on the other. Often, in "tracking," a cue would either be too long or too short. If too long, some footage would need to be removed, and ideally, the editor would make the cuts where they would be musically correct. Sometimes a piece of music would be "backtimed" in order to catch a good phrase on which to enter. If a good starting point could be found with this technique, no edits within the piece were necessary.

Obviously, anyone performing such a task as "tracking" had to be highly skilled. Not only did the edits have to be smooth and unnoticed, but where intercuts were involved (that is, cuts made somewhere within a cue to another cue) the music had to be matched according to key (or relative key) and tempo. Although the music director might be involved in the process, some "cutters" were so good that they could virtually be left alone. Such a man was Republic's Jerry Roberts. Cy Feuer states that Roberts was so facile that he would often give him free creative rein to do whatever he wanted with the music. Feuer's confidence was justified because, indeed, much of Roberts' work, with his flawless transitions and matching of cues, often made the music come out sounding like a brilliant original composition.

The orchestras supplying music for the B Western were moderately large at best. Republic, the studio that established the standard for B Western background scores, used the following instrumentation: flute/piccolo, oboe/english horn, clarinet, bass clarinet/bassoon, one or two french horns, three trumpets, two or three trombones (sometimes bass trombone and tuba), percussion (handled by one or two men), harp, six or eight violins, one or two violas, cello, string bass, piano or Novachord (an early electronic keyboard instrument). Since every studio had its own contract orchestra, and musicians were rewarded with a 52-week-a-year job, Hollywood became a mecca for instrumental artists who could also sight read and play a variety of musical styles. Thus, one can hear on the soundtracks of the period some of the world's greatest instrumental talent... and that, or course, includes the soundtracks of the B Western.

The shooting schedule for the B Western of the '30s and early '40s was often no more than ten days. As time passed, and budgets increased, orchestras grew in size and more music written especially for the picture began to be used. In the years leading up to the TV Western, and the demise of the theatrical Bs, styles changed, most notably with more dissonance being used in composing the scores.

The B-Western composer, although drawing heavily on the romanticism of the 19th century, was original in many ways, establishing a mood, a never-to-be-duplicated atmosphere bordering on a new art form. Today's film composers would do well to

APPASSIONATO DRAMATICO / Music in the B Western

study them, for there is much to be learned. William Lava once said to me, "No matter what the quality of the film that came to us, we in the music department at Republic always accepted it as a 'gem' and wrote accordingly." Cy Feuer adds, "We never wrote 'down' to the picture."

Over 50 years have passed since the strains of William Lava's *The Painted Stallion* music first fell on the ears of theater audiences. As mentioned before, this writer was one of those in 1937 who thrilled at the sound. It must have been sometime during that period that an excited boy knew he had to become a musician. Imagine that boy, as a man and professional musician in 1985, giving the downbeat for "The Painted Stallion Main Title" in front of a full orchestra playing from the original scores! That magic moment from 1937 lived again in his heart and soul.

Of course, the above story would not have been possible without the efforts of some very fine people dedicated to preserving early film music. In particular, Brigham Young University, where the Republic music archives are housed, made my labor of love even more enjoyable by graciously making available to me their vast collection of original scores. B.Y.U. offers the serious researcher access to more than 1,000 boxes of piano-conductor scores and parts, together with more than 7,000 recordings... an almost complete studio music archives. Many original pencil sketches as well as finished scores with parts and cue sheets facilitate a detailed study on many key films scored by the composers who worked at various times for Republic Pictures.

In one of our many conversations, William Lava confessed to me that in his boyhood he, too, had been "hooked" on the Western. In fact, as he put it, he would go to a theater and get lost for "days" until his folks came and literally had to drag him out. His favorite cowboy? Silent star Eddie Polo. Perhaps in his young mind, even then, he realized something was missing. Where was the music? Perhaps in his psyche, even at that young age, were the primitive beginnings of something that years hence would bear the name Lava and become "Saddle Tempo," "Black Motive" or "Riders in Pursuit." Whatever happened there, Western fans are all the better for it.

Peggy Stewart

GALS OF THE SADDLE
THE LOVELY LEADING LADIES
by Ed Hulse

Since the B Western was, more than most film forms, a star-driven genre, it's not surprising that much of what's been written by fans and historians has focused on the personalities rather than on the movies themselves. Even to this day, stars' characterizations and costumes often draw more critical attention than the stories, themes, or physical aspects of the productions. Truthfully, the B Western lends itself to this peculiar kind of scrutiny moreso than most genres; when many plots depend upon the stereotypical machinations of greedy bankers buying ranches devastated by marauding bandits, it's not surprising that favorable impressions have been (and still are) engendered by the delivery of a familiar tagline, the crease of a Stetson, the design of a shirt, or the tooling of a gunbelt.

It's fascinating, though, that while the contributions of the Western stars, sidekicks, and singing groups have all been well documented since the revival of interest in low-budget oaters, the appeal of the leading ladies in these pictures has been, if not altogether overlooked, at least undervalued and underexamined (with the exception of Jon Tuska's *The Filming of the West*, which is peppered with fetishistic references to B-Western ingenues clad in "tight riding breeches"). Granted, their charms may well have been lost on small boys yowling and bouncing in their seats at those Saturday matinees of yesteryear, but one suspects that B-Western buffs today—especially those grown-up Front Row Kids—cast more appreciative eyes upon the ingenues who adorned those films.

Unfortunately, researching the careers and lives of these actresses—especially those who worked most frequently in the independent Westerns of the '30s—is a difficult and frustrating task. Many of them (including, just to name a few, Iris Meredith, Joan Barclay, and Luana Walters) started out as bit players, chorus girls, or extras in major-studio productions. Invariably, once they realized their opportunities with the majors were limited (or when their six-month or one-year contracts ran out and were not renewed), these girls turned to Poverty Row, whose producers placed value on players who'd at least had *some* experience in front of the cameras. It wasn't uncommon for a female bit player, who'd had a few lines in a 1934 big-budget musical or comedy, to win the lead in a 1935 independent Western.

But, without the elaborate press-agentry offered by the big studios, the Western leading ladies—considered strictly ornamental in the action-oriented star vehicles—never really established their own followings. So when today's researcher dips into the annuals issued by movie-industry trade papers years ago, he's likely to find sketchy biographical entries—or, in some cases, none at all.

That leaves the researcher at the mercy of pressbook copy, which is only occasionally reliable. Or, if he's lucky, personal contact with those B-Western ingenues still living. But even interviews can be deceptive; since the youngest surviving B-Western ingenues are now in their sixties, occasional lapses of memory are to be expected. And some players—how to put this delicately—choose to proffer accounts of those halcyon days that are at variance with established facts.

So... leaving aside the historian's objectivity long enough to make some personal observations, I'd like to share some thoughts about my own favorite leading ladies of the B Western.

I've been fascinated by Luana Walters, a raven-tressed cutie with a provocative smile and ever-so-slight lisp, ever since I first saw her in *Mexicali Rose* (1939) some 20 years ago. Hardly an accomplished actress, she was certainly capable of heartfelt and, on rare occasions, dynamic performances. Luana was at her best in feisty characterizations, such as the rebellious sister of outlaw George Lloyd in *The Return of Wild Bill* (1940) and the strong-willed mountain girl in *Bad Men of the Hills* (1942), one of the better Charles Starrett-Russell Hayden outings.

Born in Los Angeles on July 22, 1912 and educated in Ramona Convent at Alhambra, California, Luana was signed at age 18 to appear in the 1930 Douglas Fairbanks starrer *Reaching for the Moon*. That same year she made a favorable impression in *The Shyster* on stage in San Francisco. An undisclosed "serious illness" forced her out of show business for two years, but she returned to the screen in bit parts in Warner Bros.' *Miss Pinkerton* and *Two Seconds* (both 1932) before winning costar billing on Tim McCoy's *The End of the Trail* (1932). In that classic B Western, her character was named Luanna, leading some fans to speculate whether or not that was her real name (especially in as much as, while trying to make a comeback in 1947, she briefly billed herself as Susan Walters).

She subsequently appeared with screen cowboys Rex Bell (1933's *The Fighting Texans*), Buck Jones (1936's *Ride 'Em Cowboy*), Tom Keene (1937's *Under Strange Flags*), Jack Randall (1938's *Where the West Begins*), Tim Holt (1942's *Thundering Hoofs*), and Don "Red" Barry (1940's *The Tulsa Kid*). Luana also undertook ingenue chores in the tyro appearances of The Range Busters (in the 1940 film of the same name) and The Rough Riders (1941's *Arizona Bound*).

Iris Meredith (l.), Wild Bill Elliott, and Luana Walters in The Return of Wild Bill *(1940).*

Although she was routinely singled out by trade reviewers as being a better actress than most sagebrush sweethearts, Luana never got the breaks she seemingly deserved. Most of her other '30s and '40s pictures were routine Poverty Row potboilers, including *The Speed Reporter* (1936, with Richard Talmadge), *Shadow of Chinatown* (1936, a serial with Bela Lugosi), and *The Corpse Vanishes* (1942, again with Lugosi). And, like several other B-Western ingenues, she occasionally dabbled in exploitation fare such as *Marijuana* (1937, an early, sensationalistic, anti-dope treatise) and *Children of Loneliness* (1936, a daring film about lesbianism that costar Jean Carmen remembers as being "pretty raw" for its day).

Luana drifted out of films after 1942 or 1943, making an ineffectual stab at a comeback in 1947, billing herself as Susan Walters for *Shoot to Kill*, a turgid crime drama in the *noir* style. Producer Alex Gordon, as he relates elsewhere in this book, used her in a couple of his '50s films, after which she more or less disappeared from view.

In the aforementioned *Return of Wild Bill* (1940), Luana shared the spotlight with Iris Meredith, Columbia's resident Western heroine, a slender, sleepy-eyed stunner who was certainly one of the most beautiful actresses to grace Saturday-matinee screens.

If pressbook biographies are to be believed, Iris (born Iris Shunn) had a much more interesting early life than any of the characters she ever played in the movies. The daughter of a sea captain, born in Massachusetts (although her *Motion Picture Almanac* entry lists Sioux City, Iowa as place of birth), Iris was taken to the Orient when she was five years old, spent one year in Singapore and three in Hangkow, China. Her father died when she was ten years old, and the family returned to the United States, settling in Los Angeles. At 17, she went to work as a cashier at Loew's State Theatre in Los Angeles to help support her mother and two younger brothers.

Accounts vary as to how Iris was "discovered." According to one source, a Columbia talent scout spotted her at Loew's and immediately had her signed by the studio, where she appeared in *The Cowboy Star* (1936) opposite Charles Starrett. But she's clearly visible in the chorus line in several Fox films of 1935, including *George White's Scandals of 1935*. Moreover, cast sheets on the Fox films (which list more players than are given screen credit) have her billed as Iris Shunn, as do early publicity stills from *Cowboy Star*, before Columbia changed her surname to Meredith.

Iris Meredith

Even though Iris worked in non-Western Columbia films (including 1938's *Those High Grey Walls* and 1939's *Beware Spooks*) and serials (1938's *The Spider's Web* and 1940's *The Green Archer*), she was most frequently seen in the Starrett films of 1938-41, in which, for the most part, she was called upon only to smile and look pretty (which wasn't difficult) while the Sons of the Pioneers sang and Starrett slugged. She seems particularly insipid in something like 1938's *Cattle Raiders*, for example, but appears to much better advantage in *The Thundering West* later that same year, partly because her character in the latter film is spunkier, and partly because she's more beautiful than ever as photographed by master cinematographer Lucien Ballard in one of his infrequent B-Western assignments.

Iris also played opposite Will Bill Elliott several times, most notably in *The Taming of the West* (1939), in the role of "Pepper," a hot-tempered firebrand. It gave her a refreshing change of pace, but apparently went unnoticed by the front office.

(It's been suggested that Iris was a victim of studio politics and unsavory casting practices, and upon leaving Columbia in 1941 she immediately went to PRC, the runt of the Hollywood litter, where she made a few forgettable films and then quit the business. In later years she showed uncommon courage by turning up at a brace of Western film festivals after several cancer operations had obliterated her beauty. Her fans were not disappointed, as she had feared; rather, they admired her all the more for appearing in public thus disfigured.)

The early years of Louise Stanley are similarly marked with intrigue and adventure. Inspired to be an actress when still a small girl, she was playing ingenue roles in a small theater in her home town of Springfield, Illinois, before she was 15. When she was 16, she ran away to St. Louis and joined a small stock company, until she was found by private detectives employed by her father, Alvin S. Keyes, Illinois's state receiver. She went back home with the detectives, but ran away to Chicago a short time later, this time getting a job on a radio program, until her anxious parents heard her on one of the broadcasts and persuaded her to return home again. A 1935 visit to Los Angeles finally launched Stanley on her picture career. This time her parents, their patience exhausted, refused to send her money. About that time Louise got a job at Paramount, and made her screen debut in *Anything Goes* (1936).

Louise made many independent Westerns, appearing frequently in the films of Jack Randall, with whom she was romantically linked. As an actress she was barely passable, but as a "looker" there were few in Westerns who could compete. She looks particularly nice in *Riders of the Rockies* (1937), a Tex Ritter Grand National, and she delivers a pretty good performance in *Gun Lords of Stirrup Basin* (1937), a nifty Bob Steele opus that, stripped of its Western accoutrements, is nothing more than a prairie *Romeo and Juliet*.

Lynn Merrick co-starred with Don "Red" Barry in 16 Republic B Westerns made between 1941 and 1943, and went on to Columbia, where she played leads in low-budget features and won supporting roles in major productions. And yet she's one of the most enigmatic of all Western leading ladies. Billed as Marilyn Merrick, she had a minor role in *Ragtime Cowboy Joe* (1940), a Johnny Mack Brown starrer for Universal that did little to attract attention to her. But the Lynn Merrick who worked with Don Barry was a talented, beautiful blonde whose com-

Louise Stanley and Bob Steele in Durango Valley Raiders *(1938).*

petent performances never suggested the condescension that some of the more gifted players allowed to creep into their characterizations. It's hard to point to specific films as being among her best, because Lynn's portrayals were consistently good. But, if pressed to name a favorite, I'd probably opt for *Outlaws of Pine Ridge* (1943). Unfortunately for B Western fans, she got her best chances in Columbia "civilian" pictures (especially 1944's *Nine Girls*, in which, cast as a snobbish sorority sister, she delivers a devastatingly funny, accurate Katharine Hepburn imitation).

Cecilia Parker got a bigger bounce from her B Western stint: She signed with M-G-M in 1937, about the best break an actress could hope for. Parker, who made her movie debut opposite George O'Brien in *The Rainbow Trail* (1931), was right out of a convent school when she entered the rough-and-tumble movie business of the '30s. But she thoroughly enjoyed making Westerns, and today recalls her favorite costars as being O'Brien, Buck Jones, Rex Bell, and John Wayne, with whom she appeared in *Riders of Destiny* (1933), the first of Monogram's "Lone Star" Westerns.

Monogram had one of Hollywood's leading equestriennes in Betty Miles, an attractive, athletic leading lady (if not much of an actress) who'd appeared in the riding sequences in *Nothing Sacred* (1937) and doubled Linda Darnell in 20th Century Fox's *Chad Hanna* (1940) immediately prior to being cast by director Spencer Bennet in *Ridin' the Cherokee Trail* (1941), a Tex Ritter starrer.

The dark-haired, silky-voiced Miles went on to appear opposite Tom Keene and The Trail Blazers in a number of early '40s Monograms, including *Riding the Sunset Trail*, *Wanderers of the West*, *Lone Star Law Men*, *Wild Horse Stampede*, *The Law Rides Again*, *Westward Bound*, and *Sonora Stagecoach*. Her appeal stemmed mainly from the fact that she was no helpless female, smothered in crinoline, who'd have to be rescued by the heroes. No, Betty dressed in buckskin jackets and tight jeans, rode like the dickens, and traded lead with most of the badguys who populated those Monogram horse operas. And, being an accomplished horsewoman, she could be photographed close up doing some pretty spectacular stunts.

There are many other B-Western ingenues who deserve mention, some of whom have backgrounds that belie their careers in low-budget Westerns. Of the girls who populated early talkie oaters, for example, Ruth Hall has always puzzled me. As an actress I find her to be stiff, and certainly not very

Lynn Merrick

Ruth Hall

passionate, but with a fascinating screen presence nonetheless. A society deb from Tallahassee, Florida, Hall was inspired to take up acting upon reading that another society girl, Francis Dee, had been selected for the lead in a major-studio feature. Believing she could go and do likewise, Hall embarked for Tampa, where Henry King was making *Hell Harbor* (1930). Impressed by Hall's dark good looks and her youthful exuberance, King signed her for a bit part. She won ingenue roles in several popular early talkies, including the 1931 Marx Brothers starrer *Monkey Business* and the 1932 Eddie Cantor spectacular *The Kid from Spain*. That same year she worked opposite John Wayne in *Ride 'Em, Cowboy*, Ken Maynard in *Dynamite Ranch* and *Fargo Express*, and Tom Mix in *Flaming Guns*. She retired early from films, settling into a long and happy married life with famed cinematographer Lee Garmes.

Dorothy Fay, a native of Prescott, Arizona, was supposedly "riding mustangs and learning to rope cattle on her uncle's Arizona ranch at the early age of 11." Reportedly, Dorothy's parents insisted on some different training, and sent her off to Chicago where she studied ballet dancing under the famous Adolph Bolm. From Chicago she went to England, learning dramatic arts in Great Britain's finest schools. The training landed her on the stage, first in England; then in summer stock in Massachusetts and later on Broadway where she appeared in the play "Good Neighbors." She arrived in Hollywood in 1938.

Dorothy appeared with Buck Jones that year in two of his lackluster Columbia releases, *The Law of the Texan* and *The Stranger from Arizona*. Shortly thereafter she appeared opposite Universal star Bob Baker in *Prairie Justie*. But she worked best with (and ultimately married) singing cowboy Tex Ritter. Dorothy's films with Tex include *Sundown on the Prairie* (1939), *Rollin' Westward* (1939), and *Rainbow Over the Range* (1940). Although she never seemed wholly at home on the range—maybe it was that precise diction of hers—Dorothy provided an engaging presence in her Western vehicles.

A more charismatic leading lady who likewise got off to a good start in pictures before winding up in B Westerns, Lois January was born in McAllen, Texas but as a young girl moved with her family to Los Angeles, where she attended the exclusive Marlborough School and, later, Virgil High School. A drama major who took piano and voice lessons from private teachers, Lois joined the prestigious Pasadena Community Players almost immediately following graduation. She played the lead in "Man of Wax" opposite Lloyd Corrigan, and was spotted by a Universal talent scout. She had a good bit role in *By Candlelight* (1934), appearing in support of Elissa Landi and Paul Lukas. She toiled in a few more Universal pictures before being dropped, and immediately went to work in cheapie Westerns. One pressbook scribbler dryly stated: "She is happiest, she says, in Westerns, loving to ride and glorying in the outdoor thrill." Even as a young woman, Lois displayed a facility with dialogue equalled by few ingenues in low-budget oaters; not that she was delivering Noel Coward lines, mind you. She was clearly the best thing in Reb Russell's *Arizona Badman* (1935), a fascinating if flawed Western stolen from the nominal star by his leading lady and Edmund Cobb, playing the titular terror. Lois made tyro Western star Bob Baker look good in *Courage of the West* (1937), which was extremely well-directed by Joseph H. Lewis, who recognized Lois' ability and utilized it in some dramatic, expressive close-ups.

She occasionally essayed "other woman" roles as well, most memorably in a 1937 Bob Steele starrer, *The Trusted Outlaw*.

Unlike many B-Western ladies of the '30s, the ingenues of the '40s tended to be contract players, some of whom were astonishingly prolific. It certainly seems, for example, that every other Republic Western made between 1944 and 1947 features Peggy Stewart in the female lead. She's in ten of the 23 Republic "Red Ryder" features, eight of Sunset Carson's 15 for the studio, and a pair of the pre-"Rocky" Allan Lane series of six. (Interestingly, she never appeared in a Republic Western starring Don "Red" Barry, to whom she was once married.)

Peggy was the perfect B Western ingenue. She delivered her lines well, handling them with just the right lightheartedness on those few occasions when comedic situations came her way. She rode well, unlike many of her contemporaries, who frequently looked as though they were about to pitch from the saddle at any minute. And, perhaps most importantly, she made her costars look good; no one would call Sunset Carson a great actor, but Peggy Stewart played their scenes together so as not to upstage him. She later freelanced for other Western producers, appearing opposite Charles Starrett, Gene Autry, Lash LaRue, Bill Elliott, and other B Western stalwarts of the post-WWII era. She was still acting in 1992, appearing in commercials and on stage in Los Angeles-based productions.

During the war years, Jennifer Holt was to Universal what Peggy Stewart was to Republic—

GALS OF THE SADDLE / The Lovely Leading Ladies

Dorothy Fay and Tex Ritter (Mr. and Mrs. Tex Ritter).

455

HOLLYWOOD CORRAL: A COMPREHENSIVE B WESTERN ROUNDUP

Irene Ware

Billie Seward

Rita Cansino (Rita Hayworth)

Carol Hughes

GALS OF THE SADDLE / The Lovely Leading Ladies

Sheila Ryan (above l.) was signed to be Gene Autry's leading lady in Mule Train, which began shooting in early November, 1949, at Lone Pine, California. Few would have guessed that Gene's sidekick Pat Buttram would literally wind up winning the girl. Sheila and Pat were married the following year. The Buttrams relax at home (top r.), and with their daughter, Kerry (above). At left is a scene from Mule Train (1950), from left, Gene Autry, Sheila Ryan and Pat Buttram.

HOLLYWOOD CORRAL: A COMPREHENSIVE B WESTERN ROUNDUP

Dale Evans

Fay McKenzie

Jennifer Holt

Lynne Roberts

GALS OF THE SADDLE / The Lovely Leading Ladies

namely, the studio's pre-eminent Western leading lady. She'd made her film debut, billed as Jacqueline Holt (her father was matinee idol Jack Holt, her brother was Western star Tim Holt), opposite William Boyd in a 1941 *Hopalong Cassidy* film, *Stick to Your Guns*. Signed to a contract by Universal in 1942, she toiled in many "civilian" pictures—mostly in bit parts—as well as in the B Westerns. She costarred with Johnny Mack Brown in one of his 1942 solo vehicles, *The Silver Bullet*, before being tagged as unit leading lady for the 1942-43 Johnny Mack Brown-Tex Ritter Westerns produced by Oliver Drake.

In the seven Brown-Ritter productions, Jennifer acquitted herself ably. She smiled prettily while the Jimmy Wakely Trio warbled, emoted earnestly when being romanced (infrequently) by Johnny or Tex, and, most impressive of all, managed to keep a straight face during Fuzzy Knight's puerile (and often adlibbed) comic-relief scenes. In later years she recalled that, although she looks at ease on horseback, she never felt entirely safe while riding, and was more than once saved from a nasty spill by other riders.

Jennifer appeared in one Universal Western starring Russell Hayden (1943's *Frontier Law*), two of Ritter's solo Universals (*Marshal of Gunsmoke* and *Oklahoma Raiders*, both 1944), and three with Rod Cameron (1944's *Riders of the Santa Fe, Beyond the Pecos* and *Renegades of the Rio Grande*, both 1945) before leaving Universal for good. Like Peggy Stewart, she freelanced at Monogram, Screen Guild, and PRC after the war, supporting Eddie Dean, Lash LaRue, Jimmy Wakely, Russell Hayden (for Screen Guild), and Johnny Mack Brown (for Monogram). The pictures got cheaper, but Jennifer got better. In fact, she delivers what's probably her best performance as the female outlaw in a 1948 Dean starrer, *The Hawk of Powder River*. Retiring from films shortly thereafter, she worked for a time in early live television before quitting show business.

There are others... Dale Evans, especially in her Rogers films of 1944-46, sexy and sassy... Fay McKenzie, bouncy, bright-eyed daughter of veteran character actors Eva and Bob McKenzie, who costarred with Gene Autry in many of his 1941-42 efforts... Lynne Roberts, who appeared opposite Roy Rogers (billed as "Mary Hart") in his 1938-39 series entries, went to 20th Century Fox in the early '40s, and returned to Westerns after the war, usually in the films of Gene Autry....

Julia Thayer (Jean Carmen) as the Rider of The Painted Stallion *(1937).*

THE MIRACLE RIDERS
COWBOYS AND CLIFFHANGERS
by Alan Barbour

There is something mildly comforting about looking back over one's life and picking out those times when fun was at a maximum and concerns at the minimum. For me, the best times came between ages eight and 12, when I spent virtually every Saturday at the Broadway Theatre in Oakland, California, watching a seemingly endless parade of serials, B Westerns and program features. I know that probably sounds like a trivial pursuit to today's "fast-track" kids who live in a world that tends to deprive them of what we used to call a "normal" childhood. Times do change, after all, so you really have to propel yourself back in time to see what made the difference.

First of all, there was no television. Kids in the late '30s and early '40s were limited to comic books (which were just really coming into their own with superheroes like Captain Marvel and Superman) and radio, which broadcast action shows like *Terry and the Pirates, Captain Midnight* and *Jack Armstrong* on a Monday-to-Friday basis. Because of school during the week, the only real chance a kid had to see exciting action was on a weekend at the theater. It was here, week after week, that we got a chance to see our heroes, bigger than life, go after the badguys on a continuing basis. The movie studios dragged us in, panting and yelling, as they put heroes from the comic pages and airwaves on that big screen.

I wish I could convey the thrill that went through us when we sat in that small theater in 1941 and suddenly *Adventures of Captain Marvel* flashed on the big screen. The entire house went wild with screaming and yelling like you couldn't believe. Oh, there was always some loud noise when the Western came on, but nothing like the din that went up for the serial. We had even been prepared in advance by having ads in *Whiz Comics* telling us about Republic's forthcoming serial, and in the second issue of *Captain Marvel Adventures* they even ran a full-page edited synopsis of Chapter One. Well, this was my first full serial (I had seen a couple of episodes of *Mysterious Doctor Satan* and I seem to recall my grandmother taking me to a Friday night show where they ran a chapter of *The Green Hornet*) and I was addicted for the next several years. How could I not be?

The studios, bless their greedy little hearts, had come up with a terrific gimmick to get audiences to come back to the theater week after week and they milked it as long as they could. Serials actually began in 1912 during the silent-film era when the newspaper feature *What Happened to Mary?* was adapted to the screen. Then came the glorious exploits of Pearl White and so many others to keep kids, and adults, too, on the edge of their collective seats. More than 250 silent serials were produced, yet due to film deterioration, only a handful have survived. The format was easily adaptable to the sound medium and continued until 1956 when television series (i.e. *The Lone Ranger, Will Bill Hickok, Sky King,*

HOLLYWOOD CORRAL: A COMPREHENSIVE B WESTERN ROUNDUP

That's Yakima Canutt under the mask, doubling for John Carroll in Zorro Rides Again *(1937). Dick Alexander is on the receiving end of the whip.*

etc.) were all the kids needed to excite themselves. Even many of the actual serials appeared on the tube. In New York, for example, in the early '50s a show called *Serial Theatre* ran a different chapter each day of the week from five Universal serials. On Monday you would have *Flash Gordon*; Tuesday, *Buck Rogers*; Wednesday, *Tim Tyler's Luck*; Thursday, *Red Barry*; and Friday, *Radio Patrol*. What a thrill it was, since I'd never seen these titles as a kid.

Each year's serial output from the studios was pretty evenly balanced as far as subject matter was concerned. There were usually one or two straight detective-type thrillers, perhaps a jungle epic or science-fiction adventure, and then...the Westerns. Westerns were a natural for serial treatment and the studios loved them. First of all, they were a little easier, on average, to make. You could utilize many natural hazards (cliffs, waterfalls, etc.) without having to spend a lot of money for special effects. Secondly, outdoor shooting in those days was considered less costly than constructing big sets on sound stages and staging lengthy dialogue scenes under the hot lights. (Rising location expenditures and increasing unionization, with attendant overtime expenses, eventually changed that, though.) In fact, costs were not a big factor in serial making. *Zorro's Black Whip* (1944), a 12-chapter Republic Western serial, was brought in for about $145,000, while *Captain Marvel*, made three years earlier, cost about the same. Republic's most expensive serial, 1943's 15-chapter *Captain America*, set the studio back only $223,000. Talk about inflation: you couldn't buy one of those elaborate one-minute television commercials for that price today.

Another reason the studios liked to do Western serials was that it enabled them to present some of the kids' favorite action stars on a weekly basis. Normally a star like Buck Jones, William Elliott, Johnny Mack Brown, etc. would only make eight films a year as their "series" output. Your theater probably would show only a few of these, so it was in the best interest of, say, Columbia to present Buck Jones in *White Eagle* (1941) and give him exposure for 15 continuous weeks. Not every great Western star made the transition from features to serials, however. Many stars considered the chapterplays demeaning and wanted no part of them. Most were simply too busy on their own eight-per-year efforts with the rest of the time being spent on personal appearance tours.

Finally, a more practical reason for doing Western serials was that the studios had built up complete libraries of stock footage that could be easily integrated into new films, saving a great deal of time and money. One of the best tipoffs that a stock-footage sequence was about to unfold in your favorite serial was when the hero or heroine changed clothes for no apparent reason. If you really want to see this sort of thing done to the maximum possible, catch the 1950 *Desperadoes of the West*, starring Richard Powers (Tom Keene). In Chapter Eight, for example, an entire shootout sequence at an oil derrick is lifted from an earlier *Three Mesquiteers* Western, *Raiders of the Range*. Long riding or chase sequences are a natural for re-use, even within the same serial. After all, kids' memories are rather short. It's hard to recall a chase in Chapter 12 that was lifted from Chapter One, which had played three months earlier.

The studios depended a lot on short memories. That's how they were able to use the same few stunt men over and over again every few chapters. Tom Steele or Dale Van Sickel would be killed as a badguy in one chapter, then pop up and get killed as another badguy two chapters later, then turn up as another character a few more episodes down the line. In *Daughter of Don Q* (1946), Van Sickel plays a villain in a recap episode and then turns up as a cop in the very same chapter. But few noticed and less cared, as long as there was plenty of action.

Over the years I attended a lot of Western and serial conventions that gave me a chance to meet many of the directors and stars of the serials. On the whole, most of them were hard-working, dedicated people who, for the most part, loved making the serials. There was a sense of comraderie and common purpose that seemed to please everyone concerned. Peggy Stewart, who costarred in many

Ray Corrigan (l.), Hoot Gibson and Hal Taliaferro in The Painted Stallion *(1937).*

HOLLYWOOD CORRAL: A COMPREHENSIVE B WESTERN ROUNDUP

Western serials, said she couldn't wait for weekends to end so that she could get back to work. Stuntmen like Tom Steele, who was Republic's chief action ace, was a terrific horseman and doubled for all of that studio's Western stars at one time or another. Tom's one complaint was that, although he never had any serious injuries, he was always getting bruised up doing "those damn horse falls."

Two of the questions I am usually asked when the subject of serials comes up are "How long did it take to make them?" and "How much money did the leads usually get?" Well, on the average during the prime era of sound serials (1937-45, for many of us), the average shooting time was from three to five weeks. *The Lone Ranger* (1938) was shot in a little over four weeks; *Zorro's Black Whip* (1944) in less than four, and *The Painted Stallion* (1937) in only three weeks. Most of the serials of the early '50s were shot in three weeks or less, thanks to the use of stock footage integrated into them. On occasion a serial like *The Lone Ranger Rides Again* (1939) could take as much as six weeks, but that was a rare exception.

As to salaries—well, that could vary all over the place. Many stars, like Kane Richmond, got only $400 a week to star in something like *Haunted Harbor* (1944)—that was the same weekly wage that stuntman Dale Van Sickel was paid to double him! A sports celebrity like "Slingin' Sammy" Baugh, bringing a well-established following to theaters for his *King of the Texas Rangers* (1941), could get $1,000 a week under special deals. Many of the supporting players were getting as little as $75 a week, including Yakima Canutt in many of his earlier Westerns. The studios were not known for being generous with a dollar.

Yet, many players who were not under studio contracts did very well by bouncing from picture to picture and studio to studio. Some of these character people, like Tom London, Ted Adams, Charles King, could be working on several films a week (sometimes even several in a day when crowd scenes were required). Republic was smart enough to lock up men like Roy Barcroft and Tom Steele under exclusive contracts in the '40s. Even though the money wasn't abundant, the work was. A 16-hour day was not unusual, and shoots often went six days a week. Spencer Bennet, one of the best serial directors, said that it was required to get the first shot "in the can" by eight o'clock every shooting day. He said they would often shoot any stray shot they could just so they could call back to the studio and say they got that first shot on schedule.

Since space doesn't permit a detailed rundown on all of the Western serials produced, let me just talk about a few of my personal favorites.

Zorro's Fighting Legion (1939) was a honey of a thriller on all counts. It had a terrific leading man, Reed Hadley, who looked great and sounded even better (although it is laughable when Yakima Canutt doubles for him in some sequences, and Zorro suddenly looks inches shorter and many pounds heavier). The villain of the piece was Don del Oro, a mysterious gold-plated masked man who wanted to hijack Mexican gold so that he could force the new Republic into bankruptcy and then step in as its new leader. There were some excellent endings, terrific riding sequences, and a superb music score composed mainly by William Lava. This 12-chapter gem is probably my favorite Western serial of them all. It still holds up in screenings today.

Daredevils of the West (1943) is a serial that probably best captures that wild "let's-wreck-the-whole-set" type of action that Republic developed in late 1941 and continued well into the decade. Formerly, fights were either wildly swinging affairs with fists flying all over the place, or incredible acrobatic sequences (usually with David Sharpe) in which crazy leaps and backflips had us all ooohing and ahhhing. Many of these early fights were done in single long-shots and unrelated intercuts. William Witney started the piece-by-piece fight sequence that he has claimed was derived from the way Busby Berkeley did his musical numbers.

Since some sets for *Daredevils of the West* covered most of an entire soundtsage, the fight action went to virtually every corner. Anything from furniture to props left standing was purely accidental. Tom Steele, who doubled for Allan Lane in this classic, said that the studio hated the bills that had to be paid for smashed props in these serials, so whenever he got the chance he would grab some bottles and breakables from any other film he was working on and bring them over to the serial sets for ultimate destruction.

Daredevils' Allan Lane was a perfect serial star. He was good-looking, very athletic and able to deliver lines effectively. He was my second favorite serial hero (Kane Richmond was my first, thanks to 1942's *Spy Smasher* and 1944's *Haunted Harbor*), and he starred in four of Republic's best serials: *King of the Royal Mounted* (1940), *King of the Mounties* (1942), *Daredevils*, and *The Tiger Woman* (1944).

Daredevils' heroine was Republic's reigning "Serial Queen," Kay Aldridge, who had scored well for the studio in *Perils of Nyoka* (1942) and would

THE MIRACLE RIDERS / Cowboys and Cliffhangers

Duncan Renaldo (l.) watches Bob Livingston accept papers from Rex Lease in The Lone Ranger Rides Again (1939). That's Eddie Dean third from the right in one of his first film roles.

Reed Hadley (l.) as Zorro, under fire with John Merton in Zorro's Fighting Legion (1939).

HOLLYWOOD CORRAL: A COMPREHENSIVE B WESTERN ROUNDUP

"Slingin' Sammy" Baugh (l.) and Duncan Renaldo pinned down by saboteurs in King of the Texas Rangers (1941).

appear with Kane Richmond in *Haunted Harbor* (1944). The serial was solo-directed by John English after his usual codirector, William Witney, entered military service. Although we usually attribute most of the action sequences to Witney in the serials he codirected with English, this serial showed that the dapper director could really do the action stuff pretty well on his own. Some of the fight sequences in this chapterplay are the best you will ever see—that is, if you *ever* see them. Much of the original negative has decomposed, and it's unlikely we will ever see the complete serial, although four complete chapters are available on videotape from various sources.

King of the Texas Rangers (1941), a 12-chapter actioner released by Republic, had All-American football star "Slingin' Sammy" Baugh trying to find his Texas Ranger father's killer and stop a band of saboteurs working for "the Leader," who was obviously a Nazi (but we weren't in the war yet, so we couldn't identify him as such). Tom Steele did much of Baugh's action stuff (with a helping hand from David Sharpe on some spectacular leaps and transfers), but the gridiron star did look good, and there were some really great chapter endings—particularly the finale for Chapter One, which had some amazing miniature work (done by Howard and Theodore Lydecker) of exploding oil derricks and storage facilities. The superb pyrotechnics done in the serials is one of the things that set Republic efforts apart from Columbia and Universal, who mainly relied on newsreel shots and really cheap miniature work. Sharpe, also doubling for costar Duncan Renaldo, had some great little action gems, and the whole serial is a delight to watch over and over again.

I didn't see too many Columbia serials when I was a kid, but in later years I saw almost all they produced. Their Western serials didn't impress me very much. There was an awful lot of riding around, albeit with some good background music, and plenty of shootouts, with hundreds and hundreds of shots being fired but with hardly anyone ever getting hit.

I guess if I were to pick one favorite from Columbia, it would be *Overland with Kit Carson* (1939), starring Will Bill Elliott. Although the rugged star appeared in *The Great Adventures of Wild Bill*

Hickok (1938) and *Valley of Vanishing Men* (1942), it is this in-betweener that is the most entertaining. *Hickok* was made too early in the Columbia cycle and really creaks, while *Vanishing Men* is often too silly to be taken even moderately seriously. Elliott was certainly one of my favorite B-Western stars, but primarily when he worked at Republic in the 1944–46 *Red Ryder* series and his earlier pairings with "Gabby" Hayes in a 1943–44 Republic series. A perfect hero type, he'd gotten his "Wild Bill" moniker from the *Hickok* serial and from the Western series he'd done at Columbia subsequently. His "I'm a peaceable man" tagline delivered in many films was a savvy warning to badguys that trouble was coming.

Overland with Kit Carson was a full 15 chapters, but every chapter seemed to be about the same. There were horse chases aplenty, and dozens of gunbattles, but fight sequences were few and far between and were often badly staged. Columbia, try as it may, could just never come up to the standards that Republic set. Thank goodness the Broadway Theatre only ran Republics!

If I have to pick a Columbia Western serial, then out of fairness I should pick a good Universal. *Riders of Death Valley* (1941) was billed as "The Million-Dollar Serial" because of a cast that included Dick Foran, Buck Jones, Charles Bickford, Leo Carillo and others, but it really wasn't so great. *Winners of the West* (1940), which also starred Foran, had some good train sequences but, again, wasn't great. So I guess I'd pick *Flaming Frontiers* (1938), with Johnny Mack Brown. It had plenty of good action, an excellent musical score, and Johnny was another of those Western stars who just seemed to satisfy all around. As far as I am concerned, he threw the most realistic-looking punch of all the cowboy stars. He had a good Western career with Universal, but when he

Dick Foran (center) in Riders of Death Valley *(1941)*.

HOLLYWOOD CORRAL: A COMPREHENSIVE B WESTERN ROUNDUP

Johnny Mack Brown, Raymond Hatton and Walter Miller in Rustlers of Red Dog *(1935).*

Tom Mix and Robert Kortman struggle in chapter eleven of The Miracle Rider *(1935).*

THE MIRACLE RIDERS / Cowboys and Cliffhangers

A rogue's gallery from Riders of Death Valley *(1941). Left to right: Roy Barcroft, Monte Blue, Charles Bickford, Lon Chaney Jr., Ethan Laidlaw, Jack Rockwell, Richard Alexander.*

went over to Monogram in 1943, everything seemed second-class. It's too bad he wasn't grabbed up by Republic in the '40s (though he did some Republic-released Westerns in 1937-38) to add to that studio's illustrious roster.

Although *Flaming Frontiers* had its share of stock footage (Universal was the worst for recycling earlier material; you saw the same Indian shot from his horse several times during this and other Western serials from the studio), it still had enough original material to make it very entertaining.

Of course, we can't leave Mascot out of the picture. Between 1929 and 1935, this studio turned out a number of Western serials featuring top stars who were a little past their glory days. Ken Maynard was acceptable in *Mystery Mountain* (1934), and Tom Mix certainly showed his age in *The Miracle Rider* (1935). However, it was a young singing cowboy by the name of Gene Autry who made a name for himself and thrilled audiences in a remarkable serial that combined traditional Western action with the science-fiction gimmick of an underground city called "Murania." The laughable part of the serial was the hook of having Gene make a daily radio broadcast in order to fulfill a contract. It certainly caused a lot of back and forth action as Gene experienced perils underground only to escape in time to make the broadcast and sing his song. The title of this epic: *The Phantom Empire*.

One of the main disappointments in this serial (as in most Mascot serials, for that matter) was the lack of a musical score. It made all the long riding sequences deadly dull. From Day One, Republic learned that it was important to use full musical scores in their chapterplays. One additional sidelight on Mascot was the fact that one of the screen's greatest Western stars of all time, John Wayne, made three serials there—1932's *Shadow of the Eagle* and *The Hurricane Express*, and 1933's *The Three Musketeers*—and none of them were Westerns.

469

Ray Whitley

CUT TO THE CHASE
SAGEBRUSH SHORT SUBJECTS
by Richard W. Bann

At one time all Westerns were short subjects. In 1903 one of the few genuine movie pioneers, Gilbert M. Anderson, essayed several roles in the history-making single-reel outdoor drama entitled *The Great Train Robbery*. In 1907 Anderson cofounded the Essanay Company and established a series of popular short Westerns, each running one or two reels in length. He also starred in many of them, and by 1911 had developed a character soon to be famous as "Broncho Billy" Anderson. For the next six years he churned out almost one short subject per week. The stage was set.

Following in Anderson's trail, two principal successors emerged: William S. Hart and Tom Mix. Both started in Western short subjects, as Anderson had, but soon progressed to feature-length films just as the motion-picture industry developed and expanded its scope. So began the star system, and as other potential Western heroes entered the field, many, like Hoot Gibson and Buck Jones, began in short-length narratives and progressed to feature-film series as their successes warranted. Thus Western shorts served as a testing ground for cowboy-star aspirants while also fulfilling a need for product demanded by exhibitors to complete a well-balanced theater program. As such, Western two-reelers remained plentiful throughout the mid '20s.

By the end of the decade, however, all Western subjects—shorts, program features, and epics—had reached a low ebb. Then, with the advent of talking pictures, the industry believed all outdoor action pictures were dead, shorts and features alike. Production was largely suspended because it was thought technically impossible and economically unfeasible to record sound in the wide-open spaces. Anyway, who wanted action when now people could talk from a screen?

The obituary for Western adventures was premature, but by the time the form was resuscitated, market conditions had changed. Western features made a comeback, all right, and soon were totally revived by the singing cowboy—but Western short subjects were a different story. They continued, in isolated cases, out of inertia, and as a response to limited market demands, but basically their importance had passed.

By the late '20s, the biggest Western names had already graduated to feature pictures. With the demand for Westerns reduced, the lesser attractions working in short subjects just couldn't make the cut during the changeover to talking pictures. Another obstacle was the Depression. Some of the Poverty Row producers grinding out low-budget short mediocrities were less well capitalized than the prestigious companies, and were casualties of the financial shakeout. So diminished demand at the box office, plus diminished supply of both stars and production companies, pretty much decimated the category of Western short subjects.

Desperate exhibitors, failing as the Depression widened, thought they could attract more customers by offering two features on the same bill. But at

HOLLYWOOD CORRAL: A COMPREHENSIVE B WESTERN ROUNDUP

what price to the traditional well-rounded program of a newsreel, a scenic, a comedy short, and maybe a serial chapter or cartoon all leading up to the feature attraction? Viewing time was finite, and this precious commodity was freed up on a theatrical program by eliminating the short product, or much of it, in favor of a second feature.

The quality and popularity of these shorts had very little to do with the situation. Double bills and so-called block booking practices (in which the majors forced theaters to buy entire blocks of A and B feature product) were simply forcing out shorts made by all except a few of the studio powers. The main reason exhibitors were playing double features was the fear that audiences would be lured to competing theaters that offered them. So it wasn't the audience (or lack of) or producers that killed short subjects, it was the exhibitors.

Producers were forced to stop making them, even though short subjects were still loved by audiences. The pre-eminent shorts producer of all time, Hal Roach, abandoned the two-reel comedy business in 1938 after 24 years. His product was better than ever, but costs were rising relative to animated cartoons, bookings decreased as the popularity of double bills grew, and profit margins narrowed. His studio could not survive producing only short product.

There were showmen who did not panic, who were solicitous of their paying customers, and who wanted to provide the best film program possible. Where there *was* a need for shorts, studios continued to produce them as a service to complement their features. M-G-M had a broad line of comedies and general information shorts that fit in well with their style of feature films. Studios like Universal, Columbia, and RKO, however, produced large blocks of Westerns in addition to their B series, general-audience pictures, and prestige features. To complement their product lines, Columbia and Universal

Al Hoxie (l.) watches helplessly as Yakima Canutt (center) and his men rob Wally Wales and Peggy Darling in Carrying the Mail *(1934).*

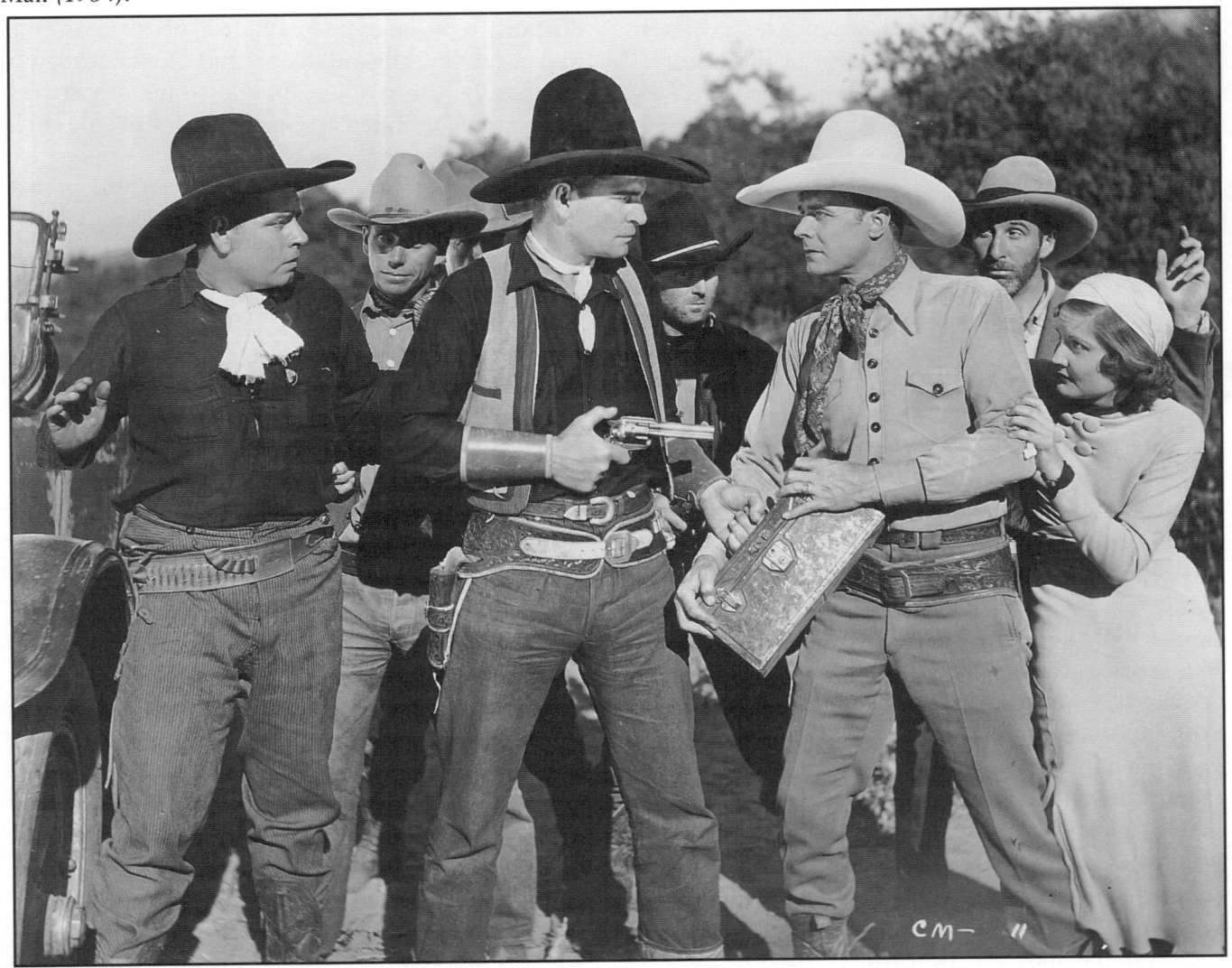

produced comedies and serials. Sometimes they were Western serials. Correspondingly, Republic offered product lines most likely to fulfill the needs of its theater circuits, which meant mostly Westerns and serials. And whatever demand remained for Western short subjects was pretty much filled by Western serial chapters.

There were oddities right from the beginning of the talkie era. In 1929, Tim McCoy, then between his silent series for M-G-M and his talkie series for Columbia, made his first talking film at Fox: a one-reel musical Western short called *A Night on the Range*. He sang around a campfire in this film, making him the first singing cowboy star (in shorts if not features). Luckily, he knew enough to quit when he was ahead.

Still, there were a few series of cowboy featurettes made during the '30s and '40s. In 1934, Wally Wales did a block of eight "high-class Westerns" (as hailed in trade ads) for William Pizor's Imperial Distributing Corporation of New York. These were strictly Poverty-Row quickies done for the states-rights market, but quite entertaining nonetheless. All were issued as three-reel subjects, but the original negatives were cut by a reel for release to the 16mm rental market. Robert Emmett Tansey directed in his usual style, and genre favorites such as Franklyn Farnum, Yakima Canutt, and Sherry Tansey were regulars. Fay McKenzie, the leading lady in *The Sundown Trail*, recalled in 1980, "I was in the ninth grade, and all of 14 years old when I made that thing. We shot it in three days." Born Floyd Alderson, star Wally Wales was a carryover from silent cheapies, and would later enjoy success in distinctive supporting and heavy roles under the name Hal Taliaferro.

Another enjoyable single-season, odd-length series was the three-reel *Bud 'n' Ben* group made by Reliable, another rock-bottom independent company, bearing the directorial imprimatur of Bernard B. Ray. Distribution was through William Steiner and the Astor Pictures exchanges. That likable fixture of low-budget Western quickies, Jack Perrin, played Bud, and pot-bellied comic Ben Corbett was, well, Ben. When Perrin was injured he was replaced by Fred Humes (himself a former star of Western short subjects at Universal during the silent days), who was in turn replaced by the aforementioned Wally Wales, here using a *fourth* screen name, Walt Williams. Then Denny Meadows essayed the cowboy chameleon, before changing *his* name to Dennis Moore. Why didn't everybody stay rooted in this series? It *couldn't* be that no one got along with Benny Corbett, a horseman and stunt double who

Jack Perrin finally tumbles to the fact that Virginia Brown Faire is a girl in Rainbow Riders *(1934).*

knocked around in Westerns for years, including more than 30 films with Hoot Gibson alone. And these half-size subjects, like the feature length Gibsons, were the closest thing to comedies in the Western market.

One series deserves mention, if only to exclude it. For its 1930-31 release schedule, Syndicate Pictures Corporation exhumed some of the silent Jack Hoxie features made nearly a decade before for Arrow Film Corporation (both companies were controlled by W. Ray Johnston, who would later establish Monogram Pictures). These were abridged to two-reel length, fitted with synchronized music-and-effects tracks, and shipped out to complement or compete with the full-sound action efforts of Ken Maynard, Buck Jones, Hoot Gibson, Tim McCoy and George O'Brien. With titles such as *Marshal of Money Mint* and *Rider from Nowhere*, a dozen of these escaped into theaters, possibly to hide in the dark.

Hitting just the right note, however, was the Ray Whitley series for RKO, combining music with comedy, and set in the west. These shorts were delightful and disarming. Their essential ingredient was the high baritone voice of Ray Whitley, who had previously appeared with the Frank Luther Trio in some Educational Pictures Western shorts in 1934 and 1935. (Whitley was also the author of Gene Autry's theme song, "Back in the Saddle.")

There was no pretense made for solid story or action values in these RKO shorts, and all the nasal-

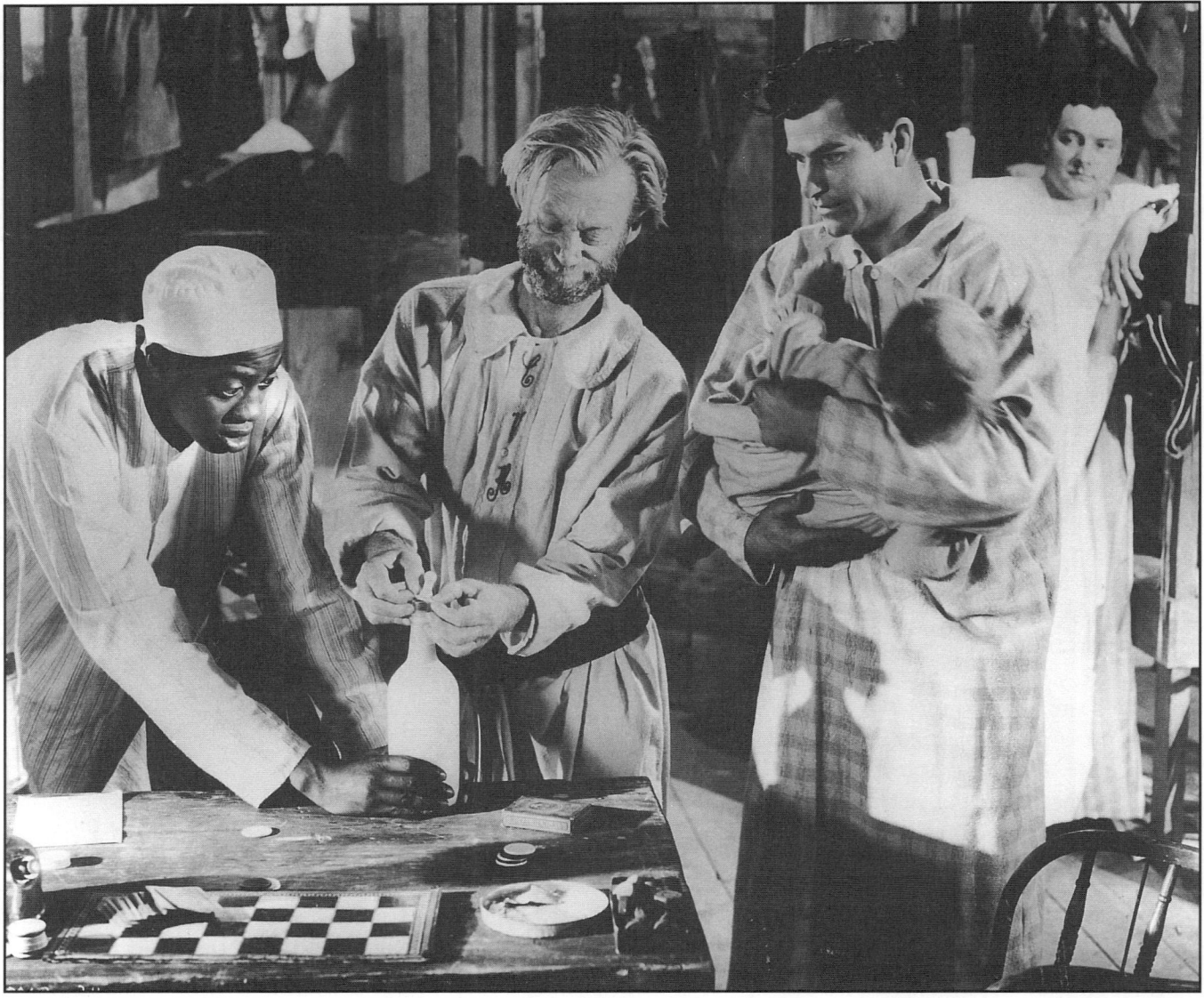
Willie Best (l.) and Al St. John help puzzled papa Ray Whitley in Prairie Papas *(1940). Willie Phelps is at right.*

but-nice Whitley had to do between his easy-to-take songs was just keep a straight face. His acting was wooden, so that was easy to do.

Molly Cures a Cowboy (1940), for instance, is a childish farce about a fat, middle-aged woman who is over-medicated by a barely villainous physician. That's the plot (by Oliver Drake, thank you). Genial character actor Dick Elliott plays the doctor. There's really no story, no action, no romance, and no dramatic conflict. But Whitley and his Six-Bar Cowboys (including Hank Worden) sing five songs, all wonderful.

Producer Lou Brock inaugurated this (by then) unique series of two-reelers in 1937. It lasted for five seasons—two shorts the first year, then four each release season thereafter—playing on RKO theater circuit programs to complement the Western action adventures of George O'Brien and Tim Holt, neither one of whom sang. Ray Whitley's 18 musical-comedy shorts made during this period were valuable units fulfilling a need because they allowed RKO to compete with singing cowboys like Gene Autry and Roy Rogers.

Even after production ceased, these musical mini-Westerns were profitably reissued to satisfy steady demand into the mid '50s. *Cupid Rides the Range* (1939) is a typical example. Shot in two days, the negative cost was $13,583.70. It was reissued the first time in 1946, and as of a 1948 year-end producer's settlement statement, this short had grossed a cumulative sum of $58,410.35. Prints and advertising costs, combined with other charges for the two releases, were $19,349.28, yielding a net profit of $25,477.37. There was a second reissue in 1954, for which earnings reports are not available. After recouping their cost, which *Cupid Rides the Range* did so well, the importance of short subjects was in setting the stage for the feature presentation, and the

CUT TO THE CHASE / Sagebrush Short Subjects

Ray Whitley and the Six-Bar Cowboys (1939)

HOLLYWOOD CORRAL: A COMPREHENSIVE B WESTERN ROUNDUP

Ray Whitley two-reelers succeeded admirably in this regard.

Employing their Vitaphone trademark, Warner Bros. made about 25 miniature Westerns between the late '30s and the late '40s. Scripts were often recycled without too much effort from the studio story department. Some were shot in black-and-white, most were in Technicolor. Some were issued with the *Technicolor Specials* brand name, some as *Broadway Brevities,* others as part of a so-called *Santa Fe Trail* series. All served as a training ground for young talent and as filler for the nearly 600 Warners theaters. Robert Shayne was kept busy doing leads. Dennis Morgan was being groomed for bigger things, and carried others. Directors such as Jean Negulesco and William McGann worked on some of these, which with titles such as *The Singing Dude* (1940) seemed a bit too clean and pretentious. Tom Tyler and Harry Woods showed up in *Gun to Gun* (1944), and it's fun to see them supported by so much impressive production value.

One short in this series, however, did not quite fit with the others: *Wells Fargo Days* (1944), which starred Dennis Moore and Louise Stanley, and was directed by action veteran Mack V. Wright. That's because it was actually produced four years earlier by Cinecolor, Inc. as *The Man from Tascosa,* and only picked up by Warners to tie in with their historical group of Western titles including *Pony Express Days* (1941), *Wagon Wheels West* (1943), and *Frontier Days* (1945). Non-theatrical distributors such as Eastin Pictures carried this short in their catalogs under its original title before the Warners pickup.

One of the most satisfying Warners Western shorts is *Ride, Cowboy, Ride* (1940), a Technicolor outing starring Dennis Morgan, Cliff "Ukelele Ike" Edwards, Maris Wrixon, and George Reeves in his pre-Superman days. Borrowing its principal plot element from the 1936 Dick Foran starrer *Land Beyond the Law,* this amiable pocket Western furthers the relationship between the two films by having Morgan warble several songs from the Foran Western, including Foran's theme, "The Prairie Is My Home." It also uses background music from the Forans, and manages the same neat blending of traditional Western action with colorful (in more ways than one) song numbers.

Also at Warner Bros., Spade Cooley, Cliff Edwards, and Bob Wills tried their respective hands at single-reel Western band shorts.

In 1940 Tex Ritter starred in a Monogram feature called *Rollin' Home to Texas,* featuring Cal Shrum's Rhythm Rangers, which in turn featured a musician named Sollie Paul "Jack" Williams. After leaving Shrum and recording a country-western song about cigarettes called "Smoke, Smoke, Smoke" (and incidentally changing his name to "Tex"), Williams was contracted by producer Will Cowan to do a series of musical Western shorts at Universal-International.

The first one was called *Tex Williams and His Western Caravan* (1947), and ran a little short of two reels. With the addition of some stock footage from the Bob Baker Universal features, the Tex Williams shorts were expanded to three reels and continued through 1950. That same year a pair of these short were spliced together as a feature entitled *Tales of the West.* Three more compilations were released through 1951.

Universal had previously enjoyed some success with a series of band shorts in the '40s, and apparently hoped to build on the Tex Williams featurettes and branch out into the country-western field. Will Cowan tried musical Western shorts such as *Frontier Frolic* (1946), featuring Bob Wills and his Texas Playboys, *Echo Ranch* (1948), featuring Red River Dave, and *Corral Cuties* (1954), featuring Tennessee Ernie Ford and Molly Bee.

Given the popularity of Western features, it was no coincidence that comedy short subjects would spoof the genre. Nearly every unit did it at least once, as witness Charley Chase in *The Tabasco Kid* (1932), Edgar Kennedy in *Westward Ho-Hum* (1941), Joe McDoakes in *So You Want to be a Cowboy* (1951), Harry Langdon in *The Fighting Parson* (1930), Buster Keaton in *The Gold Ghost* (1934), Leon Errol in *Cactus Cut-up* (1949), The Masquers Club in *Wide Open Spaces* (1931), Our Gang in *The Little Ranger* (1938), Andy Clyde in *The Cow-Catcher's Daughter* (1931), and everyone's favorite, El Brendel, in *Pistol Packin' Nitwits* (1945). The Three Stooges did Western sendups every season, remaking some, borrowing footage from the Columbia stock-shot library, and generally economizing in every department.

One of the most interesting filmmaking shortcuts involves what is perhaps Tom Tyler's first sound film, a Pathé Western comedy two-reeler called *Half Pint Polly* (1930). It was released almost simultaneously with a Pathé Western feature called *Pardon My Gun,* which starred Tom Keene (then billed as George Duryea), and used the same story and character names, shared the same production team and some of the same actors, and was staged the same way! It has been impossible to determine

Tex Williams

HOLLYWOOD CORRAL: A COMPREHENSIVE B WESTERN ROUNDUP

which was produced first, partially because, in a reversal of "tradition," neither subject used stock footage from the other.

Adding more confusion were retitled abridgements of Western feature films for the 16mm home movie market. Companies such as Castle, Official Films, and Hollywood Film Enterprises, serving the non-theatrical market, obtained licenses to issue short versions of certain Universal, PRC, and *Hopalong Cassidy* Westerns, among others. In the beginning, home-movie projectors could only accommodate one 400-foot capacity 16mm reel, which dictated the length of the abridged versions. This is how Tom Mix's six-reel feature *My Pal, the King* (1932) was transformed into *The King and the Cowboy*, running a single reel. Later, some of the PRC *Lone Rider, Texas Rangers,* and Buster Crabbe Westerns were issued as two-reelers.

Also worth noting are shorts with candid appearances showing Western film stars from a behind-the-scenes view. Tiffany's low-budget, one-reel series *The Voice of Hollywood* offered sometimes embarrassing glimpses of Western stars like Tom Mix and Ken Maynard. Paramount's similar *Hollywood on Parade* shorts spent more money, but the results with the same stars were just as awkward.

More successful was Columbia's one-reel series entitled *Screen Snapshots*, a treasure trove of fascinating behind-the-scenes material. These shorts were produced from 1920 to 1958. Today they remain largely undocumented, unseen, and unavailable. An unnamed 1940 entry offered coverage of a Palm Springs rodeo with a parade of screen cowboys enjoying the festivities, including Tom Mix, Roy Rogers, George O'Brien, William S. Hart, Gene Autry, and Buck Jones! The same short used candid footage shot during a location lunch-break on one of the Hopalong Cassidys (possibly *Doomed Caravan*),

Gaudily attired Charley Chase shares a joke with fetching Joyce Compton while Jimmy Finlayson eavesdrops in a Hal Roach/M-G-M short, Manhattan Monkey Business *(1935).*

in which narrator Hobart Cavanaugh observes Bill Boyd cautioning wife Grace Bradley, who's about to eat an onion, and quips, "If Mrs. Hoppy chaws that prairie violent, we'll *all* hop along."

My Pal Ringeye (1947) was a cross-promotional effort spotlighting Smiley Burnette, then under contract to Columbia and appearing in the Durango Kid Westerns. *Hopalong in Hoppyland* (1951) showed Boyd in full Hoppy regalia interviewing his Hollywood friends and their sometimes cooperative kids at the opening of Hoppyland, an 80-acre amusement park in Venice, California, which predated Disneyland!

Louella Parsons' daughter, Harriet, produced some *Screen Snapshots* episodes before leaving Columbia to make a similar series at Republic called *Meet the Stars*. *Meet Roy Rogers* (1941) was one such single-reel short, and offered glimpses of Rogers at home, at work, and at play. Entry number eight, and the last in the series, was *Stars Past and Present* (1941). This remarkable exercise in time travel covered the dedication of the Mabel Normand stage at Republic Pictures, once home to the Mack Sennett studio, whose "old time" stars were then united with Republic's current box-office attractions for the ceremony. Mack Sennett himself was there, as was John Wayne, and practically the entire Gene Autry company then working on *Melody Ranch*. (Autry and Rogers had previously appeared together in a 1940 M-G-M short called *Rodeo Dough*.)

The last attempt to revive the live-action theatrical short subject as a going concern was *Ken Murray's Hometown Hollywood* series in 1973. Only the tantalizing opener was released. It is fitting that the most interesting home movies Murray used were those he took of Western stars—great candid footage of Bill Boyd, Roy Rogers, and John Wayne. Most remarkable of all was the color film taken of Tom Mix, proving the story of theatrical short subjects had come back around to just about where it started, with Broncho Billy and Tom Mix.

Johnny Mack Brown and producer Alex Gordon.

HEADIN' FOR THE LAST ROUNDUP
TWILIGHT YEARS OF THE COWBOY GREATS
by Alex Gordon

When I ran the British Gene Autry Fan Club in London in the late '30s, I corresponded with many Western stars, including Ray Corrigan, George O'Brien, Tom Keene, Smiley Burnette, leading lady June Storey and, most importantly, Buck Jones. His death in the 1942 Boston night-club fire hit me hard when I read about it in London's *Daily Express* just as I was about to board a troop train.

After spending more than five years in the British Army during World War II, I got a job in New York as assistant booker for Walter Reade Theatres. This enabled me to interview the stars who passed through the city, and send those stories to British movie magazines.

I met Jack Holt at the Stork Club in 1948. He told me that when Columbia dropped him in the mid-'30s, agent George Ullman, who handled Rudolph Valentino in the '20s, arranged for Universal to give Holt a six-picture deal. Films such as *Storm over the Andes* and *Dangerous Waters* resulted. Columbia then re-signed Holt for another series of action pictures as well as the 1941 serial, *Holt of the Secret Service,* costarring Evelyn Brent. Brent had been a big star in silents and early talkies, and later played roles with Hopalong Cassidy and Buck Jones, before becoming an agent representing actors and actresses.

At the time I talked with Jack Holt, he had recently appeared with Gene Autry in *Strawberry Roan* (1948) and *Loaded Pistols* (1949). He had been considered by Monogram to replace Buck Jones in the *Rough Riders* series after Buck's death in 1942. But the studio decided to pair Johnny Mack Brown with Raymond Hatton instead, since Tim McCoy had departed the Rough Riders series before Jones' death and Rex Bell had replaced him in *Dawn on the Great Divide* (1942).

Erstwhile Rough Rider Raymond Hatton was the first actor I met with when I came to Hollywood in 1952, and he invited me to come to his house for an interview. ("We must have a bowl of soup," he suggested.) He became a regular in many movies I produced, including *The Day the World Ended, Girls in Prison, Flesh and the Spur, Shake Rattle and Rock* and *Requiem for a Gunfighter.*

Raymond loved the *Rough Riders* films, but he also appreciated his work with *The Three Mesquiteers* that featured him with John Wayne and Ray Corrigan and, later, with Bob Livingston and Duncan Renaldo. Once, while I was lunching with Ray in the Paramount commissary during the production of *Requiem for a Gunfighter,* the waitress told him that John Wayne was in the executive dining room with Hal Wallis and Henry Hathaway. "Just tell him Ray Hatton says hello," Raymond told her. A moment later John Wayne strode out and greeted him fondly. He sat down with us and reminisced for a while, obviously pleased to see his former costar, then went back to continue with discussions for *El Dorado.*

Ray talked often and fondly of his days with Cecil B. DeMille and, in particular, the 1917 production, *The Whispering Chorus,* in which he played the

HOLLYWOOD CORRAL: A COMPREHENSIVE B WESTERN ROUNDUP

Left to right: Buster Crabbe, Richard Arlen, Fuzzy Knight and Dan Duryea gather around pioneer Western star Broncho Billy Anderson between scenes of Alex Gordon's The Bounty Killer *(1965).*

lead as an apparent murderer who goes to the electric chair to save another person. Having changed his identity, his conscience does not permit him to allow the taking of a life for "his" murder, yet he cannot reveal his real identity either.

Hatton was an actor who played every role to the hilt, be it an old codger in a Western or a smalltime hood in a James Cagney Warner picture. "The frosting on the cake" is how he described the little bits and pieces he would add to a role when he had something he could get his teeth into. *In Cold Blood* would be Ray's last movie; he died very shortly after his wife's passing.

Bud Osborne and Kenne Duncan were old-timers who had worked in so many Westerns that they had forgotten the titles by the time I'd met them. Bud went back to the silent days, and was particularly fond of Tim McCoy and *The Indians Are Coming* serial. Kenne did his dastardly best at Republic and, later, with Edward D. Wood Jr. Both Western stal-

warts appeared in *The Lawless Rider,* which I produced with Johnny Carpenter.

We also had Frankie Darro and Douglas Dumbrille in supporting roles. Frankie had had a long career but was finding it hard to get work. He was a stunt fighter in *Across the Wide Missouri* with Clark Gable, and worked as a bartender in the San Fernando Valley between movie jobs. Dumbrille was a fine character actor who had been "overexposed," according to studio casting directors. I first met him at the Masquers Club with Raymond Hatton. He also appeared in my *Shake Rattle and Rock*—a movie he hated. In fact, he was quite vocal about it, and we had to calm him down to protect the sound man. He married Alan Mowbray's daughter, Mowbray being another Masquers stalwart, as was Reed Howes, who played with Anna Sten in my AIP film *Runaway Daughters*.

Tom Conway was cast as Sten's husband in that picture and director Edward L. Cahn had already shot two days when a midnight call from agent Wallace Middleton, a former actor, informed me that Conway had been rushed to the hospital and I would have to replace him by morning. Spending the night in search of a replacement, I happened on John Litel's name and requested his agent to ask him if he would show up on the set ready for work without reading the script. He studied the script in his dressing room and, half an hour later, appeared on the set and did his scenes word perfect. I've never forgotten what a pro he was. A low-budget ten-day picture would have been forced to shut down if it hadn't been for Litel.

Jack Perrin and Edmund Cobb were in this movie too. Perrin lived across from me on Carlton Way in Hollywood when I first came here. He and his wife had loud arguments throughout the week, but he was a very nice and personable man on the set and we talked often about his old Westerns and serials.

Edmund Cobb became a regular in my pictures and worked in virtually all of them starting with *Oklahoma Woman* at AIP. As he was too old to be a member of the crew in *The Atomic Submarine* at Allied Artists, I had him walk by outside the submarine base with Frank Lackteen, yet paid him as an actor, not an extra, which caused a big furor with Allied's horrible casting director Joe Rivkin. But my early-morning ambush of Allied studio head Steve Broidy worked out that little problem.

Lackteen had been a villain in silent films and a halfbreed or Indian in numerous Westerns. Many silent serials featuring him were directed by *Atomic Submarine* helmer Spencer G. Bennet. In *Requiem for a Gunfighter* Lackteen played two roles, one with a Lincolnesque beard, so he picked up a larger paycheck. In *Flesh and the Spur* he played the Indian chief, but he was ill when we made *Voodoo Woman*, and had to be replaced in the role of the native chief.

Director Spencer Bennet (in hat) calls for "Action!" on location for The Bounty Killer *(1965).*

HOLLYWOOD CORRAL: A COMPREHENSIVE B WESTERN ROUNDUP

Veteran Western and serial heavy Norman Willis was in that one, and also appeared in *The Bounty Killer*. He worked as a motorcycle policeman when not in front of the cameras. When "hit" by Rod Cameron, he took his fall with so much sincerity that I upped his salary right there on the spot.

The Bounty Killer and *Requiem for a Gunfighter*, both made in 1964, were based on screenplays by R. Alexander (my wife Ruth Gordon) from original material by Leo Gordon and Guy Tedesco. Spencer G. Bennet directed dream casts that included most of the Western old-timers still able to work in front of the cameras.

The Bounty Killer, toplining Dan Duryea and Rod Cameron, was filmed in 10 days for $194,000, with only two days of location shooting, necessitating stagebound "outdoor" scenes between Duryea and Fuzzy Knight. Everybody was afraid of the frail-looking Knight when he came to the office to discuss the role. But he came through in fine fashion and saved a disastrous half-day when veteran I. Stanford Jolley could not remember any of his lines. Fuzzy lightened up the proceedings and gave everyone time to relax, while Bennet fed the lines to Jolley one at a time, cutting it all together to make a seamless final product.

Broncho Billy Anderson was 86 years old, in a wheel chair and fitted with a hearing aid, when we persuaded him to come out of the Motion Picture Country Home for a day to shoot a cameo at Paramount for *The Bounty Killer*. A contribution to the Home, a new shirt, and a portable typewriter were his requests for pay. Elvis Presley and others working at the studio rushed to our sound stage to have their pictures taken with the screen's first cowboy star, and he had a great time. In his scene with Buster Crabbe, Billy kept missing his cue; we finally discovered that the prop man had removed his hearing aid, and he was unable to follow the director's instructions. Realizing this, I cued him from the side.

An ironic twist in this picture was the fact that Dan Duryea did not care for horses and would ride only one, which belonged to Johnny Carpenter, with whom years earlier I had made *The Lawless Rider*. So we rented that horse.

Bob Steele was in both *The Bounty Killer* and *Requiem for a Gunfighter*. One of my favorite Western stars, he had also appeared in *The Atomic Submarine*. We talked often of his early Western films. He always referred to The Three Mesquiteers as The Three Mesquiters—like mesquite—and particularly remembered strong plots from the films in which his father, Robert N. Bradbury, directed him. Bob was surprised, and pleased, when I ordered up running inserts for him in *Requiem for a Gunfighter*, something most producers and directors had not bothered with since the golden age of B Westerns.

We had to shoot Tim McCoy's scenes in two days, as he had only that short time in between touring with the Tommy Scott show, where he did his bullwhip and sharpshooting act. I first met Tim in 1952 when I interviewed him for a British magazine. Tim was the ultimate pro, word perfect on lengthy dialogue scenes and straight in the saddle. He thought horses were dumb and that women were better shots than men—they just aimed the gun and fired, he said. Tim said he loved playing the Mexican character in some of his low-budget Westerns, and fondly remembered the authenticity of his silent Metro pictures that David O. Selznick supervised.

When Rod Cameron's horse stepped into a hole and threw him (which looked like a slow-motion fall to me, with probably no harm done), Tim immediately spotted it for a bad fall. It resulted in a swollen leg and much agony for Rod, although he finished shooting the picture before going into the hospital.

Lane Chandler told me of losing out to Gary Cooper when both actors' contracts came up at Paramount after he (Chandler) had done *Red Hair* with Clara Bow. Later he lost out to Tom Tyler for the Western series that Reliable made (and that Universal released overseas). I had seen Lane in *The Hurricane Horseman, Lawless Valley*, and his other Willis Kent films, on which Bart Carré worked as assistant director and production manager and sometimes actor before coming to Republic and then American International, when that company was formed.

Some of Willis Kent's Reb Russell films had Smiley Burnette singing a song, "Reb and His Horse Rebel," over the main titles without credit. Smiley and Gene Autry had arrived and were waiting to start their films *Mystery Mountain* and *In Old Santa Fe* with Ken Maynard, and meanwhile were getting riding tips from Russell.

Girls in Prison was one of my favorites, as I was able to use a cast of great names, Western and non-Western, including Richard Denning, a fine actor and person; Adele Jergens, a great sport; Helen Gilbert, the lovely schoolteacher in *Andy Hardy Gets Spring Fever*; Mae Marsh, the memorable D.W. Griffith star; Jane Darwell, the Oscar winner from John Ford's *Grapes of Wrath*; Kermit Maynard and Edmund Cobb as prison guards; Riza Royce, ex-wife of Josef von Sternberg; and Luana Walters, leading

Bob Steele (l.) and Tim McCoy share memories for Alex Gordon's benefit while shooting Requiem for a Gunfighter *(1965).*

lady for so many great Western stars. Luana had been out of pictures, but an agent found her working at a drugstore and I cast her. She had a brief comeback in this picture and *The She Creature* before a jealous boy friend put the kibosh on further picture work.

The She Creature had several last-minute cast changes before finally shooting with Chester Morris, Marla English, Tom Conway, Ron Randell, Frank Jenks and Paul Dubov. I had Peter Lorre and Edward Arnold set for the two leads, but Lorre hated the script and refused to do it despite his agent's assurance that he was set. Arnold, who had worked for director Edward L. Cahn before in *Main Street after Dark*, died two days before our project began. I tried for John Carradine, but he had just done *The Ten Commandments* for DeMille and refused low-budget horror. I got Chester Morris, set for the Arnold role, to switch to the Lorre part and got Tom Conway, in England for a movie, to fly over to do that. Ron Randell was on his way back to his native Australia but had a week off, so I got him to take the role originally planned for Conway. AIP had a deal with Cathy Downs for top billing but when Marla English came in *she* got that, and we had to make a new two-picture deal with Downs.

I thought my big break had come when I went to Columbia to produce *The Underwater City,* a science-fiction picture to be shot in six days (including special effects) on a budget of $350,000. Frank McDonald, who had directed many good Gene Autry films, was my choice as director. Columbia refused Richard Denning for the lead and, after lengthy searches and my refusal of contractee Glenn Corbett, the studio forced William Lundigan on me. At first I had no objections. However, Lundigan had a drinking problem that caused us to go two days over budget and resulted in numerous delays on the set, because he didn't know his lines. He also called the union down on my head when I had him doubled in underwater gear to save time.

Julia Adams was a gracious leading lady in *City*, and Carl Benton Reid a good pro, but I had Basil Rathbone in mind for that role and was disappointed when he wrote me that a lecture tour would interfere. I was thrilled to sign Raymond Massey for a week, but Massey was in New York and his plane to Los Angeles was diverted to Boston during a storm, meaning a day's delay, and the studio refused to wait.

My time at Columbia gave me an insight into a major studio's problems and bureaucracy, and I began to realize that the Golden Age of Hollywood was, for many workers at the studios, not such a golden age at all. Department heads and supervisors at the major studios could be worse than Army bureaucrats, and if they wanted to hurt you they could find many ways of delaying and hindering your attempts to produce a picture on time and budget.

We had trouble finding ants to put on Marla English's legs for *Flesh and the Spur*, and I rounded up an even dozen but had to rub jam on poor Marla before they briefly wandered around. I got ace stuntman David Sharpe to double Mike Connors, and insisted on running inserts for Connors and John Agar while Kermit Maynard rode with the outlaws and did horse falls. (Kermit later became business agent for the Screen Extras Guild.)

Jack Mulhall did the same for the Screen Actors Guild after a long career as a light leading man in silents and an action star in the '30s. Jack's unlimited supply of handcuffs in *The Clutching Hand* remains a wonderful memory. He played Chester Morris' lawyer in *The She Creature*. Franklyn Farnum, Stuart Holmes, Eva Novak, Creighton Hale, Chester Conklin, all from the silent era, were fun to talk to in those AIP days. Western heavy Richard Alexander of F.W. Murnau and *Flash Gordon* fame did his bit in many of my films. The biggest villains are the nicest guys, it has been written of Fred Kohler, Harry Woods, Karloff and Rathbone and so many more,

A latter-day gathering of Western greats. Left to right: Ken Maynard, Rex Lease, Tom Keene (behind Lease), Bob Steele, Hoot Gibson, Raymond Hatton, and Guinn "Big Boy" Williams.

and this certainly applied to Dick Alexander of the Westerns. Joe Crehan, fast talking newspaper editor of Warner films, was an extra in *The Bounty Killer*. His mind gone, he was still willing to work on a movie set.

Marian Marsh and Cecilia Parker came to the AIP offices for the role in *Runaway Daughters* that ultimately went to Anna Sten, as Marla English's mother. Sten, a vastly underrated Russian star whose work deserves a new study on her own merits, rather than as an attempted Garbo/Dietrich imitation, worked beautifully on the fast schedule despite production manager Bart Carre's misgivings. Children and great names of the past were Bart's foes, his loyalty to the budget always first on his mind.

Allied Artists head Steve Broidy wouldn't allow me to use both Marshall Thompson and Arthur Franz as co-leads in *The Atomic Submarine,* because of budget limitations. Thompson said to use Franz and it worked out, because I was thus able to get Dick Foran and we had a great time discussing his Westerns and serials. At the cast party on the last day I sprung a surprise on Dick by playing his old 78 rpm recordings of "The Prairie Is My Home," "Mexicali Rose," and "Whisper While You're Waltzing" and when he heard "Rose" over the loudspeaker on the sound stage he did a terrific double take. It turned out he'd never gotten this record; it was not released in the States because of the successful Gene Autry and Bing Crosby versions. I had picked the Foran records up in London as a kid.

I always liked Audrey Dalton and Audrey Totter, and finally was able to afford the former in *Bounty Killer* and the latter in *Jet Attack*. Sam Arkoff, AIP co-head, didn't want Totter—I still don't know why—but she and John Agar made a good team for AIP. When advised that I had signed her over his objections, Sam hauled off, hit me, and knocked me down on Sunset Boulevard. He later came to my nearby office to apologize, but said that I made him so mad! Also in *Jet Attack* was bit player (now restaurateur) Nicky Blair, and to this day, whenever I visit his excellent restaurant on the Sunset Strip, Nicky tells everyone within view that I was the man who tried to make him a star!

Roy Rogers' bootprints immortalized at Grauman's Chinese Theater. Eddie Dean crouches with microphone.

WHATEVER HAPPENED TO THE SINGING COWBOY?
LIFE AFTER THE MOVIES

by Laurence Zwisohn

The *Motion Picture Herald* published an annual list of Top Ten Money Making Stars and Top Ten Money Making Western Stars which was a reflection of the box office. The Western poll was published annually from 1936 to 1954. With the exception of 1936, when Buck Jones finished first, the number one money making Western Star each year was a singing cowboy. From 1937 through 1942, Gene Autry ranked first, and from 1943 until the poll ended in 1954, Roy Rogers led the field. Among the other singing cowboys who ranked high over the years were Tex Ritter, Jimmy Wakely, Eddie Dean, Monte Hale, Rex Allen and one singing cowgirl, Dale Evans.

The end of World War II brought significant changes to the film industry. Television was about to shake the film industry much as it was when Al Jolson had proclaimed "you ain't heard nothin' yet" in the 1927 film *The Jazz Singer*.

Experimental television broadcasts had taken place as early as the late '20s and had been showcased at the 1939 World's Fair in New York by featuring cowboy singer "Red River Dave," but World War II had pushed television development into the background. With the end of the War in 1945, new energies were focused on television's possibilities. NBC and CBS had begun building nationwide television networks in the mid '40s. From a scant 14,000 television sets in 1947 the number grew to 175,000 in 1948 and jumped to over one million a year later. From there the growth was like Topsy as it just "growed and growed."

With television sets more and more a standard part of everyone's living room, programmers had to fill morning, afternoon and evening hours in a hurry. The acquistion of old movies was one of their first moves. Film studios and hundreds of old films sitting in their vaults just gathering dust and few at the studios recognized the value of these films. Television was new and untested. Videotape machines had yet to be invented and cable television was far in the future. So the studios and the independent producers and releasing companies put together packages of old films and sold them to television. A large part of these packages were Westerns and to see your favorite cowboy star all you had to do was tune them in on your television set. Afternoons and Saturday mornings found Ken Maynard, Buck Jones, Tim McCoy, Hoot Gibson, Jimmy Wakely, Eddie Dean and Hopalong Cassidy filling the screens.

As more people watched Westerns in their living rooms fewer went to the theaters. The studio dropped some stars and trimmed the budgets on even the top stars' films. The B-Western cowboy's days were numbered. By the middle of the '50s they would ride the theater screens no more. What happened to these singing cowboys?

Of all the singing cowboys, Gene Autry made the smoothest transition into television. Gene had returned to Republic Pictures in 1946 after serving in

HOLLYWOOD CORRAL: A COMPREHENSIVE B WESTERN ROUNDUP

Gene Autry relaxes in his office, circa 1974.

WHATEVER HAPPENED TO THE SINGING COWBOY? Life After the Movies

the Army Air Corps during World War II. After completing his contract at Republic, Gene formed his own production company, Flying "A" Productions, and produced his own films for release by Columbia Pictures starting in late 1947. Sensing that the singing cowboy's days in feature films were coming to an end, he began a weekly half-hour television series, *The Gene Autry Show,* in July 1950. Wrigley Chewing Gum, Gene's longtime radio sponsor, also became his television sponsor. Over the next six years eighty-five episodes were made by his Flying "A" Productions. Flying "A" also produced several other Western series including *Annie Oakley, The Range Rider* and *Buffalo Bill, Jr.*

Gene continued his long running radio series until 1956. In 1957, after 24 years with Columbia Records, Gene formed Challenge Records, the first of several labels he would own. Personal appearances had always been an important part of Gene's career and he maintained a busy schedule of theater and rodeo dates through the '50s. He also made an occasional appearance on television during the '50s.

In 1962, Gene Autry retired as a performer and recording artist to devote his energies to his various business enterprises. He owned several radio stations, had a music publishing company and owned several hotels. Golden West Broadcasting, Gene's communications company, purchased KTLA Television in Los Angeles and turned it into one of the area's top independent stations.

The investment Gene Autry is most associated with is the California Angels. In 1961, Gene acquired the rights to the American League's new expansion team. Gene had been a lifelong baseball fan and the opportunity to become an owner was something he couldn't resist. Owning both a radio and television station in Los Angeles made it a perfect fit, and the team continues to be broadcast over KMPC and televised over KTLA (although Gene has since sold the television station).

The end of the singing-cowboy films may have shifted Gene's direction but it did nothing to slow his pace or success. While other cowboys may have sung on screen before him there is no question that Gene Autry was truly the first *singing* cowboy star. Gene has earned a special place in music and film history and a warm spot in the hearts of a countless number of fans throughout the world.

Between 1962 and 1989, Gene made less than a dozen appearances as special guest on various television shows, and almost never as a performer. However, in 1989, Gene recorded the recitation "The Cowboy Code" for the Cincinnati Pops Orchestra's album *Happy Trails.* Also in January, May and October of 1989, Gene and his movie sidekick Pat Buttram hosted 105 episodes of *Melody Ranch Theatre* for the Nashville Network. Gene and Pat introduced and discussed Gene's films with various guests who had worked with them in the films. Of particular interest to Western buffs are the four shows featuring guest Roy Rogers.

Roy Rogers' transition to television had a few bumps along the way. Herbert Yates, the head of Republic Pictures, wanted to sign Roy to a new contract that would keep him with the studio beyond 1951. Roy was interested but insisted that the contract also allow him to appear on television. Yates, like all studio executives of the period, was adamant that no contract star would appear on television. This was unacceptable to Roy since the importance of television was growing by the day. They couldn't agree and so Roy completed *Pals of the Golden West* in May 1951, and concluded his 13 year stay with Republic.

Still, Herbert Yates and Republic Pictures were sitting on a treasure trove of films. It is commonly acknowledged that Republic made the best of the series Westerns and with Gene Autry and Roy

Roy and Dale in the late '70s.

HOLLYWOOD CORRAL: A COMPREHENSIVE B WESTERN ROUNDUP

Rogers had launched the medium's two biggest stars. With Gene gone and Roy about to leave, Yates announced that Republic would sell its library of films to television. However, he overlooked one important point. Several years earlier he had agreed to the inclusion of a provision in Roy Rogers' contract that gave Roy the exclusive right to his name, voice and image. It was a clause no other Hollywood actor had in his contract. Yates had thought at the time it was an insignificant gesture when he had agreed to include the provision. It allowed Roy to license his name to a wide variety of products—shirts, cap pistols, guitars, lariats, boots, pajamas, lunch boxes— the list grew larger each year until the marketing of Roy Rogers products was second only to the marketing of products bearing the image of Walt Disney's cartoon characters.

When Republic announced their plans to sell their library to television, Roy Rogers raised an objection. Selling his movies to television meant that a myriad of sponsors would advertise their wares on telecasts of Roy's films. Some of those products, such as cigarettes and beer, would not be in keeping with the image Roy had worked so hard to establish. Roy Rogers alone of all film actors had the courage (and the contract) to mount a case against his film studio. The case began in 1951 and Roy won in the lower courts. But Republic kept appealing the case.

Backed (it is believed) by the legal support of other film studios, the case progressed to the United States Supreme Court. There, in 1954, Roy's case was overturned. Few people realize the courage it took and financial cost that was incurred as Roy tried to protect his rights and control the way his image was exploited.

The seriousness of the case and the uncertainty of the final outcome made selling a Roy Rogers television series a difficult assignment. Even though Roy was still number one at the box office most advertisers, including his radio sponsors, wouldn't take the risk of having a new Roy Rogers series competing with his old films. Fortunately, Art Rush, Roy's longtime manager, found a sponsor that was willing to take the risk. Post Cereals agreed to sponsor the show and *The Roy Rogers Show* (co-starring Dale Evans) debuted in December, 1951. The program was an immediate success and stayed as a regular part of the NBC Sunday night lineup for the next six years. One hundred and one episodes were filmed, and each episode ended with Roy and Dale singing "Happy Trails," a song that has become a part of Americana. Roy's company, Frontiers Inc., also produced the *Brave Eagle* series, which was the only Western series to feature an Indian as the lead character.

At the conclusion of their series Roy and Dale continued to be very active in television. *The Chevy Show* was the highest rated show on the NBC Sunday night schedule. Dinah Shore starred in the show three weeks a month. Roy and Dale starred the fourth week. At the end of that series Roy and Dale made guest appearances on most of the variety shows that were so popular at the time. In 1962, ABC starred Roy and Dale in their own weekly variety program. Although the series won awards, the weak ABC station lineup led to a brief run for the series. Still, Roy and Dale continued to be frequent guests on other variety programs.

Just as they had during their years at Republic, Roy and Dale continued to appear at rodeos and theaters. In 1957, they signed to appear at the Ohio State Fair. Until that time state fairs did not attract frontline stars, so the signing of Roy and Dale was a challenge both for them and for the fair. Would they attract large audiences or would fairgoers be looking for the usual midway games and attractions? The results were overwhelming. The crowds were immense and soon other fairs were standing in line to book "The Roy Rogers and Dale Evans Show" which featured the Sons of the Pioneers, variety acts, Roy's Liberty horses and, of course, Trigger. Roy and Dale's fair engagements became so lucrative that many other name country and Western singing stars began seeking out state fair bookings for themselves.

Roy and Dale continued to record quite actively. They had been under contract to RCA Victor since the '40s. In the early '50s they began a series of children's recordings for Golden Records. These little yellow discs are familiar to almost all who grew up during that period. In the early '60s, Roy and Dale recorded two albums for Capitol and Roy recorded several solo albums for the label. Since then, Roy has recorded for several labels, and in 1974, came up with a nostalgic hit single "Hoppy, Gene and Me," which crossed over to the pop charts. In 1991, RCA released a new album titled *Tribute*. The album featured Roy dueting with a number of current country artists including Clint Black, Emmylou Harris, Randy Travis and Kathy Mattea. The record became the best selling album of Roy's career and was nominated for a Grammy.

In 1964, Roy and Dale moved from their home in the San Fernando Valley to Apple Valley in California's high desert where Roy opened a museum which traced his and Dale's lives and careers. In the late '70s the museum moved to expanded quarters in

WHATEVER HAPPENED TO THE SINGING COWBOY? Life After the Movies

nearby Victorville. Roy and Dale have remained active on television, personal appearances, charity work and occasional recordings.

The end of the singing-cowboy films marked the closing of one chapter but the opening of many others for Roy Rogers. Few performers have ever commanded such love and respect as has this down-to-earth man. He remains one of the most beloved of all Americans.

Tex Ritter's success as a singing cowboy came shortly after Gene Autry defined the medium. Unfortunately, Tex's early films were produced by Grand National, one of the smaller and less prestigious studios. Being smaller and less prestigious wasn't the problem, but the lack of money to mount quality productions was. As a result, Tex never achieved the full measure of success as a singing cowboy that he really deserved. Nonetheless, he ranked in the top ten at the box office seven times between 1937 and 1945. From Grand National, Tex moved over to Monogram, Columbia, Universal and finally PRC. By 1945, Tex's days as a star of singing cowboy films were coming to an end.

Although his film career ended, Tex remained very active. He and his horse White Flash performed at theaters and rodeos across the country throughout the '40s and '50s. Tex also played countless club dates and began appearing on television. He was a frequent guest on syndicated country music shows as well as being a regular on *Town Hall Party*. This long running Los Angeles country music television program had an all-star lineup that often included Merle Travis, Johnny Bond, Eddie Dean, the Collins Kids, Joe and Rose Lee Maphis and Freddie Hart. Tex became the host of *Ranch Party*, a spin-off of *Town Hall Party*, which was syndicated around the country into the early '60s.

Recording had long played a major role in Tex's

Tex Ritter entertains kids in a New Orleans hospital in 1949.

career. He began recording in 1932 when he cut several sides for the American Record Company. Between 1935 and 1939, Tex recorded for Decca. In 1942, Capitol Records was formed and one of its founders, Johnny Mercer, felt Tex was an artist he definitely wanted on the label. In June 1942, Tex cut his first sides for Capitol. He would remain with Capitol for the rest of his life, a 32-year run with the prestigious label.

In 1952 producer Stanley Kramer had completed the film *High Noon* starring Gary Cooper and Grace Kelly. Previews indicated something was lacking. The film just didn't move. Kramer asked the film's composer Dimitri Tiomkin to write a song that might energize the film. Together with lyricist Ned Washington, a song was written which Kramer used as a narrative at several points in the film. Tiomkin auditioned several singers including Tex Ritter. Rarely have singer and song fit together so well. Tex's performance of "High Noon" gave a unique feeling to the film. *High Noon* was nominated for several Academy Awards including Best Picture and won for Best Song.

One of the strangest facets of "High Noon" was that Capitol Records, Tex's label, didn't think the song was anything special and was reluctant to have him record it. After being one of the biggest record sellers during the '40s, Tex's records hadn't been selling too well at that point, so Capitol was slow in getting behind his recording. The result was that Frankie Laine wound up having the bigger hit on record. Capitol soon saw the error of their judgement and Tex's version also became a hit although not as big a record as it should have been. The success of Tex's performance of "High Noon" led to his singing the title song in several other Westerns including *The Marshal's Daughter, Wichita* and *Trooper Hook*.

By the '60s, Tex was beginning to spend a good deal of time in Nashville. He recorded there, became a member of the Grand Ole Opry and was active in the newly founded Country Music Association. In 1963, Tex was elected president of the CMA. The opportunity to host the midnight radio show on WSM, the Grand Ole Opry's station, prompted Tex to move his family to Nashville in 1965. Five years later Tex was asked to run for the United States Senate on the Republican ticket in an historically Democratic state. Jimmie Davis had twice been elected governor of Louisiana and Roy Acuff had run for governor of Tennessee. Tex took up the challenge but didn't win. So it was back to touring, recording and his radio program.

On January 2, 1974, Tex suffered a massive heart attack and died. The outpouring of sadness at the news of Tex's passing made it clear just how loved and respected he was. In a visit several years later with Johnny Bond, Tex's close friend and business partner, Tex's name came up in conversation. Johnny asked if his visitor had ever met Tex. When the visitor said he had never had the opportunity, Johnny smiled and, in a wistful manner, said, "you missed a good one."

Jimmy Wakely's road to stardom as a singing cowboy was longer than that of most of his contemporaries. Jimmy served his apprenticeship by appearing in films starring Roy Rogers, Gene Autry, William Boyd, Charles Starrett, Johnny Mack Brown and Tex Ritter before landing his own series at Monogram.

Jimmy's career in Western music had begun more than a decade earlier in Oklahoma. Inspired by the Sons of the Pioneers, Jimmy Wakely, Johnny Bond and Scotty Harrel formed the Jimmy Wakely Trio in 1937. A fortuitous meeting with Gene Autry, who was touring Oklahoma, led to a chance to work with him. Impressed with the Trio's sound, Gene asked them to come to California and appear on his *Melody Ranch* radio program. Before too long they were recording for Decca, making a series of radio transcriptions and providing musical accompaniment in a number of Western films.

Late in 1944, Jimmy was signed by Monogram to star in a series of singing cowboy films. The series continued through 1949. Fortunately for Jimmy, the end of his career as a movie singing cowboy came at a time when his success as a singer was about to reach new heights. In 1948, recording for Capitol Records, Jimmy scored with two number-one records on the country music charts. The first of these, "One Has My Name (The Other Has My Heart)," was co-written by Eddie Dean. The other was "I Love You So Much It Hurts," written by Floyd Tillman. The next year saw Jimmy's string of hits continue. The teaming of Wakely with Margaret Whiting, one of the era's most respected pop singers, resulted in "Slipping Around," a record which went to number one on the country charts and number two on the pop charts. Over the course of the next few years Jimmy's recordings, both solo and with Margaret Whiting, continued to rank high on both the pop and country charts.

Occasional country records have crossed over to the pop field almost since the beginning of the recording industry. However, Jimmy Wakely was the first country or Western artist to cross over with regularity. After leaving Capitol late in 1953, Jimmy returned to Decca. In the mid '50s, Jimmy decided to form a record company of his own. From then until his death in 1982, Jimmy produced and recorded not only himself but a considerable number of country and Western artists for his Shasta Records label. Among the artists he recorded were such old friends as Johnny Bond and Eddie Dean. Shasta became one of the record industry's most successful mail order labels.

Jimmy maintained a busy schedule of personal appearances, including frequent dates on the Las Vegas, Reno and Tahoe circuit. Instead of Western attire, Jimmy's nightclub appearances found him dressed in a tuxedo. But even on these dates Jimmy's closing song was "Cimarron," a song Johnny Bond had written back in their trio days.

In 1971, Jimmy began a weekly radio series for Armed Forces Radio. The shows consisted of interviews and records featuring many of the performers with whom Jimmy had become acquainted over the years. The series was broadcast over the European and Far East AFRS networks through 1977. For two years in 1976 and 1977 Jimmy hosted a five-day-a-week, hour-long radio program which was broadcast in Iran in the days before the Ayotollah's revolution. Jimmy produced this series at the request of the Iranian government.

Johnny Bond in 1974.

Emphysema had taken its toll on Jimmy when he finally succumbed on September 23, 1982.

Although Johhny Bond never starred as a singing cowboy, he is, for very good reason, closely identified with the genre. Johnny was featured in over two dozen films starring such Western stars as Gene Autry, Roy Rogers, William Boyd, Don Barry, Johnny Mack Brown, Tex Ritter, Charles Starrett and his old trio partner Jimmy Wakely.

Johnny's busy schedule of songwriting, recording, writing and personal appearances insured that he would be well occupied after the singing cowboy stopped riding across theater screens. Johnny began writing songs back in his native Oklahoma where his fine Western song "Cimarron" was written in 1938 and became the theme song for the Jimmy Wakely Trio. Over the years "Cimarron" has been recorded by over two dozen artists ranging from Harry James and Les Paul to the Sons of the Pioneers. Among the many other songs Johnny wrote are "I Wonder Where You Are Tonight," "I'll Step Aside," "Your Old Love Letters" and "Glad Rags." In 1943, Johnny wrote "Tomorrow Never Comes," and Ernest Tubb's recording of it became one of his signature songs. During the '60s Jim Nabors used "Tomorrow Never Comes" as the theme of his weekly television variety program.

The first recordings Johnny made were as a member of the Jimmy Wakely Trio. In 1941, Johnny began a 16-year association with Columbia Records. Although he recorded a wide variety of songs, it was with novelties that Johnny enjoyed his greatest success. Hits like "Sick, Sober and Sorry," "Put Me to Bed" and "Fat Gal" usually outsold Johnny's other recordings. In 1960, Johnny recorded "Hot Rod Lincoln" for Gene Autry's Republic label. The song became his biggest hit in quite some time and even crossed over into the pop field. Later that year Johnny signed with Starday Records in Nashville and began recording a series of outstanding albums and still came up with an occasional hit single. In November, 1964, Johnny recorded a new live version of his comedy song "Ten Little Bottles." The record quickly became the biggest hit of Johnny's career rising almost to the top of the country charts. Johnny continued to record for Starday until 1972. A few other albums for Capitol, Lamb and Lion, Shasta and CMH filled out Johnny's 36-year recording career.

The natural adjunct to songwriting is music publishing, yet few performers were involved in that field prior to the '60s. However, Johnny Bond and his close friend Tex Ritter had each started publish-

HOLLYWOOD CORRAL: A COMPREHENSIVE B WESTERN ROUNDUP

A banquet at Nudie's famous Western costume store in the early '50s. See if you can find Jock Mahoney, Bill Williams, Max Terhune, Eddie Dean, Gene Autry, Roy Rogers, Pat Buttram, Tex Ritter, Tim Spencer, and Rex Allen.

ing companies in the '40s. In 1955, Johnny and Tex formed Vidor Publications, a company that has remained in operation ever since. Vidor's first significant song was "Remember the Alamo." While Johnny and Tex sought out new material, their reputations for honesty and integrity led to their acquiring renewal rights to some important copyrights, including the Delmore Brothers' songs "Beautiful Brown Eyes" and "Blues Stay Away From Me." Johnny also helped nurture the budding talents of Harlan Howard, who went on to become one of the finest songwriters country music has ever produced. Unfortunately for Johnny and Tex, by the time Harlan's hits began flowing, he had moved to Nashville and signed with another publisher. Still, Vidor has some of his early songs and Johnny was proud of Harlan's success.

In 1952, Johnny joined the cast of *Town Hall Party*. He was there from start to finish both as a performer and as one of the show's hosts and writers. In 1964, Gene Autry brought *Melody Ranch* back as a television program on his newly purchased KTLA television station in Los Angeles. Back as one of its regular performers and writers was none other than Johnny Bond, the man who had always played the opening guitar introduction to "Back In The Saddle Again," Gene's theme song on each *Melody Ranch* radio broadcast.

With the end of *Melody Ranch* in 1970, Johnny turned his energies and creativity in yet another direction. First, he wrote the biography *The Tex Ritter Story*, which was published in 1976. Later that year, his book *Reflections: The Autobiography of Johnny Bond* was also published. Two years later saw publication of *The Recordings of Jimmie Rodgers: An Annotated Discography*. At the time of his death on June 12, 1978, Johnny was writing a history of music in Western films.

Johnny Bond was held in high regard by all who knew this quiet, unassuming man. A rare and varied talent was this fine gentleman.

Texas-born Eddie Dean's road to his own singing cowboy series was a long one. After radio and recording work in Chicago, Eddie came out to Los

WHATEVER HAPPENED TO THE SINGING COWBOY? Life After the Movies

Eddie Dean in 1980.

Monte Hale in 1985.

Angeles where he became a singer on Judy Canova's radio show, and began to land small roles in Western films. Eddie appeared in films starring William Boyd (Hopalong Cassidy), Lee Powell, Don Barry, Ken Maynard and Bob Steele. Finally, in 1944, Eddie was signed to star in his own singing cowboy series for PRC. Eddie's first four, filmed in Cinecolor, were among the first B-Western films to be made in color. Eddie's series continued through 1948.

Many of the songs featured in Eddie's films were written by him. Best remembered of these is "On The Banks of The Sunny San Juan," a song that still elicits great response at Eddie's personal appearances. The most successful song written by Eddie along with his wife Dearest and Hal Blair, was "One Has My Name (The Other Has My Heart)" which became a number one country record for Jimmy Wakely in 1948. In 1969, Jerry Lee Lewis revived the song and took it to number three on the country charts. A number of other artists including Nat King Cole recorded the song over the years. In 1954, Eddie and Hal Southern wrote "I Dreamed of a Hillbilly Heaven" which became Eddie's biggest selling single. In 1961, Tex Ritter recorded his own masterful version and took it to the top of the country charts and, surprisingly enough, into the Top 20 on the pop charts.

Eddie appeared regularly on the *Town Hall Party* television show throughout its nine-year run. Since then he has continued to make occasional recordings and remained busy with club dates throughout the country. His rich and powerful voice is still admired by all who hear him.

Monte Hale's introduction to Hollywood came as a result of his playing guitar and singing on a war bond tour of Texas in 1944. Phil Isley, Jennifer Jones' father, was handling the tour and saw how well Monte came across with audiences. He brought Monte to the attention of Republic Pictures' Herbert Yates, who offered to give Monte a screen test. The test led to a contract and in 1946, Monte began starring in his own singing cowboy series for Republic.

Monte's series continued into 1950, but by that time Republic, like the other studios, was scaling back their production. Monte, after recording a few sides for Beltone and M-G-M, decided to return to his singing career for a brief time. A few television guest roles, significant supporting roles in the films *Giant* and *The Chase* ended Monte's performing career.

Since retiring in the mid '70s, Monte has enjoyed a life of travel and relaxation. His wife, Joanne Hale, is the Executive Director of the Gene Autry Western Heritage Museum.

Western swing music played by Bob Wills and Spade Cooley was featured in a number of singing cowboy films during the '40s. The deep bass voice of Tex Williams was showcased by the Spade Cooley band and led to Tex being signed by Universal Pictures in 1949. At the time Universal didn't have a Western series in production, but they had decided

Tex Ritter and Johnny Bond.

to make a series of Western shorts and selected Tex Williams as their star. Fourteen shorts were produced in 1949 and 1950, just as the era of the singing cowboy was passing.

The end of his series of Western shorts hardly affected Tex. His orchestra, the Tex Williams Western Caravan, was busy making hit records and playing to full houses across the country. During his years with Capitol Records, Tex enjoyed hits with "Suspicion," "Life Gets Tee-Jus, Don't It," and his signature song "Smoke! Smoke! Smoke (That Cigarette)!" which reached number one on the pop charts in 1947. After a dry spell Tex began recording for Boone Records in Nashville in 1964. Before long, hits like "Too Many Tigers," "Bottom of a Mountain" and an updated version of "Smoke! Smoke! Smoke!" began scoring for Tex. In 1970, he moved over to Monument Records and soon hit with "The Night Miss Nancy Ann's Hotel For Single Girls Burned Down."

Tex continued to record for a variety of labels and maintained an active schedule of club dates throughout the country. The man so many people called friend died on October 11, 1985.

If Gene Autry was the first successful singing cowboy then Rex Allen was the last. The Arizona native actually began a life of rodeoing before he thought of a career in music and films. While sidelined by injuries received in the rodeo arena, Rex began working on radio in the unlikely locale of Trenton, New Jersey in 1943. It wasn't long before Rex's fine voice was being featured on the *National Barn Dance* in Chicago.

The combination of Rex's handsome appearance, his fine voice along with a few words of encouragement from Roy Rogers led to Rex being signed by Republic Pictures. Rarely was a performer better suited to the role of singing cowboy, but unfortunately, Rex came in at the end of the singing cowboy cycle. His series began in 1950 and within three

WHATEVER HAPPENED TO THE SINGING COWBOY? Life After the Movies

years he trailed only Roy Rogers and Gene Autry at the boxoffice. But the days of the singing cowboy ended when Rex's series ended in 1954. Republic then made an attempt at television production with Rex's series *Frontier Doctor*. The series ran for one season, but by that time Herbert Yates had lost interest in production and soon sold Republic Pictures.

So Rex and his horse Koko went back to the rodeo circuit, only this time as the headliner. Rodeos, fairs, theater engagements along with guest appearances on television kept Rex busy for the next few years. In 1961, Rex was one of five rotating hosts of the *Five Star Jubilee,* a country music variety show which was televised over NBC. Two of the other hosts were Tex Ritter and Jimmy Wakely.

Rex was one of the first artists signed by the newly formed Mercury Records in 1946. However, his biggest hit record came in 1953 when his Decca recording of "Crying in the Chapel" reached the top ten on the pop charts. In 1962, Rex scored with "Don't Go Near The Indians," which went into the top ten on the country charts. Over the years Rex, who possesses one of the finest voices in any field of music, has recorded a number of fine albums primarily for Decca and Mercury.

Just as Tex Ritter found a new career for himself by singing theme songs in Western films, so too did Rex Allen find a new off-screen role for himself. Walt Disney recognized that there were few voices richer or more mellow than Rex Allen's. Early in the '60s, Disney hired Rex to narrate one of the studio's nature films. It was the beginning of a long relationship between the Disney Studios and Rex Allen. Since then Rex has narrated countless Disney television programs and several feature films in a manner that has greatly enhanced these productions.

The Disney narration work opened yet another opportunity for Rex in voiceover work on radio and television commercials. This has oocupied the majority of Rex's time in recent years and has been the most lucrative of all his endeavors.

With the exception of a limited amount of voiceover work, Rex Allen has pretty much retired and several years ago, moved back to his native Arizona where he has always felt more comfortable.

While there were several singing cowboys who experienced varying degrees of success, Dale Evans was the only woman to make her mark in musical westerns. Too often we think of Roy Rogers and Dale Evans as a team and overlook the many accomplishments of Dale herself.

Dale Evans is the only woman to rank in the top ten western stars at the boxoffice. She accomplished this four times between 1947 and 1952. When Roy and Dale moved into television, it was Dale who wrote their theme song "Happy Trails." Dale has written many fine songs including "The Bible Tells Me So" which became a major hit in 1955.

The only child born to Roy's and Dale's marriage was a daughter named Robin. The child was afflicted with Down's syndrome and doctors at the time encouraged the parents of such children to institutionalize them since there was little that could be done to help them. Roy and Dale wouldn't consider doing such a thing to their daughter. Robin's short life (she died just before her second birthday) had such a profound effect on Roy and Dale that Dale wrote a book about Robin and her impact on the Rogers family. *Angel Unaware* has remained in print ever since and has been a source of strength and inspiration to countless families of handicapped children. Since then Dale has written almost two dozen other inspirational books including her autobiography, *The Woman at the Well.*

Dale's first solo recordings were made for Beltone and later for Majestic. In 1949, she joined RCA Victor and continued to record for them until 1958. In the 1960s, Dale began recording a number of gospel albums for Capitol and Word Records. Dale maintains a busy schedule of speaking engagements before Christian groups. She currently has a weekly television program, *A Date With Dale,* on the Trinity Broadcasting network. The combination of interviews and music with the emphasis on her Christian faith has kept Dale well occupied.

Yet through all the work in films, radio, television, personal appearances, recording, songwriting and her books, Dale managed to raise a large family. Roy and Dale have had nine children, some born to them, some adopted, but all their own. Tragedy has claimed three of their children, but the rest remain close to Roy and Dale.

And so the singing cowboy and the series western has passed into history. While singing-cowboy films may not have received their full measure of praise, there is no doubt they left a permanent mark on film history and the longevity of the careers of most singing cowboy stars shows just how talented these performers were. Few film stars of any genre became beloved the world over as Roy Rogers, Dale Evans, and Gene Autry. And few films produce such warm memories as those made by singing cowboys.

HOLLYWOOD CORRAL: A COMPREHENSIVE B WESTERN ROUNDUP

Discography

REX ALLEN

Decca DL8402	Under Western Stars
Decca DL78766	Mister Cowboy
Vocalion 73885	Golden Songs of the Golden West
Buena Vista BV3307	16 Golden Hits
Disneyland 1337	Favorite Songs
Mercury SR60719	The Faith of a Man
Mercury SR60752	Rex Allen Sings and Tells Tales
Wing SRW16324	Rex Allen
Decca DL75011	The Smooth Country Sound of Rex Allen
Decca DL75205	The Touch of God's Hand
JMI 4003	Rex Allen Sings Bony Kneed, Hairy Legged Cowboy Songs
Hacienda WWLP101	Country Songs I Love
Longhorn EJ1234	Love Gone Cold
Design DLP612	Melodies of the Plains (radio transcriptions)
Hilltop JS6009	Rex Allen Sings Western Ballads (radio transcriptions)

GENE AUTRY

Columbia HL9001	Western Classics
Columbia HL9002	Western Classics Vol. 2
Columbia CL2547	Merry Christmas
Columbia CL2568	Peter Cottontail
Columbia CL6020	Gene Autry's Western Classics
Columbia MJV82	The Story of the Nativity
Columbia MJV83	Little Johnny Pilgrem & Guffy the Goofy Gobbler
Columbia MJV94	Rusty the Rocking Horse & Bucky the Bucking Bronco
Columbia JL8001	Gene Autry at the Rodeo

GENE AUTRY (continued)

Columbia JL8009	Stampede
Columbia CL677	Gene Autry and Champion-Western Adventures
Columbia CL1575	Gene Autry's Greatest Hits
Harmony HL7332	Gene Autry's Greatest Western Hits
Harmony HL7376	Back in the Saddle Again
Harmony HL7399	You Are My Sunshine
Harmony HL9550	Rudolph the Red Nosed Reindeer and Other Children's Christmas Favorites
Columbia CS1035	Country Music Hall Of Fame Album
Encore P14380	Back in the Saddle Again
Columbia FC37465	Gene Autry
Challenge CHL600	Christmas With Gene Autry
RCA Victor LSP2623	Gene Autry's Golden Hits
Design DLPX5	Rudolph the Red Nosed Reindeer
Starday SD1038	Gene Autry's Christmas Classics
Grand Prix KXS11	Gene Autry Sings Rudolph the Red Nosed Reindeer
Republic LP1966	Holiday Time with Gene Autry
Republic R6011	South of the Border/All American Cowboy
Republic R6012	Cowboy Hall of Fame
Republic R6013	Gene Autry Favorites
Republic R6014	Live from Madison Square Garden
Republic R6017	Songs of Faith
Republic R6018	Christmas with Gene Autry
Republic R6021	Gene Autry Classics
Republic R6022	50th Anniversary
Mistletoe MLP1207	Christmastime with Gene Autry

Republic albums are radio broadcast recordings with additional instrumental accompaniment overdubbed

JOHNNY BOND

Harmony HL7308	Johnny Bond's Best
Harmony HL7353	Bottled in Bond
Starday SLP147	The Wild, Wicked But Wonderful West
Starday SLP187	Live It Up and Laugh It Up
Starday SLP227	Songs That Made Him Famous
Starday SLP298	Hot Rod Lincoln/Three Sheets in the Wind
Starday SLP333	Ten Little Bottles
Starday SLP354	Famous Hot Rodders I Have Known
Starday SLP368	The Man Who Comes Around
Starday SLP378	Bottles Up
Starday SLP388	The Branded Stock of Johnny Bond
Starday SLP402	Ten Nights in a Barroom
Starday SLP416	Drink Up and Go Home
Starday SLP444	The Best of Johnny Bond
Starday NLP2039	Sick, Sober and Sorry
Starday NLP2054	Three Sheets in the Wind
Capitol ST249	Great Songs of the Delmore Brothers (with Merle Travis)
Starday SLP456	Something Old, New, Patriotic and Blue
Starday SLP472	Here Comes the Elephants

WHATEVER HAPPENED TO THE SINGING COWBOY? Life After the Movies

JOHNNY BOND (continued)

Lamb & Lion LLC4002	How I Love Them Old Songs
Shasta LP516	Johnny Bond Rides Again
CMH 6212	The Singing Cowboy Rides Again (with Willis Brothers)
CMH 6213	The Return of the Singing Cowboy (with Willis Brothers)

EDDIE DEAN

Sage LP 1	Greater Westerns
King 686	Favorites of Eddie Dean
Sage C5	Hi-Country
Sage C16	Hillbilly Heaven
Sound LP603	Greatest Westerns
Sutton 333	I Dreamed of a Hillbilly Heaven
Shasta SH513	Sincerely, Eddie Dean
Crown CLP5258	Hillbilly Heaven
Crown CLP5434	Eddie Dean Sings
Design DLP80	Eddie Dean Sings A Tribute To Hank Williams
Shasta SH537	A Cowboy Sings Country
Crown CST320	The Golden Cowboy
Crown CST578	Little Green Apples
Crown CST581	Release Me
Crown CST583	Eddie Dean Sings Country and Western
WFC 61576	Dean of the West

DALE EVANS

Allegro Elite 4116	Dale Evans Sings
RCA Victor LPM3168	Hymns of Faith (with Roy Rogers)
RCA Victor LPM1439	Sweet Hour of Prayer (with Roy Rogers)

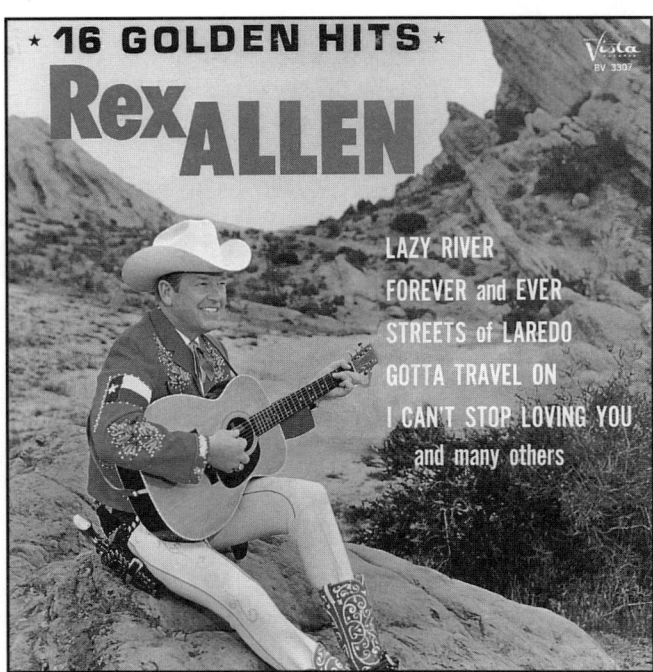

DALE EVANS (continued)

RCA Bluebird LBY1022	Jesus Loves Me (with Roy Rogers)
Golden A198:7	16 Great Songs of the Old West (with Roy Rogers)
Capitol ST1745	The Bible Tells Me So (with Roy Rogers)
Capitol ST2772	It's Real
Capitol ST2818	Christmas is Always (with Roy Rogers)
Capitol ST399	Get To Know The Lord
Word WST8566	Faith, Hope, and Charity
Word WST8589	In The Sweet By And By (with Roy Rogers)
Word WST8658	Heart of the Country
Word WST8661	Country Dale
Word WSA8761	The Good Life (with Roy Rogers)
Word WSB8803	Totally Free
Manna MS2075	Reflections of Life
Teletex C7702	Many Happy Trails (with Roy Rogers & Roy Rogers, Jr.)

TEX RITTER

MCA MCAD10188	The Country Music Hall of Fame
Capitol H4004	Cowboy Favorites
Capitol T971	Songs from the Western Screen
Capitol T1100	Psalms
Capitol ST1292	Blood on the Saddle
Capitol SW1562	The Lincoln Hymns
Capitol ST1623	Hillbilly Heaven
Capitol ST1757	Stan Kenton! Tex Ritter!
Capitol ST1910	Border Affair
Capitol ST2402	The Friendly Voice of Tex Ritter
Capitol T2595	The Best of Tex Ritter
Capitol ST2743	Sweet Land of Liberty
Capitol ST2786	Just Beyond the Moon

HOLLYWOOD CORRAL: A COMPREHENSIVE B WESTERN ROUNDUP

TEX RITTER (continued)

Capitol ST2890	Bump Tiddil Dee Bum Bum!
Capitol ST2974	Tex Ritter's Wild West
Capitol ST213	Chuck Wagon Days
Capitol ST467	Green Green Valley
Capitol ST11037	The Supercountrylegendary Tex Ritter
Capitol SKC11241	An American Legend
Capitol ST11351	Fall Away
Capitol ST11503	Comin' After Jinny
Hilltop JS6043	Tex Ritter Sings His Hits
Hilltop JS6059	Tennessee Blues
Hilltop PTP2020	My Kinda Songs
Hilltop JS6075	Love You Big as Texas
Hilltop JS6138	High Noon
Hilltop JS6155	Tex
Curb D2 77397	Tex Ritter's Greatest Hits

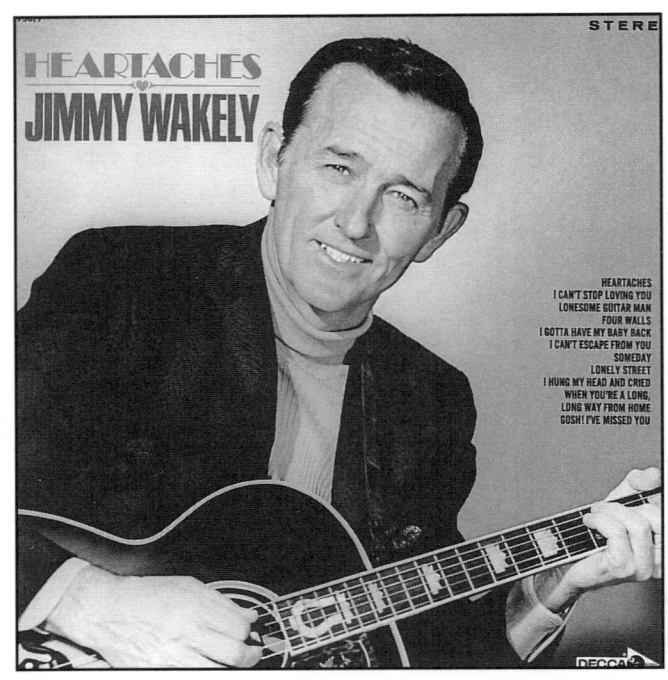

ROY ROGERS

Columbia FC38907	Roy Rogers
MCA MCAD 10548	The Country Music Hall Of Fame
RCA Victor LPM4041	Souvenir Album
RCA Victor LPM3168	Hymns of Faith (with Dale Evans)
RCA Victor LPM1439	Sweet Hour of Prayer (with Dale Evans)
RCA Camden CAL1054	Pecos Bill (w/Sons of the Pioneers)
RCA Camden CAL1074	Lore of the West (w/Dale Evans)
RCA Bluebird LBY1022	Jesus Loves Me (with Dale Evans)
RCA Camden ACL1-0953	The Best of Roy Rogers
Golden A198:7	16 Great Songs of the Old West (with Dale Evans)
Capitol ST1745	The Bible Tells Me So (with Dale Evans)

ROY ROGERS (continued)

Capitol ST2818	Christmas is Always (with Dale Evans)
Capitol ST594	The Country Side of Roy Rogers
Capitol ST785	A Man From Duck Run
Capitol ST11020	Take A Little Love
Word WST8589	In The Sweet By And By (with Dale Evans)
20th Century T467	Happy Trails to You
Word WSA8761	The Good Life (with Dale Evans)
Teletex C7702	Many Happy Trails (with Dale Evans & Roy Rogers, Jr.)
RCA 3024-2-R	Tribute

SONS OF THE PIONEERS

MCA 1563	Empty Saddles
MCAD 10090	The Country Music Hall of Fame
Harmony HL7317	The Sons of the Pioneers' Best
Columbia FC37439	Sons of the Pioneers

the above four albums include Roy Rogers as a member of the Sons of the Pioneers

Vocalion VL3715	Tumbleweed Trails
RCA Victor LPM3032	Cowboy Classics
RCA Victor LPM3095	Cowboy Hymns and Spirituals
RCA Victor LPM3162	Western Classics
RCA Victor LPM1130	25 Favorite Cowboy Songs (radio transcriptions)
RCA Victor LPM1431	How Great Thou Art
RCA Victor LPM1483	One Man's Songs
RCA Camden CAL413	Wagons West
RCA Camden CAL587	Room Full of Roses
RCA Victor LSP2118	Cool Water
RCA Victor LSP2356	Lure of the West
RCA Victor LSP2456	Tumbleweed Trail

WHATEVER HAPPENED TO THE SINGING COWBOY? Life After the Movies

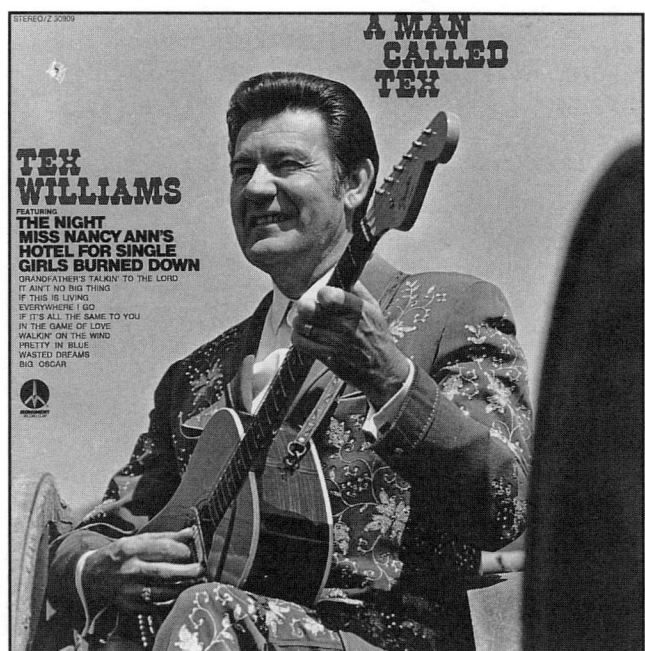

SONS OF THE PIONEERS (continued)

RCA Camden CAL723	Good Old Country Music
RCA Victor LSP2603	Our Men Out West
RCA Victor LSP2652	Hymns of the Cowboy
RCA Victor LSP2737	Trail Dust
RCA Victor LSP2855	Country Fare
RCA Victor LSP2957	Down Memory Trail
RCA Victor LSP3351	Legends of the West
RCA Victor LPM3476	The Best of the Sons of the Pioneers
RCA Victor LSP3665	The Sons of the Pioneers Sing the Songs of Bob Nolan
RCA Victor LSP3714	Campfire Favorites
RCA Victor LSP3964	South of the Border
RCA Camden CAS2205	San Antonio Rose
RCA Victor LSP4119	Tumbling Tumbleweeds
RCA Victor LSP4194	The Sons of the Pioneers Visit the South Seas
RCA Camden ADL2-0336	Riders in the Sky
RCA Victor ANL1-2332	A Country-Western Songbook
RCA Victor AYM1-4092	Let's Go West Again
RCA 9744-2-R	Tumbling Tumbleweeds–The RCA Victor Years Vol. 1
Granite GS1007	Western Country

JIMMY WAKELY

Capitol H4008	Songs of the West
Capitol H9004	Christmas on the Range
Hilltop JS6053	I'll Never Slip Around Again (with Margaret Whiting)
Decca DL8409	Santa Fe Trail
Decca DL8608	Enter, Rest and Pray
Vocalion VL3904	Big Country Songs
Vocalion VL3855	Show Me The Way
Vocalion VL3857	Here's Jimmy Wakely
MCA Coral CB20033	Blue Shadows
Decca DL75077	Heartaches
Decca DL75192	Now and Then
Dot DLP25711	Slippin' Around
Dot DLP25754	Christmas With Jimmy Wakely
Shasta LP501	Country Million Sellers
Shasta LP502	Merry Christmas
Shasta LP505	Jimmy Wakely Sings
Shasta LP511	Jimmy Wakely Country
Shasta LP512	The Jimmy Wakely Family Show
Shasta LP514	The Wakely Way With Country Hits
Shasta LP515	Jimmy Wakely On Stage
Shasta LP518	The Jimmy Wakely CBS Radio Show
Shasta LP521	The Gentle Touch
Shasta LP522	The Singing Cowboy
Shasta LP526	Western Swing and Pretty Things
Shasta LP527	Reflections
Shasta LP532	Precious Memories
Shasta LP533	An Old Fashioned Christmas
Shasta LP540	Moments to Remember

TEX WILLIAMS

RCA Camden CAL463	Tex Williams' Best
Decca DL5565	Dance-O-Rama
Decca DL4295	Country Music Time
Capitol ST1463	Smoke! Smoke! Smoke!
Shasta LP535	Best of the Best
Liberty LST7304	Tex Wiiliams in Las Vegas
Sunset SUS5144	Tex Williams
Imperial LP12309	The Voice of Authority
Boone LS1210	Two Sides of Tex Williams
Monument Z30909	A Man Called Tex
Granite GS1001	Those Lazy, Hazy Days
Frontline FLP7002	The Legendary Tex Williams
Garu GLP101	Tex Williams and California Express

Roy Rogers placed "first" in the annual polls more than any other cowboy.

BEST OF THE WEST
TOP TENS AND FAN FAVORITES
by Richard W. Bann

Suppose we could measure the worldwide theatrical and reissue grosses of B Westerns, as well as their continuing ancillary-market earnings up through, say, last weekend. This could be a leading indicator of which pictures and stars were the best, or at least the most popular. But would the results match your own personal favorites?

Fans of any kind of formal or informal public competition will forever argue over who is better or best. It's always a subjective determination. Motion picture exhibitors, however, tried to answer this question of star-power supremacy for another reason. There was an economic imperative attached to booking these pictures: Outdoor action films were not produced as art, they were manufactured as commercial products competing for time on a theater program, and for pocket change from customers. Theaters sought to play the best draws to make the most money.

During the '30s, '40s, and '50s, *Boxoffice* and *Motion Picture Herald,* two trade papers serving the motion picture industry (particularly exhibitors), attempted to assess, in an annual ordinal ranking, the theatrical drawing power of cowboy personalities—since most of them *were* personalities, singers, and rodeo champions, not actors. Which names on the marquee meant the most in paid admissions at the box office? The results of their polls have been quoted ever after by the media, especially during the '50s and '60s, when so many libraries of program Westerns were sold to television and generated an avalanche of public interest.

Trouble was, in later years these polls were usually only excerpted in fragments to illustrate how a particular Western hero was rising or falling in popularity as the result of a season's release schedule. A 1963 issue of *Screen Thrills Illustrated,* for instance, might tell us that "Ken Maynard slipped out of the top ten box office stars in 1938, the year he concluded a weak series for Grand National." He did indeed, because it was; Americans spending their entertainment nickels and dimes noticed, and so did bookkeepers counting box office receipts. Exhibitors thus voted their experience, and one of the industry's legendary big guns was sent waddling down the cinema trail.

How were these top-ten polls conducted? By whom? And where were they, anyhow? Sealed away in the National Archives? Why weren't they collected all together in one place for easy reference? Well, now we have done it once and for all.

The *Motion Picture Herald* questionnaire asked showmen to "Name, in order, the ten players whose pictures drew the largest attendance to your theaters." The results were also reported, more or less simultaneously, in two other Quigley Publishing Company annuals, *Fame,* and the *Motion Picture Almanac.*

These yearly audits of star power began in 1932, but no cowboy performers made the top ten list for the first four years. Yet Buck Jones, Tom Mix, Ken Maynard, and George O'Brien shoot-'em-ups saved plenty of Depression-era theaters that wouldn't even play the major-studio, big-budget, stage-bound talkfests. By 1935, outdoor action pictures accounted for fully 18% of total Hollywood production. That same year, three rookie saddle aces began promising careers in a great new wave of cowboy personalities: Gene Autry, Charles Starrett, and William Boyd. By this time, Westerns constituted a distinct genre worthy of special attention. So at last in 1936, a separate *Herald* poll, exclusively for Western series stars, was conducted.

Also in 1936, a competing trade paper, *Boxoffice,* in its annual publication entitled *Boxoffice Barometer,* ran an essay on the reigning sagebrush favorites among ticket buyers and theater owners. The following year *Boxoffice Barometer* followed its competition's lead and inaugurated its own popularity poll.

Neither audit of the silver screen's money-making action stars was very scientific. Exhibitors in the United States, Canada, and Britain who were subscribers to the *Motion Picture Herald* were asked to fill out ballots, based on estimated or perceived audience patronage. A correlation between box office receipts and voting was hoped for, and supposed, but was hardly rigorous. The universe of responses was presumed to include exhibitors primarily, but not every theater owner voted (in 1941 there were 16,951 movie houses operating in the United States), and many subscribers from other branches of the industry *did* vote. Exactly how many ballots were actually gathered each year was not disclosed, but the low thousands is an educated guess. Like the statistical accuracy of the contemporaneous polls which elected President Dewey, we wouldn't bet the ranch on the reliability of the *Motion Picture Herald* poll, either. In the absence of information to the contrary, however, this is the best accreditation we have for evaluating cowboy kings.

Perhaps more objective, some would argue (until studying the results) was the method used by *Boxoffice* to determine relative popularity. Their selections were computed from responses by a broad range of exhibitors, the press, and public film groups on the basis of some kind of weighted average formula.

Boxoffice sought to measure more than just theater revenue in its polls, and boasted that questionnaires were sent to "independent theater owners not subject to producer-affiliation pressure or influences." The *Motion Picture Herald* poll, on the other hand, drew not only from the independents, meaning the smaller towns and theaters playing the lower budget and states-rights product, but also from the circuit-operator vote, generally representing the film exchange centers playing mainstream and major studio product releases. Ballots from exhibitors affiliated with producers and distributors naturally carried a built-in bias.

Nevertheless, for your assessment, the tabulation of these less than totally objective popularity and drawing power polls is juxtaposed in Table 1. Proof of at least one poll's lack of precision is the fact that such twin public opinion appraisals never agreed. The rankings were nearly the same in 1948, 1949, and 1950, but never an exact match. So much for statistical accuracy. . . .

Time was when everyone took for granted that mass-produced theatrical Westerns would endure, with the same wide appeal, forever. But finally with the advent of television, market conditions changed. In its poll for 1955, *Boxoffice* noted that Rogers and Autry pictures were still booked extensively, but by that time were all reissues.

By the end of these surveys, there weren't enough active stars left to vote on. So, too, the exhibitor polls passed quietly, just as the production companies and their Western film backlogs *moved* quietly. Soon both were reincarnated with new lives and a new address: Televisionland.

Back at the outset, the popularity polls had been inaugurated coincident with the phenomenon of the singing cowboy. Sagebrush troubadours were fast displacing silent and early sound action kings of the past. Had there been a Gallup-ing Who's Who's dating back to the mid-'20s, once-durable names like Mix, Jones, Maynard, Gibson, and Fred Thomson would have dominated. By the end of 1936, when the first honor roll was published, Thomson was sadly "riding the range" (dead), others were past their prime, and Jones soon would be.

The polls had immediate impact and were closely watched by the trade. Trends were analyzed year by year. In connection with its 1938 survey, *Boxoffice* offered these remarks about the budget series Western: "While these pictures seldom reach the screens of the million-dollar palaces in the big cities, they are regulars at deluxe neighborhood houses in the metropolitan centers and in the small cities and hamlets spread from one coast to another." A dozen years later, the magazine reported, "Producers of Westerns have a product which satisfies, so they hold to the formula. Each Western is cut to pattern, full of the great open spaces and the sweep of action."

BEST OF THE WEST / Top Tens and Fan Favorites

Each year several of the leading stars took ads thanking the exhibitor trade for honoring them. In 1947, for example, one ad carried this copy: "Monogram expresses its appreciation to the exhibitors of America for again voting Johnny Mack Brown a top Western favorite at the box office." Another grateful cowboy star was pictured next to the Columbia torch lady logo, and signed his ad, "Charles Starrett—twelfth year riding for the brand."

In fact, Columbia was well represented in these surveys, placing almost as many contract performers as Monogram, RKO and Universal *combined*. But no studio dominated the action leader lists like Republic, often scoring with half the top ten attractions. In 1943, without Gene Autry, Republic earned six spots among the top ten. A posse that size could drive other producers out of the territory. (Note that leading saddle aces seldom rode the PRC prairies.)

Gene Autry was the first to appear simultaneously on both *Motion Picture Herald* polls—the Western stars, as well as the civilian stars (the original poll)—meaning he was therefore the first action star to break into the general audience top-ten ranks. In 1940, Autry rose to number four in overall motion picture drawing power, with only Mickey Rooney, Spencer Tracy and Clark Gable constituting bigger attractions. In 1941, Autry placed sixth among the top money-making stars, ahead of Gary Cooper, Bette Davis, James Cagney, and Judy Garland. He made the non-Western top ten one last time in 1942, coming in seventh. This demonstrated real Hollywood muscle.

Roy Rogers was the second crossover range rider. He finished among the general audience top-ten money-makers in both 1945 and 1946. Besides Rogers and Autry, no other Western star made both top-ten polls in the same year.

John Wayne placed in the middle of the first list in 1936. Thanks to *Stagecoach*, he cracked the *Motion Picture Herald* poll again in 1939, but just barely. Except for these two appearances, the following would be true: Gene Autry and Roy Rogers finished

All but one of the B Western stars in this photo made the Top Ten polls at least three times. (l. to r.) Sunset Carson, Bob Livingston (as a member of the Three Mesquiteers), Allan Lane, Dale Evans, Roy Rogers, Bill Elliott, and Don Barry. All were featured in Bells of Rosarita *(1945, Republic).*

HOLLYWOOD CORRAL: A COMPREHENSIVE B WESTERN ROUNDUP

TABLE 1. Annual Ordinal Ranking of Top Ten Western Box Office Attractions

Motion Picture Herald Poll	Boxoffice Poll
1936:	
1. Buck Jones	
2. George O'Brien	
3. Gene Autry	
4. William Boyd	
5. Ken Maynard	No survey as yet.
6. Dick Foran	
7. John Wayne	
8. Tim McCoy	
9. Hoot Gibson	
10. Buster Crabbe	
1937:	
1. Gene Autry	1. Gene Autry
2. William Boyd	2. George O'Brien
3. Buck Jones	3. William Boyd
4. Dick Foran	4. Buck Jones
5. George O'Brien	5. Jack Holt
6. Tex Ritter	6. Dick Foran
7. Bob Steele	7. Ken Maynard
8. Three Mesquiteers	8. Harry Carey
9. Charles Starrett	9. James Ellison
10. Ken Maynard	10. Tom Mix
1938:	
1. Gene Autry	1. Gene Autry
2. William Boyd	2. William Boyd
3. Buck Jones	3. George O'Brien
4. George O'Brien	4. Jack Holt
5. Three Mesquiteers	5. Buck Jones
6. Charles Starrett	6. Tex Ritter
7. Bob Steele	7. Ken Maynard
8. Smith Ballew	8. Roy Rogers
9. Tex Ritter	9. Harry Carey
10. Dick Foran	10. Three Mesquiteers
1939:	
1. Gene Autry	1. Gene Autry
2. William Boyd	2. William Boyd
3. Roy Rogers	3. George O'Brien
4. George O'Brien	4. Roy Rogers
5. Charles Starrett	5. Buck Jones
6. Three Mesquiteers	6. John Wayne
7. Tex Ritter	7. Charles Starrett
8. Buck Jones	8. Tex Ritter
9. John Wayne	9. Smiley Burnette
10. Bob Baker	10. Bob Livingston
1940:	
1. Gene Autry	1. Gene Autry
2. William Boyd	2. John Wayne
3. Roy Rogers	3. William Boyd
4. George O'Brien	4. George O'Brien
5. Charles Starrett	5. Roy Rogers
6. Johnny Mack Brown	6. Buck Jones
7. Tex Ritter	7. Smiley Burnette
8. Three Mesquiteers	8. Charles Starrett
9. Smiley Burnette	9. Johnny Mack Brown
10. Bill Elliott	10. Jack Holt
1941:	
1. Gene Autry	1. Gene Autry
2. William Boyd	2. William Boyd
3. Roy Rogers	3. Buck Jones
4. Charles Starrett	4. Tim Holt
5. Smiley Burnette	5. Roy Rogers
6. Tim Holt	6. Smiley Burnette
7. Johnny Mack Brown	7. Charles Starrett
8. Three Mesquiteers	8. Johnny Mack Brown
9. Bill Elliott	9. Tim McCoy
10. Tex Ritter	10. Gabby Hayes
1942:	
1. Gene Autry	1. Gene Autry
2. Roy Rogers	2. Roy Rogers
3. William Boyd	3. William Boyd
4. Smiley Burnette	4. Tim Holt
5. Charles Starrett	5. Smiley Burnette
6. Johnny Mack Brown	6. Charles Starrett
7. Bill Elliott	7. Buck Jones
8. Tim Holt	8. Johnny Mack Brown
9. Don Barry	9. Gabby Hayes
10. Three Mesquiteers	10. Tim McCoy
1943:	
1. Roy Rogers	
2. William Boyd	
3. Smiley Burnette	
4. Gabby Hayes	
5. Johnny Mack Brown	No poll conducted.
6. Tim Holt	
7. Three Mesquiteers	
8. Don Barry	
9. Bill Elliott	
10. Russell Hayden	
1944:	
1. Roy Rogers	1. Roy Rogers
2. William Boyd	2. Gene Autry
3. Smiley Burnette	3. William Boyd
4. Gabby Hayes	4. Ken Maynard
5. Bill Elliott	5. Smiley Burnette
6. Johnny Mack Brown	6. Johnny Mack Brown
7. Don Barry	7. Charles Starrett
8. Charles Starrett	8. Gabby Hayes
9. Russell Hayden	9. Hoot Gibson
10. Tex Ritter	10. Tex Ritter
1945:	
1. Roy Rogers	1. Roy Rogers
2. Gabby Hayes	2. Gene Autry
3. William Boyd	3. William Boyd
4. Bill Elliott	4. Gabby Hayes
5. Smiley Burnette	5. Bill Elliott
6. Johnny Mack Brown	6. Johnny Mack Brown
7. Charles Starrett	
8. Don Barry	
9. Tex Ritter	
10. Rod Cameron	

BEST OF THE WEST / Top Tens and Fan Favorites

TABLE 1. continued

Motion Picture Herald Poll	Boxoffice Poll
1946:	
1. Roy Rogers	1. Roy Rogers
2. Bill Elliott	2. Gene Autry
3. Gene Autry	3. Gabby Hayes
4. Gabby Hayes	4. Bill Elliott
5. Smiley Burnette	5. William Boyd
6. Charles Starrett	6. Smiley Burnette
7. Johnny Mack Brown	7. Johnny Mack Brown
8. Sunset Carson	8. Ken Maynard
9. Fuzzy Knight	9. Charles Starrett
10. Eddie Dean	10. Sons of the Pioneers
1947:	
1. Roy Rogers	1. Roy Rogers
2. Gene Autry	2. Gene Autry
3. William Boyd	3. Bill Elliott
4. Bill Elliott	4. William Boyd
5. Gabby Hayes	5. Gabby Hayes
6. Charles Starrett	6. Smiley Burnette
7. Smiley Burnette	7. Johnny Mack Brown
8. Johnny Mack Brown	8. Charles Starrett
9. Dale Evans	9. Bob Nolan
10. Eddie Dean	10. Bob Steele
1948:	
1. Roy Rogers	1. Roy Rogers
2. Gene Autry	2. Gene Autry
3. Bill Elliott	3. Gabby Hayes
4. Gabby Hayes	4. Bill Elliott
5. William Boyd	5. William Boyd
6. Charles Starrett	6. Smiley Burnette
7. Tim Holt	7. Tim Holt
8. Johnny Mack Brown	8. Charles Starrett
9. Smiley Burnette	9. Johnny Mack Brown
10. Andy Devine	10. Leo Carillo
1949:	
1. Roy Rogers	1. Roy Rogers
2. Gene Autry	2. Gene Autry
3. Gabby Hayes	3. Gabby Hayes
4. Tim Holt	4. Bill Elliott
5. Bill Elliott	5. William Boyd
6. Charles Starrett	6. Andy Devine
7. William Boyd	7. Tim Holt
8. Johnny Mack Brown	8. Smiley Burnette
9. Smiley Burnette	9. Johnny Mack Brown
10. Andy Devine	10. Leo Carillo
1950:	
1. Roy Rogers	1. Roy Rogers
2. Gene Autry	2. Gene Autry
3. Gabby Hayes	3. Gabby Hayes
4. Bill Elliott	4. William Boyd
5. William Boyd	5. Bill Elliott
6. Tim Holt	6. Tim Holt
7. Charles Starrett	7. Andy Devine
8. Johnny Mack Brown	8. Smiley Burnette
9. Smiley Burnette	9. Charles Starrett
10. Dale Evans	10. Johnny Mack Brown

TABLE 1. continued

Motion Picture Herald Poll	Boxoffice Poll
1951:	
1. Roy Rogers	1. Roy Rogers
2. Gene Autry	2. Gene Autry
3. Tim Holt	3. Gabby Hayes
4. Charles Starrett	4. Tim Holt
5. Rex Allen	5. Dale Evans
6. Bill Elliott	6. Judy Canova
7. Smiley Burnette	7. Smiley Burnette
8. Allan Lane	8. Bill Elliott
9. Dale Evans	9. Rex Allen
10. Gabby Hayes	10. Charles Starrett
1952:	
1. Roy Rogers	1. Roy Rogers
2. Gene Autry	2. Gene Autry
3. Rex Allen	3. Tim Holt
4. Bill Elliott	4. Dale Evans
5. Tim Holt	5. Bill Elliott
6. Gabby Hayes	6. Judy Canova
7. Smiley Burnette	7. Rex Allen
8. Dale Evans	8. Smiley Burnette
9. Charles Starrett	9. Vaughn Monroe
10. William Boyd	10. Charles Starrett
1953:	
1. Roy Rogers	1. Randolph Scott
2. Gene Autry	2. Roy Rogers
3. Rex Allen	3. Gene Autry
4. Bill Elliott	4. Rod Cameron
5. Allan Lane	5. George Montgomery
	6. Dale Evans
	7. Rex Allen
	8. Tim Holt
	9. Bill Elliott
	10. Judy Canova
1954:	
1. Roy Rogers	1. Randolph Scott
2. Gene Autry	2. Roy Rogers
3. Rex Allen	3. Gene Autry
4. Bill Elliott	4. Rod Cameron
5. Gabby Hayes	5. George Montgomery
	6. Dale Evans
1955:	
No poll conducted.	1. Randolph Scott
	2. Roy Rogers
	3. Rod Cameron
	4. George Montgomery
	5. Gene Autry
	6. Dale Evans

in the top ten for both civilian and Western polls, and more than once, before John Wayne was voted onto either list for the first time. That's the hard way of saying Autry and Rogers were bigger stars than most remember.

Since they rode the same trails with Autry and Rogers, it was no surprise that Smiley Burnette and Gabby Hayes were the initial two sidekicks to crash the list of reigning favorites. Burnette did it first, then Hayes. Once Burnette left Republic for Columbia, however, Hayes consistently surpassed him in the annual rankings.

The closest race for top "rider" of the range was 1937 when Autry edged another fledgling cowhand, Bill Boyd, by just five points. Although Boyd and (somewhat surprisingly) Bill Elliott demonstrated consistent and definite box office strength, it was either Autry or Rogers who topped every single poll from 1937 through 1952 in both trade publication surveys. In 1984 Autry said, "I never considered Roy competition; we both made six pictures a year and there are 52 weeks in a year. How were you going to play them at the same time? We were always friends, believe me. There was no feud. That was the Republic publicity department."

Fans will debate forever whether or not Rogers would have dethroned Autry in popularity if Gene hadn't volunteered to enter military service in 1942 (Rogers, five years younger, was deferred after failing his induction physical with a wrenched back and chronic arthritis). In any case, the names of Gene Autry, Roy Rogers, and Hopalong Cassidy on theater marquees would guarantee eager S.R.O. crowds on any Saturday, anywhere. They were the industry's big guns, in all vital respects.

The disparity between the top and lower echelon stars has blurred over time. Today we can screen a solid Ken Maynard Universal with a polished Kermit Maynard Ambassador picture and enjoy them equally, as though they were of equal status. The same for a double bill of Bob Livingston's *Covered Wagon Days* (1940) with his brother Jack Randall's

Buck Jones led the Motion Picture Herald *poll the first year and thus became the only B-Western star other than Roy Rogers or Gene Autry to be number one.*

BEST OF THE WEST / Top Tens and Fan Favorites

The Million Dollar Theatre at 3rd and Broadway in downtown Los Angeles often featured major studio B Westerns. The theater, built in 1917, is still in operation.

Covered Wagon Trails (released a couple weeks later). Yet, when these respective pairs of pictures were made, there was a dramatic difference between their relative values, their importance, and their box office potential. A caste system existed for Western personalities and filmmakers, just as it did throughout all of Hollywood.

In 1939, *Boxoffice* observed, "Since Western pictures play in entirely different situations, it is hard to compare them to other major attractions.... Very few Western program pictures play deluxe first-run houses or even the key city suburban-run houses. Accordingly we find that some of the Western series have very few bookings, and at very small film rentals, which means they are not of much importance to the industry as a whole, but used more or less as a filler attraction. However, there are some very important Westerns, such as the Bill Boyd and Gene Autry series, which get several thousand bookings and play some very important houses, in the Western and Southern districts in particular."

The *Boxoffice* general-audience, "civilian" movie-star popularity polls were divided into male and female lists. Western polls, like Western casts, were predominately "between men" only, as the Johnny Mack Brown film once said. There was one leading lady, maybe one saloon chirp, and that's it. So it was quite an achievement the year Dale Evans became the first and only Western actress (discounting the later *Boxoffice* listings for Judy Canova) to crack the top-ten survey in 1947. She *earned* the title, "Queen of the West."

Yet *Boxoffice,* just reflecting exhibitor experience, editorialized in 1951, "Who are the Western fans? Small boys, certainly. (But) little girls... are as adventuresome and even as bloodthirsty as little boys." Meaning that before they became young ladies, lots of little girls loved big cowboy stars. After all, right from the days of Tom Mix, the Western movie with its unreality and reassuring predictability has always been the greatest fairy tale made in Hollywood. So producers, distributors, and exhibitors counted on attracting boys *and* girls; they sought to attract *all* kids, and particularly the little kid left in big kids, meaning plenty of adults.

In 1950, when Bill Boyd was making regular personal appearances as Hoppy, he was constantly surrounded by fearsome crowds. *Time* magazine

HOLLYWOOD CORRAL: A COMPREHENSIVE B WESTERN ROUNDUP

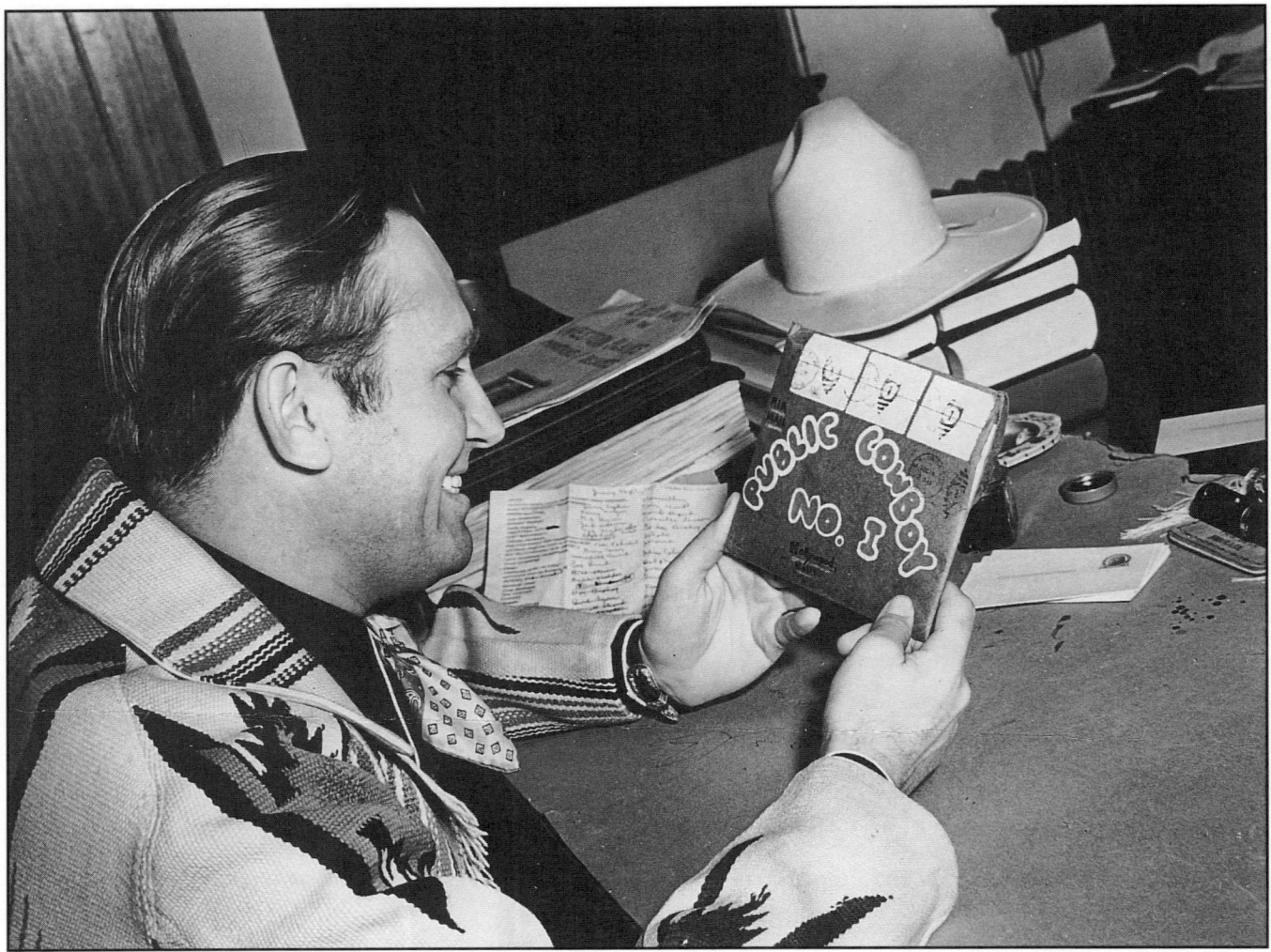

Gene Autry dominated the pre-War years and was in every poll except for the years he was in the service.

quoted his evangelistic attitude towards dealing with crowd control: "If they start pushing, I just say, 'Now kids, be good kids'—I call them all kids, grown-ups and all—and they settle down." The hard-nosed trade press, on the other hand, reported news, not mushy nostalgia; for decades they characterized Westerns as "immortal," and "the staple of the industry." At one time, and for a long time in this country, Westerns were *the* popular movie entertainment of under-age customers. In 1938, it wasn't enough for Lou Gehrig to be, well, *Lou Gehrig*. He had to try his hand as a Western movie hero.

It was truly a social and commercial phenomenon, and producers knew how to capitalize on it, and sustain it as long as possible. They knew to play the game. Stay true to heroic Western conventions; offer predictable family entertainment; deliver reassuring wish fulfillment in seven reels or less. From Buffalo Bill's wild-west shows to Buntline dime novels to Remington illustrations to simple Western movies, the public had always responded to these pure values. But in today's more "sophisticated," fast-paced world, Westerns have been superseded as popular entertainment for the masses.

Cinema highbrows have always scorned Saturday matinee Westerns. Their fierce possession of such misguided notions cannot change the fact that these films were and are enormous fun to watch and analyze. But as producer Sam Sherman says, "For those who understand, no explanation is necessary; for those who don't understand, no explanation is possible."

Besides the fun, these films offered a moral code by which impressionable youngsters were positively influenced, as witness the wonderful Randy Travis song, "Heroes and Friends." Without recognizing it at the time, these black-and-white films, with their black-and-white values, played an important role in shaping who and what we are—both as individuals and as a nation. Some argue the specter of John Wayne defines our foreign policy! Certainly President Reagan, and even Henry Kissinger pictured themselves as "cowboys."

The subtext of every unpretentious B Western

BEST OF THE WEST / Top Tens and Fan Favorites

Smiley Burnette and Gabby Hayes were the two sidekicks most often represented.

Allan Lane on a radio show in the mid-'40s promoting his latest Red Ryder film for Republic.

HOLLYWOOD CORRAL: A COMPREHENSIVE B WESTERN ROUNDUP

Republic went all out promoting Rex Allen as their new singing Western star. As a result, he was represented in the polls in each of the four years that he made films. Here he makes a personal appearance in Chicago in 1950.

screenplay (many penned by women) advocated loyalty, fair play, kindness, ambition, the work ethic, etc. How many of us learned more, from just watching these films, about honesty, chivalry, respect, and the difference between right and wrong, than from anything we heard in church or were taught in school?

As Randy Travis' song says, with some pride, he grew up with cowboys he watched on TV. He and we identified with these (apparently) virtuous stars, and they really were part of our shared extended family, providing a safe refuge, as well as inspiration. Such mythologized heroes offered dreams with powerful impact on the corners of young minds, and ultimately the American consciousness. This, as much as anything, is the *absolutely unintended* legacy left by screen attractions from Art Acord to Whip Wilson—two of the least likely names to have left lasting marks, and yet they have.

Until the B-Western era ended, youngsters flocked to theaters, cheering weekend matinees; their patronage might constitute one-third of a week's revenue. Where are all these kids today? They're not kids anymore. As the light of Western stars faded, most kids grew up and lost interest. So what does that say about the relatively few of us left who after all these years never renounced our allegiance to such humble Western favorites?

The real answer is, those of us who are not Randy Travis became collectors as a means of attaching ourselves to this pastime which had made such a permanent impression. We sought out advertising accessories, posters, still photos, arcade cards, and 16mm and now videocassette copies of the films themselves. In so doing, what happened is that we bought back our childhoods. Or tried to.

Anyhow, it seemed to this writer that it might be fun to conduct our own poll, and ask some of those

BEST OF THE WEST / Top Tens and Fan Favorites

These five B-Western stars along with Autry and Rogers dominated the polls. Clockwise (l. to r.): William Boyd, Charles Starrett, Johnny Mack Brown, Bill Elliott, and Tim Holt.

HOLLYWOOD CORRAL: A COMPREHENSIVE B WESTERN ROUNDUP

Gene Autry and Smiley Burnette disarm Duncan Renaldo as Mary Lee looks on in this scene from South of the Border *(Republic, 1939).*

grown-up kids still attracted to this field—the last of the faithful, like the last of the Duanes—to list *their* favorites. Not their favorite stars, but their favorite films. Would there be a consensus of which films are better and best? These few aficionados sampled for our poll have seen a high percentage of the 2,000 odd titles which comprise the B Western genre, and can pass an informed, if prejudiced (what else?) opinion on which films are the best, or at least their favorites.

The assignment was to choose ten titles, in order of preference, representing their ten most treasured sound series Westerns. Or, to answer the question: "If, like George O'Brien at the end of *Riders of the Purple Sage,* you find yourself totally sealed off from civilization and can only carry ten uncirculated pre-1960 Kodak stock 16mm prints (or if you have help, ten 35mm prints) to show forever against some flat cliff in the proper aspect ratio, which would they be?"

The foremost Western-film collector is a gentleman named Clyde Carroll. He tried to prepare a list while recovering from surgery, but took the task so seriously that after first selecting *South of the Border,* he could not complete his top ten. He could no more select ten titles in order than he could choose among his children and grandchildren.

There's always a troublemaker, and Sam Sherman wanted to make it easier by expanding into multiple categories of top ten lists, such as "Best Tim McCoy Western In Which He Plays A Mexican Character," "Best Reliable Western In Which The Hero Plays A Western Pulp Writer," and "Best Jack Randall Western In Which He Talks Slowly," among others. Such foolishness was not encouraged.

Some of these choices are astonishing. For his tenth favorite B Western to drag along to that desert island equipped with electrical outlets, the distinguished film historian William K. Everson has selected nothing less than *Toll of the Desert* (1935). And there *is* nothing less than *Toll of the Desert.* Apparently he wanted to have at least one rock-bottom independent, and he sure did get one. Judge the rest for yourselves. Here they are:

BEST OF THE WEST / Top Tens and Fan Favorites

Richard W. Bann, *author and archivist:*
1. *In Old Santa Fe* (1934) Ken Maynard
2. *Rider of Death Valley* (1932) Tom Mix
3. *Hop-a-long Cassidy* (1935) Hopalong Cassidy
4. *Home in Oklahoma* (1946) Roy Rogers
5. *Riders of the Purple Sage* (1931) George O'Brien
6. *Gold Mine in the Sky* (1938) Gene Autry
7. *Texas Stagecoach* (1939) Charles Starrett
8. *Mystery Ranch* (1932) George O'Brien
9. *Don't Fence Me In* (1945) Roy Rogers
10. *Death Valley Rangers* (1943) Trail Blazers

Robert Birchard, *writer and film editor:*
1. *Rider of Death Valley* (1932) Tom Mix
2. *The Lone Rider* (1930) Buck Jones
3. *Riders of the Purple Sage* (1931) George O'Brien
4. *Whispering Smith Speaks* (1936) George O'Brien
5. *The Big Show* (1936) Gene Autry
6. *Bar 20 Rides Again* (1935) William Boyd
7. *Riders of the Northwest Mounted* (1943) Russell Hayden
8. *The Idaho Kid* (1936) Rex Bell
9. *Randy Rides Alone* (1934) John Wayne
10. *Song of the Gringo* (1936) Tex Ritter

Hop-a-long Cassidy (Paramount, 1935)

Riders of the Northwest Mounted (Columbia, 1943)

Alan G. Barbour, *author and video marketing executive:*
1. *The Cherokee Flash* (1945) Sunset Carson
2. *Cheyenne Wildcat* (1944) Bill Elliott
3. *The Tulsa Kid* (1940) Don Barry
4. *Covered Wagon Days* (1940) Three Mesquiteers
5. *Mexicali Rose* (1940) Gene Autry
6. *In Old Caliente* (1939) Roy Rogers
7. *Pals of the Saddle* (1938) Three Mesquiteers
8. *Saddle Mountain Roundup* (1941) Range Busters
9. *Silver Spurs* (1943) Roy Rogers
10. *Santa Fe Uprising* (1946) Allan Lane

Eddie Brandt, *owner of Eddie Brandt's Saturday Matinee:*
1. *In Old Santa Fe* (1934) Ken Maynard
2. *Mystery Ranch* (1932) George O'Brien
3. *The Last Outlaw* (1936) Harry Carey
4. *Bells of Rosarita* (1945) Roy Rogers
5. *Eagle's Brood* (1935) Hopalong Cassidy
6. *Bitter Creek* (1954) Bill Elliott
7. *Riders of the Whistling Skull* (1937) Three Mesquiteers
8. *The Last Roundup* (1947) Gene Autry
9. *The Gunman from Bodie* (1941) Rough Riders
10. *Wyoming Outlaw* (1939) Three Mesquiteers

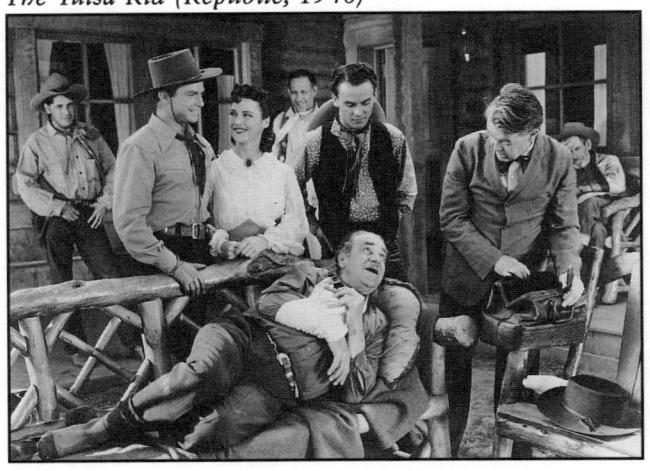

The Tulsa Kid (Republic, 1940)

The Last Outlaw (RKO, 1936)

HOLLYWOOD CORRAL: A COMPREHENSIVE B WESTERN ROUNDUP

John Cocchi, *contributor to nearly one-hundred film history books:*
1. *Hit the Saddle* (1937) Three Mesquiteers
2. *The Trail Beyond* (1934) John Wayne
3. *Texas Trail* (1937) Hopalong Cassidy
4. *Powdersmoke Range* (1935) Three Mesquiteers
5. *Mystery Ranch* (1932) George O'Brien
6. *Melody Ranch* (1940) Gene Autry
7. *Eyes of Texas* (1948) Roy Rogers
8. *Rider of Death Valley* (1932) Tom Mix
9. *In Old Santa Fe* (1934) Ken Maynard
10. *The Thrill Hunter* (1933) Buck Jones

Alex Gordon, *producer, and curator of the Gene Autry collection:*
1. *Down Mexico Way* (1941) Gene Autry
2. *The Ivory-Handled Gun* (1935) Buck Jones
3. *Everyman's Law* (1936) Johnny Mack Brown
4. *Heart of the Rockies* (1937) Three Mesquiteers
5. *Lawless Valley* (1938) George O'Brien
6. *Smokey Smith* (1935) Bob Steele
7. *Renegade Trail* (1939) Hopalong Cassidy
8. *Forbidden Trails* (1941) Rough Riders
9. *Arizona Ranger* (1948) Tim Holt
10. *The Last Musketeer* (1952) Rex Allen

The Trail Beyond (Lone Star, 1934)

Arizona Ranger (RKO, 1948)

William K. Everson, *author, historian, and professor at New York University:*
1. *Thunder Trail* (1937) Gilbert Roland
2. *Heart of the Rockies* (1937) Three Mesquiteers
3. *Bar 20 Justice* (1938) Hopalong Cassidy
4. *Moonlight on the Prairie* (1935) Dick Foran
5. *West of Carson City* (1940) Johnny Mack Brown
6. *End of the Trail* (1932) Tim McCoy
7. *End of the Trail* (1936) Jack Holt
8. *Courage of the West* (1937) Bob Baker
9. *Man from Music Mountain* (1943) Roy Rogers
10. *Toll of the Desert* (1935) Fred Kohler Jr.

Mark Heller, *co-founder of Streamline Film Archives:*
1. *Rider of Death Valley* (1932) Tom Mix
2. *Mystery Ranch* (1932) George O'Brien
3. *Riders of the Purple Sage* (1931) George O'Brien
4. *Saga of Death Valley* (1939) Roy Rogers
5. *End of the Trail* (1932) Tim McCoy
6. *Hop-a-long Cassidy* (1935) Hopalong Cassidy
7. *Down Mexico Way* (1941) Gene Autry
8. *The Deadline* (1931) Buck Jones
9. *Haunted Gold* (1932) John Wayne
10. *In Old Caliente* (1939) Roy Rogers

Courage of the West (Universal, 1937)

Saga of Death Valley (Republic, 1939)

BEST OF THE WEST / Top Tens and Fan Favorites

Ed Hulse, *writer, editor, and Cinecon Film Festival chairman:*
1. *Mystery Ranch* (1932) George O'Brien
2. *When A Man's A Man* (1935) George O'Brien
3. *Hop-a-long Cassidy* (1935) Hopalong Cassidy
4. *Rider of Death Valley* (1932) Tom Mix
5. *To The Last Man* (1933) Randolph Scott
6. *The Last Outlaw* (1936) Harry Carey
7. *Gold Mine in the Sky* (1938) Gene Autry
8. *Saga of Death Valley* (1939) Roy Rogers
9. *The Thrill Hunter* (1933) Buck Jones
10. *Riders of the Whistling Skull* (1937) Three Mesquiteers

The Thrill Hunter (Columbia, 1933)

Sam Sherman, *producer and president of Independent International Pictures Corp.:*
1. *Riders of the Whistling Skull* (1937) Three Mesquiteers
2. *The Night Riders* (1939) Three Mesquiteers
3. *When A Man's A Man* (1935) George O'Brien
4. *Hop-a-long Cassidy* (1935) Hopalong Cassidy
5. *Westbound Stage* (1939) Tex Ritter
6. *Public Cowboy No. 1* (1937) Gene Autry
7. *Frontier Pony Express* (1939) Roy Rogers
8. *Courage of the West* (1937) Bob Baker
9. *Desert Justice* (1936) Jack Perrin
10. *Cheyenne Rides Again* (1937) Tom Tyler

Westbound Stage (Monogram, 1939)

Joe Judice, *co-founder of the Cooperative Film Society of New York:*
1. *Between Men* (1935) Johnny Mack Brown
2. *Silver Bullet* (1935) Tom Tyler
3. *Riders of the Whistling Skull* (1937) Three Mesquiteers
4. *Eagle's Brood* (1935) Hopalong Cassidy
5. *Tombstone Canyon* (1932) Ken Maynard
6. *The Thrill Hunter* (1933) Buck Jones
7. *South of the Border* (1939) Gene Autry
8. *Young Bill Hickok* (1940) Roy Rogers
9. *Sunset Range* (1935) Hoot Gibson
10. *Rider of Death Valley* (1932) Tom Mix

Young Bill Hickok (Republic, 1940)

Harold Smith, *exhibitor and Western film festival sponsor:*
1. *Calling Wild Bill Elliott* (1943) Bill Elliott
2. *Wild Frontier* (1947) Allan Lane
3. *Eyes of Texas* (1948) Roy Rogers
4. *The Prescott Kid* (1934) Tim McCoy
5. *Marshal of Mesa City* (1939) George O'Brien
6. *The Lost Trail* (1945) Johnny Mack Brown
7. *Pioneers of the Frontier* (1940) Bill Elliott
8. *Missouri Outlaw* (1941) Don Barry
9. *Carolina Moon* (1940) Gene Autry
10. *Six Gun Law* (1948) Charles Starrett

Wild Frontier (Republic, 1947)

HOLLYWOOD CORRAL: A COMPREHENSIVE B WESTERN ROUNDUP

Packy Smith, *producer, publisher and original western film festival sponsor:*
1. *Outlaws of the Prairie* (1937) Charles Starrett
2. *Sioux City Sue* (1946) Gene Autry
3. *Three Men from Texas* (1940) Hopalong Cassidy
4. *Desert Vengeance* (1931) Buck Jones
5. *On the Old Spanish Trail* (1947) Roy Rogers
6. *The Light of Western Stars* (1940) Russell Hayden
7. *Song of the Gringo* (1936) Tex Ritter
8. *Riders in the Sky* (1949) Gene Autry
9. *Without Honor* (1932) Harry Carey
10. *Out California Way* (1946) Monte Hale

Finally, the most important list of all–yours:
1. _____
2. _____
3. _____
4. _____
5. _____
6. _____
7. _____
8. _____
9. _____
10. _____

Out California Way (Republic, 1946)

The 5th Avenue Theater, Nashville, Tennessee, August 4, 5 and 6, 1938.

AFTERWORD

by Roy Rogers

The *Hollywood Corral* and all these other essays sure bring back a lot of pleasant memories. From the time I first appeared on camera with the Sons of the Pioneers in 1934's *The Old Homestead* to the time I left Republic in 1951, Western movies have played an important part in my career.

You've already read about my early films as one of the Sons, appearing in some Gene Autry, Charles Starrett, and Dick Foran Westerns. And I guess by now everybody knows how I got my first starring series at Republic in 1938. We worked awful hard in those days: the series Westerns were made quick, and they were made cheap (in the beginning, anyway). We got up early in the morning—before sunup, most of the time—and drove out to those familiar locations that Dave Holland writes about. It was hot, dusty work for the most part, and we worked all day long until the last rays of the sun dropped over the horizon. Some times we worked even longer than that: I'm sure many of you have seen those early Westerns of mine, directed by Joe Kane, with scenes shot on the Republic backlot in the dead of night.

But they were *good* days, too. I sure enjoyed working with a lot of the folks you've been reading about in these pages, many of whom turned out to be close friends over the years. I got to see a few of them again during the making of our recent TV series, which I hope you've seen. And, of course, it was those early Republic Westerns that first teamed me with Dale—and that's a partnership we've been carrying on for just about a half century.

I'm also happy to see some of my co-workers get long-overdue credit here in the *Hollywood Corral*. Directors like Joe Kane and Bill Witney, writers like Sloan Nibley, stuntmen like Davy Sharpe and Joe Yrigoyen—these folks contributed an awful lot to the Western films we did at Republic, and without them I don't think those movies would've been nearly as good. Even though Herb Yates wouldn't let me hire a secretary to help with my fan mail, I've got to admit he hired people who knew how to make pretty good movies on low budgets and tight schedules! I'm especially gratified to see my old partners, the Sons of the Pioneers, covered extensively in a very well researched essay by Ken Griffis.

Of course, I was fortunate enough to be able to carry on long after the B Western disappeared in the early '50s. With all the personal appearances at circuses and rodeos, our first TV show with Dale and Pat Brady, our recording work, and in later years, my appearances at many of the Roy Rogers Restaurants around the country, I've managed to keep pretty busy in the 40 years since I last starred in a feature-film Western. And I've been delighted to see so many people visit our museum in Victorville, California, where Dale and I have displayed many of the mementos that bring back happy memories.

Over the years I've taken some good-natured ribbing about the old Westerns: about those six-shooters that never needed reloading, about the fancy outfits and rigs that "real" cowboys would never have worn, and so on. And I can assure you, we never kidded ourselves that we were making "realistic" or "historically accurate" pictures. But we *did* try to get across certain themes and messages to our audiences: Fair play, justice for all, love of animals, respect for the environment, faith in God and country. And, if you'll allow my saying so, I think we did a pretty good job, all things considered. I'd like to believe that's one of the reasons so many fans and collectors are still interested in the B Western after all these years.

Since none of us ever thought of our Western pictures as high art, it didn't really surprise us that writers and film scholars either treated them condescendingly or ignored them altogether. It was a long time before Westerns of any kind got much attention, and even then the pictures most often discussed were those made by fine directors like John Ford and Howard Hawks. Once in a while there might be some mention or maybe a picture of Gene Autry, or Bill Boyd, or myself, but not much else about what *Hollywood Corral* calls "the series Western."

I guess that's why I've been surprised from time to time about how much fans seem to know about Dale and me—especially younger fans, who were born after I stopped making pictures, and even after we did our TV show. But it seems our old Westerns made more of an impression than we thought, and that they've become part of our American folklore.

I'm proud to have been part of that tradition, and I'm delighted that Packy Smith and Ed Hulse have asked me to contribute to this worthwhile project. Here's hoping that it'll serve as a reference work for Western-movie fans for years to come.

Happy Trails!
Roy Rogers

ANNOTATED BIBLIOGRAPHY
INTRODUCTORY COMMENTS & ANNOTATIONS
by Packy Smith

Western film scholarship is a relatively new area of serious study. The body of work in English dates from 1962, with the publication of Fenin and Everson's seminal work *The Western: From Silents to Cinerama*. Prior to this ground-breaking work, a few serious attempts (mostly by French critics) at defining the parameters of the genre had appeared in film periodicals, and a few biographies of individuals closely identified with Westerns were available. But *The Western* was certainly the first popular history.

Don Miller's Hollywood Corral is concerned primarily with B Westerns, therefore the bibliography is restricted to books devoted, if not totally, at least in part to the Bs. This automatically eliminates a large number of books on Western films which either deal exclusively with the As or tend to ignore or dismiss the Bs entirely.

One of the disadvantages a serious film student faces when researching so esoteric a subject as B Westerns is that so much of the critical writing about the subject is done by apologists or fans eager to find excellence where none exists. Further, few fans have the resources available to properly research the subject. Having access to fifty Ken Maynard films, and studying these films, might make a person an expert on the *content* of the films of Ken Maynard, but it certainly does not qualify one as an expert on Ken Maynard or his films.

At present, the most useful writing about B Westerns is by fans who over a number of years of researching and writing about these films have developed into competent historians of this sub-genre. Such competent writer/researcher fans as Buck Rainey, David Rothel, and Ed Wyatt are good examples of this type of historian. If only every movie cowboy had a fan who could produce a biography as well researched and written as Wyatt's *More Than A Cowboy*, a biography of silent cowboy star Fred Thomson.

Conversely, the most damaging books and essays are also written by fans. Some seem to think that watching a few movies, reading a few books, and impressing a few friends who compliment them on their knowledge of B Westerns makes them potential film historians. So they round up all of the back issues of their favorite B Western periodicals and the few books that might have mentioned their subject cowboy, add these to the stack of pressbooks they have at hand and begin their research. They start writing by copying the passages they find most interesting, errors and all (not crediting the source), draw conclusions and make assumptions to fill in any holes, and finally, if they can't find a filmography in the limited sources at hand, they compile one from the pressbooks and *The Shoot-'Em-Ups* (again, no credit), missing at least three films because none of the sources mentioned that early in his career the subject cowboy had several unbilled bit parts in films that starred other, more popular cowboy heroes. Once the text is finished, all that remains is finding stills and lobby cards to illustrate.

HOLLYWOOD CORRAL: A COMPREHENSIVE B WESTERN ROUNDUP

At this juncture the root of the problem becomes evident. Assuming the writer finds a publisher, or publishes it himself, this poorly researched and most likely poorly written, plagiarized tome now takes its place in the body of work about its particular subject to be picked up by the next fan who decides to join the ranks of fan/writer/historians. Thus the circle starts all over again.

The point is simply that useful historical and biographical writing requires more than a passing acquaintance with a subject. Knowing how to research a subject is as important as having access to primary sources required, but not readily available. Additionally, it's fallacy to assume that all of the silver screen heroes deserve full-blown biographies. With a few exceptions, the cowboy heroes of movies had relatively brief film careers before retiring to the life of everyman (real estate salesman, car dealer, policeman, banker, rancher, etc.).

It is probable that several worthwhile books were overlooked when the following list was compiled. However, there are many books, some self-published but also a few from mainstream publishers, that have been intentionally left out for fear that inclusion might be mistaken as an implied endorsement. Most of these are so ineptly researched and written, and so sloppily produced, that they are of little value to anyone seriously interested in the subject.

Some of the most interesting interviews and data (and sometimes even scholarship) published to document the history of the B Western can be found in periodicals, when such periodicals *can* be found. Most were, and are, limited circulation tabloids and fanzines. Since so few people take this field of interest seriously, these periodicals are seldom acquired and saved for reference by libraries. As a result, end of the trail newcomers just discovering B Westerns (thanks to what could be their final roundup on cable TV) and serious film students who might seek access to this primary research will have a hard time locating these publications.

While not a part of the formalized, annotated bibliography which follows, many are worthy of at least acknowledgment here. Among the many published during the last thirty years, *Wildest Westerns, Film Fan Monthly, Screen Thrills Illustrated, Screen Facts, Those Enduring Matinee Idols, Film Collectors Registry, Views and Reviews, Western Film Collector,* and *Yesterday's Saturdays* made their contribution to sustaining interest in this genre and are worth seeking out.

Currently, *The Big Reel* (Empire Publishing Co., Madison, NC) and *Classic Images* (Muscatine, IA) offers articles of interest to B Western buffs in each monthly issue (most notable, Boyd Magers in his regular column 'Western Clippings' in *The Big Reel* offers an exhaustive assemblage of trivia about B Westerns). WOY Publications (Waynesville, NC) offers several different B Western oriented periodicals on an irregular basis. Also, there are articles and essays about B Westerns appearing on a regular basis in periodicals of all kinds, too numerous to mention here.

Adams, Les, and Buck [Bill G.] Rainey, *The Shoot-'em-Ups: The Complete Reference Guide to Westerns of the Sound Era,* Metuchen, The Scarecrow Press, 1987. 633 pps. Illustrated.
> Although not the "complete" reference promised in the title, this is *the* cornerstone book in any Western buff's library. In the fifteen years this book has been available we tend to take for granted the accessibility of this information and forget what it was like before *The Shoot-'em-Ups*. It consists of a chronological listing of all Western films made in the sound era, with cast listings, partial credits, and release dates.

Allen, Rex, as told to Paula Simpson Witt, *The Arizona Cowboy Rex Allen—My Life, Sunrise to Sunset,* Scottsdale, RexGarRus Press, 1989. 126 pps. Illustrated, with index and filmography.
> Reading this book is almost like listening to Rex tell his story. He tells all we need to know about Rex Allen presented in a way that is a pleasure to read.

Autry, Gene, with Mickey Herskowitz, *Back in the Saddle Again,* Garden City, Doubleday & Company, Inc., 1978. 252 pps. Illustrated, with index.
> One of the more eagerly awaited and ultimately more disappointing of autobiographies—the Autry story he tells is very superficial. There is nothing about the early musical influences and motivations, very little about how he came to Hollywood and who most influenced him after he got there. The definitive Autry is yet to come.

ANNOTATED BIBBLIOGRAPHY

Barbour, Alan G., *The Thrill Of It All,* New York, The MacMillan Company, 1971. 204 pps. Illustrated.
    An affectionate survey of the B Western genre told from a fan's point of view. Unpretentious and highly entertaining.

Bond, Johnny, *Reflections: The Autobiography of Johnny Bond,* JEMF Special Series, No. 8, Los Angeles, John Edwards Memorial Foundation, Inc., 1976. Illustrated, with discography and filmography.
    "Reflections" is much more accurate than "autobiography" as this is mostly about people and studios he worked with and for instead of himself.

_____. *The Tex Ritter Story,* New York, Chappell Music Co., 1975. Illustrated, with discography and filmography.
    The Ritter story told by one of his closest friends and business partner.

[Brand, Max] Easton, Robert, *Max Brand: The Big Westerner,* Norman, University of Oklahoma Press, 1970. 350 pps. Illustrated, with index.
    The life of Frederick Faust, better known by his pen name. Max Brand published over 30 million words—short stories, Westerns, historical romances, murder mysteries, plays, and poetry. His stories provided the basis for many early Tom Mix movies including the classic "Destry Rides Again." He was also the creator of Dr. Kildare.

[Brand, Max] Richardson, Darrell C., *Max Brand: The Man and His Work,* Los Angeles, Fantasy Publishing Co., 1952. 198 pps. Illustrated.
    This collection of essays is of special interest to Brand collectors because of the extensive bibliography. A great companion volume to the Easton biography.

Brownlow, Kevin, *The War, The West, And The Wilderness,* New York, Alfred A. Knopf, 1979. 602 pps. Illustrated, with index.
    The best history of the very early days of Western filmmaking (with other sections devoted to films about World War I and early documentary films), the book contains extensive interviews with movie pioneers.

Canutt, Yakima, *Stuntman: The Autobiography of Yakima Canutt* [with Oliver Drake], New York, Walker and Company, 1979. 252 pps. Illustrated, with index and filmography.
    Canutt's career as the premier stuntman is discussed in depth. Loaded with stories about his early years as John Wayne's double. More importantly, he tells the how and why stunts were done the way they were. Fascinating.

Carey, Diana Serra, *The Hollywood Posse,* Boston, Houghton Miffin Company, 1975. 268 pps. Illustrated.
    A reminiscence by silent child star "Baby Peggy" Montgomery about her father, Jack Montgomery. A good general text that is sometimes marred by spotty historical research.

Carmen, Bob, and Dan Scapperotti, *The Adventures of the Durango Kid,* Privately published, 1983. 176 ps. Illustrated.
_____. *Rex Allen, The Arizona Cowboy,* Privately published, 1982. 96 pps. Illustrated.
_____. *Roy Rogers, King of the Cowboys,* Privately published, 1979. 196 pps. Illustrated.
_____. *The Western Films of Monte Hale,* Privately published, 1984. 96 pps. Illustrated.
_____. *The Western Films of Sunset Carson,* Privately published, 1981. 72 pps. Illustrated.
    This series follows a basic format of a brief biographical essay and a chronological listing of the Western films with cast, credits, and synopsis of each film, with one to three illustrations per film. The filmographies are generally restricted to the series Westerns. For most of the stars covered in the series it is probably all that will ever be needed.

Cocchi, John, *Second Feature: The Best of the B Films,* New York, Citadel Press, 1991. 256 pps. Illustrated, with index.
    Brief but informative essays on several hundred B features, including many Westerns.

_____. *The Westerns: A Picture Quiz Book,* New York, Dover Publications, Inc., 1976. 128 pps. Illustrated, with index.
    Fun and games with B Western trivia.

Drake, Oliver, *Written and Directed by Oliver Drake,* Baldwyn, The Outlaw Press, Inc., 1990. 154 pps. Illustrated.
    The autobiography of the prolific B Western writer, producer, and director.

Drew, Bernard A. *Hopalong Cassidy: The Clarence E. Mulford Story,* Metuchen, Scarecrow Press, Inc., 1991. 307 pps. Illustrated.
    A biography of Mulford, with an overview of the films, radio, and TV series, and the comic books and strips; and a partial listing of the merchandising tie-ins.

_____. *Lawman In Scarlet: An Annotated Guide to Royal Canadian Mounted Police in Print and Performance,* Metuchen, Scarecrow Press, Inc., 1990. 296 pps. Illustrated.

Evarts, Hal G., Jr., *Skunk Ranch to Hollywood: The West of Author Hal Evarts,* Santa Barbara, Capra Press, 1989. 220 pps. Illustrated.
    A biography by writer Hal Evarts, Jr. about his father, who wrote such Western classics as "Tumbleweeds" and "The Big Trail."

Everson, William K., *A Pictorial History of the Western,* New York, The Citadel Press, 1969. 246 pps. Illustrated, with index.
    A good historical overview of Western films. When first published, it was a ground breaking extension of his first book on the subject co-authored with George Fenin.

_____. *The Hollywood Western,* New York, Citadel Press, 1992. 256 pps. Illustrated, with index.
    An expanded and updated version of the above, that regretfully incorporates many of the original errors and conclusions from the first edition.

Fenin, George, and William K. Everson, *The Western: From Silents to Cinerama,* New York, Orion Press, Inc., 1962. 362 pps. Illustrated, with index.
    The first, and in many ways still the best, overview of the Western film genre.

Fernett, Gene, *Next Time Drive Off the Cliff,* Cocoa, Cinememories Publishing Co., Inc., 1968. 205 pps. Illustrated.
    A superficial but entertaining look at the brief history of Mascot Pictures.

_____. *Poverty Row,* Satellite Beach, Coral Reef Publications, Inc., 1973. 163 pps. Illustrated.
    This volume covers several of the "poverty row" studios in a cursory manner.

Garfield, Brian, *Western Films: A Complete Guide,* New York, Da Capo Press. 2nd edition, 1988. Illustrated, with appendices and bibliography.
    Although it's hard to understand how a "complete guide" to Westerns can restrict itself to As (sort of like a "complete guide" to TV restricting its coverage to prime time programs), this is still one of the more interesting Western filmographies with critical comments on hundreds of sound Westerns. The author is an outstanding writer with a genuine understanding of the genre.

[Grey, Zane] Gruber, Frank, *Zane Grey: A Biography,* New York, The World Publishing Co., 1970. 284 pps. Illustrated, with index.
    A biography of the most popular Western novelist by a fellow Western novelist and screenwriter. Grey's novels were the basis for over 150 official screen adaptations and numerous rip-offs.

Griffis, Ken, *Hear My Song: The Story of the Celebrated Sons of the Pioneers,* Camarillo, Privately published, 1986. (revised edition), 188 pps. Illustrated, with discography.
    Bios of every member of the Sons up to 1985 as well as a complete filmography and discography.

Hagner, John G., *Falling for the Stars,* Privately published, 1964. 126 pps. Illustrated.
    One of the first books devoted exclusively to the stunt men and women. Hagner, a stuntman himself, explains how many of the stunts were done and who did them.

ANNOTATED BIBBLIOGRAPHY

Hardy, Phil, *The Encyclopedia of Western Movies,* Minneapolis, Woodbury Press, 1984. 395 pps. Illustrated, with index.
>Nice photos, but most of the information is available in other sources in a much more readable form. Limited B Western material.

Hart, William S., *My Life East and West,* Boston and New York, Houghton Miffin Co., 1929. 363 pps. Illustrated, with index.
>Hart's autobiography offers insight into his life and character, but it is highly colored and incidents of his early years especially are often romanticized.

Heide, Robert, and John Gilman, *Box-Office Buckeroos: The Cowboy Hero from the Wild West Show to the Silver Screen,* New York, Abbeville Press, 1989. 207 pps. Illustrated, with bibliography and index.
>This beautifully produced, well written history of the cowboy "hero" deals mostly with collectables surrounding the mythical cowboy originating in early Western fiction and Wild West shows, and later B Western movies.

Hitt, Jim, *The American West From Fiction Into Film,* Jefferson, McFarland & Company, Inc., 1990. 374 pps. Illustrated, with index.
>The best so far at trying to trace the source material for many Westerns and B Westerns.

Holland, Dave, *From Out of the Past, A Pictorial History of the Lone Ranger,* Granada Hills, Holland House, 1988. 444 pps. Illustrated, with index.
>A beautifully produced guide to the Lone Ranger serials, premiums, radio show, films, and television series. The definitive Lone Ranger book.

_____. *On Location in Lone Pine,* Lone Pine, Holland House, 1990. 106 pps. Illustrated, with index.
>A history of filmmaking on location in Lone Pine, California. The book touches on A films as well as many favorite B Westerns. Then and now photos, trivia, and interviews with townspeople who were actually there when these films were made make this a must for the Western buff.

Holland, Ted, *B Western Actors Encyclopedia,* Jefferson, McFarland & Co., 1989. 479 pps. Illustrated.
>Thumbnail biographies with incomplete filmographies of most of the more popular stars and character actors from the B Westerns.

Horwitz, James, *They Went Thataway,* New York, E. P. Dutton, 1976.
>A personal memoir of the author's search for the old B Western cowboys. Not bad, but doesn't add much new to the field.

Lahue, Kalton C., *Riders of the Range: The Sagebrush Heroes of the Sound Screen,* South Brunswick and New York, A. S. Barnes and Company, 1973. 259 pps. Illustrated.
_____. *Winners of the West: The Sagebrush Heroes of the Silent Screen,* South Brunswick and New York, A. S. Barnes and Company, 1970. 351 pps. Illustrated.
>Of interest only as collector's items, these books contain biographies of Western stars that are mostly unreliable and poorly researched

Langman, Larry, *A Guide To Silent Westerns,* Westport, Greenwood Press, 1992. 616 pps. Bibliography and index.
>The only thing that this book offers over other books about silent films is that it deals strictly with Westerns. More complete information on almost every film listed here is available in other sources, notably the AFI catalogues.

Leonard, John W., *Wild Bill Elliott,* Privately printed, 1976. 94 pps. Illustrated.
>The first bio/filmography of a B Western star, this book defined the style. Many that followed copied the format. A list of all of Elliott's films before his first starring role is followed by a complete Western filmography with cast and credits, release dates and a story synopsis.

HOLLYWOOD CORRAL: A COMPREHENSIVE B WESTERN ROUNDUP

Martin, Len D., *The Columbia Checklist: The Feature Films, Serials, Cartoons and Short Subjects of Columbia Pictures Corporation, 1922–1988,* Jefferson, McFarland & Co., 1991. 647 pps. Appendices, bibliography, with index.
> Checklist of 2,371 feature films (including B Westerns), 57 serials, 596 cartoons, and 76 miscellaneous shorts. Release date, running time, major personnel credits, cast and synopsis when available for each.

McClure, Arthur F., and Ken D. Jones, *Heroes, Heavies, and Sagebrush,* South Brunswick and New York, A. S. Barnes and Company, 1972. 351 pps. Illustrated.
> Thumbnail biographies of dozens of Western players. The first and still the best at putting the face with the name of many character actors of the B Western.

McCoy, Tim, with Ronald McCoy, *Tim McCoy Remembers the West,* Garden City, Doubleday.
> Autobiography of one of the great Western stars who was also a cavalry officer in the last days of the Wild West.

McDonald, Archie P. (editor), *Shooting Stars, Heroes and Heroines of Western Film,* Bloomington and Indianapolis, University of Indiana Press, 1987. 265 pps.
> Essays on the careers of several Western stars, including B Western favorites Hart, Maynard, Autry, and Wayne.

Mix, Olive Stokes, with Eric Heath, *The Fabulous Tom Mix,* Englewood Cliffs, Prentice-Hall, 1957. 177 pps. Illustrated.
> This reminiscence by Tom Mix's third of five wives is largely accurate when covering the years 1907–1915, less so in dealing with his later career.

Mix, Paul E., *The Life and Legend of Tom Mix,* New York, A. S. Barnes and Company, 1972. 206 pps. Illustrated, with index and filmography.
> A biography by a distant relative of Tom Mix that is one of the first attempts to separate the truth from the legend. The filmography is unreliable, and more recent studies are more complete. Interesting.

Mix, Tom, *The West of Yesterday,* [compiled and edited by J. B. M. Clark from interviews with the author], Los Angeles, Time-Mirror Press, 1923. 162 pps. Illustrated.
> A largely fictional "autobiography," this is the source of several of the more outlandish Tom Mix legends. Of interest primarily as a collectable.

[Mix, Tom] Birchard, Robert S., *King Cowboy: Tom Mix and the Movies,* Burbank, Riverwood Press, 1993. 265 pps. Illustrated.
> The first book to deal exclusively with Tom Mix's film career, with particular attention to the Selig Films from 1910 to 1917. Synopsis, cast and credit listings, and release dates for every known and verified short and feature is presented. The author also eliminates several titles previously credited to Mix, with the reasons he has reached his conclusions.

[Mix, Tom] Christeson, H. M. and F. M., *Tony and his Pals,* Chicago, Albert Whitman & Co., 1934. 144 pps. Illustrated.
> A book for children, but it is the best book about Tom Mix written during his lifetime.

[Mix, Tom] Nicholas, John H., *Tom Mix—Riding Up to Glory,* Oklahoma City, Persimmon Hill Books, 1980. 95 pps. Illustrated.
> Nicely produced, very superficial biography from the Cowboy Hall of Fame. Excellent photos.

[Mix, Tom], Norris, Merle G. "Bud," *The Tom Mix Book,* Waynesville, World of Yesterday, 1989. 379 pps. Illustrated.
> An imposing compilation of essays, trivia and interviews by a leading Tom Mix fan and collector. The filmography is extensive, but is somewhat unreliable on the Mix Selig films (1910–1917). However, Norris's section on the Tom Mix radio premiums provides a valuable guide for collectors.

[Mix, Tom] Seiverling, Richard F., *Tom Mix: Portrait of a Superstar,* Hershey, Keystone Enterprises, 1991. 320 pps. Illustrated.

>A grab-bag of articles about Tom Mix with special emphasis on the continuing fan interest in the Western star with a full account of the annual Tom Mix Festival that has been staged in various locations for the past dozen years. There are interesting first-hand accounts of Tom Mix's European tours in the 1930s including many rare photos of Tom on tour. The book includes a title list, but not a full filmography.

Nareau, Bob, *The "Real" Bob Steele and a Man Called "Brad,"* Mesa, Da'kine Publishing Co., 1991. 156 pps. Illustrated.

>The closest to a real biography Steele or his father is likely to ever have, this book clears up a lot of misinformation concerning the family. Of real interest to the collector and historian alike.

Nevins, Francis M., *The Films of Hopalong Cassidy,* Waynesville, The World of Yesterday Publications, 1988. 324 pps. Illustrated.

>An annotated filmography of the Hopalong Cassidy series, comparing the films to the literary source. A must for all Hoppy fans.

Okuda, Ted, *The Monogram Checklist,* Jefferson, McFarland & Company, Inc., 1987. 387 pps. Illustrated, with index.

>A filmography of Monogram Pictures, arranged chronologically. The information on some films is sketchy, but still useful to the collector and researcher.

_____. *Grand National, Producers Releasing Corporation, and Screen Guild/Lippert,* Jefferson, McFarland & Company, Inc., 1989. 241 pps. Illustrated, with index.

>What Okuda did for Monogram he does with the films of these three low-budget production/distribution companies.

Parish, James Robert, and Michael R. Pitts, *The Great Western Pictures,* Metuchen, The Scarecrow Press, 1976. 457 pps. Illustrated.

_____. *The Great Western Pictures II,* Metuchen, The Scarecrow Press, 1988. 428 pps. Illustrated.

>Two of the mass-produced volumes from the Parish movie-book mill, they gather enough information to make a worthwhile addition to a film buff's bookshelf.

Pitts, Michael R., *Western Movies, A TV and Video Guide to 4,200 Genre Films,* Jefferson, McFarland & Company, 1986. 623 pps. Bibliography, with index.

>Pitts goes solo on this one, which covers a surprisingly large number of Bs, with accurate one and two line synopsies.

Rainey, Buck [Bill G.], *Buck Jones,* Nashville, Western Film Collectors Press, 1975. 128 pps. Illustrated.

>The author's first biography of Jones is a nice collector's item. Revised and expanded in a two volume work in 1990.

_____. *The Fabulous Holts,* Nashville, Western Film Collectors Press, 1976. 216 pps. Illustrated.

>Biographies and filmographies of Jack, Tim, and Jennifer Holt.

_____. *Heroes of the Range,* Metuchen, The Scarecrow Press, 1987. 354 pps. Illustrated, with index.

>This book contains brief biographical essays of 15 of the better known B Western stars, with filmographies, by one of the most prolific and competent of the B Western writer/historians. Rainey has one flaw that becomes irritating at times; he tends to compare all of the cowboys to Buck Jones and continually shows his disdain for those who, in his opinion, don't measure up.

_____. *The Life and Films of Buck Jones—The Silent Era,* Metuchen, Scarecrow Press, 1990.

_____. *The Life and Films of Buck Jones—The Sound Era,* Metuchen, Scarecrow Press, 1991. 388 pps. Illustrated.

>Buck Rainey is the authority on Buck Jones and these two volumes are the result of many years of research.

———. *Sweethearts of the Sage,* Metuchen, The Scarecrow Press, 1992. 652 pps. Illustrated.
  Brief bios and filmographies of over 250 actresses who appeared in Western movies.

———. *They Ride Again: A Supplement to Shoot-'em-Ups,* Metuchen, The Scarecrow Press, 1990. 319 pps. Illustrated.
  Companion to the original *Shoot-'em-Ups,* corrects and updates entries from the original edition, plus entries missing from the first. Crosses from film to television.

———. *Those Fabulous Serial Heroines,* Metuchen, The Scarecrow Press, 1990. 537 pps. Illustrated.
  What he did for the Western leading ladies in *Sweethearts of the Sage,* he does here for the serial ladies.

Ricci, Mark, and Boris and Steve Zmijewsky, *The Films of John Wayne,* New York, Citadel Press, 1983. 320 pps. Illustrated.
  The definitive Wayne filmography.

Rogers, Dale Evans, *Dale, My Personal Picture Album,* Old Tappan, Fleming H. Revell, 1971. Illustrated.
  Pictorial biography, a companion to *The Woman at the Well.*

———. *The Woman at the Well,* Old Tappan, Fleming H. Revell, 1970. 191 pps.
  Dale Evans Rogers' autobiography with the emphasis on her private life and her professional career after the movies.

[Rogers, Roy] Davis, Elise Miller, *The Answer is God: The Personal Story of Dale Evans and Roy Rogers,* New York, McGraw-Hill, 1955. 243 pps. Illustrated.
  In spite of the fact that it is nearly forty years old, this remains the best biography of Evans and Rogers. It was done with the full cooperation of the principals, and was based on extensive interviews with friends and family members.

[Rogers, Roy] Rasky, Frank, *Roy Rogers, King of the Cowboys,* New York, Julian Messner, Inc., 1955. 189 pps. Illustrated.
  A superficial biography, adds no new information.

[Rogers, Roy] Roper, William R., *Roy Rogers, King of the Cowboys,* Minneapolis, T. S. Denison, 1971. 182 pps. Illustrated. Bibliography.
  One of a series of biographies for young adults, of interest primarily as a collectable.

[Rogers, Roy] Stowers, Carlton, *Happy Trails: The Story of Roy Rogers and Dale Evans,* Waco, Word Books, 1979. 213 pps. Illustrated.
  Officially, "the story of Roy and Dale in their own words written with the assistance of..." is of primary interest for the years following the end of the Davis biography (1955). This book is the source of most biographical information issued today.

Rogers, Roy Jr., *Growing Up With Roy and Dale,* Ventura, Regal Books, 1986. 206 pps. Illustrated.
  Dusty Rogers tells his story of what it was like to grow up in the family of the King of the Cowboys.

Rothel, David, *An Ambush of Ghosts, A Personal Guide to Favorite Western Locations,* Madison, Empire Publishing, 1990. 277 pps. Illustrated.
  Rothel and his friend Ken Taylor spent several years searching out and photographing specific locations used in Westerns. Must reading for anyone remotely interested in where the old Westerns were filmed.

———. *The Gene Autry Book* [revised edition], Madison, Empire Publishing, Inc., 1988. 293 pps. Illustrated, with index to filmography only.

———. *The Roy Rogers Book,* Madison, Empire Publishing, Inc., 1987. 223 pps. Illustrated, with index to filmography only.
  Reference and trivia scrapbooks that offer a wealth of information about the careers of Autry and Rogers.

ANNOTATED BIBBLIOGRAPHY

_____. *The Singing Cowboy,* New York, A. S. Barnes & Co., 1978. 272 pps. Illustrated.
  The bulk of this book consists of a series of interviews conducted by Rothel with the various singing cowboys. He has a brief biographical essay introducing each interview, followed by a filmography. Far from definitive, but the best we have to date.

_____. *Those Great Cowboy Sidekicks,* Waynesville, WOY Publications, 1984. 325 pps. Illustrated, with index.
  The only book so far devoted exclusively to Western sidekicks.

_____. *Who Was That Masked Man?* [revised edition], San Diego and New York, A. S. Barnes & Company, Inc. 1981. 280 pps. Illustrated, with index.
  The scope of Dave Holland's book on the Lone Ranger tends to dwarf all others, however this is an excellent study of the most popular masked hero ever.

Sherman, Robert F., *Quiet On The Set! Motion Picture History at the Iverson Movie Location Ranch,* Privately printed, 1984. 156 pps. Illustrated, with index.
  Although rife with errors when dealing with specific films, and many stills misidentified, this history of the Iverson family and their location ranch should be part of every library devoted to Westerns.

Speed, Maurice F., *The Western Film Annual* [published annually from 1951 through 1962], London, MacDonald and Co., Ltd. Illustrated.
  One of the best known, and most sought after publications dealing with B Westerns to come out of Great Britain, Speed's annuals contain a comprehensive listing of all Westerns released in the United Kingdom that respective year. Although slanted toward the fan, it nevertheless is a well presented, useful reference work and includes feature articles by such noted film historians as Alex Gordon and William Everson. From 1957, the title expanded to *The Western Film and TV Annual.*

Thomas, Tony, *The West That Never Was,* New York, Citadel Press, 1989. 255 pps. Illustrated.
  Essays about personal favorite Westerns from a noted film writer/researcher.

Thornton, Chuck, and David Rothel, *Allan "Rocky" Lane—Republic's Action Ace,* Madison, Empire Publishing, Inc., 1990. 181 pps. Illustrated.
  A brief bio followed by an extensive filmography of Lane's Western films.

_____. *Lash LaRue—King of the Bull Whip,* Madison, Empire Publishing, Inc., 1988. 160 pps. Illustrated.
  A brief bio with transcribed interviews, followed by a filmography of LaRue's Western films.

Tinsley, Jim Bob, *For A Cowboy Has To Sing,* Orlando, University of Central Florida Press, 1991. 330 pps. Illustrated, with index.
  Foreword by Roy Rogers and Dale Evans. The book offers in-depth essays on the music of the singing cowboys. Fascinating, and a must for the singing cowboy buff.

Tuska, Jon, *The American West in Film: Critical Approaches to the Western,* Westport, Greenwood Press, 1985. 304 pps. Illustrated, with index.
  Je n'aurai pas connu ce livre si quelqu'un ne l'avait pas mis sur mon bureau. Si vous acceptez cette poubelle que les films B de l'ouest sont une forme d'art, c'est le livre qu'il vous faut.

_____. *The Filming of the West,* Garden City, Doubleday & Company, Inc., 1976. 588 pps. Illustrated, with index.
  What should have been the best book about Western films is clouded by a pompous, overbearing prose style and an eccentric point of view. Tuska sometimes bends history to conform to his preconceived notions, and there are some just plain sloppy errors. Still, it is a fascinating book.

_____. *The Vanishing Legion: A History of Mascot Pictures, 1927–1935,* Jefferson, McFarland & Co., 1982. 224 pps. Illustrated, with index.
  Suffers from the same problems with style that all of the author's books have, but informative.

Wakely, Linda Lee, *See Ya! Up There, Baby: The Jimmy Wakely Story,* Privately published, 1992. 206 pps. Illustrated, discography, and filmography.

    A very personal biography of singing cowboy Jimmy Wakely written by his youngest daughter.

Wyatt, Edgar M., *The Hoxie Boys,* Raleigh, Wyatt Classics, Inc., 1992. 190 pps. Illustrated.

    This dual biography is as well done as Wyatt's first book. It is amazing that so much information can be compiled about the brothers after so many years. Outstanding.

_____. *More Than A Cowboy: The Life and Films of Fred Thomson,* Raleigh, Wyatt Classics, Inc., 1988. 212 pps. Illustrated, with index.

    This privately published volume is easily the best single biography of a series Western star. This book along with "The Hoxie Boys" should be on every Western film buff's shelf.

Zolotow, Maurice, *Shooting Star, A Biography of John Wayne,* New York, Simon & Schuster, 1974. 416 pps. Illustrated, with index.

    The best biography of Wayne was written by the prolific Zolotow, who sometimes worked too quickly to catch minor errors that crept into the text.

TRAIL DUST
A FILM PRESERVATION POSTSCRIPT
by Richard W. Bann

Try to find a first edition printing of *Hollywood Corral*. Try. In 1982, when Don Miller died of a heart attack caused by a diabetic infection at age 54, William K. Everson wrote a two-page eulogy for *Films In Review*. With characteristic generosity, he stated that Don's book on the B Western "was and *is* the definitive work on that genre."

Ah, but try to find a copy. For that matter, try to find a copy of lesser books devoted to the history of B Westerns (all the rest). As mentioned previously, some exceptional work in this field has been published in limited circulation periodicals. Trouble is, very few subsist as of this writing, and back issues of the others are as scarce as production values in any Range Busters adventure.

Even worse—much worse—just like the publications which sought to celebrate and memorialize them, the films themselves are silently disappearing. Destry, or Hopalong may well ride again, but someday soon, like John Wayne's "Randy," they may be riding alone. All alone.

Many B Western 35mm nitrate film negatives and master fine grain lavenders (to the extent these flammable and unstable elements still exist) are not being properly stored, cared for, and transferred to safety preservation film stock. Because of their prohibitive storage cost, or their dangerous combustible nature, or their present lack of commercial potential, original B Western preprint material continues to be purposely junked, or neglected and abandoned to certain decay and decomposition. They are turning to dust. Trail dust. Is that to be the ultimate legacy of B Westerns?

Even fans are partly to blame because of their largely uncritical acceptance of dirty, dupey, scratchy, shaky, hissy videocassettes transferred from any old 16mm projection print which may be handy.

Video is also an unstable storage medium (to say nothing of how it truncates, belittles and obliterates the pictorial beauty of these otherwise unpretentious outdoor action efforts). The objective must be the location and preservation of 35mm *film*. Video is the nitrate of the '90s, the fool's gold of the modern age.

In an earlier age, when B Westerns were originally being produced and distributed, *all* motion pictures were considered transitory, disposable entertainment. If Hollywood so regarded *City Lights* and *Wuthering Heights,* imagine where *Blazing Bullets* and *Bullets for Rustlers* fit into this hierarchy.

Today, archival fund raisers seldom make impassioned appeals to save the Tim McCoy Puritans or the Hoot Gibson Allieds. Yet B Westerns reflect popular culture and social values and are just as much a part of our national film heritage as any other film classification. Will future generations have the opportuunity to learn from them, or better, to discover and enjoy them as we have?

A savvy, well-capitalized company like Disney can afford to care for its negatives and nurture an audience for its classics by re-introducing them to successive waves of kids every seven years or so. The interest is passed along by regularly repeated ex-

HOLLYWOOD CORRAL: A COMPREHENSIVE B WESTERN ROUNDUP

posure at an impressionable age, assuring an audience for the long term.

B Westerns cannot be rediscovered if they cannot be seen, and they cannot be seen if they have not been preserved.

Try to find mint, uncut 35mm preprint material for *Eagles Brood, Riders of the Purple Sage, Come On Tarzan, Wilderness Mail, Down Mexico Way,* or any of a hundred others, including about half the PRC Westerns. Try.

No one could find them because they are all safely locked away in impressive security vaults somewhere, right? Regrettably, wrong. No one could find them, period. Not Philo Vance. Not Red Ryder. Not down Mexico way, under fiesta stars, or anywhere else, because pristine, complete 35mm elements for these films no longer exist. They are already gone. Lost. Adios, forever.

Today it costs a material amount of money—usually well in excess of $10,000 per picture—to save and preserve the unstable nitrate-based film stock common to virtually all B Westerns. Those originally produced and distributed by the major studios have a better chance for survival. Deep-pockets publicly traded corporations have an incentive, and can afford to maintain a large library. Even if only a portion of the films are successfully revived for TV syndication or video distribution, at least the rest are protected to provide security as balance sheet assets for current production financing.

As for B Westerns produced by independents, regardless of their original distribution arrangements, the prospects are less sanguine. These smaller production companies long ago disappeared over sunset range. Ownership of the physical preprint elements for the films they produced is often scattered to the winds of the wasteland and stratified among layers of disinterested heirs, storage depots, film labs, holding companies, lien holders, and prestigious archives who complain they cannot secure funding to keep themselves supplied with projector lamps, much less transfer and save all the deteriorating nitrate film.

Unless an independent film library has been acquired by a major studio, chances for proper and costly storage, preservation, restoration, and survival are not good.

Even worse, a large number of B Westerns are now in the public domain. Production companies large and small alike did not know or care enough to secure continued copyright protection for them. Again, films were disposable, perishable entertainment. Now that there is *some* interest in specialized markets, entrepeneurs are dissuaded by their inability to enjoy distribution exclusively.

Either way, a high percentage of humble Western programmers are now orphan films because there is no commercial incentive to underwrite the costly task of transferring the 35mm nitrate negatives which have survived thus far—intact and uncut—onto safety stock in order to preserve them. Already, many great Autry, Rogers, and Hopalong Cassidy films are no longer extant to these specifications.

This is a leading indicator of danger. Sad to say, but probably a hundred years from now a large share of this genre will have all but vanished without a trace. No one will have the opportunity to enjoy beautiful, complete 35mm prints (delivered via whatever state-of-the-art medium may then exist) of *Dynamite Ranch* or *Thunder Mountain,* and B Westerns, if mentioned at all, will be regarded as an entertainment relic of a quaint age—the twentieth century.

In view of what these films have meant to a comparatively small number of people, we hope some well-positioned advocates in the entertainment industry, or someone with the financial wherewithal, somewhere, somehow will prove us wrong and perceive the wisdom of seeking out and preserving these motion pictures. Before it is too late. Rekindling enthusiasm for B Westerns so as to insure their availability for future generations has been, after all, the subtext of this book.

CONTRIBUTORS

RICHARD W. BANN is film consultant to The Kirch Group of Munich, Germany. He is co-author of *Laurel & Hardy*, and the newly revised *The Little Rascals: The Life and Times of Our Gang*. In 1992, he organized a film tribute in conjunction with Hal Roach's appearance at The Berlin Film Festival, and contributed an essay to *Homage: Hal Roach*. He lives in Beverly Hills, owns the Blake Line, and continues to believe that a life immersed in great films of the past offers more than one spent mastering the U.S. tax code.

ALAN G. BARBOUR got hooked on serials as a nine-year-old in Oakland, California. It was the beginning of a lifelong love affair with that most unappreciated of all film forms; more than any other person, he is responsible for the revival of interest in classic chapterplays. The editor-publisher of *Screen Facts* magazine, a highly-regarded fanzine published in the '60s, Barbour also wrote *Days of Thrills and Adventure* and *Cliffhanger* to celebrate movie serials, and has also authored *The Thrill of It All*, *A Thousand and One Delights*, *Humphrey Bogart*, and *John Wayne*. He currently writes the "Videosyncrasy" column for *Films in Review* magazine and edits the RCA Video Club's monthly magazine.

ROBERT S. BIRCHARD is a film editor, writer, and an award-winning filmmaker. A contributing writer for *MGM: When The Lion Roars*, his book *Cecil B. DeMille—In Pursuit of the Grand Award* is scheduled for publication by Vestal Press. He has written extensively about Western films for such publications as *American Cinematographer*, *Frontier Times*, *True West*, *Westerner*, *Westways*, and *True Frontier*, and he is currently at work on a book about one of the screen's greatest cowboy stars, *King Cowboy—Tom Mix and the Movies*, to be published by Riverwood Press in the Spring of 1993.

WILLIAM K. EVERSON co-authored the seminal book on movie Westerns, *The Western: From Silents to Cinerama*, in 1962; since then he has been a tireless, passionate champion of the genre. Born in England, he came to America in 1950 and briefly worked in the film industry as a publicist. Everson, a longtime film collector whose private library numbers in the thousands, has helped preserve innumerable silent and early sound films that would otherwise have been irretrievably lost. He has taught a justifiably famous film appreciation course at New York's New School for Social Research since 1966. Among his other books on film are *The Art of W. C. Fields*, *The Films of Laurel and Hardy*, *Classics of the Horror Film*, *American Silent Film*, *Love in the Film*, and *A Pictorial History of the Western*, which was revived in 1992 as *The Hollywood Western*.

ALEX GORDON is a lifelong Western fan who actually lived his dream of meeting the great B-Western stars while producing several Westerns that featured many prominent movie cowboys. As a young British filmgoer (and childhood friend of fellow Western devotee Bill Everson), Gordon headed the U.K.'s official Gene Autry Fan Club. He came to America after the Second World War to work in the movie industry, writing and producing many low- to medium-budget genre films, most of them starring and made by Hollywood veterans of the '20s, '30s, and '40s. His films include *Bride of the Monster* (directed by cult favorite Ed Wood, Jr.), *The Atomic Submarine*, *The Bounty Killer*, and *Requiem for a Gunfighter*. While working at 20th Century-Fox, Gordon oversaw the restoration and preservation of many of that studio's classic silent and early talkie films. He is currently film archivist for one of his boyhood favorites, Gene Autry.

DOUGLAS B. GREEN has long been recognized as both a popular and scholarly writer about the history of Country and Western music. He is the author of *Country Roots*, a history of Bluegrass music, and was a contributor to *Country*, the massive history of Country music published by the Country Music Foundation. He is known to fans of the Western singing group Riders in the Sky as Ranger Doug.

KEN GRIFFIS is a recognized authority on the formative years of country and western music on the West Coast. He has written numerous articles for various historical and popular journals on western music. One of the founders of the Western Music Association and a director of the John Edwards Memorial Foundation. Griffis is the author of *Hear My Song: Story of the Celebrated Sons of the Pioneers,* the definitive history of the premier western singing group.

DAVE HOLLAND has been searching for (and finding!) movie locations for more than 30 years, taking time from such jobs as TV production manager and assistant director, theatrical press agent and newspaper reporter. The author of *On Location in Lone Pine* and *From Out of the Past: A Pictorial History of the Lone Ranger,* Holland is as much a student of the *real* West as of the *reel* West, and as such, he has explored Apache Pass, waded the Little Big Horn, and stood where Bob Ford killed Jesse James, where Buffalo Bill killed Yellow Hair, and where Billy the Kid killed Olinger. Could that be the basis of another book...? Write him at Box 1120, Lone Pine, California 93545.

ED HULSE developed an affinity for B Westerns, serials, and programmers while still in grade school. He has written dozens of articles on films for *Variety, Business Screen, Millimeter,* and other industry trade publications. Hulse covered the home video industry for the magazines *Consumer Electronics Monthly* and *Video Review* from 1980 to 1992, and his columns and reviews for the latter magazine were syndicated by the Washington Post Writers Group. Hulse also edited *Previews,* a monthly magazine distributed in video stores nationwide from 1987 to 1990. He served as Supervising Editor of *Leonard Maltin's Movie Encyclopedia* (1994 edition), and is also the author of *The Films of Betty Grable.* Hulse, a longtime film collector and archivist, also chairs Cinecon, the annual convention of the Society for Cinephiles, the oldest national film society.

JAMES KING is a composer-arranger-conductor dedicated to the task of researching and preserving the music from the B pictures of the '30s and '40s. To that end, he has produced and conducted the music for new albums featuring the music of Republic Pictures during the 1937–1942 era. All of these albums employ full orchestras of top-flight musicians playing from the original scores. For further information, write to: King Enterprises, 2635 Bahada Road, Palm Springs, California 92262.

The late **DON MILLER** was a film historian extraordinaire. He put his extensive knowledge of motion pictures to work as a researcher for such television projects as the classic *Twentieth Century,* then helped to organize the film research archives of *TV Guide.* He was a frequent contributor to various film journals and fanzines. His classic *B Movies,* a companion to *Hollywood Corral,* was recently reissued by Ballantine Books, New York.

SAMUEL M. SHERMAN became enamored with Westerns at a tender age, first in movie theaters but most voraciously on TV in the late '40s and early '50s. After graduating from the film school of the City College of New York, he edited the magazines *Wildest Westerns* and *Screen Thrills Illustrated* in the early '60s before going to work in the movie industry as a publicist, editor, and film doctor. In 1968 he co-founded Independent International Pictures Corp. and subsequently produced innumerable low-budget films, many of them directed by Al Adamson, son of B Western pioneer Denver Dixon. Sherman frequently featured Western stars—including Bob Livingston, Don "Red" Barry, and Bob Allen—in his movies, some of which are available on videotape. Although he's especially fond of his B-Western pastiche, *Blazing Stewardesses,* Sherman is perhaps best remembered for such "cult" favorites as *Satan's Sadists, Naughty Stewardesses, Dracula vs Frankenstein,* and *Horror of the Blood Monsters.*

PACKY SMITH has depended on B Westerns for his livelihood almost his entire adult life. In 1972, with two friends, he founded the first Western Film Festival in Memphis, Tennessee. He edited and published the Western Film Collector magazine in the mid '70s, and in 1977, served as Associate Producer on *Meanwhile Back At The Ranch,* a film made from clips from B Westerns. He has worked in television, serving as Associate Producer on the series *Happy Trails Theater Starring Roy Rogers and Dale Evans,* as well as the PBS special on B Westerns, *The West That Never Was.* He is currently devoting all of his time to writing, editing, and publishing books on film.

KARL THIEDE currently works for 20th Century-Fox after many years with United Artists and M-G-M in their Domestic Distribution Departments. Beginning in the business in 1963, Thiede has worked in theaters, film exchanges, and as a correspondent for *Boxoffice* Magazine. He began collecting, researching, and writing about all aspects of film in the early '60s. From 1969 to 1974, he was Research Editor for *Views and Reviews.* He has contributed financial data and filmographies for many books and articles on the film business.

LAURENCE ZWISOHN is the Director of Music Licensing at 20th Century-Fox Film Corp., and is the author of books about the music of personalities as diverse as Bing Crosby and Loretta Lynn. He has written articles on musical personalities for a number of magazines, as well as liner notes for albums and CDs released by RCA, MCA, and Columbia Records. He has produced albums of historic recordings by Fred Astaire, the Sons of the Pioneers, and Jim Reeves. Zwisohn is the author of the booklet that will accompany the historical four CD set of the Sons of the Pioneers recordings covering the period from 1945 to 1954.

INDEX

Entries in *italics* are film titles, entries in quotes are song titles, and page numbers in *italics* are photo references.

Aaker, Lee, 277, 433
Abbott and Costello, 432
Abbott, Charles, 149
ABC, 492
Abrahams, Derwin, 112–13, 168, 193, 206
Abrams, Leon, 130
Aces and Eights, 39–40
Aces Wild, 61
Acord, Art, 12, 292, 294, 301–3, 322
Across the Badlands, 170
Across the Sierras, 228
Across the Wide Missouri, 482
"Action in the Afternoon," 279
Acuff, Roy, 167, 373, 494
Adams, Betty, 268
Adams, Claire, 385
Adams, Clifton, 271
Adams, Ernie, *29*, *144*, *155*, 166, 398
Adams, Jane, *241*
Adams, Julia, 486
Adams, Ted, 165, 256, *356*, 464
Adamson, Al, 64, 311
Adamson, Victor, 309–11, *310*, 411. See also Denver Dixon
Adreon, Franklin, 193, 207
Adrian, Iris, 200
Adriot, Lucien, 70
Adventurer, The, 409
"Adventures of Bill and Bob," 43
Adventures of Don Coyote, The, 206
Adventures of Frank and Jesse James, 274
"Adventures of Kit Carson," 275
Adventures of Red Ryder, The, 212, 443
"Adventures of Rin Tin Tin," 277
Adventures of the Masked Phantom, The, 149, 411
Agar, John, 433, 486, 487

"Ages and Ages Ago," 346
"Agitato #4," 442
Albright, Wally, 37, *160*
Alden, Debra, *100*
Aldridge, Kay, 432, 464–66
Alexander, Arthur, 26, 48, 61, 237
Alexander, Max, 26, 61
Alexander, Richard, 200, *208*, *286*, *462*, 469, 484, 486, 487
Algier, Sidney, 19
Alias Billy the Kid, 216
Alias Jesse James, 135
Alias John Law, 45
Alias-the Bad Man, 23
Alice in Wonderland, 94
All Quiet on the Western Front, 108
Allan, Vic, 326
Allen, Bob, 39, *150*, *153*, 159, 225, 316, 354
Allen, Fred, 70, 91, 92, 283
Allen, Jules Verne, 334, 375
Allen, Paul, 311
Allen, Rex, 131, 135, 220–22, 223, *223*, 279, 367, 368, *368*, *369*, 373, 489, 496, 498–99, *514*
Allied Artists, 201, 232, 261, 270, 273
Allied Pictures, 19, 20, 21
Along Came Jones, 432
Along the Navajo Trail, 428
Along the Sundown Trail, 23, 359
Alvarado, Don, 178
Ambassador Pictures, 195, 197
Ambush, 433
Ameche, Don, 344
American Film Company, 294, 322, 323
American Record Company (ARC), 338, 340, 346, 364, 494
Ames, Leon, 86

Amity Pictures, 22
Anderson, Broncho Billy. *See* G. M. Anderson
Anderson, G. M., 8, 9–10, 106, 294, *294*, 309, 471, *482*, 484
Andrews, Arkansas Slim, 143, *358*
Andrews, Dana, 205
Andy Hardy Gets Spring Fever, 484
Andy Parker and the Plainsmen, 345, 365
Angel, Heather, 146
Ankrum, Morris, *109*, 112
Anna Christie, 298
"Annie Oakley" series, 275, 432, 491
"Anniversary Waltz," 364
Ansara, Michael, 279
Anthony, Stuart, 37
Apache Kid, The, 431
Apache Rose, 428, 434
Apache Trail, 284
Apache War Smoke, 284
Arbuckle, Fatty, 185
Archainbaud, George, 113, 132
Arizona, 131, 299, 309
Arizona Badman, 63, 454
Arizona Bound, 245, 246, *246*, 450
Arizona Cowboy, The, 220, 367
Arizona Cyclone (1941), 258, 403
Arizona Days, 141
Arizona Frontier, 143
Arizona Gang Busters, 41
Arizona Kid, The (1930), 203, *204*
Arizona Kid, The (1939), 127
Arizona Legend, 85–86
Arizona Legion, 444
Arizona Mahoney, 390
Arizona Raiders, The, 189–90, *189*, 390
Arizona Ranger, The, 102, 399
Arizona Roundup, 94

537

HOLLYWOOD CORRAL: A COMPREHENSIVE B WESTERN ROUNDUP

Arizona Stagecoach, 182
Arizona Terror, 23
Arizona Terrors, 213–14
Arizona Trail, 144
Arizona Whirlwind, 250, 251
Arizonian, The, 95
Arkoff, Sam, 487
Arlen, Richard, 83, 146, 190, 284, 482
Armstrong, Billy, 383
Armstrong, Robert, 36
Army Girl, 222, 444
Arness, James, 277
Arnold, Eddy, 243, 367, 373
Arnold, Edward, 485
Aronson, Max. *See* G. M. Anderson
Arrow Film Corporation, 301, 473
Arrow in the Dust, 362
Artcraft Pictures, 296, 299
Arthur J. Mix Productions, 64, 309
Arthur, Jean, 309
Ashlock, Jesse, 346
Associated Features, 352
Astor Pictures, 54, 157, 251, 268, 318, 473
Ates, Roscoe, 178, 264, *264*, 265, 372
Athens, Vi, 167
Atherton Productions, 83, 388
Atomic Submarine, The, 483, 484
Aubrey, Jimmy, *63*
Auer, Stephen, 217
August, Joseph H., 10, 82, 85, 296
Austin, Gene, 148, 357
Autry, Gene, 3, 25, 64, 97, 105, 117–22, *119*, *120*, *121*, 123, 124–27, *126*, *127*, *128*, 131–32, *132*, *133*, *134*, 137, 141, 148, 151, 159, 179, 193, 211, 213, 225, 263, 275–77, 307, 311, 315, 317, *330*, 332, 333, 334–43, *335*, *337*, *339*, *341*, *343*, *344*, 345, 348, 352–53, *353*, 355, 360, 360–62, *361*, 365, *365*, 368, 370, 371, 372, 373, 389–91, 413–14, 428, 429, 430, 432, 434, 435, 454, 459, 469, 474, 478, 479, 481, 484, *490*, 494, 495, 496, *496*, 499, 506, 507, *512*, 516
Avalanche, 389
Avenger, The, 32
Avenging Rider, The, 97
Avenging Waters, 316
Avonde, Richard, 201
Aye, Marion, 306
Aywon, 60, 301

Back in the Saddle Again, 335
"Back in the Saddle Again," 346, 372, 473, 496
Bacon, Irving, 289
Bad Girl, 19
Bad Lands, 95
Bad Man of Brimstone, The, 404
Bad Men of the Border, 240
Bad Men of the Hills, 166, 450
Badger, Clarence, 284
Badlands of Dakota, 403
Badman's Country, 191
Badman's Gold, 270

Badman's Territory, 444
Bailey, Rex, 201
Bain, Fred, 143
Baker, Bob, 146–48, *148*, 248, 249, 256, 257, 261, 349–50, *351*, 359, 360, 373, 454
Baker, Brydon, 197
Ballard, Lucien, 162, 451
Ballew, Smith, 73, 83, 146, *147*, 260, 348–49, *349*
Bancroft, George, 36
Bandit Queen, 209
Bandit Ranger, 97
Bannon, Jim, 267–68, *268*, 268, 275
Bar 20, 113
Bar 20 Justice, 280, 314
Bar 20 Rides Again, 107–8
Bar Six Cowboys, *475*
Bara, Theda, 301
Barclay, Don, *351*
Barclay, Joan, *47*, *59*
Barclay, Stephen, 215
Barcroft, Roy, 5, 127, 133, *165*, *181*, 191, 211, 213, 216, 217, 218, 219, 231, *257*, 286, *401*, 432, 464, 469
Bari, Lynn, 204
Barnett, Vince, *389*
Barrat, Robert, 95, 103, 138, 204, 392
Barrie, Mona, 247
Barry, Don "Red," 127, *128*, 130, 173, 178, 179, 186, 212–14, *212*, *213*, *214*, 217, 219, 223, 269, 270, 431, 450, 452, 495, 497, *507*
Barry, Wesley, 154, 273
Barsha, Leon, 161, 226, 239
Barton, Buzz, 55, 59, 60, *60*, 64, 154, 173, *174*, 409
Barton, Charles, 76, 189, 282, 283, 390
Bascom, Texas Rose, 270
Battling with Buffalo Bill, 42, 50
Baugh, "Slingin' Sammy," 216–17, 464, 466, *466*
Baxter, Warner, 7, 203, 204, *204*
"Be Honest With Me," 372
Beach, Rex, 297
Beacon (distributor), 62
Beaumont Productions, 64, 411
"Beautiful Brown Eyes," 496
"Beautiful Texas," 359
Beauty and the Bandit, 205, 402
Beddoe, Don, 163
Bee, Molly, *476*
Beebe, Ford, 7, 37, 39, 118, 119, 148, 159, 160, 161, 206, 255, 256, 257, 258, 269
Beecher, Elizabeth, 183
Beecher, Janet, 205
Beery, Noah, 70, 74, 82, 123, 194, 212, 213, 228, 254, 286, 390, 405
Beery, Noah, Jr., 37, 64, 74, 95, 102, 113, 127, 254, *283*, 392
Bell Boys, 362
Bell, Hank, *33*, 161
Bell, James, 222
Bell, Marjorie, 148
Bell, Rex, 12, 17, 57, *59*, 60, 60–61, 69, 247, 306, 450, 481
Bellamy, Ralph, 34, 83, 146

Bells of Capistrano, 127
Bells of Coronado, 135
Bells of Rosarita, 130, *507*
Bells of San Angelo, 133, *135*
Below the Border, 247
Beltone, 499
Ben-Hur, 10
Beneath Western Skies, 215
Bennet, Spencer, 26, 64, 142, 143, 153, 193, 207, 211, 215, 229, 230, 245, 246, 285, *285*, *398*, 401, 453, *464*, *483*, 484
Bennett, Bruce, 163, *194*. See also Herman Brix
Bennett, Raphael, 260
Bennett, Ray, *152*
Bennison, Andrew, 256
Berke, William, 54, 56, 61, 64, 101, 166, 177, 179, 195, 200, 209, 239, 269, 317–18
Bernard, Jeffrey, 205
Bernds, Edward, 87
Best Bad Man, The, 299, 307
Best, Willie, *474*
"Betsy From Pike," 332
Between Fighting Men, 23, 24
Between Men, 255
Beverly Hillbillies, 332
Beverly Pictures, 315
Beware Spooks, 451
Beyond the Last Frontier, 215
Beyond the Pecos, 459
Beyond the Purple Hills, 428
Beyond the Rio Grande, 53
Beyond the Sacramento, 227, 228
"Bible Tells Me So, The," 499
Bickford, Charles, 37, 283, 390, 467, 469
Big 4, 53, 57, 58, 59, 64
"Big Ben," 370
Big Bonanza, 366
Big Country, The, 435
Big Diamond Robbery, The, 293
Big Show, The, 120
Big Sleep, The, 47
Big Sombrero, The, 131
Big Stampede, The, 70
Big Trail, The, 67, 69, 70, 253
Billy the Kid, 47–48, 166
Billy the Kid, 70, 253–54, *254*, 404
Billy the Kid Outlawed, 48
Billy the Kid Returns, 124
"Billy the Kid" series, 188–91
Billy the Kid's Smoking Guns, 190
Biograph Company, 294
Birth of a Nation, The, 105, 113
Bishop, Kenneth, 199
Black Bandit, The, 147
Black, Clint, 492
Black Ghost, The, 64
Black Hills Express, 214
Black Market Rustlers, 183
Black Raven, The, 317
Blackmer, Sidney, 36, 110, 437
Blair, George, 211, 220, 270
Blair, Hal, 497
Blair, Nicky, 487
Blake, Bobby, 217, 218, 219, 229, 230, *230*

538

INDEX

Blake, Mary, *399*
Blake, Pamela, 267
Blane, Sally, 198–99
Blangsted, Folmer, 2, 161
Blazing Guns, 249
Blazing Stewardesses, 445
Blocked Trail, The, 181
Blue Eagle, The, 298
Blue Montana Skies, 123
Blue, Monte, 77, 127, 138, 217, 284, 405, *469*
"Blue Prairie," 334, 379
"Blue Shadows on the Trail," 360
Blue Steel, 73, 74
Bluebird, 359
"Blues Stay Away From Me," 496
Blystone, Stan, *196*
Blythe, Betty, 247
Boetticher, Oscar (Budd), 200, 283
Bogart, Humphrey, 81, 435
Boiling Point, The, 20
Bold Caballero, The, 206, 219, 444
Boles, John, 34
Bolm, Adolph, 454
Bonanza, 432
Bond, Johnny, *258,* 336, 360, 362, 363, *363,* 371, 373, 378, 493, 494, 495, *495,* 495–96, *498*
Bond, Ward, 39
Boone Records, 498
Boone, Richard, 277
Booth, Adrian, *See also* Lorna Gray, 207, 219
Booth, Delores, 311
Booth, Edwina, 61
Boots, 430
Boots and Saddles, 121–22
Boots and Saddles Productions, 140
Boots of Destiny, 26
Border Caballero, 39, 40
Border Feud, 266
Border G-Men, 417
Border Legion, The (1930), 389
Border Legion, The (1940), 392
Border Menace, 60
Border Outlaws, 270, 367
Border Patrol, 113, 428
Border Patrolman, The, 83
Border Phantom, 46
Border Rangers, 270
Border Vengeance, 63
Border Vigilantes, 112, 435
Borderline, 109
Borg, Veda Ann, 284
Born to the West, 76–77, *77,* 256, 390
Borrowed Trouble, 113–14
Borzage, Frank, 31, 215
Boss of Boomtown, 240
Boss of Bullion City, 258
Bosworth, Hobart, 197
Boteler, Wade, 37, *38*
Both Barrels Blazing, 168
Botillier, Richard, *318,* 398
"Bottom of a Mountain," 498
Bounty Killer, The, 482, *483,* 484, *487*
Bow, Clara, 61, 299, 484
Bower, Bertha H., 8

Bowers, Jesse, 245–46
Bowers, John, 194
Boxoffice, 505, 506, 511
Boxoffice Barometer, 506
Boyd, Bill "Cowboy Rambler", 235
Boyd, William, 3, 97, *104,* 105–15, *106, 107, 108, 109, 111, 112, 114, 115,* 118, 173, 235, 278, 279, *314,* 359, *406,* 415–16, 459, 479, 494, 495, 497, 506, 510, 511–12, *515*
Boyd, William (Stage), 237
Brabin, Charles, 254
Bradbury, Bill, 73, 342
Bradbury, Robert, Jr. *See* Bob Steele
Bradbury, Robert N., 43, 45, 46, 73, *73,* 74, 75, 76, 94, 141, 145, 146, 245, 255, *313,* 342, 484
Bradford, Lane, 103
Bradford, William, 129, 131, 132, 211
Bradley, Grace, 479
Brady, Matthew, 72
Brady, Pat, 127, 135, 161, 162, 277, *374,* 379, 380, 381, 382
Brand, Max, 8, 28, 79, 81, 299, 385, 386
Brand of the Devil, 238
Branded Men, 23
Brando, Marlon, 430
Brandon, Henry, 86, 127
Brannon, Fred, 193, 207, 211, 217, 218, 223, 274
"Brave Eagle" series, 279, 492
Brendel, El, 70, 476
Brennan, Walter, 39, 231
Brent, Evelyn, 95, 109, 112, 196, 205, 261, 481
Brent, George, 432
Bretherton, Howard, 97, 106, 108, 112, 113, 146, 165, 166, 181, 194, 200, 211, 214, 215, 229, 245, 247, 261
Bride of Frankenstein, The, 147, 445
Bridge, Al, 66, 161, *163,* 168, 398
Bridges, Lloyd, 228
Briskin, Irving, 315, 411
Britt, Elton, 367
Britton, Barbara, 209
Brix, Herman, 57, 146, 152. *See also* Bruce Bennett
Broadway to Cheyenne, 60
Brock, Lou, 474
Brodie, Steve, 101, 102, 483, 487
"Broken Arrow," 37, 279
Bromley, Sheila, 199
Broncho Billy, *See also* G. M. Anderson, 10, 294
"Broncho Billy" series, 294
Bronson, Betty, *343*
Bronson, Charles, 428
Bronze Buckaroo, The, 153, 352
Brooke, Hillary, 187
Brooks, Joan, 148
Brooks, Lesley, 166
Brooks, Louise, *35,* 177
Brooks, Lucius, 352
Brooks, Rand, 113, *115,* 433
Brooks, Teddy, *324*
Brothers in the Saddle, *101,* 102

Brothers of the West, 50, *51*
Brower, Otto, 19, 20, 25, 38, 39, 93, 117, 205
Brown, Harry Joe, 18, 92, 283, 306, 409
Brown, James, 277, 433
Brown, James S., Jr., 225
Brown, Johnny Mack, 45, 76, 118, 144, 148, 240, 252, 253–61, *254, 255, 256, 257, 258, 259, 260,* 268, 311, 347, 366, 390, 401, *421,* 427, 432, 459, 467–69, *468,* 479, 481, 494, 495, *515*
Brown, Milton, 378
Brown, Stanley, 164, 165, 227
Brown, Tom, 270
Browne, Fayte M., 170
Browne, Lucile, 58
Browne, Reg, 270, 275
Browne, Reno, 285
Browning, Jill, 129
Brunswick Records, 334, 337, 352, 357, 444
Bryan, Jane, 138
Bryant, Nana, 133
Buchanan, Edgar, 115, 276, 437
Buck Jones Productions, 32
Buck, Leon, 352
"Buck Parvin" series, 301
Buck Rogers, 435
Buckaroo Sheriff of Texas, 222–23
Bucko, Buck, 326
Buckskin Lady, The, 444
Buell, Jed, 139, 140, 153, 352
Buena Vista Distribution Co., 209
Buffalo Bill, 294
Buffalo Bill in Tomahawk Territory, 284
Buffalo Bill, Jr., *See also* Jay Wilsey, 12, 53, 64, 67, 173, 306, 309
"Buffalo Bill, Jr.," 275, 491
Buffalo Bill Rides Again, 284
Buffington, Adele, 174, 246, 260, 268
Bulldog Courage, 39
Bullets and Saddles, 183
Bullets for O'Hara, 404
Buntline, Ned, 8
Bupp, Tommy, 138
Burbridge, Betty, 123, 165, 166, 176, 177
Burgess, Dorothy, 203
Burnett, W. R., 61, 258
Burnette, Smiley, 25, 63, 118, *119,* 121, 122, 123, 124, 127, 131, 132, 168, *170,* 171, 215, 216, 287, 289, 340, *353,* 479, 484, 510, *513, 516*
Burns, Bob, 122
Burr, C. C., 140
Burr, Raymond, 101
Bury Me Not On The Lone Prairie, 427
Busch, Mae, 28
Bushman, Francis X., Jr., 64
Buster, Bud, 183, 256, *356*
Butler, David, 50
Butler, John K. 130, 131, 215, 222
Buttram, Pat, 132, *132,* 134, 275–76, 287, *457,* 491, *496*
Butts, Dale, 211

539

HOLLYWOOD CORRAL: A COMPREHENSIVE B WESTERN ROUNDUP

Buzzell, Eddie, 34
Buzzy and the Phantom Pinto, 157
Buzzy Rides the Range, 157
By Candlelight, 454
Byrd, Ralph, *40*, 175–76
Byron, Walter, 198, 199

"Caballero's Way, The," 203
Cabanne, Christy, 50, 51, 95, 205, 242
Cactus Cut-up, 476
Cagney, James, 240, 311, 507
Cahn, Edward L., 61, 482, 485
Caldwell, Banty, *327*
Calhoun, Rory, 83
California Frontier, 36
California Gold Rush, 231
California Mail, 139
California Trail, 32
Call of the Canyon, 126, 429
"Call of the Canyon," 334
Call of the Klondike, 201
Call of the Rockies, 215
Call the Mesquiteers, 176
Callahan, Jerry, 64
Calling Wild Bill Elliott, 229
Calvert, John, 168
Calvin, Henry, 207–9
Cameron, Rocky, 251
Cameron, Rod, 144, 240, 346, 434, 459, 484
Campeau, Frank, 79
"Can-Can," 444
Canadian Mounties vs. Atomic Invaders, 193
Canova, Judy, 364, 497
Canova, Pete, 364
Cansino, Rita. *See* Rita Hayworth
Canutt, Yakima, 12, 43, 56, 63, 72, *72*, 73, 74, 75, 128, 131, 138, 175, 178, 193, *208*, 211, 216, 218, 270, 274, *319*, *327*, 327–38, 340, 427, 462, 464, 472, 473
Canyon Ambush, 261
Canyon City, 213
"Canyon Walls," 388
Capitol Records, 347, 348, 362, 364, 365, 492, 494, 498
Caravan Trail, The, 263, 432
Carbonera, Gerard, 110
Carey, Harry, 12, 20, *21*, 49, 50, *51*, *61*, 61–62, *62*, 89, 95, 173, *174*, 300, 318, *318*, 324, *388*, 405
Carey, Olive, *324*
Carillo, Leo, 205, 467
Carlyle, Pat, 151
Carmen, Jean, 198, 451
Carmichael, Hoagy, 129
Carol, Sue, 194
Carolina Moon, 125
Carousel, 110
Carpenter, John, 270, 482
Carr, Mary, 216
Carr, Thomas, 211, 216, 232, 268, 269, 270, 271, 273, 274, 275
Carr, Trem, 45, 69, 72, 73, 76, 147, 445
Carradine, John, 85, 128, 485
Carre, Bart, 151, 484, 487

Carrillo, Leo, 37, 95, 205
Carroll, Alma, 239
Carroll, Clyde, 516
Carroll, Earl, 94
Carroll, John, 206
Carroll, Nancy, 34
Carroll, Virginia, 228, 237, 285
Carrying the Mail, 472
Carson, Ken, 382
Carson, Sunset, 130, 215–16, *215*, 216, 223, 268, 427, 454, *507*
Carver, Lynne, 260
Cary, Diana Serra, 326
Casanova, 355
Cash, Johnny, 373
Cason, John, 268
Cass County Boys, 345
Cassidy, Ed, *143*
Cassidy, Hopalong, 3, 35, 98, *104*, 105–15
Cassidy of Bar 20, 110
Castle Films, 478
Castle in the Desert, 432
Caswell, Nancy, *386*
Catlett, Walter, 127
Cattle Queen, 270, 285
Cattle Raiders, 451
Cavalier of the West, 61
Cavalry, 45–46
Cavalcade of the West, 21
"Cavalcade of the West," 279
Cavanaugh, Hobart, 87, 479
CBS, 275, 277
Ceder, Ralph, 163
Central Films, 199
Chad Hanna, 453
Challenge Records, 491
Chan, Charlie, 40, 110, 293, 432
Chandler, Helen, 80
Chandler, Lane, 53, 56, 57–58, 74, 146, 152, 188, 427, 484
Chaney, Lon, Jr., 37, 64, 120, 469
"Chant of the Wanderer," 379
Chapin, Michael, 222
Chaplin, Charlie, 10, 296
Charge of the Light Brigade, The, 138–39, 400
"Chase," 445
Chase, Alden, *188*
Chase, Charley, 476, 478
Chase, The, 366, 497
Cheney, J. Benton, 112, 167, 168, 180, 215, 229
Cherokee Flash, The, 216
Cherokee Strip, 138
Chertok, Jack, 277
Cherwin, Richard, 211
Chesebro, George, 160, *251*, 268, 286
"Chevy Show, The," 492
"Cheyenne," 443
Cheyenne Kid, The (1933), 92
Cheyenne Kid, The (1940), 155
Cheyenne Rides Again, 64
Cheyenne Wildcat, 231
Chief Thundercloud, 127, 152, 157, 249, 250, 251, 435
Chief Yowlachie, *38*, 279
Child of Manhattan, 34
Children of Loneliness, 451

China, 430
Chrisman, Pat, 299, 326, *327*
Chuck Wagon Trailers, 323
Churchill, Berton, 70
Churchill, Marguerite, 67, 70, 82
"Cimarron," 495
Cimarron, 95, 96
Cimarron City, 432
"Cimmaron, Roll On," 378
Circle of Death, 151
Cisco Kid, 7, 202, 203
Cisco Kid and the Lady, The, 204, 436
Cisco Kid Returns, The, 205, 206
"Cisco Kid" series, 203–6, 279, 403–4, 444
Cisco Kid, The, 203
Citizen Kane, 227
City for Conquest, 47
Clancy of the Mounted, 50, 193
Clark, Bobby, 153, 268
Clark, Cliff, 95
Clark, Colbert, 167, 168, 171, 242, 254
Clark, Daniel B., 12, 27, 80, 82
Clark, Frank H., 259
Clark, Harvey, 110
Clark, Steve, 241, 242, 256
Clarke, Charles, 204
Clarke, Robert, 102, 103
Clayton, Jan, 110, 200
Clearing the Range, 19
Clemens, William, 92
Clements, Zeke, 373
Clifton, Elmer, 36, 58, 59, 64, 181, 197, 198, 214, 238, 239, 258, 270
"Climb Upon My Knee," 337
Cline, Edward, 83
Cline, Robert, 191
Cline, Roscoe, 299
Cline, Wilfrid, 193
Clutching Hand, The, 486
Clyde, Andy, 95, *109*, 110, 112, 113, 115, *115*, 241, 267, 268, 287, 289, 476
Coates, Phyllis, *232*
Cobb, Edmund, 12, 53, 63, 64, 138, 161, 162, 398, 454, 483, 484
Cobb, Lee J., 110
Coburn, Buck, 151
Coburn, Walt, 385
Coby, Fred, 209
Code of the Cactus, 356
Code of the Fearless, 140
Code of the Lawless, 240, 241
Code of the Mounted, 196
Code of the Range, 161, 399
Code of the Rangers, 40
Code of the West, 100, 101, 393
Cody, Bill, 12, 53, 57, 59–60, 293, 409, 412
Coffin, Tristram, 205, 239, 247, 275
Cohen, Bennett, 216
Cohen, Sammy, 50
Cohn, Harry, 37, 39, 70, 160
Colbert, Claudette, 344
Cole, Nat King, 497
Cole, Slim, 321, *322*

540

INDEX

Coleman, C. C., Jr., 161, 163, 195, 399
Coleman, Don, 12, 306
Collins Kids, 493
Collins, Lewis D., 63, 144, 193, 231, 232, 240, 258, 267, 270, 403
Colony Pictures, 21, 26, 27
Colorado Ambush, 261
Colorado Kid, 46
Colorado Puck, 298
Colorado Ranger, 269
Colorado Serenade, 263–64, *264*, 403
Colorado Sunset, 400
Colorado Trail, The, 162
Colt Comrades, *111*, 113
Columbia, 3, 21, 25, 26, 31, 32, 34, 35, 36, 37, 38, 39, 41, 59, 64, 70, 72, 96, 97, 98, 118, 131, 144, 152, 153, 154, 158, 161, 162, 163, 164, 165, 166, 168, 170, 191, 193, 194, 195, 199, 200, 216, 225, 226, 227, 228, 229, 231, 239, 242, 267, 275, 281, 289, 306, 311, 315, 316, 318, 337, 347, 352, 357, 358, 362, 365, 367, 368, 373, 379, 397–99, 403, 404, 409, 411, 414, 466, 472–73, 507
Columbia Graphophone Company, 332
Columbia Records, 380, 491, 495
Columbo, Alberto, 211, 443
Come On, Danger (1932), 92, 93
Come On, Danger (1942), 96
Come On, Tarzan, 24
Comet Productions, 206
Coming of the Law, The, 325
Comingore, Dorothy, 227
Compson, Betty, 94
Compton, Joyce, 478
Concord Pictures, 146
Conklin, Chester, 486
Conklin, Heinie, 73
Conn, Maurice, 40, 146, 154, 195, 196, 245, 402–3, 442
Connolly, Bobby, 139
Connors, Mike, 486
Conqueror Records, 345
"Conqueror Record Time," 338
Conway, Jack, 385
Conway, Tom, 482, 485
Coogan, Jackie, 275
Cook, Elisha, 47
Cook, Joe, 76, 390
"Cool Water," 334, 375
Cooley, Marjorie, 163
Cooley, Spade, 270, 367, 476, 497
Coolidge, Dane, 8
Cooper, Gary, 13, 58, 146, 206, 387, 389, 432, 435, 484, 494, 507
Cooper, George, 145
Cooper, Inez, 200
Coote, Robert, 95
Coral Records, 362
Corbett, Ben, 40, 54, 62, 92, 247, 289, *356*, 473
Corbett, Glenn, 485
Corby, Ellen, 113
Corby, Francis, 142
Corey, Jim, *51*, 324
Coronet Pictures, 35, 36, 245

Corpse Vanishes, The, 451
Corpus Christi Bandits, 217
Corrado, Gino, *49*
Corral Cuties, 476
Corrigan, Lloyd, 454
Corrigan, Ray "Crash," 21, 77, 135, 172, 174, 175, *175*, 176, *176*, 177, *177*, 178, 181, *181*, 182, 183, 216, 433, 435, *463*, 481
Cortez, Ricardo, 83, 146, 205
Costello, Don, 230
Country Music Calvacade, 373
Country Washburn's Orchestra, 360
Courage of the North, 197
Courage of the West, 147, 350, 403, 454
Covered Wagon Days, 510
Covered Wagon, The, 28, 37
Covered Wagon Trails, 155, 511
Cow-Catcher's Daughter, The, 476
Cowan, Jerome, 128
Cowboy Canteen, 167
Cowboy and the Senorita, The, 128, 129
"Cowboy Campmeeting," 382
Cowboy Clan, The: or Tigress of Texas, 331–32
"Cowboy Code, The," 491
Cowboy Commandos, 183
Cowboy from Lonesome River, 167
"Cowboy G-Men," 275
"Cowboy Has to Sing, A," 379
Cowboy Millionaire, The, 83
Cowboy Ramblers, 332, 359
Cowboy Serenade, 126
Cowboy Star, The, 160, 161, 451
"Cowboy Tom's Roundup," 347
"Cowboy's Lament," 332
Cowboys from Texas, The, 179
Cowboys in the Clouds, 166
Cowen, Will, 270, 476
"Coyote Serenade," 382
Crabbe, Buster, 36, 48, 76, 185, 188, 189, *189*, 190, *190*, 191, 279, 283, 390, *391*, 405, 417, 433, 435, *482*, 484
Craig, James, 256, 284, 404
Cramer, Richard, 76
Crashing Thru (1939), 198
Crashing Thru (1949), 267
Crawford, "Dopey" Dick, 326–27
Crawford, Joan, 148, 253, *306*, 357, 405
Crawley Films, 277
Crehan, Joe, 138, 487
Crespinell, Bill, 364
Crimson Trail, The, 34, 35
Cripple Creek Bar-room Scene, 8
Crisp, Donald, 206
Crooked River, 269
Crooked Trail, The, 255
Crosby, Bing, 122, 379
Crossed Trails, 260
Crossfire, 93
Crouch, William Forrest, 270
Crowley, William X., 200
"Crying in the Chapel," 367, 499
Crystal Records, 364
Cummings, Irving, 81, 203

Cuneo, Lester, 295, *305*
Cunningham, Jack, 28
Cupid Rides the Range, 474
Cupid's Roundup, 299
"Curse of Capistrano, The," 206
Curtis, Dick, 161, 162, 164, 197, 227, 228, 231, 256, 398
Curtis, Donald, 165
Curtis, Ken, 207, 243, 364–65, 368, 382, *383*
Curwood, James Oliver, 74, 159, 197, 200, 247
Custer, Bob, 12, 44, 53, 57, 58, 59, 306, 409
Custer's Last Stand, 58, 59
Cyclone on Horseback, 96

Dade, Frances, 22, 23
Dalbert, Suzanne, 200
Dalhart, Vernon, 334
Dalton, Audrey, 487
Dalton Gang, The, 269
Daltons' Women, The, 267
"Dance of the Furies,"108
Dancing Lady, 357
Danger Ahead, 199
Danger Valley, 146
Dangerous Waters, 481
Dangers of the Canadian Mounted, 193
Daniel Boone, 85, 315
Daredevil's Reward, 298
Daredevils of the West, 217, 464
Darien, Frank, 110
Daring Caballero, The, 206
Daring Danger, 37
Dark Command, 127, 355, 444
Darling, Peggy, 472
Darmour, Larry, 25, 153, 159, 225, 226, 316, 317, 371, 444
Darnelly, Billy, 323
Darro, Frankie, 270, 482
Darwell, Jane, 484
Daughter of Don Q, 207, 463
Davis, Art, 41, 225, 235, 237, *356*, 359
Davis, Bette, 507
Davis Distributing, 303
Davis, Gail, *133*, 275
Davis, Jim, 279, 284
Davis, Jimmie, 166, 359, 494
Davis, Rufe, 179, 180, *180*, 359
"Davy Crockett," 279
Dawn on the Great Divide, 247, 481
Day, John, 241
Day the World Ended, The, 481
Days of Buffalo Bill, 216
Days of Jesse James, 127, 128, 212
Days of Old Cheyenne, 214
De Carlo, Yvonne, 240
De Francesco, Louis, 442
De Lay, Mel, 188
Dead Don't Dream, The, 113
Dead Game, 17
Dead Man's Gold, 266, 267
Dead Man's Gulch, 214
Dead or Alive, 238
Deadline, The (1931), 32
Deadline (1948), 268

541

Dean, Dearest, 497
Dean, Eddie, 219, 251, 263, *264*, *265*, *265*, 267, *283*, 362, 363–64, *364*, 368, 372, 373, *392*, 403, 432, *459*, *465*, 487, 489, *493*, *494*, *495*, *496*, 496–97, *497*
Dean, Jimmy, 363, 373
Death Goes North, 199, 201
"Death of Jimmy Rodgers, The," 348
Death Rides the Range, 26, *26*
"Death Valley Days," 279, 432
Death Valley Manhunt, 229
Death Valley Rangers, *250*, *433*
Decca Record Company, 344, 346, 347, 348, 357, 362, 364, 379, 494, 499
Decker, Harry, 166
"Decoy, The," 445
"Deep in the Heart of Texas," 126, 346
Deep in the Heart of Texas, 258
DeForest, Lee, 441
DeHavilland, Olivia, 430
Dehner, John, 103, 170, 217, 243
Delmore Brothers, 496
Demarest, William, 432
DeMille, Cecil B., 10, 26, 91, 105, 109, 115, 193, 298, 404, 481, 485
DeMille, Katherine, 124
Deming, Norman, 163, 226
Denning, Richard, 484, 485
Depew, Hap, 44
DeRose, Peter, 334
Derr, E. B., 94
Desciple, The, 432
Desert Gold, 189, 389, 390
Desert Justice, 56, 318
Desert Mesa, 67
Desert Passage, 103
Desert Pursuit, 270
Desert Vigilante, 170, *430*
Desmond, William, 12, 173, 197, 300
Desperado, The, 271
Desperados of the West, 217, 463
Desperate Trails, 256
Destry Rides Again, 27, 432, 446
"Destry Rides Again," 386
Detour, 317
Devil Horse, The, 131
Devil Riders, 191
Devil's Playground, The, 113
Devil's Saddle Legion, The, 139
Devil's Trail, The, 228
Devine, Andy, 133, 135, *135*, 273, *274*, 287
Dew, Eddie, 214–15, 240
DeWitt, Jack, 232
Diamond Trail, The, 60
Dick Stanley's Wild West Show, 301
Dickey, Basil, 50
Dickson, W. K. L., 8
Diege, Samuel, 64, 285
DiMaggio, Ross, 444
Diskant, George, 101
Disney, Walt, 207, 222, 499
Diversion Pictures, 21
Dix, Richard, 95, *96*, 99, 387, 393
Dixon, Denver, 64–67, 309, *310*, 311, 312, 411, 442. See also Victor Adamson

Dmytryk, Edward, 97, 151
Dodd, Jimmy, 359
Dodd, Tyler, 180
Dodge City, 432
Dodge City Trail, 161
Don Daredevil Rides Again, 207
Don Q, 206
Don Ricardo Returns, 209
Don't Fence Me In, 129
"Don't Go Near the Indians," 499
Donald M. Barry Productions, 270
Donnell, Jeff, 103
Donnelley, Bill, 322
Doomed at Sundown, 46
Doomed Caravan, 112, 203, 439
"Doomship," 444–45
Doran, Ann, 162, 398
Doss, Lloyd Thomas, 382, *383*
Dot Records, 365
"Double-Eyed Deceiver, A," 206
Douglas, Kirk, 428
Douglas, Linda, *102*
Douglas, Warren, 201
Dove, The, 95
Down Dakota Way, 135
Down Laredo Way, 222
Down Mexico Way, 126
Down Rio Grande Way, 166
Down Texas Way, 247, 248
Down the Wyoming Trail, 143
Downs, Cathy, 485
Downs, Johnny, 190, 390
Drag Harlan, 298
"Dragnet," 270
Drake, Claudia, 102
Drake, Oliver, 85, 92, 176, 238, 242, 268, 270, 417, 459, 474
Dresden, Curly, 187
Drift Fence, 189, 390
Drifter, The, 191
Drifting Along, 260, 366
Drifting Westward, 154
Drum Taps, 24, 195
Drury, James, 432
Dubin, Joseph, 211
Dubov, Paul, 485
Dude Bandit, 20
Dude Cowboy, 96
Dude Ranger, The, 83, *84*, 388
Dumbrille, Douglas, 260, 270, 283, 284, 390, 482
Duna, Steffi, 95, 110
Duncan, Julie, *182*, 237, 285
Duncan, Kenne, *186*, 211, 216, 217, 230, 231, 270, 286, 482
Duncan, Tommy, 378
Duncan, William, 12, 294, 324
Dunlap, Scott R., 37, 145, 205, 245, 259, 260, 401, 402
Dunworth, Charles, 444
Durand of the Badlands, 299
Durango Kid, 3, 167, *169*, 359
Durango Kid, The, 163, *380*
Durango Valley Raiders, 46, *452*
Durante, Jimmy, 126
Durlam, G. A., 45, 49
Duryea, Dan, 482, 484
Duryea, George, *482*, 484. See also Tom Keene

Dwan, Allan, 83, 294
Dwan, Dorothy, 299
Dwire, Earl, 62, 73, 256, 286
Dyer, Bobby, *327*
Dynamite Ranch, 24, 454

Eagle's Brood, The, 107
Eagle-Lion Corporation, 265, 267, 364
Eagles, James, 390
Earp, Wyatt, 61, 83
Eason, B. Reeves, 19, 18, 22, 25, 29, 58, 117, 123, 138, 200, 222, 240, 284
Eastin Pictures, 476
Eberson, Drew, 36
Ebsen, Buddy, 222, 289
Echo Ranch, 367, 476
Eddy, Nelson, 137, 185, 344
Edeson, Arthur, 70
Edison Co., 8, 9, 337
Edwards, Bill, 200, 270
Edwards, Cliff, 96, 164, 165, *165*, 166, 359, *359*, 476
Edwards, Edgar, 199
Eilers, Sally, *16*, 19, 81
El Diablo Rides, 47
El Paso Stampede, 219
Elam, Jack, 428
Eldredge, George, *258*
"Elfego Baca," 279
Elfelt, Clifford S., 17
Ellington, Duke, 153, 352
Elliott, Bill, 32, 130, 138, 144, 154, 166, 217, 224, 225–33, *226*, *227*, *228*, *230*, *232*, *233*, 242, 258, 270, 311, 316, 347, 365, 401, 432, 435, *450*, 451, 454, 466–67, *507*, 510, 515
Elliott, Dick, 474
Elliott, Gordon, See also Bill Elliott, 146
Ellis, Frank, *33*, 187, 248
Ellison, James (Jimmy), 106, 107, *107*, 108, 109, 261, 268, 269, *270*, 284
Eltz, Theodore von, *204*
"Empty Saddles," 334
Empty Saddles, 35, *35*, 445
End of the Trail, The (1932), 34, 37–38, *38*, 450
End of the Trail (1936), 281
English, John, 129, 131, 132, 133, 141, 152, 176, 180, 194, 196, 197, 206, 211, 212, 214, 215, 216, 217, 229, 466
English, Marla, 485, 486, 487
Equity Productions, 149, 267
Erickson, A. F., 79, 80
Erikson, Leif, *391*
Errol, Leon, 476
Erskine, Laurie York, 197
Escape From Fort Bravo, 433
Essanay Film Company, 10, 294, 471
Este Productions Inc., 314, 415
Estrella, Esther, 237
Evans, Dale, 129, *130*, 133, 219, 277, 366, 428, 458, 459, 489, 491, 492, 499, *507*, 511

INDEX

Evans, Douglas, *260*
"Everlasting Hills of Oklahoma," 382
Evers, Ann, *176*
Everson, William K., 311, 332, 342
"Everything I Have Is Yours," 148
Eyes of Texas, 133

Fair Warning, 81
Fairbanks, Douglas, 206, 296, 299, 435
Fairbanks, William, *305*
Faire, Virginia Brown, *473*
Falkenberg, Jinx, 142, 152
False Colors, 113
Fame, 505
Fangs of the Arctic, 201
"Fanny Moore," 332
Fargo, 232, *232*
Fargo Express, 24, 454
Farnum, Dustin, 296, 297, 298, 300
Farnum, Franklin, 53, 173, *304*, *473*, 486
Farnum, William, 12, 135, 151, 173, 235, 255, 258, 296, 297, *297*, 297–98, *335*, 386, 387
Farr, Hugh, 120, *120*, 374, 377, 379, *379*, 380, 382–83, *383*
Farr, Karl, 374, 378–79, *379*, 380, 383, *383*
Farrar, Geraldine, 296
Farrell, Tommy, 268
Fast on the Draw, 269
"Fat Gal," 495
"Fat" Jones Stable, 329
Fay, Dorothy, *144*, 285, *285*, 355, 454, *455*
Faye, Randall, 230–31
Faylen, Frank, 138
Fellows, Edith, 28, 127
Felton, Earl, 127
Fenin, George, 332
Fennelly, Vincent M., 231, 270
Feud of the Range, 46–47
Feudin' Rhythm, 367
Feuer and Martin Productions, 444
Feuer, Cy, 211, 444, 447
Fiddlin' Buckaroo, 24
Field, Virginia, 204
Fielding, Romaine, 294
Fields Brothers Marvelous Medicine Show, 336
Fields, Stanley, 81, 146
Fields, W. C., 163
Fier, Jack, 166
$50,000 Reward, 17–18
Fig Leaves, 79
Fightin' Buckaroo, 358
Fighting Bill Carson, 191
Fighting Caravans, 389
Fighting Champ, The, 45
Fighting for Gold, 299
Fighting for Justice, 38
Fighting Frontier, 97
Fighting Fury, 64
Fighting Lawman, The, 270
Fighting Mad, 198, *198*
Fighting Parson (1930), 476
Fighting Parson, The (1933), 20

Fighting Ranger, The, 32
Fighting Redhead, The, 268
Fighting Seabees, The, 430
Fighting Shadows, 39, 193
Fighting Texans, The, 60, 450
Fighting Through, 65
Fighting to Live, 64
Fighting Trooper, The, 195
Fighting with Kit Carson, 254
Film Booking Offices (FBO), 15, 27, 43, 48, 91, 306, 408
Filming of the West, The, 332
Finlayson, Jimmy, 478
Finley, Evelyn, 183, *190*, 241, 285
Finney, Ed, 140, 141, 142, 143, 155, 311, *312*, 347, 354, 402
Firebrand Jordan, 58
Firebrands of Arizona, 216
First National, 15, 18, 19, 22, 24, 70, 137, 306, 409, 411
Fisher, Shug, 382
Fisk, William, 415
Fiske, Richard, 161, 227
Five Bad Men, 64
Five Star Jubilee, 499
Fix, Paul, 34, 72
Flame of the West, 260
Flaming Bullets, 238, 348
Flaming Frontiers, 256, 467–69
Flaming Guns, 27, 29, 435, 454
Flaming Lead, 26
Fleming, Alice, 217, 229
Fleming, Victor, 69
Flesh and the Spur, 481, 483, 486
Fletcher, Curley, 326
Fletcher, Tex, 148–49, *149*, 279, 357
Flying A Productions, 132, 275, 294, 491
Flynn, Emmett, 11
Flynn, Errol, 50, 430, 435
Foley, Red, 354, 358
Fonda, Henry, 83, 433
Fontaine, Jacqueline, 267
Fool's Gold, 113
For the Service, 35
Foran, Dick, 37, 105, 137, 138–39, *139*, 141, 194, 225, 328, 344, *344*, 345, 357, 404, 428, 467, *467*, 487
Forbes, John, 270
Forbidden Trails, 245, 246–47
Forbidden Valley, 64
Ford, Francis, 95
Ford, John (Jack), 10, 11, 31, 50, 56, 61, 77, 79, 80, 81, 83, 87, 95, 298, 300, 432, 433, 434
Ford, Philip, 211, 219, 220, 222
Ford, Tennessee Ernie, 476
Forest, Patsey de, *300*
Forlorn River, 189
Forman, Carol, *101*
Fort Apache, 433
Fort Savage Raiders, 170
40 Guns to Apache Pass, 435
Forty Thieves, 113
FortyNiners, The, 49
Foster, Lewis R., 209
Foster, Norman, 204, 209
Foster, Preston, 284
Four For Texas, 428

Four Tones, 352
Fourth Horseman, The, 28, 82
Fowley, Douglas, 110, *111*, 200
Fox Film Corporation, 7, 11, 12, 15, 19, 27, 28, 31, 35, 60, 69, 70, 72, 79, 80, 83, 85, 87, 91, 95, 138, 203, 204, 281, 293, 295, 297, 298–99, 300, 306, 315, 326, 387, 388, 389, 403–4, 407, 408, 411, 413, 442
Fox, Wallace, 44, 49, 50, 95, 154, 173, 206, 215, 240, 241, 259
Fox, William, 298
Foy, Bryan, 137, 138, 193
Foy, Charley, 137
Foy, Eddie, 137
Foy, Eddie, Jr., 137
Foy Willing and the Riders of the Purple Sage, 345
Francis, Noel, 28
Francks, Don, 277
Franklin, Joe, *310*
Franklin, Paul, 166
Franz, Arthur, 487
Fraser, Harry, 20, 21, 26, 48, 56, 59, 60, 61, 69, 139, 148, 152, 193, 219, 238, 243, 318, 357
Frazee, Jane, 133, 167, 284, *370*
Frazer, Robert, 92, 247
Freighters of Destiny, 91, 95
French, Charles K., 322
French, Ted, 297, 299, 300, 321, 322–23, 329, *329*
Freuler, John R., 49, 53, 57
Freulich, Henry, 170
Friedhofer, 110
Friedlander, Louis, 37, 64, 255
Frisco, Joe, 123
Frome, Milton, 285
Frontier Crusader, 41, *41*
Frontier Days, 476
"Frontier Doctor," 279, 367, 499
Frontier Feud, 259
Frontier Frolic, 476
Frontier Fury, 166
Frontier Investigator, 218
Frontier Law, 239, 459
Frontier Marshal (1934), 83
"Frontier Marshal" series, 359
Frontier Marshals, 237
Frontier Outlaws, 191
Frontier Outpost, 170
Frontier Phantom, The, 267
Frontier Pony Express, 124
Frontier Scout, 186, *186*, 355
Frontier Town, 141–42
Frontier Vengeance, 213
Frontiers Inc., 492
Frontiers of '49, 226
Frontiersmen, The, 110
Frost, Terry, *180*
Frye, Kathy, 260
Fu Manchu, 86
Fugitive from Sonora, 214
Fugitive Valley, 182
Fuller, Robert, 435
Fulton, Lou, *41*
Furness, Betty, 93
"Fury," 277

543

Futter, Walter, 21
Fuzzy Settles Down, 191

Gable, Clark, 105, 254, 284, 482, 507
Gallant Defender, 159, 160
Gallant Fool, The, 45
Galloping Dynamite, 196
Galloping Romeo, 45
Galloping Thru, 49
Gambling Terror, The, 256
Gangelin, Paul, 130
Gangs of Sonora, 180
Garbo, Greta, 253
Garfield, Herman, 312
Garland, Judy, 507
Garmes, Lee, 24, 454
Garralaga, Martin, 205
Garrett, Pat, 124
Gasnier, Louis, 199
Gates, Nancy, 99
Gatzert, Nate, 153, 225
Gaucho Serenade, 125
Gauchos of El Dorado, 180, *180*
Gay Amigo, The, 206
Gay Bandit of the Border, The, 82
Gay Caballero, The (1932), 82, *82*,
Gay Caballero, The (1940), 205
Gay Cavalier, The, 205
Gay, Nancy, 215
Gay Ranchero, The, 133, *370*, 429
Geary, Bud, *180*, 211, 230, *230*, 231, 286
Gehrig, Lou, 146, *349*, 512
Gene Autry Productions, 365
"Gene Autry Show, The," 491
Gennett Company, 337
Gentleman from Arizona, 219
Gentleman from Texas, 402
Gentlemen With Guns, 191
George White's Scandals of 1935, 451
Geraghty, Gerald, 113, 131, 135, 222
Geraghty, Maurice, 166
Ghost Guns, 259
Ghost of Zorro, 207
Ghost Rider, The, 259
Ghost Town, 62
Ghost Town Gold, 174
Ghost Town Law, 247, *247*
Ghost Town Raiders, 148
Ghost Valley, 91
Giant, 346, 366, 497
Gibbons, Floyd, 113
Gibson, Edmund (Hoot), 12, 15, *16*, 17, *17*, 18, 19–21, *20*, *21*, 27, 29, 32, 34, 45, 49, 50, 79, 92, 173, 174, 216, 244, 248, 249, *249*, 250, *250*, 251, *251*, 294, 295, 300–301, *301*, 306, 350, 401, 408–9, *413*, 463, 471, 473, 486
Gibson, Helen, 300
Gibson, Tom, 155
Gifford, Frances, 112
Gilbert, Helen, 484
Gill, Tom, 82
Gillette, James, 236
Gillis, Bill, *324*
Gilman, Fred, *305*, 306
Gilmore, Stuart, 103
Gilroy, Bert, 85, 95, 97, 417

Gilstrap, Jack, 323
Girl and the Gambler, The, 95
Girl From Frisco, The, 301
Girl from San Lorenzo, The, 206
Girls in Prison, 481, 484
Girty, Simon, 85
Gittens, Wyndham, 64, 164
"Give Me a Home in Oklahoma," 357
Givot, George, 113
"Glad Rags," 495
Glasser, Albert, 205, 444
Glasser, Bernard, 87
Gleason, James, 105
Glennon, Bert, 45, 194
Glickman, Mort, 211, 445
Go West Young Lady, 358
God's Country and the Man, 94
Gold Ghost, The, 476
Gold Is Where You Find It, 240
Gold Mine in the Sky, 353, 355, 443
"Gold Mine in the Sky," 372
Gold Raiders, 87
"Gold Rush, The," 445
Golden West Broadcasting, 491
Golden West Cowboys, 347, 355
Golden West, The, 83, 388
Goldstein, Leonard, 35
Goldstone, Phil, 22
Goldwyn, Sam, 385
Good, Frank B., 12, 83, 85
Goodfriend, Pliny, 50
Goodkind, Saul A., 256
Gordon, Alex, 451, 479, 485
Gordon, C. Henry, 82, 392
Gordon, Leo, 484
Gordon of Ghost City, 427
Gordon, Stan, 445
Gorss, Sol, 241
Graham, Fred, 133, 211
Grand Canyon Trail, 133–35
Grand National Pictures, 21, 26, 46, 60, 64, 95, 141, 142, 148, 149, 185, 186, 197, 198, 284–85, 311, 347, 357, 371, 411, 493, 505
Grande, Nick, *410*
Grant, Cary, 435
Grant, Frances, *339*
Grant, Kirby, 86, 177, *199*, 200, *200*, 240, *241*, 263, 275
Grant, Norton, 215
Granville, Bonita, 138, 274
Grapes of Wrath, 484
Graves, Ralph, *177*, 178
Gray, Lawrence, 196
Gray, Lorna, See also Adrian Booth, 177, 207
Gray, Louis, 127, 179, 215, 242
Grayson, Donald, 161, 350, *354*
Great Adventures of Wild Bill Hickok, The, 225, 466–67
Great K & A Train Robbery, The, 299, 429
Great Meadow, The, 254
Great Stagecoach Robbery, The, 230
Great Train Robbery, The, 8–9, 193, 231, 293, 331, 429, 471
Greatest Show on Earth, The, 115
Green, Alfred E., 125

Green Archer, The, 451
Green Grow the Lilacs, 346–47
Greene, Angela, 205
Greene, Duke, 211
Greene, Walter, 266
Greenhalgh, Jack, 97, 191
Greer, Jane, 101
Gregory, Jackson, 215
Grey, Harry, 127, 179, 211
Grey, Shirley, 39
Grey, Zane, 8, 76, 79, 81, 82, 83, 94, 98, 99, 101, 102, 105, 153, 159, 189, 193, 194, 197, 235, 281, 282, 283, 284, 293, 298, 331, 386–93
Gribbon, Harry, 70
Griffis, Ken, 371
Griffith, D. W., 10, 105, 294
Griffith, James, 131
Grissell, Wallace A., 100, 207, 217, 230
Guest Wife, 344
Guihan, Frances, 161
Guilfoye, Paul, 95, 392
Guizar, Tito, 133, 206, *370*, 429
Gun Brothers, 191
Gun Code, 41
Gun Fire, 60
Gun Grit, 54, 318
Gun Justice, 25
Gun Law, 85
Gun Lords of the Stirrup Basin, 3–4, 452
Gun Play, 62
Gun Smoke, 151
Gun Smugglers, 102
Gun to Gun, 476
Gun Town, 240
Gunfighters of Abilene, 191
Gunfighters of the Northwest, 193
Gunfire, 270
Gunga Din, 437
Gunman from Bodie, 245, 246
Gunners and Guns, 64, 411
Guns and Guitars, 119
Guns in the Dark, 256
Guns of the Pecos, 443
"Gunsmoke," 243, 277, 365, 382, 432
Gunsmoke Ranch, 435
Gunsmoke Trail, 402–3
"Guys and Dolls," 444
Gwynne, Anne, 201, 257, 267

Haade, William, 214, *230*
Hackel, A. W., 45, 46, 76, 255
Hackett, Karl, 187, 237, 256
Hadley, Reed, 103, 206, 207, 284, 464, 465
Hagney, Frank, 70, 187
Hail to the Rangers, 166
Hair-Trigger Casey, 56, 318
Hajos, Karl, 444
Hale, Barbara, 99, *99*
Hale, Creighton, 486
Hale, Georgia, 390
Hale, Joanna, 497
Hale, Monte, *134*, 135, 219, 220, *220*, 221, 222, *222*, 223, 263,

INDEX

365–66, *366*, 367, 368, 434, 489, 497, *497*, 497–98
Haley, Earl, 64, 219
Half Pint Polly, 476
Hall, Ethel, 299
Hall, Harry, 377
Hall, Jon, 160
Hall, Norman S., 168, 214, 217
Hall, Raymond E., 339
Hall, Ruth, *23*, 24, 70, *453*, 453–54
Hall, Thurston, 99
Hamblen, Stuart, 379
Hamilton, Neil, 217
Hammond, Victor, 251
Hampton, Orville, 284
Hands Across the Border, 128–29, 130, 428
Hands Off, 11
"Happy Rovin' Cowboy," 375
"Happy Trails," 492, 499
Hard Hombre, 20
Hard Rock Harrigan, 83
Hardin, Ira, 352
Harding, Tex, 167, 168, 359
Hardy, Oliver, 140
Hardy, Sam, 173, 174
Harlan, Kenneth, 249, *249*
Harlan, Otis, 28, 70
Harlan, Russell, 106–7
Harlem on the Prairie, 153, 352
Harlem Rides the Range, 352
Harmony Trail, 251, 332
Harper, Patricia, 183
Harrell, Scotty, *258*, 378, 494
Harris, Emmylou, 492
Harris, Roy, 258
Harrison's Reports, 13
Hart, Freddie, 493
Hart, John, 274
Hart, Maria, 285
Hart, Mary, 124
Hart, Neal, 301, *304, 324,* 326
Hart, William S., 9, 10, 28, 61, 80, 94, 97, 164, 232, 233, *254,* 260, 289, 295–97, 298, 370, 432, 471, 478
Hartley, Hashknife, 21
Harvey, Harry, 140
Hathaway, Henry, 110, 282, 389
Hatton, Raymond, 124, *125,* 178, 179, *179,* 189, 190, 245, 246, *246, 247, 247,* 248, 255, 259, 260, *260,* 261, 267, 268, *288,* 390, *421,* 430, 468, 481–82, 486
Haunted Gold, 70
Haunted Harbor, 464, 466
Haunted Ranch, 182
Haunted Trails, 268
"Have Gun–Will Travel," 277, 365
Hawaiian Buckaroo, 146, 349
Hawk of Powder River, The, 265, 459
Hawkins, Georgia, 112
Hawks, Howard, 47, 79
Hawks, J. G., 296
Haycox, Ernest, 235
Hayden, Russell, 106, *108,* 109, *109,* 112, 144, 165, *165,* 166, 170, *192,* 200, *201,* 239, *239,* 240, 266, 268, 269, 275, 283, 318, 358, 392, 459

Hayden, Sterling, 362
Haydon, Julie, 92, 93
Hayes, "Gabby," 25, 45, 74, 107, *107,* 108, *108,* 110, 123–24, *125,* 126, 127, 129, *129, 130,* 191, 229, 230, 255, 279, *280,* 289, 427, 430, 510, *513*
Hayes, Linda, 127
Hayworth, Rita, 86, *87,* 89, 92, 175, *417,* 456
Hazards of Helen, 300
Headin' East, 36
"Headin' For the Home Corral," 382
Headin' for the Rio Grande, 347
Headin' North, 44
Headin' South, 299
Healey, Myron, 261
Heart of Arizona, 314
Heart of Texas Ryan, 320
Heart of the Golden West, 127, 360, 400
Heart of the North, 193
Heart of the Rio Grande, 126
Heart of the Rockies (1937), 175, 401
Heart of the Rockies (1951), 135
Heart of the West, 203
Hecht, Ben, 26
Heflin, Van, 96
Heinz, Ray, 63
Heisler, Stuart, 274
Hell Harbor, 454
Hell Town, 77, 390
Hell's Angels, 400
Hell's Hinges, 10, 297
Hell-Fire Austin, 23
Hellfire, 231
Hello Trouble, 32
Hemisphere Pictures, Inc., 312
Henabery, Joseph E., 113
Henderson, Kelo, 275
Hendricks, Ben, *195*
Henry, Bill, 193
Henry, Buzzy, 157
Henry, Charlotte, 94
Henry, Gloria, 170
Henry, Robert B., 157
"Heritage of the Desert," 387
Heritage of the Desert, 389, 392
Herman, Al, 25, 62, 142, 143, 197, 237, 312
"Heroes and Friends," 510
Heroes of the Alamo, 152
Heroes of the Flames, 37
Heroes of the Hills, 176
Heroes of the Saddle, 179
Heyburn, Weldon, 82, *82,* 249
Hi-Yo Silver!, 152
Hidden Gold, 27, 28, 411
Hidden Valley, 45
Hidden Valley Days, 367
Hidden Valley Outlaws, 229
Higgin, Howard, 105
High Noon, 3, 145, 432, 494
"High Noon," 348, 494
High Sierra, 435
High Speed, 34
Hill, Billy, 334
Hill, George, 254
Hill, Riley, 261

Hill, Robert, 26, 37, 50, 64, 92, 94
"Hillbilly Heaven," 348
Hillie, Verna, 74, *389,* 390
Hills of Old Wyoming, 104, 109
Hillyer, Lambert, 10, 32, 34, 97, 163, 164, 165, 195, 205, 228, 241, 245, 259, 260, 268, 296, 297, 298, 299, 401
Hines, Johnny, 140
Hirliman, George, 83, 85, 315, 413, 442
Hirsch, William W., 411
His Brother's Ghost, 191
His Family Tree, 350
His Fighting Blood, 196
Hit the Saddle, 175
Hitler's Children, 97
Hittin' the Trail, 143, 313
Hodgins, Earle, 152, 153, 289
Hoedown, 367
Hoerl, Arthur, 182
Hoffman, John, 284
Hoffman, M. H., 19, 26
Hogan, James, 189
Hogg, Curley, 377
Holden, William, 433
Holloway, Sterling, 131, 219, 289
Hollywood Barn Dance, 358–59
Hollywood Cowboy, 85, 315
Hollywood Film Enterprises, 478
Hollywood on Parade, 478
"Hollywood Posse, The," 326
Hollywood Productions, 352
Hollywood Roundup, 36
Hollywood TV Service, 279
Holm, Eleanor, 148
Holmes, "PeeWee," *327*
Holmes, Stuart, 28, 486
Holt, Jack, 70, 89, 102, 131, 135, 267, 269, 281, *384,* 387, 390, 435, 481
Holt, Jennifer, 200, 258, 437, 454–59, *458*
Holt of the Secret Service, 481
Holt, Tim, 89, *90,* 91, 92, 95, 97, *98, 101,* 102, 101–3, *103,* 232, 263, 359, *393, 394, 395,* 413, *423,* 450, 474, *515*
Holy Terror, A, 81
Homans, Robert, 353
Home in Wyomin', 126
Home on the Prairie, 123, 400
"Home on the Range," 181, 332, 333–34
Home on the Range, 219, 366
Homes, Geoffrey, 271
Honor of the Mounted, 193
Honor of the West, 148
Hoosier Hot Shots, 123, 242, 243, 365
Hop-a-long Cassidy, 106
Hopalong Cassidy, 276
Hopalong Cassidy Enters, 115
Hopalong Cassidy Returns, 108, 112, 346
"Hopalong Cassidy" series, 275, 279, 312–14, 404–5, 415–16
Hopalong in Hoppyland, 479
Hopalong Rides Along, 110

Hope, Bob, 132, 135
"Hoppy, Gene and Me," 492
Hoppy Serves A Writ, 113
Hopton, Russell, 196
Horne, James W., 37, 193, 245
Horner, Robert J., 54, 60, 442
Horton, Robert, 284
Hostile Country, 269
"Hot Rod Lincoln," 495
Houston, George, 185, 186, 187, *188,* 197, *355–57, 356*
Houston, Norman, 98, 99, 100, 102–3, 110
"How Come Do You Do Me Like You Do?", 357
How the West Was Won, 435
Howard, David, 25, 64, 80, 82, 83, 85, 86, 87, 89, 95–96, 404, 417
Howard, Harlan, 496
Howe, Dorothy. *See* Virginia Vale
Howes, Reed, 306, 482
Howlin, Olin, 289
Hoxie, Al, 301, 472
Hoxie, Jack, 4, 12, 62–63, 293, 301, *303*
Hughes, Carol, *122,* 123, 127, *456*
Hughes, Kay, 165–66
Hughes, Mary Beth, 205, 284
Hull, Warren, 198
Humberstone, H. Bruce, 204
Humes, Fred, 12, 57, 306, 473
Hunnicutt, Arthur, 166
Hunt, Anent, 101
Hunt, Eleanor, 73, 74, 196
Hunt, J. Roy, 97, 101
Hunt, Marsha, 76, 190, 283, 390
Hunt, Roy, 85
Hunter, Dick, 327, *327*
Hunter, Rudolph, 352
Hurley, Harold, 390
Hurricane Express, 430, 469
Hurricane Horseman, The, 58, 484
Hurst, Paul, 28, 70, 95, 196, 220
Huston, John, 101
Huston, Walter, 258
Hutchinson, Charles, 64, 197
Hyer, Martha, 102, 284, *394*

"I Dreamed of a Hillbilly Heaven," 364, 497
"I Hang My Head and Cry," 346
I Killed Bill Hickok, 270
I Killed Geronimo, 284
"I Love You So Much (It Hurts Me)," 362, 494
I Shot Billy the Kid, 270
"I Still Do," 365
"I Wonder Where You Are Tonight," 495
"I'll Remember April," 139
"I'll Step Aside," 495
"I'm an Old Cowhand," 122
"I'm Coming Home," 357
Idaho, 127, 128
Imhof, Roger, *437*
Imperial Distributing Corporation, 312, 473
In Cold Blood, 482
In Early Arizona, 225–26

In Line of Duty, 194
In Old Arizona, 7, 79, 203
In Old Caliente, 124, *124*
In Old Cheyenne, 58
In Old Colorado, 112
In Old Mexico, 205, 314, *314*
In Old Montana, 140
In Old Monterey, 123, 124
In Old Santa Fe, 25, 117, 315, 332, 342, 368, 413, 484
In the Days of Buffalo Bill, 303
In The San Fernando Valley, 294
Ince, Thomas, 7, 10, 295, 444
Independent-International Picture Corporation, 311, 312
Indian Agent, 102
Indian Territory, 131
Indians Are Coming, The, 37, 482
Ingraham, Lloyd, 322
Ingram, Jack, *94, 171,* 186, 197, 239, 241, 286
International Cowboys, 376
Invasion of the Body Snatchers, 429
Irish Gringo, The, 151
Iron Horse, The, 79, 80
Iron Mountain Trail, 222
Irwin, Jack, 64
Isabell, Henry, 323
Isley, Phil, 497
Isley, Phyllis, 178
"It Makes No Difference Now," 359, 372
Ivano, Paul, 21
Ivory-Handled Gun, The, 35, 258

Jack and His Texas Outlaws, 376
Jack Schwarz Productions, 87
Jack Wrather Productions, 274, 277
Jackson, Marion, 18
Jacobs, Harrison, 110
Jacobs, William, 138
Jamboree, 358
James, Alan, *See also* Alvin J. Neitz, 23–24, 35, 40, 146, 154, 197, 216, 248, 256
James, Harry, 495
James, John, 242
Janssen, Eilene, 222
January, Lois, *40,* 47, 147, 285, 454
Jarrett, Art, 148, 186, *187,* 357
Jarrett, Dan, 80, 146
Jazz Singer, The, 332, 489
"Jealous Heart," 348
"Jeannine, I Dream of Lilac Time," 337
Jeep Herders, 241
Jeffreys, Anne, 99, 229
Jeffries, Herb, 152–53, 350–52
Jenkins, Gordon, 129
Jenks, Frank, 270, 485
Jenks, Si, 289
Jennings, Dev, 77
Jennings, Waylon, 373
Jergens, Adele, 138, 139, 270, 344, 484
Jerome, M. K., 138, 139, 344
"Jesse James," 332
Jesse James, 429
Jesse James at Bay, 127, 428

Jesse James Jr., 214
Jesse James Rides Again, 274
Jet Attack, 487
"Jimmie the Kid," 338
Jimmy Wakely Trio, 345, 494
Jimmy Wilson's Catfish String Band, 337
"Jingle, Jangle, Jingle," 348
John Paul Revere, 215
Johnson, Ben, 56
Johnson, Chubby, 219, 289
Johnson, Laraine (Day), 86, 417
Johnson, Noble, 127
Johnson, Raymond K., 47, 140, 155
Johnson, Rome, 383
Johnston, W. Ray, 53
Jolley, I. Sanford, 186, *190,* 200, 237, 238, 246, *246,* 247, *247,* 249, 286, *356,* 484
Jolson, Al, 332, 489
Jones, Buck, 3, 12, 17, 20, 31–37, *33, 34, 35, 36,* 38, 40, 41, 70, 146, 158, 161, 166, 193, 245, 248, 253, 258, 289, 295, 300, *300,* 325, 349, 401, 403, 408, 409, 411–13, 427, 428, 432, 434, 450, 454, 462, 467, 471, 473, 478, 481, 489, *510*
Jones, Dick, 138, 146, 275
Jones, Ed, 321
Jones, Gordon, *134,* 135, 222, 289
Jones, Harry O., 45
Jones, Jennifer, 178
Jordan, Sid, *320,* 324, *324,* 325, *325,* 326
Jory, Victor, 112, 113, 283–84, *283, 392, 392*
Joy, Leonard, 337
Juarez, 432
"Jubilation Jamboree," 382
Julius Caesar, 430
Jungle Jim, 428, 433

Kahn, Edward L., 191
Kahn, Richard C., 153, 157
Kalem Company, 300, 301
Kane, Joseph, *13,* 76, 118, 120, 121, 122, 123, 124, 127, 129, 174, 175, 191, 211, 212, 231
Kangaroo Kid, The, 284
Kansas Territory, 232
Kansas Terrors, The, 178–79, 232
Karlan, Richard, 201
Karloff, Boris, 58, 153, 435, 486
Karno troupe, 10
Karns, Roscoe, 217
Katzman, Sam, 40, 50, 191, 315, 316, 317, 442, 444
Kavanaugh, Frances, 249
Keaton, Buster, 21, 476
Keays, Vernon, 144, 168, 240, 242, 251
Keene, Tom, 40, 76, 91–95, *92, 93, 94, 95,* 102, 118, 135, 142, 182, 189, 217, 283, 390, 405, 417, 432, 450, 453, 463, 476, 486
Keith, Brian, 277
Keith, Ian, 231
Keith, Rosalind, 86, 161
Kellaway, Alec, 284

INDEX

Keller, Harry, 211, 219, 222
Kelley, George, 168, 170
Kelly, Grace, 494
Kelly, Paul, 83, 146
Kelso, Ed, 112, 141
"Ken Murray's Hometown Hollywood," 479
Kendall, Cy, 76
Kennedy, Bill, 193
Kennedy, Burt, 283
Kennedy, Douglas, 277
Kennedy, Edgar, 93, 476
Kennedy, Tom, 390
Kennis, Dan, 311
Kent, Dorothea, 199
Kent, Robert, 194
Kent, Travis, 207
Kent, Willis, 58, 63
Kenton, Erle C., 281
Kenyon, Gwen, 205
Kerrigan, J. Warren, 294, 304
Kesterson, George (Whitey), See also Art Mix, 64, 295, 309
Keyes, Evelyn, 227, 228
Kid Courageous, 45
Kid from Arizona, The, 54
Kid from Broken Gun, The, 171
Kid from Spain, The, 454
Kilenyi, Edward, 442
"Killer, The," 385
Killy, Edward, 86, 92, 95, 96, 98, 99, 100
Kimbrough, John, 235, 393, 403
Kinematrade Releasing Co., 58
King and the Cowboy, The, 478
King, Billy, 108
King, Brad, 112, 113
King, Charlie, 22, 23, 26–27, 28, 43, 46, 47, 48, 94, 141, 144, 167, 186, 196, 197, 225, 226, 237, 238, 256, 259, 264, 286, 356, 433, 464
King, Henry, 323, 385, 429, 454
King, Jerry, 378
King, Joe, 138
King, John "Dusty," 64, 181, 182, 182, 183, 219, 358
King, Louis, 31, 83, 138
King of Dodge City, 228, 228
King of the Arena, 24
King of the Bandits, 205
King of the Bullwhip, 267
King of the Cowboys, 128
King of the Khyber Rifles, 435
King of the Mounties, 194, 464
King of the Pecos, 76
King of the Royal Mounted, 194, 464
King of the Sierras, 64
King of the Stallions, 157
King of the Texas Rangers, 216, 464, 466, 466
King of the Wild Horses, 64
King, Pee Wee, 347, 355
King Solomon of Broadway, 357
King's Men, 283, 392
Kirby, Jay, 11, 113, 241
Kirk, Jack, 66, 75
Kirkland, Muriel, 390
Kirkwood, James, 81
Kline, Benjamin, 12, 166

Knapp, Evalyn, 25
Knickerbocker Buckaroo, The, 299
Knight, Fuzzy, 141, 144, 147, 191, 222, 232, 240, 241, 256, 257, 258, 268, 288, 390, 459, 482, 484
Knights of the Range, 283, 392
Knott, Lydia, 32
Kohler, Fred, 28, 28, 63, 79, 83, 85, 196, 286, 486
Kohler, Fred, Jr., 64, 85, 162
Kolb, Clarence, 95
Kortman, Bob, 24, 60, 187, 256, 286, 318
Krafft, John, 190
Kramer, Stanley, 145, 494
Krasne, Phil, 197, 198, 205, 206
Kraushaar, Raoul, 211
Kress, Harold, 284
Krusada, Carl, 155
Kruse, J. Henry, 50
Kyne, Peter B., 10, 197

L'Estrange, Dick, 157
La Plante, Laura, 70
La Rue, Al (Lash), 168, 188, 262, 263–67, 265, 266, 454, 459
La Rue, Jack, 205, 217, 249, 390
Lackteen, Frank, 483
Ladd, Alan, 392, 430
Lady and Gent, 36
Laemmle, Carl, 19, 22, 27, 31, 311
Laemmle, Carl, Jr., 19, 22, 27, 31, 333
Laemmle, Edward, 28, 254
Laidlaw, Ethan, 469
Laine, Frankie, 494
Lair, John, 354
Lait, Jack, Jr., 86
Lake, Stuart, 83
Lamont, Charles, 139
Lamour, Dorothy, 113
Land Beyond the Law, 138, 476
Land of Hunted Men, 182
Land of the Fighting Men, 146
Land of the Open Range, 96
Landers, Lew, 37, 95, 101, 102, 103, 167
Landis, Carol, 177, 178
Lane, Allan "Rocky", 95, 130, 134, 135, 193, 210, 217–18, 218, 219, 219, 222, 223, 231, 434, 464, 507, 513
Lane, Nora, 25, 39, 40, 285
Lane, Rosemary, 242
Lane, Yancey, 151
Lang, Charles, 200, 201
Langan, Glenn, 270
Langdon, Harry, 476
Langford, Frances, 146
Lanham, Roy, 383
Lanning, Reggie, 128, 129, 133, 135, 207, 211
Laramie, 284, 367
Laramie Trail, The, 215
LaRoy, Rita, 81
Larson, Keith, 279
Larue, Frank, 41, 124, 226, 255
"Lasca," 370
Lasca of the Rio Grande, 254

Last Bandit, The, 231, 435
Last Days of Boot Hill, 168
Last Frontier, The, 64
Last of the Clintons, 61
Last of the Duanes, The (1919), 298
Last of the Duanes, The (1930), 81, 387
Last of the Duanes, The (1941), 235, 392
Last of the Pony Riders, 132, 368
Last of the Warrens, The, 45
Last of the Wild Horses, 284
Last Outlaw, The, 20, 21, 50, 95, 345
Last Round-Up, The (1934), 389
Last Round-Up, The (1947), 131
"Last Roundup, The," 334, 348
"Last Trail, The," 388
Last Trail, The, 388
Laurel and Hardy, 432
Laurel, Stan, 10
Laurenz, John, 101
Lauter, Harry, 270, 275
Lava, William, 207, 211, 443, 447, 464
Law and Order (1932), 61 286
Law and Order (1940), 257–58
Law and Order (1942), 190
Law Beyond the Range, 39
Law Comes to Texas, The, 226
Law Men, 259
Law of the .45s, 62, 173
Law of the Northwest, 195
Law of the Pampas, 110, 435, 437
Law of the Range, The, 258, 306
Law of the Saddle, 188
Law of the Texan, The, 36, 454
Law of the Wild, 58
Law Rides Again, The, 249, 453
Law West of Tombstone, The, 95
Lawless Rider, The, 482
Lawless Code, 242, 362
Lawless Eighties, The, 191
Lawless Nineties, The, 76
Lawless Plainsmen, 166
Lawless Range, 76
Lawless Rider, The, 270, 275, 484
Lawless Valley (1932), 484
Lawless Valley (1938), 64, 85, 86, 399
Lawman Is Born, A, 255
Layne, Tracy, 119, 340
Le Borg, Reginald, 206
Le Picard, Marcel, 249
Le Saint, Edward, 160, 161, 398
Lease, Rex, 58–59, 146, 152, 182, 465, 486
Leather Burners, 113, 427
Lederman, D. Ross, 32, 34, 37, 39, 48, 70, 85, 138, 228, 345
Lee, Mary, 125, 127, 516
Lee, Pinky, 135
Leeds, Andrea, 197
Leeds, Herbert I., 203, 205
Lees, Antoinette, 197
LeFevre, Jack, 377
Left-Handed Law, 35
Legend of the Lone Ranger, The, 434
Leichter, Mitchell, 64
Leipold, John, 110

547

Leonard, L. G., 35
Leone, Pedro, *324*
LePicard, Marcel, 142, 143, 249
Leslie, Nan, 101, 102
Lesser, Sol, 31, 64, 83, 146, 153, 194, 306, 315, 349, 385–86, 388, 403, 409, 411, 413, 442
Let 'Er Buck!, 275
Let Freedom Ring, 404
Letz, George, 152. See also George Montgomery
Levering, Joseph, 153–54, 225
Levi-Taylor, William, 331
Levine, Nat, 25, 29, 117, 118, 119, 137, 311, 314–15, 332–33, 339, 340, 342, 344, 413
Lewis, David, 92
Lewis, George, 207, *209*, 267, 268
Lewis, Jerry Lee, 497
Lewis, Joseph H., 147, 163, 227, 258, 283, 398, 403, 454
Liberty Pictures, 20, 345
Liebert, Billy, 383
"Life Gets Tee-Jus, Don't It," 498
"Life's Weary Ways," 339
"Light Mysterioso," 444
Light of the Western Stars, The, 389
Light of Western Stars, The, 283, *392*, 392,
Lightcrust Doughboys, 378
Lightnin' Bill Carson, 40
Lightnin' Smith's Return, 64
Lightning Bill, 64
Lightning Bryce, 301
Lightning Guns, 170
Lightning Range, 64
Lightning Warrior, The, 432
Lippert Pictures, 209, 268, 269
Lippert, Robert L., 284, 312
Litel, John, 483
"Little Joe the Wrangler," 331
"Little Old Sod Shanty on the Claim, The," 333
Little Ranger, The, 476
Little Train Robbery, The, 9
Littlefield, Lucien, 77, *77*
Litvak, Anatole, 47
Lively, William, 41, 153
Lives of a Bengal Lancer, 432
Livingston, Robert, 4, 77, 123, 130, 145, 152, 167, 174, 175, *175*, 177, 178, 179, *179*, 180, 185, 187, 188, *188*, 206, 215, 219, 223, 315, 317, 350, 432, 435, *465*, 481, *507*
Llano Kid, The, 206
Lloyd, Frank, 256
Loaded Pistols, 131, 481
Locher, Charles, 160
Lockwood, Alyn, 270
Loggia, Robert, 279
Lomax, John Avery, 331, 334
Lombard, Carole, *204*
London Music Halls, 10
London, Tom, *54*, 132, 187, 216, 217, *218*, 247, 248, 286, 326, 464
Lone Prairie, The, 239
Lone Ranger and the Lost City of Gold, The, 274

Lone Ranger Rides Again, The, 152, 428, 434, 443, 464, *465*
"Lone Ranger" series, 138, 186–88, 235, 274
Lone Ranger, The, 31, 57–58, *152*, 212, 274, 428, 429, 443, 464
Lone Rider, The, 31
"Lone Rider" series, 186–88
Lone Rider Fights Back, The, 187
Lone Rider Rides On, The, 187, 355
Lone Star Law Men, 453
Lone Star Raiders, 179
Lone Star Ranger (1930), 79, 80, 235, 387, 393
Lone Star Ranger (1942), 235, 393, 395
"Lone Star" series, 69
Lone Star Trail, The, 258
"Lone Star Trail," 332
Lone Texas Ranger, The, 230
Lone Trail, The, 58
"Lonely River," 346
Long, Jimmy, 338
Long, Long Trailer, The, 435
Long, Walter, 94
Longenecker, Bert, 145
Longhorn, The, 231
Lord, Marjorie, *233*
Lorre, Peter, 485
Lost Canyon, 110
Lost Patrol, The, 95
"Love Sends a Little Gift of Roses," 364
"Love Song of the Waterfall," 334, 379
Lovering, Otho, 189
Lowe, Edmund, 203
Lowery, Robert, 247, 269
Loyd, Beverly, 129
Lubin Manufacturing Company, 9, 294
Luby, S. Roy, 46, 63, 181, 182, 183, 255
Lucky Cisco Kid, 204
Lucky Larrigan, 60
Lucky Texan, The, 72, 74
Luddington, Nick, 415
Luddy, Barbara, 44
Luden, Jack, 59, 153, 154, *154*, 225, 316
Lugosi, Bela, 451
Lumberjack, 113
Lund, Lucille, *65*
Lundigan, William, 284, 485–86
Lupton, John, 279
Lure of the Wasteland, 219
Lydecker, Howard, 466
Lydecker, Theodore, 466
Lyden, Pierce, *218*
Lyles, A. C., 289
Lynn, Emmett, 95, 96, 167, 214, *218*, 264, 267, 271, 432
Lyons, Cliff, 119
Lyons, Collette, 178
Lyons, Edgar, 196

MacArthur, Charles, 26
MacBurnie, John, 211
MacDonald, Edmund, 205

MacDonald, J. Farrell, 79, *80*, 196, *283*, *392*, 392
MacDonald, Jeanette, 137
MacDonald, Kenneth, 63, 161, 163, 167, 398
MacDonald, Wallace, *23*, 299
MacDonald, William Colt, 49, 173, 385
Mace, Wynn, *327*
MacFadden, Hamilton, 28, 81, 82
MacGowan, Kenneth, 203
Mack, Betty, 49
Mack, Cactus, 75, 326
Mack, Helen, 24
Mack Sennett Studio, *415*
Mack, William, 95
MacKenna of the Mounted, 33
MacLane, Barton, 217, 390
MacRae, Henry, 29, 37
Madison, Guy, 273, 274
Magnificent Ambersons, The, 97
Mahoney, Jock, 193, 275, 284, *496*. See also Jacques O'Mahoney
Main, Marjorie, 127
Main Street before Dark, 485
"Main Title #3," 445
Majestic Pictures, 62, 105, 364, 499
Malcolm Brown Pictures, Inc., 411
Mallory, Boots, 173
Malone, Bill, 335
Maloney, Leo, 7, 12–13, *13*, 53, 293, 295, *307*, 322
Malvern, Paul, 69, 72, 73, 106
Mama Runs Wild, 357
Mamoulian, Rouben, 206
Man from Death Valley, The, 49, *49*
Man from Guntown, The, 39
Man from Hell's Edges, 45
Man from Montana, 403
Man from Monterey, The, 72
Man from Music Mountain, The (1938), 129, 414
Man from Music Mountain, The (1943), 129, 400
Man from Painted Post, The, 299
Man from Rainbow Valley, 219
Man from Sundown, The, 163
Man from Tascosa, The, 476
Man from Texas, The, 143
Man from Thunder River, The, 229, *229*
Man from Tumbleweeds, The, 227
Man from Utah, The, 74
Man of Action, 39
Man of the Forest, The, 384, 389, *389*, 390
Man Who Won, The, 300, 332
Man with the Steel Whip, 207
Manhattan Melodrama, 284
Manhattan Moon, 357
Manning, Hope, 120
Mannors, Sheila, 138, *345*
Mapes, Ted, 170, *220*, 241
Maphis, Joe, 493
Maphis, Rose Lee, 493
Marcus, Lee, 417
Marijuana, 451
Marin, Edwin L., 216
Marion, Beth, 316

INDEX

Maris, Mona, 32
Mark of Zorro, The, 206, 299, 432
Marked for Murder, 238
Marked Men, 186
Marked Trails, 250–51
Markowski, Vincent, 408. See also Tom Tyler
Marksman, The, 270
Marsh, Mae, 484
Marsh, Marian, 487
Marshal of Amarillo, 219
Marshal of Cripple Creek, 217
Marshal of Gunsmoke, 144, 459
Marshal of Heldorado, 269
Marshal of Mesa City, 86
Marshal of Money Mint, 473
Marshal of Reno, 230
Marshal's Daughter, The, 494
Marshall, Anthony, 183
Marshall, George, 51, 295, *324*
Marta, Jack, 76, 129, 133, 211
Martel, June, 123
Martin, Chris-Pin, 204, 205, 206, *207*, 284
Martin, Dean, 428
Martin, John, 273
Martin, Richard, 99, 101, *101*, 103, *103*, 206, 289, 393, *393*, 395
Martin, Scoop, 326
Martinelli, Tony, 133
Marvin, Frank, 118, *119*, 336–37, 338, 340, *353*, 360, 373
Marvin, Johnny, 336, 337, 338, 339
Mascot Pictures, 21, 25, 29, 45, 48, 58, 61, 70, 72, 117, 131, 166, 167, 254, 314, 315, 333, 368, 469
Masked Rider, The, 258
Mason, LeRoy (Roy), *84*, 146, 157, 196, 286, *351*, 432
Masquers Club, 476
Massey, Raymond, 486
Mattea, Kathy, 492
Mattox, Walt, 251, 268
Maverick, The, 232
Mayer, Ray, 173
Maynard, Ken, 12, *14*, 15, 17–18, *18*, 19, 20, 21–27, *23*, *25*, 26, 29, 34, 35, 39, 40, 45, 54, 57, 58, 70, 79, 117, 118, 137, 153, 158, 193, 225, 244, 248, 249, *249*, 250, *250*, 251, *251*, 293, 300, *302*, 306, *306*, 316, 326, *332*, 332–33, 340, 342, 350, 368, 371, *398*, 401, 403, 409, 437, 454, 469, 473, 478, 484, 486, 497, 505
Maynard, Kermit, 24, 135, 177, 178, 195, *195*, *196*, 197, 217, 237, *238*, 256, 484, 486
Mayo, Frank, 22
McCarey, Ray, 21
McCarroll, Frank, *256*
McCarthy, J. P., 44, 45, 49, 60, 61, 62, 141, 205, 250, 251
McCarthy, Kevin, 429
McClintock, Harry, 373
McConville, Bernard, 417
McCord, Ted, 18, 23, 24, 35, 92
McCoy, Tim, 4, 12, 17, 20, 22, 24, 30, 31, 34, 37–41, *38*, *39*, 40, 41, 50, 59, 70, 95, 153, 158, 166, 191, 193, 245, 246, *246*, 247, *247*, 248, *248*, 278, 279, 306, *306*, 309, 315, 401, 409, *410*, 411, *412*, *416*, 473, 481, 482, 484, *485*
McCulley, Johnston, 46, 112, 203, 209
McDoakes, Joe, 476
McDonald, Francis, *44*, 95, 103, 194, 219, 267
McDonald, Frank 102, 125, 130, 131, 138, 199, 201, 273, 485
McGann, William, 476
McGlynn, Frank, Jr., 76, 82, *106*, 428
McGowan, Dorrell, 231
McGowan, J. P., 24, 44, 49, 53, 58, 72, 123, 146, 231
McGowan, Robert, 21
McGowan, Stuart, 231
McGraw, Charles, 133
McGuire, John, 133
McHugh, Frank, 72
McIntyre, Christine, 247, 261
McKay, Wanda, 237
McKee, Lafe, 22, 23, *140*
McKenzie, Fay, 26, *458*, 459, 473
McLaglen, Victor, 82, 432
McMasters, Jimmy, *378*
McQuarrie, Murdock, 247
McTaggart, Bud, 190
"Mechanical Montage," 444
Medico of Painted Springs, 164
Meet Roy Rogers, 479
Meet the Stars, 479
Mehaffey, Blanche, 194
Meins, Gus, 146
Melford, George, 20, 39, 160
Melody Lingers On, The, 355
Melody of the Plains, 140
Melody Ranch, 126, 373
"Melody Ranch," 362, 373, 494, 496
"Melody Ranch Theatre," 491
Melody Trail, 119, 345
Melton, Frank, 176
Men Are Like That, 70
Men of Texas, 403
Men of the Plains, 59
Men With Steel Faces, 126
Men Without Law, 31, 32
Mercer, Johnny, 122, 494
Mercury Pictures, 315, 352, 364, 365, 367
Mercury Records, 499
Meredith, Iris, *160*, 161, 162, *163*, 164, *164*, 227, *228*, *255*, 256, 398, *450*, 451, 451–52
Merrick, George, 58
Merrick, Lynn, 452–53, *453*
Mersch, Mary, *386*
Merton, John, *40*, 183, *196*, 197, 255, 286, *465*
Mesquite Buckaroo, 47
Messinger, Gertrude, *61*
Metro, 284
Metropolitan Pictures, 46, 47
Mexicali Kid, The, 154
Mexicali Rose, 123, 450
"Mexicali Rose," 348, 487
Meyer, Abe, 442, 444

Meyer Synchronizing Service, Ltd., 442, 444
MGM, 4, 22, 35, 37, 137, 148, 178, 254, 275, 284, 306, 311, 365, 404, 472
Middleton, Charles, 82–83, *106*, 161
Middleton, Wallace, 483
Miles, Betty, *249*, 285, 453
Milestone, Lewis, 47, 108
Miljan, John, 417
Miller, Ann, 126
Miller, Baldy, 326
Miller, "Bear Valley Charlie," 327
Miller Brothers 101 Ranch Show, 294, 295, 301, 324
Miller, Ernest, 20, 211
Miller, F. E., 153
Miller, Virgil, 147
Miller, Walter, 24, *25*, 468
Miller, Winston, 164, 195
Millican, James, 284
Mills Brothers, 167
Milner, Victor, *296*, *301*
Milton, George, 190, 191
Mine with the Iron Door, The, 385, 386
Miracle Rider, The, 29, *29*, 468, 469
Miss Pinkerton, 450
"Mississippi River Blues," 339
Mitchell, Frank, 228, 257
Mitchum, Robert, 97–98, 98–99, *99*, 100, *111*, 113, 215, 258, *258*, 393, *393*, 428
Mix, Art, *See also* George Kesterson, 64, 161, 162, 173, 188, 309, 326
Mix, Ruth, 15, 60, 285
Mix, Tom, 3, *8*, 10–12, 15, 17, 20, 27–29, *27*, 28, *29*, 31, 40, 58, 64, 80, 81, 82, 91, 166, 193, 235, 294–95, 298, 298–99, 299–300, 306, 307, 309, *320*, 323, 324, *325*, *325*, 326, 327, 386, 387, 403, 408, 411, 429, 432, 437, 454, *468*, 469, 471, 478, 479
"Modern Cinderella," 363
Mojave Firebrand, 229
Molly Cures a Cowboy, 474
Mollycoddle, The, 299
Monarch, 49
Monkey Business, 454
Monkey Madness, 317
Monogram, 40, 41, 45, 46, 48, 53, 59, 60, 69, 72, 74, 75, 76, 94, 95, 117, 142, 144, 145, 146, 148, 154, 155, 166, 181, 182, 194, 197, 198, 200, 201, 205, 231, 232, 240, 241, 242, 245, 248, 250, 253, 255, 258, 259, 260, 261, 267, 270, 273, 275, 311, 342, 347, 350, 358, 362, 364, 399, 401–3, 411, 473, 494
Montana, Monte, 151, 401
Montana Moon, 405
Montez, Maria, 258
Montgomery, "Baby Peggy," (Diana Sera Carey), 326
Montgomery, George, 57, 191, 204, 235, *238*, *353*, 393, 403. See also George Letz
Montgomery, Jack, 326

Monument Records, 498
Moon Rider, The, 303
Moonlight on the Prairie, 138, 344, 345, *345,* 404
Moore, Clayton, 103, 207, *271,* 274, 284, 427, 429, 435
Moore, Constance, 147
Moore, Dennis, 144, 182, 187, 188, *188,* 240, 241, 242, 247, 267, 268, 473, 476
Moore, Grace, 39, 153
Moore, Pauline, 127, 217, 257
Moran, Peggy, 257
Moran, Polly, 177
Moreland, Mantan, 153
Moreno, Antonio, 80
Morgan, Dennis, 87, 476
Morgan, George, 32
Morgan, William, 126, 127
Morgan's Last Raid, 410
Morison, Patricia, 205, 284
Morris, Adrian, 173
Morris, Chester, 485
Morris, Stephen, 109
Morris, Wayne, 138, 270, 284, 368
Morrison, Chuck, *62, 318*
Morrison, Jim, 294
Morrison, Marion, See also John Wayne, 326
Morrison, Pete, 53, 294, 300, 301, 305, 323
Morse, T. O., 209
Morton, Arthur, 85
Motion Picture Almanac, 505
Motion Picture Herald, 505, 506, 507
Mountain Justice, 19
Mountain Rhythm, 121, 123
Mounted Fury, 194
Movitone Music Corporation, 442
Mowbray, Alan, 206, 482
Mule Train, 131
Mulford, Clarence, 8, 105, 314, 385, 386
Mulhall, Jack, 200, 486
Mummy, The, 435
Mummy's Hand, The, 51
Murder on the Yukon, 199
Muriettak, Joaquin, 32
Murnau, F. W., 79
Murphy, Audie, 386, 432, 435
Murphy, Horace, 141, *256, 351*
Murray, "Dutchman," 323
Murray, James, 194
Murray, Zon, 286
Musuraca, Nick, 70, 97, 101
"My Alabama Home," 338
"My Blue Heaven," 148, 357
My Darling Clementine, 83
"My Dreaming of You," 338
"My Life East and West," 295
"My Little Buckaroo," 139
My Pal Ringeye, 479
My Pal, the King, 27, 28, 478
My Pal Trigger, 130–31, *131,* 366
Mysterious Avenger, 159, 160
"Mysterious Dr. Satan Main Title," 445
Mysterious Rider (1933), 389
Mysterious Rider (1942), 190

Mysterious Rider, The (1938), 283, 390, 405
"Mystery at Spanish Hacienda," 215
Mystery Man, 113
Mystery Mountain, 25, 117, 413, 432, 469, 484
Mystery of the Hooded Horseman, The, 136, 141
Mystery Ranch (1933), 63, 385
Mystery Ranch (1934), 83
Myton, Fred, 34, 153, 214, 417

Nabors, Jim, 495
Naish, J. Carrol, 39, 390, *391*
Nallie, Luther, 383
Narrow Trail, The, 297
Nashville Girl, 373
Nashville Rebel, 373
National Barn Dance, 338, 349, 350, 363, 367, 373
National Screen Service, 442
Natteford, Jack, 20, 174, 315
Nawahi, Bennie, 376
Nazarro, Cliff, 140, 242, 284
Nazarro, Ray, 168, 170
NBC, 115, 277, 279, 492
"Ne-Ha-Nee," 382
Neal, Frances, 92, 96
Neal, Tom, 201, 267, 269
Near the Rainbow's End, 44
Near Trail's End, 44
'Neath Arizona Skies, 319
'Neath Canadian Skies, 200
Negulesco, Jean, 240, 476
Neill, Noel, 267, 270
Neill, Roy William, 32
Neitz, Alvin J., See also Allan James, 23, 57, 58
Nelson, Bobby, 59, 91
Nelson, Jack, 60
Nelson, Sam, 97, 161, 163, 164, 195, 225, 226, 227, 228
Neufeld, Sigmund, 153, 191, 235, 317, 417
Neufeld, Stan, 317
Neumann, Harry, 18, 20, 259
Neumann, Kurt, 28, 36
Nevada (1936), 189, 390, *391,* 405
Nevada (1944), 97–99, 393, *393*
Nevada Badmen, 269
New Frontier (1935), 76
New Frontier (1939), 178, *396*
New Moon, 355
New York Motion Picture Corporation, 294, 295, 301
Newfield, Sam, 26, 39, 40, 41, 46, 47, 140, 148, 153, 160, 175, 185, 186, 188, 189, 190, 191, 196, 198, 235, 237, 255, 284, 317, 417. See also Sherman Scott
Newill, James, 144, 157, 197, *198,* 199, 235, 237, 238, 359–60, 438
Newman, Joe, 284
Newmeyer, Fred, 140
Nibley, Sloan, 133
Niblo, Fred, 206
Nichols, Bill "Slumber," 375–76
Nichols, Dudley, 95
Nigh, William, 22, 61, 205

"Night Horseman, The," 386
Night Horsemen, The, 299
"Night Miss Nancy Ann's Motel For Single Girls Burned Down, The," 498
"Night on the Desert," 334
Night on the Range, A, 473
Night Riders, The, 177–78
Night Train to Memphis, 373
Nightclass, 61
Nine Girls, 453
Nixon, Marion, *301*
Nobles, William, 121, 174, 211
"Nobody's Darling," 348
"Nobody's Darling But Mine," 359
Nolan, Bob, 118, 120, 161, 162, 163, *164,* 219, 334, 350, 355, 357, *374, 375,* 376, 377, *377,* 378, 379, 380, 381, 382
Nolan, Lloyd, 284
Norris, Edward, 61, 200
North from the Lone Star, 228
North of the Border, 200, *201*
North of the Rio Grande, 109–10
North of the Rockies, 228
North of the Yukon, 195
Northern Frontier, 195–96, *196*
Northern Patrol, 199, 201
Northwest Mounted Police, 193
Northwest Rangers, 284
Northwest Territory, 201
Northwest Trail, 193
Nosler, Lloyd, 49, 93
Nothing Sacred, 453
Novak, Eva, 486
Nowlin, Herman, *327*

O'Brian, Hugh, 222
O'Brien, Billy, 74
O'Brien, Dave, 144, 157, 190, 198, *198,* 199, 235, 237, *238, 238,* 248, 285
O'Brien, George, 31, 64, 78, 79–89, *80, 81, 82, 84, 85, 86, 87, 88, 89,* 91, 92, 95, 102, 146, 235, 293, 295, 298, 315, 325, 386, 387, 388, 400, 403, 413, 417, 422, 425, 453, 473, 474, 478
O'Connell, L. W., 193
O'Connor, Donald, 37
O'Day, Nell, 257, 285
O'Donnell, Joseph, 187, 191
O'Driscoll, Martha, 95, 97
O'Flynn, Damian, 220
O'Hara, Maureen, 435
O'Hearn, Eileen, 164, 165
O'Mahoney, Jacques, 170, 171. See also Jock Mahoney
O'Malley of the Mounted, 80
O'Neal, Anne, 113–14
O'Sullivan, Maureen, 83, 388
O-Bar-O Cowboys, 376
Oakie, Jack, 80
Oakman, Wheeler, 37, 146, 160, 164, 196, 197, 286, 412
Of Mice and Men, 47
Official Films, 478
Oh Susannah, 339

INDEX

Okeh Record Co., 346
Oklahoma, 360
Oklahoma Badlands, 218
Oklahoma Blues, 242
Oklahoma Frontier, 148, 257, 445
Oklahoma Kid, The, 240, 404
Oklahoma Outlaws, 240
Oklahoma Raiders, 459
Oklahoma Renegades, 179
Oklahoma Riders, 144
Oklahoma Woman, 483
Old Barn Dance, The, 122, 123, 443
Old Chisholm Trail, The, 257
"Old Chisholm Trail, The," 333
Old Corral, The, 64, 120, *120*
Old Homestead, The, 345, 355
Old Louisiana, 417
Old Mexico, 110
Old Oklahoma Plains, 222
Old Oregon Trail, The, 310, 311
"Old Spinning Wheel, The," 334
Old Texas Trail, The, 240
Old West, The, 132
Old Wyoming Trail, The, 161, 350, 354, 430
"On the Banks of the Sunny San Juan," 251, 364, 497
On the Old Spanish Trail, 133
"One Has My Name (the Other Has My Heart)," 362, 364, 494, 497
One Man Justice, 161
"Open Range Ahead," 379
Oregon Trail, The, 76, 216, 256
"Oregon Trail, The," 334
Orion Pictures, 317
Orlebeck, Lester, *4*, 179, 180
Ormand, Ron, 266, 267, 269
Osborne, Bud, *144*, 241, 268, 270, 324, 482
Our Daily Bread, 93
Our Gang, 476
Out California Way, 219, 366
Outlaw Country, 267
Outlaw Deputy, The, 39
Outlaw Express, 351, 445
Outlaw Tamer, 58
Outlaw Trail, 250
Outlaw Treasure, 270
Outlaws of Boulder Pass, 187, 355, 356
Outlaws of Pine Ridge, 214, 453
Outlaws of Sonora, 401, 443
Outlaws of Stampede Pass, 259
Outlaws of Texas, 268
Outlaws of the Desert, 113, 428, 435
Outlaws of the Panhandle, 164, 357
Outlaws of the Prairie, 161
Outlaws of the Rockies, 168
Outlaws of the Sonora, 176
Outpost of the Mounties, 195, 379
Over the Santa Fe Trail, 242–43
"Over the Santa Fe Trail," 375
Overland Bound, 7, 13, *13*, 53, 56, 79, 293
Overland Express, The, 36
Overland Stage Raiders, 177
Overland Stagecoach, 187–88, *188*
Overland To Deadwood, 166

Overland with Kit Carson, 226, 466–67
Owen, Reginald, 83
Owen, Virginia, 102
Ox Bow Incident, The, 432

Padjeon, Jack, 12
Pagano, Jo, 113
Page, Bradley, 95
Page, Dorothy, 284–85, 357
Paid to Love, 79
Paige, Robert, 161
Painted Desert, 105
Painted Stallion, The, 21, 216, 443, 447, 460, *463*, 464
Painted Trail, The, 94–95
Palm Springs, 146, 349
Pals of the Golden West, 135, 368, 491
Pals of the Pecos, 4
Pals of the Saddle, 177
Panamint's Bad Man, 146, 349
Paramount, 13, 36, 58, 70, 76, 77, 86, 94, 105, 107, 108, 110, 113, 122, 146, 153, 189, 190, 196, 240, 254, 256, 281–82, 283, 289, 312–14, 387, 389, 393, 404–5, 407, 408, 415, 416
Pardon My Gun, 476
Park Avenue Logger, 315
Parker, Cecilia, 24, 71, 73, 82, 83, 85, 146, 285, 453, 487
Parker, Ed, 211
Parker, Fess, 279
Parker, Jean, 392
Parker, Norton S., 110, 112, 127, 147
Parker, Tom, 364
Parker, Willard, 275
Parks, Larry, 228
Paroled to Die, 46
Parrish, Helen, 200
Parsons, Harriet, 479
Parsons, Lindsley, 69, *142*, 200, 201, 270, 311, *313*, 327
Partners, 91
Partners of the Plains, 110
Partners of the Trail (1931), 49, *50*
Partners of the Trail (1944), 259
"Pastoral," 445
Pathe, 43, 91, 105, 139, 311, 345
Paton, Stuart, 58, 194
Patrick, Dorothy, 103
Patrick, Gail, 390
Patten, Bill, 326
Patterson, John, 77
Paul, Les, 495
Pawley, William, 163, 199
Pawnee Bill, 294, 328
Peck, Gregory, 435
Peckinpah, Sam, 157, 277
Pecos Kid, The, 64
Pelletier, Gilles, 277
Pembroke, Scott, 76
Pendleton, Nat, 23
Perez, Paul, 161
Perils of Nyoka, The, 432, 464
Perils of the Royal Mounted, 193
Perkins, John, 277
Perkins, Kenneth, 70, 270

Perrin, Jack, 12, 53–56, *54*, 57, *63*, 153, 301, *304*, 318, 409, 473, *473*, 483
Perry, Harvey, 241
Perry, Joan, 160
Perryman, Lloyd, *374*, 380, 382, 383, *383*
Peter B. Kyne Productions, 159
Peterson, Gus, 142
Phantom Cowboy, The (1935), 60
Phantom Cowboy, The (1941), 213
Phantom Empire, 117, 125–26, 427
Phantom Gold, 154
Phantom Horseman, The, 303
Phantom of the Desert, 53
Phantom of the Plains, 231, 431
Phantom of the West, 48
Phantom Patrol, 197
Phantom Plainsmen, 180
Phantom Ranger, 40
Phantom Stallion, The, 222, 368
Phantom Valley, 168
Pickens, Slim, 222, *222*, 223
Picker, Sidney, 217
Pickford, Mary, 296
Pidgeon, Walter, 127
Piel, Ed, 73, 152
Pierce, Webb, 368
Pierson, Carl, 76
Pillow, Bob, 321, 329
Pine-Thomas, 190, 191
Pinto Canyon, 47
Pioneer Justice, 266
Pioneer Marshal, 220
Pioneer Trail, 154
Pioneer Trio, 355, 375, 377. *See also* Sons of the Pioneers
Pioneers of the Frontier, 227
Pioneers of the West, 179
Pioneers, The, 143, 312, 358
Pirates on Horseback, 109, 112, 435
Pirates on the Prairie, 97
Pistol Packin' Nitwits, 476
Pizor, Irwin, 312
Pizor, William, *310*, 312
Plainsman, The, 109
Planet Films, 241
Poland, Joseph, 232, 261
Pollard, Snub, 141
Pony Express Days, 476
Porter, Cole, 129
Porter, Edwin S., 8, 9
Porter, William Sydney, 203
Post, Charles A., 49
Powder River, 83
Powder River Rustlers, 219
Powdersmoke Range, 20, 49, 50, 62, 95, 173, 173–74, *174*
Powell, Lee, 57, 148, 152, *152*, 186, 187, *187*, 235, 237, *237*, 359, 497
Powell, William, 284
Power, Tyrone, 206, 435, 437
Powers, Richard. *See* Tom Keene
Prairie Gunsmoke, 228
"Prairie Is My Home, The," 105, 476, 487
Prairie Justice, 454
Prairie Law, 86
Prairie Outlaws, 265

551

HOLLYWOOD CORRAL: A COMPREHENSIVE B WESTERN ROUNDUP

Prairie Pals, 237
Prairie Poppas, 474
Prairie Roundup, 170
Prairie Rustlers, 190, 417
Prairie Schooners, 227–28
Prairie Stranger, 165
Presidio Pictures, 13
Presley, Elvis, 484
Preston, John, 197
Preston, Robert, 435
Price, Hal, *41,* 46, 241
Price, Stanley, 188, 268
Pride of the Plains, 215
Pride of the West, 110, 314, 435
Prima, Louis, 123
Principal Company, 146, 153
"Prisoner for Life," 332
"Prisoner's Song, The," 337
Producers Distributing Corporation, 40
Producers Releasing Corporation (PRC), 41, 47, 48, 91, 140, 144, 153, 157, 185, 186, 187, 188, 190, 191, 197, 199, 215, 219, 235, 238, 245, 263, 265, 279, 317, 347, 355, 364, 373, 403, 445, 451, 507
Prosser, Hugh, *241*
Pryor, Roger, 205
Public Cowboy No. 1, 335
Puglia, Frank, 124
Puritan Pictures, 39, 40, 159, 245
Purple Vigilantes, The, 176, 443
"Put Me To Bed," 494
Pyle, Denver, 103
Pyle, Ernie, 100

Quillan, Marie, 92
Quinn, Anthony, 430

"R.C.M.P.," 277
Raboch, Al, 35
Rachmil, Lewis J., 113
Racketeers of the Range, 85, 399, 444
Radford, Rad, *392*
Rafferty, Chito, 99, 100, *103*
Ragtime Cowboy Joe, 452
Raiders of Sunset Pass, 215
Raiders of the Range, 463
Raiders of the South, 260–61
Rainbow Over the Range, 454
Rainbow Ranch, 60
Rainbow Riders, 473
Rainbow Trail, The, 81, 82, 298, 299, 388, 453
Rainbow's End, 20
Raine, William McLeod, 8
Raksin, David, 445
Raison, Milton, 190, 222
Ralston, Esther, 390, 405
"Ranch Party," 493
Randall, Bob, 317
Randall, Jack, 3, 137, 142, *145,* 145–46, 154, 155, *155,* 285, 344, 350, 351, 402, 431, 450, 452
Randell, Ron, 485
Randy Rides Alone, 69
"Range Busters" series, 181–83
Range Feud, 70
Range Law, 22

"Range Rider, The," 275, 432, 491
Range War, 437
Rangers' Roundup, 140
Rangers Take Over, The, 237, 359
Rangle River, 284
Ranown Productions, 283
Rathbone, Basil, 486
Rathmell, John, 181
Rawhide, 146, 349, *349,* 437
Rawlins, John, 102
Rawlins, Monte, 149
Rawlinson, Herbert, *111,* 127, 217, 300
Ray, Albert, 255, 256
Ray, Allene, 53
Ray, Bernard B., 46, 50, 54, 58, 284, 442, 473
Rayart, 195, 306
Raye, Martha, 123
RCA Victor, 359, 382, 492, 499
Reaching for the Moon, 450
Real Glory, The, 432
Real Thing In Cowboys, The, 295
Realart, 267
"Reb and His Horse Rebel," 484
Rebel City, 232, 233
Reckless Ranger, 153
"Recreation of Brian Kent, The," 386
Red Blood of Courage, 195, 196
Red Desert, 269
Red Hair, 484
Red Raiders, The, 22, 409
Red Rider, The, 37
Red River, 3
Red River Dave, 270, 367, 476, 489
Red River Range, 177
Red River Robin Hood, 97
Red River Valley (1941), 127, 357, 381
Red Rope, The, 46
"Red Ryder" series, 212, 229–31, 267
Red Seal, 370
Redskins and Redheads, 367
Reed, Arthur, 22, 191, 197
Reed, Donna, 284
Reed, Marshall, 241, 261
Reed, Walter, 103
Reeves, Bob, 306
Reeves, Del, 373
Reeves, George, *111,* 113, 476
Regas, George, *195*
Reid, Carl Benton, 486
Reid, Wallace, 294
Reliable Pictures, 46, 50, 58, 473, 484
Renaldo, Duncan, 61, 178, 179, *179,* 180, *202,* 205, 206, *206,* 209, 217, *277,* 279, 428, 465, 466, *466,* 481, *516*
Renegade Ranger, The, 86, 87, 89, 92, 400, 444
Renegade Trail, 112
Renegades of the Rio Grande, 459
Renegades of the West, 92, 93
"Renfrew of the Royal Mounted" series, 197, 205, 359
Repp, Ed Earl, 171
Republic, 21, 43, 45, 46, 57, 75, 76, 77, 85, 86, 95, 98, 117, 118, 119, 120, 121, 122, 123, 124, 125, 127, 128, 129, 130, 131, 132, 135, 137, 148, 152, 153, 166, 173, 174, 175, 176, 177, 178, 179, 181, 186, 187, 188, 191, 193, 194, 203, 206, 207, 211, 213, 214, 215, 216, 217, 219, 220, 222, 223, 225, 229, 230, 231, 240, 245, 253, 255, 261, 263, 268, 274, 279, 285, 289, 311, 314, 315, 316–17, 318, 340, 342, 348, 352–53, 353, 354, 355, 365, 371, 373, 380, 381, 382, 399–401, 411, 413, 414, 443, 444, 446, 447, 464, 466, 473, 479, 492, 499, 507
Requiem for a Gunfighter, 481, 483, 484, 485
Resolute, 60
Return of Daniel Boone, The, 228
Return of Draw Egan, The, 403
Return of the Cisco Kid, The, 204
Return of the Durango Kid, The, 168
Return of Wild Bill, The, 226, 227, 450, *450,* 451
Return of Wildfire, The, 284
Revenge Rider, The, 39
Revier, Dorothy, 32
Reynolds, Craig, 99
Reynolds, Don Kay, 267, *268*
Reynolds, Lynn, 11–12
Reynolds, Marjorie, 86, 88, 127, *142*
Rhinehart, Dick, 362
Rhodes, Jane, 190
Rhythm of the Rio Grande, 143
Rhythm on the Range, 122
Rhythm Rangers, 476
Rice, Frank, 289
Richards, Addison, *95,* 138
Richards, Rusty, 383
Richmond, Kane, 204, 464, 466
Richmond, Warner, 145, *145,* 256, 286
Rickson, Joe, *307, 322, 323, 324*
Riddle Gawne, 296
Riddle Ranch, 64
Ride, Cowboy, Ride, 476
Ride 'Em Cowboy (1932), 70, 454
Ride 'Em Cowboy (1936), 35, 450
Ride 'Em Cowboy (1942), 139, 432
Ride 'Em Cowgirl, 285, 357
Ride, Ranger, Ride, 342
Ride, Ryder, Ride, 267
"Ride, Vaqueros, Ride," 428
Rider from Nowhere, 473
Rider of Death Valley, 28, *28,* 37
Riders from Nowhere, 155
Riders in the Dawn, 350
Riders in the Sky, 131–32, *132*
Riders of Death Valley, 428, 437, 467, *467*
Riders of Destiny, 71, 73, 342, 453
Riders of Pecos Basin, 403
Riders of the Badlands, 165, *165*
Riders of the Black Hills, 176
Riders of the Cactus, 55
Riders of the Dawn (1937), 145, 145–46, 402, 431
Riders of the Deadline, 111, 113
Riders of the Desert, 45
Riders of the Frontier, 143

INDEX

Riders of the Golden Gulch, 64
Riders of the Hills, 176
Riders of the Northland, 166
Riders of the Northwest Mounted, 200
Riders of the Pony Express, 243
Riders of the Purple Sage (1918), 297–98, *386*
Riders of the Purple Sage (1925), *438*
Riders of the Purple Sage (1931), 78, 81, *235*, *236*, 388, 392
Riders of the Purple Sage (1941), 235, 236, 392, 403
Riders of the Purple Sage (book), 331, 387
"Riders of the Purple Sage" Foy Willing (singing group), 135, *367*
Riders of the Range, 103, *103*
Riders of the Rio, 58
Riders of the Rio Grande, 181
Riders of the Rockies, 141, 452
Riders of the Santa Fe, 459
Riders of the Timberline, 113
Riders of the West, 247
Ridges, Stanley, 110
"Ridin' Down the Canyon," 118
Ridin' Law, 53
Ridin' the Cherokee Trail, 453
Ridin' the Trail, 140
Ridin' West, 358
Riding Actors Association of Hollywood, 326
Riding Avenger, The, 21
Riding the California Trail, 205
Riding the Sunset Trail, 453
Riding Tornado, The, 37
Riesenfeld, Hugo, 85, 442
Rim of the Canyon, 131
Rimfire, 284
"Rin Tin Tin," 433
Rio Grande (1938), 162
Rio Grande (1949), 268
Rio Grande Raiders, 216
Ripcord, 365
Ritter, Dorothy, 311–12
Ritter, Tex, 3, 40, 64, 95, 118, 137, *136*, 141–45, *142*, *143*, *144*, 155, 167, 228, *228*, 235, 238, *238*, 240, 258, *258*, 261, 311, *312*, 344, 346–48, *348*, 354, 357, 358, *358*, 359, 360, 362, 368, 371, 402, 432, 454, *455*, 476, 489, *493*, 493–94, *495*, *496*, *497*, *498*, *499*
Rivero, Julian, 152
Rivkin, Joe, 483
RKO, 20, 43, 44, 48, 49, 50, 61, 64, 79, 83, 85, 86, 87, 89, 91, 92, 93, 95, 97, 98, 99, 100, 101, 118, 145, 173, 174, 240, 281, 289, 315, 346, 350, 359, 393, 395, 399, 408, 413, 428, 443, 472
Roach, Hal, 113, 472
Road Agent, 139
Roarin' Guns, 39
Roarin' Lead, 175, 317
Roarin' Ranch, 19
Roaring Guns, 240
Roaring Rangers, 168
Roaring Timbers, 398, 404

Robbers Roost, 83, 388
Robbins, Marty, 373
Robbins, "Skeeter" Bill, 20
Roberts, Bob, 64
Roberts, Jerry, 446
Roberts, Lee, 261, 268
Roberts, Lynn, 124, 201, 205, 236, *428*, *458*, 459
Robertson, Willard, 82
Robertson, William, 28
Robin Hood of Monterey, 205, 207
Robin Hood of Texas, 131, 365
Robins, Sam, 190
Robinson, Casey, 92–93
Rockwell, Jack, 20, 161, 237, 469
Rocky Mountain Mystery, 282, *282*
Rocky Mountain Rangers, 432
Rocky Mountaineers, 375, 376
Rocky Rhodes, 35
Rodeo Dough, 479
Rodeo King and the Senorita, 222
Rodeo Rhythm, 140
Rodgers, Jimmie, 336, 338, 375
Rodriguez, Estelita, *370*
Rodriguez, Johnny, 373
Roemheld, Heinz, 442
Rogell, Al, 28, 161, *302*, 303, 306, 409
Rogers, Charles R., 92, 306
Rogers, Jimmy, 113
Rogers, Roy, 3, 5, *116*, 118, 120, *120*, 122, 123–24, *124*, *125*, 127–31, *128*, *129*, *130*, 132–35, *134*, *135*, 160, 176, 179, 211, 213, 217, 219, 220, 277, 317, 334, 348, 349, 350, 352, 353–55, *354*, *355*, 357, 360, 362, 365, 366, 368, *368*, *370*, 381, *381*, 382, 414, 427, 428, 430, 431, 434, 459, 474, 478, 479, 489, 491, *491*–93, 494, 495, 496, 498, 499, *504*, 507, *507*. See also Leonard Sly
Rogers, Will, 11, 62
Roland, Gilbert, 76, 205, 207, 283, 284, 390, *391*, 402, 405
Roll Along, Cowboy, 146
Roll, Thunder, Roll, 267
Rollin' Home to Texas, 476
Rollin' Plains, 142
Rollin' Westward, 454
Roman, Ruth, 251
Romance of the Rio Grande, 205
Romance of the Rockies, 93, 94
Romance of the West, 53
Romance Rides the Range, 139, 345
Romero, Cesar, 204, 205, 403, 432
"Room Full of Roses," 365
Rooney, Mickey, 28, 507
Roosevelt, Buddy, 12, 53, 64, 120, 173, 187, 306, 309
Root, Wells, 206
Rootin' Tootin' Rhythm, 121, 400
Roping a Bride, 323
Roping a Sweetheart, 323
Roscoe, Alan, 23
Rose, Fred, 336, 346
Rose, Jackson, 24
Rosen, Phil, 22, 28, 45, 95, 205, 254
Rosson, Art, 18, 19, 26, 27

"Rough Rider" series, 245–47, 402
Rough Riders of Cheyenne, 427
Rough Riders' Roundup, 124
Rough Romance, 80
Roundup Time in Texas, 430
"Roundup's Done," 332
Rouverol, Jean, 95
Rovin' Tumbleweeds, 124
Roy Knapp Juvenile Riders, 140
"Roy Rogers Show, The," 492
Royal, Charles Francis, 162, 255
Royal Mounted Patrol, The, 194, 195
Royal Mounted Rides Again, The, 193, 350
Royal West Productions, 270
Royce, Riza, 484
Rubel, James L., 164, 165
Rubin, Benny, 199
Ruffner, Robert Clyde "Kinney," *327*, *328*, 328–29
Ruggles, Wesley, 131
Ruick, Barbara, 284
Runaway Daughters, 487
Rush, Art, 492
"Rushing Riders Hurry," 444
Russell, Reb, 57, 63–64, *65*, *66*, 386
Russell, William, 12, 297, 298
Rustler's Roundup, 29
Rustler's Valley, 110
Rustlers, 102
Rustlers of Devil's Canyon, 218
Rustlers of Red Dog, 255, 468
Rutherford, Ann, 76, 119, *335*
Ryan, Joe, 295
Ryan, Sheila, 205, *395*, *457*

Saddle Buster, The, 91–92, 93
Saddle Hawk, The, 301
Saddle Leather Law, 167
Saddle Mountain Roundup, 182
Saddle Pals, 131
Saddle Serenade, 242, 362
Saddlemates, 180
Saga of Death Valley, 212, 362
Sage and Sand, 364
Sagebrush Family Trails West, The, 153
Sagebrush Law, 97
Sagebrush Politics, 64
Sagebrush Trail, 74, 427, 429
Sagebrush Troubadour, 119–20, 345
Saint Johnson, 61
Sais, Marin, 267, 301
Saland, Nat, 315
Sale, Chic, 282
Salkow, Sidney, 191
Salle, Michael, 243
Sam Fox Library, 442
Sam Fox Publishing Company, 442
Sampson, Teddy, 299
Samuels, Henri, 58
San Antonio, 50, 432
"San Antonio Rose," 358
San Fernando Valley, 129
"Sandman Lullaby, A," 382
Santa Fe Saddlemates, 216
Santa Fe Scouts, 181
Santa Fe Stampede, 172, 177, 178
"Santa Fe Trail Westerns," 240

553

HOLLYWOOD CORRAL: A COMPREHENSIVE B WESTERN ROUNDUP

Santa Fe Uprising, 217
Santell, Alfred, 203
Santley, Joseph, 126
Santschi, Tom, 79, 297
Sanucci, Frank, 147, 181, 182, 402, 445
Satan's Cradle, 206
Satherley, Art, 336, 338, 339, 352, 354, 380
Sauers, Joseph, 39. See also Joe Sawyer
Savage, Ann, 239
Sawtell, Paul, 98, 444
Sawyer, Joe, 138, 277. See also Joseph Sauers
Saylor, Syd, 141, 174, *175*, 289
Sayre, George W., 190
Scarlet River, 93
Schaefer, Armand, 29, 58, 60, 74, 118–19, 131, 254
Schlesinger, Leon, 411
Schlom, Herman, 98, 99, 101, 395
Schneiderman, George, 80, 81, 82
Scholl, Jack, 138, 139, 344
Schroeder, Doris, 106
Schroeder, Edward, 108
Scott, Ewing, 36, 85, 176, 315
Scott, Fred, 137, 139–40, *140*, 141, *141*, 185, 344, 345–46, *346*
Scott, Lester, Jr., 309
Scott, Nathan, 211
Scott, Randolph, 76, 83, 97, 170, 281–83, *282*, 283, 389, 390, 405, 435, 437
Scott, Sherman, 47, 317. See also Sam Newfield
Scotto, Aubrey, 146
Screen Gems, 275, 277
Screen Guild Productions, 200, 266, 267, 268, 284, 312
Screen Snapshots, 478–79
Screen Thrills Illustrated, 505
Searchers, The, 430
Sears, Alan, 161, *162*, 286
Sears, Barbara, 240
Sears, Fred F., 170, 171, 191, 289
Seas Beneath, The, 81
Sebastian, Dorothy, *410*
Second Fiddle to an Old Guitar, 373
Secret of the Wastelands, 112–13
Secret Patrol, 161, *195*
Secret Six, The, 254
Sedgwick, Edward, 17, 30, *301*
Sedgwick, Eileen, *307*
Sedgwick, Josei, *301*
Seiler, Lewis, 83, 193
Seitz, George B., 32, 34, 70, 274–75
Selander, Les, 35, 96, 97, 102, 103, 110, 112, 113, 131, 211, 215, 217, 219, 230, 231, 274, 283, 284, *314*, 401
Selig Polyscope Company, 11, 294, 295, 298, 324
Selig, William N., 294
Sellon, Charles, 70
Selman, David, 39, 159, 161, 193
Seltzer, Charles Alden, 298
Selznick, David O., 92, 409
Semels, Harry, 44

Sennett, Mack, 10, 22, 112, 479
"Sergeant Preston of the Yukon," 277
Seward, Billie, 39
Seymour, Dan, 200
Shackleford, Robert, 264
Shadow of Chinatown, 451
Shadow of the Eagle, 469
Shadow Ranch, 31
Shadows on the Sage, 180, 359
Shaff, Monroe, 35
Shake Rattle and Rock, 481, 482
Shane, 3
Shannon, Jack, *401*
Sharpe, David, 62, 133, *135*, 155–57, 156, *158*, 164, 165, 178, 182, *183*, 211, 263, 264, 464, 466, 486
Sharpe, Roy, 323
Shasta, 362, 364, 495
Shayne, Robert, 240, 476
She Creature, The, 485, 486
Sheffield, Reginald, 49
Sheldon, Forrest, 22, 23, 58, 196
Sheldon, Kathryn, 246
Sheldon, Norman, 268
Shepard, Elaine, 197
Sheridan, Ann, 196
Sheriff of Cimarron, 215, 216
Sheriff of Las Vegas, 230, 231
Sheriff of Medicine Bow, The, 261
Sheriff of Redwood Valley, 231
Sheriff of Sage Valley, 190
Sheriff of Sundown, 217
Sheriff of Witchita, 219
Sherman, George, 123, 124, 125, 176, 177, 178, 179, 211, 213, 214, 315
Sherman, Harry, 35, 96, 101, 105, 106, 107, 108, 109, 110, 113, 206, 240, 283, 314, 390, 404, *406*, 415, 416
Sherman, Sam, 445, 512, 516
Sherry, J. Barney, 294
Shilkret, Nat, 337, 443
Shipman, Barry, 170, 171
Shoot to Kill, 451
Shooting High, 125
Shooting Star, 355
Shore, Dinah, 492
Short, Luke, 8
Showdown, The (1940), 110, 439
Showdown, The (1950), 231
Shrum, Cal, 476
Shuford, Andy, 59
Shumate, Harold, 93, 161, 281
Shumway, Walter, 326
"Sick, Sober and Sorry," 495
Sickner, William, 273
Siegel, Moe, 342
Siegel, Sol, 123, 315, 352, 354, 381
"Sierry Petes," 333
Sign of the Wolf, 58
Sign of Zorro, The, 209
Silent Conflict, 113, *115*
"Silk Stockings," 444
Silver Bandit, The, 270, 367
"Silver Bells," 362
Silver Bullet, The, 258, 459
Silver City Bonanza, 220–22
Silver City Kid, 217
Silver on the Sage, 110

Silver Spurs, 128
Silver Stallion, 155, *156*
Silver Trail, The, 58
Silver Trails, 242, 243
Silver Treasures, 431
Silverheels, Jay, 200, 274, 429
Simmons, Dick, 207, 277
Simpson, Earl, *327*
Simpson, Russell, 201, *286*, *343*
Sinatra, Frank, 364, 428
Sing Me A Song of Texas, 242
Singer Jim McKee, 297
Singin' Sandy, 73, *342*
Singing Buckaroo, The, 141
Singing Cowboy, The, 120, 345
Singing Cowgirl, The, 285, 357
Singing Dude, The, 476
Singing Vagabond, The, 342
Single-Handed Sanders, 49
Sioux City Sue, 131, 365, 428
Six Feet Four, 298
Six Gun Rhythm, 357
Six Shootin' Sheriff, 26
Six-Gun Gold, 96, 98
Six-Gun Gospel, 259
Six-Gun Rhythm, 148, *149*, 279, 357
Six-Gun Trail, 40
Sky Bandits, 199
Sky High, 166, 299
"Sky King," 275
Sleeper, Martha, 96
"Slipping Around," 362, 494
Sly, Leonard, 334, 375, 376–77, *377*, 379, 380–81. See also Roy Rogers
Small, Edward, 191
Small, Louise, *140*
Smith, Carl, 368
Smith, Cliff, 10, 64, 256, 326
Smith, H. Allen, 127
Smith, Noel, 138
Smith, Pete, 157
Smith, Raymond "Colorado Cotton," 327, *327*
Smith, Tom, 321, *322*
Smith, Tucson, 49, 173
Smoke Lightning, 388
"Smoke! Smoke! Smoke!", 367, 498
Smoking Guns, 24
Smoky Canyon, 171
Snell, Earle, 22, 217, 231
Snow Dog, 201
Snow White and the Seven Dwarfs, 373
So You Want to Be a Cowboy, 476
Somewhere in Sonora, 72
Son of a Badman, 267
Son of Davy Crockett, The, 228
Son of Oklahoma, 45
Son of Paleface, 135
Son of Roaring Dan, 257
Son of the Border, 93
Son of the Renegade, 270
Son of Zorro, 207
Sondergaard, Gale, 206
Song of Old Wyoming, 263
"Song of the Bandit," 334
Song of the Buckaroo, 142–43
Song of the Caballero, 19
Song of the Gringo, 141, 347

INDEX

"Song of the Prairie," 334
Song of the Range, 241, 362
Song of the Saddle, 138
Song of the Sierras, 362
Song of the Trail, 196, 197
Song of the Wasteland, 363
Songs and Bullets, 346, 357
Songs and Saddles, 148
Songs of the Cowboys, 331
"Sonny Boy," 337
Sonora Stagecoach, 250, 453
Sons of the Pioneers, 3, 118, 120, 122, 123, 127, 135, 138, 160, 161, 162, 163, 164, 219, 243, 277, 334, 345, 350, 352, 354, *354,* 355, 357, 360, 365, 371, 374, 375–83, 378, 379, 380, 381, 382, 383, 495
Sons of the Saddle, 19
Sooter, Rudy, 377
South of Arizona, 162
South of Monterey, 205
South of Santa Fe, 45
South of the Border, 125, *126,* 434, 516
"South of the Border," 372
South of the Chisholm Trail, 168
South of the Rio Grande, 32, 205
Southern, Hal, 497
Sowards, George, 326
Space, Arthur, 220
Spackman, Spike, 326
Spade Cooley's Orchestra, 345
Spanish Trail, 133
Spectrum Pictures, 59, 139, 140
Speed Reporter, The, 451
Spencer, Richard, 162, 296
Spencer, Tim, 120, 162, 334, *374,* 376, 377, 378, 379, *379,* 382, *496*
Sperling, Milton, 203
Spider's Web, The, 451
Spoilers of the Range, 164
Spoilers of the West, 409
Spoilers, The, 297
Spoor, George K., 10, 294
Sprague, Carl T., 331, 375
Spriggens, Deuce, 382
Springsteen, R. G., 211, 217, 219, 220, 231
Springtime in Texas, 242
Springtime in the Rockies, 122, 443
Springtime in the Sierras, 133
"Springtime on the Range Today," 382
Spy Smasher, 464
Square Dance Jubilee, 373
Square Shooter, The, 300
"Squaw Man, The," 293, 298
St. John, Al ('Fuzzy'), 44, 48, *48,* 73, 140, 148, 173, 184, 185, 186, 187, 188, 189, 190, *190,* 191, 199, 214, 255, 265, 266, 267, 289, 317, *356,* 417, 474
Stafford, Jo, 365
Stage Door Canteen, 215
Stage & Screen Attractions, 197
Stage to Chino, 86, *89*
Stage to Mesa City, 437
Stagecoach, 3, 5, 50, 77, 89, 178, 270, 284, 430, 434, 507

Stagecoach Buckaroo, 403
Stagecoach Kid, 102
Stairs of Sand, 389
"Stairs of Sand," 390
Stallion Canyon, 243
Stampede, 160
Stan Laurel Productions, 140
Stand Up and Cheer, 344
Standard Recording Company, 378
Stanley, Forrest, 28, *28*
Stanley, Louise, 146, 199, 240, *452,* *452,* 476
Stanton, Robert, 86, 200
Star of Texas, 270
Star Packer, The, 74, 402
Starday Records, 495
Stardust on the Sage, 127
Starlight over Texas, 142
Starling, Pat, 268
Starrett, Charles, 2, 3, 96, 97, 118, 122, 158, *158,* 160, *160,* 161, *162,* 163, *163,* 164, *164,* 165, *165,* 166, 167, *167,* 168, *169,* 170, *170,* 171, *171,* 173, 194, 194–95, *195,* 216, 225, 232, 239, 253, 284, 318, 355, 357, 359, 379, 398, *399,* 431, 451, 454, 494, 495, 506, *515*
Stars over Arizona, 146, *351*
Stars Past and Present, 479
Start Cheering, 161
Staub, Ralph, 123, 199
"Stealthy Footsteps," 444
Steele, Bob, 4, *4,* 12, 17, 43–48, *44,* 46, 47, 48, 50, 51, 69, 74, 91, 127, 173, *174,* 179, 180, *180,* 186, 188, 190, 193, 216, 219, 231, 241, *250,* 250, 251, *251,* 263, 266, 269, 293, 306, *333,* 401, *433,* *452,* 464, 466, 484, 485, 486, 497
Steele, Tom, 211, 431
Steinbeck, John, 47
Steiner, William, 473
Sten, Anna, 482, 487
Stengler, Mack, 107, 113
Stepping In Society, 366
Stern, Alfred, 237
Sternberg, Joseph von, 484
"Steve Donovan, Western Marshal," 277
Stevens, George, 51
Stevens, Jean, 168
Stevens, Louis, 127
Stevens, Robert, 193
Stevens, Rose Anne, 166
Stewart, Edward White, 385
Stewart, Eleanor, *109*
Stewart, James, 386, 432
Stewart, Peggy, 129, *216,* 285, *285,* 448, 454, 463–64
Stewart, Peter, 40–41, 47, 317. *See also* Sam Newfield
Stick To Your Guns, 113, 459
Stirling, Linda, 207, 209, 216, 285
Stockman Joe, 309
Stoloff, Ben, 27
Stoloff, Morris, 445
Stone, George E., 138, *345*
Stone, Milburn, 127, 198, 201
Storey, June, *121,* 125

Storey, Tom, 64
"Stories of the Century," 279
"Stories of the West," 278
"Storm and War," 444
Storm, Gale, 127
Storm over the Andes, 481
Stormy, 64
Story of G.I. Joe, The, 100, 432
Stout, Archie, 44, 72, 73, 76, 106, 108, 109
Straight Shootin', 434
Strang, Harry, *258*
Strange, Glenn, *33, 75, 188,* 237, 248, 326
Strange, Robert, 243
Stranger from Arizona, The, 36, 454
Stranger from Pecos, 259
Strawberry Roan, The, 24, 131, 332, 481
Streets of Ghost Town, 171
Stroheim, Erich von, 303
Struss, Karl, 283, 390, 405
Sturges, Preston, 34
Stutenroth, Gene, 218
Sudden Bill Dorn, 35
Sullivan, C. Gardner, 10, 296
Summerville, Slim, 229, 242
Sun Valley Cyclone, 231
Sundown Jim, 235
Sundown on the Prairie, 144, 454
Sundown Riders, 241
Sundown Saunders, 46
Sundown Trail, 92
Sundown Valley, 166–67
Sunrise, 79
Sunset in El Dorado, 130, 217, 432
Sunset of Power, 35
Sunset Pass, 101, 389, 393, 405
Sunset Pictures, 64, 152, 301
Sunset Range, 16, 20
Sunset Trail, 110
Superior, 57, 59
Supreme Pictures, 45, 57, 59, 253, 255, 256, 261, 315
"Suspicion," 498
Sutter's Gold, 445
Sutton, Kay, 86
Swander, Don, 346
Swander, June, 346
"Sweetheart of the Cimarron," 339
"Sweethearts or Strangers," 359
Swifty, 21
Swing in the Saddle, 367
Switzer, Carl, 222
Syndicate Pictures, 44, 45, 48, 53, 58, 64, 473
Syndicate-Monogram, 306

"T. B. Blues," 338
Tabasco Kid, The, 476
"Take Me Back to My Boots and Saddles," 372
Take Me Back to Oklahoma, 358, *358*
Talbot, Helen, *213,* 217
Talbot, Lyle, 87, 240, 267
"Tales of the Texas Rangers," 275
Tales of the West, 270–71, 476
"Tales of the West," 367

555

HOLLYWOOD CORRAL: A COMPREHENSIVE B WESTERN ROUNDUP

Taliaferro, Hal, 112, 127, 152, 153, 154, 161, 226, 427, 463. *See also* Wally Wales and Walt Williams
Talk of the Town, 51
Tall in the Saddle, 216
Tall T, The, 437
Talmadge, Richard, 241, 270, 451
Taming of the West, 226, 451
Tannen, William, 103
Tansey, John, 53, 58
Tansey, Robert, 53, 57, 58, 94, 95, 146, 154, 182, 197, 219, 248, 249, 250, 251, 263, 264, 270, 285, 473
Tansey, Sherry, *94*, 473
Target, 103
Tashlin, Frank, 135
Taurog, Norman, 122
Taylor, Al, 92
Taylor, Dub, 166, 167, 168, 214, 227, 228, 239, 242, *242*, *243*, 288
Taylor, Forrest, *41*, *148*, 351
Taylor, Grant, 284
Taylor, Kent, 283
Taylor, Ray, 35, 37, 50, 141, 146, 174, 193, 195, 206, 216, 240, 256, 257, 258, 264, 265, 266, 267, 284, 403
Taylor, Robert, 433
Tedesco, Guy, 484
Telegraph Trail, The, 72
Temple, Shirley, 282, 343, 390, 432
"Ten Little Bottles," 495
Tenney, Jack, 123
Tenting Tonight on the Old Camp Ground, 258
Terhune, Max, 124, 167, 172, 174, 175, *176*, 177, 178, 181, 182, *183*, 217, 251, 261, 349, 359, 435, 496
Terrell, Ken, 211
Terror of Tiny Town, The, 153
Terror Trail, 29, 427
Terrors on Horseback, 191
Terry, Ethelind, 141
Terry, Ruth, 127, 129
Tetzlaff, Ted, 32
Tex Rides with the Boy Scouts, 141, 142
"Tex Ritter Story, The," 496
Tex Williams and His Western Caravan, 476
Texans Never Cry, 133
Texas Bad Man, The, 28
Texas Buddies, 44
Texas Cyclone, 39, 70
Texas Lawman, 261
Texas Manhunt, 237, 359
Texas Marshall, The, *41*, 359
Texas Outlaws, 377
Texas Pioneers, 59
Texas Playboys, 345, 358, *358*
Texas Ranger, The, 32
Texas Renegades, 40–41
Texas Stampede, 162
Texas Terrors, 213
Texas to Bataan, 182
Texas Trail, 108, 435
Texas Trouble Shooters, 182
Thackery, Bud, 129, 211, 215
"That Pioneer Mother of Mine," 382

"That Silver Haired Daddy of Mine," 105, 338, 340, 348
Thayer, Julia, *460*
"There's a New Moon Over My Shoulder," 348
"There's an Empty Cot in the Bunkhouse Tonight," 348
They Died With Their Boots On, 430
Thin Man, The, 35
"This Ain't The Same Old Range," 379
Thomas, Augustus, 70
Thomas, Jameson, 199
Thomas, Jerry, 264, 265, 267
Thomas, Shy, 326
Thompson, Allen, 36
Thompson, Marshall, 487
Thompson, William, 151
Thomson, Fred, 12, *12*, 91, *302*, 306, 408
Thomson, Kenneth, 107
Thorpe, Jim, 138, 197
Thorpe, N. Howard, 331
Thorpe, Richard, 19, 58, 284
Those High Grey Walls, 451
3 Desperate Men, 284
Three Godfathers, 435
Three Jumps Ahead, 434
Three Men from Texas, 110, 435
Three Mesquiteers, 3, 4, 48, 49, 51, 62, 77, 123, 124, 173–83, *175*, 188, 211, 318, 359, 484
Three Muskateers, The, 469
Three Stooges, 87, 476
Three Texas Steers, 177, 178
Thrill Hunter, The, *33*, 34
Thumbs Up, 355
Thunder Mountain (1936), 388–89, 394, 395
Thunder Mountain (1947), 83, *85*, 101–2
Thunder Over Texas, 62
Thunder Over the Prairie, 164
Thunder River Feud, 182
Thunder Town, 48
Thunder Trail, 283, 390, 391, 405
Thundering Herd, The, 282, *388*, 389, 390
Thundering Hoofs, 96, 306, 450
Thundering Trail, The, 267
Thundering Trails, 180–81
Thundering West, The, 451
Tiffany Pictures, 15, 21, 22, 23, 44, 45, 58, 416
Tiffany-Stahl, 306
Tiger Woman, The, 464
Tillman, Floyd, 494
Timber Stampede, 88
Timber Terrors, 197
"Timber Trail," 379
Timber War, 196
Timely Tunes, 338
Tinling, James, 235, 404
Tiomkin, Dimitri, 494
To the Last Man, 282, 389, 390, 395, 405
Toler, Sidney, 110
Toll Gate, The, 297
Toll of the Desert, 64

Tombragel, Maurice, 269
Tombstone Canyon, 24
Tomlin, Pinky, 242
Tommy Dorsey's Orchestra, 364
"Tomorrow Never Comes," 495
Tone, Franchot, 432, 435
Tonto Rim, 102
"Too Late," 359, 362
"Too Many Tigers," 498
Topeka, 232, 403
Tornado in the Saddle, A, 239
Totman, Wellyn, 45
Totter, Audrey, 487
Tovar, Lupita, *126*
"Town Hall Party," 493, 496
Townley, Jack, 32, 123, 130, 131
Tracy Rides, 50
Tracy, Spencer, 507
Trader Horn, 61
Trail Beyond, The, 74
"Trail Blazers" series, 248–51, 445
Trail Drive, 24
"Trail Drive, The," 332
Trail Dust, 107, 109
Trail Guide, 102
Trail of Kit Carson, 217
Trail of Robin Hood, 134, 135
Trail of Terror, 238
Trail of the Hawk, 151
Trail of the Lonesome Pine, 110
"Trail of the Lonesome Pine, The," 295
Trail of the Mounties, 200
Trail of the Vigilantes, 446
Trail of the Yukon, 200
Trail Riders, 183
Trail to Gunsight, 240
Trail to San Antone, 131, 435
Trailin', 81
Trailin' North, 45
Trailin' Trouble, 17, 26
Trailin' West, 404
Trailing Double Trouble, 181, *181*
Trails of the Wild, 196
Train to Tombstone, 270
Trapped, 161
Travelin' On, 9
Travis, Merle, 346, 362, 373, 493
Travis, Randy, 492, 512
Treachery Rides the Range, 138
Treasure of the Sierra Madre, The, 101
Trevor, Claire, 127
Triangle, 10, 296, 299
"Tribute," 492
Trigger Law, 251
Trigger Pals, 148, 186, *187*, 357
Trigger Smith, 154
Trigger Trail, 240
Trigger Tricks, 16, 19
Trigger Trio, 175–76
Triggerman, 261
Triple Justice, 87, 422
Trop, Jack, 312–14, *314*, 415–16
Tropper Hook, 494
Trouble in Sundown, 86
Trouble in Texas, 141
Trusted Outlaw, The, 47, 454
Tryon, Glenn, 95, 259

INDEX

Tubb, Ernest, 166, 358–59
Tucker, Forrest, 435
Tucker, Melville, 220
Tucson Raiders, 230, *230*
Tulsa Kid, The, 212, *213*, 450
Tumbledown Ranch in Arizona, 181–82
Tumbleweed Trail, 237
"Tumbleweed Trail," 375
Tumbleweeds, 10
Tumbling River, 299
Tumbling Tumbleweeds, 118–19, 137, 159, 315, 344, 345, 414
"Tumbling Tumbleweeds," 162, 307, 334, 348, 364–65, 375, 378, 381
Turner, George, 207, 217
Turpin, Ben, 58
Turpin, Dick, 12
Tuska, Jon, 332, 340, 343–44, 371
Tuttle, W. C., 21, 92, 385
"Tweedle-O-Twill," 372
Twelvetrees, Helen, 36
20th-Century Fox, 83, 125, 146, 153, 204, 205, 207, 235, 315, 349
"26 Men," 275
Twilight on the Rio Grande, 131
Twilight on the Trail, 113
Twist, John, 95
Two Gun Law, 161, 398
Two Gun Man from Harlem, 153, 352
'Two Gun" of the Tumblewood, 322
Two Gun Troubador, 140
Two Guns and a Badge, 271, 368
Two Seconds, 450
Two-Fisted Justice, 49
Two-Fisted Law, 37, 70
Two-Fisted Rangers, 163, 357
Two-Fisted Sheriff, 161
Two-Fisted Stranger, 168
Two-Gun Justice, 40
Two-Gun Sheriff, 162, 213
Tycoon, 435
"Tying Knots in the Devil's Tail," 333
Tyler, Tom, 12, 17, 20, 31, 42, 43, 44, 46, 48–51, *49*, *50*, *51*, 56, 57, 63, 64, 91, 95, 103, 112, 135, 173, *174*, 177, 178, 180, *180*, 193, 229, 240, 242, 268, 293, 306, 392, 408, 476, 484. See also Vincent Markowski
Tyrell, John, 161

UCLA Film & Television Archive, 393
Ullman, Dan, 231, 232, 268
Ullman, George, 481
Uncensored Movies, 11
Unconquered Bandit, 50
Under Mexicali Stars, 220
Under Nevada Skies, 260
Under Strange Flags, 450
Under Texas Skies, 53, 58, 59
"Under The Double Eagle," 359
Under the Tonto Rim (1933), 389, 393
Under the Tonto Rim (1947), 101, 395, 399
Under Western Skies, 353, 443

Under Western Stars, 122, *123*, 355, 414
Undercover, 160
Undercover Man, 113
Underground Rustlers, 182
Underwater City, The, 485
Unexpected Guest, 113
United Artists, 10, 113, 205, 311, 415, 416
Universal, 7, 15–17, 18, 19, 20, 21, 22, 24, 27, 29, 31, 32, 35, 37, 38, 53, 54, 60, 61, 64, 76, 77, 82, 98, 139, 144, 146, 147, 148, 163, 193, 200, 215, 239, 240, 245, 253, 254, 255, 256, 257, 261, 275, 294, 300, 301, 303, 306, 311, 316, 333, 344, 346, 347, 349, 350, 367, 403, 408, *408*, 411, 443, 445, 446, 466, 469, 472–73, 484
Universal-International, 240
Unknown, The, 386
Unknown Valley, 32
Unmarried, 36, 37
Untamed, The, 299
"Untamed, The," 386
Utah, 129, 427, 435
"Utah Carrol," 332
Utah Kid, The, 58, 251
Utah Trail, 142
Utah Wagon Train, 222

Vague, Vera, 126, 167
Vale, Virginia, 86, 87, *89*
Valentino, 113
Valiant Hombre, The, 206
Valley of Fire, 134
Valley of Hunted Men, 180
Valley of Terror, 197
Valley of the Lawless, 255
Valley of the Sun, 51
Valley of Vanishing Men, 229, 467
Vallin, Rick, 201
Van Beuren Corporation, 64
Van Dyke, LeRoy, 373
Van Dyke, W. S. "Woody", 31, 35, 284
Van Enger, Charles, 32, 258
Van Sickel, Dale, 211, 241, 463, 464
"Vanishing American, The," 387
Vanishing Frontier, 254
Vanishing Outpost, The, 267
Vanishing Westerner, The, 220
Venable, Evelyn, 110, 204, 392
Vengeance of Rannah, The, 57
Vengeance of the West, 32
Venturini, Edward D., 110, 206, *314*
Verdugo, Elena, 201
Vernon, Wally, 214, 217, 269
Via Pony Express, 63
Victor Talking Machine Co., 334, 347, 348, 352, 357
Victory Pictures, 40, 50, 245, 315
Vidor, Charles, 95
Vidor, King, 70, 93, 94, 253, 254, *254*, 404
Vidor Publications, 496
Vigilantes Are Coming, The, 206
Vigilantes of Boomtown, 217
Vigilantes of Dodge City, 230

Viking, The, 160
Vinton, Victoria, *57*, *141*
Violent Men, The, 435
"Virginian, The," 277
Virginian, The, 8, 13, 69, 298, 331, 432
"Virginian, The" (play), 293
Visaroff, Michael, 24
Vitagraph, 137
Viva Cisco Kid, 204
"Voice of Hollywood" series, 15, 478
Voodoo Woman, 483

Waco, 232
Wade, Russell, 240–41
Wade, Tom, 50
Waggner, George, 147, 148
Wagon Tracks West, 229
Wagon Trail, 61
Wagon Train, 95, 97
"Wagon Wheels," 334
Wagon Wheels West, 476
Wagons Westward, 37
Wakely, Jimmy, 166, 167, 214, *233*, 235, 241–42, *242*, *243*, 258, 260, 362, 363, *363*, 367, 368, 378, 432, 459, 489, 494–95, 497, 499
Wales, Wally, See also Hal Taliaferro and Walt Williams, 12, *55*, 56–57, 58, 62, 173, *174*, 293, 295, 306, 317, 472, 473
Walker, Francis, 228
Walker, Terry, 164
Wall Street Cowboy, 124, *125*, 127, 430
Wallace, Beryl, *93*, 94, 197
Wallace, Lew, 10
Wallace, Morgan, *85*
Waller, Eddie, 277
Waller, Eddy, 219, *219*, 288, 289
Walsh, Raoul, 69, 127, 203
Walt Disney Studios, 443
Walters, Luana, 38, 226, 227, 248, 285, 450, 450–51, 484–85
Walthall, Henry B., 21, 70, 72
Walton, Douglas, 95
Wanderers of the Wasteland, 100, 393
Wanderers of the West, 453
Wanger, Walter, 77, 146
Ward, John, *196*
Ward, Luci, 177, 195
Warde, Anthony, *201*
Warde, Tony, 200
Ware. Irene, *456*
Warner Brothers, 4, 70, 72, 81, 87, 92, 101, 120, 137, 138, 139, 193, 225, 239–40, 344, 404, 429, 432, 443, 476
Warner, H. B., 25
Warner, John, 62
Warren, Dale, 382, 383
Warren, James, *100*, 100–101, 263, 393, *395*
Warrenton, Gil, 21
Warwick Films, 199
Washburn, Bryant, 151
Washington Cowboy, 353, 414
Washington, Ned, 494
Water Rustlers, 285, 357

HOLLYWOOD CORRAL: A COMPREHENSIVE B WESTERN ROUNDUP

Waters, John, *384*
Watkin, Pierre, *125*
Watkins, Linda, 82
Watt, Nate, 108, 109, 110, 179, 213, 270
Watts, Twinkie, 214, 217
Waxman, Franz, 445
Way of the West, 57
"Way Out There," 334, 375
Wayne, John, *See also* Marion Morrison, 17, *39*, *43*, *45*, *57*, *67*, *69–77*, *71*, *72*, *73*, *74*, *75*, 77, 80, 92, 97, 106, 117, 118, 127, 129, 137, 146, *172*, *176–77*, *177*, *178*, 215, 216, 253, 256, 295, 306, 326, 342, 344, 355, *359*, *365*, *390*, *396*, 401, *402*, 411, 427, 428, 430, 433, 434, 435, 454, 469, 479, 481, *507*, 510
Weaver Brothers & Elviry, 127
Weaver, Marjorie, 204
Webb, Harry S., 46, 47, 48, 50, 53, 54, 58, 64, 155
Webb, Ira, 266
Webb, Roy, 444
Wee Willie Winkie, 432
Weeks, George W., 181
Weisses, 58
Weissmuller, Johnny, 191, 428
Welch, Niles, *81*
Welles, Orson, 97, 227
Wellman, William A., 31, 100
Wells Fargo, 256, 437
Wells Fargo Days, 240, 476
Wells, Jacqueline, 127
Wells, Ted, 12, 60, 241
Wentworth, Martha, 217
Wentz, Roby, 152
Werker, Alfred, 81, 82
West, Joseph. *See* George Waggner
West, Mae, 255
West of Abilene, 163
West of Carson City, 257, 403
West of Cheyenne, 48, 162
West of Cimarron, 180
West of Dodge City, 168, 170
West of Rainbow's End, 40
West of Sonora, 168, 169
West of Texas, 238
West of the Brazos, 269
West of the Divide, 74, *74*
West of the Law, 247
West of the Pecos (1934), 95, 96
West of the Pecos (1945), 99, *99*, 102, 393
West of the Rockies, 64
West of Tombstone, 166
West to Glory, 264–65
West, Wally, 67
Westbound Mail, 2, 161
Western Adventure Productions, 266, 267
Western Courage, 26
Western Cyclone, 191
Western Frontier, 25
Western Gold, 146, 349
Western Jamboree, 123
Western Terror, 157
Western Trail, 148

"Westerner, The," 277
Weston, Dick. *See* Roy Rogers
Westward Bound, 53, 64, 244, 250, 453
Westward Ho!, 75, 75–76, 428, 435
Westward Ho-Hum, 476
Whalen, Michael, 267, 270
What Every Woman Wants, 315
Wheels of Destiny, 24
"Wheels of Destiny," 332
When a Man Sees Red, 35
When a Man's a Man, 83, 385, 386
"When It's Springtime in the Rockies," 372
"When My Sugar Walks Down the Street," 357
"When Payday Rolls Around," 379
"When the Work's All Done This Fall," 331, 332
"When You Wish Upon a Star," 359
Where the Buffalo Roam, 142
Where the North Begins, 200
Where the West Begins, 146, 450
Where Trails Divide, 94
Wherever the Grass Grows, 240
Whipper, Leigh, 127
Whirlin' Horseman, 26
Whirlwind Rider, The, 67
'Whisper While You're Waltzing," 487
Whispering Chorus, The, 481
Whispering Skull, The, 238
Whispering Smith Speaks, 83
Whistling Bullets, 197
Whitaker, Slim, 40, 92, *154*, *186*
White, Dan, 167
White Eagle (1934), 34, 38, 245
White Eagle (1941), 37, 245, 462
White, Eddy, 127, 133
White, Edward J., 214, 222
White Heat, 431
White, Jacqueline, 103
White, John I., 333–34
White, Lee "Lasses," 96, 98, 102, 241, *363*, 423
White Rider, The, 309
White Stallion, 251
White, Stewart Edward, 8, 83
Whitely, Ray, 85, 86, 95, 98, 240, 336, 346, *346*, 347, 354, 355, 357, 400, 417, 423, 470, 473, 474, *474*, 475
Whiting, Margaret, 362, 494
Wichita, 494
Wide Open Spaces, 476
Wide Open Town, 112
Wiere Brothers, 129
Wild and Wooly, 299
"Wild Bill Hickok," 273–74, *274*
Wild Brian Kent, 315, 386
Wild Bunch, The, 157
Wild Country, 372
Wild Frontier, The, 219, 220
Wild Gold, 437
Wild, Harry, 85, 97, 98, 99
Wild Horse, 19
Wild Horse Ambush, 223
Wild Horse Mesa, 389, 393, 395
Wild Horse Range, 155
Wild Horse Rodeo, 123, 176, 315, 443

Wild Horse Roundup, 197
Wild Horse Rustlers, 188
Wild Horse Stampede, 248, 249, 350, 453
Wild Mustang, 318
Wild West, 264, 265, *265*
Wild West Days, 256, 445
Wild West Whopee, 54
Wildcat Saunders, 54, 56, 318
Wildcat Trooper, 197
Wilderness Mail, 196
Wilderness Trail, The, 295
Wildfire, 219, 263, 266
Wilke, Bob, 217, 427
Wilkerson, Guy, 144, 157, 235, 237, 238
Willat, Irvin, 297
Williams, Ann, 338–39
Williams, Bill, 99, 275, 496
Williams, Bob, 215, 218, 220, 230
Williams, Guinn "Big Boy," 37, 62, 63, 95, 99, 127, 167, 173, *174*, 242, 281, 328, 393, *393*, 486
Williams, Guy, 207
Williams, Hank, 368
Williams, Lester, 64, 318. *See also* William Berke
Williams, Roger, *57*, 62
Williams, Sollie, 476
Williams, Tex, 270, 271, 367, 477, 497–98
Williams, Walt, *See also* Wally Wales, 57
Willing, Foy, 135, *367*
Willis, Norman, 161, *180*, 286, 484
Wills, Bob, 239, 345, 357–58, *358*, 378, 476, 497
Wills, Chill, 85, 95
Wilsey, Jay, *See also* Buffalo Bill, Jr., *308*, *319*, 409
Wilson, Cherry, 92
Wilson, Dorothy, 83, 93
Wilson, Lois, 28
Wilson, Stanley, 211
Wilson, Whip, 242, 243, 267–68, 269, 432
Wilson, Woodrow, 62
"Wind," 379
Windjammer, 315
Winds of the Wasteland, 76
Windsor, Marie, 231
Winners of the West, 467
Winning of Barbara Worth, The, 385
Winters, Linda, 227
Wister, Owen, 8, 293, 331
Withers, Grant, 36, 219, 427
Withers, Jane, 125
Witney, William, 133, 135, 152, 176, 179, 194, 206, 209, 211, 212, 214, 216, 222, 399, 401, 429, 435, 464, 466
Wohl, Herman, 151
Wolf Call, 402
Wolf Hunters, The, 200, *200*, 201
Wolfe, Bud, 211
Wolves of the Range, 188
Wood, Britt, 110, 166
Wood, Edward D., Jr., 482
Wood, Harlene, 197

INDEX

Wood, Natalie, 430
Woodbury, Joan, 127, 205, 260
Woods, Donald, 392
Woods, Harry, 58, 99, 102, 124, 127, 153, 154, 160, 205, 216, 225, 247, 255, 260, 286, 286, 476, 486
Worden, Hank, *143, 144*, 474
World Wide Pictures, 21, 23, 24, 45, 54
Wormser, Richard, 218, 219
"Worried Mind, A," 359
Worth, Harry, 108
Wright, Harold Bell, 385–86
Wright, Mack, 70, 72, 76, 120, 121, 175, 206, 211, 225, 240, 476
Wright, Tenny, 70, 72
Wrixon, Maris, 476
Wurtzel, Sol, 204
"Wyatt Earp," 432
Wynter, Dana, 429
Wyoming, 409
Wyoming Hurricane, 239
Wyoming Outlaw, 178, 212, 213
Wyoming Roundup, 268

Wyoming Whirlwind, 56
Wyoming Wildcat, 213

Xydias, Anthony J., 64, 152

Yaconelli, Frank, 95, 154
Yates, Herbert J., 117, 122, 123, 127, 315, 317, 340, 342, 348, 352, 353, 360, 365, 366, 414, 444, 491, 497, 498
Yellow Contraband, 307
Yellow Dust, 95
"Yellow Rose of Texas," 348
Yellow Sky, 432
Yodelin' Kid from Pine Ridge, 343
York, Duke, 201
Yost, Robert, 190
"You Are My Sunshine," 359, 372
"You Two Timed Me One Time Too Often," 348
Young Bill Hickok, 127
Young Blood, 45
Young Buffalo Bill, 127
Young, Carleton, *48*, 190
Young, Clarence Upton, 95

Young, Faron, 373
Young, Jack, 24
Young, Loretta, 199, 432
Young, Polly Ann, *34, 74*, 199
Young, Victor, 110, 444
"Your Old Love Letters," 495
Yrigoyen, Joe, 211, 435
Yucca Productions, 268
Yukon Flight, 199
Yukon Manhunt, 201

Zahler, Lee, 238, 403, 442, 444–45
Zamecnik, J. S., 442
Zanuck, Darryl, 203
"Zebra Dun," 332
Ziehm, Arthur, 140
Zimmerman, Fred, 145
"Zorro," 279, 443
Zorro Rides Again, 206, *208*, 443, 462
"Zorro" series, 206–9
Zorro's Black Whip, 207, 209, 462, 464
Zorro's Fighting Legion, 206–7, 443, 464, 465